HYPERBOLES

HARVARD STUDIES IN COMPARATIVE LITERATURE
FOUNDED BY WILLIAM HENRY SCHOFIELD

52

Eloquentia Fortitudine præ-
ftantior.

Arcum læua tenet.rigidam fert dextera clauam,
Contegit & Nemees corpora nuda leo.
Herculis hæc igitur facies.non conuenit illud
Quòd uetus & senio tempora cana gerit.
Quid quòd lingua illi leuibus traiecta cathenis,
Quæis fiſſa facileis allicit aure uiros?
An'ne quòd Alciden lingua non robore Galli
Præſtantem,populis iura dediſſe ferunt?
Cedunt arma togæ,& quamuis duriſſima corda
Eloquio pollens ad sua uota trahit.

"Eloquence, surpassing strength"
from Andrea Alciato, *Emblemata* (1550)
Courtesy of Houghton Library (Typ.515.50.132)

HYPERBOLES

The Rhetoric of Excess
in
Baroque Literature and Thought

Christopher D. Johnson

Harvard University Department of Comparative Literature
Distributed by Harvard University Press
Cambridge, Massachusetts, and London, England
2010

The font used in this book is Poliphilus, based on the typeface first developed by Aldus Manutius in 1499 for the *Hypnerotomachia Poliphili*.

PRINTED IN THE UNITED STATES OF AMERICA

FIRST PRINTING

ISBN 978-0-674-05331-1 (cl.)
ISBN 978-0-674-05333-5 (pa.)

Acknowledgments

This book has been long in the making. I would like to thank my family for their boundless understanding and love as I wrestled with its protean forms. I wish also to thank and acknowledge the many generous, learned persons who offered instruction and encouragement as it progressed. Daniel Javitch, Ernest Gilman, Mary Carruthers, Ken Krabbenhoft, Elizabeth Duquette, Tom Conley, Regina Schwartz, and Reg Gibbons critiqued earlier versions; while Timothy Reiss, James Engell, James Iffland, Bill Todd, Susan Suleiman, Luis Girón-Negrón, Marc Shell, Christopher Krebs, John Hamilton, Daniel Selcer, Brady Bowman, Marty Cohen, Mary Gaylord, Stanley Cavell, and numerous colleagues and students at Harvard helped and provoked me to refine the work. For their patience, innumerable insights, and timely cries of "Coraggio!" I am truly grateful. But if a big book is a big evil, as Callimachus insisted long ago, then the fault is mine alone.

Contents

HYPERBOLES

Introduction

> The proper METHOD for studying poetry and
> good letters is the method of contemporary biologists,
> that is careful first-hand examination of the matter, and
> continual COMPARISON of one 'slide'
> or specimen with another.
> — Ezra Pound, *ABC of Reading*

I

In "The Decay of Lying," Oscar Wilde describes three stages in the history of art. The second, most vital stage — the one corresponding to what has come to be called the Baroque — occurs when "[a]rt itself is really a form of exaggeration; and selection, which is the very spirit of art, is nothing more than an intensified mode of over-emphasis."[1] At once formalist and historicist, this claim is also a fine exaggeration itself, one meant to turn Victorian tastes on their head. Following Wilde's cue, Pound's prescription on "METHOD," but also responding to various post-structuralist attempts to explicate the dynamics of rhetorical, aesthetic, and material excess, this book reads hyperbole as the audacious but often subtle, the sublime but sometimes ironic, engine of Baroque literature and thought. My aim in the following pages is to offer a voluminous, wide-ranging defense of the figure George Puttenham in 1589 dubs the "lowd lyar" and "the over reacher," this most infamous of tropes, whose name most literary criticism dares not praise, and whose existence the history of philosophy largely ignores.[2]

In Greek ὑπερβολή literally means an "overshooting," as does its Latin cognate *superiectio*.[3] Aristotle, Quintilian, and their Renaissance and Baroque successors ambivalently treat such "overshooting" as a form of artful exaggeration that gives vividness, energy, and marvelousness to a speech or poem, but which also may lead to charges that the hyperbolist lacks control of his art.[4] As either a metaphoric or discursive figure of rhetoric in which the writer selfconsciously exaggerates a thought, feeling, or image, hyperbole encourages, or some would say forces, the reader to find the intended figurative meaning rather than accepting the apparent or literal meaning. The hyperbolist perceives an extraordinary, outrageous, ridiculous, or ineffable *res* (thing, event, feeling, idea), while his or her *verba* (words, speech, language) strain discursive limits, analogical frameworks, and literary and rhetorical conventions, to represent that *res*. In Linnaean terms, *excess* is the order, *bombast* and *hyperbole* the genera, and within the genus *hyperbole*, one finds various species: metaphoric hyperbole, discursive hyperbole, hyperbole ruled by allegory, hyperbole as litote, and hyperbole that verges on irony, catachresis, or paradox.

Hyperbole is "bolder" [*audacioris*] than the other tropes, Quintilian declares, for in order to create the "incredible" [*ultra fidem*] it risks that the readerauditor will mistake its impossibility and take the sign for the thing itself. But the poetorator may also be at fault, and with "unmeasured" [*ultra modum*] rhetoric create laughter or disgust where none is intended.[5] As opposed to the mere purveyor of bombast, the Baroque hyperbolist, ever conscious of rhetorical precepts, and skillfully manipulating literary traditions and forms, solicits complicity rather than mockery. Shakespeare is a hyperbolist; Falstaff is not.

This book investigates the art of exaggeration where it is most ordinary and extraordinary: in Baroque literature and philosophy. By Baroque I mean at once a literary style, a period concept, and a fundamental *Weltanschauung* that describes the transitional period in European culture from the Renaissance to the Enlightenment.[6] In the most schematic terms, I take the Baroque to describe a literary style and intellectual disposition that flourish between 1575 and 1690, or from Tasso's *Gerusalemme liberata* to Sor Juana Inés de la Cruz's *Primero sueño*. While the Baroque style peaks at different times in different countries, and often assumes quite varied local characteristics, it is generally marked by rhetorical sophistication, excess, and play. Ingenious, unusual metaphors and conceits, as well as a predilection for figures such as paradox, antithesis, and paronomasia distinguish Baroque poetry and prose. More than trying to persuade or simply please, the Baroque style tends to court surprise, admiration (*admiratio*), and, depending on the author, skepticism or belief. Favorite themes in Baroque literature and thought include the pleasure of the

senses, metamorphosis, mutability, disillusionment, melancholy, inexpressibility, and infinity. With this said, my use of the term is more inductive than
deductive: what I mean by Baroque will in large part be defined by how hyperbole helps define the concept. As Deleuze writes in *The Fold*:

> It would seem strange for one to deny the existence of the Baroque as one
> would deny Unicorns or Pink Elephants. Because in these cases the con-
> cept is given, while in the case of the Baroque it is rather one of know-
> ing whether one can invent a concept capable of giving (or not) its
> existence. Irregular pearls exist, but the Baroque has no reason to exist
> without a concept that forms this reason itself. It's easy to render the
> Baroque non-existent; one only has to stop proposing its concept.[7]

While Baroque writing tends to trumpet its own literariness and belatedness, the Baroque hyperbolist's abuse of commonplaces, received traditions
and forms, and, above all, of literal truths, even as it may flirt with affectation, absurdity, and aporia, often creates real conceptual novelty and powerful
emotive effect. The favorite figure of diverse personalities writing in sundry
circumstances — Shakespeare dramatizing human perfidy and woe for a Jacobean audience, Descartes, in Holland, fashioning a philosophical method
out of radical doubt, Sor Juana depicting her failure to gain absolute knowledge in a Mexican convent cell — hyperbole proves a chameleon figure, a vehicle for extreme disillusionment and enthusiastic thaumaturgy. Hyperbole, in
brief, is a "master trope," one that vies with metaphor, metonymy, synecdoche,
and irony for our attention.[8]

If exaggeration has often been taken to epitomize Baroque aesthetics, then
Gérard Genette's brief essay on the poetry of Jean de Sponde (1557–1595),
"Hyperboles," contains, monad-like, many of the questions unfolded in my
book.[9] Observing that Sponde's hyperboles tend to compare the self's desires with either far-fetched cosmological or historical terms, Genette writes:
". . . on appellerait *hyperboles* les effets par lesquels le langage . . . rapproche
comme par effraction des réalités naturellement éloignées dans le contraste et
la discontinuité" [. . . *one may call* hyperboles *the effects by which language . . .
draws closer through contrast and discontinuity, as if by burglary, realities naturally far-
removed*]. Extending the spatial metaphor, he then localizes hyperbole's power:
". . . d'envoyer (ou d'aller chercher) aussi loin que possible quelque chose
qu'il faut bien appeler la pensée" [*to send forth (or to send searching) as far a possible*

something that one must indeed call thought]. But Genette's final sentence provokes the most: "Ce mode hyperbolique de l'esprit n'a⁄t⁄il pas ses raisons — que le bon sens ignore, et que la raison veut connaître?" [*Does not this hyperbolic mode of thought (wit) have its reasons, which commonsense ignores and which reason wishes to know?*].[10] What, then, are hyperbole's "reasons" or "motives" and what do they promise to teach our "reason"? And why is the Baroque the best place to look for these "reasons"?

Hyperbole, theorists from Quintilian to Genette agree, is uniquely suited to represent extraordinary things, experiences, and events. Acclaimed by Quintilian for its "boldness" and "elegant straining of the truth," by Henry Peacham for its "reach" and "compass," and by Baltasar Gracián for its ex⁄pression of "the impossible," hyperbole may serve as more than a mere trope of exaggeration or diminution.[11] It may function as a figure of thought in⁄forming a conceit, fueling a speech, even shaping a novel, or, as Quintilian comments about Socrates and irony, describing an entire life. Yet to succeed in persuading or astounding, and to avoid being charged with the grievous sty⁄listic sin of *cacozelia*, or "perverse, excessive affectation," hyperbole must be somehow grounded in the real, in some commonly held opinion, or shared ex⁄perience. As Harry Levin shows in his study of Marlowe's dramatic "over⁄reaching," and Brian Vickers contends in his reading of hyperbole in Donne's *Songs and Sonets*, the hyperbolist's motives can be wildly diverse.[12] External events (a comet's appearance in the night sky, a king's ascension or fall), po⁄etic traditions (Petrarchism, Senecan drama), poetic genres (the sonnet, epi⁄thalamium, the picaresque novel), the passions (wonder, grief, outrage), and the desire to give expression to ideas (eternity, the perfection of the universe, the uniqueness of love, God's omnipotence, the *cogito*) can all occasion hyper⁄bole. But such motives may also be muddied or mixed. Stanley Cavell dis⁄covers in his reading of Shakespearean tragedy that characters such as Lear or Cleopatra seek the same absolute responses from people that Descartes would skeptically demand of ideas.[13] Alternately, Sor Juana and Pascal turn to hyperbole to demarcate the limits of certainty as well as their own rhetori⁄cal powers.

At its most potent and dynamic, Baroque hyperbole is more than a figure of style: it is a mode of thought, a way of being. Even when it takes the seem⁄ingly transparent form of an invidious comparison, we discover that to com⁄pare invidiously can be to place inordinate, potentially untenable weight on the writer's subjectivity. The hyperbolist measures the tension between the ideal and the real, the distance between the word and world. Hyperbole helps mark the limits of objective and subjective representation in the historical moment when the earth was being mapped, the cosmos reordered, nations forged, and as Bloom and Foucault contend, the "human" or modern individual invented. An understanding of the dynamics of hyperbole is thus crucial to appreciating a period marked by contradictory feelings of novelty and belatedness, radical skepticism, and an excessive love of spectacle. Like its "silver" Latin counterpart and its current incarnation as the Neo-Baroque, the seventeenth-century Baroque is an age in which verbal rhetoric (like the visual rhetoric of anamorphosis and chiaroscuro) makes keenly felt the epistemological strain caused by the perceived gulf between seeming and being. And while most scholars treat as axiomatic how rhetorical culture was instrumental in forging the subtleties of Petrarchism, Shakespearean drama, Cartesian philosophy, and Pascalian mysticism, that hyperbole frequently proves quite dialogic (even when the conversation is with an absent or disdainful beloved, or when that beloved is God) runs counter to critical orthodoxy, which generally regards it as facile or mendacious. Joshua Scodel persuasively argues that a fertile literary and philosophic dialectic occurs between competing visions of excess and the mean throughout early modernity.[14] But hyperbole, I would add, also functions dialectically in late Renaissance poetry because the reader, well versed in the dynamics of poetic *imitatio*, knew how to hear and interpret its excess, and thus straddle its literal and figurative meanings. Hyperboles did not spring fully formed from the poet's imagination like Athena from Zeus' head; rather, they were inherited, then adapted, that they might outdo their predecessors and therefore continue to astonish their recipients.

The hyperbolist constructs his readers as much as he awaits them, which is another way of saying that the history of hyperbole is also the history of its reception. Because of the dramatic gap the hyperbolist creates between language and the world, between figurative and literal truth, strong demands are made on judgment as well as taste. While the hyperbolist's attacks on convention astonish and sometimes disturb, these also frequently achieve the conceptual effect of suggesting the insufficiency or inexhaustibility of meaning. To ensure his extravagant claims are mediated, therefore, the hyperbolist appeals to the reader's knowledge, experience, and common sense. But these resources prove less common, more in need of cultivation, than Descartes, for one, famously assumes. When Jacques, in *As You Like It*, mockingly declares "All the world's a stage, and all the men and women merely players," an Elizabethan

audience understood such a hyperbolic commonplace in various ways depending on their class, gender, and education; while a student of literary *topoi* like
E. R. Curtius detects echoes of Petronius; but school children attending a
performance in Central Park might simply delight at the prospect of a world
reduced to a plaything. As with the interpretation of irony, how hyperbole is
received depends inordinately upon one's disposition. Homer masterfully uses
hyperbole to give expression to Achilles' epic anger, but Aristotle reading
Homer with the law court in mind brands it as "adolescent." Disturbed by
the form of hyperbolic skepticism that Descartes employs to deduce the *cogito*,
his contemporary, Pierre Gassendi, refuses or is unable to hear it as provisional
and thus balks at accepting the Cartesian method. In brief, as Rosaline remarks in *Love's Labour's Lost*: "A jest's prosperity lies in the ear / Of him that
hears it, never in the tongues / Of him that makes it."

II

When Virgil in the opening lines of the *Aeneid* portrays Juno's wrath against
his hero, when he pits Aeneas' laments against the storm's anger, he turns to
hyperbole to heighten his rhetoric:

> Talia iactanti stridens Aquilone procella
> velum adversa ferit, fluctusque ad sidera tollit . . . (1.102–103)

> As he flings forth such words, a gust, shrieking from the North, strikes
> full on his sail and lifts the waves to heaven . . .[15]

Virgil's hyperbole (*superiectio*) answers but also overwhelms the "flinging"
[*iactanti*] words of Aeneas, who has yet to comprehend, let alone measure up
to his fate. In describing a physical impossibility pitting the cosmos against
human ambition this verse also sets in motion the epic's remarkable chain of
hyperboles that will culminate with an angry, mountain-like Aeneas (12.697–
703) mercilessly sending the once overreaching but now suppliant Turnus
"beneath the shadows" [*sub umbras*].

When Robert Burton at the end of "Democritus to the Reader" (1628)
brings his rhetorical whirlwind to a momentary close — *The Anatomy of
Melancholy* with its encyclopedic scope and intricate Ramist framework has yet
to begin in earnest — he employs a more discursive form of hyperbole:

I owe thee nothing (Reader), I look for no favour at thy hands, I am independent, I fear not. No, I recant, I will not, I care, I fear, I confess my
fault, acknowledge a great offence, — *motos praestat componere fluctus* [it is
better to calm the troubled waves] I have overshot myself, I have spoken
foolishly, rashly, unadvisedly, absurdly, I have anatomized my own folly.[16]

After some hundred pages, in which he describes how "all the world is mad,"
portrayed an apocryphal Democritus in exquisite detail, diagnosed the sorry
state of political affairs in England, and sketched a utopian commonwealth,
Burton lets the mask of Democritus fall. In so doing, his larger project of
anatomy, with all its scientific pretensions, is reduced to self-consciously paradoxical hyperbole. His flagrant "offence" has been against the arbiters of
rhetorical decorum who require moderation and frown upon unnecessary
amplification and digression. But his more furtive offence, one that goes to the
heart of my study of hyperbole and its subjective subtleties, cosmographical
pretensions, and intertextual echoes, is to invoke Virgil as an authority in defense of his newfound but certainly facetious restraint. Plucked from Neptune's speech that comes just after the verses I quoted above, the borrowed
phrase promises only a false respite from the verbal and phenomenal *fluctus* to
come — both in Virgil's epic and Burton's anatomy. It invests hyperbole with
precise literary and historical ironies.

Burton has two targets: a disapproving reader ("Thou thyself art the subject of my discourse") and his own rhetorical *ethos*. At the very end of "Democritus to the Reader," after invoking apologies borrowed from Seneca,
Ariosto, and Julius Caesar Scaliger, he turns to Juvenal and Horace's *Ars poetica* in one final, ambivalent attempt to excuse his overshooting:

… tis a most difficult thing to keep an even tone, a perpetuall tenor, and
not sometimes to lash out; *difficile est Satyram non scribere*, there be so many
objects to divert, inward perturbations to molest, and the very best may
sometimes erre, *aliquandò bonus dormitat Homerus*, it is impossible not in so
much to overshoot …[17]

In highlighting the objective ("so many objects") and subjective ("inward
perturbations") causes for his excess, Burton neatly identifies the two principal motives that will fuel much of the rhetoric examined in this book. But in

eschewing responsibility for his sins against decorum and taste, Burton also challenges his readers to appropriate his hyperbole for themselves.

A "throwing-beyond," like the spear that Lucretius, in one of his *adu-nata*, or exercises in the counterfactual, urges his readers to throw beyond the edge of finite space (". . . siquis procurrat ad oras / ultimus extremas iacitque volatile telum"), hyperbole often precipitates a heuristic experience in which imaginative and cognitive limits are tested.[18] At the same time, as rhetorical amplification, hyperbole can produce palpable material and discursive *copia*. This "*copia* of word and thought," championed first by Erasmus in the Renaissance and lately by Terence Cave, signals at once rhetorical, material, and conceptual abundance.[19] But it may also mark the lack of other means of signification. As Pascal observes: "Figure porte présence et absence." Hyperbolic *copia* (not a pleonasm) may thus make epistemological, even ontological claims about the immanence, or lack thereof, of the real. Conversely, just as nowadays one struggles to parse the multifarious *hype* flooding the media flooding our daily lives, readers of Baroque hyperbole had and still have to rely on all kinds of knowledge and experience to judge the excessive language that tries to represent remarkable truths.[20]

In the early eighteenth century, César Chesneau Dumarsais equates *excès* with hyperbole, though this is to conflate tenor with vehicle.[21] Excess corresponds to the extraordinary idea or emotional effect (*affectus*) produced, while hyperbole is the linguistic means to achieve this. As a metaphor or conceit, hyperbole can be a swift "wingéd chariot" of wit, but as a discursive figure integral to the success of classical and Renaissance epic, Erasmian eloquence, Burtonian satire, Shakespearean tragedy, Pascalian apology, as well as the viability of the Cartesian method, it can be narrative, dialogic, or structural. In brief, whether it assumes metaphoric or discursive form, hyperbole requires semantic analysis.

If we imagine a speaker confronted with the task of expressing an extraordinary event, and if we accept the logic of catachresis, which tends to represent extraordinary qualities in far-fetched quantitative terms (i.e., a storm is so fierce that the ocean's waves rise to the stars), then a continuum emerges, a reductive but hopefully heuristic continuum, in which the *quantity of expressibility* in a linguistic act might be gauged:

$$\text{silence} \rightarrow \text{litote} \rightarrow \text{verisimilitude} \rightarrow \text{hyperbole} \rightarrow \text{silence}$$

With silence either nothing is worth being expressed or the *res* is perceived as being too much for speech even to begin. With litote the speaker suggests that speech is insufficient to represent the *res* by ironically settling for understatement or too little speech. With the realistic ambitions of a verisimilar style correspondences between word and world are cultivated. With hyperbole the speaker again suggests that language is poorly suited to represent the *res*, but now he opts for too much, exaggerated, or conceptually audacious speech. And finally, with silence the superfluity or insufficiency of speech is again encountered. If, however, silence is reached after the speaker tries and, perhaps, exhausts other forms of expression, the quality of that silence has been altered. As Sor Juana puts it: ". . . el callar no es no haber que decir, sino no caber en las voces lo mucho que hay que decir" [*silence is not having nothing to say, rather it is words not containing all that there is to say*].[22] Accordingly, in the book's latter chapters, I ask how the silence urged by Wittgenstein's muchdebated last proposition in the *Tractatus*, which responds to certain circumstances such as "the mystical" [*das Mystische*], differs from the silence before the first proposition, or even those silences between the propositions. Such difference helps us understand, I argue, how Cordelia's silence ("Love and be silent") at the beginning of *Lear* has been mediated by the Fool's litotes and the old King's hyperboles, such that by the time we experience the play's climactic "general woe" all speech seems superfluous.

To judge what kinds of aesthetic, cognitive, or ethical claims the hyperbolist makes, they need to be read in ways that allow meanings to accumulate around them in addition to the meanings they themselves promise — Nietzsche's prescription "to read slowly" [*langsam lesen*] is never more acute than in the case of hyperbole. For to discern between literal and figurative meanings, or as an Augustinian reader might put it, to distinguish between the husk and the kernel, the contexts and paratexts that inform and frame such rhetoric should be charitably examined. This is why I engage at length in the latter half of the book Cavell's claim that philosophy and the language of philosophy ought to respond to the myriad ways people ordinarily speak, and that they may sometimes passionately utter ordinary words of great significance.[23] Obviously, people ordinarily use hyperbole; but that poets and philosophers may wish to create an exceptional rhetorical and conceptual space where the extraordinary and ordinary are both in view, and that hyperbole helps to create the cognitive dissonance for that to occur, are less commonly appreciated.

III

In *On Bullshit*, Harry Frankfurt contends that bullshit is so effective because it manages to remain ambiguous, often even to the bullshitters themselves, who sometimes cannot or care not to distinguish between truth and lies.[24] The same ambiguity, I find, holds true for the best of Baroque hyperbole. To begin to describe this ambiguity, and in order to provide an initial theoretical ground- ing for the book's close readings, I wish here to consider briefly the semantic relations between hyperbole and irony, and then adumbrate a few of the rhetor- ical, aesthetic, and philosophical aspects of Baroque hyperbole.

Eric Gans discovers a fundamental dichotomy between hyperbole and irony.[25] Looking beyond the text to the author's intentionality and the work's reception, Gans argues that whereas hyperbole posits a referent, irony denies one. He thus treats hyperbole and its initial deceptiveness that instigates the reader's search for intended meaning as emblematic of how all literature pro- duces meaning. Hyperbole creates a "temporal reality" whose play of quanti- ties dissolves when we realize its content's fictiveness. The work ("l'œuvre littéraire"), on the contrary, qualitatively confuses the real and the fictive in an a priori manner, and thus for Gans is the true object of hermeneutics. In the course of reading the work, unlike in the interpretation of hyperbole, one does not return to the "real" to determine the "exact [*juste*] value of literary dis- course."[26] Instead, the work, like irony, provides its own referent even if its meaning ("sens") remains ungraspable. Hyperbole thus becomes a kind of realism opposed to irony's subjectivity. Yet for all this schema's structuralist clarity, I would show in the course of this book that it rarely obtains in the Baroque, where often the very motive of the hyperbolist is to disrupt the reader's "bons sens" and to confuse discursive boundaries, where language and figura- tion are highly self-referential, and where the referent often concerns the mar- velous and the supernatural.

Laurent Perrin reads irony and hyperbole as figures that make subtle dis- cursive claims about reality: irony cannot be reduced to mere "antiphrase," while the semantic excess produced by hyperbole requires exacting hermeneu- tic labor.[27] The interpreter of both tropes relies on the principle of pertinence, a principle grounded in the notion of shared cultural experiences, to select what "effects" are intended. In distinguishing though between the two tropes, Perrin dramatically expands the usual equation that makes hyperbole's play with quantities the basis for its qualitative meaning, such that it now applies

to all the other tropes save one: "In fact, every non-ironic tropological statement [*énonce*] is fundamentally hyperbolic . . . every qualitative deformation
with a metaphoric or metonymic aim harbors a quantitative deformation of
reality."[28] Creating in this way an absolute antithesis between hyperbolic and
ironic tropes, Perrin insists that the former aims at communication even if it is
momentarily illocutionary, while the latter frustrates communication and underscores the impossibility of communication. Irony is "irreparable," whereas
hyperbole creates only a "temporary, transitory" disruption between expression and communication.[29] The hyperbolist uses the disruption of literal sense
to communicate what could not have been otherwise communicated; he persists in wanting the reader to believe an extraordinary "idée."

But what if the violence caused by the initial "détour" cannot be healed?
Perrin appears to take for granted that the context in which the enunciation is
made can always be made to provide the information needed to reconcile the
illocutionary aspects of hyperbole with locutionary ones. When the hyperbolist relies on a context that is obscure, unstable, or self-reflexive, then, as I
shall show in this book's close readings, hyperbole may verge on irony and
paradox. In other words, the interpretative task is greatly complicated in those
literary and philosophic contexts that prize open-ended heuresis (discovery
and invention) over communication. Furthermore, like much of Baroque literature, and like the Longinian sublime, hyperbole does not always aim to
persuade.[30] Sometimes it would astonish or create other emotional or cognitive effects. Sometimes the hyperbolist cultivates lasting ambiguity. To assert
"only an unfortunate [*malheureuse*] hyperbole can be confused with an irony"
is to deny Montaigne, Donne, and Quevedo one of their principal rhetorical
weapons.[31] Like Romantic irony as described by Friedrich Schlegel (and later
revisited by Paul de Man), Baroque hyperbole often explores subjective limits
of representation in the face of the infinite. It tends to seize upon those immeasurable objective referents that cosmography and history supply, and that
induced a widespread sense of cultural and epistemological crisis in the
Baroque.

Because of these rhetorical and semantic qualities, the hyperboles in this
book should induce us to rethink the nature of taste and aesthetic judgment.
The disjunction between what hyperbole does — flirt with the irrational, the
tasteless, the affected — and what most literary criticism has tried to do —
establish rational, tasteful, natural criteria for making aesthetic judgments —
should give pause to anyone who would make taste the principal judge of the

hyperbolic. As Samuel Johnson's critique of the English metaphysical poets in the "Life of Cowley" confirms, taste can form the central obstacle to an ap⁄ preciation of hyperboles, even if they belong to a poet such as Donne whom the critic otherwise admires. Likewise, it is a curious atavism in contemporary literary criticism that the objections offered by the dictates of taste continue to pervert readings of hyperbole.[32]

Johnson's assertion that "what [the metaphysical poets] wanted . . . of the sublime they endeavored to supply by hyperbole" spurs another task of this book: namely, to read the hyperbolic with and against the sublime.[33] The hy⁄ perbolist does a trapeze act without a net, now flying upward to great heights, now hurtling ignominiously downward toward the ridiculous. As Longinus advises those thirsting for the sublime, the hyperbolist frequently draws on ex⁄ traordinary emotion to excuse his rhetoric; he, too, sublimates enormous quantities into wonderful qualities and affects. Alternately, the hyperbolist de⁄ lights in mapping the liminal space where the claims of science yield to the power of myth. While Longinus describes Plato or the author of Genesis as sublimely representing the greatest phenomena of nature, many early modern writers exploit the discoveries described by explorers and astronomers to fash⁄ ion what Frank Lestringant dubs "cosmographical hyperbole."[34] For others, like Pascal, such objective hyperbole is literarily too much and yet not enough. Signaling the failure of signs and *scientia*, it is made to turn against, decon⁄ struct itself; and, in the process, physical space yields to metaphysical space.

Hyperbolic amplification proves a means of exhausting or mocking re⁄ ceived ideas, including the idea(l) of decorum. An ethical as well as a rhetor⁄ ical concept, decorum is anchored in the notion of proportionality. And when, for example, Rabelais attacks decorum in his famous catalogue of the myriad ways to wipe one's ass, hyperbolic *copia* becomes a centrifugal vehicle for ex⁄ ploring one's being⁄in⁄the⁄world. In his study of the carnivalesque in Rabelais, Mikhail Bakhtin theorizes this remarkable species of hyperbole. Powered by the "material body principle" whereby individual bodily functions, especially digestive ones, are made public, a "banquet for all the world," "positive hy⁄ perbolism" is a complex aesthetic phenomenon. To explicate this hyperbolism, Bakhtin examines the "deep ambivalence of the grotesque," which precludes making the satiric its "essential attribute."[35] He explains:

> A grotesque world in which only the inappropriate is exaggerated is only quantitatively large, but qualitatively it is extremely poor, colorless,

and far from gay . . . What would such a world have in common with Rabelais' merry and rich universe? Satire alone would not suffice to ex plain even the positive pathos of the quantitative exaggeration, not to speak of its qualitative wealth.[36]

To remedy this, Bakhtin asserts the ontological, even cosmological value of the grotesque; the grotesque is a form of "becoming" that erases distinctions between "objects and phenomena," between the individual body and "the whole."[37] Fueled by hyperbole, the grotesque mode has universalist aspira tions, even as it would rewrite the macrocosmic/microcosmic analogy in de cidedly ludic, material terms:

> . . . the grotesque body is cosmic and universal . . . It reflects the cosmic hierarchy. This body can merge with various natural phenomena, with mountains, rivers, seas, islands, and continents. It can fill the entire uni verse . . . We must take into consideration the importance of cosmic ter ror, the fear of the immeasurable, the infinitely powerful . . . In the sphere of imagery cosmic fear (as any other fear) is defeated by laughter. Therefore dung and urine, as cosmic matter that can be interpreted bod ily, play an important part in these images. They appear in hyperbolic quantities and cosmic dimensions. Cosmic catastrophe represented in the material bodily lower stratum is degraded, humanized, and trans formed into grotesque monsters. Terror is conquered by laughter.[38]

Laughter at "hyperbolic quantities" assuages metaphysical dread, though at the cost of traditional notions of literary genre and decorum. Bakhtin acknowledges, however, that Rabelais may be exceptional in this regard. Thus with Francisco de Quevedo, Rabelais's closest Baroque counterpart in the cultivation of the grotesque, such "hyperbolic qualities" often serve more reactionary than lib eratory ends. Quevedo's satiric epideixis rarely yields redemptive laughter; in stead, his extravagant mockery skewers hypocrisy and the poet's own follies. Those burlesque moments in which he seems to be pursing purely ludic or aesthetic ends are subsumed by the larger, ethical effort to create a certain dis illusioned wisdom (*sapientia*) or melancholy in the reader. As we shall see, such extreme disillusionment (*desengaño*) riddles much of Spanish Baroque culture.

In the nineteenth century, Pierre Fontanier observes that hyperbole may "augmente ou diminue les choses avec excès . . ."[39] Fontanier, who copies, comments on, and supplements Dumarsais, is instrumental in the recent structuralist approaches to hyperbole of Gans, Perrin, and Genette. Fontanier also corrects Dumarsais' improbable insistence that hyperbole is alien to French writing, as he folds hyperbole into his larger argument that catachresis underlies all tropological acts. Given pride of place in his treatise, hyperbole steps in where metaphor and other tropes fear to tread. That the hyperbolist overshoots his mark indicates a necessary failure.

A nother reader of Fontanier, Jacques Derrida, deepens this claim in his essay on philosophic metaphor, "White Mythology," which in its final pages also reveals itself to be an essay on philosophic hyperbole. In other words, the logic of the *supplément* in Derrida's thinking may be said to depend on the Enlightenment logic of catachresis. In *Of Grammatology*, Derrida initially defines the *supplément* as what writing adds to speech. But then he adds: "Writing is dangerous from the moment that representation there claims to be presence and the sign of the thing itself."[40] Echoing diagnoses that we will see of Baroque epistemological crises, Derrida links the origin of this supplement to the perception of disorder in or unavailability of nature: "When Nature, as selfproximity, comes to be forbidden or interrupted, when speech fails to protect presence, writing becomes necessary. It must *be added* to the word urgently."[41] The supplement is thus phenomenological as well as linguistic. It signals both an addition and a lack. First, it points to an originary, natural being:

> The supplement adds itself, it is a surplus, a plenitude enriching another plenitude, the *fullest measure* of presence. It cumulates and accumulates presence. It is thus that art, *technè*, image, convention, etc., come as supplements to nature and are rich with this entire cumulating function.[42]

But in the next breath it marks the place where nonbeing haunts:

> . . . the supplement supplements. It adds only to replace. It intervenes or insinuates itself *intheplaceof*; if it fills, it is as if one fills a void. If it represents and makes an image, it is by the anterior default of a presence . . . As substitute, it is not simply added to the positivity of presence, it produces no relief, its place is assigned in the structure by the mark of emptiness. Somewhere, something can be filled up *of itself*, can accomplish itself, only by allowing itself to be filled through sign and proxy. The sign is always the supplement of the thing itself.[43]

Terminology aside, Derrida describes here a familiar dialectic to those versed in the early-modern debates concerning the proper balance between *natura* and *ars*. Nature is presence but presence ruined by original sin and thus in need of the remedies supplied by art. The most extreme remedy that Baroque dis-course provides to this fallen condition comes, I would argue, in the form of literary and philosophical hyperbole. Such hyperbole institutes a metaphysics of presence and absence in which the gap between signifier and signified is manneristically decreased and increased. What Derrida calls the "economy of *différance*" manifests itself in the now ludic, now pathetic, dialectics of ex-cess and dearth fostered by the hyperbolic conceit and discursive *copia*. Or, as I shall argue in my reading of Descartes' hyperbolic skepticism, his ex-haustion of the verisimilar is an exercise in *amplificatio*, where the intended re-sult is decidedly centripetal, that is, toward the construction of an absolutist *cogito*.

Early modern Spanish has its own version of the *supplément* in the seman-tic tension between the verbs *carecer* (to lack) and *encarecer* (to exaggerate). Gracián in his theory of witty exaggeration (*encarecimiento*) endows the hyper-bolic conceit with transcendent powers while underscoring its dangerously close affinity with paradox. But if the motto of the Spanish Baroque hyper-bolist is, as I shall suggest, *plus ultra* [yet farther], this, like the Senecan "satis non est," also vehemently insists on *realia* outside of the text.[44] In the context of his reading of Rousseau, Derrida can plausibly assert that "there has never been anything but writing"; similarly, the modes of poetic imitation that Thomas Greene, for instance, so ably traces in *The Light in Troy*, confirm just how inbred, how intertextual, late Renaissance texts can be. Yet however much it participates in the dynamics of literary imitation, hyperbole consis-tently proves, to appropriate another Derridean term, "exorbitant."[45] Its suc-cess with readers depends on the existence or perceived existence of a *res* beyond the mere play of signifiers. In this sense, it is contingent like most rhet-oric on its ties with what Husserl and Blumenberg call the "lifeworld," with a community of readers, and with a shared ethics of decorum. But contin-gency, I shall argue, may also mean the need of a lyric poet to please a patron, the plight of a philosopher in a stove-heated room, or the travails of a mystic responding to the new cosmography. It includes the experience of subjective voices trying to give objective form to extraordinary perceptions. Hyperbole's metaphysical "raisons" are grounded in this crux, which can be described as an inability to be content with what Renaissance theologians call *accommodation*,

or, conversely, as a dissatisfaction with the necessary but vain attempt to accumulate language and thoughts to represent the ineffable. The hyperbolist flirts
with apophasis (an ironic surrender of language), but then tends to veer
toward cataphasis (the embrace of all of language's resources). As I contend
in my reading of Pascal and Wittgenstein below, this dual temptation is one
of the hyperbolist's primary fates.

IV

In the book that first made the Baroque a viable concept for historians of
thought and style, Heinrich Wölfflin's *Renaissance and Baroque* (1888), an entry
by Quatremère de Quincy from the *Encyclopédie méthodique* (1788) is quoted to
confirm the degree to which taste can forestall analysis: ". . . baroque, adjectif
en architecture, est une nuance du bizarre. Il en est, si on veut, le raffinement,
où s'il était possible de le dire, l'abus . . . il en est le superlatif. L'idée du baroque
entraîne avec soi celle du ridicule poussée à l'excès."[46] Wölfflin started the rebellion against such summary judgments, but the revolution in taste, or, better yet, the effort to obviate the dictates of taste, has been accomplished by the
likes of Strich, Benjamin, Alonso, Rousset, Wellek, and, more recently, Barner,
Maravall, Deleuze, and Buci-Glucksmann. Thus while the Baroque style no
longer needs to be defended, inexplicably, given the still vibrant specter of
such of "excès," no full-scale defense has been made of the Baroque's most
baroque figure. This book tries to remedy that lack.

By forcing readers to waver between credulity and incredulity, Baroque
hyperbole points to its own artifice and rhetoricality. Its frequent effect is akin
to what Emanuele Tesauro, in his treatise on poetic wit, *The Aristotelian Telescope* (1654), describes as the cognitive experience of surprise, delight, and
disappointment when interpreting the conceit (*concetto*). Exemplifying this experience, are these lines from "A Pastoral Courtship" by Thomas Randolph
(1605–1635):

> Blush you at this, pretty one stay,
> And I will take that kisse away.
> Thus with a second, and that too
> A third wipes of [f]; so will we goe
> To numbers that the starrs out run,
> And all the Atoms in the Sun.[47]

An imitation and inversion of Catullus V ("Vivamus, mea Lesbia") by way of some three hundred years of Petrarchism and a renewed appetite for the Lucretian notion of an infinite universe comprised of infinitesimal atoms, Randolph's hyperbole, like many cultivated by Labé, Donne, Quevedo, and other belated Petrarchists, wavers between self-mockery and earnest epideixis. Its quantities strain to bridge the gap between microcosm and macrocosm and thereby leave the reader wavering indefinitely between laughter, admiration, and scorn.

When Quintilian in his discussion of hyperbole asserts that it is prefer-able to produce an "excess" of language than a dearth when one has to speak about incredible things, he anticipates the same tension between words and things that Erasmus, Bacon, and others inscribe at the center of early modern debates about signification.[48] Moreover, rhetoric that makes claims about the extraordinary nature of things in late Renaissance science and philoso-phy, whether it belongs to Copernicus, Descartes, or Athanasius Kircher, thoroughly relies on verbal ornament to foster and condition belief. Alter-nately, while the principal themes and experiences figured by the period's hyperbolists — such as doubt, change, decentering, inconstancy, vertigo, the void, infinity, and revelation — are often frankly thaumaturgical, hyperbolists also question and subvert inherited ideals such as Petrarchan love, imperial glory, and humanist learning. Cast by most Renaissance theorists as ethically suspect, the "overreacher," as Levin's 1952 study of Marlowe showed, can be the means of evoking complex moral sentiments. Likewise, if the verse of Mar-vell, Quevedo, Gryphius, Marino, or Saint-Amant corresponds to a historical moment when crisis and change are the norm, then hyperbole is one of the most acute and persuasive ways poets possess of responding to this turmoil.

In still broader terms, Baroque hyperbole helps goad as well as represent the dissolution of the analogical worldview. Surprisingly heuristic, hyper-boles may be read as seismic markers that help chart the early modern "rup-ture" between what Foucault calls an *epistēmē* of resemblance and one of measure, identity, and difference.[49] This shift from a sixteenth-century uni-verse experienced and interpreted through analogy and other figures of re-semblance, to a late seventeenth-century cosmos in which language becomes increasingly "transparent" and ontologically suspect, is filled with "ruptures" that clearly call for hyperbole.[50] And while it may seem intuitively obvious that hyperbole is a figure well-suited for epochs when realism and other aesthetics grounded in a perception of order, proportionality, and continuity no longer satisfy, the causality of this relation should not be taken for granted. Instead, as I hope my close readings of texts in this book demonstrate, hyperbole may well breed the very disorder it would represent. Furthermore, by offering the extravagant Don Quixote, a "man alienated in analogy," as a symbol of this change, Foucault implicitly points not only to the plight of the Baroque hy-perbolist, but also to that of the scholar of Baroque hyperboles.[51] When or whether to make windmills into giants, ornament into invention, or rhetoric into philosophy, is a challenge frequently faced in the pages of this book.

Just as it is fiendishly difficult to write about metaphor without resorting to metaphor, a study of hyperbole, especially of its more discursive forms, risks the logical and stylistic faults of becoming hyperbolic or, more precisely, excessive. In the late Renaissance, poetic *copia* frequently generates exegetical *copia*; but a latecomer intent on making the complex workings of hyperbole transparent, has four additional centuries of critical opprobrium through which to sift. My decision to read some of the most canonical Baroque texts for their hyperboles — the idea being that if the hyperbolic in *Lear*, the *Soledad primera*, or the *Meditations* could be shown to be an object worthy of inquiry, then by metonymy the rhetoric of the whole period might be reassessed — inevitably engages another bevy of critical voices. Etymologically, to exem-plify is to extract an idea from a given amplitude, to take a part from a whole. But just as the hyperbolist delights in blurring discursive and disciplinary boundaries, *exempla* of hyperbole tend to grow conceptually larger upon ex-amination. In this sense, hyperbole proves a kind of Wittgensteinian "lan-guage game," a "form of life" resisting paraphrase and so requiring multiple, shifting perspectives.

From Homer to García Márquez, hyperbolists have hyperbolized their antecedents. But what Curtius defines as the dynamics of *Überbietung* (outdo-ing) becomes especially crucial to the process of literary *imitatio* in epochs like early imperial Rome, Carolingian France, late Renaissance Europe, and, ar-guably our own, when classical (or modernist) currents appear to have run their course and thus have ceded to more mannered, ironic, and fantastic forms of representation.[52] It is this book's contention, then, that at their most sophisticated, literary hyperbolists give expression to this historical conscious-ness and signal to readers how and where to situate themselves as they under-take interpretation.

After three initial chapters in which I mine classical, Renaissance, and

Baroque rhetorics and poetics for views on hyperbole, chapters four through eight explore how the extravagant poetics of Petrarchism is remade with self-conscious urgency and irony in the Spanish Baroque by Góngora, Quevedo, and Sor Juana. For in a dynamic already adumbrated by Quintilian, Aristotle, and the poets that exemplify their rhetorical ideals, Petrarchist rhetoric vividly underscores the ways in which the hyperboles of predecessors are at once necessary and insufficient. Then, prompted in part by Stanley Cavell's ordinary language criticism, I turn in chapters nine to eleven to a reading of hyperbole in Shakespearean drama in the light of Cartesian skepticism. I also consider here how hyperbole functions in Senecan drama in order better to examine how this aspect of the Senecan legacy is refashioned in *King Lear* where *superiectio* and *superbia* (pride) converge to produce a spectacle of rhetorical excess made all the more jarring by a dearth of any obvious metaphysical meaning. Chapters twelve through fifteen are dedicated to a critique of philosophical hyperbole as practiced by Descartes against the backdrop of the rhetorical tradition and Neo-Skepticism, and then by Pascal who hyperbolizes, on the one hand, in the light of Descartes's enormous claims on behalf of his own reason and, on the other, in the shadow of the language and gestures of negative theology. Finally, the last chapter contemplates how the kindred philosophies of Cavell and Wittgenstein condemn hyperbolic absolutism in the wake of the Kantian sublime. Ironically, their critiques of hyperbolic reason prove immensely illuminating, for in describing the cardinals dangers of the hyperbolic they linger in their encounter with it and thereby ascribe to it subtleties and pitfalls that its friends sometimes take for granted. This is partly the reason for my unorthodox reading in the book's last chapter of Wittgenstein as a philosopher of the hyperbolic despite his avowed distaste for the language of the "frozen sublime." Again, because at its most dynamic hyperbole can be quite dialogic, it is critical to give space to voices like those of Aristotle, Samuel Johnson, and Nicolas Boileau who would proscribe or tame the excess of the hyperbolist. Ultimately, though, it turns out that hyperbolists themselves often perform this critique most forcefully. Shakespeare gives the hypebolic Lear the skeptical Fool and Kent to teach his audience to "see better"; Cervantes has the phlegmatic Sancho accompany Quixote and his credulous vision; Pascal makes Descartes's *cogito* the starting point for his own hyperbolic journey of faith. While Burton, in tirelessly amplifying his melancholy, figures his readers as the final arbiters of why "it is impossible not in so much to overshoot."

Chapter One

Classical Theories of Hyperbole

O lucrum ingens, o insperatum gaudium!
— Leonardo Bruni, in a 1416 letter to Poggio Bracciolini
after the latter discovered a complete manuscript
of the *Institutio oratoria.*

STYLE AND DECORUM

In Revolutionary France, the *Garde nationale* had engraved on their sabres a line by Lucan: "datos, ne quisquam serviat, enses" [*swords are given, lest any man be a slave*].[1] Borrowed from one of the poet's many fine hyperboles against tyranny, this ornamental inscription points to a fundamental truth about the persuasive power of language. Oratory without eloquence, Quintilian observes, is as worthless "as a sword that is put up and will not come out of its scabbard."[2] In 1549 Joachim Du Bellay refashions the same image in his *Deffence et illustration de la langue françoyse* to champion the style of the Pléiade: "Mais quant à l'élocution ... sans laquelle toutes autres choses restent comme inutiles et semblables à un glaive encore couvert de sa gaine ... [*But as for style ... without which all other things remain as if useless and like a sword still covered by its sheath ...*]."[3] And while this axiom about style's preeminence has proven an enduring one, so has its corollary: a politician, poet, or philosopher who would master the ornaments of style is always in danger of unintentionally falling upon his sword. How Alciato describes Ajax's fury, in the emblem *Insani gladius*, applies exactly to the unwary stylist: "errat ab ictu | consiliique impos in sua damna ruit" [*his stroke errs | and, without deliberation, he rushes to his ruin*].[4]

Never is this cautionary tale more apt than when it comes to hyperbole. Of all the questions addressed by classical and Renaissance theorists of rhe/ torical ornament, none is more complicated or contentious than how to use hyperbole. The virtues and vices ascribed to hyperbole epitomize the difficulty of finding a proper style. While style (*elocutio*), more than invention, arrange/ ment, delivery, or memory is that element in every oration that most severely tests a speaker's talent, skill, and character (*ethos*). Conversely, the trickiest task of the *doctor*, as Quintilian dubs the theorist and teacher of rhetoric (10.1.15), is to make aesthetic and ethical judgments about an oration's force, clarity, and tastefulness. But how does one judge what style is most effective, tasteful, or moving in a speech or a poem? Since rhetoric attends to circum/ stance (*kairos*) much more than any other liberal art, how is it possible to es/ tablish fixed or objective standards of judgment? Which ornaments are to be used, and in what circumstances and given which subjects? How much li/ cense should nature (or natural talent) have and how much recourse should there be to art(ifice)? More specifically still, if the creation of a persuasive metaphor or stirring hyperbole depends more on natural ability than any teachable precept, is not one reduced to pointing to the ineffable when trying to objectify a decorous, persuasive style?

Attempting to answer such questions, the *doctores* try to put the question of *elocutio* on firmer footing. All agree that a style must possess, in one form or another, what the Greeks term *to prepon* (the seemly), or what the Romans call *proprietas* (propriety). Each theorist tries to establish through precepts and ex/ amples what such decorum might be. Many would also deduce general rules on the "proper" relation between style and subject matter. Yet notwithstand/ ing these myriad, valiant efforts, the concept of decorum, that quintessential stylistic virtue, dubbed by Milton "the grand masterpiece to observe," has re/ mained necessarily vague and elusive.[5] For if rhetoric is to respond to the va/ garies of human affairs, style must reflect this mutability. More to the point, when the subject or circumstances of a speech concerns the extraordinary, out/ rageous, sublime, or pathetic, the stylist tries to mirror and represent this ex/ ceptionality. As a result the principle of decorum will often seem strained if not entirely broken as the orator or poet resorts to excessive stylistic means to signify what he sees, feels, or thinks.

Nonetheless, I wish to argue that the principle of decorum — even if it turns out to be a rather paradoxical kind of decorum — still shapes the species of rhetorical excess that I shall group within the genus *hyperbole*. Indeed, only by first examining the crucial concept of decorum can the *affectus*, the reception, of hyperbole be gauged. An understanding of decorum, in turn, depends on appreciating the complexities of the rhetorical enterprise, which I take to be an immanently humanist response to the exigencies of the world and other people. Homer and Góngora do not nod when they hyperbolize, but rather are making extraordinary claims to rhetorically savvy readers as to how things are or seem. And yet Hamlet's promise before he goes to speak to his mother in her chambers also suggests the difficulties the hyperbolist faces in realizing his intentions: "I will speak daggers to her but use none."

From Greek antiquity through the European Baroque, the making and interpreting of poetry (by this I mean all literary arts) is rooted in the rhetorical tradition. All the poets discussed in this book studied rhetoric; their poems and the poetry they read depend on the techniques of invention and ornamentation, the theory of styles, as well as the notions of furnishing proof and creating *affectus* taught in the rhetorical handbooks. This is not to say, however, that the validity of this wholesale transference goes unchallenged. Quintilian and Cicero repeatedly stress that what is appropriate for the poet may be inappropriate for the orator. While the bolder stylistic devices are often denied the orator, in practice, theorists of rhetoric often muddle or ignore the question of what is proper to each *ars*. Sometimes also they consciously conflate the rules for different discourses. George Kennedy describes this conflation when he discusses *letteraturizzazione* or " . . . the tendency of rhetoric to shift its focus from persuasion to narration, from civic to personal contexts, and from discourse to literature, including poetry. Such slippage can be observed in the Hellenistic period, in the Roman Empire, in medieval France, and in the sixteenth and eighteenth centuries throughout Europe."[6]

This "slippage" explains why the prescriptions of Quintilian or Erasmus can help illuminate the poetry of Lucan or Sor Juana, or even the discourse of Descartes. But it is also the hallmark of much modern, structuralist, and post-structuralist literary scholarship, which wittingly or not relies on oral rhetoric's legacy to analyze literary texts. *Letteraturizzazione* runs like Ariadne's thread through the labyrinthine turns in twentieth-century criticism: from the philological comparatism of Spitzer, Auerbach, and Curtius, through the New Criticism of Empson, Richards, and Brooks, the structuralism of Jakobson and Genette, the deconstruction of de Man and Derrida, up to the avowedly neo⁄rhetorical criticism of Fumaroli, Plett, and Vickers. It is essential, then, to keep an eye on this thread as the threats against decorum and taste posed by that minotaur of tropes, hyperbole, are encoun⁄ tered. Only in this way will it become evident why a certain species of hostile critical excess, one blind to the extent to which rhetorical, poetic, and philo⁄ sophical concerns can be interwoven, invariably accompanies the most daring forms of poetic and conceptual excess.

Style is the element in the art (*technē*) of persuasion most amenable to individual expression. It is also the aspect most susceptible to historical and social forces. Not only may a Gorgias, Cicero, Corneille, or Martin Luther King Jr. set an example that those with less genius and originality may fol⁄ low, but circumstance — a war, the discovery of a "new" world, a tyrant's whims — may help determine what constitutes decorous eloquence in a par⁄ ticular time and place. Alternately, changes in style may also be ascribed to in⁄ ternal, formalist dynamics, that is, to the cycles of innovation, perfection, and exhaustion evident in most literary traditions. Livy and Lucretius struggle to forge novel means of expression in Latin out of the Hellenic legacy; Augus⁄ tan orators and poets aim at *mediocritas* and clarity of expression, while their Neoteric and Imperial successors prize more elaborate, enigmatic forms of ornamentation; Petrarch's fourteenth⁄century vernacular verse gives rise to a tribe of imitators who, in subsequent centuries, turn to increasingly manner⁄ ist means to renovate and exhaust their model's imagery.

As for interpretation and reception, because most poetics from antiquity to the Baroque are prescriptive (rather than analytic), the question of a proper style often seems inseparable from what beginning in the Enlightenment will be framed as the question of taste. It is of course true that each age and culture acquires its own particular notions of what constitutes good taste; yet when it concerns rhetoric, judgments of taste are also contingent on the perception of how a speech corresponds to character and circumstance. In one of his epis⁄ tles to Lucilius, Seneca compares the well⁄regulated mind with a king, and a "cupidus" [*greedy*] mind lacking in self⁄control with a tyrant. By adapting this venerable Stoic conceit, he is reminding his correspondent that any crite⁄ ria for a decorous style must include the orator's character (*animus*), or what Aristotle dubs his *ethos*. To sharpen this ethical point, he offers this striking analogy between an excessive love of rhetorical ornament and an overindul⁄ gence of food:

Look at our kitchens and our cooks milling around so many fires: can
you believe that all that bustle is to prepare food for just one stomach?
Look at our wine — cellars and our barns full of the grape — harvests
of many generations: can you believe that wines of so many vintages are
stored for just one stomach? Look at all the estates where the land is being tilled, the thousands of farmers who are plowing and digging: can
you believe that both Sicily and Africa are being cultivated for just one
stomach [*unum videri putas ventrum cui et in Sicilia et in Africa servitur*]? We
shall recover our senses and moderate our desires if each man assesses
himself and measures his body, realizing that he cannot hold much or
hold it for long.[7]

Fusing the Stoic ethic of moderation and the virtues of a moderate *elocutio*,
Seneca ironically hyperbolizes the taste for stylistic excess. But besides confirming the power of hyperbole as an ethical scourge and potential form of
amplification, Seneca's culinary-digestive metaphorics suggests the difficulties of establishing objective criteria for taste. Not accidentally, Kant will try
to solve this same crux in his critical philosophy as he mediates between the
claims of reason and the pull of the senses. For to make judgments about
whether an aesthetic object (be it an oration or an ocean) is beautiful, jejune,
trivial, or sublime is to create a conflict or "antinomy" between what pleases
or displeases the individual and what is perceived as a universal principle of
taste.[8] In other words, the difficulties of fixing notions of propriety and decorum belong as well to the perennial philosophical task of extracting the unity
of abstract truth out of empirical, phenomenological multiplicity. While the
idea that subject matter and style must somehow be proportionate seems fairly
fixed throughout the history of rhetoric, judgments about what is proportionate or measured are as varied as the objects judged. Such undulations are still
more extreme in the history of poetic taste. Horace, in the beginning of the
Ars poetica chides the laughable monstrosities produced by poets who abandon the mean, while in the next generation, Ovid makes such *monstra* the subject of his belated epic. Similarly, throughout early modernity partisans of
differing vernacular styles make caricatures out of Homer and Virgil in the
attempt to forge tastes and expectations.

Meanwhile, like anthropologists fetishizing the traits of an exotic culture,
theorists of rhetoric have long tried to account for the uncanny attraction that
poetry's bolder, more florid styles exert on aspiring orators, even as they have

insisted on irredeemable differences between the two discourses. Aristotle per-force makes the *Rhetoric* overlap with the *Poetics* on questions of style, though it is frequently unclear in the former to what extent his prescriptions might apply to poets.[9] To illustrate insights on the orator's proper style, the *Rhetoric* borrows numerous passages from Homer; almost all Roman, medieval, and Renaissance *doctores* engage in similar larceny. Most *rhetors*, moreover, adopt a far more haphazard approach to poetics than Aristotle. While Quintilian and Cicero urge prospective orators to read the poets for lessons in invention, and while poets are recommended for their ability to delight an audience with their stories (*narrationes*), often in the next breath their abuse of credulity is blamed.[10] Poets are lauded for their skillful use of figures like metaphor, metonymy, hyperbaton, anaphora, and hyperbole. Yet just as frequently re-straint is urged in the use of such ornaments.[11] Quintilian's practice of citing Virgil, Cicero, Ovid, Homer, and a host of other Greek and Roman writers to illustrate now a perspicacious, now a faulty style transforms the *Institutio* into an intertextual cornucopia, even as he ironically cautions in light of con-temporary tastes: "We borrow figures or metaphors from the most decadent [*a corruptissimo*] of poets, and take it that the unique sign of genius is needing a genius to understand us [*tum demum ingeniosi scilicet si ad intellegendos nos opus sit ingenio*] (8.Pr.25).[12] Orators who are too "poetic" risk being considered frigid, bombastic, or even "insane."[13] Hermeneutic difficulty should be shunned. Thus the pragmatic Quintilian advises:

> . . . let us remember that the orator should not follow the poet in everything — neither in his freedom of vocabulary, nor in his license to develop figures . . . [poetry] aims exclusively for pleasure and pursues this by inventing things that are not only untrue but also unbelievable [*eamque fingendo non falsa modo sed etiam quaedam incredibilia sectatur*] . . . (10.1.28)

This warning about poetry's falsity and ability to represent the incredible implicitly shapes, as we shall see, his treatment of hyperbole. Alternately, this ambivalence on the part of the *rhetors* toward poetic ornament confirms the undeveloped state of poetics — poetry could thus be freely ransacked — as well as the need to account for all forms of rhetoric no matter how extreme. Dismissing with one hand the excesses of poets, with the other more practical hand, the theorists pick their pockets. Aristotle, Cicero, and Quintilian quote so often and copiously from poets and dramatists that one wonders at times whether they are trying to train orators in poetic decorum or make poets conform to rhetorical decorum.

The use of poetry to exemplify oratory belongs to the more general attempt to develop an objective yardstick to gauge the line between rhetorical decorum and poetic excess. To this end, Aristotle introduces the key notion of *to prepon*.[14] Theophrastus offers his influential theory of the three styles.[15] Cicero treads a middle path between Asianism and Atticism by promoting *claritas*. And Quintilian champions an ethical *perspicuitas*. Yet each shuttles between oratory and poetry for their paradigms of decorous eloquence. While this is partially because verse is more memorable than prose and so more pedagogically useful, as a kind of mean, decorum is best illustrated by the juxtaposition of the most ingenious and atrocious examples. To arrive at a notion of decorum (or taste), the negative and the extreme are necessary starting points. Decorum is a dialectical concept; and as Walter Benjamin insists in his study of German Baroque drama: "Vom Extremen geht der Begriff aus" [*From extremity the concept emerges*].[16]

But decorum is also an aesthetic and ethical concept. It consists in attuning style with the nature of the subject matter, the circumstances of the speech, and the character of the speaker and audience. All the virtues of style — such as clarity, vividness, correctness, and variety — contribute to decorum. Aesthetically, decorum appeals to the notions of harmony and proportion.[17] Style must correspond with subject matter. When discussing the nature of the gods, elevated diction and sophisticated figures of thought should be used. A decorous speaker in the courtroom shows good judgment and inspires trust by avoiding excessive artifice. As Aristotle observes throughout the *Rhetoric*, the orator must not imperil his *ethos* by adopting a style incommensurate with his age, position, or audience. A venerable senator ought not engage in lighthearted satire or use overly impassioned language. A crowd in the marketplace should not be wooed with learned allusions.

CICERO'S COSMOS

An unapologetic champion of rhetoric's supremacy over the other *artes*, Cicero lauds the art of persuasion as the culmination of all human endeavors. Adumbrating in *De oratore* (55 BCE) the "incredible vastness and difficulty" of oratory [*rei quamdam incredibilem magnitudinem, ac difficultatem*] (1.16–17), he urges orators to acquire a broad education in the sciences and arts.[18] This lofty

epistemological ideal will inspire Quintilian's encyclopedic efforts, Augustine's assimilation of the classical legacy into Christian hermeneutics, and
most importantly for our purposes, become an engine of Renaissance humanism.[19] Even so, Ernesto Grassi notes that Cicero's ideal is also thoroughly
pragmatic, as it would make knowledge available to an orator's *usus* whenever
it might be needed.[20] Cicero, that is, would reanimate Isocrates' failed attempt
to reunite philosophy and rhetoric in the wake of Plato's attacks against the
latter in the *Gorgias* and *Phaedrus*. As such his *scientia* draws on the Stoics, who
declared rhetoric to be a virtue if the *sapiens* assumes the role of orator.[21] And
while Stoicism also counseled the orator to prize brevity and argue only the
facts without embellishment, in broadening this rather narrow view of the
rhetorical enterprise in his theory and practice, Cicero never abandons its ethical and philosophical concerns.

The orator aspires to the learning of the philosopher, while in other respects the orator and the poet are nearly indistinguishable:

> The truth is that the poet is a very near kinsmen of the orator, rather
> more heavily fettered as regards rhythm, but with ampler freedom in his
> choice of words, while in the use of many sorts of ornament he is his
> ally and almost his counterpart; in one respect at all events something
> like identity exists, since he sets no boundaries or limits to his claims,
> such as would prevent him from ranging whither he will with the same
> freedom and license as the other [*nullis ut terminus circumscribat aut definiat
> ius suum, quo minus ei liceat eadem illa facultate et copia vagari, qua velit*].[22]

This has important implications for the study of hyperbole. For if, as Cicero
suggests, among all the *officia oratoris* rousing the emotions is the highest
achievement, and if mastery of the grand style sets the great orator apart from
the mediocre one, then an oration favoring the grand style, with its copious,
bold use of figures, its impassioned delivery, its straining after enormous affect,
and search for sublimity ("nullis ut terminus circumscribat"), flirts most perilously with the indecorousness associated with hyperbole.[23]

When decorum is lost, however, through excessive or inappropriate use
of ornament, the most grievous stylistic sin occurs: *cacozelia*. A catch-all term,
cacozelia or *affectatio* serves as the very name of stylistic, mannered excess.[24] In
De oratore Cicero blames metaphors that do not appeal to the senses, especially
sight; he chides "dissimilitudo" in metaphorical expressions, such as "the

huge arches of heaven" [*coeli ingentes fornices*] where the arch and the notion of the globe are conceptually at odds; and he discourages especially daring, obscure, and "disfigured" [*deformis*] metaphors — the last clearly pointing to hyperbole, as in "a hurricane of revelry" or, inversely, "the reveling of the hurricane" (3.160–166). Indeed, frequently when Cicero contemplates the hyperbolic there appears the specter of *cacozelia* and the suggestion of the unethical. He pointedly blames, for example, the comic poets for their immoral, exaggerated depiction of the passions in love scenes.[25] Yet when addressing prospective jurists (*Top. 45*), he reluctantly permits the use of "imaginary examples": ". . . in this area orators and philosophers have license to make dumb things talk, to raise dead people from the underworld, to speak of something which cannot possibly happen, in order to magnify or minimize something — this is called hyperbole — and to do many other strange things [*ut aliquid quod fieri nullo modo possit augendae rei gratia dicatur, aut minuendae, quae hyperbole dicitur, multa alia mirabilia*]."[26]

Cicero's conservative stance toward decorum is partially grounded in his cosmology, and his perception of nature's objective, orderly laws. Translating the Greek *cosmos* as *ornatus*, he makes nature the model that orators must follow to achieve utility, dignity, and beauty of style:

> . . . in oratory as in most matters, nature has contrived with incredible skill [*incredibiliter*] that the thing possessing most utility also have the greatest amount of dignity, and, indeed, frequently of beauty also. We observe that for the safety and security of the universe this whole ordered world of nature is so constituted that the sky is a round vault, with the earth at its centre, held stationary by its own force and stress; and that the sun travels around . . . Take the trees: in these the trunk, the branches and lastly the leaves are all without exception designed so as to keep and preserve their own nature, yet nowhere is there any part that is not beautiful . . . The same is the case in regard to all the divisions of a speech [*partibus orationis*] . . . so that a certain agreeableness and charm follow from utility and almost necessity.[27] (3.178–181)

Since nature is beauty's greatest source and the most palpable evidence of divinity, the poet and the orator 'naturally' imitate it in their compositions. Alternately, as readers of Sophocles or Seneca can attest, tumult in the physical universe is usually reflected in the upsetting of the principle of decorum — a mimetic, ontological phenomenon that will acquire new, urgent force in the late Renaissance. In other words, this perception of decorum involves a real analogy between rhetoric and nature. Cicero grounds aesthetic judgments about a speech's decorum in objective principles of harmony and order, principles 'naturally' preferable to those of chaos and disproportionality. With this said, for the Neo-Stoic Cicero, events in or ideas about the physical realm are easily transferred to the ethical realm and vice versa.

As decorum acquires these ontological and mimetic valences, it also becomes synonymous with compromise. The balance between *ars* and *ingenium* is an essential mark of decorum for Cicero. In his own rhetoric he aims to reconcile Atticism, which emphasizes brevity, *ingenium*, and would imitate common, unadorned speech, and Asianism, which encourages elaborate figuration and symmetrical syntax.[28] Decorum, finally, often marches under the Horatian banner of *ars est celare artem*. A speaker, for example, who would seem aggrieved and vengeful, would be indecorous if he painstakingly cultivated ornament. Thus while Cicero regards metaphor as preeminently capable of lending beauty and sublimity to poetry and prose, it is also the greatest potential destroyer of decorum.[29] This ambivalence is increased when hyperbole joins metaphor. Potentially adding novelty, vividness, and force to a speech, the far-fetched claims of hyperbolic metaphor can make the speaker seem indecorous, unnatural, unethical, and irrational.

QUINTILIAN, ORATORY, AND ORNAMENT

Institutio oratoria (88 CE) offers antiquity's most exhaustive treatment of oral and written rhetoric. More even than the *Rhetorica ad Herennium, De inventione, De oratore,* and *Brutus,* the *Institutio* served as the primary source for the teaching of classical rhetoric in the late Renaissance. Owing in part to his cautious temperament and relatively belated historical position, Marcus Fabius Quintilianus offers a fairly dispassionate, objective treatment of the art of persuasion.[30] He is also the first theorist to consider extensively the psychological basis and appeal of many of the tropes and figures. His importance to Renaissance poetics — both in theory and practice — is immense. Poggio discovers a complete *Institutio* in 1416, which spurs its adoption into the humanist curriculum.[31] But Quintilian's influence in the schoolroom waxes with the advent of the anti-Ciceronian movement in the sixteenth and early part of the seventeenth century. In short, the Christian humanism of Erasmus and the subsequent flowering of vernacular literatures would be difficult to conceive without Quintilian. More generally still, in the slow but seemingly inexorable shift from primary to secondary rhetoric — including the emergence of literary criticism as a separate discipline — Quintilian remains a constant and clear presence. Figures as diverse as Geoffrey de Vinsauf, Valla, Erasmus, Montaigne, Agricola, Guzmán, Puttenham, Blair, and in the last century Burke, Frye, and Barthes all claim Quintilian as a guide as they map the convergences of rhetoric and literature (and sometimes philosophy).[32]

Quintilian teaches rhetoric in a time overripe with rhetoric, when poets, such as Statius and Lucan, make their witty hexameters sag with excessive figuration and erudition. By the time Quintilian writes his treatise, the ideal of eloquence married to martial valor — emblemized by Homer's portrayal of Achilles who learns the arts of persuasion and war from Phoinix — already spurs nostalgia.[33] His views on stylistic propriety and Roman literature can thus often seem rather conservative, or even at times somewhat reactionary. Rejecting the Senecan vogue for *sententiae* and extreme *brevitas* bordering on obscurity, Quintilian steers his readers back, at least in questions of style, to prescriptions for a rounder, more balanced style as embodied by Cicero's compromise between Atticism and Asianism.

With his pragmatic approach to rhetoric, Quintilian rejects the influence in imperial Rome of the declamation schools with their penchant for bizarre, exaggerated themes and their love of mannerist, affected styles.[34] History and poetry, especially that of Homer and his epigones, furnished the declaimers with extravagant subjects. Encyclopedic works, such as Valerius Maximus' *Facta ac dicta memorabilia*, likewise supplied recondite materials. In response, Quintilian compares their specious style to the false, effeminate beauties of eunuchs.[35] He urges instead that style "be manly, strong, and chaste. It must not favour effeminate smoothness or the false covering of cosmetics; it must shine with health and vigour" [*virilis et fortis et sanctus sit nec effeminatam levitatem et fuco ementitum colorem amet: sanguine et viribus niteat*] (8.3.67).[36]

Quintilian wrote a now-lost treatise, *De causis corruptae eloquentiae*, to which he alludes repeatedly in the *Institutio*. At the end of his treatment of hyperbole, refusing to amplify further, he thus refers instead to "eo libro, quo causas corruptae eloquentiae reddabamus."[37] Further, that *De causis* reportedly traced the insidious relation between the *declamationes* and the period's many mannerist poets raises the question of how the canon of literary works assembled in Book 10 of the *Institutio* should be read.[38] There Quintilian argues that studying written texts may facilitate the learning of oral rhetoric. Assuming the role of the *grammaticus*, who knows how to write correctly and to judge *poetarum ennarationes*, he carefully chooses which works should serve as proper models, even as he further blurs the lines between the discursive arts (10.1.17).[39] For example, Homer is prescribed for his unsurpassed ability to invest great themes with "sublimity" and to handle small themes with "propriety" (10.1.49). Also recommended are Terence, Lucretius, Horace, and Virgil; but, not surprisingly, Ovid, Lucan, and Seneca are treated less enthusiastically. Made by a pedagogue anxious to shape his young charges' tastes, such criticism epitomizes the conception of rhetoric as a measured, moral activity. Put another way, that Ovid, Lucan, Seneca, and their contemporary Statius, came partly to be renowned for their ingenious hyperboles suggests that artful *superiectio* was assimilated only with great difficulty into the rhetorical enterprise.[40]

Statius in particular shared the declaimers' predilection for seizing upon new, bizarre, or trivial topics and representing them in a difficult, obscure, or exaggerated manner. As a result his epic, epideictic machinery often feels incommensurate with its subject matter. At once witty and absurd, his description of an equestrian statue of Domitian in the *Silvae* (1.1–45), whose sword is "as large as the blade with which Orion threatens and terrifies the winter stars" [*magnus quanto mucrone minatur | noctibus hibernis et sidera terret Orion*], or that of a Malean mountain in the *Thebiad* (2.32–54), whose summit is so tall that it is immune from wind and rain, so that the stars use it as a resting place ("*stat sublimis apex ventosque imbresque serenus | despicit et tantum fessis insiditur astris.*"), provokes both admiration and laughter. One imagines that such hyperboles were read or heard (Statius was a skilled recitator) with scorn by Quintilian.

Is there any room, though, for such self-conscious exaggeration in the *Institutio*'s seminal, if conservative accounts of rhetoric and poetry? More particularly, how might its discussion of hyperbole help us interpret the overreachings of a dramatist like Seneca or that of a Baroque reader of Seneca, like Quevedo? To begin to answer these questions and, more urgently still, to avoid what Genette aptly terms a "rhétorique restreinte," Quintilian's take on the hyperbolic needs to be viewed as belonging to the broad, syncretic, insistently practical vision of rhetoric charted in the *Institutio*.[41] In this way alone can the danger of constructing a Procrustean bed with hyperbole be forstalled. Only then can a theory of hyperbole, and the aesthetic, ethical, and philosophical problems native to it, be properly delineated.

Rhetoric is the art of shaping the whole person. It teaches (male) citizens how to speak and act; it prepares them for lives in the *res publica* — this despite the limited possibilities of applying the Ciceronian ideal in an imperial era. Superficially, Quintilian's model orator, the *vir bonus dicendi peritus*, resembles Plato's ideal at the end of the *Gorgias*, where Socrates urges rhetoric be em-ployed to improve morality and promote justice. Instead of making rhetoric subservient to metaphysics, though, Quintilian is happy to let it serve practi-cal ethics. By defining rhetoric as the *scientia dicendi bene* (8.Pr.6), he shows himself more indebted to the Stoic ethical philosophers, Chrysippus and Cleanthes, than to any Neo-Platonic or Aristotelian vision of eloquence.[42] For him a rhetorical education offers a modest version of *paideia*; it teaches young men how to appropriate their cultural legacy, it forms their taste, and it cultivates moral and civic virtues. The orator is thus superior to the philoso-pher because he is active (1.Pr.10) — a claim that will help shape Renaissance humanism.[43] Surrounded by mannerist excess and determined to combat the reigning opinion that rhetoric had suffered an inalterable decline, Quintilian offers a vigorous, voluminous defense of the art of persuasion.

The exposition of the *Institutio* follows the traditional five-part division of rhetoric into invention, arrangement, style, delivery, and memory. Before focusing though on the question of style in Book 8, Quintilian helpfully reviews the previous seven books on invention and arrangement. First, he re-peats the idea that the *res* of a speech determines whether the deliberative, forensic (juridical), or demonstrative (epideictic) genre should be adopted; for only after this determination is made can the process of invention, or the find-ing and elaboration of arguments, begin. Invention (*stasis*) seeks to answer three questions: "is it? what is it? how is it?" [*sit? quid sit? quale sit?*]. In epideic-tic verse or oratory the answer to the question *quale sit?* involves judgments of quality and quantity. To praise or blame, the orator first must discover and, to some extent at least, understand the extraordinary nature of his subject before he ornaments, let alone exaggerates it (3.7.25).[44] Invention is thus where rhet-oric proves most philosophical, if also sometimes, as we shall see, most hyper-bolic and imaginative.

A speech is arranged into five parts: exordium, narration, proof, refuta-tion, and peroration.[45] Intriguingly, the discussion in Book 6 of the means of awakening emotion (*pathos, adfectus*) begins just after Quintilian has explained that in the peroration (and exordium) the necessary balance between recount-ing facts and awakening emotions may tip toward the latter: ". . . here, if any-where, we are allowed to release the whole flood of our eloquence [*totos eloquentiae aperire fontes licet]* . . . we can use grand and ornate words and thoughts" (6.1.51–52). Poignantly exemplifying this skewed balance is his own proemium to Book 6 where he mourns the death of his son (6.Pr.12). This affecting moment eventually precipitates an attempt to distinguish be/ tween *pathos* and *ethos* — the latter being tentatively defined as the more con/ stant and thus ethical stance adopted by the speaker and communicated to the audience. Like keeping decorum, maintaining *ethos* relies somewhat on dis/ semblance: "The great virtue in expressing it lies in making it seem that every/ thing flows from the nature of the facts and the persons, so that the speaker's character [*mores*] shines through his speech and is somehow recognized" (6.2.13). Echoing Aristotle, Horace, and Cicero, Quintilian then adds that the best *ethos* consists in being truly moved by — rather than just feigning — one's emotions (6.2.26). In this way enough vividness (*enargeia*) is produced such that an audience never begins to suspect the speaker's motives even when his rhetoric may call attention to itself (6.2.32).

Style is "the most difficult part of the whole work" (8.Pr.13). Style dis/ tinguishes a great orator from a capable one, as the former spurns "effeminate" and affected attention to individual words and phrases (8.3.7). By avoiding obscurity, the best stylists give language its maximum significance and econ/ omy. Accordingly, propriety (*proprietas*) and clarity (*perspicuitas*) are the chief stylistic virtues (8.2.22). Virtuous *elocutio* excites admiration in the learned and wins the favor of the masses, since ornament appeals to a universal desire for pleasure (*delectatio*) (8.3.5). In a rare effusive moment, Quintilian cites the exemplary Cicero to highlight the potential *adfectus* of a well/ornamented speech:

> . . . it was the sublimity and the splendour, the elegance and the author/ itative manner that evoked that storm of applause . . . Those present, I suspect, did not know what they were doing, their applause did not come from choice or judgment, they were possessed by a sort of frenzy, lost all sense of where they were, and burst out in that ecstasy of delight [*in hunc voluptatis adfectum*]. (8.3.3–4)

This brief glimpse of the orator as a sublime enthusiast is quickly tempered though by more sober accounts.[46] For every stylistic vice there exists a corre/ sponding virtue (8.3.7). Emphasizing *utilitas* here and throughout, Quintil/ ian insists that the orator adapt to his audience's capacities and his subject's

demands. True, in panegyric, the orator will seek to dazzle with bold, ostentatious ornaments, but in deliberative and forensic oratory fewer figures and
more sober diction are required (8.3.11–14). Yet even the panegyrist must not
allow the taste for novelty or excess to endanger his *ethos*. Thus we are warned:

> ... if we seem to have taken a risk in inventing a word [*si quid periculosius
> finxisse videbimur*], we should protect ourselves by some palliative expres-
> sion [*remediis*]: "so to say," "if I may so put it" ... The same precaution
> is useful with overbold metaphors; indeed anything can be said safely if
> the qualms we feel about it make it clear that our judgement is not at
> fault. The Greeks have an extremely neat piece of advice on this subject:
> "Be the first to criticize your own exaggeration ὑπερβολή." (8.3.37)

The handbooks call such proleptic blame a *remedium*. As we shall see, such *remedia* are critical to the subtlest workings of hyperbole in literature and philosophy. The more sophisticated and subjective hyperbole becomes, the more
elaborate *remedia* become. For instance, Shakespeare uses contingencies of plot
to provide his characters with *remedia*, while Descartes is the first to blame his
own hyperbole, though only after he has used it to establish absolute certainty.

Characteristically cautious, just when Quintilian implies that the orator
may sometimes transgress the rules of decorum as long as it is done consciously, he begins a discussion of stylistic faults. As with Cicero, the most
grievous is *cacozelia*, broadly defined here as "perverse affectation" [*mala adfectatio*] and

> a fault found in every type of style. The same name covers the turgid, the
> trivial, the luscious, the redundant, the far-fetched, and the extravagant
> [*tumida et pusilla et praedulcia et abundantia et arcessita et exultantia*] In short, it
> is the name given to whatever goes beyond the demands of good style
> [*quidquid est ultra virtutem*], whenever the mind shows a lack of judge-
> ment ... It is the worst of all faults of eloquence, because the rest are due
> to failure to avoid them, whereas this is deliberately sought. (8.3.56)

Cacozelia thus encompasses every fault of excess caused by insincerity, pretence, ambition, or faulty judgment. It signals a distortion of the relation between subject and style, between things and words. And, not surprisingly,
it is the charge leveled most often against hyperbolists. Under the rubric of

cacozelia Quintilian lambastes tapinosis, "by which the importance [*magni-tudo*] or dignity of something is diminished," as seen in the line: "There is a rocky wart upon the mountain's head" (8.3.48). Likewise, an opposite fault is "giving small things extravagant names" [*parvis dare excedentia modum nomina*], though if such hyperbole deliberately solicits laughter, it is grudgingly allowed (8.3.48).

TROPES AND FIGURES

While hyperbole, irony, allegory, simile, synecdoche, and metonymy are all termed tropes, Quintilian praises metaphor as the "commonest" and "by far the most beautiful [*longe pulcherrimus*]" of the tropes.[47] Effectively spurning what has come to be called the substitution theory of tropes, he asserts "that it is not only the forms of words that undergo change, but also the forms of sentences and of Composition" (8.6.2). This last claim appears to lend metaphor (and hyperbolic metaphor) more subtle semantic powers and "virtues" than would be the case if a trope was limited only, say, to the substitution of the word "mountain" for "Ajax." Metaphor thus plays an essential semantic and aesthetic role:

> Copiam quoque sermonis auget permutando aut mutuando quae non habet, quodque est difficillimum, praestat ne ulli rei nomen deesse videatur. (8.6.5)

> It also adds to the resources of language by exchanges or borrowings to supply its deficiencies, and (hardest task of all) it ensures that nothing goes without a name.

The task of catachresis, of providing a word or expression for something that lacks one (i.e., "the leg of a chair"), is here conflated with metaphor's ability to produce *copia*. Indeed, Patricia Parker observes that as *abusio* catachresis was frequently used to name the *audacia* of an overly bold or far-fetched metaphor.[48] In either case, she finds that such use and abuse undermine's the orator's claim to mastery: "The violent intrusions of catachresis and the possibility of transferences that, unwilled, subvert the very model of the controlling subject, are the gothic underside of the mastery of metaphor, the uncanny other of its will to control."[49] Similarly, I will argue below that hyperbole, which Quintilian describes as "bolder" [*audacioris*] than other tropes, often functions as a catachrestic vehicle for the most desperate, unspeakable emotions and thoughts; for if metaphor usurps the role of catachresis, one would expect hyperbole, which seeks to provide a "nomen" for extraordinary and ineffable things, to be even more eager to overstep its role.

Quintilian identifies four kinds of metaphorical transference.[50] His example of the fourth kind, the substitution of an animate for an inanimate thing, is neatly hyperbolic: "Araxes [a river], who spurns bridges" (*Aeneid*, 8.728). In particular, "a wonderfully sublime effect is produced if the subject is elevated by a bold and hazardous metaphor" [*Praecipueque ex his oritur mira sublimitas, quae audaci et proxime periculum translatione tolluntur*] (8.6.11). As for its decorum, metaphor should be neither too great nor too little for its subject; it must not be "ugly" [*deformis*], as in "the state was neutered by Africanus' death" or "Glaucia, the excrement of the Senate" (8.6.15).[51] Certain metaphors appropriate for poetry are too allegorical, enigmatic, or "disproportionate" [*dissimilis*] for oratory's practical needs (8.6.14–18), for poetic metaphor aims to please more than to teach. And despite metaphor's valuable ability to create *copia*, Quintilian cautions, in what could serve as a gloss on Lucan's extended geographical conceits or Seneca's remarkable cosmographical metaphors: "Excessive amounts [*copia*] of metaphor, especially of the same species, are also a fault" (8.6.16–17).

Metaphor is "more concise" than a simile, which is defined as a "comparison" rather than a substitution (8.6.8–9).[52] A simile can make a thing "sublime, colorful, attractive, or striking" [*sublimen, floridam, iucundam, mirabilem*]; also, "[t]he more remote the source of the simile, the more novelty it produces and the more unexpected it is" (8.3.74).[53] But always suspicious of rhetorical extremes, in his next breath Quintilian effectively precludes hyperbolic similes by noting that "common" [*vulgaria*] similes create "trust" [*fidem*], while the licentious use of more complex similes by "certain declaimers" is "corrupt" (8.3.75). This emphasis on *fides* distinguishes the use of simile from the use of hyperbole whose proper subject matter we will see presently is the *ultra fidem*. As for synecdoche, it adds variety and allows us to understand "many things from one." It may be more freely applied by poets than orators, although it is commonly found in everyday speech (8.6.19). In other words, with its "liberty of number," synecdoche often trespasses on hyperbole. To say "mast" when you mean ship, or that "the Roman won the battle" when you mean an army of Romans, may be read as hyperbolic diminution or augmentation. Indeed, as Philip Hardie meticulously demonstrates, synecdoche has a complex and fruitful relationship with Virgilian hyperbole.[54] Finally, closely related to synecdoche is metonymy, "which is the substitution of one name for another" (8.6.23). One of the instances of metonymy — "sixty thousand were killed at Cannae by Hannibal" — savors strongly of hyperbole. Yet after culling examples from Virgil and Horace, Quintilian is keen to limit metonymy's use in oratory.[55] Thus while Richard Lanham views the metonymist as skillfully manipulating and distorting physical quantities, as artfully transposing normal, spatial scale, and as purposefully confusing cause and effect, Quintilian, as will be the case with many of his Renaissance successors, would limit the metonymist's scope as he tries to keep the hyperbolic genie in the bottle.[56]

Irony, allegory, and hyperbole energize and amplify a speech, while their reception involves a complex bargain between speaker and audience, poet and reader. To begin with, Quintilian casts irony as a species of allegory.[57] Like the allegorist, an ironist intends the opposite of what is said. Elliptically defined as a means by which "contrary things are shown" [*contraria ostendun- tur*], irony relies upon a savvy audience erudite and experienced enough to parse the speaker's meaning (8.6.54).[58] Given the difficulties of discerning the speaker's *voluntas*, the audience has a decisive role in determining irony's efficacy. This task is further complicated by the historical and cultural contexts informing an oration. In brief, Quintilian's treatment of irony underscores how the complications and contingencies of rhetoric and tropology may include those of everyday life, and not just those found in the schools or on Parnassus. Thus for the ironic hyperbolist sometimes it "is permissible to blame with a pretence of praise and to praise with a pretence of blame" (8.6.55).[59] Satiric epideixis is valid because, Quintilian's examples imply, history is filled with characters whose virtues and vices strain language's ability to represent them.

Later, in his treatment of the figures (*schema*), Quintilian observes that irony can be treated as a figure of thought as well as a trope (9.1.3). His definition of the figures — "a purposeful deviation [*cum ratione mutatio*] in sense or language from the ordinary simple form" — buttresses the claim that an ironic style may be a figured one (9.1.11).[60] The trope of irony is "more open" [*apertior*] or obvious and more concise than the figure (9.2.45); the former usually concerns the change of individual words, as when Cicero calls Catiline's friend a "virum bonum." But the figured form of irony is more subtle, discursive, and therefore understandable only if the entire speech and its attendant circumstances are examined:

In the Figure . . . the pretence involves the whole meaning, and is transparent rather than openly avowed [*in figura totius voluntatis fictio est, ap-
parens magis quam confessa*], so that, whereas, in the Trope the contrast is
between words and words, here it is between the meaning and the
words, <and the Figure can cover> whole passages and sometimes the
entire shape of the Cause. Indeed, a whole life may be held to illustrate
Irony, as was thought of Socrates, who was called *eiron* . . . (9.2.46–47)

The distinction between irony as trope and figure, together with the undeveloped but unmistakable implication that allegory could be regarded as a figure
of thought, suggest that hyperbole too may be employed in a discursive, non-
tropological manner. Hyperbole also places strong emphasis on the speaker's
voluntas and the audience's judgment, and as with irony, hyperbole, we are
offhandedly told, "may involve both things and words" [*rebus fit et verbis*]
(9.1.5). Furthermore, the rich suggestion that a whole man's life may be described by a single figure of thought — a notion finely mined by Kierkegaard
in *The Concept of Irony* — suggests that hyperbole too may help shape a *Lebens-
philosophie*. It makes one wonder, indeed, who are those poets and thinkers
whose lives "illustrate" hyperbole.

THE VIRTUES AND VICES OF HYPERBOLE

Quintilian's treatment of hyperbole is more systematic, serious, and ultimately
far richer in complications and implications than anything offered by Cicero
or Aristotle.[61] It also provides late Renaissance rhetoric and poetics with many
of the terms, concepts, and sometimes even the script, for their treatment of
our figure. Yet while the view of the orator in the *Institutio* is broad and deep
enough to give voice to the ornamental, affective, conceptual, and even social
value of exaggeration, the case for hyperbole at the finale of the eighth book is
made with real ambivalence. Here Quintilian charts hyperbole's virtues and
vices as he indicates how it helps define the limits of rhetoric, rhetoric's shared
boundaries with poetry, and, implicitly, the very possibility of certain theological and philosophical discourses. For these reasons, and given their cardinal influence on early modern treatments of the subject, Quintilian's insights
have almost monadic importance for this book.

The discussion of hyperbole serves as a peroration crowning his exhaustive treatment of the tropes: "I have left Hyperbole, which belongs to a bolder

kind of Ornament, to the last" [*Hyperbolen audacioris ornatus summo loco posui*] (8.6.67).[62] Hyperbole has the taint of vice and excess. It fits poorly with the ideal of a judicious, sober style. It potentially most threatens his intention to write a treatise teaching decorous eloquence. Because of its overuse in the declamation schools, its ability to deceive, its refusal to be categorized only as a trope, and, above all, because of its potential indecorousness hyperbole is saved for last.

The discussion begins laconically enough:

> Est haec decens veri superiectio: virtus eius ex diverso par augendi atque minuendi; fit pluribus modis.

> It is an appropriate exaggeration of the truth. It has an equal value in the opposite functions of Amplification and Attentuation. There are various forms.

Literally a "decorous throwing-beyond of the truth," *superiectio*, as the objective genitive implies, never completely departs the realm of the truth — it just stretches and strains its borders.[63] Whatever "truth" was present or perceived before the hyperbolist sets to work is still present, but now its semantic range has been altered. Meanwhile, the emphasis on augmentation and diminution points to hyperbole's potential in various genres ("pluribus modis") to serve as a figure of thought and not just as a metaphor.

The "truth" of hyperbole may be different than, even opposed to, mimetic truths. Indeed, hyperbole enjoys a looser, more flexible decorum than the other tropes:

> We may say more than the facts [*plus facto dicimus*]: "As he vomited, he filled his lap and the whole platform with gobbets of food," or "Twin rocks that threaten skywards" [*Geminique minantur | In caelum scopuli*].

With these examples, neither of which is strictly tropological, Quintilian indicates the two terminal directions of the hyperbolic: the grotesque and sublime. He hints how a satirist might employ a hyperbole to disfigure a subject and how an allegorist might adapt hyperbole to reach ineffable heights. The first example from the *Philippics* (2.25.63) elicits laughter and revulsion, but it is also prompted by outrage at Marcus Antonius' — Shakespeare's Mark Antony — perceived betrayal of the Republic. Notably, just before this phrase occurs Cicero acknowledges his audience's potential incredulity: "Quid est? num mentior?" (2.25.61). Alternately, he strengthens his *ethos* by underscoring his extraordinary anger: "O rem non modo visu foedam, sed etiam auditu!"[64] The second hyperbole, from the *Aeneid* (1.162–63), provokes *admiratio* as it strains to express the great fear and doubt that the exiled Trojans, having just survived a tempest, feel as they gaze at the forbidding Libyan coast. Taken together these examples confirm that hyperbole is not limited to a single literary genre or rhetorical situation. Both the orator in political battle and the epic poet recounting mythological events need hyperbole. And while there will be tendency of Renaissance theorists to limit hyperbole to the grand style of epic or panegyric, it may be that this is partially due to the brevity of their discussions, rather than indicating a definitive stance on hyperbole's scope. For, as the Ciceronian example suggests, hyperbole becomes increasingly undecidable and thus dynamic as the hyperbolist ventures beyond traditional confines.

Three other instances from the *Aeneid* are then quickly cited to establish how a theme may be exalted. But because the terminology is somewhat confusing and the analysis often succinct to the point of obscurity, it is worth trying to unfold the implications of Quintilian's claims. First comes an example of hyperbole by simile (*per similitudinem*), though as quoted it seems more concise than a simile proper: "credas innare revulsas / Cycladas" (*Aen.* 8.691–92) [*You would think that they were Cyclades uprooted and afloat*]. When the full period is contemplated, it becomes evident that the single hyperbolic image quoted by Quintilian is part of a larger, exaggerated discourse in which Virgil involves the reader ("credas") in his search for the appropriate metaphor.[65] The hyperbole belongs to the ekphrastic description of Aeneas' shield, an outbidding of Homer's description of Achilles' shield, and a part of the scene where Virgil-Vulcan provides Aeneas with the military and rhetorical ornaments to found Rome. Containing in vivid microcosm Rome's entire history and described as a "clipei non enarrible textum," a texture, a text, a weapon, not to be narrated, the shield is the poem's most hyperbolic object.[66] A confusion of images, an impossible artifact, a series of dense ekphrases, or a string of *adunata*, the shield is designed to awe the reader and Aeneas. The passage from which Quintilian quotes portrays the Battle of Actium and Antony's ships:

una omnes ruere ac totum spumare reductis
convolsum remis rostrisque tridentibus aequor.
alta petunt; pelago credas innare revolsas
Cyclades aut montis concurrere montibus altos:
tanta mole viri turritis puppibus instant.
stuppea flamma manu telisque volatile ferrum
spargitur, arva nova Neptunia caede rubescunt. (8.689–695)

On they came at speed, all together, and the whole surface of the sea was churned to foam by the pull of the oars and the bow/waves from their triple beaks. They steered for the high sea and you would have thought the Cycliadic Islands had been torn loose again and were floating on the ocean, or that the mountains were colliding with mountains, to see men in action on those ships with their massive turreted sterns, showering blazing torches of tow and flying steel as the fresh blood began to redden the furrows of Neptune's fields.[67]

Playing with quantitative extremes ("una omnes ruere ac totum"), Virgil fashions here what Samuel Johnson would call a conceit of "confused mag/nificence." As if the poet could not decide which hyperbole would be more impressive, Antony's ships become "either" uprooted islands or mountains fighting other mountains while everything floats atop the foaming, convuls/ing sea. No wonder Aeneas stands stunned by the shield's panoply of heroes. He remains, as Milton will write of an "overawed" Satan observing the beau/tiful Eve, "abstracted" and "stupidely good" (*Paradise Lost*, 8.729–731). Re/figuring the notion of ascent, Virgil portrays an "ignarus" Aeneas "attolens" a destiny he is doomed never to understand. But taught by the shield's exag/gerated visual rhetoric to admire and imitate as far as he is able, Aeneas can at least begin to act.

The second example is hyperbole by comparison (*per comparationem*): "Fulminis ocior alis" [*Swifter even than the lightning's wings*] (*Aen.* 5.319). The full phrase is "et ventis et fulminis ocior alis" and concerns Nisus' speed in a footrace — a footrace he is about to lose by slipping in a puddle of sacrificial blood. The Virgilian irony of this last image aside, here we see how *compara/tio*, as Lausberg indicates, might itself be given to *Überbietung*.[68]

More dynamic still is the third example, or hyperbole "by some kind of signs" [*signis quasi quibusdam*]:

illa vel intactae segetis per summa volaret
gramina nec teneras cursu laesisset aristas . . . (*Aen.* 7.808–809)

Over the top shoots of the untouched corn / she flew and, running,
never bruised the ears . . .

These "signs" describing Camilla's superhuman prowess should be read discursively. Not limited to the metaphor (i.e., "volaret") or even the sentence, the
hyperbole is extended over four lines as the poet makes his case for Camilla's
exceptionality. The manner in which Virgil completes the hyperbole clarifies
Quintilian's curious reading of the *signa*:

vel mare per medium fluctu suspensa tumenti
ferret iter celeris nec tingueret aequore plantas. (*Aen.* 7.810–811)

or rushed across the middle of the sea, suspended above the waves, nor
would her swift feet touch the water.[69]

With such syntactic complexity and narrative energy, hyperbole functions
more properly as a figure of thought than a trope. These lines are also characteristic of hyperbole in other ways. First, they come at the climax of Book 7
and so, as in a peroration, they create *pathos* where the reader most expects it.
Second, they use nature as an objective basis for the exaggeration. Third, they
point to the conceptual and allegorical promise of hyperbole, for Camilla is
endowed here with nearly divine status.

To summarize, Quintilian delineates five species of hyperbole. Three are
tropological: hyperbole by simile, comparison, and metaphor.[70] Two are discursive or figures of thought: hyperbole by exaggerating the facts and by "certain signs." Together they confirm Volkmann's insight that the hyperbolist
often exploits other tropes and figures to achieve a desired effect.[71] Like allegory and irony, hyperbole is a kind of *Übertrope*. It is able to control, enhance,
and often subvert the function of other tropes. As Quintilian remarks: "One
hyperbole is sometimes enhanced by the addition of another" (8.6.70). Indeed, often one hyperbole does not suffice, and the speaker seems compelled,
for reasons I shall explore later, to outdo or supersede an initial hyperbole
with one or more increasingly exaggerated hyperboles — a phenomenon that

might be dubbed hyperbole's chain-reaction effect. Quintilian cites one such chain reaction from the *Second Philippic* where Antony is condemned:

> Quae Charybdis tam vorax? Charybdis dico? Quae si fuit, fuit animal unum: Oceanus, medius fidius, vix videtur tot res, tam dissipatas, tam distantibus in locis positas, tam cito absorbere potuisse. (*Phil.* 2.27.67)

> What Charybdis is so greedy? Charybdis, do I say? If ever there was a Charybdis, she was only one animal. No: the Ocean, heaven help us, could hardly have swallowed up so many things, so widely scattered, in such distant places, and so quickly.

In the wake of Homer the figure of Charybdis had become increasingly commonplace; hence Cicero quickly disqualifies his initial comparison as insufficient to express Antony's monstrosity. He chooses instead to invoke the Titan, Oceanus. Yet even the specter of the all-absorbing sea is inadequate to express Antony's voraciousness or to satiate Cicero's outrage. In terms of syntax, the repetition of "tam" along with the "vix" clause are highly characteristic of hyperbolic formulations in Latin prose and verse. Finally, this passage exemplifies how the monstrous is one of the hyperbolist's most characteristic subjects.

Referring next to a lost work of Pindar, "foremost of lyric poets," Quintilian underscores the metaphorical power of hyperbole (8.6.71). Pindar furnishes an "exquisitam . . . figuram" celebrating the onslaught of Hercules as "non igni nec ventis nec mari, sed fulmini dicit similem fuisse, ut illa minora, hoc par esset" [*not like the fire nor like the winds nor like the sea, but like the lightning*]. Underscored here is the vividness of the poet's ornamentation and how the trope "crescit" [*grows*] by piling one hyperbole atop another. By casting the lightning bolt as the only true equivalent of Hercules' speed and power, Pindar rejects lesser, though still hyperbolic, metaphors in order to endow his subject with the greatest possible brilliance. He ultimately makes the term of comparison equal, or logically adequate ("par"), to the mythological signified. In other words, Hercules' mythic-heroic stature requires hyperbole; it is decorous, even logical to borrow from nature's macrocosmic grandeur to find adequate expression for extraordinary human qualities. And by making the reader privy to his search for an adequate metaphor, Pindar literally attaches to his hyperbole a conceptual justification, if not also a hermeneutic, just as Cicero does when he implicitly rejects the Charybdis metaphor as insufficient and trite.

Frequently revealing the inadequacy of metaphor, the hyperbolist exploits and transgresses the limits of the reader's credulity by flirting with extravagant or "frigid" metaphors defying easy interpretation. Furthermore, while each of these examples has a psychological justification — Cicero's is propelled by anger, Pindar's by awe — each turns to nature as an objective source for its imagery. Similarly, Quintilian notes that "hyperbole by attenuation" can be effective, as in Virgil's *Eclogues* where starving sheep are described: "hardly [*vix*] adhering to bones." Insisting on this ludic aspect of hyperbole, he hints that hyperbole may avail itself of irony as well. Again, many of these examples indicate that hyperbole sometimes must be interpreted not just as a trope, but also as a sophisticated, discursive figure of thought. In demanding such an interpretation, the hyperbolist constantly puts his *ethos* at risk, as he depends on the reader's good will and ability to decide how his inventions are received. But fortunately, the reader's task is made easier by hyperbole's reliance on objective standards of greatness such as provided by nature and mythology. Most everyone has experienced a storm or seen a shooting star; and for a contemporary inhabitant of Sicily, the mighty, fiery heights of Aetna were still synonymous with the might of Hephaestus and the Cyclopses who labored in its bowels. Gazing at the volcano, one saw not only a natural marvel, but also the fury of Enceladus, who after his failed rebellion, is entombed by Zeus beneath its flanks. Such gigantomachy is objective in that it was common cultural property throughout antiquity.

In sum, there are two principal justifications for hyperbole. First, the speaker is moved in some extraordinary manner. Second, some incredible subject calls for expression. Both psychological (interior) and phenomenological (exterior) motives depend upon the existence of an outrageous or extraordinary *res*.[72] Yet whether this responsiveness to the matter at hand takes the hyperbolist beyond the concerns of *elocutio* and into the more conceptual realm of *inventio* is a question skirted by Quintilian. Whether hyperbole is heuristic as well as ornamental will have to be addressed elsewhere.

Quintilian next turns to an unknown work ascribed to Cicero for a humorous hyperbole in which the orator puns on *funda* (a sling) and *fundus* (a farm): "fundam Vetto vocat quem possit mittere funda / ni tamen exciderit, qui cava funda patet" [*Vetto calls it a farm, but he could throw it from a sling, unless it fell through where the sling's pouch is open*]. The gloss, though, immediately urges restraint. Having now established that hyperbole is proper to poetry and oratory, that it may provoke wonder and laughter, he warns prospective orators:

> Sed huius quoque rei servetur mensura quaedam. Quamvis est enim omnis hyperbole ultra fidem, non tamen esse debet ultra modum, nec alia via magis in cacozelian itur.
>
> Piget referre plurima hinc orta vitia, cum praesertim minime sint ignota et obscura. Monere satis est mentiri hyperbolen, nec ita ut men-dacio fallere velit. Quo magis intuendum est, quousque deceat extollere quod nobis non creditur. Pervenit haec res frequentissime ad risum; qui si captatus est, urbanitatis, sin aliter, stultitiae nomen adsequitur.
>
> Est autem in usu vulgo quoque et inter ineruditos et apud rustiscos, videlicet quia natura est omnibus augendi res vel minuendi cupiditas in-sita nec quisquam vero contentus est. (8.6.73–75)

But even here, a certain sense of proportion is necessary. Though every Hyperbole surpasses belief, it must not be beyond all reason; there is no surer route to cacozelia.

I feel it distasteful to report the many faults arising from this Trope, especially as they are by no means unfamiliar or obscure. It is enough to remind the reader that Hyperbole is a liar, but does not lie to deceive. We must therefore consider all the more carefully how far it is appropriate to exaggerate a thing which is not to believed. The attempt very often raises a laugh. If that is what was aimed at, it comes to be called wit; if not, folly.

It is in ordinary use, too, among the uneducated and with country people, no doubt because everybody has a natural desire to exaggerate or minimize things, and no one is satisfied with the truth.

These are foundational insights for any prospective theory of hyperbole. Pointing both to rhetoric's content (*ultra fidem*) and its form (*non tamen esse debet ultra modum*), Quintilian situates the successful hyperbolist squarely within his vision of the orator who can transform any subject into eloquent, decorous speech. Hyperbole must have measure ("mensura quaedam") even as it repre-sents the immeasurable. A "certain" quantitative relation must exist for a qualitative judgment to be made. The hyperbolist thus follows a difficult, if not paradoxical, "via." If one has to speak about the "ultra fidem," then this must be done credibly and without *cacozelia*. While a *vir bonus dicendi peritus* risks stylistic sins when he hyperbolizes, he may also ethically exploit the power of exaggeration. Moreover, hyperbole has a unique psychological function. It satisfies the universal thirst for strangeness, sublimity, and novelty. And by attaching such importance to the audience's feelings and thoughts, Quintilian underscores how potentially suspicious ears receive hyperbole. Here, then, we glimpse the genesis of a possible reception theory of hyperbole.

Quintilian's own exaggerations suggest further implications. He employs a timely litote inflected with hyperbole and irony to describe hyperbole's faults as "minime . . . ignota et obscura" (8.6.74). Likewise, he selfconsciously begs off blaming hyperbole, declaring simply: "Monere satis est mentiri hyperbolen nec ita, ut mendacio fallere velit" [*It is enough to warn that to hyperbolize is to lie, but not thereby mendaciously to want to deceive*].[73] The word play on "mentiri" and "mendacio" suggests how difficult it is for the hyperbolist to play the liar without mendacity. Either naively or purposefully, he distances his words from the literal truth in order to represent extraordinary truths. Echoing Plato's already ancient charge that the orator, like the poet, is a liar, Quintilian reifies the gap between language and reality just as he describes a way of bridging it. The hyperbolist walks the razor's edge between satisfying a basic human need and appearing utterly foolish, between giving sublime pleasure and seeming a mendacious liar. To do so he must have a judicious sense of what and when to exaggerate ("deceat extollere"). And given the use of *intueor*, presumably this sense is more innate than learned. But unfortunately, Quintilian's crucial insight here into the universal *cupiditas* of the human psyche, its need for exaggerated, ornamented truths, does not distinguish between what pleases and persuades sophisticated, urbane readers and what moves the unpolished ones ("rusticos").[74]

Likewise, it is with regrettable brevity that the discussion abruptly shifts from hyperbole's potential to produce laughter to its potential to signal complex truths. What such a dynamic might mean is teasingly touched upon in his concluding thoughts:

Tum est hyperbole virtus cum res ipsa de qua loquendum est naturalem modum excessit: conceditur enim amplius dicere, quia dici quantum est non potest, meliusque ultra quam citra stat oratio. (8.7.75–76)

Hyperbole only has positive value when the thing about which we have to speak transcends the ordinary limits of nature. We are then allowed to amplify, because the real size of the thing cannot be expressed, and it is better to go too far than not to go far enough.

An a priori, ethical, and phenomenological justification for hyperbole, these sentences will form the bedrock for most Renaissance attempts to describe hyperbole. At the beginning of Book 8, metaphor is called a stylistic "virtus," and now at its conclusion hyperbole too becomes a "virtus," for like metaphor, it produces *copia*. But whereas metaphor may add beauty and brilliance to an oration, hyperbole is assigned no such explicit aesthetic function. Instead, the hyperbolist risks a stylistic *vitium* on account of the extraordinary nature of the "res ipsa." It is the content itself, the signified of the hyperbole, that forces one ("de qua loquendum est") to exaggerate and lie. When the *res* "surpasses the ordinary limits of nature" [*naturalem modum excessit*], when it is *ultra modum*, then language must somehow keep pace with reality. While Quintilian warns earlier not to make ornament *ultra fidem*, or prey to the charge of *cacozelia*, here he proposes a notion of decorum loosened by the need to give vivid, truthful expression to the sometimes extraordinary nature of things. This paradoxical need, a need more often claimed by the philosophers and poets than by rhetoricians, induces Quintilian to violate his standard prescriptions against stylistic excess. By definition exceptional, the *ultra fidem* calls for exceptional rhetoric.

Of no small importance is the way the "incredible" is represented in quantitative terms. We are urged to overshoot such a *res* rather than undershoot it: ". . . quia dici quantum est non potest, meliusque ultra quam citra stat oratio." The "quantum" here corresponds to the subject matter, but "speech" [*oratio*] is not capable of giving *ratio* to this quantity. Thus the vague but infinitely suggestive formula, "better more than less" [*meliusque ultra quam citra*], is prescribed. Since rhetoric, unlike philosophy, aims at the possible ("potest") and not the ideal, the orator makes more concessions ("conceditur") to the real, to the situation at hand. But the hyperbolist must still navigate between his perception of an extraordinary "res ipsa" and an audience that must be persuaded and pleased. For him *veritas* is neither absolute nor fixed — it is contingent, mutable, and thus sometimes exceptional. Therefore, Quintilian offers the axiom that rhetorical excess is preferable to dearth, but with the corollary that this excess be measured. That the hyperbolist cheats literal facts to compass a larger truth is a necessary evil. Such cheating has its benefits as well as its risks, for laughter solicited or unsolicited may result when the audience gauges the abyss the speaker creates between literal and figurative meaning.

In brief, hyperbole is something of a monster (*monstrum*) given Quintilian's dictum casting nature as the most capable teacher of eloquence:

> We have only to watch nature and follow her [*naturam intueamur, hanc se quamur*]. All eloquence is about the activities of life, every man applies whatever he hears to his own experience, and the mind finds it easiest to accept what it can recognize. (8.3.71)

Perhaps this explains why hyperbole is saved for last in the discussion of ornament. Hyperbole ultimately fails to follow his ideal of nature or, at least, his ideal of natural speech. Or it perilously follows nature when nature becomes excessive or chaotic. Always reluctant to praise "excess," Quintilian takes a last jab at hyperbole in the final two sentences of Book 8. After noting in the penultimate sentence that we may hyperbolize when faced with some extraordinary subject, he declares curtly in the last sentence that he has said enough ("Conceditur enim amplius dicere . . ."). There is always room to say more, but not apparently when it comes to hyperbole.

All of this raises various epistemological and ethical difficulties. What truth claims does the orator make when faced with incredible or *ultra fidem* subject matter? Is Quintilian sharply distinguishing here between the aims of the practical orator and those pursued in philosophy? Why does he assume that the audience clearly perceives the hyperbolist's *voluntas*? What kind of ethical understanding, what bargain, would Quintilian make with the lying hyperbolist? Will the hyperbolist turn out to be as trustworthy as Cicero railing against Cataline's treacheries? Will he be as deserving of belief as Yahweh promising Abraham that his descendents will outnumber the desert sands? Or perhaps he will prove as duplicitous as Shakespeare's Richard the Third, "Hell's black intelligencer." In the wake of Quintilian, how do we hear the hyperboles of the Petrarchan lover, of Descartes doubting in his *poêle*, or of Sor Juana dreaming of absolute knowledge?

HYPERBOLIC AMPLIFICATION

Whether amplification can be a decorous species of hyperbole is also a critical question, especially as we look forward to the dynamics of Baroque prose. Recall that in his discussion of hyperbole as a trope, Quintilian states: "virtus eius ex diverso par augendi atque minuendi" (8.6.67); but this is preceded by the remarkable claim that "the whole power of the orator lies in amplification and attenuation" [*vis oratoris omnis in augendo minuendoque consistit*] (8.3.89). Distinguishing then between methods concerned "with things or with words" [*rebus et verbis*], he refers to his discussion of invention for the former and now promises to explicate "style" [*elocutio*] as amplification. In practice, however, the "force" of amplification confounds any attempt to separate words from things — a lesson that Erasmus will strongly reinforce with his influential treatise *De utraque verborum ac rerum copia*.

Like hyperbole, amplification is prescribed when one wishes to augment or diminish a subject. The motives for amplification thus rest on the same axiom concerning the insufficiency of plain, unadorned truth that invites hyperbole. Comprising numerous figures of thought that create repetition, parallelism, variation, and digression, skillful *amplificatio* cultivates linguistic and conceptual abundance. To structure his discussion, Quintilian delineates four principal species of amplification or *auxesis*: augmentation, comparison, reasoning, and accumulation (*incrementum, comparatio, ratiocinatio, congeries*).

Augmentation is the rhetorical equivalent of mountain climbing:

> Incrementum est potentissimum cum magna videntur etiam quae inferiora sunt. Id aut uno gradu fit aut pluribus et pervenit non modo ad summum sed interim quodammodo supra summum. (8.4.3)

> Increment is most powerful when even comparatively insignificant things are made to seem important. This is done either by one step or by several; the process not only goes to the top, it sometimes in a sense goes beyond it.

To indicate the orator's skill in elevating a subject, however banal it might be, Quintilian depends on spatial and quantitative catachreses ("magna . . . inferiora . . . gradu . . . supra summum").[75] *Incrementum* magnifies the worth of a subject by methodically adducing all possible related facts; by exhausting the vocabulary potentially related to a subject; by comparing the subject to a superlative; by showing that nothing greater can be conceived, as when someone says: "You beat your mother? What more need I say? You beat your mother . . ."; or, finally, "when a succession of details, each stronger than the last, occurs in a continuous passage without any break in the sentence"

(8.4.4–80).[76] Lausberg thus aptly calls *incrementum* a "heightening of *eviden-tia*."[77] A cardinal feature of classical prose and poetry, it proves fundamental also for Baroque prose writers such as Quevedo and Browne as they plumb satiric depths and scale transcendent heights.

The second type of amplification, *comparatio*, increases a lesser thing's importance by implying a logical connection with a greater thing, as when Cicero says to Catiline: "If my slaves feared me as all your fellow-citizens fear you, I should think I ought to leave my house" (*Catil.* 1.7.17). As a form of exaggeration, *comparatio* at first glance resembles an enthymeme, as it creates a tendentious logical inference to enhance the quality of someone or something (8.4.11). And though Quintilian warns that *comparatio* is not a method of proof but merely an ornament, a means of amplifying a subject point by point (*partes partibus comparari*), here again the line between proof and ornament blurs, for though such amplification does not seek to answer the question *quid sit?*, it does, we learn, address the question *quale sit?* — one of the methods of producing proof.

The third kind of amplification, "inference" [*ratiocinatio*], likewise con-flates invention and ornament. Here "[o]ne thing is magnified to augment an-other, and a transition is made by inference to the thing we wish to emphasize" [*ut aliud crescat, aliud augetur, inde ad id quod extolli volumus ratione transitur*] (8.4.15–16). The more extreme forms of inference rely on the emotional atmosphere created by the orator-poet, thereby allowing more extravagant claims to gain credence. For instance, the fantastic verses describing how Aeolus unleashes the wind — "cavum conversa cuspide montem / impulit in latus; ac venti ve-lut agmine facto / . . . ruunt" (*Aen.* 1.81–83) — provides the necessary an-tecedent for the *amplificatio* of the magnificent tempest that follows. Likewise, by praising the Gauls, a speaker elevates Caesar who conquers the Gauls. Or if the orator first minimizes some "outrageous event" [*res atrocissimas*], for which the audience normally would feel "the greatest antipathy," then he may exploit this reversal to magnify, say, a crime which otherwise would be beyond comparison (8.4.19). By describing first the enormous shield of Ajax and the "spear-shaft of Achilles hewn in the forests of Pelion," Homer lends his he-roes glory (8.4.24). Similarly, in a gesture that Góngora will marvelously im-itate, Virgil's description of the "pinus" [*pine tree*], which the Cyclops uses as a staff, enhances the subsequent effect when he describes the horror produced by the monster. In short, the aims of such magnification are nearly indistinguishable from those of hyperbole as a trope. Quintilian in fact compares *emphasis* to *ratiocinatio*, but affirms that "emphasis is a matter of suggestive words, and this of suggestive things; it is therefore the more potent, inasmuch as things carry more weight than words [*tantoque plus valet quanto res ipsa verbis est firmior*]" (8.4.26). Like hyperbole, then, this species of amplification owes its ultimate justification to the subject, the *res ipsa* (which may include emotion, *adfectus*, as well), rather than the need for verbal brilliance.

Accumulation ("congeries . . . verborum ac sententiarum") is the fourth species of amplification (8.4.26). Through such syntactic accumulation a feeling of abundance is conveyed. The inverse of this creation of *copia* is the principle of attenuation ("ratio minunendi"). An essential weapon in the satirist's arsenal, such attenuation produces the effect of a descent (8.4.28), such that a thing or person's worth is methodically diminished. An early modern example might be the vituperation that Anne and Queen Margaret direct against the eponymous villain in *Richard III*: "Thou elvish-marked abortive, rooting hog, / Thou that wast sealed in thy nativity / Thou slave of nature, and the son of hell; / Thou slander of thy heavy mother's womb, / Thou loathed issue of thy father's loins, / Thou rag of honour, thou detested —" (1.3.228–233).

Finally, at the outset of his discussion of amplification (8.4.1), Quintilian hints at a fifth method in which one word is substituted for another within a long period, as when Cicero calls an "impudent woman" [*impudicam*] a "prostitute" [*meretricem*] (8.4.2). Though we are not told how this relates to metonymy, such substitution is more prosaic and less economical than the trope, as it is conventionally accompanied by figures of speech such as parison and antithesis. Cicero's denunciation of Verres is cited (*Verr.* 1.3.9) to show the methodical progression from bad to worse:

> We have brought before your court not a thief, but a plunderer; not an adulterer, but a stormer of women's virtues; not a committer of sacrilege, but the avowed enemy of all sacred things and religious observances; not an assassin, but a bloodthirsty butcher of our fellow-citizens and our allies. (8.4.2–3)

Like Pindar's "exquisitam figuram" discussed in the section on hyperbole proper, Cicero's period asserts, then methodically rejects, possible comparisons. It, too, self-consciously displays the mechanics of debasement, though its parataxis and anaphora draw more attention to syntax than to tropological substitution.

Given all this, no wonder Quintilian coyly remarks at the end of his treat-ment of amplification:

> I know that some may think Hyperbole also to be a species of amplifi-cation [*quibusdam speciem amplificationis hyperbolen quoque*], for it too works both ways. But as it goes beyond our present subject, I postpone it till we come to Tropes. (8.4.29)

More than just being another way of increasing or diminishing the value of a *res*, hyperbole may encompass or control the various kinds of amplification discussed above. In sum, to borrow Kenneth Burke's moniker, Quintilian treats hyperbole as a kind of "master trope," especially as its use frequently in-volves the other master tropes, metaphor, metonymy, synecdoche, and irony. The aims of hyperbole and amplification are often similar: to move and teach the audience/reader with the extraordinary nature of things, events, feelings, and ideas. And if amplification creates a less acute, more sustained effect, this is also the goal of some of the figures of thought that stress repetition, or that, like irony, function over an entire discourse. Hyperbole, in short, thrives as both a trope and a discursive figure of thought. But Quintilian, never very in-terested in quibbling over definitions, would probably have balked at these dis-tinctions. Having tried to slay, or at least tame, the hydra-hyperbole at the end of Book 8, he does not prevent its heads from growing elsewhere.

ARISTOTLE: WONDER AND ADOLESCENCE

Quintilian is not the only *doctor* to express extreme ambivalence about hyper-bole. As in most aspects of the rhetorical enterprise, Aristotle sets the tone and introduces many of the concepts concerning hyperbole that later thinkers, in-cluding Quintilian, grapple with when discussing the most natural and arti-ficial of tropes. But Aristotle particularly deserves attention for the manner in which he firmly ties hyperbole to his philosophically rich treatment of meta-phor.[78] The chapters in the *Rhetoric* on metaphor mark the moment in his corpus where philosophy and, what would now be called psychology and literary criticism have their most fruitful commerce. Refashioning the cardi-nal notion of *energeia* from the *Physics* and *Metaphysics* to capture the strangely alluring, truth-producing power of metaphor, Aristotle sets the stage for his discussion of hyperbole that follows immediately afterward. It turns out, however, that the part he assigns hyperbole is minor one, more of a character sketch than a fully realized role.

Introducing late in book three of the *Rhetoric* (1410b) the important notion of *asteia* or "wit," Aristotle observes: "To achieve urbanity in style one should . . . aim at three things: metaphor, antithesis, actualization [*energeia*]."[79] Urbanity is most effectively realized by metaphor whose unique power of "bringing-before-the-eyes" [*pro ommatōn poiein*] naturally pleases and facilitates learning. When a successful metaphor permits such visualization, the auditor experiences "motion" and the unique "surprise" of discovery; for either the inanimate has been made animate ("the ruthless stone"), or qualities from one object has been transferred to another ("the arrow flew").[80] Earlier in Book 3 Aristotle writes: "Metaphor especially has clarity and sweetness and strangeness, and its use cannot be learned from someone else."[81] Homer's metaphors especially achieve this decorous *energeia*. When the poet writes "the point sped eagerly through his breast," we see and understand more keenly an arrow's swift and deadly flight.

Metaphor's unique ability to teach is traced partly to how it surprises and delights, and partly to how it finds similarity amidst difference. It depends, Richard Moran comments, on the audience's prior disposition to be pleased and its willingness to experience actively the "liveliness" and contradictions inherent in metaphor.[82] This disposition derives not only from the rhetorical situation but also — Aristotle insists, dabbling in what would now be called cognitive psychology — from our natural thirst and admiration for the foreign and exotic:

> To deviate [from prevailing usage] makes language seem more elevated; for people feel the same in regard to style [*lexis*] as they do in regard to strangers [*tous xenous*] compared with citizens. As a result, one should make the language unfamiliar [*xenēn*], for people are admirers of what is far off [*apontōn*], and what is marvelous is sweet. (1404b)

This remarkable analogy appears, paradoxically, to derive from Aristotle's notion of the mean that grounds his moral philosophy.[83] In an observation that I take to describe the analytic power of hyperbole as well, Aristotle writes:

... metaphors should be transferred from things that are related but not obviously so, as in philosophy, too, it is characteristic of a well-directed mind to observe the likeness even in things very different.[84] (1412a)

Metaphor and metaphoric hyperbole can be employed judiciously to balance the far off and the familiar, thereby producing knowledge.[85] They also produce such knowledge more swiftly than more discursive language: "... knowledge [*mathesis*] results more from contrast but is quicker in brief form" (1412b). Brevity is not only the soul of wit, but metaphoric wit has real epistemological value.

While in the *Rhetoric* ornament combined with proof and a suitable *ethos* work to persuade an audience, in the *Poetics* (1450a) "reversals and recognitions" are "the greatest things by which tragedy guides the soul [*psuchagōgei*]."[86] When metaphor is discussed in the *Poetics* (1457b, 1459a), underscored is the poet's natural ability to discern similarities required to make good metaphors. And though Aristotle generally seems more interested there in classifying metaphor than explaining its reach or worth, still, one of the four kinds of *epiphora* or transference described is clearly hyperbolic, even if it is not what nowadays would be called a metaphor. To illustrate the metaphorical transference from species to genus, the *Iliad* (2.272) is quoted: "Surely Odysseus has done ten thousand good things." Then Aristotle comments: "For ten thousand [*myria*] is many [*poly*] and in this place it is used in the place of many." Homer's sentence does not depend on the "notion of resemblance," even though it retains the surprise and heuristic force that metaphor employs to engage the judgment.[87] It is based rather on the quantitative play native to hyperbole. Yet a larger question remains: given that such unmeasured contrasts appeal to a reader's judgment and so precipitate learning, why has Aristotle confined metaphor and, implicitly, hyperbole to the realm of style (*lexis*)? Why should these tropes be separated from the tasks of invention and producing proof?

Distinguishing at the outset of Book 3 of the *Rhetoric* between poetic *lexis* and rhetorical *lexis*, Aristotle insists that while the unfamiliar and the far off are naturally prized, especially in diction, the orator must ensure that his style is "clear" and "appropriate" [*prepon*] (1404b). What is appropriate for the poet is often blameworthy for the orator, as the latter must try to create and maintain a believable *ethos*. Thus Aristotle devotes much of the third chapter of Book 3 to "the frigidities" or *ta psykhra*. There he blames, anticipating Quintilian but also Renaissance critics of Góngora and Donne, frigidity in metaphor as either causing unlooked for laughter, or as being "too lofty or tragic" for the situation.[88]

With his emphasis on propriety, no wonder Aristotle reluctantly praises hyperbole. Hyperbole may be "effective" or "acceptable," but it is appropriate only for adolescents and angry speakers (1413a). Because hyperbole exhibits "vehemence" [*sphrodrotēta*], it belongs most properly to the young, or those who naturally "overdo" things.[89] Instead of justifying hyperbole by pointing to the *res ipsa*, Aristotle links it to the orator's emotions (*pathē*). Still, his dis/cussion of hyperbole begins empirically enough:

> Effective hyperboles are also metaphors; for example, of a man with a black eye [one might say], "You would have thought him a basket of mul/berries," for his face is somewhat purple, but there is much exaggeration. And in *like* this or that there is hyperbole differing in the form of expres/sion [*lexis*]: "Like Philammon boxing the punching ball" (you would think him to be Philammon fighting a sack) "He has legs like stringy parsley" (you would think him to have parsley for legs, so stringy they are). (1413a)

Limited to a metaphor and two similes, the phrases cited are exaggerated and pleasantly humorous, but not particularly audacious or ingenious. Initially, then, hyperbole seems merely a device in a comedian's or satirist's bag of tricks. It points to an excess of a certain physical quality, for example, color or thinness. We may also infer that wonder or mockery is what justifies the exag/gerations here. And while these examples certainly bring contrasting things before the eyes, without more context it is difficult to say how much they teach. A soldier or farmer might say any one these phrases (save, perhaps, for the learned allusion to Philammon). Also, there is no sense that hyperbole could be a figure of thought. Hyperbole seems reduced to a narrow trope. It does not seem to have implications for philosophy comparable to those that Martin Heidegger, Paul Ricoeur, and Glenn Most find in other aspects of the *Rhetoric*.

But then, in another of the *Rhetoric's* frustratingly abrupt transitions, Ar/istotle offers a more general evaluation of hyperbole that leaves the ludic and, in a certain sense, undermines it. Now emotion fuels hyperbole:

> Hyperboles are adolescent [*meirakiōdeis*], for they exhibit vehemence. Therefore those in anger, mostly speak them . . .[90]

Is "adolescent" meant literally? The comment at 1413b ("... it is inappropriate for an older man to speak [in hyperbole]") implies that it is. The text continues by citing two verse passages from the mouth of that angry young man,
Achilles, who passionately refuses to accept the Achaians' entreaties to rejoin
the fight:

> not if he gave me gifts as many as the sand or dust is . . . (9.385)

> Nor will I marry a daughter of Atreus' son, Agamemnon,
> not if she challenged Aphrodite the golden for loveliness,
> not if she matched the work of her hands with grey-eyed Athene . . .
> (9.388–390)

But only if these lines are read in the context of the entire passage, can
Homer's hyperbolic genius in portraying Achilles' enormous wrath be appreciated:

> I hate his gifts. I hold him as light as the strip of a splinter.
> Not if he gave me ten times as much, and twenty times over
> as he possesses now, not if more should come from elsewhere,
> or gave all that is brought in to Orchomenos, all that is brought in
> to Thebes of Egypt, where the greatest possessions lie up in houses,
> Thebes of a hundred gates, where through each of the gates two hundred
> fighting men come forth to war with horses and chariots;
> not if he gave me gifts as many as the sand or dust is,
> not even so would Agamemnon have his way with my spirit
> until he made good to me all this heartrending insolence.
> Nor will I marry a daughter of Atreus' son, Agamemnon,
> not if she challenged Aphrodite the golden for loveliness,
> not if she matched the work of her hands with grey-eyed Athene;
> not even so will I marry her; let him pick some other Achaian,
> one who is to his liking and is kinglier than I am. (9.378–392)[91]

Homer's use of anaphora to propel the hyperboles mimics the way an angry
man neglects to alter his syntax in the heat of emotion. The passage is also remarkable for the way hyperbole works as a form of diminution as well as exaggeration. Indeed, if hyperbole is a necessary ornament, it seems that its

propriety here comes from Achilles' extraordinary situation and feelings. His age matters little. Taught the art of speaking well by Phionix, Achilles is not the most eloquent Achaian, but he effects moments of great *energeia* in his speeches. Hyperbole achieves what *enargeia* cannot — it is impossible to visu- alize so many gifts or the spectacle of Thebes. Further, the larger speech in which these hyperboles are embedded is itself an exemplary oration, arranged into four parts, ornamented with numerous other figures besides hyperbole, and powered by a series of irrefutable arguments that leaves his listeners "stricken to silence in amazement at his words."[92] As Homer wryly comments: "[h]e had spoken to them very strongly" (9.430–431). Phionix responds to his former student's vehement speech with a long oration concerning honor and ruin that, despite its eloquence, has little real effect on Achilles or the narrative. Achilles' hyperboles, on the contrary, epitomize the epic's theme of incomparable anger. Indeed, a kind of enthymeme might be constructed as a way of reading the epic: (a) hyperbole is anger's favorite trope; (b) anger is the theme of the *Iliad*; (c) the *Iliad* is an extended hyperbole.

Aristotle's final comments on hyperbole, which Cope-Sandys identify as possibly spurious,[93] allude to the excesses of the Sophists, orators who greatly influenced students of rhetoric in Aristotle's lifetime:

(The Attic orators especially use [hyperbole]). Thus, it is inappropriate for an older man to speak [in hyperbole]. (1413b)

Apparently a reference to Isocrates and his "school," this is at odds with an earlier moment in the *Rhetoric* (1418b) where Isocrates exemplifies how the or- ator's use of "invective" and the emotional style may be decorous:

Double words and frequent epithets and especially unfamiliar words suit one speaking passionately: for it is excusable that an angry person calls a wrong "heaven-high" or "monstrous." And [this can be done] when a speaker holds the audience in his control and causes them to be stirred either by praise or blame or hate or love, as Isocrates does at the end of the *Panegyricus* . . . Those who are impassioned mouth such ut- terances, and audiences clearly accept them because they are in a similar mood. That is why [this emotional style] is suited to poetry, too, for po- etry is inspired. It should be used as described — or in mockery [*eirōneia*] as Gorgias did and as in the *Phaedrus*. (1408b)

Encompassing epideictic oratory, poetry, Platonic dialogue, and satire, Aristotle underscores how the hyperbolist's *ethos* is crucial in helping him persuade. Yet even as Isocrates, Gorgias, Socrates, and presumably the tragedians
as well are excused for their overreaching, Aristotle urges them also to excuse
their excess beforehand: "There is a commonly used defense for every hyperbole: The speaker should preempt criticism; for something seems true when
the speaker does not conceal what he is doing" (1408b). In urging such a
remedium, Aristotle reiterates his concern that the hyperbolist risks abandoning
an ethical mean. Nonetheless, *remedia* are at odds with the passionate, vehement state of mind that is supposed to produce hyperbole in the first place.
Achilles is too angry to say "if you will" or "if I may say so" before he scorns
the gifts of Agamemnon whom he holds as "light as the strip of a splinter."

To summarize, for Aristotle, as will be the case later for Demetrius in his
influential treatise *On Style*, the only explicit justification of hyperbole is the
intensity of the speaker's emotional state.[94] Although we are offered two comic
examples, it is unclear how they show "vehemence." Aristotle's citation of
Homer is puzzling. Are Homer's hyperboles "adolescent"? Or does Aristotle
mean that Achilles is being portrayed as "adolescent" through his use of this
trope? And if so, how does this prove the *energeia* of Homer's verse and so allow the poet to escape the calumny of being dubbed "adolescent" too? In
short, it remains unclear just to what extent the hyperbolist's sacrifice of propriety prevents him from enjoying the rhetorical and philosophical virtues of
metaphor. In the *Nicomachean Ethics* (1095a) it is affirmed that young men are
too passionate to study moral philosophy. Should one conclude therefore that
hyperboles are unphilosophical? Given Aristotle's perfunctory, slightly dismissive treatment of hyperbole, together with hyperbole's inherent lack of
proportion and measure, the overshooting trope, despite Homer's use of it
and its undeniable *energeia*, appears to be unsuitable for moving most audiences. But perhaps this is due to the different duties of the orator and poet.
What a shame, then, that Aristotle does not specifically address the risks and
rewards of hyperbole in the *Poetics* when he comments on the value of the paralogism: "The wondrous is pleasant, and the sign of this is that in report-
ing everyone adds things as if to be gratifying. Homer is especially effective
in teaching everyone else how they must speak in falsehoods; this is the paralogism" (1460a). Is it the epic form and Homer's genius that excuse such
lies, or is it our own desire for excess and amazement? Is a paralogism a form

of hyperbolic reason particular to poetry? Aristotle cryptically suggests that the "Bath Scene" in the *Odyssey* (19.386ff) exemplifies such misreason — the very scene that Erich Auerbach makes the starting point for his incomparable history of the mimetic representation of reality in the Western literary tradition.[95]

Paul Ricoeur calls the discussion in the beginning of chapter eleven of "bringingbeforethe eyes" and *energeia* the "most enigmatic passage of the *Rhetoric*."[96] But the finale of the same chapter, where Aristotle's dismissively treats hyperbole, is only slightly less puzzling. Moreover, though it may be perilous to ignore Ricoeur's reading of metaphor in the *Poetics* as essentially "mimetic" versus the "persuasive" function it is assigned in the *Rhetoric*, for reasons that will become clearer as this book progresses, this distinction seems untenable in the extreme case of hyperbolic metaphor in which imitation and "the probable" [*to eikos*] are usurped by the improbable and the impossible.

LONGINUS: HYPERBOLE AND THE SUBLIME

The author of *On the Sublime*, usually identified as Cassius Longinus, amplifies and deepens the Aristotelian idea that the speaker's emotional state chiefly justifies hyperbole. In so doing, *Peri hypsos* gives hyperbole novel literary and philosophical currency.[97] While the treatise as it stands dedicates one truncated section to critiquing hyperbole, elsewhere Longinus, despite his caveats, frequently conflates the hyperbolic and the sublime. Not only are numerous remarkable hyperboles enlisted to describe the reach and power of the sublime, but this eloquent, lacunaeridden text relies on various species of rhetorical excess when lauding a particular passage or author for sublimity. In this way, *On the Sublime* at once exemplifies and theorizes the risks and rewards of hyperbole. Or as Alexander Pope observes, Longinus "*is himself* the great *Sublime* he draws."[98]

Adapting many of the terms and ideas native to rhetorical theory and practice in his examination of sublimity in written texts, Longinus also enacts the *letteraturizzazione* of rhetoric, which we saw Kennedy describe in my introduction. Though he initially announces that he is writing for "public speakers" (4), most of his attention is given to what would now be called literature or secondary rhetoric, albeit written largely in the grand style.[99] Further, for all his reliance on the rhetorical tradition, Longinus also devalues the virtues of a sophisticated rhetorical technique when he affirms that nature alone, in the form of a writer's natural talent, makes the difference between fame-producing sublimity and ignominious frigidity. Works with "greatness of soul" [*megalophrosunēs*] that occasionally fail in the pursuit of the sublime are far more valuable than literature that achieves an impeccable mediocrity (33). Offering, arguably, the strongest defiance in antiquity to the tyranny of keeping decorum, *Peri hypsos* shifts critical attention toward content (*dianoia*) and away from rhetorical expectations. By prizing, or at least excusing, the excesses of great-souled poets, Longinus justifies the conceptual straining native to hyperbole.

Such justification is rooted in the fact that the sublime and hyperbolic share a great deal of characteristic content. For instance, in a remarkable digression defending Plato's style (35.4–5), Longinus sketches a kind of topographical map of nature's marvels:

> Look at life from all sides and see how in all things the extraordinary, the great [*mega*], the beautiful stand supreme, and you will soon realize what we were born for. So it is by some natural instinct that we admire, not the small streams, clear and useful as they are, but the Nile, the Danube, the Rhine, and above all the Ocean. The little fire we kindle for ourselves keeps clear and steady, yet we do not therefore regard it with more amazement [*thaumazomen*] than the fires of Heaven, which are often darkened, or think it more wonderful than the craters of Etna in eruption, hurling up rocks and whole hills from their depths and sometimes shooting forth rivers that earthborn, spontaneous fire. But on all such matters I would only say this, that what is useful or necessary is easily obtained by man; it is always the unusual [*paradoxon*] which wins our wonder [*thaumaston*].

Nature's enormous scale, as embodied by mighty rivers, the ocean, the sun, stars, eclipses, and erupting volcanoes, provides the objective cause, the mimetic motive, for the writer's thirst for the sublime. But Longinus' diction also points to the sublime's subjective or psychological appeal; nature itself has a thaumaturgical effect that "writers of genius" [*logois megalophuōn*] (36.1), and here Longinus himself, are driven to emulate. In other words, the representation of "greatness" (*megethos*) is regarded from both within and without, from a subjective and objective perspective. Moreover, Longinus suggests a real analogy between nature's greatness and the greatness of genius. It is but a small step, then, to contend that if nature is perceived as hyperbolic, hyper-bolic writing about nature should follow suit.

The celebration of the "unusual" above also recalls Quintilian's empha-sis on the *ultra fidem* and Aristotle's stress on extraordinary emotion in their dis-cussions of hyperbole. Still, it would be erroneous to conflate directly the hyperbolic with the sublime. Longinus warns that bombast and bathos often masquerade as sublimity (7.1–3), and that hyperbole can either boost or de-base the sublime (5). He focuses on hyperbole in section 38; but one of the six lacunae riddling the text occurs in the midst of his discussion. As a result, *Peri hypsos* tells us much more about why hyperbole should be blamed than why it should be praised. In order to evaluate, therefore, what remains of his treatment of hyperbole, it makes sense first to consider his discussion of the sublime proper. There the affinities and differences that hyperbole has with the sublime be-come manifest. And, on a meta-rhetorical level, the role hyperbole plays in the exegesis and exemplification of the sublime greatly illuminates.

In section 8, five sources of sublimity are delineated: "the power of grand conceptions," "the inspiration of vehement emotion," and the mastery of three aspects of *lexis*: figures of thought and speech, noble diction, and digni-fied word arrangement. And while the first two sources are indispensable, and are the kernel of what Longinus dubs natural "genius" [*ta megalophuē*], he also urges writers to use stylistic helps, which, when used with "good judgment," can guarantee the sublime (2.2). Significantly, unlike efforts at invention or proof, attempts to create the sublime through "a consummate excellence and distinction of language" need not be embodied by an entire discourse, but rather, "like a bolt of lightning," can occur in flashes of brilliance (1.3–4). Moreover, while the sublime bestows "fame" on those who know how to pro-duce it, its subject matter, like that of hyperbole, is often fame itself or those qualities, persons, and events deserving epideixis.

Anticipating also the future autonomy of literary theory, Longinus as-serts that to aim for sublimity is to ignore the chief aim of practical rhetoric:

> For the effect of genius is not to persuade the audience but rather to trans-port them out of themselves [*all' eis ekstasin agei ta uperphua*]. Invariably what inspires wonder [*ekplēxei*], with its power of amazing us [*to thauma-sion*], always prevails over what is merely convincing and pleasing. (1.4)

Thaumaturgy and *ekstasis* rather than persuasion are the goals of the sublime writer, even as the "wonder" he would produce is always in danger of be/ coming bathetic.[100] It must, therefore, know a certain restraint:

> We must remember also that mere grandeur runs the greatest risk if left to itself without the stay and ballast of scientific method and abandoned to the impetus of uninstructed temerity. For genius needs the curb as of/ ten as the spur. (2.2)

Just as the excesses of hyperbole may yield *cacozelia*, the desire for sublime grandeur often causes tumidity, puerility and, most grievously, frigidity. The passion for novelty especially leads writers astray. A playwright, probably Aeschylus, is lambasted as "despicable" for his empty bombast, while phrases of his near contemporary Callisthenes are branded as "meteōra" [*lofty but empty*] (3.1–2).[101] The overzealous pursuit of novelty also may lead the writer astray, especially when using hyperbole (5). By contrast, the sublime is grounded in knowledge and experience; if its *dianoia*, the thought informing it, bears re/ peated scrutiny, then the writer has succeeded. If the grandeur of the thought is universal, if it appeals to judgment as well as the imagination, then the chance of failure is greatly lessened. To illustrate a sublime passage derived from a great thought and "quite without emotion," Longinus in 8.2 quotes "daring lies" from the *Odyssey*:

> Ossa then up on Olympus they strove to set, then upon Ossa
> Pelion, ashiver with leaves, to build them a ladder to Heaven; (11.315–316)

Only to add that a "still greater exaggeration" occurs in the subsequent line:

> And they would have done it as well.

On the heels of this gigantomachic hyperbole, he then cites verses from the *Il/ iad* where Homer "magnifies the powers of heaven":

> Far as a man can see with his eyes in the shadowy distance,
> Keeping his watch on a hilltop, agaze o'er the winedark ocean,
> So far leap at a bound the high/neighing horses of heaven. (5.770–772)

Noting that Homer avoids any pathos here, Longinus celebrates "the cosmic interval" [*kosmikō diastēmati*] measuring the leap of divine horses. Such a span, he suggests after the large lacuna at 9.4, also measures Homer's greatness. Commenting on the same passage in the *Iliad* (4.442) discussed by Demetrius above, where Strife "plants her head in the sky" while her feet stride over a shrunken earth, Longinus writes: "One might say too that this measured the stature not of Strife so much as Homer." Thus if in terms of content this "cosmic interval" resembles the hyperbolic, then like the subtlest hyperboles it also self-consciously measures the limits of poetic form and expression.

The themes of gigantomachy and titanomachy, in other words, provide the hyperbolist aiming at the sublime the perfect occasion to reflect on the limits of his overreaching art. This is further underscored when Longinus in 9.6 conflates two passages from the *Iliad* (21.388 and 20.61–65) to create a "marvelous" picture of the Battle of the Gods. Here "the earth is split to its foundations, hell itself is laid bare, the whole universe sundered and turned upside down; and meanwhile everything, heaven and hell, mortal and immortal alike, share in the conflict and danger of the battle." While producing "terror" (an emotion that in the eighteenth century will be associated with the negative sublime), such a passage would be utterly "irreligious" if not read "allegorically" (9.7). By glossing Homer in this way, Longinus 'saves' him from his own hyperboles, just as another Alexandrian, Ptolemy, 'saves' the astronomical calculations of earlier Greek and Persian astronomers by adding epicycles and eccentricities. Allegory alone excuses excessive exaggeration, or, more negatively, the hyperbolic becomes the sublime manqué.[102]

Nevertheless, to crown his exegesis of Homeric sublimity, Longinus resorts to two hyperbolic conceits. First, considering the change of style from the *Iliad* to the *Odyssey*, he comments: ". . . in the *Odyssey* one may liken Homer to the setting sun: the grandeur remains without the intensity . . . It is rather as though the Ocean had retreated into itself and lay quiet within its own confines" (9.13). The inexplicable fact of Homer's genius is precisely the kind of *res ipsa* Quintilian made proper to hyperbole; but here Longinus measures it with the "cosmic interval" of the sublime. Second, to illustrate how the sublime may be created by intense emotion, Sappho's fr. 31 is cited, where the "density" of her "passion of love" finds skillful expression in a kind of anatomical catalogue of contradictory sensations.[103] Commenting that "she displays not a single emotion, but whole congeries of emotions," Longinus makes the sublime synonymous with the expression of copious feelings. But then addressing the danger of simply conflating amplification and the sub-lime, he makes this important qualification: "Sublimity lies in elevation, am-plification rather in amount" (12.1). Amplification, as exemplified by Cicero, who is compared to "a widespread conflagration, rolling around and devour-ing all around it," exhausts a theme by "accumulating all the aspects and top-ics inherent in a subject"; whereas sublimity, as exemplified by Demosthenes, may be conveyed through a single, momentary idea. On the other end of the emotional spectrum, the description of the *megethos* cultivated by Demos-thenes recalls how Aristotle makes "vehemence" proper to the hyperbolist: "Our countryman with his violence, yes, and his speed, his force, his terrific power of rhetoric, burns, as it were, and scatters everything before him, and therefore may be compared to a flash of lightning or a thunderbolt" (12.4).[104] Aristotle blames the "adolescent" [*meirakiōdeis*] hyperbolist; but Longinus, valuing sudden affect and the appearance of spontaneity, warns against over-elaboration and thus "puerility" [*meirakiōdes*] when cultivating the sublime (3.4).

Presumably a subspecies of sublimity derived from great thoughts, the imitation of great authors offers another source of sublimity (13–14). With Homer as his preeminent model, Longinus recommends the cultivating of el-evation by borrowing and reworking themes and techniques from the past's great authors. This prescription, we shall see in the next chapter, resembles E. R. Curtius's notion of "outbidding" [*Überbietung*], as the poet-orator seeks to imitate and outdo canonical authors and texts when it involves a *topos* or com-monplace. Given the towering stature that such models have in the eyes of their imitators, it is no accident, Longinus implies, that an exaggerated use of tropes and figures is often the means chosen when attempting to repeat and surpass such elevation. Nor should it be surprising to discover the hyperbolic where the attempt fails.

As for the use of figures to create the sublime, Longinus' various pre-scriptions may be boiled down to the Horatian *ars est celare artem*. One should appear to write in an unpremeditated fashion or ensure that one's figures achieve such brilliance and sublimity that they blind readers to the possibility that they are being manipulated. Again, if the emotion is intense enough or the thought grand enough, no excuse is needed for the excessive use of figures, since hearts or minds will already be swayed.[105] Yet obviously, such excess en-tails great risks; for if the pathos or subject matter of a speech or poem fails to amaze, its figures and all their artifice will be laid bare to skeptical eyes.

Thus regarding metaphor, Longinus recommends a highly metaphorical style only "when emotion sweeps on like a flood and carries the multitude of metaphors as an inevitable consequence" (32.1). Rejecting Aristotle and Quintilian's insistence that the use of audacious or numerous metaphors be softened by *remedia*, he insists that "strong and timely emotion and genuine sublimity" will protect the author from censure (32.4). Inherent in the use of metaphor, however, is the temptation of "excess" [*to ametron*] (32.7).[106] Plato himself is guilty of this as "he is often carried away by a sort of Bacchic possession in his writing . . ." Such excess may also result from "harsh and intemperate metaphor and allegorical bombast [*allegorikon stomphon*]" (32.7). Curiously though, in the next section Longinus offers his celebrated defense of a daring but sometimes flawed style, over a smooth, unblemished, but ultimately mediocre *lexis*: just as the beautiful but dangerous "heights" are to be preferred over the safe but unremarkable plains, likewise, because of their "greatness of mind," Homer is preferable to Apollonius, Pindar to Bacchylides, and Demosthenes, with his "consummate form, sublime intensity, living emotion, redundance, readiness, speed . . . and his own unapproachable vehemence and power," to Hyperides, notwithstanding the latter's untold store of "polished wit" (33–34). Writers of genius, Longinus concludes with fitting hyperbole, are "above the mortal range . . . sublimity lifts them near the mighty mind of god" (36.1).

Due to a two-page lacuna in the manuscript at the outset of his discussion of comparisons and similes and ending somewhere in his discussion of hyperbole, the first thing we learn about hyperbole is its potential for failure:

> . . . Laughable also are such things as "if you do not carry your brains trodden down in your heels" (Demosthenes, *Oration* 7.45). One must know, then, where to draw the line in each case. The hyperbole [*uperbolēn*] is sometimes ruined by overshooting [*uperteinomena*] the mark. Overdo the strain and the thing sags, and often produces the opposite effect to the thing intended.[107] (38.1)

The semantic play on what is "over" or "beyond" enacts the difficulty of controlling the trajectory of hyperbole. Like Aristotle, Longinus makes unintended laughter the chief consequence of not reaching the proper "heights." Yet at the end of his truncated discussion, the desire to solicit laughter, an "emotion based on pleasure," is made to justify comic, "incredible" [*apistian*], hyperboles (38.5–6). Like Quintilian, then, Longinus stresses the versatility of hyperbole, the fact that it may be more than a momentary trope, and that sometimes it can be nearly indistinguishable from amplification:

> Hyperbole may tend to belittle as well as magnify: the common element in both is a strain on the facts. In a sense too vilification is an amplifica⁄ tion of the low and trivial. (38.6)

Such satiric amplification, though, does not aim at the sublime. And when a hyperbolist does strive for the sublime — Isocrates in the *Panegyricus* is cited as exemplary — he can fall "into unaccountable puerility through his desire to amplify everything" (38.2). Isocrates is blamed, moreover, because he alerts readers at the outset of his discourse that he intends to strain credulity. Once again, Longinus urges concealment instead of apology:

> Perhaps then, as we said above of figures, the best hyperbole is the one which conceals the very fact of its being hyperbole. And this happens when it is uttered under stress of emotion to suit the circumstances of a great crisis. (38.3)

Adducing an example from Thucydides, he comments: "That a drink of mud and gore should yet still be worth fighting for is made credible only by the height of the emotions [*tou pathous*] that the circumstances arouse."[108] A sim⁄ ilar emphasis on the emotions is found in a passage by Herodotus:

> Here you may well ask what is meant actually "fighting with teeth" against armed men or being "buried" with missiles; yet it carries cre⁄ dence . . . because Herodotus does not seem to have introduced the inci⁄ dent to justify the hyperbole, but the hyperbole for the sake of the incident. As I am never tired of saying, to atone for a daring phrase the univer⁄ sal specific is found in actions and feelings that almost make one beside oneself. (38.4)

The hyperbolist, therefore, grounds his exaggeration in the universality of a grand, but specific thought — here the courage of the Spartans at Thermopylae — that however objective and historically accurate, also man⁄ ages to cause a certain *ekstaseos* in the reader. And while it might be discon⁄

certing to some historiographers to see the two most celebrated Greek historians quoted in defense of hyperbole, Longinus demonstrates thereby not only hyperbole's reach beyond epic poetry but also the interdependence of *dianoia* and *pathos* as the hyperbolic verges on the sublime. Finally, this dialectic between thought and feeling in his fragmented treatment of hyperbole mirrors the treatise as a whole, for as the final surviving lines of *Peri hypsos* indicate, the emotions (*pathē*) were to be his last topic.[108] But, maddeningly, this section, like what presumably was Longinus' praise of hyperbole at the beginning of section 38, is now lost.

Chapter Two

Renaissance Theories of Hyperbole

> Now the stoics consider themselves next thing in this world
> to deities. But give me a triple or a quadruple stoic, or if
> you choose a six-hundred fold stoic, yet in this matter, just
> think if he won't have to shave off his beard which is his
> special badge of wisdom . . . lower his lofty expression,
> smooth out his forehead, set aside his hard and fast dogmas,
> and talk a bit of nonsense, verging even on madness.
>
> — Erasmus, *The Praise of Folly*

CURTIUS: INEXPRESSIBILITY AND OUTDOING

Envisioning *European Literature and the Latin Middle Ages* (1948) as a "*Nova Rhetorica*," E. R. Curtius crystallizes in his "magnificent book" many con-cepts that remain unformed in classical treatments of hyperbole.[1] Tracing the cardinal phenomena of *outbidding* and *inexpressibility* in the chapter he titles "Poetry and Rhetoric," Curtius sketches the subtle dynamics of hyperbole and imitation in classical and medieval verse.[2] Marshalling a host of exam-ples, he demonstrates how, despite the shifting contingencies of time, place, and taste, certain topics (*topoi*) invariably invite the invention of poetic hyper-bolists, whose task is largely epideictic. But for Curtius, such hyperbole is es-sential not only to medieval literature but also to the "mannerism" he discovers throughout Western literary history. Thus when he considers the style of Calderón, Gracián, and Shakespeare, he rejects the term "Baroque" as his-torically myopic and conceptually confusing; instead, he sees in such manner-ists proof that the resources of the rhetorical tradition — be it in the courts of seventeenth-century Europe, the cloisters of twelfth-century France, or the

villas of Imperial Rome — provide writers with the most vital means to re⁄
new their literary cultures. Given this synchrony, Curtius's topical, intertex⁄
tual approach to hyperbole can help us bridge the gap between ancient
rhetoric and poetics and their early modern counterparts.[3]

Adapting Hermogenes' claim that all poetry is essentially panegyric,
Curtius views the medieval poet as essentially an orator refashioning the com⁄
monplaces and techniques of practical and public eloquence derived from
Cicero and the *Rhetorica ad Herennium*.[4] Yet without the restraining presence
of a circumspect audience trained in forensic and deliberative rhetoric, Mero⁄
vingian and Carolingian panegyrists were freer than their classical counterparts
to refine their art of exaggeration. Starting with standard *topoi* for praising a
ruler (for example, Trojan lineage), these poets eagerly pursue novel paths of
invention. And while this liberty of expression may also derive from the les⁄
sons of medieval handbooks, such as Geoffrey de Vinsauf's *Poetria nova*,
which taught *ars versificandi* and *ars dictandi*, Curtius tends to treat the poet more
as an orator than a scribe. Alternately, the writers of the *Lives of the Saints* mix
"panegyrical and ecclesiastical elements" in their metrical *encomia*.[5] Spaniards,
following Isidore, inaugurate a tradition of praising the virtues of their native
land that incorporates epic elements into the panegyric. With such intertextu⁄
ality fundamental to their invention, even as poets fashion specific *laudes* for
their own cities and countries, certain topics and schema (*formula laudes*) yield
mannerist extremes. Likewise, though Curtius omits them in "Poetry and
Rhetoric," the dynamics of imitation and outdoing among the troubadours as
they praise their beloved (*midons*) and their own skill in "finding" such praise
closely resembles the practice of these panegyric poets.

Of greatest interest to Curtius are the topics associated with personal eu⁄
logy, for here the "inexpressibility *topoi*" prove most innovative and detailed.[6]
By visiting these, the poet, whether by convention, false modesty, or a genuine
sense of inadequacy, emphasizes the "inability to cope with the subject." The
poet ostensibly, ostentatiously, searches for the ultimate term of comparison
by ransacking all history and literature only to admit that he has failed to dis⁄
cover the perfect, unique expression for the subject at hand. In metarhetorical
terms, he admits or feigns the impossibility of comparison even as he com⁄
pares. If the person to be eulogized surpasses the gods in power, wisdom, or
beauty, what more can be said? Drawing on a wealth of vivid examples,
Curtius adumbrates how "inexpressibility *topoi*" become mannerisms in late
Antiquity, are assiduously revisited in medieval verse, and are revived,

adapted, and transformed in the late Renaissance. From Homer onward eulo⁄
gizing poets have claimed that they, like their predecessors, are unequal to the
task at hand, or that they set down only a small part (*pauca e multis*) of what
they wish to say, or that "all sing the praises" of the person or thing being cele⁄
brated or mourned, or that the "whole earth" and all of time join the poet in
praise.[7] Subspecies of these *topoi* are the innumerability *topoi* in which the orator⁄
poet uses huge numbers or quantities to mimic the arithmetician's ability to
suggest infinite or enormous quantities. In chapter one we saw an example of
this from the *Iliad* (9.378–392), but Spenser's "Bower of Bliss" episode of *The
Faerie Queene* (2.12.23) provides a vivid early modern version of the same ges⁄
ture when he blames the creatures of Vice: "All these, and thousands many
more, / And more deforméd Monsters thousand fold, / With dreadfull noise,
and hollow rumbling rore, / Came rushing in the fomy waves enrold . . ."

Because inexpressibility *topoi* often rely on formulas such as *omnis sexus et
aetas*, and given the historical dynamics of imitation, the panegyrist's use of
hyperbole is constantly in danger of becoming conventional or clichéd. What
Curtius dubs the "India *topos*" neatly exemplifies this. A poet, like Fortuna⁄
tus, who claims that all peoples, places, and times sing somebody's praises
might boast that the object of praise

> . . . is known in India or Thule. To be known in India is obviously the
> greatest of fame. India — coupled, if need be, with Thule — is indeed
> the farthest corner of the world . . . It serves *pars pro toto* for "the whole
> earth." This pre⁄eminence of India was attested by Virgil. Had he not
> made Anchises prophesy (*Aeneid*, VI, 794) that Augustus would ex⁄
> tend his rule over the Indians? But when the ruler is incapable of ruling
> his own soul, what boots it "if ever distant India trembles before his
> power, if Thule serves him"? Thus Boethius taught (*Consolatio*, III, 5)
> and found a crowd of imitators, among them Fortunatus. So we can make
> the topos "all sing his praises" yield a subdivision: the "India topos."[8]

The exotic, the marginal, and the fantastic — embodied here by a specific
slice of *terra incognita* — become familiar to readers even as they persist in being
what Aristotle would call "alien" [*allotrios*]. But as such alterity wanes from
overuse, poets are forced to recast the *topos* to seek a new topographical source
of the *ultra fidem*. Thus in early modernity Donne and Camões mined the
newly discovered dimensions of the earth and cosmos to lend such "inex⁄

pressibility *topoi*" novel force and reach. While their sophisticated readers, attuned to the dynamics of *imitatio*, expected and prized such gestures.

That Curtius's insights on medieval verse apply to periods in the classical
and Renaissance literary tradition is confirmed in the context of his discussion
of, arguably, the most self-reflective *topos* of panegyric, *Überbietung*:

> If a person or thing is to be "eulogized" one points out that he or it sur-
> passes anything of the kind and to this end employs a special form of
> comparison, which I call "outdoing." On the basis of a comparison
> with famous examples provided by tradition, the superiority, even the
> uniqueness, of the person or thing to be praised is established. In Latin
> poetry Statius is the first to make this a manner.[9]

A more sophisticated form of what Demetrius calls "hyperbole by superiority," *Überbietung* ("outbidding," "outdoing"), Curtius contends, is one of the
chief engines of medieval encomium. A question of invention as well as style,
an outbidding occurs when a panegyric poet claims his subject surpasses in
worth all previous subjects that have been lauded.[10] In formal terms, *Überbietung* generates ever more *ultra modum* rhetoric — the eulogized subject inevitably becomes itself a new standard of measure and thus a new topic to
be outbid. The history of Petrarchism, I would add, is also a history of outbidding.

Curtius's examples point, however, to the risks such audacious rhetoric
poses for the poet's *ethos*. Noting a contradiction between Statius' praise of
Lucan's poetry as "outdoing" all other verse and more critical claims Statius
makes elsewhere, Curtius asks: "Is hyperbolical panegyric ethically permissible?"[11] By way of an answer to this crucial question, he first observes that
medieval poets are "conscious" of such dilemmas and so either excuse the
hyperbole or, like Peter the Venerable, defend their exaggerated style in more
general terms.[12] But then he adds a new justification, one mouthed also by
many Renaissance rhetors: "Its [panegyric's] chief trope is hyperbole. The
hyperbolic style is authorized not only by the pagan writers but also by the entire Bible."[13] By citing Scripture as the ultimate *auctoritas*, Curtius indicates
that Christian hyperbolists, unlike their classical predecessors, possess a priori
authorization for their exaggerations. This is certainly the case throughout
the Renaissance, as the Bible, with its metaphysical content and constant calls
for credence, proves a particularly fertile and orthodox source of exemplary

hyperboles for the handbooks. Furthermore, medieval theologians who prefer the *via negativa*, like Meister Eckhart, Bernard of Clairvaux, and Julian of Norwich, keep alive the mystical tradition of Pseudo-Dionysius by renovat-ing the hyperboles and paradoxes integral to apophatic and cataphatic speech. Such renovation will in turn inform the attempts of San Juan de la Cruz, Pascal, Sor Juana, and other late Renaissance writers to express mystical ex-periences.

More mundanely, the panegyric poet protects his *ethos* by following cer-tain conventions that allow him to show awareness of his predecessors even as he outdoes them.[14] The tradition itself becomes a kind of *redemium*. Neverthe-less, because of their tireless efforts to set subject and style above previous *enco-mia*, medieval and Renaissance panegyrists are often charged with the same grievous stylistic sins with which Quintilian reproaches the declaimers. That panegyric, as it uses and abuses literary conventions, might lead to mannerist excess and rhetorical artifice seems obvious. A more endemic danger, how-ever, is that panegyric's chief trope, hyperbole, is itself a form of outbidding of more restrained figures. A poem risks being called trite if it fails to outbid its predecessors, while hyperbole often invites charges of "frigidity" and ab-surdity. The hyperbolic poet tries to outbid all other poets, but he also tries to outdo all other hyperboles whether they belong to others or are his own in-vention. For example, in the second, *Iliadic* half of the *Aeneid*, Virgil grapples with the need to outbid in the many battle scenes the cosmological hyperboles that dominate the poem's first half, which takes as its model the *Odyssey*. The much-maligned comparison of Aeneas (12.701–703) to various mountains ("quantus Athos aut quantus Eryx aut ipse coruscis / cum fremit ilicibus quantus gaudetque nivali / vertice se attollens pater Appenninus ad auras.") is Virgil's last sortie in a complex struggle with literary tradition and his own invention. Likewise, much of the *agon* in Sor Juana's *Primero sueño* consists in its secondariness, that is, its debts to Gongorist hyperbole and the discov-ery that her own efforts at outdoing are insufficient in light of her subject matter.

In more formal terms, hyperbole used in a poem's proemium demands to be outbid in its peroration. Like metaphor, hyperbole must surprise if it is to satisfy the reader's desire for novelty and strangeness. Hyperbole helps consti-tute panegyric, which demands excessive novelty if its praises are to seem sin-cere, or at the very least, ingenious. But this dynamic, as we shall see, often becomes still more complicated (and fertile) when it occurs in other genres.

The *Überbietung* inherent in Elizabethan Petrarchism, for example, merges with that of Senecan drama to produce some of Shakespeare's most com, pelling rhetoric. That Lucan's portrayal of Erictho's necromancy has prece, dents in Homer and Virgil, and successors in Dante, D'Aubigné, and Goethe, is fascinating, but its real importance lies in what it reveals about the rhetorical and conceptual limits of epic representation and how those limits are shaped by certain historical factors. The richest hyperboles, the ones that seem to repeat, such as those powering the *world upside,down topos*, cannot be read in synchronic isolation. Nor can their effectiveness or indecorousness be fairly judged without asking what they seek to outbid or how they themselves were later outbid. In short, a hyperbole is not a felicitous literary hyperbole if it does not up the ante each time. The meticulous network of examples and allusions woven by Curtius argues that to read "outbidding" in any period of literary history, diachronic attention must be paid to philologic and stylistic genealogies. Only in this way can the subtleties of hyperbole as a vehicle for the poet's idealism (or skepticism) be judged.

RENAISSANCE HUMANISM AND RHETORIC

It is impossible to understand the many fates of hyperbole in the Renaissance without an appreciation of the inextricable links between rhetoric and the other *studia humanitatis*, or of the aesthetic and social implications of the rhetor, ical *curricula*, or the way that Ramist reorganization of rhetoric and dialectic helps shape developments in philosophic thought. Nor, more generally, can one fully appreciate the extent to which the orator's resources (especially *inven, tio* and *elocutio*) become integral to the poet's task of moving, teaching, and de, lighting without tracing in detail how individual thinkers such as Valla, Vida, Tasso, Wilson, and Ramus rethink the functions of the discursive arts in late fifteenth, and sixteenth,century culture. For accounts of these crucial aspects of the history of rhetoric and their place in the history of ideas, how, ever, I must send readers elsewhere.[15] Bernard Weinberg's exhaustive study of *Cinquecento* literary criticism confirms the highly syncretic nature of Re, naissance poetics, as Italian theorists try to reconcile the classical rhetorical legacy with the claims of Aristotle's *Poetics*, Neo,Platonic philosophy, and Horatian precepts, as well as with the emergence of new literary genres and tastes.[16] The myriad ways criticism written in sixteenth,century Italy, both in the vernacular and Latin, influences critics elsewhere on the continent and those writing in subsequent generations, have been ably traced by Fumaroli,

Vickers, Meerhoff, Murphy, and others.[17] Alternately, the rise of Ramism
with its Balkanization of the rhetorical enterprise and its attempt to strip poets, orators, and historians of the ability to convey the proper method of
thinking, has, Walter Ong argues, the unintended consequence of giving
even more power to the figures of rhetoric as a popular means of persuasion.[18]
Thus David Renaker observes of Robert Burton's method: "Everything that
Ramus had sought to banish — digressiveness, inconsistency, *copia*, the fusion
of rhetoric with dialectic — ran riot over and through the meticulous pattern
of his 'method.'"[19] This is to say that rhetoric well into the seventeenth century, whether in its primary or secondary forms, still provides poetics with its
fundamental "Rezeptionästhetik."[20] The question, though, is what this aesthetic looks like when it comes to hyperbole. As the rhetorical legacy is remade by Renaissance, then Baroque thinkers and poets, how does hyperbole
fare in theory and practice?

Desiderius Erasmus, J. C. Scaliger, and Baltasar Gracián exemplify
strikingly different responses to the questions the classical *rhetors* raise about
hyperbole and its relation to decorum, the *ultra fidem*, amplification, and related matters. Erasmus shifts the relationship of style and invention to promote
the influential ideal of *copia* as eloquence, an ideal that effectively encourages
Christian humanists to cultivate forms of hyperbolic excess. Writing in the
orthodox, cinquecento vein of trying to reconcile Plato, Aristotle, and Horace's ideas on form and style, Scaliger resists the pull of the vernacular and
the marvelous to produce instead an encyclopedic vision of Neo-Latin poetics. Scaliger treats hyperbole as a figure of quantity governed by the poet's
philosophic *prudentia*. Yet at the same time its powers are unleashed in the
critic's excessive zeal to champion Virgil as the unrivaled neoclassical model
for imitation. Finally, Gracián transforms the aesthetics of disproportionality
into a constitutive element of his theory of Baroque wit such that the hyperbolic conceit gains real aesthetic, philosophic, and theological currency. With
Gracián, witty exaggeration becomes a refined mode of understanding and
expression. In brief, by attending to how these theorists follow and diverge
from their classical counterparts, we will be in a much better position to appreciate and evaluate the complex history of imitation, invention, and *letteraturizzazione* in the Baroque period — whether in Spanish lyric poetry, Jacobean
drama, or French philosophy — as it concerns hyperbole.

ERASMIAN *COPIA*

When it comes to hyperbole, Erasmus (1466/69–1536) warily practices what he teaches. A foe of slavish neo-Ciceronian imitation, a reluctant flatterer of princes, but also the Renaissance's most celebrated mock encomiast, Erasmus teaches and models a form of discursive hyperbole that boldly marries ampli-fication with invention. His celebrated philological rigor and antipathy to dogmatism spur him to cultivate a vision of copious eloquence in service of a new breed of humanism. And if this eloquence sometime flirts with hyper-bolic extremes, it also spurns those who thirst for linguistic purity and ideo-logical absolutes. In *Ciceronianus sive de optimo genero dicendi* (1528), Erasmus has Cicero's sixteenth-century epigones discredit themselves with their laugh-able excesses in *imitatio*.[21] In the *Panegyricus*, an epideictic oration in honor of Philip the Handsome's return to Brussels in 1504, he skillfully if somewhat reluctantly pursues traditional epideixis.[22] And as the author of the immensely influential *De duplici copia verborum ac rerum commentarii duo* (1512; final, author-ized edition, 1534), he describes and performs a kind of discursive excess that will fuel much of Baroque prose. For Erasmus, to cultivate *copia* is to favor abundance over brevity, ingenuity over mere communication.

Inheriting the philological riches of Italian humanism, but suspicious of some of its more pagan elements, Erasmus offers his numerous European readers compelling new methods to accomplish aspects of the *translatio stu-diorum*. His *De ratione studii*, for example, originally published along with *De copia* and designed for his friend John Colet's use at St. Paul's School in Lon-don, is modeled directly on the *Institutio oratoria*. With this said, its condensed contents and concern not to corrupt Colet's young charges with unseemly or superfluous material pave the way for the pragmatic stance toward the study of antiquity and the use of rhetorical and literary models that will characterize most of the handbooks written in Northern European countries in the six-teenth century.[23]

Jean Chomarat has persuasively argued that Erasmus was more of a grammarian, rhetor, and orator than a theologian.[24] In this respect, Lorenzo Valla exercised the most immediate influence on Erasmian rhetoric. Valla's *Elegantiae linguae latinae* (1471) adumbrates many of the prescriptions fleshed out in *De copia*, and it helps persuade Erasmus that Quintilian (and not Cic-ero) is the most important classical author for aspiring Christian humanists.[25] Valla's insistence on the merits of Latin over the vernacular is also imitated by

Erasmus, although ironically the effect of the latter's teaching on *copia* will be felt most strongly in vernacular literature. Meanwhile, as his comments in the *Défense* confirm, Du Bellay at least learned Erasmus's cardinal lesson concern-ing *copia*: namely, that it must derive from an understanding of *res* as well as from a mastery of style and imitation of classical models:

> Se compose donc celui que voudra enrichir sa langue à l'imitation des meilleurs auteurs grecs et latins: et à toutes leurs plus grandes vertus, comme à un certain but, dirige la pointe de son style. Car il n'y a point de doute que la plus grande part de l'artifice ne soit contenue en l'imita-tion, et tout ainsi que ce fut le plus loable aux anciens de bien inventer, aussi est-ce le plus utile de bien imiter, même à ceux dont la langue n'est encore bien copieuse et riche. Mais entende celui qui voudra imiter, que ce n'est chose facile de bien suivre les vertus d'un bon auteur, et quasi comme se transformer en lui . . . Je dis ceci, pource qu'il y en a beaucoup en toutes langues qui, sans pénétrer aux plus cachées et intérieures par-ties de l'auteur qu'ils se sont proposé, s'adaptent seulement au premier re-gard, et, s'amusant à la beauté des mots, perdent la force des choses.[26]

The tension here may be anachronistically described as between those who would merely *copy* and those who understand the Erasmian lesson that *copia* means true eloquence. As Terence Cave argues in his invaluable study of how the desire for *copia* helps shape sixteenth-century French literature, this tension has an intriguing etymological basis, not to mention important consequences for post-structuralist approaches to Renaissance *écriture*.[27] But rather than cov-ering ground already well surveyed, I would show how *De copia* identifies, de-scribes, and teaches its readers to interpret species of discursive hyperbole that will thrive throughout the Baroque.

Taking as his starting point Quintilian's brief discussion concerning *copia verborum ac rerum* (10.1.5–6), Erasmus initially represents *copia* as having as much to do with things as with words.[28] Indeed, the close connection and fre-quent conflation of what is proper to the *copia* of words and what belongs to the *copia* of things is maintained throughout the treatise, which, not acciden-tally, also serves as an encyclopedic storehouse (*thesaurus*) of humanist learn-ing. This conflation also may explain why Erasmus inverts the usual expository order for handbooks: book one is dedicated to figures of style, whereas book two treats what is traditionally classified as methods of invention. Further,

rather than dividing rhetoric into its five parts to be analyzed separately, Erasmus incorporates them in a largely ad hoc manner into his description and
performance of *copia*.[29] For example, the stasis theory that takes up much of
the middle books in the *Institutio* is first made explicit only when Erasmus
turns, late in Book II, to the tenth "method of embellishing" [*ratio locuple-
tandi*], a method of amplifying based "on inventing as many propositions as
possible," that is "rhetorical propositions or themes, which are demonstrated
to be true by the exposition of arguments."[30] Reaffirming Quintilian's belief
(5.10.119–121) that such *heurisis* relies on native *ingenium* as much as technique, Erasmus proleptically rejects the Ramist insistence on separating invention (dialectic) from style (rhetoric).[31] Not that he dismisses the need for
logical rigor; instead, copious invention requires the faculties of imagination
and reason to work in consort. Likewise, experience helps as much as *scientia*.[32] Determined to teach the proper *ratio* for cultivating *copia*, Erasmus effectively lays down a gauntlet for Ramus and Descartes whose methods will try
to separate *res* from *verba*.[33] And if ultimately Erasmus subordinates the rigorous claims of dialectic to the more humanist, contingent rewards offered by
rhetoric, then Ramus unequivocally subordinates rhetoric to dialectic —
though his dialectic has so many holes in it, that Ong for one, asserts that it ultimately leans on rhetoric's persuasive powers.[34] In other words, in *De copia* the
battle between *ratio* (method, reason) and *oratio* (speech, rhetoric) is already
joined, and the insistence by Cicero and the early Italian humanists such as
Pico that such a struggle is unnecessary has been forgotten.

Copia can mean "abundance," "plenty," "quantity" or "resources." In a
rhetorical context it is synonymous with "eloquence" and the "ability" needed
to produce it.[35] It can have starkly material, even sensual connotations, as in
Ovid's play on the myth of Amaltheia and the horn of plenty (*cornucopia*) in
Metamorphoses (9.86–88): ". . . divesque meo Bona Copia cornu est."[36] But
usually *copia* denotes a *facilitas* that creates subtler *affectus* in the audience. As
its etymology (*co-ops*, "with the goddess Ops") and martial connotations (in
the plural it is the Roman word for "troops") suggest, *copia* can appeal to the
auditor-reader in many different ways.[37] Above all, Erasmus emphasizes the
cognitive pull of *copia* as it lends *varietas* to a speech, an invaluable ability
lauded with fitting hyperbole:

> Variety is so powerful in every sphere that there is absolutely nothing,
> however brilliant, which is not dimmed if not commended by variety.

Nature above all delights in variety; in all this huge concourse of things, she has left nothing anywhere unpainted by her wonderful technique of variety [*quod non admirabili quodam varietatis artificio de pinxerit*]. Just as the eyes fasten themselves on some new spectacle, so the mind is always look, ing round for some fresh object of interest. If it is offered a monotonous succession of similarities, it very soon wearies and turns its attention else, where . . . This disaster can easily be avoided by someone who has it at his fingertips to turn [*vertere*] one idea into more shapes than Proteus himself is supposed to have turned into [*quam Proteus ipse se transformasse dicitur*] . . . We shall also find [this form of exercise] of great assistance in commenting on authors, translating books from foreign languages, and writing verse [*in scribendo carmine*]. (1.8)

In brief, *copia* produces eloquence as well as understanding. Sometimes it is synonymous with ornament itself, but it is also described in 1.9 as a faculty of mind, a now logical, now imaginative way of thinking about the world.[38] Cave suggests that it effectively replaces the classical notion of *amplificatio*, al, beit in a manner that the amplified *res* refers more to a "word,thing" than an "object,thing." Thus "the sign of Proteus" invoked here and elsewhere in the treatise "is not simply a pedagogical marker, but a generative principle with wide,ranging functions."[39] In this way, the cultivation of *copia* — at least in the sixteenth,century writing of Rabelais, Ronsard, Montaigne, and, as I will argue later, in the poetry and prose of the Spanish Baroque — precipitates a centripetal, transformative process wherein all the stuff of the world is enlisted to increase the self,consciousness of the poet,orator.

Like hyperbole, however, *copia* invites failure as well as success. Fittingly, the title of Erasmus's first chapter is: *Periculosam esse Copiae affectationem*. This danger resembles the *periculum* that Quintilian ascribes to hyperbole, for as Erasmus's many examples strive to illustrate, decorum and *ethos* remain urgent concerns, especially for the Christian humanist.[40] Attempts at *copia* built on ignorance of the *res* or *copia* that deforms the oration by being inopportune (as in some panegyric), tasteless (as in some satire), or obscure (as in some poetry) are faulted. Empty or bathetic loquacity must be assiduously avoided.

And yet, "if we are not instructed in these techniques [of creating *copia*], we shall often be found unintelligible, harsh, or even totally unable to express ourselves." Moreover, if pupils are to learn how to achieve *copia*, "everything must be exaggerated" in their training. Adapting Quintilian's observations

(2.4.3–8) on the preferability of training students to produce too much *copia* rather than too little ("Facile remedium est ubertatis, sterilia nullo labore vin-cuntur."), Erasmus proves more liberal than his teacher: "It does not worry me that certain writers have been blamed for excessive or misjudged fullness of diction. Quintilian censures Stesichorus for overabundant and extravagant expression [*nimis effusam et redundatem copiam*], while at the same time admitting that is a fault that cannot be absolutely avoided."[41] In brief, the only ways to learn *copia* are by reading and translating other authors, by relying on memory, and by practicing the use (and flirting with the abuse) of such figures as pe-riphrasis, metaphor, metalepsis, auxesis, and hyperbole.

Initially, Erasmus treats hyperbole as simply another means of creating copious, elegant variation. His definition of *superlatio* is standard fare:

> In this, as Seneca says, we reach the truth by saying something which is obviously false. Hyperbole says more than the situation warrants, yet the truth can be inferred from the falsehood: for example, he could split rocks with his never-ending chatter; to touch heaven with one's finger; swifter than the wings of the thunder; I shall strike the stars with my ex-alted head.[42] (1.73)

Only in his subsequent definition of meiosis (*diminutio*) does he begin to break new ground: "*Diminutio* too can sometimes involve hyperbole: 'they scarce cling to their bones'; 'shorter than a pygmy'; 'he has less than nothing.' But . . . I shall have something to say about this type when I reach the proper place."[43] That place is "On methods of varying superlative expressions" [*Quibus modis superlativum variamus*] (1.46), which, fittingly, is one of the longest chapters in book one.[44] Following shorter chapters prescribing ways to in-crease the effect of a word-idea (1.41), "Making the comparative more em-phatic" (1.43) and "Making the superlative more emphatic" (1.44)[45], this chapter illustrates the various ways to make and vary superlative statements. These include: "using a verb or positive adjective modified by an adverb" (e.g., *vir minime doctus*); employing the comparative (e.g., *nullo inferior*); using certain verbs (e.g., *vincit omnes candore*); choosing modifiers like *unicus, solus, singularis* (e.g., *unice te amat*); employing certain syntactical constructions with *tam, quam, quantum potest, quoad fieri potest*; asking rhetorical questions (e.g., *quis hoc uno facundior?*); making absolute statements (e.g., *domus celebratur ita ut cum maxime* (Cicero)); or mixing metonymy with hyperbole, "like calling a very cruel man an Atreus . . . or comparisons that involve hyperbole: whiter than snow, more barbaric than a Scythian, more talkative than a jackdaw or turtle-dove." Of this last type, Erasmus notes that it depends on "some substance re-markable for a quality in question, such as whiter than snow, blacker than pitch." Fusing and confusing notions of quality and quantity, he thus makes an empirical understanding of the nature of things constitutive of the success of a superlative expression. Alternately, the use of metonymy — calling a mon-strous person, a monster; or "a dissolute person, a running sore" — requires a talent for forging abstractions.

Following these prescriptions, Erasmus offers an astonishing litany of quotations, taken largely from classical literature and his own *Adages*, to illus-trate the many paths available to the hyperbolist who would make the extraor-dinary seem immanent. (Indeed, as with many of his texts, Erasmus seizes the occasions of subsequent editions of *De copia* to expand greatly the book's con-tents.[46]) He shows how certain nouns used with a comparative can yield a su-perlative idea: "more stormy than the Adriatic, more bibulous than a sponge, thirstier than the sands"; then, how hyperbole can result from repeating the stem of the same word: "more garrulous than garrulity, uglier than ugliness." This is similar in kind to saying: "more mutable than Proteus, more change-able than Empusa, . . . madder than Ajax, craftier than Ulysses, uglier than Thersites . . . obscurer than Heraclitus, more learned than Aristarchus."[47] Other superlative expressions play on the "names of living creatures" such as "more melodious than a nightingale, more deadly than a viper." Still others require knowledge of "occupations" ("more brutal than a hangman . . . more severe than an Areopagite"), or are adjectives derived from specific nouns ("a vultrine stomach, a foxy mind, leonine ferocity, Thrasonian boasting, De-mean harshness, Stentorian voice, Ciceronian eloquence"). In sum, for these exaggerations to be called eloquent, writer and reader must be able to draw upon a shared store of knowledge provided by sundry humanist traditions.

Erasmus in 1.33 also effectively resolves Quintilian's hesitation whether *amplificatio* should be considered a form of hyperbole where he regales his readers with two virtuoso demonstrations of how to vary a sentence with dif-ferent diction and figures.[48] The one hundred fifty variations on the sentence, "Your letter has delighted me very much" [*tuae litterae me magnopere delectarunt*], and two hundred variations on, "Always, as long as I live, I shall remember you" [*semper dum vivam, tui meminero*], are recast to show "the Protean variety of shapes" possible in ordinary expressions.[49] Decidedly different from the jejune exercises promoted by Roman declaimers, neither set of variations digresses far from the original sentence. Nor do they follow the patterns of amplification Quintilian describes when he prescribes *incrementum, comparatio, ratiocinatio*, and *congeries* — these will be handled later (2.10) when Erasmus turns to inven/ tion proper. The two sets of variations instead represent a species of discursive hyperbole in two principal senses. First, the words *magnopere* and *semper* verge, respectively, on the superlative and the absolute. Second, and more importantly, in demonstrating the astonishing extent to which a thought can be repeated and yet varied without losing its decorum, Erasmus proves how the writer's *ingenium* creates a field of play in prose as ample as that traditionally given to verse.[50]

As for how diction may verge on hyperbole, his gloss on the word *magnopere*, offered before the variations on the first sentence begin, is illuminat/ ing. It can mean:

> . . . greatly, intensely, extremely, wonderfully, marvelously, extraordinar/ ily (synonym); mightily, hugely, superlatively, exceedingly, singularly (*aux/ esis* heightening); in no scant measure, on no small scale, in no common manner (opposites and negatives); it is impossible to say how much, it is beyond belief [*incredibile dictu*], I could not finds words to express (these and similar expressions are on the way to hyperbole) [*atque id genus alia Hyberbolen sapiunt*].[51]

One of the variations proper is: "Your brief missive flooded me with inex/ pressible joy." This uses "metaphor," Erasmus notes, though like many of the other sentences, it also strongly savors of hyperbole. Alternately, another vari/ ation employs metonymy, metaphor, and hyperbole: "Your letter was pure honey to me." Another replaces *magnopere* with an *incrementum* of sorts: "There is no pleasure, no delight, that I would willingly compare with your letter." Similarly, in the second set of variations, the "not particularly fertile or suggestive" sentence becomes most vivid and moving when the variation pivots on the word *semper*: "While any drop of blood retains its warmth in this feeble frame, the memory of More will never grow cold in my heart." Re/ calling here and throughout this second set his beloved friend, Sir Thomas More, who will be executed in 1535, Erasmus hints that his rhetorical virtu/ osity has a real *res* motivating it. The field of play, in other words, is also a field of mourning; "death" figures in many of the variations, as if Erasmus is

self-consciously touching upon the *aere perennius topos* even while accomplish-
ing the more mundane task of instructing schoolboys.

Fittingly, to begin Book II, which is explicitly dedicated to teaching
methods of amplification, Erasmus chooses to exemplify the first method of
extending and dividing a thought by amplifying the phrase: "He lost all
worldly goods through extravagance" [*Rem universam luxu perdidit*].[52] Implicitly warning against the dangers of a certain kind of excess in life even while
producing eloquent *copia*, he now would show that abundance of thought is
distinct from abundance of speech, and that the former can clarify and so improve the latter. Yet though Erasmus warns repeatedly against creating "a
mass of unorganized material," his own text frequently flirts with such shapeless excess.[53] The fact that the monstrous and the strange often provide him
with subject matter may be excused given the tastes of his young readers. But
that he himself seems to revel in testing decorum's boundaries points to a more
fundamental tension. In the fifth method of amplification, which describes
how to create *enargeia* or *evidentia*, Erasmus ornaments Quintilian's precepts
with a cornucopia of fantastic examples from his wide-ranging reading of
classical literature and history. Joining the serious business of the *rhetor* with a
more subjective, aesthetic desire to entertain and perhaps move his reader
("Verum quum tota res ad voluptatem spectat . . ."), he enthusiastically recommends for imitation some of the most extravagant, ingenious moments in
Homer, Virgil, Ovid, Plutarch, Pliny, and Lucan.[54] From descriptions of
"whirlwinds, storms, and shipwrecks," to those of "prodigies, eclipses of the
sun, snowstorms, torrential rain, lightning flashes," and "living creatures"
such as the "porcupine" and the "phoenix," to a "a chariot, a Colossus, a
pyramid, or anything else the description of which would afford delight,"
Erasmus unfolds the marvels of nature and antiquity.[55] And though he insists,
as he catches his breath, that it is best to have seen these things with one's own
eyes in order to describe them well, the kinds of prosopopeia, topographia,
and chronographia he adumbrates are almost all based on imitation of classical models. Thus Cave observes that such *copia* suspends the distinction between truth and falsity: "the real and the imaginary are allowed to slide
together and contaminate one another; the things which appear in their verbal
surface have discarded the signs of their provenance and are happy to masquerade as words."[56] But that this disregard for truth claims will also be
echoed in Gracián's and Tesauro's theories of the conceit again suggests that
hyperbole's main task may be expression rather than representation.

Such contamination also occurs in one of the subsections of the eleventh method of amplification, which putatively covers the production of proof (*pistis*). Initially insisting that "[m]ost of these are derived from the circum-stances of the case, which cover persons or things [*rei*]," the subsequent dis-cussion of employing commonplaces, examples, parables, images, maxims, fables, and fictions, rather than appealing to the student's experience or un-derstanding of the *res* itself, relies instead on Erasmus's ability to ransack the overstuffed *thesaurus* of humanist knowledge. Moreover, much of the material found there can be freely amplified and exaggerated.[57] Nonetheless, when handling fictional examples and narratives, or comparisons in epideictic ora-tory, the orator is advised to carefully qualify his material by appealing, for instance, to authority or by employing allegory. In this respect, despite under-scoring several times in the treatise's closing pages that he is not writing a rhetorical handbook, Erasmus remains wary, or wants to seem wary, of upset-ting rhetorical decorum. So when he does finally mention oratory's offices — "to inform, to give pleasure, to influence" — he grants the orator who chooses to practice *brevitas* only the task of providing information.[58] The "laconic," Attic orator, Erasmus ironically observes, "must shun all figures that would make his speech sonorous, splendid, vehement, elaborate, or delightful."[59] Conversely, the copious orator can command attention, dispel boredom, gen-erate good will, stir passions, overcome prejudice, foster belief, and create real and lasting pleasure.[60] Granted, the copious style has its own vices as well as virtues; but its faults may be excused, even redeemed, on the occasion when the orator has more subjective, artistic motivations:

> I would also advise you not to express yourself with equal fullness at all points . . . So leaving aside the things that do not naturally lend them-selves to fullness of expression, choose the most fertile and easily handled topics, unless of course one wants to try one's hand or demonstrate one's cleverness on occasion, and make an elephant out of a fly, as the saying goes. Thus Favorinus eulogizes fever, Synesius baldness, myself folly (in my *Moriae encomium*) . . .[61]

In this way, all the prescriptions for cultivating *copia* are directed toward a certain kind of literary practice, one in which self-conscious ingenuity and artistry are prized over the keeping of decorum. And in justifying his most fa-mous literary work, published a year before *De copia*, Erasmus helps precipitate the Renaissance and Baroque vogue for mock encomia, while also indicating how the rhetoric of (dis)praise can question its own form and function.

Making ironic, hyperbolic elephants out of flies is not just to increase or distort quantities. It is a task at the heart of the late humanist response to an at/ mosphere of violent religious controversy between competing orthodoxies. As Thomas Conley observes, one may well view the "humanist rhetorical perspective" as embodied by Erasmus as synonymous with the "controversial/ ist cast of mind."[62] For in having Folly (*Stultitia*) praise folly and mock wis/ dom, Erasmus's mock epideixis masterfully argues both sides of the question (*utramque partem*). The reader, in turn, is left with the enormous, Tantalean challenge of making sense of the hilarious, but undecidable hyperboles of Erasmus's foolish speaker:

> Who can explain me better than I can myself — unless, perhaps, some/ one who knows me better than I do? Actually, I think what I am doing here is more decent [*non paulo . . . modestius*] than what the common ruck of pundits and patricians do when, under cover of a certain perverse mock modesty, they hire some servile rhetorician or limber/tongued poet [*rhetorem quenpiam palponem vel poetam vaniloquum*], and bribe him literally to pour forth their praises, praises [*laudes*] that are nothing but flat/out lies [*mere mendacia*]. While the recipient of all this adulation spreads his borrowed plumes and raise his crest aloft like a peacock, the barefaced orator expatiates, comparing his good/for/nothing subject to some god or other, and proposing him as the absolute model of all the virtues [*ab/ solutum omnium virtutum exemplar*], especially those of which they both know he doesn't possess a "single grain." Still, the speaker doesn't hesi/ tate to deck his crow in borrowed plumes, to "whitewash his Ethiopian," or finally to "puff up his gnat to the size of an elephant." In any case, I'm following the advice of that trite old proverb that says a man is en/ titled to praise himself when there's nobody else to do it.[63]

In the barest terms, *The Praise of Folly* is a *declamatio* performing a paradox. Erasmus can and does point to classical models to excuse the "frivolity of the argument and the absurdity of the jokes," as well as to protect his *ethos*, though this does not make his satire one whit less sharp.[64] Situating Erasmus's text within the rhetorical tradition of the mock encomium and then alongside *De*

copia itself, Marcel Tetel describes the enormous hermeneutic labor facing the
reader in this way: "Par définition, l'éloge paradoxal opte pour le *mundus inver-*
sus, afin de mettre en question la conduite et la pensée de l'homme. D'autre
part, l'éloge paradoxal par sa portée hyperbolique interroge le lecteur sur la
signification, ou les significations qu'il faut conférer à ce texte . . ."[65] Tetel's
own reading discovers a "logorrhée" in Dame Folly, who "se plaît à dégoiser
un débit surchargé, à exhiber une *rhetorica perpetua*, car pour guérir les fous, il
faut une démence verbale et non une *rhetorica precisa* . . ." *Copia* is thus made to
widen performatively, deliberately the space between words and things. Erasmus's prosopopeia institutes "anamorphotic play," which "veut faire rire et
faire penser, mêler l'hyperbole au fait, mystifier au moyen de la *copia*, mentir et
dire vrai selon des perspectives interchangeables, c'est-à-dire, selon des op-
tiques différentes."[66] Moreover, that title and text pun heavily on the dedi-
catee's name, Thomas More, and that Erasmus does not spare scholars like
himself from mockery, further preclude finding a stable perspective from
which one might interpret such exaggeration. In other words, as in *De copia*,
appeals to experience, decorum, or even logic are ultimately outstripped by the
momentum or force of the writing itself. Literary *copia*, here propelled by a
persona whose *ethos* is itself the subject of the discourse, becomes "decent"
only because it is predicated on "flat-out lies." It becomes an extravagant joke
with no discernible punch line and no stable referent; to hyperbolize is to tell
and not to tell enormous truths in one eloquent breath.[67]

SCALIGER'S ENCYCLOPEDIA

Curtius's call in 1948 for scholars to mine the riches of the Latin Middle
Ages has recently been echoed, or more accurately, paralleled by Christopher
Celenza, whose *Lost Italian Renaissance* makes a forceful case for a renewed
engagement with neo-Latin texts of the Italian Renaissance.[68] To make sense
of the "difference between diachrony and synchrony, between philosophical
historicism and philosophical idealism" in twentieth-century approaches to
Italian humanism, Celenza urges not only renewed attention to the social and
cultural circumstances informing our scholarship, but also that we look back
to the Renaissance itself for the roots of this dichotomy.[69] In strategically casting Eugenio Garin and Lorenzo Valla as historicists, and P. O. Kristeller and
Marsilio Ficino as idealists, Celenza offers a promising dialectic with which
to approach historical figures whose debts and contributions to the neo-Latin

tradition may be more ambiguous or marginal than the paradigmatic Valla or Ficino.

One such figure is Julius Caesar Scaliger (1484–1558) who, born in Padua, led an itinerant life chasing patronage as he variously tried to salvage and renew aspects of the scholastic and Aristotelian legacies. Spending most of his adulthood in France, Scaliger gained some measure of early fame due to an invective against Erasmus's anti-Ciceronianism and then late in life as the erudite but bilious foe of Cardano's natural philosophy.[70] Aside from such polemics, Scaliger was renowned in his own time and in subsequent generations for variously promoting the value of *experimenta* over mere *auctorita* in his neo-Latin books on medicine, botany, and natural philosophy. Conversely, his *Poetices libri septem* (1561; reprinted 1586, 1594; revised editions 1607, 1617) is an unrepentant encyclopedia of neo-Aristotelian poetics that, given the concurrent rise of vernacular poetries and the advent of more philologically oriented criticism, can only be viewed as something of an "anachronism."[71] The *Poetices*, that is, was written just as the champions of vernacular poetry such as Du Bellay, Sébillet, Speroni, and Herrera were successfully pleading their case. Another historical irony is that his son, Joseph Scaliger, became one of the pioneers of "scientific," philological criticism destined to challenge the neo-Aristotelian emphasis on genre, verisimilitude, and ethical *affectus* so prevalent in sixteenth-century literary theory.[72]

Yet Scaliger is important for this study because he represents in its more sophisticated if long-winded form the orthodoxy that keeping verisimilitude was the poet's most important task. For all of its derivativeness, frequent superficiality, and many internal contradictions, the *Poetices* remains a valuable *thesaurus* for understanding the state and direction of late Renaissance poetics. As Luc Dietz, principal editor, translator, and commentator of the invaluable German-Latin edition of the *Poetices* concludes, it is "the most extensive treatment of poetics in the sixteenth century."[73] More specifically, Scaliger's Herculean attempt to give precise definitions and pertinent examples of all poetic genres, meters, and figures, to construct a synthetic, tabular order that would encompass the entire poetic enterprise, and to situate stylistics within a larger theory of representation and what Heinrich Plett sees as "a general ontology of the work of art" possesses at once real philologic rigor, philosophic depth, and all the faults and contradictions of an approach marked by extreme, syncretic abstraction.[74]

Spurning the dialogic approach of other Neo-Latin literary criticism, such as Girolamo Vida's highly influential *De arte poetica* (1527) and Antonio Minturno's *De poeta* (1559), Scaliger's *Poetices* adopts a single, authoritative voice to reconcile Aristotelian prescriptions and terminology, Neo-Platonic claims regarding poetic inspiration and form, and the Horatian emphasis on the poet's ethical role. More broadly speaking, the ways in which Scaliger lends the study of poetry and poetics analytic precision and ethical gravitas are his book's greatest contribution to Renaissance literary criticism.[75] While attending to many technical and formal issues, he also gives poetry, and the rhetorical assumptions and techniques thoroughly informing his theory of poetic style, a strong ethical cast, and thus ultimately an ontological one as well.[76] Thus it is worth recalling, *pace* Weinberg, that the question of whether and how poetics was conceived as a distinctive *ars* is critical, for it largely determines what kinds of questions will be asked and to a great extent what kinds of answers will be found.[77] Like Horace, Scaliger would have the poet pleasantly teach right moral action: "... the goal of poetics is not imitation, but pleasant learning [*doctrina iucunda*], through which the characters of souls [*mores animorum*] may be led to appropriate reason, so that in this way man may succeed to perfect deeds, which is called beatitude."[78]

The poet's virtuous use of figures, Scaliger insists, must be guided by *prudentia*, a claim Dietz regards as a novel attempt to "combine Aristotelian psychology with classical rhetoric."[79] Significantly, such syncreticism shifts the notion of decorum from the external, social sphere to an interior, psychological one. As such, it will find its Baroque counterpart in Gracián and Tesauro's theories of wit where the remnants of Aristotelian psychology are applied to analyses of the poetic faculty of *ingenium*. Indeed, Scaliger also reveals a venerable, Neo-Platonic strain in his conception of the poet as a creator and lawgiver, who aims to improve upon if not overstep nature and its bounds. There are numerous poetic genres, he asserts, such as "lyric poetry, scholia, paeans, elegies, epigrams, satires, sylvae, epithalamia, hymns, and others in which there is no imitation, but only bare *epangelia*, that is narration or explication of the emotions, which only originate from the ingenuity of the singer, not from a represented person."[80] In this sense, the source of these genres and their corresponding *affectus* are subjective, for the individual poet relies on his own *ingenium* and not, as a narrow Aristotelian view would have it, a mere *imitatio* of the world.

Entitled *Idea*, Book Three purports to deal with the "philosophic" bases for poetry as a form of invention. (Book Four, *Parasceve* or "Preparation," covers *elocutio* or, as Scaliger confusingly terms it, *dispositio*; here he demonstrates how the figures and tropes, various types of style, and even different meters can be prudently employed.) The longest of the seven books — it comprises about a quarter of the whole — it also is "the most theoretically demanding [*anspruchsvollste*] and contains the ripest, most complex and original thinking of Scaliger on the art of poetry's essence and function."[81] Putatively, the chief topic here is *imitatio* and its proper object; but to prepare his discussion of imitation as invention, Scaliger first distinguishes between "thing" and "word."[82] Whereas *res* may also include the metrical "material" of Book 2, the first chapter of the third book undertakes a more metaphysical inquiry into the nature of ideas (*res*) as they come to be represented in words:

> Things themselves are the goal of speech; words are their signs [*Res autem ipsae finis sunt orationis, quarum verba notae sunt*]. Wherefore words receive from objects themselves that form, through which they are precisely what they are. On this account we have entitled this book *Idea*; not because I commit the error of believing with the Platonists that words are created essentially from the nature of things themselves, but because in speech we show not the things themselves, but rather how the qualities and quantities of things are in such and such manner. Thus just as "Socrates" is the idea of an image, so is "Troy" the image of Homer's *Iliad*.[83]

Despite his protests to the contrary here, Scaliger's use of *Idea* does retain a strong NeoPlatonic flavor. Thus Anne Moss comments upon the tensions in Scaliger's treatment of *verba et res*, and underscores the tensions in the theory of representation that underlie it:

> Perhaps the basic question to which Scaliger addresses himself is the division in poetic writing between *verba* and *res*. This was a pedagogic simplification inherited from the rhetoricians, but recent discussion had emphasized and complicated it, pulling in one direction towards a theory of literature as selfreferring, autonomous discourse, as in Fracastoro and even Vida, and in the other direction towards literature as a trans

parent medium through which the things it is said to imitate, especially moral things, are clearly perceived.[84]

For example, Scaliger is keen throughout 3.1 to establish the *habitus* of a thing or a person, by which he means its fixed nature, quality, or condition. In this way, a person's character or mores, expressed through words as much as deeds, may become an object of imitation as well as a *res* pointing to more permanent truths.

It is in this ambiguous light that Scaliger's account of the poetic figures should be read. For while the individual poet discovers how to apply figures to a subject, such invention clearly assumes an a priori, external, and thus stable reality. In one of the key passages grounding the philosophical claims of his poetics, Scaliger neatly maps the cognitive and ontological basis for this two-way street:

> A figure is an admissible delineation of concepts which are in the mind and which differs from common usage [*Figura est notionum quae in mente sunt tolerabilis delineatio, alia ab usu communi*]. I call concepts the external forms of things, which are conveyed through the senses to be represented in the mind. These external forms have the same contours as the things themselves [*Harum specierum lineamenta communia sunt qualia in rebus ipsis*]. Therefore when the eyes of an angry man are bloodshot, then I interpret them in my imagination and say, on account of their similarity [*a similitudine*] with flames, that they are enflamed and that fire flashes from them.[85]

The creation of this metaphor *a similtudine* seems to occur, Scaliger's passive constructions suggest, with hardly any poetic agency. The activity of the senses simply leads via a "tolerabilis delineatio" to a *notio*, which the figure represents. Though not a very inspired vision, it does potentially open the door to more conceited verse. For example, in *Troilus and Cressida*, Troilus exclaims: "Inflamed with Venus. Never did young man fancy / With so eternal and so fixed a soul" (5.2.165–166). Here the metaphor is based on the similarity of internal or abstract qualities: the lover's fiery humor and the commonplace concerning Venus. Or Scaliger could have quoted Virgil's description of "accensa" Dido (4.364). But to be fair his aim here is to delineate a reliable theory of the *figura* — ample space will be devoted to examples in Books 5 and 6. Thus the fascinating if rather scholastic description of how the mind forms figures, which follows this initial definition, tries to explicate how the "features" or "contours" [*lineamenta*] of an object form a superficial "sketch" [*delineatio*] of the object such that it is adequately, quantitatively, if only ana-logically represented to the "soul" [*animam*].[86] This makes all the more sur-prising his subsequent, Neo-Platonic comparison of this process to how angels move the heavenly spheres without becoming adulterated by their materiality; though the idea seems to be that the discovery of figures is a spiritual as well as mental process guaranteed by the divine ordering of the world. Finally, Scaliger allows that this process requires human "scientias" to succeed. He divides these into *dialectica, grammatica*, and then a third species consisting of "*oratoria, historica, poetica*" — each having figures proper to them (so that di-alectics, for instance, has the syllogism).

In this respect, the figure of hyperbole, though potentially justifiable in the light of Aristotelian and Platonic philosophy, belongs principally to the tra-ditional *ars* of rhetoric.[87] In describing this art, after outlining the cardinal virtues of style (3.24–28) — *prudentia, efficacia, varietas*, and *suavitas* [prudence, actuality, variety, and pleasantness] — Scaliger divides all the figures (3.31) into categories corresponding roughly to quantitative and qualitative judg-ments: "A figure signifies either what is or the opposite" [*Significatur aut id quod est aut contrarium*]. The former is quantitative, as in *tractatio* (an exact descrip-tion), *detractio* (an understated description), and *hyperbole* (an overstated de-scription), while the latter is qualitative, as in *allegory*.[88] Accordingly, when hyperbole becomes the focus (3.73), it is presented as the first of those figures "which express more than may be in the thing/idea" [*quibus plus quam in re sit designatur*]. Scaliger's gloss emphasizes this quantitative excess:

Ὑπερβολήν Aristotles in Quaestionibus accipit pro utroque excessu, quive ad exuberantiam quive ad defectum tendat; quippe utroque ex-cedi medium sive mediocritatem. Nos eum tantum excessum dicimus, qui redundantium denotat. Id figurae nomen est, quoties rem rerum am-bitu aut maiore natura extollimus. Cicero superlata, Graeci superiecta maiore vi vocis.[89]

Aristotle in the *Problemata* regards *hyperbole* as an excess on two accounts: it either tends towards an abundance or towards a lack; but in both cases the mean or moderation is exceeded. We speak here only of that excess

denoting superfluity. Hyperbole is the name of the figure we use whenever we extol a thing by ascribing a greater compass or nature to it. Cicero calls it "over-stepping"; the Greeks, more forcefully, call it
"over-throwing."

Here *excessus* retains something of its negative, classical Latin connotation of
"digression" or "deviation" in that the hyperbolist dangerously abandons the
"mean." But it also acquires a more positive connotation as the hyperbolist's
manipulation of quantities now "tends" or "strains" to represent "abundance"
or "lack." Hyperbole is not itself excessive, but rather the means to represent
excess. It neatly expresses an unnatural state of affairs ("Sane maior natura
attribuitur"), such as when Virgil portrays the horses of Turnus: "Qui candore nives, anteirent, cursibus auras" (*Aeneid*, 12.84). Scaliger's five examples,
all taken from the *Aeneid* (the others are 5.451, 2.488, 2.105, 7.808–811) and
all ubiquitous in classical textbooks, confirm that hyperbole may be a form of
prudent "attribution" when discussing a "thing" such as a "cry" that "mounts
to heaven," or Camilla's foot speed. Also notable here, especially as we look
forward to the excesses of Baroque prose, is how Scaliger immediately folds
hyperbole into his subsequent treatment of digression:

Atque unius quidem rei natura cum augescit praeter modum, hyperbole
est, cum vero additur aliquid praeter propositum, ita ut excedamus ab in-
stituta oratione, ecbasis dicitur a Graecis, Latine digressio sive egressio.[90]

When the essence of a single thing is heightened beyond measure, it is
hyperbole. When in comparison something is said beyond the proposition at hand, so that we exceed the original scope of the speech, the
Greeks call this *ecbasis*; in Latin it is called *digressio* or *egressio*.

Digression, a figure of thought, in this way is cast as another form of quantitative rhetorical "excess," one that surpasses "modum" on account of the "nature
of the thing," but now one that also "exceeds" the bounds of the "already-
begun speech." In this way, Scaliger extends Quintilian's dialectic of *ultra
modum* and *ultra fidem* to include amplification.

And just as the twelve books of the *Institutio* offer the aspiring orator a
complete and carefully structured education so that potentially dangerous models of imitation are only treated in detail in the last books, only after Scaliger's

more abstract ideas and prescriptions have presumably been digested does the
Poetices turn to examination of possible models of imitation for the aspiring
poet. In still more theoretical terms, the invidious comparisons of Homer
with Virgil that comprise a good deal of Book 5 (*Criticus*) and the historical
review of what poetry is fitting for imitation in Book 6 (*Hypercriticus*) neatly
correspond to Celenza's dichotomy between synchronic and diachronic criticism. With this said, Scaliger also dissolves the dichotomy. These two books,
that is, prove that practical criticism is the principal means Scaliger finds to
negotiate the seemingly futile task of "saving" Aristotelian theory and Neo-
Latin poetry just at the moment when they were otherwise losing their efficacy.[91] Thus it is worth recalling how Weinberg emphasizes not only the
syncretism and acuity of cinquecento poetic theory but also its dynamic, dialectical relation to practical criticism. The interaction of these two strands, he
suggests, may be the most outstanding feature of sixteenth-century Italian
thinking about literature.

Throughout Books 5 and 6 of the *Poetices* the theory refined in the earlier
books is consistently qualified by epideictic attention to the poetic practices of
Virgil. Indeed, as his criticism becomes increasingly epideictic, even at times
hyperbolic, *prudentia* is frequently sacrificed. Exemplary of this is how *Hypercriticus* concludes with an encomium to "Virgil's divinity," which transforms
him into the superhuman "measure" that frames and so limits the theorist's efforts.[92] Noteworthy also is how Scaliger gives pride of place in Book 6 to the
recentiores (the Neo-Latin poets beginning with Petrarch), only to use his
analysis of these poets to begin the arduous but necessary process of working
his way back through late classical literary history to the Augustan ideal.[93]
One relevant example of his comparatist method must suffice: in "Tempes-
tas," one of the chapters dedicated to comparing the treatment of different
topoi by various poets, Scaliger begins by lauding as painterly verses "ex divini
viri," that is, from Virgil's storm scene in the *Aeneid*, 1.84–91.[94] Then he cites
lines from the *Metamorphoses* (11.481–501) where Ovid describes the tempest
that will doom Ceyx and his men, only to judge them "ineffectual" and "exceedingly hasty" [*nimis propere*]. Turning next to Lucan's account of the storm
threatening Caesar in Book 5 of *De bello civili*, he cites lines 598–614, and
comments: "beyond these hyperboles are these laughable ones" [*Praeter has
hyperbolas illa ridicula*]. This points to lines 615–626, which he also quotes.
Then, echoing Horace's polemic at the end of the *Ars poetica*, he pauses to
exclaim:

You see what inanities these are [*Vides, quas inanitates*]. For when did it oc⁄
cur that hard things could be constrained by soft ones? This is entirely
vacuous, and belongs to a madman rather than a poet [*Vasta omnia et in⁄
sani potius quam poetae*]. In this way these people pass over what Virgil left
behind, as if it had proven of little worth, while they pursue what they
think he had neglected or not known. They earn blackened reputations
through their importunate sedulity [*acquirunt damna nominis sui importuna
sedulitate*] . . .⁹⁵

Besides decrying Lucan's audacious, almost surrealistic conceits, and blam⁄
ing any attempt to outdo Virgil in order to pursue places of invention not ex⁄
plored by the master, Scaliger makes the hyperbolic the mark of the insane
and morally suspect ("importuna sedulitate"). But then, as if he had not yet
clinched his argument, he quotes more from the storm scene to condemn the
way Lucan's "monstrosities" [*monstra*] distract the mind of even the "more
prudent" [*prudentioribus*] readers. Finally, after adducing numerous other neg⁄
ative examples mostly from Ovid and Statius, he closes the chapter by ap⁄
proving a passage by Valerius Flaccus, who wisely contents himself to imitate
slavishly Virgil ("ad Maronis imitationem totum"). In brief, this and a slew
of other instances of what constitutes proper imitation confirms that what
Cicero is for Renaissance Ciceronians, Virgil is for the suddenly less than
prudent Scaliger.

Thus notwithstanding its anachronistic aspects, Scaliger's approach to
poetics neatly exemplifies how certain ingenious, daring, or even novel species
of hyperbole are received by learned readers before the revolution in style ef⁄
fected by Baroque poets, which will later be defended by theorists like Gracián
and Tesauro. Scaliger's desire to make poetic language as apt as possible to
serve as "lineaments" for timeless truths limits how far hyperbole and poetic
invention can go. His insistence on such a narrow canon also confirms that
the poetic hyperbolist has not yet been granted real subjective license. And
while Erasmus's prescriptions for creating *copia* in Latin translated easily to
vernacular practices, the impact of Scaliger's encyclopedia of poetics was far
more ambiguous. More cited than read, the *Poetices* exercised some influence
on Sidney, Peacham, and Jonson in England, on Optiz in Germany, on Vos⁄
sius and Heinsius in Holland, on Herrera, Pinciano, and Gracián in Spain,
and it may have helped shape the notions of verisimilitude, *affectus*, decorum
(*bienséance*), and the three unities (time, place, and action) that come to be

synonymous with French *doctrine classique.*[96] Dietz, however, is unequivocal when he concludes that the "resonance" of the *Poetices* is "rather more *quanti-tative* than qualitative." In other words, even when Renaissance readers try to assess its doctrines they do so very selectively and without taking into account the whole or their philosophical underpinnings. And as for Scaliger's erudite treatment of the trope whose task is to deform quantities in order to express ex-traordinary qualities, it continues to be emblematic of the cautious, even wary approach toward hyperbole well into the seventeenth century. But by then with the undisputed rule of the vernacular literatures and with it the rise of Baroque styles in poetry and prose, Scaliger's theoretical *prudentia* is thrown to the wind.

Chapter Three

Baroque Theories of Hyperbole

How witty's ruine?
— John Donne, *First Anniversarie*

BEYOND TASTE

Responding to the witty style of Góngora, Marino, Lope, Camões, Garcilaso, and other authors from the immediately preceding generations, and
canonizing the renewed taste in Baroque Europe for the subtleties of Martial
and his Silver Latin peers, Baltasar Gracián's theory of witty exaggeration in
Agudeza y arte de ingenio (1642; revised, amplified edition in 1648) makes enormous aesthetic and epistemological claims. Without parallel in seventeenth-
century England and France, the *Agudeza* attempts to explain the cognitive
experience of wit, even as it makes this experience integral to the perception
of beauty and truth. Trading prescription for description and analysis, Gracián
celebrates the poet's ingenious ability to express novel, ideal, difficult, even impossible truths by showing how the figures inherited from the rhetorical tradition may function as the raw "material," the semantic building blocks, from
which conceits (*conceptos*) may be constructed. A poetics of invention that
struggles to give new legitimacy to the ingenious writer's subjective fancies and
thirst for objective correspondences, a poetics that seizes the middle ground
between dialectics and rhetoric, the *Agudeza* is, all exaggeration aside, unprecedented in the history of literary criticism and theory.

Embedded in his wide-ranging theory of wit and the poetic conceit, the
chapters in the *Agudeza* dedicated to explaining how the hyperbolic conceit differs from a mere "rhetorical hyperbole" are immensely important for any interpretation of the conceptual riches of hyperbole in Spanish and other Baroque

literatures.[1] For Gracián, the hyperbolic conceit, or *agudeza por exageración* (wit by exaggeration), like all the forms of wit described and exemplified in the *Agudeza*, is much more than simple ornament. It is cast rather as a nearly di-vine "act of the understanding" whose ability to express surprising truths is guaranteed by a universe in which "correspondences" are still the rule. Con-versely, such witty exaggeration is fostered by a literary culture that rewards artifice, ingenuity, and not a little sophistry — a culture that by and large re-jects the traditional aesthetics of proportionality. The witty hyperbolist self-consciously gives novel, astonishing expression to thoughts, feelings, objects, events, and circumstances. Borrowing elements from the rhetorical and scholas-tic traditions, even as he discards most of their aims and rules, Gracián's hy-perbolist skillfully balances the creation of *engaño* and *desengaño* in pursuit of the "impossible." And while such cognitive demands are made by most forms of wit in the *Agudeza*, what makes "encarecimientos conceptuosos" especially compelling is how Gracián appropriates rhetoric's riskiest trope to transcend rhetoric and show how the ingenious poet can express universal if also ulti-mately subjective truths.

This praise of exaggeration is all the more striking for how it defies the precept Gracián formulates in *Oráculo manual y arte de prudencia*, his treatise on courtliness:

> *Nunca exagerar.* Gran asunto de la atención, no hablar por superlativos, ya por no exponerse a ofender la verdad, ya por no desdorar su cordura. Son las exageraciones prodigalidades de la estimación, y dan indicio de la cortedad del conocimiento y del gusto. Despierta vivamente a la cu-riosidad la alabança, pica el deseo, y después, si no corresponde el valor al aprecio, como de ordinario acontece, rebuelve la expectación contra el engaño y despícase en el menosprecio de lo celebrado y del que celebró. Anda, pues, el cuerdo mui detenido, y quiere más pecar de corto que de largo. Son raras las eminencias: témplese la estimación. El encarecer es ramo de mentir, y piérdese en ello el crédito de buen gusto, que es grande, y el de entendido, que es mayor.[2]

> *Never exaggerate.* A great topic worthy of attention: in order not to risk offending the truth or devaluing one's wisdom, do not speak in su-perlatives. Exaggerations are prodigalities of esteem, and they indicate a lack of knowledge and taste. Praise energetically awakens curiosity, it spurs desire, and afterward, if the thing's value does not correspond

with the appreciation, as ordinarily happens, expectation turns upon the deceit and avenges itself in scorn of the thing celebrated and the one who celebrated it. The wise man thus proceeds very cautiously and would rather underdo things than overdo them. Eminent things are scarce. May you temper esteem. Exaggeration is a branch of lying; and you will lose the credit of men of good taste thereby, which is a great loss, and that of men of understanding, which is greater.

The invocation here of "buen gusto" is critical as it seems to place exaggera-tion within the scope of aesthetic judgments. Yet like Castiglione before him, Gracián is writing ethical prescriptions for humanists playing the courtier in dangerous if not cynical times.[3] Thus the aesthetic value, to say nothing of the philosophical value, of such rhetoric is ignored in favor of its immediate cul-tural currency. Intriguingly, Hans-Georg Gadamer reads Gracián as a fore-runner to Kant in trying to establish a concept of taste that is born from sensual experience and yet also that appeals to a communal notion of *Bildung*. Gadamer focuses on Gracián's moral writings directed to a courtly audience to show why judgments of taste tend to be formulated in the negative.[4] With this noted, like Anthony Cascardi after him, Gadamer neglects the *Agudeza* where Gracián, I would argue, creates an alternate, no "como de ordinario" community of taste, one steeped in a *culto* literary tradition and practice, and where *encarecer* is not *mentir*, or an "indicio de la cortedad del conocimiento y del gusto," but rather a refined means of reaching difficult truths.[5]

Devoting a chapter to Gracián in *ELLMA*, Curtius observes: "Gracián's originality [in the *Agudeza*] consists precisely in the fact that he, first and alone, declares the system of antique rhetoric to be insufficient and supplements it by a new discipline, for which he claims systematic validity . . . But it is not a poetics, as is sometimes said."[6] In the wake of the first great wave of Span-ish Baroque poetry and prose, and in the midst of Calderón's long career, Gracián subordinates the art of persuasion to the art of producing wit — a wide-ranging art that transcends the orthodox concerns we saw in Scaliger's poetics, skirts the cinquecento debate on the verisimilar and the marvelous, and assumes that the poet through his wit (*ingenio*) possesses a unique under-standing of the nature of things. Gracián's observation that the "ancients" limited their inquiries by treating wit only through the lens of logic and rhet-oric, that is, either as a kind of syllogism or trope, while not entirely accurate, is symptomatic of the desire for a theoretical response to recent poetic practice

that characterizes the best of Baroque literary criticism.[7] Wit as described by
Gracián resembles what Samuel Johnson will later dub in "Cowley," the art
of cultivating *discordia concors*, or "a combination of dissimilar images or discovery of occult resemblances in things apparently unlike."[8] But unlike Johnson, who saw the pursuit of wit as a detour from the poet's task to imitate
nature and thus as a frivolous burden on the reader, Gracián celebrates the cultivation of wit as the acme of poetics and the reader's most urgent task.

TESAURO'S PYRAMID OF WIT

Gracián's efforts to provide a philosophically rigorous theory of the conceit are
mirrored in Italy where Matteo Pelligrini's *Delle acutezze, che altrimenti spiriti,
vivezze e concetti si appellano* (1639), Pietro Sforza Pallavicino's, *Considerationi sopra
l'arte dello stile e del dialogo* (1646), and Emanuele Tesauro's *Il Cannocchiale aristotelico* (1654, first edition; 1670, expanded, final edition) variously try to delineate a poetics of wit that would break with the strictures of the classical tradition
in order to account for recent poetic practice.[9] Indeed, just as Gracián is inspired
by the *culto* Góngora, Lope, and other Spanish wits, and just as the theorists of
the cinquecento are provoked by the practice of Ariosto and Tasso, these seicento writers respond to the witty excesses of *Marinismo*.

Tesauro's encyclopedic treatise, "cette bible du conceptisme," is thus par-
ticulary important to help us situate and evaluate Gracián's efforts.[10] The
seventeenth century's most systematic, comprehensive defense of metaphor
and poetic ingenuity, *The Aristotelian Telescope* is also its most theoretically
ambitious, as it seeks to reconcile the marvelous claims of wit (*argutia*) with
neo-Aristotelian conceptions of how reason (*ratio*) functions and the perspectivism heralded by Galileo's discoveries. Such ambition is emblemized even
in the treatise's title, which conflates the new science's most controversial tool
with Aristotle's authority. Likewise, the frontispiece of the 1670 edition depicts a seated woman, *poesis*, looking through a telescope aimed at the sun covered with spots, while the figure of Aristotle stands beside her guiding her
observations.[11] On a banderole is inscribed "egregio in corpore," a phrase
borrowed from Horace's *Satires*: "atqui si vitiis mediocribus ac mea paucis /
mendosa est natura, ailoqui recta, velut si / egregio inspersos reprendas corpore naevos . . ." [*if my nature, otherwise virtuous, be found faulty for small, ordinary
things, as if you were censuring the scattered moles on a well-formed body . . .*] (1.6.65–
67). The superlunary, in other words, blemished by sublunary imperfection,
instead of hindering Tesauro's poetics, inspires wit's heroic, epistemological

efforts. Rather than finding eternal truths, wit discovers novel, ingenious ways of representing a fallen world. Thus a second woman, *pictura*, sits next to *poe-sis* and self-absorbedly executes an anamorphotic painting — another em-blem of Tesauro's claim that wit should be cultivated in all artistic spheres.

The treatise itself systematically categorizes and analyzes wit's myriad lin-guistic and visual (de)formations. Prompted by Marino's dictum — È del poeta il fin la maraviglia: / parlo dell'eccelente e non del goffo; / chi non sa far stupir, vada alla striglia!" [*The end of the poet is to cause wonder: I speak of the ex-cellent poet and not the clumsy one; he who is not able to amaze, let him go to the stables!*][12] — Tesauro constructs a now prescriptive, now analytic theory of wit that would transform Marino's insight into "un pien teatro di meraviglie" [*a theater full of wonders*] open to anyone willing to follow Tesauro's script.[13] To achieve this spectacle he dramatically expands Aristotle's account of metaphor into a complex, three-tiered, ascending system through which the witty poet spurns the tasks of creating verisimilitude and discovering objec-tive truths and relations in order to explore instead the subjective limits of metaphoric thought. As the poet ascends this pyramid of wit, he approaches, almost in the manner of Dante's pilgrim, the "suprema gloria delle composi-tioni' ngegnose."[14]

For Tesauro metaphor is the principle vehicle of ingenious signification. In his encyclopedic hands, metaphor's scope becomes enormous as it effec-tively absorbs the functions of the other major tropes. No longer simply a trope of substitution or analogy as per Aristotle, it becomes "une Métaphore superlative" whose *energeia* acquires explicit philosophical value.[15] Metaphor is "the most acute of figures," for it "riflessivamente penetra & investiga le più astruse notioni per accoppiarle: & dove quelle vestono i Concetti di parole: questa veste le parole medesime di Concetti" [*reflexively penetrates and investi-gates the most abstract notions in order to connect them; and whereas other figures dress Conceits with words, metaphor dresses words themselves with Conceits*]. Metaphor thus constantly flirts with conceptual "excess" [*il troppo*]; indeed, Tesauro's no-tion of decorum encourages far-fetched comparisons.[16] As a "simple metaphor," "metaphorical proposition," and "metaphorical argument," metaphor corre-sponds, respectively, to the intellect's three operations: apprehension, judg-ment, and syllogistic reasoning.[17] Yet wit ultimately does not aim to produce *scientia* or objective truths. Sharing a deceptive similarity with the motions of dialectic, metaphoric wit remains essentially a heuristic experience dedicated to producing novel ideas rather than logically consistent ones. The acts of thought accomplished by the *ingegno* involve analytic *perspicacia* and synthetic *versabilitá*, but not necessarily verifiable truth claims.[18] As J. W. van Hook observes, the mind follows the model of Aristotelian faculty psychology, as described in the *Rhetoric*, such that it is able "volar" [*to fly*] between categories of thought, such as quality, quantity, place, and time, to produce "Argomenti."[19] And as wit's sharpest instrument, metaphor deserves boundless praise for "portando à volo la nostra mente da un genere all' altro; ci fà travedere in una sola parola più di un' obietto" [*carrying in flight our mind from one class of thing to another, so that we glimpse in a single word more than a single object*].[20] Nor does it necessarily appeal to empirical truths. Eugenio Donato argues that, for all its acuity of thought, such metaphoric wit is "basically arbitrary," a form of aesthetic play.[21] Furthermore, the highest *argomenti* of wit tend to be "fallacious" or paralogical.[22] Relying on Aristotle, while also exploring territory left untouched by the "rhetorical schools," Tesauro asserts: ". . . io dico, le *Perfette Argutezze*, & gli' ngeniosi *Concetti*; non esser' altro che ARGOMENTI URBANAMENTE FALLACI" [. . . *I say*, perfect wit *and ingenious* conceits, *are nothing other than URBANELY FALLACIOUS ARGUMENTS*].[23] Poets are liars, as Sidney (and Plato) might say, but the reader knows this, or should know this, before he takes the bait. Inevitably though, the marvelous effect of such "urbane fallacies" also includes a whiff of Baroque disillusionment:

> . . . ad udirle sorprendono l'Intelletto, parendo concludenti di primo incontro; ma esaminate, si risolvono in una *vana Fallacia*: come le mele del Mar Negro, di veduta son belle, & colorite: ma se le mordi, ti lasciano le fauci piene di cenere & di fumo.

> . . . upon hearing one of them, it surprises the mind, appearing conclusive at the first encounter, but upon examination, it resolves into an *empty fallacy* like Black Sea apples — they look beautiful and colorful, but if you bite into them, your jaws drop full of ash and smoke.[24]

Rather than making any universal truth claims, the conceit precipitates a complex experience of admiration and cognitive dissonance. If we seek in it stable or lasting truths, we court disappointment; instead, wit signals a new form of poetic subjectivity for poet and reader. As Pellegrini puts it: ". . . it is the power of the forming wit [*ingegno*] itself which is the principal object of our admiration."[25]

The chief of Tesauro's many distinctions concerning the faculty of *in-gegno* is the initial division of metaphor into eight species: "di somiglianza," "di laconismo," "di equivoco," "di hipotiposi," "di hiperbole," "di lacon-simo," "di oppositione," and significantly, "di decettione."[26] While Virgil's phrase *instar montis equum* ("a horse like a mountain") initially exemplifies metaphor with hyperbole, in his subsequent discussion of this fifth species of metaphor, Tesauro nimbly defends hyperbole by rethinking the most tired of Petrarchan metaphors. Thus instead of calling love a fire, employing thereby a *simplice hiperbole*, we may call it "a portable furnace, a torch of a vixen . . . a lightning bolt of Cupid, an ignited feeling, a living bomb, a volcano of the breast, an eternal pyre, a torrid zone, another sphere of fire, an empyrean ves-sel, a deluge of flame, a living inferno . . ."[27] All kinds of "signs" taken from "natural or artificial substances," whether "real or imagined," may be ad-duced to produce such hyperboles. Moreover, metaphoric hyperbole can have a semantic force greater than a simple trope's. Such is the case with Marino's comic poem on a large nose, where "our poet" writes "che faceva OMBRA fino à Marocco."[28] Likewise, borrowing again from Aristotle, Tesauro cites Achilles' indignant refusal to parley with Agamemnon in the *Iliad*, 9.378–92 ("Not even if the . . ."), which I discussed in chapter one. Examples from Cicero, Ovid, Seneca, Plautus, Aristophanes, jokes from *Commedia dell'arte*, flatteries of monarchs, and epithets earned by philosophers (Pico is "la FENICE degli' ngegni") are also adduced to demonstrate how hyperbole ef-fects "augmentation" or "diminution," praise or blame.[29] But if all this seems rather mechanical, earlier in the treatise, Tesauro notes that the "passions" also may sharpen wit. Or, more precisely, that the intellect, when altered by the passions, may "strangely alter" them in turn, "accrescendole et accoppiandole, ne fabrica iperbolici e capricciosamente figurati concetti . . ." [*intensifying and joining them, it forges hyperbolic and bizarrely figured conceits*].[30]

The second, higher form of ingenious hyperbole Tesauro dubs *propositioni hiperboliche*. Resembling more a continued metaphor — one often verging on allegory — than a conceit proper, this kind of hyperbole appeals to the judg-ment and is produced by exaggerating *quantita* ("Vesuvius is a little spark of that flame."), *qualita sensibli* and *qualita spirituali* ("He is a lightning bolt with-out thunder."), *relationi di simiglianza ò contrarieta* ("A paragon of that fire, every other fire is snow: the inferno of Enceladus is a delight."), *attioni e passioni* ("So much is that ardor, that it can almost melt diamonds and cook salaman- ders . . ."), *luogo e movimento* ("It is a miracle that such a flame does not fly to its sphere."), or *tempo* ("That breast is the altar of eternity where perpetual fire is Love.").[31] By mining these "categories" of thought, the poet and the object of his wit are "gigantified." Exemplifying this are two epigrams by Martial (8.33, 11.18), which Tesauro cites and carefully annotates according to his schema.[32] Conversely, another "genus" of hyperbole, *conclusioni hiperboliche, & incredibili*, is subdivided according to "great thoughts" such as the "divine, na- ture, the world, eternity, fate, fame, fortune, victory, triumph, empire, [and] impossible things [*cosi impossibili*]." Such "conclusions" are cultivated "per dare una spinta agli' ngegni sonnacchiosi: come per inalzare i concetti sopra l'opinione, balzandogli oltre al credible: & per rendergli dilettevoli con la Maraviglia di un' ardita e arguta menzogna; che non è creduta, e pur piace" [*to incite sleepy wits: thus to raise conceits above common opinion, leaping beyond the cred- ible, and thereby rendering them delightful with the Marvelous of a passionate and witty lie, which is not believed, yet greatly pleases*].[33] This "leaping" also uncharacteristi- cally prompts Tesauro to allow considerations of content to creep into his dis- cussion. Thus he recommends Claudian's panegyrics of rulers and their empire; and, looking forward to the final chapters of the treatise where *impre- sas* are discussed, he includes extravagant mottos of famous rulers (i.e., *Domino Orbis Terrarum*).

But again Tesauro is more interested in the formal qualities of hyperbole as a kind of metaphor than in any typical content it might have — in this his approach is diametrically opposed to the history of hyperbolic *topoi* sketched by Curtius. Extracting from the *Rhetoric* and *Poetics* reasons to laud hyper- bole, Tesauro treats it as a means of creating "maraviglie."[34] In this respect he leans heavily on the passage from the twenty-fourth chapter of the *Poetics*, which I discussed in chapter one, where Aristotle praises Homer's paralo- gisms. But for Tesauro it is not the license afforded by the epic that justifies such paralogisms; instead it is the "Autore, che per forza dell' Argutia ti fan credible l'incredible" [*author, who by the dint of wit makes the credible seem incredible to you*], together with the cognitive and aesthetic pleasures afforded by the sharpness of Homer's wit, which spur us to accept the paralogism's irrational and nonversimilar aspects.[35]

Yet for all his praise of such exaggeration, only the third and highest species of wit, which forges "true conceits" [*veri concetti*] with *urbanely fallacious arguments*, involves the intellect's power to draw inferences. These conceits alone merit "the name of wit [*Argutia*]." Whether in the form of poetic *pointes*, epigrams, quick rejoinders, or emblems, these conceits convey the "force of in-genious argument" and therefore truly astonish if not ultimately persuade. To demonstrate the spiritual value of such wit for hyperbolists, Tesauro meditates on the verse from Luke (22:44) describing Christ's agony of doubt in the Garden of Gethsamene: "Factus est sudor eius sicut guttae sanguinis" [*His sweat became like great drops of blood*]. More transparent, though, is his explana-tion of how, "given a theme, to fabricate an enthymeme-like argument out of hyperbole." Here his starting point is Martial's verses on a "bee that dies in amber" [*apis in electro moritur*]. Tesauro comments: "Hyperbolically you could call such a gem [*gemma*], a TREASURE [*THESAURUS*], by an excess of esteem. Consequently you could argue: *This little bee has the most foolish avarice: for in order to acquire treasure, it dies*" [Stolidissima istius Apicula avaritia est: quae Thesaurum ut potiatur, perit].[36] The paralogism thus begins with the probable premise that the bee is hungry, then turns on the polysemy of *gemma*, which can mean a "jewel" (of amber) as well as a flower's "bud," and then concludes that the bee is a greedy fool. Combine this with the play on *potior* and *potare*, and we see how the bee's inability to detect semantic richness is just as fatal as its greed. In brief, with this and numerous other examples Tesauro confirms the degree to which the hyperbolist flirts with sophistry in order to produce marvelous thoughts. As for the reader, Roland Barthes highlights the peculiar aesthetic pleasures produced by such tenuous logic:

> The enthymeme has the pleasures of a progress, of a journey: one sets out from a point which has no need to be proved and from there one pro-ceeds toward another point which does need to be proved; one has the agreeable feeling (even if under duress) of discovering something new by a natural kind of contagion, of capillarity which extends the known (the opinable) toward the unknown.[37]

GRACIÁN CONCEIVES THE CONCEIT

Like Tesauro, who represents the sky as "a vast cerulean Shield, on which skillful Nature draws what she meditates: forming heroical Devices, and mys-terious and witty Symbols of her secrets," Gracián hopes to make the cosmos the objective justification for his theory of wit.[38] In the event, however, his poetics mainly celebrates the mind's subjective powers — both of the witty author and his readers. The resourceful *ingenio* produces subtlety and difficulty where before there was none, and in this it prefers artifice and idiosyncrasy over nature and convention: ". . . no se puede negar arte donde reina tanto la dificultad" [*art cannot be denied where such difficulty reigns*].[39]

Writing after the fierce style wars over Góngora's *culteranismo* had calmed somewhat, Gracián is able to achieve a more detached, panoptic perspective on the question of hyperbole than did previous generations. In comparison with Gracián's, other late Spanish Renaissance discussions of hyperbole are rather superficial and unsystematic. Although hyperbole is often instrumental to their praise of poetry and poetic inspiration, little thought is given to exag-geration as a form of invention. This is certainly the case with Juan Huarte de San Juan's *Examen de ingenios para las ciencias* (1575), Alonso López Pinciano's *Filosofía antigua poética* (1596), Luis Alfonso de Caravallo's *Cisne de Apollo* (1602), and Luis Carillo y Sotomayor's *Libro de la erudición poética* (1611).[40] In-deed, while Huarte offers a theory of the imagination that will have lasting in-fluence in the seventeenth century — Burton and Descartes engage it — and Carillo defends the *docto*, difficult style in the most extravagant, syncretic man-ner, hyperbole as an engine of thought and style receives scant consideration.

Rejecting the temptation of casting his treatise as an extended allegory ("Pudiera haber dado a este volumen la forma de alguna alegoría . . ." [*I could have given this volume the form of some allegory*]), Gracián chooses generally to teach by example rather than precept: "Es este ser uno de aquellos que son más conocidos a bulto, y menos a precisión, déjase percibir, no definir . . ." [*Wit's being is one of those more known in bulk, and less by detail; it lets itself be perceived, not defined. . .*].[41] Consequently, the *Agudeza* reads like an anthology of conceited Spanish, Portuguese, and Italian verse. Its pages are also filled with examples from and thus the authority of Augustine, Horace, Caesar, Ovid, Tacitus, and Martial. The *Epigrams* especially epitomize the faculty of wit Gracián prizes. And having been born in Iberia, Martial becomes still more exem-plary of the talents Gracián would promote.[42] Likewise, that many of the treatise's Latin examples are followed by translations by Gracián's friend, Manuel de Salinas, indicates that the examination of poetic *agudeza* is part of a larger attempt to reconcile the classical poetic and rhetorical legacies with specific contemporary conditions — Gracián would call them "circunstan-cias" [*circumstances, contingencies*] — native to Spain and its literary culture.

Such syncretism extends to the treatise's attempts at defining wit and providing theoretical arguments to defend it. Yet in offering philosophic justifications for *agudeza*, Gracián curiously ignores canonical poetic and rhetorical
theory. Infrequently mentioned, the precepts of Quintilian, Cicero, and Aristotle are applied idiosyncratically and fitfully. This is to say that like Sidney,
Gracián is writing principally for poets and about poetry. He too assumes
Aristotle's dictum that poetry is the most universal and so philosophic of the
arts. But in narrowing his focus to wit's dynamics, Gracián also remakes
Aristotelian accounts of how the mind's faculties operate as he draws heavily
on neo-scholastic notions concerning the discovery of correspondences. Alternately, he shows a deep sympathy with Neo-Platonic theories of representation and the value of difficulty, theories present already in Augustine and
León Hebreo, but which also consistently inform the reigning, *culto* literary
aesthetic in Spain.[43] Such Neo-Platonism fuels the ecstatic claims made in the
opening chapters: "Si el percibir la agudeza acreditada de águila, el producirla empeñará en angel; empleo de querubines, y elevación de hombres,
que nos remonta a extravagante jerarquía" [*If perceiving wit lends credit to the
eagle, producing it indebts us to an angel; employment of cherubim, and elevation of men,
which raises us towards an extravagant hierarchy*].[44] In brief, Gracián's "teórica fla-
mante" [*novel theory*] has strong metaphysical pretensions. In the first *Discourse*,
subtitled "Panegírico al arte y al objeto," *agudeza* is celebrated as "pasto del
alma" [*fodder for the soul*]. Its "works," he intimates, possess real theological
currency:

Son cuerpos vivos sus obras, con alma conceptuosa; que los otros son
cadáveres que yacen en sepulcros de polvo, comidos de polilla. Pequeño
cuerpo de Crisólogo encierra espíritu gigante; breve *Panegírico* de Plinio,
se mide con la eternidad. Tiene cada potencia un rey entre sus actos, y un
otro entre sus objectos; entre los de la mente, reina el concepto, triunfa la
agudeza ... Entendimiento sin agudeza ni conceptos, es sol sin luz, sin
rayos, y cuantos brillan en las celestes lumbreras son materiales con los
del ingenio.[45]

Its works are living bodies with conceited souls; for the others are cadav-
ers that lie in dusty sepulchres, eaten by moths. The small body of St.
Peter Chrysologus contains a gigantic spirit; the brief *Panegyric of Trajan*
by Pliny the Younger is measured against eternity. Every potentiality has

a king amongst its actions and another one amongst its objects; amongst those of the mind, the conceit rules, wit triumphs . . . Understanding without wit or conceits, is a sun without light, without rays, and as many celestial lights shine in the sky, there are materials for ingenuity's conceits.

By brazenly insisting on wit's ability to actualize potentiality, to furnish en-lightenment if not also revelation, Gracián envisions it as the principal con-ceptual means by which the subjective mind closes the gap between the real and ideal.[46] And in describing the mind's innate, intuitive power to produce concepts and juggle abstract ideas, he carefully explicates how the conceit's cognitive demands and rewards surpass what traditional rhetoric and poetics ascribe to plain metaphor. It is thus far more than a question of nomenclature when Gracián asserts in *Discourse XX*:

> Son los tropos y figuras retóricas materia y como fundamento para que sobre ellos levante sus primores la agudeza, y lo que la retórica tiene por formalidad, esta nuestra arte por materia sobre que echa el esmalte de su artificio. No pasan algunos por concepto el encarecimiento así a secas: dicen no ser más que un hipérbole retórico, sin el picante de la agudeza viva y verdadera . . .[47]

> The tropes and rhetorical figures are the material with and like the foun-dation atop which wit can erect its outstanding artifices. And what rhet-oric takes as its form, our art considers to be the material upon which it applies the enamel of its artifice. Thus some do not count mere exagger-ation as a conceit; they say it is nothing more than a rhetorical hyperbole, without the spice of true and lively wit . . .

Without the "picante" and "esmalte" added by the *concepto*, hyperbole invites all the calumnies that eloquence without content conventionally attracts.[48] As a mere trope hyperbole is simply semantic raw material, like any simple metaphor or figured bit of language, that awaits "nuestra arte"; alone it makes no meaningful, lively demands on the hermeneut.

To grasp, however, what constitutes a hyperbolic conceit, first we have to grapple with Gracián's exegesis of the *concepto* proper. Confusingly, to begin the treatise he offers three separate definitions of the conceit. The first concerns the relation between art and understanding:

> Consiste, pues, este artificio conceptuouso, en una primorosa concor⸗
> dancia, en una armónica correlacíon entre dos o tres cognoscibles ex⸗
> tremos, expresada por un acto del entendimiento.[49]

> This conceptual artifice thus consists in an excellent concordance
> (agreement), in a harmonic correlation, between two or three knowable
> extremes, expressed by an act of the understanding.

An "act of the understanding," the conceit at once correlates and expresses
correspondences between a given set of "extremes." Rather than settling for
mere representation, it creates relations as well as finding already existing ones.
Such an act depends on the poet's native *ingenio*, while demanding also the
mastery of a certain "artifice." Keen to ascertain the extent to which metaphor
and the other tropes used to produce conceits may help us invent, discover, or
even judge something about a subject matter rather than just adorning it,
Gracián muddles the traditional boundaries separating rhetoric, poetry, and
philosophy. With its emphasis on invention and understanding, his theory of
the conceit marks a fundamental, epistemological fault line, as well as signal⸗
ing a new kind of literary theory, one that hails the poet's subjective imagina⸗
tion as the primary engine of literary creation. Quixote's *ingenium* may have led
him wildly astray, to mistake windmills for giants, inns for castles, but Gracián
insists that the witty, *culto* ways he mediates between "knowable extremes" is
not only grounded in truth, but is the thinker's highest calling.

Like many late Renaissance cosmologies, his theory assumes that God
has granted human understanding the ability to make the *cosmos* accessible to
human *logos*.[50] Schooled in scholastic logic and yet the proud inheritor of the
recent legacy of *conceptismo* and *culteranismo*, Gracián makes the *ingenio* the ar⸗
biter of the most difficult, novel, and paradoxical questions that thinking —
whether it be poetic, political or philosophical thinking — might raise. In
this sense his task is far different than his Spanish predecessors such as Juan de
Guzmán, who, writing for an audience of prospective sermonizers in the
Primera parte de la Rhetorica (1589), is at pains even to distinguish between
comparison and simile.[51] Still, T. E. May makes the case that Gracián either
cannot be bothered or does not have the conceptual means to distinguish con⸗
sistently between the faculties of understanding involved in the *concepto*.[52] It is
indeed often difficult to know whether by *entendimiento* Gracián means solely
the faculty of intuition that conceives correspondences, or whether it also

includes the ability to draw deductive inferences. He insists that the conceit differs from the syllogism, and yet certain forms of wit necessarily involve the faculty of judgment. Moreover, Gracián unequivocally asserts: "No se contenta el
ingenio con sola la verdad, como el juicio, sino que aspira a la hermosura" [*Ingenuity is not content only with the truth, like judgment, but rather it aspires to beauty*].[53]
That this pursuit of beauty may sometimes obviate scrupulous attention to literal, empirical truths proves essential to his theory of witty exaggeration.

Nevertheless, to interpret a conceit may require considerable empirical
knowledge, together with substantial skills in intuitive and deductive reasoning. A conceit's "knowable extremes" may include abstract ideas, feigned
emotions, material objects, and subjects proper to history or literature. To discover the "harmonious correlation" that the poet has already discovered between such terms requires real invention on the reader's part. Bucking the
Ramist stampede in Northern Europe, Gracián refuses to divorce the process
of invention from analysis and cultivation of poetic style. The third, most ambitious definition of the *concepto* undergirds this refusal:

> Es un acto del entendimiento, que exprime la correspondencia que se
> halla entre los objetos. La misma consonancia o correlación artificiosa
> exprimida, es la sutileza objetiva, como se ve, o se admira, en este céle-
> bre soneto, que, en competencia de otros muchos a la rosa, cantó don
> Luis de Góngora:
>
> > Ayer naciste, y morirás mañana;
> > Para tan breve ser, ¿quién te dió vida?
> > Para vivir tan poco, estás lucida,
> > Y para nada ser, estás lozana.
> > Si tu hermosura te engañó más vana,
> > Bien presto la verás desvanecida,
> > Porque en esa hermosura está escondida
> > La ocasión de morir muerte temprana.
> > Cuando te corte la robusta mano,
> > Ley de agricultura permitida,
> > Grosero aliento acabará tu suerte.
> > No salgas, que te aguarda algún tirano;
> > Dilata tu nacer para tu vida,
> > Que anticipas tu ser para tu muerte.

> Esta correspondencia es genérica a todos los conceptos, y abraza todo el
> artificio del ingenio, que aunque éste sea tal vez por contraposición y dis/
> onancia, aquello mismo es artificiosa conexión de los objectos.[54]

> It is an act of the understanding, which expresses the correspondence
> that is found between objects. The consonance itself or harmonious cor/
> relation that is expressed, is the objective subtlety, as is seen, or admired,
> in this celebrated sonnet, which, competing with many others concern/
> ing the rose, Don Luis de Góngora sings:
>
>> Yesterday you were born, and tomorrow you will die; for a being so
>> ephemeral, who gave you life? For living so briefly, you are brilliant,
>> and for being nothing, you are praised. If your extremely vain
>> beauty deceived you, very soon you will see it faded; because in that
>> beauty is hidden the occasion of dying an early death. When the
>> robust hand picks you — by farming's valid law — a rude breath
>> will complete your fate. Do not bud, for some tyrant awaits you;
>> may you delay your birth for your life's sake, for you hasten your be/
>> ing for death's sake.
>
> This correspondence is common to all conceits, and embraces all the ar/
> tifice of ingenuity; and though here it may be by comparison and disso/
> nance, this too is an artificial connection of the objects.

Gracián here gives aesthetic value and philosophical rigor to the characteristi/
cally Baroque strategy of playing with phenomenological extremes to discover
some metaphysical or psychological truth. Conversely, the phrase "sutileza
objectiva" proleptically works to remove the taint of caprice and solipsism
some twentieth/century readers associate with Baroque poetry. It also implic/
itly excuses the difficulty inherent in discovering ("se halla") meaning in such
"contraposición y disonancia." Góngora is admirable not because he elo/
quently renovates poetic commonplaces about the rose, but because his artifi/
cial play of differences yields new insight. In this sense, Gracián's use of the
verb *exprimir* may be somewhat deceptive for English readers. Conventionally
translated as "to express," it is less a question here of pure self/expression than
of discovering an ingenious artifice "to squeeze out," "extract," or "solicit"
from a set of "objects" such that beauty (a "correlación armoniosa exprim/
ida") and understanding result.[55] Confronted with the task of producing new
knowledge out of "extremos cognoscibles," the *ingenio* tries to *ex/press* and

thus to master such difference. But in so doing, as "sutileza objectiva" implies, each conceit also strives to be an objective ordering or "squeezing" of the cos-mos. Further, when one considers the many kinds of *agudeza* in Gracián's trea-tise, it becomes evident that wit is perceived as much as a state of being as a way of perceiving the world. This is to say that the search for "correspon-dences" in a subject (*res*), be it a rose, St. Peter's cowardice, or the sadness of a shepherd descending from a mountain with his flocks, is made possible by a real, or what might be called a phenomenological connection between mind and world, a connection Gracián assumes but never really explicates. This re-mains true even when correspondences rely on disproportion rather than pro-portion (the two main types of conceits) and when the links between mind and world seem highly tenuous and artificial.[56]

While the expression of correspondences is native to all forms of under-standing,[57] in *Discurso III*, Gracián delineates four privileged kinds of *agudeza* by which the mind perceives correspondences and so expresses new meanings:

> La primera es de correlación y conveniencia de un término a otro, y aquí entran las proporciones, improporciones, semejanzas, paridades, alusiones, etc. La segunda es de ponderación juiciosa sutil, y a ésta se reducen cri-sis, paradojas, exageraciones, sentencias, desempeños, etc. La tercera es de raciocinación, y a ésta pertenecen los misterios, reparos, ilaciones, pruebas, etc. La cuarta es de invención, y comprehende las ficciones, es-tratagemas, invenciones en acción y dicho, etc.[58]

> The first is that of correlation and agreement of one term with another, and here are included proportions, disproportions, similitudes, compar-isons, allusions, etc. The second is subtle, judicious ponderation, and this consists of empirical judgments, paradoxes, exaggerations, maxims, ripostes, etc. The third is that of ratiocinations, and to this belongs mys-teries, objections (warnings), illations, proofs, etc. The fourth is inven-tion, and it compasses fictions, stratagems, and inventions in action and speech, etc.

Each species of wit signals a different cognitive experience wherein sundry images, sensations, circumstances, and ideas may be transformed into artistic, abstract thoughts. In each the witty mind apprehends the world, although the objects that the *ingenio* "squeezes" may be purely linguistic or "fictions" created by the mind. Thus puns and etymological wordplay can also yield *conceptos*.[59] Alternately, wit's fourth species usually occurs in the world and not on the page — it largely concerns the actions and stratagems of royalty, statesman, and courtiers.[60] Summarizing this schema, Arturo Zárate Ruiz argues that the establishment of correspondences does not initially aim to produce judg-ments or inferences — two other possibilities the scholastics pursued — but primarily to permit "the apprehension of new ideas."[61] To forge poetic con-ceits is to create new ideas, an aim different from medieval logic which tried to organize synthetically the mind's already present thoughts.

Much of the genius that Aristotle ascribes to style Gracián reascribes, broadly speaking, to invention — whether it belong to the poet or the theorist. The opening sentences of *Discourse I* read:

> Fácil es adelentar lo comenzado; arduo el inventar, y después de tanto, cerca de insuperable; aunque no todo lo que se prosigue se adelanta. Hallaron los antiguos métodos al siligismo, arte al tropo; sellaron la agudeza . . . remitiéndola a sola la valentía del ingenio . . . No pasaban a observarla, con que no se halla reflexión, cuanto menos definición.

> To advance the already begun is easy; to invent is arduous, and after so much, almost insuperable, although not everything that continues ad-vances. The ancients discovered methods for the syllogism, an art for the trope; they sealed up wit . . . ascribing it only to the bravery of the in-genious faculty of the mind . . . They did not pause to observe it, so that they offered no reflections on it, let alone a definition.

Eschewing strictly logical ("siligismo") or rhetorical ("tropo") aims, Gra-cián's self-assigned task on behalf of writing and thought is to remedy this the-oretical lack by assigning *ingenio* its proper scope and heritage. I will discuss presently how this occurs in the first two species of wit, but it is worth not-ing here that the third and fourth types may belong to courtiers, theologians, mystics, novelists, generals, as well as to poets and orators. *Raciocinación*, or ar-gumentative wit, provides proof and resolves disputes not by offering a defin-itive judgment (*juicio*) about a puzzling state of affairs but by offering an artistic, plausible solution.[62] As distinct from other species of wit, *invención* does not occur solely in the linguistic sphere. Rather than pretending to solve a problem or discover "correspondences" between deeds, things, or language, it crystallizes the witty situation in a tangible form.[63] A capacious category, such invention may include anamorphotic paintings, extravagant stage machinery, parables, allegories, dramas, jokes, emblems, *impresas*, pantomime, military strategy, gardening, and even religious ritual. Diogenes the Cynic's ostentatious daytime search with a torch in his hand for a single good man exemplifies an "[i]ngenioso encarecimiento" [*ingenious exaggeration*] belonging to this wit.[64] Other examples of such invention might include Cortés's replacement of the Aztec Templo Mayor in Tenoctitlán with a cathedral, Horapollo's hieroglyphs, Alciato's emblems, the courtly masques in Jacobean England, or Calderón's *autos*.[65]

SPECIES OF WIT

While Benedetto Croce chastises Gracián for not hewing to the categories established early in the treatise, that the ultimate design and execution of the *Agudeza* is not as neat as Gracián's fourfold scheme promises can also be interpreted as proof of wit's refusal to obey rigid precepts.[66] Gracián approaches the ingenious writer's restless mind in a scholastic, a priori fashion, but it quickly proves a subject too copious and subtle to be bound by any single category or method. Thus more generously than Croce, T. E. May regards Gracián's various, shifting classificatory schema as forms of critical ingenuity.[67]

There is general agreement, however, that as the treatise progresses a fundamental division emerges between conceits based on proportion and those exploiting disproportion.[68] As for the former, Gracián remains loyal to Aristotle's dictum in the *Rhetoric* (3.11) that it is the mark of the philosophically acute mind to perceive resemblances in dissimilar things. Considering *correlación* (correlation), the first species of *ingenio*, he urges the poet to discover "terminos extremos" [*extreme terms*] that when joined skillfully together, can yield a new, acute thought. In practice, though, the circumstances attending the terms of a comparison often prove crucial as well to the conceit's ingenuity. Such circumstances complicate and add subtlety to the corresponding terms. They also prevent *agudeza* from becoming just a reified judgment about universal qualities. By taking into account circumstance, wit responds to the contingency and mutability native to human affairs and natural phenomena. In the following example of a *concepto de proporción* from a *romance* by Góngora, the felicitous circumstance of a cruel woman having been born in a country famous for its snakes creates an "intellectual symmetry" between corresponding terms — the idea of cruelty and a particular woman:

> Extremo de las hermosas
> Y extremo de las crueles;
> Hija al fin de sus arenas
> Engendradoras de sierpes.[69]

Extreme in beautiful things and extreme in cruel ones; daughter, in sum,
of her sands, progenitors of serpents.

The poem's "extremes" thus wittily resolve in the coincidence of character
and natural-historical circumstance.

As for conceits based on disproportion, these create differences in kind
between terms conventionally regarded as similar. Engines of mannerist verse,
whether in imperial Rome, Carolingian France, or Baroque Spain, such conceits aspire to "perfection" of thought rather than "beauty."[70] With these conceits the reigning precept is: "Cuando es mayor la repugnancia, hace más
conceptuosa la improporción" [*When the incompatibility is greater, it makes the disproportion more conceited*].[71] Gracián discovers such heuristic dissonance in an
exquisite Petrarchist poem by Lope de Vega.[72]

Contemplating a snow-blanketed volcano, finding no solace in a lazy
river's waters, no hope in spring, and no pleasure in birdsong, Lope invites us
to admire his play of contraries and, Gracián argues, to grant that the lover's
psychology is a "circunstancia" that occasions and justifies such play. Conversely, the *pointes* in Luis de León's "Canción real al desengaño" confirm the
grave but no less astonishing — *admiratio* being the primary aesthetic pleasure
granted by Gracián in the treatise — potential of this kind of *agudeza*.[73] Other
examples from St. Augustine, Martial, Marino, and Camões show how the
cultivation of *repugnancia*, *disonancia*, and other kinds of *contrariedad* is essential
to the creation of wit and to ensuring that the understanding fostered by wit
can be as encompassing as possible. Thus May cites Saint Teresa's "muero,
porque no muero" [*I die, because I do not die*] as confirming how the conceit need
not be based on similitude; as the initial hyperbole of *muero* is put in a causal
but antithetical relation to *no muero*, a relation that ultimately expresses "a simple truth about a state of feeling."[74]

To these two fundamental species of the conceit a third basic type is
added: ponderation, which accomplishes the judicious "weighing" of extremes. Now contraries are either ponderously reduced to a witty *pointe* that
harmonizes terms previously held in "suspension," or they resolve a "mystery"

fostered by their juxtaposition. Confusingly though, Gracián then distinguishes between these types of ponderation and the second major genre of
agudeza dubbed "ponderación juiciosa sutil," which, as I outlined above, "se
reducen a crisis, paradojas, exageraciones, sentencias, desempeños."[75] Unlike
wit produced by swiftly or slowly "squeezing" correspondences, witty ponderation finds novel meaning in terms already chosen or established. Now the
poet judiciously tries to renovate old topics and whatever wit might still lodge
there.[76] Akin to the dynamics of "outbidding," such ponderation contains
both subjective and objective aspects. For to discover and prize what is new,
extravagant, or difficult depends on subjective standards of convention and
taste. Yet ponderation must not eschew all plausibility; the poet has to point to
the world, to objective circumstances and shared cultural experiences, to provide proof or ground for the extraordinary. In this, Gracián largely agrees
with earlier theorists of hyperbole, as he also urges psychological as well as
empirical justification for rhetorical overreaching. Indeed, *juiciosa* may be a
misnomer for such "weighing" of terms, for the *ingenio* is often responsible for
importing some condition, circumstance, or doubt that scrambles the "ordinary" terms of correspondence. Likewise, the *ingenio* often reacts to its own extraordinary emotions or the perception of something extraordinary in the
world, and so purposefully defies judicious, decorous expression.

EXAGGERATED WIT

As tempting as the notion of "cognoscibles extremos" may be to students of
hyperbole, when Gracián turns his attention to exaggeration it quickly becomes clear that extremity is not simply synonymous with exaggeration. Beginning with *Discourse XIX*, "De la agudeza por exageración" [*On wit by
exaggeration*], Gracián treats witty exaggeration as uniquely expressing the
ideal and the "impossible":

> Poco es ya discurrir lo posible, si no se trasciende a lo imposible. Las
> demás agudezas dicen lo que es, ésta lo que pudiera ser; ni se contenta
> con eso, sino que se arroja a lo repugnante.[77]

> To discourse about the possible is nothing much, if it does not transcend
> toward the impossible. The other forms of wit say what is, this one what
> could be. It is not content with that either, but rather it boldly leaps after
> the incompatible.

With echoes of Demetrius ("lo imposible") and Quintilian ("no se contenta con eso . . ."), Gracián gives "exageración" a technical meaning specific to his notion of the witty poet who plays fast and loose with logic to convey sub-jective insights. The special status ascribed to such exaggeration in those *Dis-courses* (XIX–XXII) dedicated to exaggerated wit further distances his treatise from the handbook notions of decorum that traditionally restrain the practi-cal orator.[78] In the best Aristotelian manner, Gracián encourages the poet to aim at the ideal ("lo que pudiera ser"); but as champion of the *conceptista* style, he also embraces "lo repugnante."

Strikingly, both qualities are discovered in these verses of Horace, his first example of *encarecimiento ingenioso*:

> Iustum et tenacem propositi virum
> non civium ardor prava iubentium,
>   non vultus instantis tyranni
>   mente quatit solida neque Auster,
> dux inquieti turbidus Hadriae,
> nec fulminantis magna manus Iovis;
>   si fractus illabatur orbis,
>   impavidum ferient ruinae. (*Odes*, 3.3.1–8)

Not the crooked ardor of a cowered people, nor the face of a threatening tyrant, shakes the just man, tenacious in purpose, from his firm resolve; nor the east wind, boisterous ruler of the unquiet Adriatic; nor the great hand of Jove with its lightning bolts; if the world should break and fall, the ruins would leave him undaunted.

The cosmic hyperbole of a "crashing sky" unable to disturb the virtuous man's Stoic certainty is justified, Gracián insists, by the "ocasión, que en las extraordinarias ha de ser el pensar y el decir extraordinario" [*occasion, for in extraordinary circumstances, thinking and speaking must be extraordinary*]. But unlike Seamus Heaney's recent imitation of *Ode* 1.34 in the aftermath of the Sep-tember 11 attacks ("Anything can happen. You know how Jupiter / Will mostly wait for clouds to gather head / Before he hurls the lightning? . . .), Horace underscores, Gracián insists, on "la seguridad de la virtud y la intre-pidez de la buena conciencia" [*virtue's assurance and a good conscience's intrepid-ity*].[79] In this way Horace, whose siren at the beginning of *De arte poetica* comes to emblemize in the Renaissance the mismatch of style and subject, serves as the unlikely, ethical spokesman for the Baroque hyperbolic conceit.[80] Like Longinus and Hermogenes, Gracián exemplifies hyperbole with verses exploiting the confusion of the terrestrial and celestial spheres. And while the contrast between the leader's microcosmic calm and the surrounding macrocosmic chaos borders on the sublime, Gracián seems less concerned with creating cosmic grandeur than with highlighting the extraordinary *mens* anchoring these lines. In this respect, he proleptically converts into praise Samuel Johnson's blame of the Metaphysical poets: "What they wanted however of the sublime they endeavored to supply by hyperbole . . ."[81]

Again, ingenuity necessarily belongs to the reader as well. *Discourse VII* starts with the declaration: "La verdad, cuanto más dificultosa, es más agradable" [*Truth, the more difficult, the more pleasant it is*].[82] To exemplify this cardinal precept, Gracián reads the opening lines of *De bello civili* as pondering, "con la bizarría que acostumbra, la disonancia de la sangrienta guerra civil" [*with its customary splendor, the dissonance of the bloody civil war*].[83] But then "the grave Lucan" in lines 33–38 offers a "hiperbólica salida" [*a hyperbolic* pointe] in which martial excesses are justified by how they allow the fates to pave the way for Nero's accession. This in turn is supplemented by the "excelente paridad" [*excellent comparison*] of the war with the gigantomachy that paves the way for Jupiter's triumph.

Just as Lucan excels among epic poets in hyperbolic wit, Lope de Vega, whom contemporaries dubbed a "monstruo del ingenio," is incomparable when it comes to comic exaggeration. Further, by insisting on such a range of examples, Gracián raises hyperbole from its lowly status as superficial ornament and tired commonplace, and endows it instead with the conceit's full epistemological potential. His own catachrestic metaphors are telling in this regard: "En la misma verdad puede haber exageración, subiendo de una eminencia en otra el objeto, dándole el aumento por la artificiosa gradación" [*In truth itself there can be exaggeration, which raises the object from one eminence to another, augmenting it by an artificial gradation*].[84] Such truths may include the beloved's beauty, the Virgin's grace, or as with Lucan, history's course. In other words, witty hyperbole puts ordinary truths at risk:

> No escrupulea en la verdad este género de sutileza, déjase llevar de la ponderación y atiende sólo a encarecer la grandeza del objeto, o en panegiri o en sátira.[85]

> This genre of subtlety does not scruple about truth; whether in pane-
> gyric or satire, it lets itself by borne by the ponderation and attends only
> to exaggerating the object's greatness.

By pointing to the genres, panegyric and satire, most accommodating to
such lying wit, Gracián initially grounds its reception in what Jauss calls
a "horizon of expectation." We embrace hyperbolic wit, because genre demands it. Meanwhile, the striking phrase, "No escrupulea en la verdad,"
recalls and implicitly rejects the classical debates concerning the ethics of hyperbole. This also explains why in the third Discourse *agudeza por exageración*
is placed under the rubric of *ponderación judiciosa sutil*. To employ judiciously
exaggerated wit in these genres is less to make judgments about truth or falsity than to enter into theatres of aesthetic judgment where a poet's extraordinary rhetoric can be tested against the immanent exigencies of circumstance.
Moreover, in culling witty hyperboles from numerous genres and kinds of
discourse to explicate his theory of exaggeration, Gracián greatly broadens
the range of circumstances available to the witty hyperbolist to include
"feigned" as well as real (historical, empirical) ones. All of this suggests that
the most valuable but difficult *res* is the power of the *ingenio* itself to understand "extremes." For *agudeza por exageración* expresses impossibility not only
in light of objects found in the world but also in terms of language itself. Thus
Mercedes Blanco, in her definitive study of Gracián and *conceptisme* in Europe, reads "agudeza por exageración" as extending the limits of linguistic
expression:

> Indeed, this statute [which makes exaggeration into a conceit] is justi-
> fied if one admits there exists wit, in Gracián's sense, where a novel ex-
> pression [*une tournure verbale*] gives proof of the powers native to
> discourse. Exaggeration is a *conceit* since it proves that everything can be
> said, not only the real, but also that which is merely possible, and even
> the contradictory and the impossible [*le contradictoire et l'impossible*]; and
> the *ingenio* makes a show of itself through the fortitude with which it
> meets the challenge of the impossible.[86]

Underscoring the defiance of trying to represent "le contradictoire et l'impossible," Blanco casts the hyperbolic conceit primarily as an exercise in poetic
self-reflection and self-discovery.

Such subjectivity obtains even when an external *res* grounds the conceit. Sicily's remarkable fertility, for instance, inspires this infamous hyperbole from Góngora's *Fábula de Polifemo y Galatea*:

> Sicilia, en cuanto oculta, en cuanto ofrece,
> Copa es de Baco, huerte de Pomona:
> Tanto de frutas ésta la enriquece,
> Cuanto aquél de racimos la corona.
> En carro que estival trillo parece,
> A sus campañas Ceres no perdona,
> De cuyas siempre fértiles espigas
> Las provincias de Europa son hormigas.[87]

Sicily, for the quantities it hides and the quantities it offers, is the cup of Bacchus, orchard of Pomona; the latter enriches it with as many fruits as the former crowns it with grape vines. In a car that seems like a summer thresher, Ceres does not pardon her fields, for whose always fertile ears of wheat the provinces of Europe are like ants.

While the last two lines yield the *concepto* proper, the entire verse is a hyperbolic figure of thought exploring the conditions or *circunstancias* in which wit can prosper. The parallelism, parison, and diction of quantity ("Tanto . . . Cuanto . . .") in the first four lines foster what Gracián elsewhere calls *suspensión*, and hence prepare the way for the final *salida*, wherein everything is diminished save the principal subject which is suddenly elevated. In this octave about *copia*, the final transformation of nation states into insects is prefigured by the copious transformations accomplished by nature and its divinities. Thus Gracián recommends, using this poem and Martial's praise of Caesar as examples, "encarecimientos conglobados, que digan entre sí correspondencia y vayan en proporción aumentando el objecto y concepto" [*conglomerated exaggerations, which express from amongst their parts correspondence and which proportionally increase the object and the conceit*].[88] As a means of furnishing proof, such methodical augmentation tends to seize upon ordinary or "inconveniente" [*accidental*] details instead of remarkable ones to propel the conceit's logic forward and eventually create novelty.

Similarly, the cultivation of Erasmian *copia* can provide the raw material, the "fundamento," with which hyperbolic wit works to elevate a subject:

Mayor sutileza contiene la exageración, cuando se forma entre dos extremos; ponderando en cada uno la dificultad, realza mucho la suspensión y la duda de la deliberación a uno de entrambos, y exprímese la
oposición, encareciendo el inconveniente que hay en cualquiera dellos.[89]

Exaggeration contains greater subtlety, when it is formed between two
extremes; pondering the difficulty in each one enhances greatly the suspense and doubt in the consideration of both, and it expresses their opposition, exaggerating what is accidental in either of them.

Exemplifying this is a "sublime epigrama" by the recently deceased don Carlos, "serenísimo héroe, Infante gloriosísimo de Espana" [*most serene hero, most
glorious Prince of Spain*], in which the lover's simultaneous silence and desire to
complain of his treatment at the beloved's hands are pondered until yielding
in the final line: "... si callo mi mal, dos veces muero" [*if I do not speak my ill,
I die twice over*]. But perhaps more intriguing than the verse or Gracián's reading is the way he wittily embeds courtly epideixis into a theoretical discourse
on exaggeration's virtues. Read against the economic and social *declinación*
characterizing seventeenth-century Spain, such panegyric reminds us that
Gracián's theory of wit belongs, however ambivalently, to his larger project of
shaping and diffusing the style and mores of courtly culture, or what Cascardi aptly describes as the "authority of taste." In this sense, hyperbole becomes a weapon against skepticism, rather than a cause for incredulity.

In formal terms, hyperbolic wit is most effective when it exploits other
tropes and figures: "A más de su propia agudeza, suele la exageración valerse
de las otras especies, que la realzan mucho" [*More than its own wit, exaggeration
tends to avail itself of other species of wit, which enhances it greatly*].[90] Gracián's first
example of such piggybacking comes from that "filósofo en verso, Andres
Alciato," who uses "contraposición entre la eloquencia y el valor, entre el
saber y el poder" [*antithesis between eloquence and valor, knowledge and power*] to
sharpen the wit of a "conceptuoso emblema" in which the aged Hercules,
who Renaissance writers cast as trading his physical strength and prowess for
eloquence, now becomes the occasion for celebrating Baroque hyperbole.
And though Gracián only cites the subscript, it is the entire emblem, including its superscript ("Eloquentia fortitudine praestantior" [*Eloquence superior to
strength*]) and image, that creates the antithesis between Hercules' youthful

arms and the chains of eloquence he uses as an old man to force the "durissima corda" [*hardest of hearts*].[91] Likewise, another poem ironically turns the hours into years, even as it makes the years "breves" [*brief*]; while verses by Martial employ an "exagerada antítesis" to show how Caesar's brilliant presence transforms night into day. Reading another poem in which Martial elaborately celebrates the lush beauty of Vesuvius' slopes only suddenly to contrast it in the final lines with the pain that the flames from its eruption causes the "Su-peri" [*gods*], he insists that the greater the difficulty of the "hiperbólica salida," the more ingenious the entire poem. In sum, then, Gracián prizes how, when informed by a conceit, rhetorical figures increase linguistic and conceptual difficulty and thus help sharpen the understanding.

While valuing difficulty in this way ignores conventional classical and Renaissance notions of poetic decorum, like Quintilian, Gracián at least par-tially justifies the wit of exaggeration by what happens in the world:

> Requiérese, pues, que alguna circunstancia especial dé motivo y ocasión al encarecimiento, para que no sea libremente dicho, sino con funda-mento, que es darle alma al concebir . . . Cuanto la circunstancia es más especial y prodigiosa da pie para el encarecimiento mayor.[92]

> It is necessary, hence, that some special circumstance provides the motive and occasion for exaggeration, so that it not be arbitrarily said, but rather with a foundation, which gives it the spirit to forge conceits . . . When the circumstance is very unique and prodigious it provides the footing for greater exaggeration.

The extraordinary in human and natural history serve as "motive and occa-sion" for exaggeration. Supernatural events may spark the hyperbolist, as in the "special circumstance" of Christ's suffering on the cross as described in Scripture, which not only excuses but "obliga a la exageración" [*obligates the exaggeration*] from John 19:34 of "Et continuo exivit sanguis et aqua" [*and at once there came out blood and water*].[93] Alternately, the witty hyperbolist may also "sometimes" feign circumstances, as we will see in Góngora's *Polifemo*. Or, as we shall discover in Sor Juana's *Primero sueño*, she may even ransack the dreamworld for material, thus pushing *encarecimiento* further toward the fantastic or *fantasía*.[94] Also, the wit inherent in language itself may sometimes precipitate exaggeration: an amorous poem by Lope is lauded for an "exageración" prompted in part by a pun. But whether theological, imagined, or linguistic, the contingency prompting witty exaggeration, "ha de ser extraordinaria" [*must be extraordinary*] to produce an extraordinary result.

Only in *Discourso XXI*, "De los encarecimientos condicionales fingidos y ayudados" [*On conditional, feigned, and assisted exaggerations*], does Gracián betray any sustained concern for the exaggerating poet's credibility. Given the conditional quality of this form of exaggeration, a timely moderation is urged:

> Lo que unas veces se arroja la exageración, otras veces se detiene y se modera, que como de sí es tan sobresaliente, necesita en algunas ocasiones de templarse, y aunque dice mucho, pero no todo lo que iba a decir.[95]

> What sometimes fuels the exaggeration, other times curbs and moderates it, since it is in itself so striking, it needs sometimes to be tempered. And though the exaggeration says a great deal, it does not say all that it was going to say.

In this manner, the ingenious hyperbolist may mean more than is said, even when what has been said is already exaggerated, as in these verses cited from Góngora:

> Yerbas le aplica a sus llagas,
> Que si no sanan entonces,
> En virtud de tales manos,
> *Lisonjean los dolores.*[96]

(Love) applies herbs to his wounds, which if they aren't cured right away, by virtue of such hands, *soothe the pains.*

Here a form of Góngora's infamous *si . . . no* construction, which earned so much contempt from contemporaries, is defended as offering a subtler solution than if the poet had claimed that her hands "entirely cured the pain." Similarly, Gracián praises "exageración por negación" which allows the poet to deny the very hyperboles he has just enumerated. Adducing also examples of witty prose exaggeration, he celebrates the mannerist prose of Apuleius with a long quotation, cites once again from Pliny the Younger's *Panegyric of*

Trajan, and recommends the apophatic rhetoric of Dionysius the Areopagite — rhetoric which I will discuss at length in the chapters on Pascal.[97]
Then he highlights this gem from J. C. Scaliger who places a prosopopeia in
the mouth of the city of Memphis:

> Africa cur posita est vobis pars tertia mundi?
> Tertia quando Orbis pars ego sola forem.[98]
>
> Why have you made Africa the third part of the world? When I alone
> could be the third part.

Geographical or more properly cosmographical conceits like these provide
Gracián with many of his most vivid examples of successful *agudeza por exageración*. Reading another poem, which concludes with an "impossibility"
that "pide al mar y a la tierra que pasen más adelante sus limites, para que
puedan caber los de la Monarquía española" [*requests the sea and earth to overstep
their limits, so that those of the Spanish monarchy might fit*] he proves how a witty
hyperbole refreshes a political commonplace such as the motto *Plus ultra* and,
I would add, revisits an ancient literary *topos*, namely, Virgil's "imperium sine
fine dedi."[99] Such wit may squeeze the ordinary or commonplace but it may
also outdo the literary hyperboles preceding it. And while Gracián suggests
that sometimes the poet should make explicit reference to the incredulity of his
claims, other times, however, "se fingen los afectos, el engaño, la credulidad
imposible para más exagerar" [*feelings, deceit, and credulity are feigned in order to exaggerate more*].[100]
     All this means that whatever strategy the exaggerating poet adopts neces-
sarily depends for its ultimate success on readers having the experience, erudition, will (*voluntad*), and *ingenio* to recognize the exaggeration as a vehicle for
the poet's understanding. The readers to whom Gracián directs his treatise
were already well versed in the conventions of exaggeration, such as those belonging to Petrarchism and courtly epideixis. As such the rules of decorum
and allusion for a *conceptista* hyperbolist are considerably slacker than they
would be if Gracián were writing for someone who needed to persuade the *in-
culto* masses or obdurate rulers. Spurning the caveats offered by the handbook
writers, or for that matter his own advice to courtiers in the *Oráculo manual*, in
Discurso XXII, "De las ponderaciones juiciosas, críticas y sentenciosas por ex-
ageracíon" [*On judicious, critical, and aphoristic ponderations by exaggeration*], he
supplies a broad, psychological justification for hyperbolic wit:

Así como el ingenio en los grandes objetos no satisface, sino con un relevante encarecimiento, así en la voluntad suele ser tanta la intensión del afecto que no se satisface con menos que con una exagerada pon-deración.[101]

Thus as ingenuity is not satisfied with great objects without a relevant exaggeration, likewise it is common that the intensity of feeling in the will is so great that it is not satisfied with anything less than an exagger-ated ponderation.

Camões is exemplary in this regard, as is Garcilaso who exaggerates, in a son-net cited by Gracián, with "dulzura y agudeza" [*sweetness and wit*] the "tiranía de sus pasiones" [*the tyranny of his passions*]. An example of Garcilaso's nimble reworking of Petrarchist commonplaces is also cited to indicate how the hy-perbolist balances the demands of convention and the need to create novel forms of invention. Likewise, a sonnet by Góngora begins in an obviously Petrarchan manner, yet by the time the *reparo* is reached, the poet's "furia in-fernal," his jealousy, can no longer be sent back to its proper place:

> *Más no cabrás allá, que pues ha tanto*
> *Que comes de ti mismo, y no te acabas,*
> *Mayor debes ser que el mismo infierno.*[102]

But you will not fit there [in the kingdom of terror], *for since you have eaten your-self for so long, and you still are not finished, you must be greater than Hell itself.*

The way the hyperbole savors here of paradox speaks to the more general Baroque tendency to exaggerate to the point, the witty *pointe*, of paradox. This tendency lends hyperbole intellectual and metaphysical value as it helps map the tensions between *Weltsucht* and *Weltflucht*, tensions that Leo Spitzer regards as emblemizing the Baroque *Weltanschauung*.[103] But it also causes the limits of witty signification to be questioned. As the reader navigates between what Keats calls a "fine excess" of language and what post-structuralist theory often sees as a failure of signification, the possibility of producing understanding — the conceit's first and greatest promise — is put at risk.[104]

No wonder, then, that Gracián follows his discussion of *agudeza por ex-ageración* with a consideration of *la agudeza paradoja*.[105] Witty paradox is par-tially justified by the greatness of the subject matter, but we are also repeatedly urged to consider the world's inherent ineffability. Thus while on a metarhetorical level Gracián's definition of paradox leans on hyperbole ("Son las paradojas monstruos de la verdad . . ." [*Paradoxes are the monsters of truth . . .*]), more importantly, paradox represents another method of conceptualizing the impossible and the extraordinary. Indeed, hyperbole and paradox often share the same methods and subject matter. Exaggeration is fundamental to both as is evidenced by many of his examples and confirmed by the declaration: "Tienen por fundamento estas agudezas el mismo que los encarecimientos ingeniosos, porque son especie de exageración, y la más extravagante y sobresaliente" [*Witty paradoxes have as their foundation the same thing as ingenious exaggerations, since they are a species of exaggeration, and the most extravagant and striking*].[106] Such praise is tempered, however, by the awareness that paradox may abuse too much the understanding. Paradox exploits and defies logic to a far greater degree than its cousin, hyperbole, which produces greater emotional "admiración y enseñanza" [*admiration and teaching*].[107] Skeptical of the new cosmology, Gracián curiously makes witty paradoxes, "por ser menos escrupolosas" [*for being less scrupulous*], most proper to natural philosophy.[108] The Copernican universe, "fabricado al revés" [*constructed backwards*] is one such paradox and so prompts this warning:

> Las paradojas han de ser como la sal, raras y plausibles, que como son opiniones escrupulosas, y así desacreditadas, no pueden dar reputación; y muchas arguyen destemplanza en el ingenio, y si en el juicio, peor.[109]

> Paradoxes have to be like salt, exceptional and fitting, since they are doubtful opinions; and thus discredited, they cannot win good repute; and many of them suggest an unbalance in the imagination, and still worse, in the judgment.

Nowhere does Gracián ascribe such "destemplanza" to witty exaggeration. Instead, witty exaggeration is granted the license not to scruple with the truth, as its impossibility creates more admiration than confusion.

In sum, then, while Gracián's championing of hyperbolic wit owes fundamental formal debts to the rhetorical and scholastic traditions, it is the exemplary practice of the early imperial Latin poets and late Spanish Renaissance poets and prose writers that fuels the aesthetics of his treatise. His slightly belated position moulds his taste for "encarecimiento," but it also permits him detachedly to separate the messy, compromised world in "crisis," which he represents with the subtlest powers of Baroque allegory in *El Crit-icón*, from the green, textual world of the *Agudeza* where extremities can be reconciled and understood through wit's play. While his treatment of hyper-bole is framed, even haunted, by the specter of paradox, this is less a fully realized theoretical stance and more a sign that even as the poet and the poet's defender strain after the ideal, hyperbole proves "impossible." Rhetoric aims to deceive, *engañar*, but exaggerated *agudeza*, an integral part of the art of cre-ating new understanding, aims to enlighten, *desengañar*, a fallen world.[110]

Chapter Four

Yonder: Spanish Baroque Hyperboles

PLUS ULTRA

Nowhere is the question of limits — rhetorical, empirical, and cognitive limits — more sublimely posed than in Dante's enigmatic portrayal of Ulysses' last voyage. Unequivocally condemned in Hell's eighth circle as a "false counselor" for the trick of the Trojan horse, Ulysses reappears later in the *Inferno* to speak as an exile, overreaching hero, and self-styled victim of his own hubris:

> When I took leave of Circe . . . not tenderness for a son, nor filial duty toward my agèd father, nor the love I owed Penelope that would have made her glad, could overcome the fervor that was mine to gain experience of the world and learn about man's vices, and his worth. And so I set forth on the open deep with but a single ship and that handful of shipmates who had not deserted me . . . I and my shipmates had grown old and slow by the time we reached the narrow strait where Hercules marked off the limits, warning all men to go no farther [*dov' Ercule segnò li suoi riguardi, | acciò che l'uom più oltre non si metta*] . . . "O brothers," I said, "who, in the course of a hundred thousand perils, at last have reached the west . . . do not yourselves deny experience [*esperïenza*] following the sun . . . You were not born to live like brutes, but to pursue virtue and knowledge." . . . and we set out our stern to sunrise, in our mad flight [*folle volo*] we turned our oars to wings . . .[1] (26.90–125)

After five months of their "folle volo" to reach the antipodes, and within sight of a "mountain, distant, dark and dim," Ulysses and his crew, as their "joy . . . turned to grief," perish in a sudden "whirlwind."[2] In this manner, even while condemning him for his sins, Dante grants enormous, epic dignity to Ulysses, who in his "orazion picciola" (26.122) seems almost proud to suffer for "esperïenza" and "virtute e canoscenza." Exceedingly ambitious to sail "yet farther" [*più oltre*], Ulysses also desires salvation; for the mountain he sees in the distance is Purgatory. But having nearly conquered geographic space, there is little he can do about providential time. His burning desires — Dante has him speak from within a fire — are clearly premature. The episode, in short, has a tragic feel, one that will help assure its *Nachleben* in the early modern imagination. As Hans Blumenberg observes, Dante's Ulysses is fated to become a symbolic avatar of the theoretical *curiositas* that in subsequent centuries fuels the voyages of discovery and the scientific revolution, a *curiositas* that I would show in this and subsequent chapters becomes the marvelous, protean object of Baroque skepticism and hyperbole.[3]

Ubiquitous in the sixteenth century as the imperial motto of Charles V, the phrase *Plus ultra* [yet farther] originates in this episode of the *Inferno*.[4] Inscribed on a banderole hung between a pair of columns rising from the sea or floating in space, this motto became part of a device (*impresa*) long interpreted to have it origins in the Herculean *topos* warning sailors not to venture beyond the Straits of Gibraltar. Indeed, thanks largely to this emblem Charles was figured as outbidding Hercules, the classical exemplar of bravery and fortitude. Charles's overseas empire has made him, as one contemporary put it, "un nouvel Hercule, un nouvel Atlas."[5] Likewise, the Italian humanist, Girolamo Ruscelli, finds an analogue to *Plus ultra* in the *Aeneid* where Virgil, thinking of Africa, writes: "Extra anni solisque vias" (6.796).[6] That Philip II subsequently fuses this latter verse with *Plus ultra* to yield the emblem "Ultra anni solisque vias" confirms again how, as with Virgil's "imperium sine fine dedit," a literary hyperbole can signal political and terrestrial hegemony.[7] Subject to the dynamics of *translatio studii* as well as those of *translatio imperii*, *Plus ultra* acquires both classical authority and the contemporary weight of secular authority.

As the phrase's motley grammar suggests, the "plus" is a *calque* from the French *plus oultre*, which in turn comes from a translation of Dante's "più oltre non."[8] Emblazoned on the flag of the ship that carried Charles to Spain in 1517, the French version of the phrase, not surprisingly, offended Spanish sensibilities and so was quickly translated into a more neutral Latin. But for all its apparent antiquity, *Plus ultra* has no identifiable classical source, nor was it derived from any adage such as *Non plus ultra* or *Nec plus ultra*, neither of which have precedents in relation to the Pillars of Hercules.[9] Nevertheless, with the defeat of the Aztecs in 1520, and the Incas in 1533, *Plus ultra* came to be regarded as the divinely inspired, emblematic phrase of geographical and imperial ambition. Most famously, Francisco Lopéz de Gómara, in his *Historia general de las Indias* (1552), dedicates his book to the elderly Charles by vaunting:

> Quiso Dios descobrir las Indias en vuestro tiempo y a vuestros vasallos, para que convirtiésedes a santa ley . . . Comenzaron las conquistas de indios acabada la de moros, porque siempre guerreasen españoles contra infieles; otorgó la conquista y conversion el papa; tomastes por letra *Plus ultra* dando a entender el señorio de Nuevo-Mundo.[10]

> God wanted the Indies to be discovered in your age and by your vassals, so that the Indies would be converted to Holy Law . . . The conquests of the Indians began, when that of the Moors was complete, so that the Spanish might always war against infidels. The Pope awarded the conquest and conversion; you take as your device *Plus ultra*, meaning the lordship of the New World.

Even as such praise blends political ideology and Catholic theology it depends on the Renaissance rhetoric of *admiratio*, which drawing on classical and medieval models such as Pliny and Mandeville, cultivated a thirst for the new and the marvelous. As Lopéz de Gómara unequivocally declares:

> La mayor cosa después de la creación del mundo, sacando la encarnación y muerte del que lo crió, es el descubrimiento de Indias; y así las llaman Nuevo Mundo. Y no tanto te dicen nuevo por ser nuevamente hallado, cuanto por ser grandísimo y casi tan grande como el viejo, que contiene a Europa, África y Asia. También se puede llamar nuevo por ser todas sus cosas diferentísimas de las del nuestro.[11]

> The greatest thing after the world's creation, save the incarnation and death of He who created it, is the discovery of the Indies, which thus they call the New World. And they say "new" not so much for being newly discovered, but more for being extremely large, almost as large as the old, which contains Europe, Africa, and Asia. Also it may be called "new" because all of its things are extremely different from those in our own world.

Here hyperbole promotes cosmography and historiography as well as the interests of theology and empire; it helps produce what Henri Lefebvre calls
"dominated space."[12] No wonder, then, that *Plus ultra* became ubiquitous in
insignia, emblems, and other signs of imperial power. By the mid-sixteenth
century, "Charles's motto had become a universal symbol for limitless ambition."[13] Yet circumspection regarding the *topos* had already begun decades
earlier when Erasmus cast the Pillars as a warning against overweening ambition. In one of his *Adages*, *Ad Herculis columnas* (3.5.24), he quotes Pindar,
Aristophanes, and others to suggest the limits of terrestrial and, interestingly,
allegorical ambition.[14] Alternately, Bartolomé de Las Casas tries to give the
phrase a utopian, spiritual meaning when, during his famous debates with
Sepúlveda at the imperial court, he attacks the inhuman treatment of the *indios*.[15] And there is "Le passage de Gibraltar" (1637), a "caprice héroï-
comique" by the French poet Saint-Amant in which drunken sailors mock
Atlas and Hercules before engaging the Spanish fleet in battle.[16] *Plus ultra*, in
short, becomes a hyperbole ready for any occasion.

Much more than a philological or historical footnote, the *topos* of *Plus ultra* offers readers of Spanish Baroque poetry a hermeneutic thread to unravel
the uses and abuses of hyperbole. It is visited with particular subtlety by Luis
de Góngora and Francisco de Quevedo to help represent the moral dangers
associated with overseas navigation. In their verse *Plus ultra* effectively becomes *Nec plus ultra*, and hyperbole serves at once as a moral scourge, an occasion to examine the dynamics of literary imitation, and a sophisticated
vehicle for their own dissenting subjectivities. Pushed to the margins by their
temperaments and the difficulty of winning favor at court, Góngora and
Quevedo cultivate exquisite forms of poetic excess to voice their subjective
dislocation. This metamorphosis of imperial hyperbolism into the language
of radical poetic and philosophical subjectivity finds its most remarkable avatar,
however, at the end of the century and on another continent. In Sor Juana
Inés de la Cruz's *Primero sueño*, *Plus ultra* emblemizes the hyperbolic attempt
to exploit a nearly exhausted Baroque aesthetic to conquer the same epistemological ground as Bacon and Descartes map with their new philosophies. But
that Sor Juana also allows herself to experience thereby a real cognitive defeat
proves to be the greatest marvel of all produced by a Baroque hyperbolist.

This is not the place to analyze in detail why the "crisis of consciousness"
in the early seventeenth century assumed particularly extravagant forms in
Spain. I do wish, though, to suggest that by the time Cervantes publishes the

first part of *Don Quijote* (1605) the imperial *Plus ultra* had lost much of its positive epideictic force. Just as the mad, audacious idealism of a *caballero andante* yields to Alonso Quijada's deathbed regrets, by the beginning of the century Spain had belatedly begun to contemplate the real and spiritual costs of the imperial ideal. Early seventeenth-century Spanish society, saddled with enormous debt, an ossified monarchy, and riven by class conflict, largely traded the expansive outlook of previous generations for scathing forms of introspection. Sixteenth-century optimism had become fin-de-siècle pessimism. With the defeat of the Invincible Armada, the many successes of English pirates, the war in Flanders, the Catalan revolt, and the general realization that the economy and political culture were in need of radical reforms, poets, dramatists, and *arbitristas* (zealous reformers who produced numerous, often voluminous treatises prescribing remedies, some practical, others quite fantastic) increasingly dedicated their writings to self-reflection and critique.

The prominent *arbitrista* Martin González de Cellorigo laments, in his *Memorial de la política necessaria* (1600), Spain's dwindling population, which has caused "nuestra República a decaer tanto de su florido estado" [*our Republic to decline so much from its flourishing state*].[17] Such demographic decline in turn is partially traced to the paradox of an economy grown dependent on precious metals: ". . . lo que más ha hecho daño a estos Reinos, es que las mismas riquezas que han entrado son las que los han empobrecido" [*what has most damaged these Kingdoms is that the same wealth that has entered them has impoverished them*].[18] But the fact that both Cervantes and Quevedo devote considerable energy to satirizing *arbitristas* like Cellorigo further confirms what José Antonio Maravall describes as the pervasive social consciousness of "crisis" dominating Baroque Spain.[19] Literature reflects and sharpens this sense of cultural crisis, even if, as Maravall forcefully argues, it is complicit with its rhetoric of *escarmiento* (warning) and *prudencia* (prudence) in maintaining the authoritarian status quo: ". . . beneath its sometimes hallucinating excesses and exaggerations, it was a culture whose disorder somehow made sense, was regulated and under control."[20] Conversely, as Maravall acknowledges, the attempts of poets like Góngora and Quevedo to discover the linguistic means to express "disorder" also help to deepen the very crisis they decry.

Meanwhile, the mathematical and physical sciences had fallen into relative neglect. After an initial enthusiasm for Copernicanism before the turn of the century — especially in Diego de Zuñiga's writings — Spain experienced a reactionary backlash that greatly limited the acceptance of the scientific "novedades" to a marginalized few. The forward-looking Academia de Matemáticas in Madrid had ceased to function by 1625; and with the official condemnation of Galileo in 1633, the attack on heliocentrism received the sanction of both Church and State.[21] This helps partially explain why the role played by the new sciences in Quevedo and Góngora's poetry is rather slight in comparison to their role, say, in the poetry of Du Bartas or Donne. And while geometric imagery and conceits sometimes assume vital heuristic and thaumaturgical functions for Spanish hyperbolists, this kind of spatial representation is less ubiquitous than with their English or French counterparts. To furnish their *ultra fidem* content, Spanish Baroque poets tend instead to prefer the geographical *copia* produced by the voyages of discovery to the more abstract victories claimed by astronomers.[22] And in the wake of Camões's *Os Lusiades* (1572), they saw how terrestrial space could become a political and ethical phenomenon as well as a literary one.

More generally still, with its emphasis on the mutability and superficiality of earthly things, and with its devotion to exploring its protagonists' self-deception and melancholy, much of Spanish Baroque literature feasts on the self-reflexive theme of overreaching. As imperial, amorous, societal, and spiritual overreaching become central thematic concerns, hyperbole is relieved of its more traditional epideictic tasks and is transformed into a potent, often double-edged, ethical scourge emphasizing the perils of *engaño* and the necessity of *desengaño*. This dialectic of *engaño* and *desengaño* proves fundamental to the invention of Spanish hyperbolists, as do the related themes of *atrevimiento* (audacity) and *codicia* (greed), on the one hand, and, on the other, *desaliento* (despondency) and *despeñamiento* (literally, a "precipitous descent," but figuratively, a "sudden, disastrous collapse").[23] Despite the antiquity of these themes — or perhaps because of their central, venerable role in Judeo-Christian culture — the representation of excessive desire and the subsequent ruin that usually accompanies it is ubiquitous in all genres of early modern Spanish literature, from the picaresque novel and *comedia* to the *auto sacramental*. The aesthetic *asombro* (wonder) produced by the ruinous effects of *atrevimiento* and *codicia* works to frighten and warn as well as to teach and delight. Just as the treatises of the *arbitristas* eagerly denounce the debilitating effects of an overextended empire, divisions between the classes, and the erosion of traditional values, literary hyperbolists seem to delight in blaming unbridled desire and ambition while self-reflexively contemplating their own conceptual and stylistic excesses.

In *La vida es sueño* (1635), for example, even as Calderón fashions the allegorical creature Segismundo whose bestial appetites know no limits, his own
dramatic art cultivates *asombro* through the *atrevido* manner it depicts his hero's
overreaching, fall, and redemption. When Segismundo, with his self-described
"ojos hidrópicos" [*dropsical eyes*] (227), reflects on his ambition, the audience
is enticed by the "cristales" and "jaspe" he envisions, while it is also invited to
condemn his *atrevimiento*:

> ¡Ah, cielos,
> qué bien hacéis en quitarme
> la libertad, porque fuera
> contra vosotros gigante
> que, para quebrar al sol
> esos vidrios y cristales,
> sobre cimientos de piedra,
> pusiera montes de jaspe!²⁴ (328–335)

Ah, heavens, you do well in taking liberty from me; because otherwise
there'd be a giant against you, who to destroy these glasses and crystals to
the ground, would place mountains of jasper atop foundations of stone.

Segismundo uses such language and conceits to condemn moral transgres-
sions, but in doing so he blatantly endangers his own *ethos* as well as that of
the dramatist who dreamed him. This same dilemma is acutely exemplified by
the career of Juan de Jáuregui who as a young man loudly condemns Góngora as "atrevido," but who, years later, becomes himself a Gongorist epigone
when he translates Lucan's *De bello civili*. Given aporias such as these, the relative willingness or ability of the overreaching poet to judge, or at the very
least, experience his or her own overreaching will be a chief focus of these
chapters. What signs or *señas* do hyperbolists give to show an awareness of this
dilemma? Or to put it another way, how does the aesthetic appetite for semantic and conceptual excess translate into ethical or epistemological insight?

READING EXCESS

The manifold hyperbole in Spanish Baroque poetry defies any single
hermeneutic. Most infamously, Góngora's exorbitant *culto* style cagily dares
readers to mock its excesses. His hyperbolic metamorphosis of a quotidian,
pastoral world into an ideal, poetic idiolect in the *Soledades* immediately pro-

voked contemporaries to charge him with all manner of crimes against taste, with ignorance of classical models, and in terms of his *ethos*, with mendacity, degeneracy, irreligiosity, even insanity. In this way, as with Samuel Johnson's treatment of Donne and the Metaphysicals, the question of taste and the often unexamined perception that hyperbole is unnatural or a betrayal of classical literary models, occluded and still largely occludes the possibility that hyper-bole be treated as an object of serious, critical interpretation. Not only has the hyperbolist's role as critic of society and self still not been properly mapped, but readers of Gongorist and Quevedian hyperbole generally have not been prepared or willing to do the hermeneutic labor, the philologic and semantic spadework, to realize the extent of its intertextual and conceptual riches.

One exception to this is Paul Julian Smith who argues that Spanish Golden Age poets have a unique predilection for "verbal and conceptual overloading."[25] Leaning on Scaliger, Herrera, and El Pinciano, as well as the Derridean *supplément*, Smith challenges what has conventionally been seen as a shift from sixteenth-century plainness and theoretical dependency to seventeenth-century excess and autonomy.[26] He defends the semantic excesses of late Renaissance and Baroque Spanish writers given the axiom that the per-ception of nature can yield a model for poetic disorder as well as order. If the poet's aim is no longer to imitate nature but to supplement it, then nature's ex-cesses, whether in the form of storms, earthquakes, prodigies, or *grotescos*, may be rightly said to provoke the hyperbolist. More particularly, the *silva* — that quintessential Baroque strophic form in which lines of eleven and eight feet may freely alternate and rhyme according to various patterns — points etymo-logically to the idea of dark forests and thus also to disorder and obscurity in nature.[27] In this Smith implicitly agrees with Antonio Carreño who reads the "metric disorder" of the *silva* as upsetting and reshaping the cosmic, ontolog-ical order traditionally created by analogy and similitude in Spanish Baroque poetry.[28] For Smith, Góngora is exemplary in his respect, as the *silvas* of his *Soledades*, with their disdain for ordinary speech, demonstrate the impossibil-ity of directly imitating nature and therefore making art itself the object of im-itation. Such "supplementarity" is not a break with the immediate past but suggests rather "Góngora's newness is one of quantity, rather than quality."[29] Ultimately, however, Smith is more concerned with the "graphic brilliance" of Góngora's language than the specific excesses of diction, periphrasis, hy-perbaton, or metaphor. Focusing more on the figure of *enargeia* than hyperbole, he quickly, too quickly perhaps, folds the hyperbolic into the long-standing, critical debate over the virtues of obscurity.[30] For, as I will argue below, it is by no means obvious that the visual should be chief hermeneutic concern in reading Góngora's most difficult verse, especially if Aristotelian or even Auerbachian *mimêsis* is not being pursued there. With this said, Smith's book dramatically changes the nature of the debate, at least in Anglo-American circles, on the role of clarity and decorum in seventeenth-century Spanish poetics. It also opens the door for readings like my own that take the stylistic and semantic aspects of poetic excess as starting points rather than stumbling blocks.

Jorge Luis Borges urges a more suspicious hermeneutic when he reads Góngora's hyperboles. In a short essay, "La metáfora," Borges observes how metaphor tends to lose its connection to things and emotions in certain historical periods such as the Baroque. When this occurs they become "objetos verbales, puro e independientes como un cristal o como un anillo de plata" [*verbal objects, pure and independent like a crystal or a silver ring*]. The mannerist metaphors in Ariosto, Baudelaire, or the Icelandic sagas may impress, even astound, "pero nada revelan o communican" [*but they reveal or communicate nothing*]. And while Borges insists here and elsewhere that there are only a "few patterns" for metaphor to follow — such as the analogy between a woman and a flower, or life and a dream, or God and an infinite sphere whose center is everywhere and circumference nowhere — nonetheless: ". . . los modos de indicar o insinuar estas secretas simpátias de los conceptos resultan, de hecho ilimitados. Su virtud o flaqueza está en las palabras" [*the means of indicating or insinuating these secret sympathies of conceits turn out to be in fact unlimited. The virtue or weakness of metaphor is in the words*].[31] To sharpen his point, Borges cites a metaphor shared by Dante and Góngora:

> . . . el curioso verso en que Dante (*Purgatorio*, I, 13), para definir el cielo oriental invoca una piedra oriental, una piedra límpida en cuyo nombre está, por venturoso azar, el Oriente: *Dolce color d'oriental zaffiro*, es, más allá de cualquier duda, admirable; no así el de Góngora (*Soledad*, I, 6): *En campos de zafiros pace estrellas*, que es, si no me equivoco, una mera grosería, un mero énfasis. Algún día se escribirá la historia de la metáfora y sabremos la verdad y el error que estas conjeturas encierran.[32]

> . . . the curious verse in which Dante (*Purgatory*, I, 13), in order to define the oriental sky, invokes an oriental stone, a limpid stone in whose name, by happy chance, is the Orient: *Dolce color d'oriental zaffiro*, is beyond any

doubt, an admirable one. This is not the case with Góngora's (*Soledad,* I, 6): *En campos de zafiros pace estrellas,* which is, if I am not mistaken, a mere vulgarity, mere emphasis. Some day the history of metaphor will be written and we will know the truth and error contained in these conjectures.

But such a critical "history," I would contend, is already partially inscribed in Góngora's own *imitatio.* In other words, whether or not it engages Dante directly, this metaphor deserves to be judged for its "virtud o flaqueza" only in the context of the intratextual and intertextual web in which it moves.

Góngora's "mera grosería" belongs to the opening lines of the *Soledad primera* (1612), a poem heralding a new poetic genre, the pastoral epic:

> Era del año la estación florida
> en que el mentido robador de Europa
> (media luna las armas de su frente,
> y el Sol todos los rayos de su pelo),
> luciente honor del cielo,
> en campos de zafiro pace estrellas . . .[33]

It was the year's florid season, in which the celestial bull, lying thief of Europa's virtue — with the horns of his brow adorned by a half moon and all the sun ray's on his coat — shining honor of the sky, in sapphire fields grazes on stars . . .[34]

Jupiter here is at once the deceitful rapist of Europa, a mythic bull transformed into the constellation of Taurus whose luminous parts, in turn, are conflated into the sun and moon, the planet Jupiter ("luciente honor del cielo"), and a cosmographic pederast (the subsequent lines compare the poem's protagonist to Jupiter's Ganymede) who, in the offending hyperbole, "grazes" upon "stars" growing in "sapphire fields." That this hyperbole already had a long "history" entirely distinct from Dante's paronomastic conceit is confirmed, for instance, by the way Lucan, in his epic's proemium, relying on models inherited from Virgil and Ovid, transforms Nero into an obese, celestial Jupiter threatening to disrupt the cosmos. One of Góngora's contemporary commentators, Pellicer, in addition to indicating this and various other literary sources, points to sundry cosmographic observations of Pliny, Cicero, and Aristotle to buttress the decorum of the almost surreal image of a bovine

god feeding upon stars.[35] In terms of the larger role it plays in the poem's initial semantic field, however, the hyperbole repeats and amplifies the gesture of
the first two lines in which nature's beauties and bounty are juxtaposed with
some form of violence. Also, like many of his epic predecessors, Góngora
conflates science with myth. He accomplishes this in an exacting, not merely
emphatic manner; the presence of both the sun and moon in these lines suggests it must be late afternoon, and hence Jupiter might indeed have been visible in a sapphire sky while the stars would still be blotted out.[36] Instead of
Dante's "eastern sky," then, the poem begins with an extravagant westward
glance towards the soon-to-be-setting sun.

    More strikingly still, Borges strangely ignores Góngora's efforts to elicit
the "secretas simpátias de los conceptos" with his hyperbole. For in the poem's
labyrinthine logic, hyperbole helps create a whole tissue of mythic, if not hermetic comparisons that place Góngora's pilgrim (*peregrino*) in a world riddled
by extravagant correspondences:

> cuando el que ministrar podía la copa
> a Júpiter mejor que el garzón de Ida,
> náufrago, y desdeñado sobre ausente,
> lagrimosas de amor dulces querellas
>   da al mar; que condolido,
>   fué a las ondas, fué al viento
>   el mísero gemido,
> segundo de Arión dulce instrumento. (7–14)

> when he, one worthier to serve as cupbearer to Jupiter than Ganymede,
> shipwrecked and disdained, besides being absent (from his lover), gives
> his tearful, sweet complaints to the sea; because the sea sympathized, the
> miserable moaning was to the waves and wind the sweet instrument of a
> second Arion.

By invidiously comparing the once avian Ganymede to the pilgrim grieving
his amorous misfortunes, and then the shipwrecked ("náufrago") pilgrim to
the shipwrecked Arion, Góngora quickly teaches his readers how complex
and self-referential metaphoric epideixis can be. In reshaping the Petrarchan
commonplace of the lover's tears finding sympathy in the sea, Góngora also
ingeniously insists on how his own "dulce instrumento," like Arion's, gives
pleasing form to grief ("dulces querellas"). But perhaps the chilly reception

of this hyperbole concerns neither Góngora the sly poet *provocateur* nor Borges the universal reader; perhaps it should be chalked up to differences in taste. Perhaps Borges, who always preferred Quevedo to Góngora, and who in his youth even playfully intimated that Quevedo's soul had transmigrated into his own, decided to make an earlier time's style wars his own.[37] With the resurrection of Góngora's reputation in the 1920s by Dámaso Alonso, Jorge Guillén, Rafael Alberti, and others, the Cordoban was once again in fashion, and Borges deeply despised fashion in literature. Finally, his critique curiously echoes those of Góngora's implacable contemporary critics. Lope de Vega, for example, famously laments: ". . . siendo ellas tan intrincadas y escabrosas, como V.m. y sus comentadores conocen, son tan superficiales sus misterios que, entendiendo todos lo que quieren decir, ninguno entiende lo que dicen" [*since the* Soledades *are so convoluted and scabrous, as you and their commentators well know, their mysteries are so superficial that, everyone understanding what they want to say, no one understands what they do say*].[38]

Before considering though how the dynamics of Góngora's reception speak to the larger issue of how the concept of taste has dominated the reception of hyperbole, I would recall how Gracián's philosophically rich treatment of various forms of *agudeza por encarecimiento* rescues hyperbole from its customary critical opprobrium. Add to this the ways in which Gracián's own mastery of hyperbole is put to more skeptical uses, and we begin to see how the extreme, conceited rhetoric against imperial overreaching may serve as the moral counterpart to the ideology of *Plus ultra*. A quick glance at *El Criticón* (1651), his allegoric, proto-*Bildungsroman*, reveals a text subtly overflowing with hyperbolic metaphor and amplification. In its opening pages, after a brief panegyric to Philip II and his empire, Gracián, remaking the classical polemic against navigation, punningly inveighs against the *audacia* of the first man who sailed the sea:

> ¡Oh, tirano mil veces de todo el ser humano, aquel primero, que con escandolosa temeridad fió su vida en un frágil leño al inconstante elemento. Vestido dicen que tuvo el pecho de aceros, mas yo digo que revestido de yerros

> O, tyrant a thousand time over all humanity, that first one, who with scandalous temerity trusted his life on a fragile piece of wood to that inconstant element. He was clothed, they say, with a breast of steel, but I say that he was covered with errors.[39]

A few sentences later, his outraged wit visits some of the Baroque's most hyperbolic *topoi*:

> Perdonaron los áspides a Alcides, las tempestades a César, los aceros a
> Alejandro y las balas a Carlos V. Mas ¡ay!, que, como andan encade-
> nadas las desdichas, unas a otras se introducen, y el acabarse una es de or-
> dinario el engendrarse otra mayor. Cuando creyó hallarse en el seguro
> regazo de aquella madre común, volvió de nuevo a temer que, enfureci-
> das las olas, le arrebataban para estrellarle en uno de aquellas escollos,
> duras entrañas de su fortuna. Tántalo de la tierra, huyéndosele de entre
> las manos, cuando más segura la creía, que un desdichado, no sólo no
> halla agua en el mar, pero ni tierra en la tierra.[40]

> The asps spared Hercules, the tempests Caesar, the swords Alexander,
> and the bullets Charles V. But, ah, how misfortunes come enchained;
> new ones follow others, and usually when one ceases it engenders an-
> other greater one. When a man believed that a safe lap on that common
> mother had been found, he started to fear again that the enraged waves
> would snatch him to be destroyed on one of those reefs, harsh entrails of
> his fortune. Tantalus of the earth, which flees from between his fingers,
> the more he believed the earth safe — what a miserable person — he
> finds not only no water in the sea, but no earth on the earth.

Compounding paradox ("no halla agua en el mar"), metaphor ("duras en-
trañas de su fortuna"), and the panegyric commonplaces associated with
Alexander and Caesar to show the extraordinary, hyperbolic violence of the
sea, Gracián methodically makes the sailor less fortunate than that paragon of
misfortune, Tantalus. And when the naïve Andrenio subsequently rescues a
shipwrecked Critilo ("náufrago, monstruo de la Naturaleza y de la suerte"),
the latter, as he teaches the former the art of speech, also illustrates hyperbole's
essential epistemological and ethical role:

> . . . si aunque todos los entendimientos de los hombres que ha habido ni
> habrá, se juntaran antes a trazar esta gran máquina del mundo y se les
> consultara cómo había de ser, jámas pudieran atinar a disponerla! ¿Que
> digo el Universo? Las más mínima flor, un mosquito, no supieran for-
> marlo. Sola la infinita sabiduría de aquel Supremo Hacedor pudo hallar
> el modo, el orden y el concierto de tan hermosa y perenne variedad.[41]

... even if all the minds of men that have been or will be came together beforehand to sketch this world's great construction, and they were consulted about how it should be, never would they hit upon how to do it! But why do I say the universe? The tiniest flower, a mosquito, they would not know how to form. Only the infinite knowledge of that Supreme Maker could find the means, order, and harmony of such beautiful and perennial variety.

Critilo elicits wonder at nature's "perennial variety" even as he cools Andrenio's nascent passion for knowledge. With Pascalian rigor, brevity, and wit, he charts the limits of human knowledge in the light of the "la infinita sabiduría" of God. Epistemologically chastened, Gracián's *tabula rasa* is welcomed into the world. On closer inspection, though, the entire world depicted in *El Criticón* is already a fallen one, a breeding place for late Renaissance skepticism. It is all the more remarkable, then, that language, as this hyperbolic meiosis confirms, somehow still retains its efficacy:

Todo cuanto inventó la industria humana ha sido perniciosamente fatal y en daño de sí misma: la pólvora es un horrible estrago de las vidas, instrumento de su mayor ruina, y una nave ni es otro que un ataúd anticipado.[42]

All that human ingenuity invented has been perniciously fatal and damaging to itself: gunpowder is a horrible devastation of lives, an instrument of its greatest ruin, and a ship is nothing but an eager coffin.

While Gracián gives *non plus ultra* a positive spin later in the novel when he dubs Charles V "el *non plus ultra* de los Césares," the themes of *desengaño* and world-weariness come to undermine any secular claims of glory. Conversely, that these themes and the melancholy, if ultimately orthodox central allegory of *El Criticón* become commonplaces in seventeenth-century Spanish literature makes the manner in which Sor Juana subsequently ignores Critilo's hyperbolic warning that much more surprising.[43] By ingeniously expressing the heroic if ultimately pyrrhic desire for certain knowledge about herself and this "gran máquina del mundo," poetic wit in the *Primero sueño* strives to fulfill the redemptive promise Gracián ascribes to it in the *Agudeza*.

The tensions between *Weltsucht* and *Weltflucht*, or the ways that the allures of the senses and the promise of transcendence conflict, are nowhere more acutely exemplified than in Calderón's dramas. For instance, *El mágico prodigioso*

(1637) takes as its starting point Pliny's absolute, inscrutable maxim, in the *Historia naturalis* (2.7) that the divine is "totus est sensus, totus visus, totus au﹣ ditus, totus animae, totus animi, totus sui," which Calderón renders as "Dios es una bondad suma, / una esencia, una sustancia, / todo vista y todo manos" [*God is the greatest good, / an essence, a substance, / all seeing and all doing*] (169– 171).[44] With this frame in place the main character of the *comedia religiosa*, Cipriano, can chart a trajectory "de un extremo en otro extremo" [*from one ex﹣ treme to another*], from his seduction of an innocent woman to his Faustian bar﹣ gain with the Demonio to trade his "alma" for knowledge of "magia."[45] All of which eventually yields this skeptical realization:

> . . . o con extraños tormentos
> acrisole mi constancia;
> que yo rendido y resuelto
> a padecer dos mil muertos
> estoy, porque a saber llego
> que, sin el gran Dios que busco,
> que adoro y que reverencio,
> las humanas glorias son
> polvo, humo, ceniza y viento. (2936–2944)

. . . or with strange torments let me refine my constancy; for I am de﹣ feated and resolved to suffer two thousand deaths; because I have come to know that, without the might of God which I seek, which I adore and revere, human glories are dust, smoke, ash, and wind.

Cipriano's extreme *skepsis* is thus followed by one last "atrevimiento" — his sudden, public conversion to Christianity. This transpires even as Calderón orchestrates the play's *peripeteia* by anaphorically debasing the earthly creation to yield another, greater reality:

> No tiene
> tantas estrellas el cielo,
> tantas arenas el mar,
> tantas centellas el fuego,
> tantos átomos el día,
> ni tantas plumas el viento,
> como Él perdona pecados. (3019–3025)

The sky does not have as many stars, the sea as many grains of sand, fire as many sparks, the day as many atoms, nor the wind as many feathers, as He pardons sins.

In this manner Calderón's *comedia religiosa* transforms rhetorical overreaching into a ineffable, fleeting vision of divine omnipotence. That hyperbolic skep-ticism can be converted into this type of theological straining suggests one possible solution to the subjective turmoil that riddles the verse of Góngora, Quevedo, and Sor Juana. In his first incarnation, Cipriano is a Marlovian overreacher of the type described so acutely by Harry Levin. But Calderón's resolution of the *comedia* and his curbing of Cipriano's Faustian desires also represent a decidedly more programmatic, if also gnostic worldview.[46]

IMITATION AND COURTLINESS

In the course of this and the next four chapters, several worldviews charac-teristic of Baroque Spanish hyperbolists are explored. These may be charac-terized as: the *Icarean*, or the desire to soar toward the celestial sphere, a desire often accompanied by the Platonic urge for eternal wisdom and beauty; the *Atlantean*, or the need to look down upon humanity and the world thereby achieving distant or novel perspectives; the *Faustian*, or the thirst for profane power and knowledge; and the *Columbian*, or the hunger for terrestrial domi-nation via seafaring and conquest. As heuristically useful as these terms may be, of course in actual practice these different modes frequently merge. For instance, while the perils of seafaring and the attendant classical trope of the ship as soul is a theme explored by most Spanish hyperbolists, this *Co-lumbian* perspective is inextricably linked in Quevedo's moral poetry with the *Faustian* desire for knowledge and riches at the expense of one's own salvation.

Put another way, the period's hyperbolic *topoi* tend to assume a monu-mental, even iconic role in the dynamics of literary *imitatio*. Setting the stage for hyperbolists to come, Garcilaso, for example, (re)introduces via Ovid, Sannazaro, and Tansillo, the *Icarean* theme in *Soneto XII*:

> Si para refrenar este deseo
> loco, imposible, vano, temeroso,
> y guarecer de un mal tan peligroso,
> que es darme a entender yo lo que no creo,

> no me aprovecha verme cual me veo,
> o muy aventurado o muy medroso,
> en tanta confusion que nunca oso
> fiar el mal de mí que lo poseo,
>   ¿qué me ha de aprovechar ver la pintura
> d'aquel que con las alas derretidas
> cayendo, fama y nombre al mar ha dado,
>   y la del que su fuego y su locura
> llora entre aquellas plantas conocidas,
> apenas en el agua resfrïado?[47]

If to curb this insane, impossible, vain, frightened desire, and to cure an ill so dangerous, since it convinces me of things I don't believe, [and] it does not profit me to see myself as I am — whether very daring or very afraid — in so much confusion that I never believe I possess this ill that I have, why must it profit me to see the painting of the one that, falling with melted wings, has given the sea his fame and name; and the painting of him who, barely cooled by the water, laments his fire and madness amidst those famous trees?

Just as this psychologically complex self-portrait is driven by a chain of paratactic, contradictory adjectives — a chain which Francisco de Herrera in his *Anotaciones a la poesía de Garcilaso* (1580) describes suggestively as an "*amontonamiento* de vozes que tienen varia significación" [a piling up *of words that have various meanings*] — the sonnet's entire theme may well be the impossibility of reconciling understanding with belief and "deseo."[48] Given the pernicious examples of Icarus and Phaethon, the poet, beset by his own perilous syntax — the sonnet is a single sentence — as well as the extravagant "mal" that possesses him, dares not ("nunca oso") realize with visual images ("verme") the extent of his plight. Instead, he places himself in the paradoxical but immanently Petrarchan position of verbally publicizing his will's insufficiency. In effect, Garcilaso would poetically imitate a painter's representation of the same scene: "porque la poesía es pintura que habla . . . porque si ellos se atrevieron a cosas impossibles, él osa lo mesmo" [*because poetry is painting that speaks . . . because painters dared impossible things, he dares the same*].[49] The chief vehicle of this verbal impossibility, Herrera adds, glossing the phrase "fiar el mal," is hyperbole:

Ipérbole. Los romanos le dieron por nombre *superlación*, o *ecesso*, o *crecimiento*, que sobrepuja la verdad por causa de acrecentar or deminuir alguna cosa. O, como siente Escalígero, es ecesso i sobra que denota redundancia, cuando levantamos una cosa con circuito de cosas o con mayor naturaleza que la suya propria. Podemos llamalla en nuestra lengua *engrandecimiento*, i es buena demostración d'ella este lugar, porque ninguna cosa ay que fiemos de nosotros.[50]

Hyperbole. The Romans named it *exaggeration*, or *excess*, or *increase*. It exceeds the truth in order to enhance or diminish some thing. Or, as Scaliger felt, it is excess and superfluity that denotes redundancy when we heighten a thing via surrounding things or with a greater nature than belongs to it. We may call it in our language *augmentation*, and a good demonstration of it is this instance, because there is no thing that we trust about ourselves.

The hyperbolic poet dares what the lover cannot: "fix the ill" in its proper place by exceeding ("sobrepuja") the truth.[51] Yet in glossing the skeptical commonplaces concerning existence's mutability, Herrera also refuses to grant the possibility of self-knowledge. In this way, poetic subjectivity becomes the "cosa," the *res*, justifying hyperbole. Herrera's annotation thus interprets the amplification accomplished by the "*amontonamiento* de voces" in line two as a part of the same rhetorical aim that the conceptual "*crecimiento*" in line eight pursues. Garcilaso's extreme rhetoric of self-doubt, in other words, transforms him into an "osado español" [*daring Spaniard*], to borrow from Herrera's longest and most famous gloss, in the field of poetry, even if he hyperbolically fails to "fix" the evil besetting him.[52]

Given Garcilaso's (and Herrera's) enormous influence on Spanish verse, not surprisingly Góngora in the *Soledad segunda* experiments with the same mythic theme. Here the pilgrim, recounting his flight from court and a disdainful beloved, wraps himself in the *Icarean* allegory and, like Garcilaso, makes that *Ur*-overreacher a figure for the poet and his impossible tasks:

> "Audaz mi pensamiento
> el Cenit escaló, plumas vestido,
>   cuyo vuelo atrevido,
> si no ha dado su nombre a tus espumas,

      de sus vestidas plumas
conservarán el desvanecimiento
los anales diáfanos del viento."
      "Esta pues culpa mía
el timón alternar menos seguro
      y el báculo mas duro
un lustro ha hecho a mi dudosa mano,
      solicitando en vano
las alas sepultar de mi osadía
donde el Sol nace o donde muere el día."[53] (137–150)

Audacious, dressed in humble feathers, my thought scaled the sky's highest part, and if its daring flight had not given, falling into the sea, its fame to your foam, the wind's diaphanous annals would have conserved the memory of its feathers' vanity. It is my fault that I have, during five years, alternated, in my indecisive hand, the most instable rudder with the hardest staff, vainly seeking death, punishment of my audacity, either in the Orient or Occident.

Góngora's metaphor comparing the "bold flight" of his "thought" to Icarus' audacity is sharpened and so distinguished from Garcilaso's by the marvelous conceit transforming "plumas," the feathers on the tragic hero's wings, into writing instruments vainly recording "the vanity" of his deeds in "the wind's diaphanous annals." Such "anales" allude to his own poetic practice while emblemizing also the risks facing the daring, hyperbolic poet. Not content though with having metapoetically remade the *Icarean* theme, Góngora has the pilgrim on account of his "culpa," trade his wings for a "timón" and a "báculo," and then seek the earth's horizontal limits. Like Homer's Odysseus, whose final task is to journey to a *terra incognita* where the inhabitants know nothing of navigation and so where he might plant an oar in homage to Poseidon, the pilgrim also faces an epic, if vain task — he must travel for five years ["un lustro"] chasing the sun and so outdo Dante's Ulysses who travels westwards for a mere five months.

    The pathos of his plight then leads the pilgrim, who has already been shipwrecked once, to this solipsistic hyperbole eight lines later:

      "Naufragio ya segundo,
    o filos pongan de homicida hierro

> fin duro a mi destierro;
> tan generosa fe, no facíl onda,
> no poca tierra esconda:
> urna suya el Océano profundo,
> y obeliscos los montes sean del mundo." (158–164)

Whatever may be the cruel fate of my exile, whether a second shipwreck or the edge of some homicidal sword, such generous faith like my own will not remain buried beneath scant earth or a simple wave; may its urn be the deep sea, and its obelisks all the world's mountains.

The lover's "tan generosa fe" can only be measured by the exaggerated scale provided by topographical space and epic time (what Bakhtin calls a *chrono-tope*), and in the process obelisks become mountains and an urn contains the sea. While these hyperboles are accompanied by hyperbaton, ellipsis, litote, periphrasis and other elements of Góngora's infamous style, I wish to under-score here the curious persistence at the end of these finely balanced lines of the Petrarchan mode with all its exaggerated sense of self-suffering. For the student of hyperbole, what is most interesting about Góngora's *obra* is not how Petrarchism influences Góngora — studies on this are already legion, and Petrarchism was as fundamental to poets like Góngora as the air they breathed — but how Gongorism infects and exaggerates Petrarchism through the bold, *culto* offices of hyperbole. Refiguring the Pillars of Hercules as the "obelisks" limiting his faith, the poet relies on the exaggerated scale provided by geographic space and epic time to measure not terrestrial or imperial ambi-tion, but rather idealized erotic longing. In this way, the *Plus ultra topos* is ulti-mately transformed into a trope of interiority for Góngora. The world and its spaces provide neither riches nor fame, but only the metaphoric material for the poet's linguistic desires, moral concerns, and transcendent yearnings. Thus even as the Petrarchan lover's semantic stances constitute the most im-posing tradition for Spanish Baroque poetry, a sophisticated counter-tradition of rejecting and refashioning Petrarchism also keeps epic pretensions at bay.

This partly explains why in these chapters on the Spanish Baroque I treat as illusory the critical abyss dividing Góngora's use of hyperbole to create aes-thetic beauty and glorify an agrarian ideal from Sor Juana's use of hyperbole to explore the limits of human reason and imagination. While Góngora may seem simply to apply *superlatio* like costly paint to the sensual, often fantastic, world of his pilgrim, like his fellow hyperbolists he too, as Robert Jammes and John Beverley learnedly insist, dedicates his poetic language to the supremely difficult conceptual task of expressing the inexpressible and objec-tifying the subjective.[54] For her part, Sor Juana elaborately mimics most of Góngora's *culto* gestures in the *Sueño*, but she also refines them to serve sophis-ticated philosophic ends. Meanwhile, with his enormous spiritual and stylis-tic debts to Stoicism, Quevedo presents a different hermeneutic challenge. Besides his often extravagant reworking of the clichéd conceits of an already exaggerated Petrarchism, Quevedo in his *Sueños*, his moral poems, and in-deed in most of his *obra*, hyperbolically exposes hypocrisy and vice. In this he implicitly rejects the Stoic doctrine of *ataraxia* or tranquility while insisting, like Seneca and Lucan, that the moral and physical universes are ontologi-cally intertwined. Given all this, together with Calderón's many theological hyperboles and Gracián's revalorization of *exageración*, we begin to see how *su-perlación* in Spanish Baroque literature might shed its putative status as a mere ornament of style and become instead an essential vehicle of invention.

Close readings of Spanish Baroque hyperbole may yield other fruit. Nowadays, in the wake of Lezama Lima, Sarduy, Deleuze, and Buci-Glucksmann, and with the phrase "Neo-Baroque" threatening to acquire the same attenuated ubiquity that "Baroque" experienced earlier in the last cen-tury, it is all the more urgent to determine if and how some of the more recent, exuberant claims for excess and multiplicity can be grounded in readings of the canonical texts that are said to provide their original justification.[55] More specifically, it is high time to reevaluate Dámaso Alonso's 1927 observation that hyperbole is "uno de los puntos en que su poesía está más distante de la nuestra, y adonde el gusto moderno más se resiste a acompañarle" [*is one of the aspects in which Góngora's poetry is most distant from our own, and where modern taste balks most in accompanying him*].[56] While Alonso's seminal essay "Claridad y belleza de las *Soledades*," as well as his exhaustive work on the *Polifemo*, were instrumental in preparing the way for a critical appreciation of Góngora's po-etry, his cursory, superficial treatment of hyperbole may well reflect his desire to protect his newly resurrected poet from a hostile academy's slings and ar-rows. Or, more problematically, it is simply emblematic of his tastes. To take the case of Góngora further, our own generation's most accomplished *gongorista*, Robert Jammes, also appears reluctant to call a hyperbole a hyperbole.[57] He convincingly judges Góngora's occasional, largely epideictic verse to be the least brilliant in his *obra*, but implied in his criticism is that excessive hyper-bole, in the form of clichéd *laudes* and exaggerated emotions, irredeemably disfigures the poet's style. Still, the fact that Góngora's efforts in conventional poetic epideixis form a substantial part of it his *obra*, as it does likewise with Quevedo and Sor Juana — nearly half of her work is encomiastic — argues for a greater engagement with the occasional verse of these poets and what Daniel Javitch calls the complex dynamics of "the theory and practice of courtliness."[58]

Góngora, Quevedo, Calderón, and Sor Juana were all perforce courtiers as well as poets. As his dedicatory verses to the Duque de Béjar make abundantly clear, Góngora pens his *Soledades* with his eyes fixed avidly on the court.[59] Quevedo's luck with patrons fluctuated wildly throughout his career: early on he hitched his star to the Duque de Osuna, who entrusted the poet with various diplomatic missions, but Quevedo also shared his disgrace when he fell in 1620. Likewise, Quevedo successfully wooed with his writings Philip III's favorite the Conde-Duque de Olivares only eventually to lose favor and suffer imprisonment during his final years. Sor Juana depends on the favor of patrons and patronesses for the very right to publish; when she loses this protection, her pen falls silent. In short, these poets embraced the language of epideixis as opportunity and necessity. Their mastery of the rhetorical subtleties of praise and blame was fundamental to their social identity as poets but also to their myriad conceptual explorations of the limits of linguistic expression.

A sonnet to Philip IV illustrates one aspect of Quevedo's subtle, often somewhat subversive mastery of the conventions of praise. His detailed gigantomachic and star-scaling imagery paints a witty, vivid picture of a timorous god surrounded by deadly enemies:

> No siempre tienen paz las siempre hermosas
> estrellas en el coro azul ardiente;
> y, si es posible, Jove omnipotente
> publican que temió guerras furiosas.
>
> Cuando armó las cien manos bellicosas
> Tifeo con cien montes, insolente,
> víboras de la greña de su frente
> atónitas lamieron a las Osas.
>
> Si habitan en el cielo mal seguras
> las estrellas, y en él teme el Tonante,
> ¿qué extrañas guerras, tú, qué paz procuras?

> Vibre tu mano el rayo fulminante:
> castigarás soberbias y locuras,
> y, si militas, volverás triunfante.[60]

The always beautiful stars in the burning, blue choir do not always have peace; and, if it is possible, they make known that omnipotent Jove, feared furious wars. When insolent Typhon armed his hundred bellicose hands with a hundred mountains, the thundering vipers in the tangle of his forehead licked the Bears. If the stars dwell insecurely in the sky, and if the Thunderer is afraid there, why are wars alien to you, what peace do you procure? Let the fulminating bolt vibrate in your hand: you will punish pride and madness, and if you militate, you'll return triumphant.

Playing in the second quatrain on Virgil's portrait of the rebellious Titan in the *Aeneid* (6.598), as well as the commonplace that bears lick newly born cubs into their proper shape, Quevedo fashions the ingenious image of chthonic snakes shaping the constellations of Ursa major and Ursa minor. With such ambiguity but also caution ("si es possible . . . Si habitan"), the poet compares and contrasts Jove's plight to Philip's. And when he poses the *culto* question (*extrañar* may mean "to avoid" as well as "to make someone feel strange") designed to urge Philip to war, it is answered by the thunderous final tercet, which for all its martial surety and mythographic hyperbole, still hints, with the play of "Vibre" on the earlier "víboras," at less than heroic deeds.

Quevedo's poetic *obra*, notwithstanding its multiplicity of theme and mastery of diverse poetic forms, is proof for Hermogenes' claim that all poetry is essentially epideictic. In his stirring *silva*, "Himno a las estrellas," he begins by praising the stars ("ejército de oro . . . Argos divino de cristal y fuego . . ."), continues with an epic description of their mythic origins ("os aborta Saturno, Jove, o Marte"), but ends by beseeching them not to forget "la pena de amor" and his own plight ("desatado en humo").[61] Alternately, in a series of sonnets (#284–288), he fulsomely praises Lope de Vega, but in another sequence (#825–841) mercilessly satirizes his rival, Góngora. That a similar dynamic of praise and blame is palpable in his love poetry, religious verse, and popular and burlesque lyrics (where, though, the cynic's barbs decidedly prevail), suggests again the difficulty if not impossibility of divorcing the specific task of epideixis from poetics more generally.

To adduce a final example, Sor Juana's numerous efforts dedicated to cele-brating her patronesses' virtues uncannily echo her own straining toward spir-itual perfection and the metaphysical absolutes in the *Primero sueño*. In "Esmera su respetuoso amor hablando a un Retrato," the Geronimite nun swiftly, per-haps too swiftly to elict sympathy, reaches the limits of expressibility:

> COPIA divina, en quien veo
> desvanecido al pincel,
> de ver que ha llegado él
> donde no pudo el deseo;
> alto, soberano empleo
> de más que humano talento;
> exenta de atrevimiento,
> pues tu beldad increíble,
> como excede a lo posible,
> no la alcanza el pensamiento.
>   ¿Qué pincel tan soberano
> fué a copiarte suficiente?
> ¿Qué numen movió la mente?
> ¿Qué virtud rigió la mano?
> No se alabe el Arte, vano,
> que te formó peregrino:
> pues en tu beldad convino,
> para formar un portento,
> fuese humano el instrumento
> pero el impulso, divino.[62]

Divine *copia*, in which I see the vainglorious paintbrush has arrived where desire could not. Elevated, sovereign employment of more than human talent; exempt from audacity, since your incredible beauty, as ex-ceeding the possible, cannot be reached by thought. What brush so sov-ereign was sufficient to copy you? What divinity moved the mind? What virtue governed the hand? The peregrine art that formed you is not praised in vain; for to form a portent with your beauty, a human tool was needed, but the impulse was divine.

Metapoetically reflecting on the difficulty of finding the correct form ("formó . . . formar") for such "copia divina," Sor Juana reifies here the belated hyperbolist's predicament. To copy ("copiarte") the devotional object is not "sufficient"; at best she can lament her merely "human ability." But if this ges-ture also seems to smack of mere flattery or worse, we might postpone a ver-dict until we have traversed the oneirocritical labyrinth she dubs her *Sueño*. There she will employ much the same diction and eventually be forced to adopt a similar stance of the frustrated artist who enflamed by a "deseo" for aesthetic perfection comes to realize the paucity of expressive means. There, however, the poetic object at hand will not be the patronage of a *marquesa*, but rather her audacious mind trying to refigure the abundance and aporias of language itself.

Chapter Five

Góngora's Art of Abundance

Todo vivir en el reino de la poesía *in extremis*,
aporta la configuración de vivir de salvación,
paradojal, hiperbólico . . .

— José Lezama Lima,
"Sierpe de Don Luis de Góngora"

POLIFEMO: A PETRARCHAN GIGANTOMACHY

For the botanist of Baroque hyperbole, the myriad species of poetic excess cultivated in Góngora's *Fábula de Polifemo and Galatea* (1612) defy easy classification. And, as Robert Jammes observes, there is more than a little folly in trying to say something new about a poem that has already occasioned such a cornucopia of criticism.[1] Fortunately, given Antonio Vilanova's voluminous source study and commentary — 1,753 pages on 504 lines of verse — I can spare the reader a rehearsal of how Góngora's hyperboles in his poem about monstrous love literally stand upon the shoulders of classical and Renaissance giants.[2] My aim instead is to explore the specific aesthetic and ethical effects of what Lezama Lima calls Góngora's "poesía *in extremis*." A poem that Ignacio Navarrete calls "the most effective upending of Petrarchism in the Spanish Golden Age,"[3] the *Polifemo*, I contend, stages a Petrarchan gigantomachy moralizing the themes of *copia* and *codicia* even as it self-consciously commits all kinds of stylistic crimes against traditional poetic decorum. Góngora toys with the Petrarchan legacy, turning the genre, its characteristic rhetorical gestures and *topoi*, in the direction of parody.[4] In part this is due to his "metalepsis" of numerous traditions and sources.[5] In syncretizing and sublimating

Petrarch, Ovid, Tasso, Marino, as well as his immediate Spanish predecessors, Garcilaso and Herrera, Góngora comments on the fate of literary imitation when the already distorted object of imitation is largely literature itself.
Yet if his poem's extravagant conceits sometimes mock their own excesses as
well as those of the poetic tradition, then remarkably they also manage to affirm the ethical nature of the poet's subjective pursuit of the ineffable.

As might be expected, the lines devoted to the beautiful nymph, Galatea,
her disdain for the monster Polyphemus, and her desire for the comely youth,
Acis, are the parts of the *Polifemo* borrowing most heavily from the Petrarchan
patois. Frequently resorting to *culto* diction like "cristal" and "nieve" to represent Galatea's physical beauty, Góngora employs these commonplace metaphors as semantic building block, or what Gracián calls a *fundamento*, to
construct larger, hyperbolic conceits. For instance, to elevate Galatea and
Acis to their proper mythic status in octave 24, he exaggerates their physical
qualities only to find improbable correspondences for these qualities in nature:

> (polvo el cabello, húmidas centellas,
> si no ardientes aljófares, sudando)
> llegó Acis; y, de ambas luces bellas
> dulce Occidente viendo al sueño blando,
> su boca dio, y sus ojos cuanto pudo,
> al sonoro cristal, al cristal mudo.[6] (187–192)

> dust in his hair, sweating humid sparks, if not burning pearls, Acis ar-
> rived; and seeing that soft sleep had hidden, like the west hides the sun,
> Galatea's two beautiful lights, he gave his mouth to the sonorous crystal,
> as much as his eyes gazing at the mute crystal would let him.

The characteristic "si . . . no" construction forms a *remedium* subtly introducing the conceit of "burning irregular pearls" which fuses the sweat and passion of Acis — a compelling emblem for Góngora's Baroque aesthetics. By
following it then with a more obscure hyperbole in which the sleep closing
Galatea's eyes is compared to the western horizon swallowing the sun, Góngora aspires to larger cosmographical themes (these verses are preceded by two
lines playing marvelously on the dog star, *canicula*). But this yields, by metalepsis and parataxis, renewed attention to the body, as Acis slakes his thirst
in a stream ("sonoro cristal") and tries to catch a glimpse of the sleeping
Galatea's skin ("cristal mudo"). And by prefacing this last hyperbole with

the more probable metonymy of "crystal" for water, the poet gracefully transforms all the objects in the scene into jewel-like substances.

In octave 23, Góngora prepares the way for such harmonious but still exaggerated correspondences by methodically, quantitatively, analyzing Galatea's
place in nature:

> La fugitiva ninfa, en tanto, donde
> hurta un laurel su tronco al sol ardiente,
> tantos jazmines cuanta hierba esconde
> la nieve de sus miembros, da una fuente.
> Dulce se queja, dulce le responde
> un ruiseñor a otro, y dulcemente
> al sueño da sus ojos a la armonía,
> por no abrasar con tres soles el día. (177–184)

Meanwhile, the fleeing nymph stops by a spring, where a laurel tree
steals its trunk from the burning sun, and where (lying down) she gives
as many jasmines to the spring as the grass hides her limbs' snow. One
nightingale's sweet plaints are sweetly answered by another, and the
sweet harmony lulls her eyes to sleep, so as not to scorch the day with
three suns.

Here a nap becomes a cosmic event, and because of it the world is saved from
a holocaust. Out of the stanza's surprising confusion of visual and acoustic
imagery, the idea emerges that nature's unsurpassable beauty and "armonía"
are the only measures worthy of the nymph. Conversely, the quantitative diction ("en tanto . . . tantos") and the carefully balanced syntax ("Dulce . . .
dulce") have the rigor almost of a mathematical equation, one that also produces an extremely sensual *agudeza*. After citing and dismissing Salcedo Coronel's interpretation of lines 179–180, Vilanova comments: "Encierra este
pasaje uno de los más indescifrables misterios de la obra gongorina" [*this passage
contains one of the most indecipherable mysteries in Góngora's works*]. His subsequent
gloss (which informs my English paraphrase) reads these oblique hyperboles
as imitating Petrarch's *canzone* 160: "Qual miracolo è quel, quando tra l'erba /
quasi un fior siede, over quand'ella preme / col suo candido seno un verde
cespo!" But then, with some assistance from Pellicer, he adds still more exegetical *copia* to Góngora's extravagant scene by discovering other sundry sources
including Euripides, Seneca, Petrarch, Ariosto, Tasso, Marino, Montemayor,

and Lope de Vega.[7] Such are the joys of the "crítica hidrolica" as Antonio Carreira has dubbed it.[8]

While inspiring critics to dig, Góngora by the poem's end all but aban-dons the search for pastoral harmony. In one of the most memorable, if in-conclusive, sexual encounters in Spanish Baroque literature, an awakened Galatea lies with Acis, only to initially reject his advances: "con desvíos . . . suaves, / a su audacia los términos limita" [*with gentle diversions, she fixes limits to his audacity*] (322–323). But less cautious than his protagonists, Góngora re-works the *nieve* and *cristal* conceits as he compares Acis' lust with Tantalus' thirst:

> Entre las ondas y la fruta, imita
> Acis al siempre ayuno en penas graves:
> que, en tanta gloria, infierno son no breve,
> fugitivo cristal, pomos de nieve. (325–328)

Between the waves and the fruit, Acis imitates the grave pains of the always-famished one: for, in the face of such glory, her fleeing crystal, her apples of snow, are a not-fleeting Hell.

Imitating himself numerous literary and mythological precedents, Góngora, with a superb litote ("infierno son no breve"), distorts an ephemeral desire into an eternal punishment. As Jammes observes, here the poet explores the characters' psychology and "intensa voluptuosidad."[9] And if for Góngora such extravagant psychological and poetic desires prove standard fare, the metamorphoses that occurs at the poem's very end, where the blood of the murdered Acis becomes "cristal . . . puro" [*pure crystal*] (496) and later "líquido aljófar" [*liquid pearl*] (500), suggest that he seeks an immutable form for mutable phenomena. Indeed, relatively straightforward hyperboles like these are rarely allowed to stand syntactically or semantically alone. A few lines earlier another hyperbole is offered whereby the murder weapon is trans-formed with such metonymic force that the poet himself seems to become a kind of rhetorical Cyclops disfiguring the physical world:

> Con vïolencia desgajó infinita,
> la mayor punta de la excelsa roca,
> que al joven, sobre quien la precipita,
> urna es mucha, pirámide no poca. (489–492)

With infinite violence he broke off the biggest point of the towering peak, which for young Acis, on whom it falls, is quite an urn and not a little pyramid.

The first two lines posit what Gracián calls "cognoscibles extremos" — the Cyclops's violence and the mountaintop — while the last two lines, conclud' ing with a marvelous, slightly paradoxical syncrisis, finds some proportion (albeit a gigantic one) and meaning in the death of Acis.

As might be expected, Góngora cannot be bothered even to hew to the il' lusion of decorum when it comes to that "mortal horror" of Sicily, Polifemo, who, ever since he dined on Odysseus' men in the *Odyssey*, and Ovid trans' formed him into a monster in love, has provoked poets to extremes.[10] Though only approximately a third of the poem is dedicated to the Cyclops, Góngora reserves his most disproportionate hyperboles for him. The *discordia concors* of a hideously misshapen creature enamored with an unsurpassed beauty is ren' dered with extravagant topographic conceits mixing detailed physical de' scription and a tone of moral outrage to solicit the reader's admiration.[11] In an image that anticipates many in the *Soledad primera*, the monster's passion trans' lates directly into cartographic overreaching:

> "Polifemo te llama, no te escondas;
> que tanto esposo admira la ribera
> cual otro no vio Febo, más robusto,
> del perezoso Volga al Indo adusto." (405–408)

"Polyphemus calls you, do not hide; for the seashore admires such a great spouse, and from the lazy Volga to the scorched Indus, Phoebus has not seen any other more robust."

Refashioning the "India *topos*" identified by Curtius, Góngora'Polifemo wittily recharts terrestrial limits on the basis of the Petrarchan and climatic extremes of hot and cold — the Volga was considered a synecdoche for the *Septentrión* or Hyperboria.[12] Yet despite his Baroque mastery of space, Polifemo is doomed by literary history never to gain the material object of his desire.

Put another way, from its outset Góngora inserts the poem with its Sicil' ian setting into a gigantomachic frame: ". . . bóveda o de las fraguas de Vul' cano, / o tumba de los huesos de Tifeo" [*Vulcan's vault or forge, or the tomb of Typhon's bones*] (27–28). And while Virgil in the *Aeneid* made Sicily on

account of its natural features and gigantomachic heritage into a locus requiring hyperbole, Góngora has it yield a more solipsistic species of material and
semantic *copia*. Polifemo boasts:

> "Pastor soy, mas tan rico de ganados
> que los valles impido más vacíos,
> los cerros desaperezco levantados
> y los caudales seco de los rios;
> no los que, de sus ubres desatados,
> o derivados de los ojos míos,
> leche corren y lágrimas; que iguales
> en número a mis bienes son mis males." (385–392)

"I am a shepherd, but one so rich in herds that I choke the emptiest val-
leys, make disappear the highest hills, and dry up the riches of rivers; but
never dry are those flowing riches of milk unleashed from their udders,
or those flowing tears coming from my eyes; for equal in number are my
boons and banes."

By no means an isolated image or equation, this dramatic pastoral snapshot
amplifies the description of Sicily in octave 18, which ends "de cuyas siempre
fértiles espigas / las provincias de Europa son hormigas" [*to whose always fertile
ears (of wheat) / the provinces of Europe are like ants*], a conceit that we saw
Gracián praise as exemplary of *agudeza por exageración* that diminishes its terms
in order to elevate its principal subject.[13] Such meoisis further confirms how
an exaggerated, poetic topography can reflect and distort an outsized self-
consciousness.

  Although he may be a shepherd to a "copia bella" (47) of goats, Polifemo
chiefly symbolizes the dangers inherent in the attempt to upset, supplant, and
supplement the natural order of things. Nature's *copia* thus methodically acquires monstrous connotations:

> Un monte era de miembros eminente
> este (que, de Neptuno hijo fiero,
> de un ojo ilustra el orbe de su frente,
> émulo casi del mayor lucero)
> cíclope, a quien el pino más valiente,
> bastón, le obedecía, tan ligero,

y al grave peso junco tan delgado
que un día era bastón y otro cayado.
   Negro el cabello, imitador undoso
de las obscuras aguas del Leteo,
al veinto que lo peina proceloso,
vuela sin orden, pende sin aseo;
un torrente es su barba impetüoso,
que (adusto hijo de este Pirineo)
su pecho inunda, o tarde, o mal, o en vano
surcada aun de los dedos de su mano. (49–64)

A lofty mountain he was with limbs (who, fierce son of Neptune, illuminates the orb of his forehead with one eye; emulating almost the greatest light), this cyclops, whom the strongest pine tree, a light staff, obeyed;
and with his enormous weight it was like a skinny reed, which one day
was a staff, another a shepherd's crook. His black hair, wavy imitator of
Lethe's obscure waters, hangs unkempt, flies without order in the tempestuous wind combing it; his beard is an impetuous torrent, which
(scorched son of the Pyrenees) inundates his breast, and is plowed,
whether belatedly, or badly, or in vain, by his hand's fingers.

With their superb detail octaves 6 and 7 manage perversely to refashion the
microcosmic-macrocosmic *blasón* favored by Petrarch, his epigones, and the
grand rhétoriquers. In the first octave, subtly comparing ("émulo casi") Polifemo's eye ("el orbe") to the sun, Góngora depends on a *copia* of sources to
stitch together and so ultimately defend these lines and his portrait of man become mountain. Thus poetic tradition, especially when tethered to Homer,
Virgil, and Ovid, helps sanctions what otherwise might be condemned as
mere affectation or folly. Salcedo Coronel, one of Góngora's early commentators, locates "este hipérbole" in the *Aeneid* (3.635–637), where the Cyclopean
eye is "lumen . . . ingens . . . Argolici clipei aut Phoebeae lampadis instar."
Andrés Cuesta cites *Metamorphoses* (13.851–853), where Ovid takes Virgil's
shield metaphor above and conflates it, I think, with the "clipei non enarrible
textum" (8.625) — a text literally impossible to narrate — to produce these
lines: "Unum est in media lumen mihi fronte, sed instar / Ingentis clipei.
quid? non haec omnia magnus / Sol videre e caelo? soli tamen unicus orbis"
[*A single light there is in the middle of my forehead, but it stands there like a huge shield.
And what of it? Does not the great Sun see all these things from the sky, and yet the sun*

has but a single orb]. This is not to say, though, that Góngora lacks his own in-vention. To illustrate further the monster's enormous power and weight, he subjugates even the "más valiente" pinetree to the Cyclops, forcing it to serve dutifully as a "light staff" before it is further debased to a "reed," which, by the octave's end, finally becomes a "cane."[14] In terms of syntax, the hyperbole's precision depends upon the anaphora ("tan ... tan"), which, like a series of steps, guides the reader as the native grandeur of the "pino" precipitously de-clines. Salcedo Coronel rightly celebrates this octave as a "Hermosíssimo hipérbole, y en que se excedió a si mismo. Imitó en este lugar a Virgilio, pero con tanta ventaja suya, que lo confesarán los antiguos, y no la negarán los modernos escritores" [*A most beautiful hyperbole, and one which exceeds itself. Gón-gora imitates here Virgil, but with such advantage to himself, that the ancients would have confessed it, and the moderns will not deny it*].[15] Hyperbole thus produces poetic fame and novelty; it promotes the cultural worth of vernacular poetry and spurs critical excess.

The use of hyperbaton further heightens the difficulty of interpreting these octaves. Generally speaking, hyperbaton pretends to function only syn-tactically, whereas hyperbole seems to operate largely in a semantic fashion. Upon closer inspection, though, these functions often merge. Just as hyper-bole is literally a "throwing-beyond" of the truth, hyperbaton is a "passing-over." (The Greek noun ὑπερβατός in addition to meaning "transposed" can mean what is "*accessible* (to trespassers).")[16] The over-stepping of normal syn-tax, far from always conveying a feeling of artifice or affectation, often lends the poetry of Góngora (and Sor Juana) an improvised, heuristic air, as if the mind were too jumbled by and involved in thought and experience to care about normal syntactical order. Thus in these lines, with the exaggerated predicate preceding the subject, "cíclope," Góngora temporarily suspends the possibil-ity of judging the meaning and decorum of his exaggerations. Or, perhaps, the analogous disordering, disfiguring functions of hyperbole and hyperbaton derive from the singular perception that the chaotic world — as embodied by the Cyclops — requires disorder and indecorousness on the page.[17]

In octave 7, leaning on hyperbaton, Góngora hyperbolically amplifies what Vilanova calls the "deshumanización" of Polifemo. Initially, in the apos-trophe (57–58), his hair, "imitator ... of the obscure waters of Lethe," seems bound to an infernal, classical myth, but then in the next lines it abruptly "flies" when combed by the "tempestuous" wind.[18] This play of high and low — another recurring characteristic of hyperbole that will assume its most sophisticated conceptual form in Sor Juana and Pascal — continues in the next quatrain where his beard is cast as an "impetuous torrent" descending from his mountain-top/head to "flood" his chest.[19] Playing upon the catachrestic *surcar* — to plow a field or plow the waves — Góngora transforms Polifemo's "fingers" into a ship, a ship ultimately at the mercy of the elements. At war with himself, the Cyclops's tempestuous passion corresponds nicely with his extreme, outward appearance, though it also owes a great deal to Góngora's weird logic of metaphor and metonymy. By refashioning the microcosmic-macrocosmic conceit into a kind of gigantomachic *blasón*, Góngora refigures the Cyclops as a synecdoche of all that is awesome, chthonic, and chaotic in nature. Such is hyperbole's compass that death's mystery, the mountain's sublimity, the storm's rage, and the sea's unpredictability are all ingeniously embodied in the portrait of the monster's hair and beard.

Finally, the appearance of a *náufrago* in lines 425–456 is intimately connected to the motifs of *copia, codicia* and *atrevimiento*. Like Sicily itself, the shipwreck described in octave 55 produces *copia* ("cuantas vomitó [the sea] riquezas"). But if Sicily's material cornucopia is benign, Polifemo's soothing music only temporarily dampens the violence implicit in the shipwreck and its exotic "treasures." The "horrenda . . . relación" [*horrible tale*] of the *náufrago* interpolated into the Cyclops' own narration is literally interrupted by Góngora in octave 59, which begins "Su horrenda voz . . ." [*His horrible voice*]. This persistence of horror amidst such plenty — Bacchus is invoked in line 468 — indicates the poem's fundamental conceptual and ethical tensions. While identifying Polifemo with nature's enormous wealth and power, Góngora still blames his hero for an excessive and thus unnatural desire for the well-proportioned Galatea. In more metapoetic terms, the conflict between the hyperboles describing his physique, riches, and sorrow and those describing Galatea's beauty are irreconcilable.

But how does such semantic tension effect the poem's final *propositio*? If I am correct to call it a Petrarchan gigantomachy, then Góngora himself ought to be identified with Polifemo the overreaching lover.[20] It is the Cyclops who achieves the *Atlantean* perspective to compose a "dulce" song in octave 44, who provokes Góngora to invoke the muses' aid in octave 45, and who exclaims in the finest, belated, Petrarchan manner in octave 46:

> "¡Oh bella Galatea, más süave
> que los claveles que tronchó la aurora;

> blanca más que las plumas de aquel ave
> que dulce muere y en las aguas mora;
> igual en pompa al pájaro que, grave,
> su manto azul de tantos ojos dora
> cuantas el celestial zafiro estrellas!
> ¡Oh tú, que en dos incluyes las más bellas!" (361–368)

"O beautiful Galatea, gentler than the carnations that the dawn plucks; whiter than the feathers of that bird which dies sweetly and dwells on the waters; equal in pomp to the grave bird, whose blue mantle gilds as many eyes as the celestial sapphire does stars! O you, whose two eyes contain the most beautiful stars."

By making the singer a greedy, boastful monster in possession of an *ingenio* capable of such exacting invidious comparisons, Góngora mocks the entire *ethos* of the Petrarchan enterprise. In calling attention to his monster's ability to transform reality, to equate the number and beauty of the "stars" in the "celestial zafiro" with the peacock's "eyes," he underscores also the grotesque impossibility of such desire. Further exemplifying this parodic effect is octave 49 where the monster's grief verges decidedly on bathos.

Commenting on these verses, Alonso makes Góngora's "monstruosa hipérbole" characteristic of the Baroque style and the imitation of classical models; but he ignores any parodic effects.[21] By contrast, his most virulent contemporary critics, while generally dismissing Góngora's astonishing wit, often regarded his *culto* verse as mere self-promotion. Echoing the Aristotelian critique of hyperbole, Pedro de Valencia, after condemning Góngora's "pensamiento hiperbólico" and "juvenil" use of ornament, writes:

> Qué, pues, es lo que llamo juvenil? (porque es de mozos y novicios). Un pensamiento escolástico de estudiantes y bisoños, que de pura curiosidad y compostura viene a parar en frialdad, y resbalan y caen en este género con el apetito de lo extraordinario y pulido, y principalmente de lo sabroso, y dan al través en los bajíos de lo figurado, trópico y afectado o cacocelo.[22]

> Well, what am I calling juvenile (or what is proper to boys and novices)? Scholastic thought of students and rookies, which starting from pure curiosity and circumspection comes to a halt in frigidity, and slips and falls in this genre of writing because of an appetite for the extraordinary and

the ornate; and, especially, they tumble from the tasteful into the shallows of the figurative, tropological, affected, or indecorous.

For his detractors, Góngora himself is an object worthy of satire. But they imprudently dismiss the possibility that he risks their opprobrium to remap the world following the prescriptions of a radical critique of desire. Or that, as Paul Celan affirms in his *Meridian* address, given the impossibility of ever achieving the "absolute poem," one can at least make the "exorbitant claim" that "the poem would then be the place where all tropes and metaphors want to be led ad absurdum."[23]

EGO AND ETHICS IN THE *SOLEDADES*

In Terence Cave's influential account of sixteenth-century French writing (*écriture*), *The Cornucopian Text*, the creation of conceptual and linguistic *copia* signals the writer's "self-awareness" of the fragmentary nature of his imitation and the "centrifugality" of his subjectivity.[24] Leaning heavily on Erasmus's *De copia*, Cave's readings of the *copia* cultivated by Rabelais, Ronsard, and Montaigne reveal how such "prodigality" exhausts and ironizes many traditional Renaissance literary *topoi*.[25] Similarly, I read Góngora's cornucopian *Soledad primera* and equally prodigal but unfinished *Soledad segunda* as challenging the Petrarchan legacy in part by remapping the ideology of *Plus ultra*. Building also on the rich legacy of Garcilaso's three eclogues (1543) and the classical tradition of pastoral poetics, the *Soledades* (1612) reimagine Petrarchism with a form of *imitatio* that riddles every material and linguistic object with inexplicable abundance. Briefly put, the bevy of *cultismos* and *conceptos* dominating the poems create a solipsistic, even narcissistic universe wherein poetic and erotic desire, turned inward upon themselves, are able to yield significant ethical and aesthetic questions that would never have occurred in a strictly Petrarchan context. Though long chided for an almost immoral lack of poetic decorum — a contemporary, Francisco Cascales, brands him the "Mohammed of Spain's poetry" — Góngora, in these two genre-defying poems, fashions a complex critique of Spain's imperial project. His praise of bucolic life is largely ethical;[26] while his hyperbolism in the so-called navigation-*exkursus* of the *Soledad primera* hinges on the critical commonplace that the extremes of ambition and greed explored there are answered by the ideal *mediocritas* promoted in the poems' pastoral and piscatory sections. In my reading,

then, of this remarkable *digressio*, I see Góngora's extreme rhetoric of mourning, outrage, and wonder, with all its hyperbolic, conceited play, as offering an
ironic, self-consciously subjective response to Spanish imperial ideology, with
all its objective, verisimilar pretensions. Góngora rails against the overstep-
ping of limits ("los términos saber todos no quiere," 1.409), but in so doing
slyly invites the charge that his poetic *copia* overreaches most of all. As John
Beverley argues, this apparent paradox contains a possible solution: "The
danger, as in the crisis of empire itself, is that ambitious desire will produce
transgression and perversion. But the other side of the wager is the possibility
of a language of *discovery*. The economics of art replace here the economics of
an imperial project that has become problematic . . ."[27] Yet if Góngora's language proves heuristic, even ethical in the course of the *Soledades*, then this also
depends inordinately on readers, like Beverley, Jammes, and, more recently,
Joaquín Roses Lozano, willing to accept the poet's "wager" and able to convert his hyperbolic currency.[28]

Góngora's cultivation of *copia* and difficulty through Latinate and Ital-
ianate diction, allusion, periphrasis, metaphor, hyperbole, as well as his infamous mastery of hyperbaton and ellipsis, unleashed an avalanche of critical
opprobrium from his first commentators and critics. Hostile texts published
or circulated soon after the publication of the *Soledades* included Francisco
Fernández de Córdoba's "Parecer de Don Francisco de Córdoba acerca de
las *Soledades* a instancia de su autor," Pedro de Valencia's "Carta escrita a don
Luis de Góngora en censura de sus poesías," Francisco Cascales's epistles in
the *Cartas filológicas*, and two acerbic letters by Lope de Vega.[29]

Córdoba regrets that the poems' "materia" is not "más grave, heroica" and
that Góngora balked at writing a true epic.[30] Adducing myriad authorities,
including Aristotle, Horace, Quintilian, Minturno, and Scaliger, Córdoba
chiefly blames the poet's obscure style. As for hyperbole, leaning on Quintilian, he notes that its ubiquity leads to *cacozelia*. He then perceptively if sar-
donically asks: "¿Todo ha de ser sumo, ir por esos cielos, o por los abismos? . . .
¿cómo se ha de ver lo grande, sin oposición de lo pequeño? Si todo es en grado
superlativo; ¿qué harán del positivo y comparativo los pobres gramáticos?"
[*Must everything be supreme, go through the heavens, or through abysses? . . . How is the
large to be seen, without the opposition of the small? If everything is in the superlative degree, what will poor grammarians make of the positive and the comparative?*].[31] Likewise, Valencia, who was best known as an *arbitrista* and whom Góngora

invited to read a manuscript version of the poems in 1613, compares Góngora's style in the *Soledades* unfavorably with the *obscuritas* of Pindar and Ovid.
He also evokes Longinus' treatise on the sublime to chasten Góngora as well
as citing Demetrius' caution about hyperbole and reproach of the Neo-
Homeric poet who had goats browsing on the rock the Cyclops hurled at
Odysseus' ship. For his part, Cascales in two epistles repeatedly blames the
obscurity of Góngora's "crético laberinto" [*Cretan labyrinth*], his "palabras
trastornadas con catacreses y metáforas licenciosas" [*contorted words with catachreses and licentious metaphors*], and the general "caos de esta poesía" [*chaos of
this poetry*].[32] Stoking the ever-simmering debate on the relative values of *res et
verba*, Cascales allows "peregrino pensamiento" [*peregrine* (i.e., outlandish)
thinking] but not "el modo de hablar peregrino," which he defines partly as the
using of Latinate syntax in Spanish, for such syntax "es violentar a la naturaleza y engendrar monstruosidades" [*is to do violence to nature and engender monstrosities*], and partly as the excessive use of tropes to the point of creating mere
enigmas.[33] Most famously, Lope de Vega pens his so-called "Carta de un
amigo" (1615), which, while recognizing the novelty of Góngora's style,
cagily blames the poet for publishing the poems in the first place. Góngora's
incomprehensible language, Lope muses, fosters the belief that the poet has
taken hold of "algún ramalazo de la desdicha de Babel" [*some branch of the misfortune of Babel*] and therefore of not having "participado de la gracia de Pen-
tecostés" [*participated in the grace of Pentecost*].[34]

While Góngora, as we shall presently see, is not shy in defending himself
against these and other calumnies, he is also assisted by a motley collection of
learned partisans. Well after Góngora's friend, Andrés de Almansa y Mendoza
shepherded the manuscript of the *Soledades* through the largely incredulous
court in 1614, José Pellicer de Salas y Tovar offers a wide-ranging defense of
and commentary on the poet's work and life, *Lecciones solemnes a las obras de Don
Luis de Góngora y Argote, Pindaro Andaluz, Principe de los poëtas liricos de España*
(1630).[35] As Pellicer's subtitle and focus on the poet's most difficult works
suggest, he seems to want to do for Góngora what Herrera accomplished for
Garcilaso: namely, weave an encyclopedic web of authorities and *realia* about
the poet to ensure his canonical status and value for vernacular imitators. And
while it is remarkable how little Pellicer explicates Góngora's *ornatus* given the
bevy of treatises attacking the style of this "Pindaro Eruditisimo Cordoves,"
still his commentary helpfully traces numerous possible historiographic and

literary sources for Góngora's *imitatio*. In offering, moreover, an erudite if rather conventional theological defense of the Spanish imperial project in the course of his exegesis of the navigation-*exkursus*, Pellicer endows the poem's hyperboles with a scholarly gravitas previously absent from the debate; this, despite largely ignoring their conceptual acuity.

Most forcefully of all Góngora's defenders, José García de Salcedo Coronel, in editing *Soledades de D. Luis de Góngora* (1636), celebrates the poet's "osadia" in becoming a vernacular, poetic model for subsequent generations.[36] Nor does he hesitate to praise Góngora's *copia* as surpassing the ancients':

> Vea pues el mas riguroso censor de las obras de nuestro Poeta con quanta atencion siguiò la autoridad de los antiguos Escritores en ilustracion de nuestro idioma, valiendose de licencias que le han enriquezido, y de metaforas que marvillosamente le adornan, sin que en esta parte conozca ventajas en ninguno de los antiguos, pues nadie usò mas propiamente dellas, ni las continuò con mayor decoro.[37]

> Let the most rigorous judge of our poet's work consider with what attention he follows the authority of the ancient writers as he illuminates our language, validating the liberties that have enriched it, and the metaphors that marvelously adorn it, without in this regard ceding advantage to any of the ancients, since nobody used them more properly, nor developed them with greater decorum.

In anchoring Góngora's defense in the notion of "decoro," Salcedo Coronel expands his claims for the text beyond a purely literary or textual orbit. For again, decorum may be defined not only by how a text meets generic expectations, but also by how it answers the exigencies of readers and of their world.

Exemplifying the most common twentieth-century critical stance toward the *Soledades*, a stance that tends to read Góngora as an early modern avatar of "l'art pour l'art," as a Spanish Mallarmé, Helmut Hatzfeld maintains that the poet's remarkable penchant for ornamental *copia* is inimical to any ethical stance, ironic or otherwise. In contrast to Cervantes's *copia* Góngora's is said to signal only aesthetic self-awareness, or as Hatzfeld terms it, the aesthetic values of mannerism. Seconding Spitzer's stress on the *lascivo* in the *Soledades*, Hatzfeld juxtaposes Góngora's "actitud amoral" and "pseudo-grandeza" with Cervantes's "humor" and "grandeza barroca."[38] Similarly, the ambivalence of Dámaso Alonso toward the ability of hyperbole to produce decorous *copia* is unmistakable. In "Hipérboles," a brief section of "Claridad y belleza de las *Soledades*," Alonso affirms:

> Góngora no quiere que ni una sola de las hermosuras que presenta admita término de comparación. En éste otro modo de elevar lo natural a plano astético, particularmente grato a la poesía renacentista, y aquí, como siempre, Góngora está situado al cabo de la serie de poetas del siglo XIV. Nunca se detiene ante un hipérbole, por caprichosa o absurda que sea . . . Enorme abundancía de ejemplos.[39]

> Góngora does not wish that even one of the beauties that he offers should admit of comparison. This is another manner of elevating the natural to the aesthetic plane, one particularly pleasing to Renaissance poetry. And here, as always, Góngora is situated at the end of a series of sixteenth-century poets. Never does he balk at a hyperbole, no matter how capricious or absurd it may be . . . There is an enormous abundance of examples.

By chiding Góngora's lack of self-control and therefore also his *ethos* when it comes to hyperbole, Alonso spreads the blame around (that is, all late Renaissance poets did the same) and suggests that Góngora was particularly devoted to the figure given its potent ability to "elevate" nature toward art. Nevertheless, neither Hatzfeld nor Alonso seriously consider the possibility that Góngora may at times use hyperbole not only to aestheticize nature but also to underscore the "absurdity" or "capriciousness" of human artifice in this and other arenas. Indeed, being "caprichosa" may be an end in itself. Or at least Juan Huarte de San Juan thought so in his influential *Examen de ingenios para las ciencias* (1580). Here Huarte distinguishes between "ingenios inventivos [que] llamen en lengua toscana caprichosos, por semejanza que tienen con la cabra en el andar y pacer" [*inventive wits called in Italian* caprichosos, *for the similarity they have with the goat in moving and grazing*] and those sheep-like *ingenios* who disdain novelties, are content with a single thought, and so follow the lead of others.[40] Huarte's goat may be regarded as the very model for the solitary, audacious pilgrim-poet:

> Esta jamás huelga por lo llano; siempre es amiga de andar a sus solas por los riscos y alturas, y asomarse a grandes profundidades; por donde no sigue vereda ninguna ni quiere caminar con compañia . . . jamás huelga

en ninguna contemplación, todo es andar inquieta buscando cosas nuevas que saber y entender.[41]

It never delights in the plain; it is always keen to go alone along the crags and heights, and to lean out over great depths; it goes where it follows no path nor does it want to walk accompanied by others . . . it never delights in any contemplation; it always goes discontentedly seeking new things to know and understand.

We will see that Huarte's imagery nicely prefigures the volatile pastoral dynamics explored by Góngora in the *Soledades*. Conversely, his physiological, even deterministic ideas about the nature of genius and wit go some way to indicating why a certain caution should be observed in branding Góngora's hyperbolism merely *précieux*.

CAMÕES'S EXAMPLE

Immediately attacked from all sides for his new, exaggerated, *culto* style, Góngora remained absent from court until 1617 (he left Madrid in 1609). Retired to his farm near Córdoba, he had ample opportunity to contemplate all things pastoral. Biographical fallacies aside, the aestheticization of the bucolic life, the theme of solitude, and the abandonment of love as a topic in the *Soledades* do correspond neatly with Góngora's personal situation during these years. Moreover, the navigation theme has, ever since Horace, often been accompanied by a certain contempt for the court and princes.[42] Yet while Jammes, Beverley, and Maravall have been crucial in reminding readers of Góngora and his Baroque contemporaries of the ways literature can be symptomatic of complex social and cultural forces, such considerations should not eclipse the synchronic aspects of Góngora's engagement with literary history.

Specifically, as students of Gongorist hyperbole we should consider, however briefly, Luis de Camões's epic poem *Os Lusiades* (1572) and how its protean rhetoric charting Vasco da Gama's voyage to India prefigures aspects of the "navigation" *exkursus*. Three passages are particularly vital: 1) the speech of the Old Man of Belém contra navigation; 2) the description and prophecies of the giant Adamastor as the Cape of Storms; 3) Camões's reflections on the "truth" of his poem versus the exaggeration and grandiloquence of classical epic.

At the end of Canto 4, just after da Gama and his men have prayed at church for good fortune in their voyage and just before embarking on their ships (whose promise Camões compares to the Argo which was transformed into "estrelas" for its heroic efforts), "um velho de aspeito venerando" [*an old man with a venerable air*] emerges from the crowd gathered to see them off.[43] This old man immediately, mockingly, denounces their presumption: "Ó glória de mandar! ó vã cobiça / Desta vaidade a quem chamamos fama!" [*Oh, the glory of command! Oh, the vain thirsting / after what we call fame!*]. His polemic (stanzas 95–104) not only provides a chilling, moralizing frame for the Canto and the voyage, both of which constitute the poem's narrative core, but the manner in which it appropriates classical forerunners such as Homer, Apollonius, Valerius Flaccus, Lucan, and Horace suggests the extent to which Renaissance notions of *translatio imperii* may be marvelously, if darkly intertwined with the riches of *translatio studii*. More particularly, his imprecation against the folly of seeking distant lands when enemies lurk much closer to home ("Deixas criar às portas o inimigo / Por ires buscar outro de tão longe . . ." [*You allow an enemy to grow at your gates / in order to go looking for another far away*]) recalls the speech warning against civil war that Lucan puts in the mouth of one of Rome's older citizens (2.68–233). But it also curiously inverts Lucan's own declamation at the beginning of the *Pharsalia* (1.8–23) where he decries the civil war as a missed opportunity to extend empire's boundaries. Similarly, Camões rethinks Horace's *Ode* 1.3 where the commonplaces contra navigation are given their most influential lyric form ("Nequiquam deus abscidit / prudens Oceano dissociabili / terras, si tamen impiae / non tangenda rates transiliunt vada . . ."). He does so by amplifying Horace's sentiments, while also explicitly comparing the ode's cast of overreachers, Prometheus, Phaethon, and Icarus, with their early modern imitators. This latter crew, however, refuses to profit from their classical forerunners:

> "Nenhum cometimento alto e nefando,
> Por fogo, ferro, água, calma e frio,
> Deixa intentado a humana gèraçao!
> Mísera sorte! Estranha condiçao!" (4.104)

"No undertaking great or nefarious, concerning fire, sword, water, heat, or cold, will man leave untried! Miserable fate, strange condition!"

Such strangeness acquires a cosmographical dimension in the second episode I wish to rehearse. Lying at the very center of *Os Lusiades*, the celebrated prosopopeia of Adamastor as the Cape of Storms (or Cape of Good

Hope) offers Góngora's readers a formidable gigantomachic model for Polifemo as well as a preliminary lesson how hyperbole can be simultaneously
ethical, historical, mythic, and cosmographic. Borrowing from classical precedents and perhaps Rabelais as well, Camões has da Gama paint the most hor-
rendous portrait of geography become flesh:

> Não acabava, quando uma figura
> Se nos mostra no ar, robusta e válida,
> De disforme e grandíssima estatura,
> O rosto carregado, a barba esquálida,
> Os olhos encovados, e a postura
> Medonha e má, e a cor terrena e pálida,
> Cheios de terra e crespos os cabelos,
> A boca negra, os dentes amarelos.
> > Tão grande era de membros, que bem posso
> > Certificar-te que este ero o segundo
> > De Rodes estranhíssimho Colosso,
> > Que um dos sete milagres foi do mundo. (5.39–40)

I hardly finished speaking, when a robust and valiant figure showed itself in the air. Deformed and of enormous stature, with a heavy jowl, a
squalid beard, hollow eyes, and an expression that was gruesome or
worse; its complexion earthen and pale, its curly hair matted with clay,
its black mouth with yellow teeth. So great was its limbs I swear that you
would believe he was the strangest, second Colossus of Rhodes, one of
the world's seven wonders.

How Camões wants the appearance of this "estranhíssimho," hyperbolic
"figura" to be judged is made clear by da Gama's terrified reaction, but also by
the giant's subsequent discourse lengthily excoriating the mariners' "sobejo
atrevimento." Part Cassandra and part Anchises, Adamastor acknowledges
the extraordinary audacity of the Portuguese ("Ó gente ousada . . . navegar
meus longos mares ousas"), yet he quickly represents it as unnatural (". . . vens
ver os segredos escondidos / Da natureza e do húmido elemento"), and therefore predicts numerous nautical catastrophes.

That Camões makes this hideous giant the proleptic chronicler of Portuguese history is ingenious enough, but that he also transforms him into an
Ovidian monster in love (especially in stanzas 55–56 with their debts to Meta-

morphoses V and *Heroides* X) marvelously abuses the reader's credulity. Like da
Gama, Camões seeks novelty, fame, and to outbid the ancients. To accomplish
this he rewrites classical mythology in a manner that sublimates Renaissance
cartography into epic poetry.[44] In response to da Gama's query, Adamastor
identifies himself:

> "Eu sou aquele oculto e grande Cabo
> A quem chamais vós outros Tormentório,
> Qui nunca a Ptolomeu, Pompónio, Estrabo,
> Plínio, e quantos passaram fui notório.
> Aqui toda a africana costa acabo
> Neste meu nunca visto promontório,
> Que pera o Pólo Antárctico se estende,
> A quem vossa ousadia tanto ofende.
>   Fui dos filhos aspérrimos da Terra,
> Qual Encélado, Egeu e o Centimano;
> Chamei-me Adamastor, e fui na guerra
> Contra o que vibra os raios de Vulcano." (5.50–51)

"I am that hidden and great Cape, which you Portuguese call the Cape
of Storms, of which neither Ptolemy, Pomponius, Strabo, Pliny, nor
any other ancient ever knew. Here the African coast reaches its end with
this my never-before-seen promontory, which extends towards the South
Pole, and which your audacity greatly offends. I was one of those un-
couth sons of the Earth, along with Enceladus, Briareus, and Aegeon; I
am called Adamastor, and we made war against the one who shakes
Vulcan's lightning bolts."

By transforming one of the ancient Greek *gigantes* into a learned, but ethical
scourge ("vossa ousadia tanto ofende") vainly warning against the overreaching of early modern explorers, Camões neatly weaves da Gama and his men
into an exorbitant, mythic fabric in the same breath as he charts Portuguese
history. A prosopopeia of mute nature, the horrific Adamastor, for all his outrage, is ultimately unable to persuade da Gama to forsake his navigation.

The third moment in *Os Lusiades* essential to an understanding of some
of the rich ambiguities inherent in Góngora's hyperbolism occurs also in
Canto 5. Here da Gama, having just ended his long account (which includes
the Adamastor episode) of the voyage from Portugal until his ships' arrival at

the Kingdom of Malindi (on the east coast of Africa, near Abyssinia), appraises his own exploits. In doing so, he becomes the mouthpiece for Camões's poetic achievements as well:

> "Esse que bebeu tanto da água Aónia,
> Sobre quem têm contenda peregrina,
> Entre si, Rodes, Smirna e Colofónia,
> Atenas, Ios, Argo e Salamina;
> Essoutro que esclarece toda Ausónia,
> A cuja voz altíssona e divina,
> Ouvindo, o pátrio Míncio se adormece,
> Mas o Tibre co som se ensorberbece;
>
>   Cantem, louvem e escrevam sempre extremos
> Desses seus Semideuses, e encareçam,
> Fingindo magas Circes, Polifemos,
> Sirenas que co canto os adormeçam;
> Dêm-lhe mais navegar à vela e remos
> Os Cícones e a terra onde se esqueçam
> Os companheiros, em gostando o loto;
> Dêm-lhe perder nas águas o piloto;
>
>   Ventos soltos lhe finjam e imaginem
> Dos odres, e Calipsos namoradas;
> Harpias que o manjar lhe contaminem;
> Descer às sombras nuas já passadas;
> Que por muito e por muito que se afinem
> Nestas fábulas vãs, tão bem sonhadas,
> A verdade que eu conto, nua e pura,
> Vence toda grandíloca escritura!" (5.87–89)

"He who drank deeply from Ionian water, the peregrine poet for whom Rhodes, Smyrna, Colophon, Athens, Chios, Argo, and Salamais have contended; that other who enlightens all of Ausonia, and on account of whom, when they hear his high-sounding, divine voice, the waters of his native Mincius fall asleep, but the Tiber with the sound swells with pride — let these two sing about and praise their semi-divine beings, and let them exaggerate, inventing magicians, Circes, Polyphemuses, and Sirens who make you men go to sleep; let them navigate further with sail and oar, to the Cicones and the land where they leave their companions to taste the lotus; let them lose their pilot in the sea, and imagine and feign winds loosened from bags, and enamored Calypsos, Harpies who foul their food, and to descend to the naked shades of the newly dead: Yet however they try and try to polish their empty fables, so well dreamed, truly, the tale I tell is naked and pure, and defeats all grandiloquent writing."

Invidiously comparing Homer, Virgil, and their "sombras nuas já passadas" with his own "verdade . . . nua e pura," Camões-da Gama engages directly the cinquecento debate fostered by Cinthio, Minturno, Tasso, and others on the relative virtues of the marvelous and the verisimilar in the epic. His sly if simple solution is first to demand appreciation for the ways classical epic cul-tivated *admiratio*, and only then to appeal to the reader to grant that his empiri-cal and historical knowledge of these voyages is unimpeachable.[45] His *ethos*, in other words, putatively disdains hyperbole ("e encareçam") and "toda grandíloca escritura" because the *res* of his belated epic speaks for itself. Now if the disingenuous nature of such a stance is immediately confirmed by the Adamastor episode with its far-fetched rhetoric and debts to classical literature and myth, then it might also be conceded that in the historical part of his speech the giant did speak "verdade . . . nua e pura" to da Gama and his men even if they could not, as was the case with Aeneas in the underworld, have been expected to understand it. To them it was incomprehensible hyperbole and the speaker a monster, but to Camões's readers it was already history. As will be the case with Góngora, Camões depends on such perspectivism and anachronism to help his epic teach and delight. But unlike Góngora, he can also rely on the *ethos* of firsthand experience to defend his credulity:

> Os casos vi, que os rudos marinheiros,
> Que têm por mestra a longa experiência,
> Contam por certos sempre e verdaideiros,
> Julgando as cousas só pola aparência,
> E que os que têm juízos mais inteiros,
> Que só por puro engenho e por ciência
> Vêm do mundo os segredos escondidos,
> Julgam por falsos ou mal entendidos.[46] (5.17)

I saw these events, which coarse mariners, who have as their teacher long experience, take always to be certain and true, judging things solely by appearances, and which those with judgments more complete, who use only pure intuition and science to see the world's hidden secrets, judge as false or badly understood.

That the infamously *culto* Góngora becomes an avid, credulous reader of these "rudos" mariners is not surprising given the canonical status quickly attained by *Os Lusíades*. More remarkable, however, is the manner in which he extravagantly imitates the ambivalent mixture of pessimism and idealism concerning the imperial project riddling Camões's epic. In what follows, then, I argue that Góngora remakes with great sophistication literary models written in the grand style such as *Os Lusíades*, even as he endows hyperbole with startling, ethical force and idiosyncratic, ironic energy.[47]

MAPPING HYPERBOLE

To limit what Alonso dubs the "[e]norme abundancía de ejemplos" of hyperbole in the poems my focus will be on the polemic against navigation in lines 366–502 of the *Soledad primera*.[48] A startling *digressio* given the bucolic scenes that precede and follow it, this discourse, spoken by a "montañés prolijo" [*a prolix highlander*], a "[p]olítico serrano, de canas grave" [*a grave, politic, white-haired mountain dweller*], is sparked by the sudden appearance of the *náufrago* who reminds the old man of his dead son drowned at sea. Grief, in this way, calls for and partially excuses exaggerated rhetoric; the *pathos* of the situation protects, at least partially, the mourning father's *ethos*.[49] In this respect, Góngora improves on Camões's Old Man of Bélem whose declamation seems untethered to any personal circumstance. Alternately, *desengaño* with imperialism's bitter fruits also motivates Góngora's rhetoric. Playing upon the classical commonplace that the Iron Age was associated with navigation, a commonplace lately reinforced by the Armada's defeat and Spain's continual financial crisis despite the bounty of precious metals brought back by the King's ships (but all-too-frequently transferred directly to the accounts of foreign bankers), the *exkursus* also gives voice to strong historical and political currents.[50]

In terms of literary *imitatio*, along with Camões's *Lusíades* the most important models for what Beverley dubs an "epica trágica in miniatura de la Conquista" are Seneca's *Medea*, Virgil's fourth *Eclogue*, and Horace's *Odes* 1.4, 1.14.[51] This later poem ("O navis...") — famously interpreted by Quintilian (8.6.44) as a political allegory warning against the dangers faced by the ship of state from civil wars, or, as others have read it, as an allegory in which an older woman is about to reembark on love's stormy seas — resonates with particular force in Góngora's figuration of *codicia* as a kind of erotic madness for empire.[52] Further, the dedicatory stanzas to the Conde urg-ing him to leave the hunt and listen to Góngora's verse neatly rework the Ho-ratian *recusatio* of epic poetry in favor of lyric forms. They also cast the entire poem into an allegorical framework where the re-creational powers of verse ("pasos . . . errante . . . otros inspirados") displace the hunt's martial allure. The ambition Góngora expresses at the outset of the *Polifemo* ("si la mía puede ofrecer tanto / clarín (y de la Fama no segundo), / tu nombre oirán los térmi-nos del mundo" [*if my muse can muster such a clarion (one not inferior to Fame's call), the ends of the earth will hear your name*]) is given still more convoluted form in the thirty-seven lines opening the *Soledad primera*, by the end of which Euterpe's pastoral flute replaces the "trompa" of "Fama." Ambiguously imitating the panegyric *fama* cultivated in classical epic, Góngora, following also Garcilaso and Herrera's lyric examples, makes *letras* usurp the place of increasingly im-potent *armas*.

In more conceptual terms, Hans Blumenberg in *Shipwreck with Spectator* demonstrates how the rich metaphorics associated with sea voyages and ship-wrecks form a fundamental "paradigm" not only for humanity's relation to the world but also to our ability to theorize that world. Taking as his starting point the proem to Book II of Lucretius' *De rerum natura* where the poet celebrates the spectator's *ataraxia*, or tranquility, who watches the misfortune of ship-wrecked people drowning at sea, Blumenberg charts the rich history of an imaginative *topos* to which philosopher and poets consistently return to make sense of their relation to the "Lifeworld" and their own cultural-historical po-sition. And if the kind of detachment urged by Lucretius proves untenable for the likes of Montaigne, Voltaire, and Goethe, this is because, Blumenberg suggests, the metaphorics of the sea voyage and shipwreck historically becomes less an opportunity to reflect on the relations between humanity and nature and more an occasion to heighten one's self-consciousness. "Shipwreck," he writes after considering Horace's Ode 1.4, "as seen by a survivor, is the figure of an initial philosophical experience."[53] In this sense, by having the old man (a vicarious shipwreck survivor) speak to the shipwrecked pilgrim (and the reader), Góngora undermines whatever Stoic tranquility the enframing bu-colic scenes might afford. Readers are instead invited to reflect on the force and violence of metaphor itself, which here becomes hyperbolic to draw attention to itself and its limited ability to provide analogies satisfying enough to explain humanity's place and role in the world.

This is not to say that the disastrous consequences of the voyages of discovery and conquest are the only motives for Góngora's hyperboles. His daring conceits and numerous mythological allusions foster also considerable
asombro at the feats of the overreaching Spanish mariners. At moments he
adopts what Stephen Greenblatt, reading Columbus's descriptions of his arrival in the New World, calls the rhetoric of the marvelous: ". . . it is not simply the recognition of the unusual the constitutes a marvel, but a certain
excess, a hyperbolic intensity, a sense of awed delight. The marvelous for
Columbus usually involves then a surpassing of the measure but not in the direction of the monstrous or grotesque; rather, a heightening of impressions
until they reach a kind of perfection."[54] In this sense the act of discovery (and
later of conquest) is in many respects "discursive."[55] And while a closer look
at the *Diaro* and *Cartas* confirms how the marvelous serves less as an ornament
and more as a source for invention itself — the explorer needed for various
personal and political reasons to make his discoveries seem as extraordinary
as possible — still no exigency can completely explain Columbus's bizarre
comparison of the world's shape to a woman's breast:

> Fallé que no era redondo en la forma que escriben, salvo que es de la
> forma de una pera que sea toda muy redonda, salvo allí donde tiene el
> pezón, que allí tiene más alto, o como tiene una pelota muy redonda y en
> lugar de ella fuese como una teta de mujer allí puesta, y que esta parte de
> este sea la más alta y más proxima al cielo . . .

> I found that the world was not round in the form that they describe,
> rather that it has the form of a pear, which is all very round, save that
> where it has the stem, that part is higher; or like a very round ball on one
> part of which there was placed a woman's breast, and that this part
> would be highest and nearest to the sky.[56]

From world to pear to ball to breast, Columbus's futile search for the appropriate analogy exemplifies the cognitive and rhetorical difficulties Renaissance
Europeans had in representing and evaluating the *ultra fidem* experience of the
nuevo mundo.

Also, Greenblatt notwithstanding, the "surpassing of the measure" by those Spanish hyperbolists who no longer shared Columbus's idealism frequently verges on the "monstrous or grotesque." The first note struck by the old man in the navigation-*exkursus* is decidedly grim:

> "¿Cual tigre, la más fiera
>   que clima infamó Hircano,
>   dió el primer alimento
> al que, ya deste o de aquel mar, primero
>   surcó labrador fiero
> el campo undoso en mal nacido pino,
>   vaga Clicie del viento,
> en telas hecho antes que en flor el lino?" (366–373)

"What tiger, the fiercest one that made Hircanian climes infamous, suckled the man, fierce peasant who, for the first time, plowed the wavy field of this or that sea in an ill-born pine tree, a mobile Clytie of the wind, transformed into sails of linen rather than into a flower?"

Heightened by the verb *infamar*, his outraged, incredulous tone sets the stage for a lengthy, negative epideixis, which Pellicer aptly refers to as an "execración."[57] And while it would be silly to deny the wild improbability of such *culto* rhetoric coming from a peasant's mouth, Góngora seems far more interested in cultivating the semantic *copia* and exploring the mythic if ultimately untenable correspondences to be gleaned from this unnatural act of plowing the sea than he is in maintaining the vestiges of verisimilitude. The mixture of the exotic ("Hircano"), mythic ("Clicie"), and quotidian ("labrador," "mar," "viento") typifies Góngora's style. As for metaphor, here Polifemo's "pino" is given a new, more transgressive task: now instead of serving as a cane it becomes a "mal nacido" shipmast. Beloved by classical hyperbolists, this conflation of the nautical and terrestrial ("campo undoso"), while recalling the portrait of the Cyclops in the *Polifemo* ("Negro el cabello, imitador undoso / de las obscuras aguas del Leteo . . ."), prefigures as well the liminal aspects of the coastal theme in the *Soledad segunda*. It is also brilliantly amplified in the conceit drawing from the *Metamorphoses* (4.256–273) where Clytie — a sea nymph whose love was spurned by Apollo, and who was changed into a sunflower or *heliotrope* for her pains — is compared with a ship's sail that turns or, if you will, tropes with the wind. Not content with a mere flower of rhetoric, Góngora creates an *auratrope* that heightens the poem's *energeia* rather than its *enargeia*. This is to say that the disastrous spectacle of navigation is too great to be visualized. Indeed, what Derrida identifies as metaphor's fate in philosophical texts obtains not just for the *Clicie* metaphor but for all the bold conceits in the *Soledades*: "L'héliotrope peut toujours se relever ... Ce supplément de code qui traverse son champ, en déplace sans cesse la clôture, brouille la ligne, ouvre le cercle, aucune ontologie n'aura pu le reduire."[58] In this sense, the *poiesis* of the *Soledades* expresses more the phenomenology of the poet thinking than it tries to make any objective claim to represent the nature of things.

But if invoking Derrida seems far-fetched, Góngora himself suggests how the reigning idealism inherent in a visual, deictic poetics threatens the kind of hermeneutic his poetry requires. As he writes in the *Carta en respuesta*:

> ... en dos maneras considero me ha sido honorosa esta poesía; si entendida para los doctos, causarme ha autoridad siendo lance forzoso venerar que nuestra lengua a costa de mi trabajo haya llegado a la perfección y alteza de la latina ... Demás que honra me ha causado hacerme oscuro a los ignorantes, que [es] la distinción de los hombres doctos, hablar de manera que a ellos les parezca griego; pues no se han de dar las piedras preciosas a animales de cerda. ... pues si deleitar el entendimiento es darle razones que le concluyan y se midan con su contento, descubierto lo que está debajo de esos tropos, por fuerza el entendimiento ha de quedar convencido, y convencido, satisfecho: demás que, como el fin del entendimiento es hacer presa en verdades, que por eso no le satisface nada, si no es la primera verdad, conforme a aquella sentencia de san Agustín; *Inquietum est cor nostrum, donec requiescat in te*, en tanto quedará más deleitado cuanto, obligándole a la especulación por la obscuridad de la obra, fuera hallando debajo de las sombras de la obscuridad asimilaciones a su concepto.[59]

> ... I consider this poetry to have given me honor in two ways: if understood by the learned, it has earned me authority, since it is indubitably an occasion to admire that our language through my labor has reached the perfection and height of Latin ... Further, I have earned honor by making myself obscure to the ignorant, to speak in a manner that seems Greek to them, which is the mark of learned men; one must not give

pearls to swine . . . for to delight the understanding is to give it reasons that may convince it and satisfy it; having discovered what is beneath those tropes, the understanding perforce is convinced, and therefore sat- isfied. Further, as the goal of the understanding is to take truths prisoner, therefore it is in no way satisfied, if it does not have essential truth, ac- cording to that maxim of St. Augustine, *Inquietum est cor nostrum, donec requiescat in te*, in so far as someone will remain more delighted when, ob- ligating him to speculate because of the work's obscurity, he finds him- self discovering beneath the shadows of obscurity similarities to his own conceit.

Having detailed Góngora's debts in this letter to Augustine and Luis Carillo y Sotomayor elsewhere, I want to emphasize here the philosophical and, more strictly, theological value Góngora assigns to his conceited style.[60] Poetic difficulty and obscurity provoke spiritually valuable hermeneutic labor on the reader's part. What appears at first glance to be merely obscure turns out to be a "concepto" pointing to "la primera verdad." Consequently, like his other difficult figures and tropes, his hyperboles are liable to be "piedras preciosas" wasted on porcine "ignorantes."

With this said, Góngora obviously also revels in his ability "to delight" his readers and thereby fulfill one of the principal Horatian offices. The next period in the *exkursus* amplifies the Hircanian tiger's ferocity until it becomes a sea "monstruo" whose bellicosity outbids even that of the Homeric heroes:

> "Más armas introdujo este marino
> monstruo, escamado de robustas hayas,
> a las que tanto mar divide playas,
>   que confusión y fuego
> al Frigio muro el otro leño Griego." (374–378)

"This marine monster, whose scales are robust beeches, brought more arms to remote shores, separated by so much sea, than the confusion and fire brought to the walls of Troy by that other Greek piece of wood."

Here the *techné* of navigation becomes the new epic theme as Góngora's "ar- mas" effectively rewrite Virgil's "Arma virumque cano . . ." More insidious than Odysseus' legendary guile, the ability to sail the sea renders a single, anonymous ship more powerful than "el otro leño Griego."[61] Pellicer glosses the subsequent lines alluding to the magnetic compass with a lengthy explica- tion of its origins and use such that Góngora is placed in direct dialogue with a mob of ancient and early modern cosmographers from Eratosthenes and Pliny to Isaac Casaubon and Gregorio García.[62] In terms of syntax, though, these lines balance on the phrase "tanto mar," which neatly "divide" the dis- tant shores of Góngora's expanded world. They offer in this way a sophisti- cated, Baroque reworking of the antinavigation *topos*, such that the novel *res* of the voyages of discovery now quantitatively, and so also qualitatively, sup- plant epic poetry's old subject matter.

Góngora continues his audacious interweaving of new and old dis- courses in lines 379–396. These feature a virtuoso series of periphrases mix- ing nautical vocabulary ("Náutica industria") and mythic language ("Marte," "Aurora"), together with an ironic Petrarchan insistence on the radical unique- ness of the lover's passion:

> "En esta pues fiándose atractiva,
> del Norte amante dura, alado roble,
> no hay tormentoso cabo que no doble,
> ni isla hoy a su vuelo fugitiva." (393–396)

"Trusting, then, in this harsh, magnetic lover of the North, the winged oak knows no stormy cape that it cannot round, nor island now that can escape its flight."

As surprising as this apparently parodic version of the Horatian conceit of ship as lover might feel at first, the subsequent string of negations emphatically underscores how no place is beyond the sails of the overreaching "winged oak." Having played previously on the mutability of the compass's motion, Góngora now fixes the ship's attraction to an eroticized North Star. But then, after alluding to Tifis, Palinurus, and Hercules (who, with his eponymous pillars, disdainfully "cierra" [*encloses*] the Mediterranean into an "estanque" [*pond*]), he ominously inscribes the *Plus ultra* motif into his lyric geography. The "Piloto . . . Codicia" outbids all the great Captains of myth and epic, as he subjugates the limits of terrestrial space to his will. He impels the voyages, respectively, of Columbus (413–429), Pizarro (430–446), Vasco da Gama

(447–465), and Magellan (466–502). Though ultimately it is Greed and his "selvas inconstantes" — a wonderful metonymy for the explorers' ships — that outflank the reach and wisdom of "el Sol":

> "Piloto hoy la Codicia, no de errantes
> árboles, mas de selvas inconstantes,
> al padre de las aguas Oceano,
>   de cuya monarquía
>   el Sol, que cada dia
> nace en sus ondas y en su ondas muere,
> los términos saber todos no quiere —
> dejó primero de su espuma cano,
>   sin admitir segundo
> en inculcar sus límites al mundo. (403–412)

"Nowadays Greed is the captain, not of wandering trees, but of mutable forests; and it has been the first to whiten the hairs of the father of the Ocean with its foam (a father whose monarchy the sun, which each day is born and dies in its waves, refuses to acknowledge all its boundaries), without admitting a rival in inculcating limits on the world."

Góngora imagines here "the limits of the Earth" by figuratively and syntactically confusing the proper place of the elements. As Salcedo Coronel comments: "Para ponderar D. Luis la vasta inmensidad del Oceano, se valio deste hiperbole, no como soñò alguno, porque el Sol ignore alguna parte del, pues en Noruega, y mar elado que el dize no alcança el Sol, ay dia de tres meses" [*In order to ponder the Ocean's vast immensity, Góngora avails himself of this hyperbole, not because as some imagine the sun does not know some part of the ocean, since in Norway and the frozen sea where he says the sun does not reach, the day may last three months*].[63] In other words, Góngora sacrifices verisimilitude to make an ethical point. The ocean and its "monarchy" are at odds with the earth's "forests" and the "sun" whose death Greed causes. But if Greed, "pilot" of "mutable" forests, plays the anti-hero here, then Góngora himself is the true captain of *silvas inconstantes*. Reordering the abundance of the limitless world ("los términos saber todos no quiere") and implicitly also Virgil's *imperium sine fine* with such figures as the marvelous chiasmus in line 408, the metonymy of "espuma cano," as well as the striking hyperbaton of the first six lines, Góngora gives the hyperbole dominating this strophe an unrivaled syntactic and rhetorical complexity. As for the tenor of the allegory, Greed ("sin . . . segundo") imposes its limits on a world too big even for the sun to compass. Not only does Greed remake the most brilliant Neo-Platonic symbol, but then Neptune is "violated" by Columbus's three ships, whose "banderas / siempre gloriosas, siempre tremolantes" [*banners always glorious, always fluttering*] defy the "plumas ciento" [hundred feathers] (i.e., the arrows) of the Caribbean natives. Intriguingly, in contrast to Góngora's *chiaroscuro* treatment of Columbus, Pellicer, in his extensive notes, in addition to making the explorer a reader of Seneca's *Medea* and the Book of Isaiah celebrates him in unambiguous, providential terms: "A este Sanson Español, a este Gedeon en cuyo pecho resplandece el vellon de oro . . . dio el cielo esta expedicion como a Primogenito de su Iglesia, y Rey Catholico sobre todos" [*To this Spanish Samson, to this Gideon on whose breast shines a golden fleece . . . Heaven specially granted this expedition as if a primogeniture from the Church and the Catholic King*].[64] And while he follows this with a brief consideration of voices objecting to and defending the practices of the Spanish empire, such as Hugo Grotius, Las Casas, and Sepúlveda, the "disputa" is clearly "resuelta" in Pellicer's conservative view.[65]

For his part, even as Góngora inveighs against *codicia*, he does not refrain from praising, almost alchemizing, the conquered land and sea:

> "el Istmo que al Océano divide,
> y sierpe de cristal, juntar le impide
> la cabeza del Norte coronada
> con la que ilustra el Sur cola escamada
> de Antárticas estrellas." (425–429)

"the isthmus that divides the Ocean and impedes it, as if it were a crystal serpent, from joining its head, crowned by the North Star, with its tail, illuminated by the Southern Cross and whose scales are the Antarctic stars."

The meaning here is not entirely clear, and Góngora's defenders and detractors have long quibbled over maps and the question of verisimilitude.[66] Is this a grotesque? A warning? Both? He offers us a bejeweled monster, but, all in all, it is still a monster. Fascinated by this oceanic creature, the Cuban poet, novelist, and sometime critic, José Lezama Lima transforms it into a metonym for both poems in his 1951 essay, "Sierpe de Don Luis de Góngora." And while Lezama Lima does not address these verses directly in his oblique, but infinitely suggestive, Neo-Gongorist meditation, he does eloquently reanimate the heliotrope:

> Góngora culmina posiblemente en todas las lenguas románicas el venci-miento de la prueba heliotrópica. Su índice de luminosidad fija el centro por donde penetra el rayo metáforico y su tiempo de permanencia dentro de haz luminoso. Gracias a ese tiempo lucífugo cobra el único sentido, el endurecimiento del logos poético, por el cual no ofrece el rejuego de las mutaciones interpretativas, sino el único sentido que no se alcanza.[67]

> Arguably, Góngora brings to a climax in all the romance languages the defeat of the heliotropic proof. His degree of luminosity fixes the center through which the metaphoric lightning bolt can penetrate as well as its time of permanence within the luminous deed. Thanks to this lucifu-gous time he obtains the unique meaning, the hardening of the poetic *logos*, through which it does not offer the replay of interpretative muta-tions, but rather that unique meaning which is not reached.

It is doubtful that Keats read Góngora, yet when Cortés and his men stand on that peak in Darien in "On First Looking into Chapman's Homer," gazing out on Góngora's crystal serpent and at each other "with a wild surmise," why should it be surprising, given the universal motion of this heliotrope, that the poet, now a nineteenth-century Englishman, repeats this gesture of inex-pressibility?

The aesthetic wonders produced by this *Atlantean* perspective aside, Gón-gora never loses sight of the ethical. Moving from the geographic to the human, the *exkursus* continues with a comparison of the Spanish lust for "metales homicidas" [*homicidal metals*] with the goldlust of Midas — prompting even Pellicer to chide "la execrable hambre del oro" [*execrable hunger for gold*].[68] Blaming the Portuguese inability to read the hyperbolic, moralizing "señas" left by the dead Spaniards, the poet laments:

> "No le bastó después a este elemento
> conducir Orcas, alistar Ballenas,
> murarse de montañas espumosas,
> infamar blanqueando sus arenas
> con tantas del primer atrevimiento

> señas, aun a los buitres lastimosas,
> para con estas lastimosas señas
> temeridades enfrenar segundas." (435–442)

"Afterward, it was not enough that this element (water) mustered orcas and whales, walled itself in with foamy mountains, shamed its sands, whitening them with so many signs of the first audacity, piteous even to the vultures, in order with these woeful signs to curb subsequent temerities."

In the end even the vultures feel pity for their suppers! Echoing the story of Jonah and the whale, but also recalling Garcilaso's *Soneto XI*, these verses regale the reader with whales and vultures — both extremes of nature — even as they stress, by repeating "señas," the failure of semiosis itself. In term of the poem's metapoetics, then, these lines underscore the moral necessity of Góngora's hyperboles and linguistic excesses, while the repetition of "lastimosas" emphasizes the *pathos* involved in the failure of signification. If the material "signs of the first audacity" found on the beaches are not sufficient to warn the foolhardy, then the poet will. The series of infinitive verbs ending with "infamar" propels the invective and echoes the old man's opening lines (367); but in terms of metaphor, the conventional metonomy of "montañas espumosas" is superbly refashioned with the earthen "murarse," and the notion of the bones "blanqueando" beaches on far-flung shores is charged with striking *enargeia*. This last image also prefigures one of the poem's most ingenious if vilified hyperboles:

> virgen tan bella, que hacer podría
> tórrida la Noruega con dos soles,
> y blanca la Etiopa con dos manos.[69] (783–785)

virgin so beautiful, that you could make Norway torrid with two suns, and Ethiopia white with two hands [by placing them over your eyes].

While the conceit of bones whitening the already white beaches further exaggerates the old *topos* of the blood of fallen soldiers turning red the waters of a river or sea, these magnificently absurd lines, with their visual chiasmus of black and white, underscore the extent to which the hyperbolic is fundamental to Góngora's understanding, or, at the very least representation of nature, geography, and cosmology. Though they come later in poem, in a wedding hymn in the style of Catullus 64, sung by one of the "zagalejas" [*shep-herdesses*], this tercet, like the lines above, also seek hyperbolic analogies or metonymies between humanity and the cosmos. In other words, the effects of beauty or greed are so extreme, not due principally to the poet's caprice, but because nature is perceived as feeling extreme outrage or sympathy with the human actors who inhabit its stage.

Turning back, then, to the *exkursus*, our astonishment grows as Góngora figures Camões's principal epic subject (and narrator), Vasco da Gama's voyage around the Cape of Good Hope to India.[70] Addressed directly, da Gama becomes the successful cosmographical wooer, an improbable Petrarchan lover who has Aeolus (447–450) and the Phoenix (461–465) as allies, and who gains the prize where others have failed:

> "Tantos luego Astronómicos presagios
> frustrados, tanta Náutica doctrina,
> debajo de la Zona aun más vecina
> al Sol, calmas vencidas y naufragios,
> los reinos de la Aurora al fin besaste,
> cuyos purpúreos senos perlas netas,
>   cuyas minas secretas
> hoy te guardan su más precioso engaste." (453–460)

"Then, having confounded so many astronomical predictions, so much nautical doctrine, below the (terrestrial) zone closest to the sun, having defeated the doldrums and shipwrecks, you kissed finally Dawn's king-doms, whose violet breasts safeguard for you limpid pearls, whose se-cret mines safeguard for you the most precious setting (gold) for these pearls."

The apparent optimism of these lines, in which failure is methodically over-come ("Tantos . . . tanta") and beauty made superlative ("más precioso"), in which the geography of Africa and the Orient ("los reinos de la Aurora al fin besaste") are transformed into an idealized beloved's erotic parts, would seem to mark a change in the poet's attitude. Likewise, when the old man considers Magellan's voyage in subsequent verses, the metonymic "pino," pre-viously "mal nacido," is now "glorïoso" and an "inmortal memoria." The undeniable success of the first circumnavigation spurs him momentarily to view all the oceans as one ("siempre uno"). Cast now as a lover, the encircling sea "bese" [*kisses*] the pillars of Hercules and the dawn's "escarlata" [*scarlet*] carpet.

But then sounding a darker note, Góngora makes the "glorioso pino" an "émulo vago del ardiente coche del Sol" — an allusion to Phaeton's fate. Likewise, the amorous imagery suddenly becomes insidious in the description of the Philippine islands:

> "cuyo número, ya que no lascivo,
> por lo bello agradable y por lo vario
> la dulce confusión hacer podía,
> que en los blancos estanques del Eurota
> la virginal desnuda montería,
> haciendo escollos o de mármol Pario
> o de terso marfil sus miembros bellos,
> que pudo bien Acteón perderse en ellos." (483–490)

"whose multitude, while not lascivious, had such pleasant beauty and variety that it was able to create the (same) sweet confusion, which the virginal hunting (party) disrobing in the white ponds of the Eurotas created, making reefs either of Parian marble or of smooth ivory with their beautiful limbs, which no wonder caused Actaeon to go to his perdition in them."

In the course of this remarkably sensual prosopopeia of geographic space, lasciviousness gives way to the mythic threat of violence. The bathing Diana's limbs, compared to the whitest marble from Paros, threaten a "dulce confusión" and, implicitly, a fatal shipwreck. The comparison also confirms the dangers of the (merely) visual image.[71] For on the heels of this image, Góngora mouths the commonplace that "especias" sought in Asia cause unbridled "apetito," which explains, in turn, why the sailors' *atrevimiento* in visiting these places produces yet more illusory desires.

The old man concludes his discourse by invoking his dead son, "del alma . . . la mejor prenda, / cuya memoria es buitre de pesares" [*the greatest pledge of his soul, / whose memory is a vulture of sorrows*]. This graphic hyperbole alludes to the fate of that Ur-overreacher Prometheus, though it also may derive from *De rerum natura* (5.992–993) where Lucretius, describing the dangers faced by primitive humanity, portrays how wild beasts hunted primitive man who: "... nemora ac montis gemitu silvasque replebat, / viva videns vivo sepeliri viscera busto" [*filled the woods, mountains, and forests with groaning, seeing his living flesh in a living tomb entombed*].[72] In other words, the imagery in the old man's *silvas* is far more venerable than the hairs on his head: to grieve and to blame is to supplement literary history. It is also to try and to fail to account for loss. The vehemence of this vulture conceit — these are his last words and so should be regarded as his peroration — complements the twin hyperboles signaling closure:

> En suspiros con esto,
> y en más anegó lágrimas el resto
> de su discurso el montañés prolijo,
> que el viento su caudal, el mar su hijo. (503–506)

With this, the verbose mountaineer flooded the rest of his speech with more sighs than the wind had overwhelming his treasure and more tears than the sea had drowning his son.

The old man's prolixity is matched only by his grief. These final, enframing verses (especially the last line with its neat parison deceptively suggesting equanimity) again insist on the urgent conceptual task of establishing some manner of correspondence, however hyperbolic, between an individual's subjective desires (and fears) and the objective forces in the world. Yet if the old man's sighs and tears surpass in quantity the wind and water that sink his son's ship, this event also annihilates, literally drowns ("annegó) the possibility of further "discurso" — at least for him. His sighs and tears mark the site where hyperbole ends and silence begins. Ultimately, it is this exorbitant rhetorical space, where "dulce confusión" is the rule for the reader, rather than the physical or historical space of the *orbis terrarum*, that marks the boundaries of Góngora's invention.

JÁUREGUI'S CURE

If I have read Góngora's hyperboles appreciatively, even sometimes enthusiastically, then Juan de Jáuregui, a young contemporary of Góngora, would teach us to read them with derision. His "Antidoto contra la pestilente poesía de las *Soledades*," condemns Gongorist hyperbole in the course of a withering, often witty diatribe that begins with some scatological calumnies and goes on to attack, amongst other faults, the poet's anachronisms, obscurity, repetitive diction, privileging of sound over sense, and use of a heroic style for mean subjects.[73] As for Góngora's hyperboles, the trenchant and unforgiving quality of Jáuregui's critique can be traced in part anyway to its reliance on authorities such as Horace, Cicero, and Scaliger. These arbiters of taste are read as promoting the dictum *ars est celare artem*, a dictum that Góngora is seen as unwisely flaunting. And because Jáuregui's learned screed is arguably the most extreme entry in the bitter controversy immediately following the publication of the *Soledades*, it merits attention as a text in its own right. Not only does the "Antidoto" exemplify a certain species of critical hyperbolism, or how difficult it is to chastise poetic *atrevimiento* without resorting to satiric extremes (and so create another kind of indecorousness), it also helps sharpen the ethical and literary historical stakes involved in Góngora's overreaching.

Asserting that Góngora's poetry is contra "razón" and "costumbre," Jáuregui blames the Cordoban's frigid style, or his "mil caminos desvariados o frías" [*thousand delirious or frigid paths*]; his lack of verisimilitude, exemplified by his faulty understanding of astronomy and logic; and, most severely, the inordinate demands his difficult and obscure style makes on readers. Góngora's penchant for *opposita juxta repposita* [*juxtaposed remote, opposite things*], as embodied by the dual hyperboles we saw above ("Virgen tan bella, que hacer podría / tórrida la Noruega con dos soles, / y blanca la Ethiopia con dos manos . . ."), are such "raterías" [*depravities*] Jáuregui exclaims, that "me confundan la inteligencía" [*they confound my understanding*].[74] But Góngora is also condemned in the light of literary history. His search for stylistic novelty compares unfavorably with Statius' *Thebiad*, arguably antiquity's most villified epic, on account of its licentious use of figures like hyperbole:

> Pero dejemos la pureza de el gran Virgilio, de quien Vm. es Antípoda, y vamos a Estacio Papinio, que es tenido por áspero y atrevidísimo, osaré apostar que no se halla en toda la *Tebaida* tan espantoso grimazo como el menor de los que Vm. emprende.[75]

> But let us leave aside the purity of the great Virgil, of whom you are the Antipode, and let us consider Statius, who is held to be uncouth and most daring. I would wager that nowhere in all of the *Thebiad* is there such horrible foreshortening like the least one you undertake.

This intriguing invocation of painterly technique ("grimazo") to condemn Góngora is not, however, part of a consistent aesthetic philosophy. For more invidious comparisons follow as the mannerist verse of Tasso and Martial is used to cudgel Góngora. All of which leads Jáuregui to conclude:

> Vm. no sólo desprecia la severidad de nuestra poca licencia, mas excede a cuantos usaron los más atrevidos Poetas del mundo en todas lenguas, sin parecerse en sus versos a ninguno de todos ellos.[76]

> You not only disdain the severity of our limited license, but you excede by a great deal the license used by the most daring poets in all languages, without resembling any of them in your verses.

Then he learnedly, if ironically, amplifies such singularity:

> Así que en este no puede haber medianía, o Vm. es el único que ha en-
> tendido esta facultad desde el principio de los siglos haste el día hoy, o el
> que más la ha ignorado:
>> solis nosse Deos, et coeli numina vobis,
>> aut solis nescire datum . . .
> Esto dijo Lucano a los Druidas por la singular extravagancia de sus ri-
> tos. Yo pienso que los que Vm. introduce en su Poesía no son más católi-
> cos que los de aquella gente . . . los más de estos versos no tienen siquiera
> alta armonía y hinchazón de palabras, ni siempre siguen aquella obscura
> extravagancia de terribles frases y formas tan remotas de el lenguaje
> común, antes, en medio de sus temeridades, se dejan caer infinitas veces
> con unos modos . . .[77]

> Thus in this you are unable to find any mean, or you are the only one to have understood this faculty from the beginning of time to today, or you are he who most has ignored it: *to you alone is granted to know, or not to know, the gods and celestial powers.* Lucan says this to the Druids because of the singular extravagance of their rituals. I think that the extravagances you introduce in your poetry are no more Catholic than those people's . . . most of these verses do not even have harmony or swelling of words; nor do they always follow that obscure extravagance of terrible phrases and forms utterly remote from common language, rather, in the midst of their temerities, they fall to pieces infinite times through various mannerisms . . .

In citing the hyperbolic Lucan to compare invidiously Góngora's poetics with the "singular extravagance" of Druidic rituals, Jáuregui improbably presents himself as an authority on decorous extravagance. Ignoring the beam in his own eye, he charges Góngora with morally suspect excess ("aquella obscura extravagancia de terribles frases"). But if Góngora has violated the law of decorum ("nuestra poca licencia"), his conceits, prosody and diction are all indicted without, seemingly, the least concession on Jáuregui's part that certain, exemplary citizens of antiquity are really Góngora's partners in crime. Instead, Quintilian's notion of what constitutes proper *copia* is invoked to seal the verdict: "Nam secretae et extra vulgarem usum positae, ideoque magis nobiles: ut novitate aurem excitant, ita copia saciant . . ."[78]

But beyond chastising Góngora's *copia* of meticulously obtained obscurities, Jáuregui levels the even graver charge of "malicia" against the poet's stylistic innovations. This clearly implies that the poet intends to deceive his readers. Jáuregui, in short, would undercut anyone like Jammes or myself who might claim that the *Soledades* possess a strong ethical intent. Specifically, in his discussion of hyperbole, the tone of moral disgust is fueled by the perceived disproportion between Góngora's rhetoric and the common things it describes:

> Algunas exageraciones usa Vm. tan disformes y desproporcionadas, que no se pueden comportar, como llamar a la cecina de macho: *Purpúreos hilos es de gran fina.* Al pavo negro, siendo ave grosera, le nombra Vm.: . . . *esplendor de el Occidente.*[79]

> Some of the exaggerations you use are so misshapen and disproportionate that they cannot be endured; such as calling dried goat meat: *Violet threads of great fineness*; or you call the turkey, a grotesque bird, *the splendor of the Occident.*

Admittedly, read by themselves, these instances and the nine others he adduces do verge on the absurd. But in lampooning the transformation of "any liquid" into "nectar" or of country girls into "seraphs," Jáuregui levels a more serious, complex charge: namely, in transforming so often quotidian things into aesthetic objects, Góngora leaves himself and his readers no room to appreciate differences or to represent true, epic grandeur:

> ¿Quién ha de sufrir tan descompasadas y molestas hipérboles? Porque el navegante se asoma a mirar un valle, dice: *Muda la admiración, habla*

callando. No le queda a Vm. qué decir cuando la muerte mísera del Magno Pompeyo o algún espectáculo semejante.[80]

Who needs to suffer such unmeasured and troublesome hyperboles? Because the shipwrecked sailor admiringly regards a valley, you say: *Admiration grows mute, speaks silently*. Thus nothing remains for you to say about the miserable death of the Great Pompey or another similar spectacle.

The allusion is to the grand, elegiac rhetoric at the end of book eight of Lucan's *De bello civili*. But of course Lucan himself is thoroughly guilty of this putative sin — the extravagant description of travails of Cato's march through the Libyan desert and the horrific catalogue of snakes follow this "espectáculo." More obviously still, there is not a hint anywhere here or in the entire treatise that Jáuregui has pondered the ludic or even satiric power of such rhetoric except as it might be turned against the reputedly unwitting poet, or, more intriguingly, "to mock the reader" [*hacer burlas de nosotros*]. And yet if I am right to argue that Góngora devotes at least part of his invention to critiquing the cost of empire, then in this theme and in its attendant hyperboles the ironic ambivalences of Lucan's epic should also be felt. In this sense, it is not the *culto* reader who is mocked, but the ordinary ideas about empire of an ordinary reader. Moreover, it certainly gives one pause to watch Lucan become the standard against which all other hyperbolists are to be measured, as Lucan's epic tissue of hyperboles is itself distorted almost beyond recognition by Jáuregui in his bombastic, Neo-Gongorist 1630 translation.[81] And while it is probably time wasted to dwell on the Freudian aspects of the younger Jáuregui's need to savage the man who within a decade will father Jáuregui's own exaggerated style, there is something highly perverse and blinkered about using Lucan and Statius as models of decorum with which to cudgel Góngora.

Finally, Góngora's navigation-*exkursus* particularly offends Jáuregui's taste: "El discurso de navagaciones, que hace aquel viejo, es generalmente horrendo y bronquísamente relatado, tanto que hará dar de cabeza por las paredes a cualquier hombre de juicio" [*The discourse of the sea voyages, which that old man gives, is generally horribly and raspingly related; so much so that any man of judgment will bang his head against the wall*].[82] Blaming its geographical and ethnographical inaccuracies, as well as its many rhetorical ellipses, Jáuregui also condemns Góngora's deformzation, or hyperbolizing of space in lines 425–429:

> Preciosa manera de darse a entender. No tiene el mundo pieza como esta sierpe de cristal, partida por medio con su cabeza y su cola y todo su re‑caudo.[83]

> What a precious manner to make oneself understood. The world has no part like this crystal serpent, divided in half with its head and tail and all its jewels.

Such preciosity verges on mockery, Jáuregui concludes. The difficulty of the nautical digression, in other words, is not worth the reader's effort for nothing reasonable or dignified informs it: ". . . vemos juntamente en el tratarlo mar‑avillosas confusiones y ceguedades" [*we see all at once in its treatment marvelous confusions and blindnesses*].[84] But besides the fact that anyone consulting a con‑temporary map would have encountered any number of sea monsters fantas‑tically sporting in the oceans, it never occurs to the bilious critic that the simultaneous cultivation of confusion, blindness, and the marvelous may be precisely the poet's aim.

As for the rhetoric itself of the "Antidoto," it repeatedly relies on various hyperbolic *topoi*: "Querer ahora señalar todos los lugares obscuros, broncos y escabros, sería no acabar jamás . . ." [*To want now to signal all the obscure, rough, and scabrous places would be never to finish*].[85] Yet even if this is read as a conven‑tional gesture of inexpressibility, by the end of his treatise Jáuregui seems gen‑uinely exhausted by contemplating Góngora's *copia*:

> Bastantísimamente hemos manifestado cuán perniciosas son estas *Soledades* por todos cuatro costados; así será bien no cansarnos más, aunque sin duda pudiéramos descubrir redoblados errores que los apuntados. Y con ser tan pestilente y perjudicial esta obra, es aún peor (si peor puede ser) el *Polifemo*, y no lo tomamos por asunto porque, habiéndolo Vm. escrito primero, no creyese alguno que se había enmendado mucho en las *Sol‑edades*.[86]

> We have made most sufficiently manifest how pernicious these *Solitudes* are from every angle; thus it is well not to weary ourselves more, al‑though undoubtedly we could discover twice as many errors than those already indicated. And this work being so pestilent and pernicious, the

> *Polifemo* (if possible) is even worse. And we don't make it our subject since, having been written first, nobody believes that you improved upon it much in the *Solitudes*.

What is "worse" [*peor*] is left to the reader's imagination. Or to quote Lear when he quibbles with his daughters about the number of knights he is to retain: "Not being the worst / Stands in some rank of praise." Like Lear's pun on "rank," Jáuregui's ill-meaning reticence in regard to his potential antidote to the *Polifemo* indicates just how noisome and aporetic critical epideixis can be.

Chapter Six

Quevedo's Poetics of Disillusion

> He was, to be sure, born to flourish, if he flourished,
> during a decadence of national prestige, a falling away
> immediately following the golden age of Spanish literature
> which had seen such men as de León, Góngora, and
> Lope de Vega at their peak. Even at that, Quevedo's
> temper was too unbridled for those restraints that
> might have made him supreme.
>
> — William Carlos Williams, Introduction to
> Francisco de Quevedo, *The Dog & the Fever*

SKEPTICISM, SATIRE, AND PANEGYRIC

As the principal force behind the neo-Stoic revival in early seventeenth-century Spain, Francisco de Quevedo y Villegas brings venerable philosophical concerns to bear on Petrarchan and Imperial commonplaces. His devotion to the Belgian humanist, Justus Lipsius, together with the aesthetic and ethical kinship he feels with early imperial Roman poets such as Seneca, Propertius, and Lucan, explain in part why Quevedo, much more consistently than Góngora, makes greed, hypocrisy, and audacity central themes in his writings. And though like Góngora he proves a sophisticated, iconoclastic, and at times ironic *bricoleur* of literary traditions, rather than sublimating and purifying poetic *copia* to create an ideal space of self-reflection, Quevedo tends to sharpen his language and conceits to yield extreme ethical *pointes* that undermine not only the rhetoric of amorous and imperial overreaching but also underscore the contingent and contradictory nature of his poetic striving. His wide-ranging *escritura*, which includes most genres with the notable exceptions of tragic drama and pastoral romance, is one in which, as Claudio Guillén phrases it, "jamás descansa el dinamismo implícito en el hiperbólico pesimismo cristiano" [*the implicit dynamism in the hyperbolic, Christian pessimism never rests*].[1] In more mundane terms, Quevedo's neo-Petrarchist conceits are taken to such self-consciously fantastic extremes that they come to have the same *propositio* as the anti-Petrarchist conceits in his burlesque verse and those describing the pursuit of material riches in his moral poetry. Add to this dynamic his many reactionary political and cultural views, along with the mordant but often ludic tone that pervades much of his writing, and the difficulty of appraising Quevedo's rhetorical *ethos* becomes obvious. Still, my intention in this chapter is to sketch one aspect of this *ethos* in the light of the idea that the conceptual tensions between the roles of satirist and Petrarchist become sharpest and most fruitful when Quevedo forces imperial and amorous hyperboles to critique themselves.

Quevedo's *obra* is fueled by epideixis in all its myriad forms. His mastery of the dynamics of praise and blame secure him a (tenuous) place, during various stages in his career, near to power at court, make him an influential player in various political and theological controversies, and help him to become one of his culture's sharpest critics.[2] Never lacking passionate motives, Quevedo careens constantly between the most extravagant praise and the fiercest satire. For example, his blinkered antipathy for Góngora's *culto* style informs some of his wittiest, scatological satires. These carnivalesque lines are from a sonnet titled, "Contra don Luis de Góngora y su poesía":

> Este cíclope, no sicilïano,
> del microcosmo sí, orbe postrero;
> esta antípoda faz, cuyo hemisfero
> zona divide en término italiano;
> este círculo vivo en todo plano . . . [#832]

This non-Sicilian cyclops, a microcosmic, posterior orb; this antipodal face, whose hemisphere is divided in Italian style; this circle living in plain view . . .

Transforming Góngora into a microcosmic ass with monstrous if mythic connotations, only then punningly to anatomize him as an all-encompassing asshole ("este círculo"), Quevedo manages to mimic and mock Góngora's

singular style and themes — the cartographic conceit likely plays on Góngora's "el Istmo que al Oceano divide" in the *Soledad primera*. Subtler, if less
ribald is the charge in the prose treatise, *Aguja de navegar cultos con la receta de
hacer* Soledades *en un día* [Compass to Navigate *Cultos* with the Recipe to
Make *Soledades* in One Day] (1631), that Góngora and his *cultísmo* style me-
chanically hyperbolize reality for purely sensational reasons:

> En la platería de los cultos hay hechos cristales fugitivos para arroyos, y
> montes de cristal para las espumas, y campos de zafir para los mares y
> margen de esmeraldas para los praditos. Para las facciones de la mujeres
> hay gargantas de plata bruñida y trenzas de oro para cabellos, y labios de
> coral y de rubíes para jetas y hocicos . . . pechos de diamantes para pe-
> chos, y estrellas coruscantes para ojos, y infinito nácar para las mejillas.[3]

> In the *culto* silversmithy are made fugitive crystals for streams, and moun-
> tains of crystal for sea foam, and fields of sapphire for seas, and strips of
> emeralds for little meadows. For the features of women there are throats
> of polished silver and locks of gold for hair, and lips of coral and of ru-
> bies for mugs and snouts . . . breasts of diamonds for breasts, and
> sparkling stars for eyes, and infinite mother-of-pearl for cheeks.

Strictly speaking, this indictment is accurate enough, for as we saw, Góngora frequently disdains to give quotidian objects their proper name. It also resembles Jáuregui's critique and prefigures Borges's insistence that Góngora's
metaphors are superficial, derivative, and indecorous. Yet like Borges, Quevedo
willfully ignores here the conceptual or discursive claims that such continual
hyperbole might make. Nor does Quevedo permit Góngora or his poetic
metalepsis of the world any self-awareness, ironic or otherwise. Instead, his
"silversmithy" is figured as a mendacious place dedicated to producing poetry
designed simply to frustrate the serious reader.

That Quevedo himself is a master of *culto* diction, artificial syntax, and
neo-Petrarchan conceits undermines in a more fundamental manner the charges
in *Aguja de navegar cultos*. Indeed, as Vilanova, Parker, Blanco, and others have
strenuously argued, a hard and fast distinction between *conceptismo* and *culteranismo* is untenable; the wealth of conceits in the *Polifemo* and *Soledades* and
the cornucopia of *cultismos* in Quevedo's love poetry and *silvas* void the usefulness of such monikers.[4] Still, as Huarte might have observed, Quevedo's
bilious *ingenio* rarely lets him to luxuriate contentedly in the kind of linguistic

and imagined, material abundance favored by Góngora. Instead, in numerous sonnets, such as "Bastábale al clavel verse vencido" [#303], his inclina-
tion to use exaggerated, *culto* diction for self-reflexive, ironic ends undermines
the Gongorist style from inside. Holding a carnation in her mouth, a beloved
who wants revenge on her floral competitor accidentally bites her lip with her
"white pearls," thus provoking this wry conceit: "Sangre vertió tu boca sober-
ana, / porque, roja victoria, amaneciese / llanto al clavel y risa a la mañana"
[*Your sovereign mouth spilled blood, so that, red victory, grief would dawn with the carnation and smiles with the morning*]. Quevedo's play here with emotions, colors,
and body parts, some of which are named directly, others which are alchem-
ized, barely veils signs of violence and hints of sexual promiscuity, signs and
hints that work to threaten the Petrarchan ideal.

Quevedo's readers, in short, are trained to adopt a skeptical stance vis-à-
vis poetic traditions and tastes. In his 1631 dedicatory epistle for an edition he
prepared of Fray Luis de León's poetry, Quevedo presents Fray Luis's style
as the remedy for Góngora's *culteranismo*.[5] In what amounts to a lesson in
hermeneutics, he stresses the "desengaño" of the savvy reader who deciphers
the *culto* poet's enigmas only to find the *res* wanting. And while the notion of
Fray Luis as an avatar of *conceptismo* makes perfect sense, given the Augustinian's devotion to allegorical conceits and metonymical reasoning (see *De los
nombres de Cristo*), to contrast his "casta" [*chaste*] and "ni ambiciosa ... ni
tenebrosa" [*neither ambitious ... nor shadowy*] diction with the "codicia" of those
who model their writing on the "informe y fanfarrona parlería de Asia"
[*formless and boasting verbosity of Asia*] is to distort again the differences between
conceptismo and *culteranismo*, or what was in the early seventeenth century sometimes labeled the Attic and Asian styles.[6]

Quevedo's enthusiasm for Lucan likewise proves the difficulty of judging
the style wars some four hundred years after the fact. In the course of his
learned defense of the theology and style of the Book of Job, *La constancia y pa-
ciencia del Santo Job* (1641), he portrays Job as a kind of Stoic saint, and compares favorably the Book's "eloquencia, copia, hermosura y propriedad" with
that cultivated by Virgil and Lucan. Praising and quoting Lucan also gives
him the occasion to take a swipe at Scaliger:

Mi Lucano, que en ingenio, agudeza y sentencias éticas y políticas excedió, no sólo a los poetas, sino los historiadores y oradores ... Julio
Scalígero (que en su Poética censura con el odio a la nación española, no

con el juicio) por esta abundancia llama a Lucano demasiadamente ambicioso, y superfluo con ostentación sobrada. No de otra manera mur-
mura el mendigo invidioso la opulencia der rico.[7]

My Lucan, who in genius, wit and ethical and political maxims exceeds, not only the poets, but also the historians and orators . . . Julius
Scaliger (who in his *Poetics* hatefully, injudiciously censures the Spanish
nation), in the same way that the envious beggar murmurs against the
rich man's opulence, calls Lucan for this abundance overly ambitious
and superfluous with his excessive ostentation.

Lucan's "abundancia," along with his *ingenium*, Stoic ethical concerns, opposition to tyranny, not to mention his Iberian origins all make him exemplary.[8]
And if the phrase "demasiadamente ambicioso, y superfluo con ostentación
sobrada" neatly condenses the traditional critique of Lucan's hyperbolic style,
it also captures, despite Quevedo's protestations, something of why "Mi Lucano" may be said to have "exceeded" historians, orators, and other poets.

"[M]enos un hombre que una dilatada y compleja literatura" [*Less a man
than an expansive and complex literature*] as Borges memorably dubs him, Quevedo requires from his readers a broader cultural and historical horizon than
does Góngora.[9] To appreciate fully Quevedo's celebrated poem on a man's
nose, "A un hombre de gran nariz," ideally one would be able to juggle
knowledge of the Greek and Latin satirical traditions with a familiarity with
the entire lexical range of contemporary Spanish (from the most *culto* expression to the jargon, *germanía*, of thieves and prostitutes), as well as having a taste
for exaggerated metaphors and *conceptos*:

> Érase un hombre a una nariz pegado,
> érase una nariz superlativa,
> érase una alquitara medio viva,
> érase un peje espada mal barbado;
>   era un reloj de sol mal encarado,
> érase un elefante boca arriba,
> érase una nariz sayón y escriba,
> Un Ovidio Nasón mal narigado.
>   Érase el espolón de una galera,
> érase una pirámide de Egito,
> los doce tribus de narices era;

> érase un naricísimo infinito,
> frisón archinariz, caratulera,
> sabañón garrafal, morado y frito. [#513]

There was a man glued to a nose; it was a superlative nose; it was a beaker half bubbling; it was a swordfish badly shaven; it was a sundial badly-positioned; it was an upturned elephant's trunk; it was a nose of an executioner, a scribe; a snuffling Ovidius Nosus. It was a galley's battering ram; it was an Egyptian pyramid; it was a twelve-tribe nose; it was an infinitely big nose; a Frisian arch-nose, a comedian's mask, a fried, purple, scabrous morello-cherry.

As difficult as it is to tread the line here separating mockery and admiration, if we laugh at this "battering ram of a galley . . . Egyptian pyramid . . . infinitely big nose," it is largely because we appreciate the conceptual and material differences between Quevedo's rhetoric and what normally passes for reality. We allow, that is, metaphor to become hyperbole. As Lía Schwartz Lerner observes, in Quevedian satire "metaphor is the figure that permits the impossible, anomalous to be said; it is a form of transgressing the system's semantic restrictions."[10] But this sonnet also demands a delight in paranomasia ("Ovidio Nasón") and a certain complicity in, or at least knowledge of, anti-Semitic commonplaces to which Quevedo all too often resorts in his writings. More generally, the reader is asked to suspend judgment while the paratactic predications accumulate to compass this extraordinary object. At the same time, Quevedo mocks his culture's mania for encomia and the *blasón*, a mania in which he and Góngora fervently participated.[11]

While Alonso's impassioned attempt to make Don Francisco into a tortured existentialist *avant la lettre* now feels somewhat overplayed, Quevedo's art certainly engages with the messy realities of his world and own psyche to a degree rarely attempted by Góngora.[12] As his hyperboles repeatedly verge toward satire (often of the scatological kind), Quevedo vividly embodies Bakhtin's claims in his book on Rabelais concerning the objective, potentially infinite character of the grotesque. Stressing "the aspiration to abundance and to a universal spirit" in such images, or what he calls "their positive hyperbolism," Bakhtin claims "all that is bodily becomes grandiose, exaggerated, immeasurable. This exaggeration has a positive, assertive character. The leading themes of these images of bodily life are fertility, growth, and a brimming overabundance . . . The material bodily principle is the triumphant, festive principle, it is a 'banquet for all the world.' This character is preserved to a considerable degree in Renaissance literature, and most fully, of course, in Rab-elais."[13] As a close look at his burlesque poems and satiric prose works such as the *Sueños* would confirm, Quevedian satire also consistently embraces this "material bodily principle." Yet Quevedo's "banquet" is also somewhat fune-real, furnished, if you well, with cold meats, thriftily leftover from happier oc-casions, and which when tried leave a decidedly acrid taste in the mouth.

As might be expected given his tumultuous relations with the Spanish court and various patrons, Quevedo's epideictic verse is filled with that now furtive, now ostentatious transformative alchemy native to panegyric.[14] Such metamorphosis, however, proves to be a process by which Quevedo expresses his desire for self-transformation as well. George Mariscal comments that even as Quevedo's "courtly lyric" represents the "discursive elaboration of early modern aristocratic subjectivity" in its most contradictory aspects, the poet also makes his subjected position the basis for a fluid, sometimes subversive sense of self.[15] At its best, then, such occasional poetry nimbly treads the blurry, often ironic lines between flattery, critique, and introspection, as the poet dutifully but ingeniously visits most of the hyperbolic *topoi* expected in panegyric. Most famously, "Elogio al Duque de Lerma" [#237], dubbed a "Canción Pindárica" by José Antonio González de Salas, Quevedo's friend and literary executor, visits the inexpressibility *topos* and borrows from Virgil's first *Georgic*, even as it would outdo the praise of classical heroes such as Caesar and Alexander. Quevedo also slyly rewrites here the classical gigan-tomachy by placing the Duke on the same footing as victorious Jupiter; but in doing so, by the poem's end he introduces a curious strain of agonistic violence:

> ¡Oh, cómo ufanos
> vuestros padres y abuelos soberanos
> que España armados vio (de la manera
> que a Jove los gigantes,
> soberbio parto de la parda tierra,
> que, fulminados, yacen fulminantes)
> escarmiento a la guerra,
> darán, de vos, en nietos esforzados,
> sus hechos, y sus nombres heredados! (Epode II, 13–21)

Oh, your proud fathers and sovereign grandfathers, who Spain saw armed (in the manner that the giants, the dun earth's arrogant brood, who, fulminated, lie fulminating, [saw] Jove), would give a warning about war, through you, in valiant descendents, their deeds, and their inherited names.

The punning "manera" in which Lerma's "sovereign" [*soberanos*] ancestors are compared to the "arrogant" [*soberbio*] brood of giants reduced to subjection by Jove's witty lightning bolts ("fulminados, yacen fulminantes") is as astonishing as it is grim. While celebrating his martial powers, it slyly urges Lerma to be a peacemaker as well. An encomiastic occasion for Quevedo to try his skills in invention and elocution, this Pindaric imitation proffers a timely *escarmiento* to any of his countrymen able and willing to listen.

Analogous complications and ambivalences riddle most of his epideictic verse. Although he embraces the cause of reform in the 1620s, generally Quevedo proves a fiercely nostalgic defender of what he perceives to be vanishing values. His patrons thus often feared his pen's pointed, satiric zeal as much as they courted its witty praises.[16] A sonnet written to the recently deceased Duke of Osuna, nicely exemplifies this dialectic of praise and blame. Honoring his onetime patron, who died while imprisoned by his enemies, Quevedo creates real pathos with his version of the pathetic fallacy:

> Faltar pudo su patria al grande Osuna,
> pero no a su defensa sus hazañas;
> diéronle muerte y cárcel las Españas,
> de quien él hizo esclava la Fortuna.
>
> Lloraron sus invidias una a una
> con las proprias naciones las extrañas;
> su tumba son de Flandes las campañas,
> y su epitafio la sangrienta luna.
>
> En sus exequias encendió al Vesubio
> Parténope, y Trinacria al Mongibelo;
> el llanto militar creció en diluvio.
>
> Diole el mejor lugar Marte en su cielo;
> la Mosa, el Rhin, el Tajo y el Danubio
> murmuran con dolor su desconsuelo. [#223]

His country may have failed the great Osuna, but his deeds in his defense did not; Spain gave him death and prison, though he made Fortune her slave. His own nation along with foreign lands wept tears of envy, one by one; his tomb is Flemish fields, and his epitaph the bloody moon. For his funeral Naples ignited Vesuvius, Sicily Etna; martial grief became a flood. Mars gave him the best place in the heavens; the Mosel, Rhine, Tagus, and Danube inconsolably murmur their grief.

Osuna's fall is sympathetically mourned by all nations, the "bloody moon," the constellations, and the Earth's great rivers. And while Borges celebrates the image of "su epitafio la sangrienta luna" for its "esplendida eficacia," the student of hyperbole can revel in the remarkable compass of these conceits as the European map is remade in the light of Osuna's spectacular disgrace.[17] In fashioning also the volcano hyperbole, Quevedo neatly transfers his own fury at the thankless way Osuna was treated onto objective, universal nature. Conversely, that the poem ends with the verb *murmurar* suggests a more subjective stance. For as Cervantes vividly portrays in his novela, "El coloquio de los perros," murmuring is the chief rhetorical act of cynics and those who feel marginalized by society.

Quevedo's "defensa" of Osuna's virtue after it was no longer politically expedient also speaks to his vision of the poet as a moral scourge and repository of ancient wisdom. Quevedo's debts to NeoStoic thought, and, in particular, Justus Lipsius, are immense. Henry Ettinghausen's valuable study of the poet's neoStoicism dwells largely on the philosophical aspects of this debt, though it also ties doctrinal questions to the poet's biography: "It would almost be strange had Francisco de Quevedo not been attracted by the Stoics' consolation for misfortune and exhortations to selfreliance. His life was dogged by continual reverses of fortune: ill health, penury, imprisonment, lawsuits, and a disastrously shortlived marriage to an elderly widow punctuated a brilliant career as a diplomat and writer."[18] In other words, the manner in which nature and the Gods react to Osuna's fate ought not be dismissed as mere hyperbolic convention, but rather should be read as a Baroque adaptation of the Stoic notion of *sumpatheia*, a philosophical concept that helps the likes of Seneca and Lucan literally and figuratively link the physical and ethical spheres with such astonishing effect. For instance, just as Lucan makes all of nature grieve for the fallen Pompey: "Situs est, qua terra extrema refuso / Pendet in Oceano; Romanum nomen et omne / Imperium Magno tumuli est modus . . ." (8.797–799), Quevedo, in a prosopopeia to Columbus [#236] spoken from the explorer's graveside by a piece of wood from one of his ships, universalizes the act of mourning: "la gente / tanta agua ha de verter con tierno ojos, / que al mar nos vuelva a entrambos con el llanto" [*people will have to spill so much water with tender eyes that grief will return us both to the sea*]. And while Quevedo's hyperbole here is emblematic of his *imitatio* of neoteric and imperial Latin poetry, it also suggests how difficult it was for Quevedo (as it was for Lucan) to hew to the Stoic ideal of *apatheia* (tranquility).[19]

OUTDOING PETRARCH

In his *poesías amorosas*, grouped under the heading *Erato* by González de Salas, Quevedo's imitation relies largely on a different source. Petrarchism here becomes the material that Quevedo exaggerates and attenuates to the furthest limits of credulity. Or to borrow a line from Donne, the presence of Petrarch in his amorous verse often feels "like gold to aery thinness beat." More acutely concerned with the cognitive play of *engaño* and *desengaño* than Góngora, Quevedo's hyperboles are powered more by *conceptos* than exorbitant amplification, distorted syntaxis, and semantic overreaching. This helps explain why he brands Góngora's descriptions of Galatea as "airosa de hipérboles" [*inflated with hyperboles*].[20] Like Donne, to whom he has often been compared, Quevedo's exaggerated wit is intensely self-critical and restless.[21] But if Donne's *Songs and sonnets* smell of the boudoir, Quevedo's love poetry, as was apparently his passion, is more calculated. Both poets reach for the stars and imagine the flames of Hell, but Quevedo is more content with perfecting inherited lyric forms. Many of his love sonnets, with their peregrine, far-fetched comparisons, which only yield their ingenious *pointes* in the concluding lines, explore the subtleties of the passions as if feeling were a formal enigma rather than an actual experience. Finely sophistic, the writing subject ransacks the world and myth for objects and exemplars that will allow him to establish imagined correspondences between his own extreme, contradictory feelings and his beloved's incomparable worth, her parts, her virtues, and of course her disdain. Comparing himself to a speck of dust or a mountain, to Tantalus, Orpheus, or Hercules, his beloved to Venus, the sky, a sepulcher, or, more paradoxically, to a "deidad y cárcel" [*divinity and prison*], Quevedo, as is the Petrarchist's wont, involves the entire macrocosm in his passion. But like Donne, by constantly drawing the reader's attention to the speaker's *persona* and *ingenium*, as well as his intertextual debts to previous poetic voices, Quevedo ironically underscores the extreme artifice involved in such subjectivity. Moreover, as Navarrete argues in his reading of the celebrated lyric sequence, *Canta sola a Lisi y la amorosa pasión de su amante* [#442–511], by imbuing it with the same moral concerns as his metaphysical poetry and juxtaposing it with his bur‑ lesque poetry, Quevedo undermines the semantic gestures and cultural values associated with the Petrarchan tradition.[22] In still more general terms, his Neo‑Petrarchan verse epitomizes Borges's definition of the Baroque as "a style which deliberately exhausts (or tries to exhaust) all its possibilities and which borders on its own parody."[23]

Many of the titles González de Salas gives to his friend's poems explicitly stress their artful exaggeration and hence determination to provoke the reader's *asombro*.[24] And while this may be traced partly to an editor's critical epideixis, these titles labor to lend Quevedo's hyperboles further conceptual currency and rigor.[25] In a sonnet Salas titles "Compara con el Etna las propriedades de su amor" [#293], Quevedo methodically humanizes his addressee, a volcano, only then to usurp its extreme, monstrous qualities as his own:

> Ostentas, de prodigios coronado,
> sepulcro fulminante, monte aleve,
> las hazañas del fuego y de la nieve,
> y el incendio en los yelos hospedado.
>
> Arde el hibierno en llamas erizado,
> y el fuego lluvias y granizos bebe;
> truena, si gimes; si respiras, llueve
> en cenizas tu cuerpo derramado.
>
> Si yo fuera a tanto mal nacido,
> no tuvieras, ¡oh Etna!, semejante:
> fueras hermoso monstro sin segundo.
>
> Mas como en alta nieve ardo encendido,
> soy Encélado vivo y Etna amante,
> y ardiente imitación de ti en el mundo.[26]

Crowned with marvels, you boast, fulminating sepulchre, treacherous peak, of great deeds of fire and snow, of a pyre lodged in ice. The win‑ ter burns in curling flames, and the fire imbibes the rain and hail; you groan, there's thunder; you breathe, it rains your body scattered in ash. If I had been born to less misfortune, you, my Etna, would have no equal: you'd be a beautiful, peerless monster. But since in lofty snow I

burn inflamed, I am Enceladus revived and Etna's lover, and your burn⁄
ing likeness in the world.

By remaking throughout the Petrarchan antitheses of fire and ice, and then by
identifying himself in the *pointe* with the tribulations of Enceladus (a Titan
whom Zeus punished by burying beneath Aetna), Quevedo neatly renders
the Petrarchan mise⁄en⁄scène on a cosmographic, mythic, if also somewhat
ridiculous scale.[27] Indeed, as oxymoron ("hermoso monstro") mixes with
prosopopeia ("si gimes; si respiras"), and as octet yields to sestet, we realize
that the real *furor* belongs neither to the volcano nor to a lover, but rather to the
poet discovering in the sonnet's narrow bounds an ingenious way to represent
the hyperbolic poetics of "ardiente imitación." The striking conceit of the
volcano exhaling or vomiting its own transformed body also figures the fate
of the belated Petrarchan poet who disdains verisimilitude and conventional
decorum. Calling attention chiefly to his now fiery, now frigid wit, and risk⁄
ing throughout *grotesquerie* and stylistic *cacozelia*, Quevedo's self⁄conscious
mastery of hyperbole stages a mini⁄narrative of solipsistic marvels and amorous
desengaño.[28]

Read as a sequence, the Neo⁄Petrarchan poems in *Canta sola a Lisi* mas⁄
terfully refine this exaggerated aesthetics of wonder and disillusion. They offer
what Roland Greene might call Quevedo's most sustained "fiction," or at⁄
tempt to explore and exploit the formal qualities of a lyric sequence to dis⁄
cover and then represent the poet's subjective place within a larger cultural
and historical matrix.[29] From the incomparable beauty of the sequence's ful⁄
crum, "Cerrar podrá mis ojos la postrera" [#472], to the more conventional
"Miro este monte que envejece enero" [#503], Quevedo dutifully visits, skill⁄
fully embraces, and then ambivalently exaggerates the *topoi* associated with
Petrarchan poetry and hyperbole.[30] That in the process he composes what is
widely regarded as the *Siglo de Oro*'s most accomplished sequence of love
sonnets, despite the fact that his biography paints a far less courtly picture of
Quevedo's amorous experiences, argues less for his rhetoric's disingenuous⁄
ness than for the aesthetic desire to perfect a poetic form (here the sonnet and
the sonnet sequence) and to address the larger conceptual and ethical ques⁄
tions traditionally raised by that form. Commenting on "Cerrar podrá mis
ojos la postrera," Claudio Guillén, accordingly, permits himself to be infected
by the poet's hyperbole: "Quevedo adopts the exorbitant conceit of mad, eter⁄
nal love and, in just a few verses, measured and unmeasured at the same time,

in a lightning bolt of audacity, goes further than everyone and no one. *Plus ul-tra*: Quevedo is the one who goes further, the hyperbole of a literature."[31]

Similarly, just as Erasmus made them his model for a collection of adages, Hercules' unbidden labors are the model for Quevedo's Petrarchan "trabajos":

> Si el cuerpo reluciente que en Oeta
> se desnudó, en ceniza desatado
> Hércules, y de celos fulminado
> (ansí lo quiso Amor), murió cometa,
>   le volviera a habitar aquella inquieta
> alma, que dejó el mundo descansado
> de monstros y portentos, y el osado
> brazo armaran la clava y la saeta,
>   sólo en mi corazón hallara fieras,
> que todos sus trabajos renovaran,
> leones y centauros y quimeras.
>   El *Non Plus Ultra* suyo restauraran
> sus dos columnas, si en tus dos esferas,
> Lisi, el fin de las luces señalaran.[32] [#452]

If the shining body, which undressed itself on Oeta, which reduced Hercules to ashes, who blitzed by jealousy (so Love wished it), died like a comet, should return to inhabit that unquiet soul, which left the world cleansed of monsters and portents, and if the daring arm took up the club and spear, in my heart alone would he find beasts, lions, centaurs, and chimeras that would renew all his labors. He would restore his two pillars of *Non plus ultra*, if your two spheres, Lisi, would mark the lim-its of (star)light.

By initially lauding Hercules' deeds and then resurrecting him from ashes to have him battle with his heart's "monstros," Quevedo subtly transfers Her-culean glory to himself. But by reshaping the conceit to make his beloved's closed eyes ("dos esferas") the restoration of the pillars of Hercules with their warning to sailors, he also unexpectedly transforms the hyperbole into a warning against imprudent lovers like himself who are blind to certain *señas*. This emphasis on fruitless signs recalls Góngora's hyperbole in the *Soledad primera* (435–443) where the funereal *señas* on the shore fail to warn audacious sailors; but it also literalizes what Demetrius defines as hyperbole "by certain signs." The failure of *señas*, whether natural, mythic, or artificial, precipitates the hyperbolic. In this respect, Quevedo forces the reader to engage the text and the world in order to secure meaning from these poems. Or as Gracián would have it, Quevedo the hyperbolist demands the reader make an act of judgment where before there was only a commonplace, ignorance, or passivity.

Although the poems in *Canta sola a Lisi* make enormous conceptual claims about the self, world, and their interaction, there are numerous moments in this sequence where Quevedo dwells chiefly upon the precarious ambiguity of his own rhetoric. In this respect, his ambivalent Petrarchism resembles the species of irony Paul de Man's discovers in Baudelaire's *œuvre*. Considering the process of ironic *dédoublement* portrayed in "De l'essence du rire," de Man observes: "The reflective disjunction not only occurs *by means* of language as a privileged category, but it transfers the self out of the empirical world into a world constituted out of, and in, language — a language that it finds in the world like one entity among others, but that remains unique in being the only entity by means of which it can differentiate itself from the world."[33] An analogous "reflective disjunction" occurs in Quevedo's constant dialectic of exaggeration and self-reflection, which ironizes the Petrarchan enterprise by transforming it into the only available semantic field for the poet's desires, and then, significantly, testing that field against the world such as he finds it. And if in the process of such experimentation, the boundaries normally distinguishing "self" from "the empirical world" blur or disappear, then the reader also loses any stable, autonomous *realia* against which to measure Quevedo's hyperboles.

Exemplary of this shift is the first quatrain of "Si mis párpados, Lisi, labios fueran" [#448], which takes the conceited style to almost surrealist lengths as it imagines a possible world:

> Si mis párpados, Lisi, labios fueran,
> besos fueran los rayos visüales
> de mis ojos, que al sol miran caudales
> águilas, y besaran más que vieran.

If my eyelids, Lisi, were lips, kisses like visual beams would come from my eyes, which like royal eagles gazing sunward, would kiss more than they see.

Playing with the Neoplatonic emphasis on the lover's eyes and the mystic language they traditionally speak, Quevedo inverts the mind-body hierarchy and
muses upon eyelids that kiss the sun, i.e., Lisi, with a constancy matched by
"royal eagles," creatures thought to be able to look upon the sun without
averting their eyes. The tenuous, subjunctive, purely linguistic quality of this
desire ("fueran . . . fueran . . . besaran . . . vieran") is further heightened in
the sonnet's concluding lines as the poet's fragmented "mudos . . . ardores"
[*mute . . . ardors*] paradoxically strive "verse unidos, / y en público, secretos, los
amores" [*to see themselves joined publicly in secret passion*]. The only place where
eyelids may even begin to realize kissing and enjoying ("gozaran") their desired object is in the sonnet's unique, but unreal fourteen-line space.

A still more dramatic version of this aestheticized frustration is the magnificent sonnet "En crespa tempestad del oro undoso" [#449] where the poet's
heart swims the stormy seas of the beloved's hair. Compared in swift succession to Leander, Icarus, the Phoenix, Midas, and finally to Tantalus, his
"corazón" is more metonymy than muscle. Tempering the Rabelesian disproportionality of the initial conceit — one thinks of the passage in *Pantagruel*
(2.32) read brilliantly by Auerbach where the narrator explores the world inside the giant's mouth — with a remarkable economy of syntax and imagery
that manages to crowd in such mob of allegorical figures, Quevedo's wit ultimately succeeds in focusing our attention on the paradoxical "pretensión" of
the speaker who represents his heart in the last tercet as:

> Avaro y rico y pobre, en el tesoro,
> el castigo y la hambre imita a Midas,
> Tántalo en fugitiva fuente de oro.

Greedy and rich and poor, it imitates Midas in punishment and hunger;
Tantalus with his fleeing fount of gold.

With the aid of polysyndeton and ellipsis, the "gold" of the beloved's hair in
the first line becomes the dangerous but still desired "fleeing fount of gold,"
which the poet, by metalepsis, but also, putatively, without any say in the matter, "imitates."[34] Even a poem, then, as extravagantly sensuous as this, is complicated by moral and metapoetic concerns. Like Garcilaso in his twelfth
sonnet and Góngora in the *Soledad segunda* (137–150), Quevedo explicitly
identifies the lover's mythic overreaching with his own poetic efforts.

When it comes to the legacy of Petrarchism, Quevedo proves much more devoted than his rivals in imitation to amplifying and exaggerating its commonplaces until they verge on or cross over into satire. One madrigal, "Bostezó Floris, y su mano hermosa" [#405], flirts with both blasphemy and *preciosité* as the beloved's hand covering a yawn is represented as "crucificando en labios carmesíes" [*crucifying with crimson lips*] its fingers. In a *romance*, "Aquí, donde, tus peñascos" [#437], Quevedo popularizes the *culto* hyperbole to parodic extremes: *"Mas, ¿qué descanso espero, | si a Jacinta dejé y ausente muero, | aquí, donde mis llantos y mis penas | crecen el mar y exceden las arenas?"* [But what rest do I expect, if, having left Jacinta, I die absent, here where my weeping and pain make the sea increase and exceed the sands?]. More obviously still, in the numerous poems Blecua classifies as *poemas satíricos y burlescos*, Quevedo with great rancor and still greater wit systematically inverts Petrarchan values: the beloved is an elaborate fraud hiding behind a parapet of dresses and cosmetics, or the lover is a gigantic fool feeding his vanity; but above all, women are hyperbolically portrayed as little better than whores offering illusory pleasures. Still, the greatest pleasure of all clearly belongs to Quevedo, who takes enormous delight in fashioning extravagant *burlas* out of the literary tradition.

FIGURAS

Quevedo's laughter can be enormously self-reflexive. As such, it aims partially at unmasking the nature, appeal, and limitations of figuration; indeed, at times it seems to insist on the hypocrisy inherent in all figures. In making *codicia* and *atrevimiento* central motifs throughout his *obra*, Quevedo also doggedly reflects on the task of figuring immanent if unpleasant truths. In his most celebrated prose works, the picaresque novel *La vida del Buscón llamado don Pablos* (1626) and the satiric, eschatological *Sueños* (first published 1627), *codicia* is repeatedly and variously figured as a kind of *hipócresia* (hypocrisy). Sharply etching the enormous gaps between society's grandiose appearances and its motley, often grotesque realities, between its orthodox ideologies of church and state and the material chaos and confusion of everyday life, Quevedo frequently contemplates the necessity of satirical critique. For example, in *El alguacil endemoniado* (dedicated to the Conde de Lemos, "Presidente de Indias"), responding to the narrator's query whether there are kings in Hell, the title character insists: "Todo el infierno es figuras, y hay muchos, porque el poder, libertad y mando les hace sacar a las virtudes de su medio, y llegan los vicios a su extremo . . ." [*All Hell is figures, and many exist there because power, liberty, and command displace the virtues from their mean, and so vices become extreme*].[35] That one of these extreme vices is "codicia,"[36] and that Covarrubias glosses *figuras* as "ciertos modos y términos de hablar extraordinarios" [*certain ways and terms with which to speak extraordinarily*], and *figura* as an "hombre de humor y extravagante" [*a man of extravagant humor* (in the sense of the four humors)], again suggest how essential and yet risky figurative language is in the task of representing extraordinary realities.[37]

More strikingly still, in *El mundo por de dentro* (dedicated to the Duque de Osuna), after citing Francisco Sánchez's 1580 treatise, *Quod nihil scitur*, Quevedo gives flesh to Sánchez's philosophical skepticism by making his mouthpiece "un viejo venerable en sus canas, maltratado, roto por mil partes el vestido y pisado" [*a mistreated old man with venerable white hair, with clothes torn and trampled in a thousand places*], though still "severo y digno de respeto" [*serious and worthy of respect*] — a walking allegory whom Quevedo dubs simply *Desengaño*. Playing a role akin to Góngora's "[p]olítico serrano, de canas grave," this figure immediately points to the equivocal objects of his scorn: "Si tú quieres, hijo, ver el mundo, ven conmigo, que yo te llevaré a la calle mayor, que es adonde salen todas las figuras . . . Yo te enseñaré el mundo como es: que tú no alcanzas a ver sino lo que parece" [*If you wish, my son, to see the world, come with me, for I'll bring you to the main avenue, where all the world's figures come out . . . I will show you the world as it is: which you will not manage to see except as it appears*].[38] The world is figured because it is illusory, a valley of shadows. But because the "calle mayor" belongs to the Baroque metropolis, it goes by a sophisticated name:

> — ¿Y cómo se llama — dije yo — la calle mayor del mundo donde hemos de ir?
> — Llámase — respondió — Hipocresía.[39]

> "And what is the name," I said, "of the world's main avenue that we must visit?"
> "It's called," he responded, "Hypocrisy."

A sin that easily lends itself to the figures of antithesis, irony, and especially hyperbole, hypocrisy functions as a ubiquitous if moving target in Quevedo's *obra*. Yet as Schwartz Lerner indicates in her reading of the semantic aspects of Quevedian satire, an ethical and so eschatological *terminus* also exists for his protean rhetoric: "In the system of Quevedian satire, the infernal is always the *non plus ultra* of physical, moral, or spiritual horror. Everything hyperbolically disagreeable and condemnable is demonic."[40]

Similarly, in "Sobre el arte de Quevedo en el *Buscón*," Leo Spitzer underscores this ethical concern with hypocrisy to defend Quevedo's exaggerated rhetoric as a means of figuring the real. However, in emphasizing Quevedo's hyperbolic play with proportions and numbers, Spitzer also calls attention to the aporetic aspects of such figuration: "It cannot be accidental that precisely *this* type of comparison greatly abounds in Quevedo: the *more . . . than* whose arithmetic quality converts thus into a sign of boasting, numerical exaggeration, but also of that supernatural and illusory grandeur so pursued by the Baroque."[41] In other words, figures of excess often go beyond the needs of *enargeia*. They express the "supernatural," the irrational, and the surreal. Spitzer's examples confirm that it is often impossible — and such impossibility is precisely the point — to visualize Quevedo's descriptions: "Miren el todo trapos como muñeca de niñas, más triste que pastelería en Cuaresma, con más agujeros que una flauta y más remiendos que una pía y más manchas que un jaspe y más puntos que un libro de música . . ." [*Look at him all rags like a girl's doll, sadder than a pastry shop in Lent, with more holes than a flute and more patches than a piebald horse and more veins than a piece of jasper and more pitches-stitches than a book of music*].[42] Such discursive hyperbole fuels Quevedo's skeptical critique of the human condition and confirms that decorous *figuras* are incapable of revealing the nature, the essence, of things because, in part at least, it is mere appearance. His vivid experiments in the picaresque and his vertiginous, eschatological fantasies collected under the rubric of the *Sueños* acutely mine the gap between appearance and reality, between *verba et res*, in ways that emphasize also his unique rhetorical *ethos* in a mutable and actively hostile world.

NAVIGATING DISILLUSION

Quevedo's balancing act is carried to further subjective and political extremes when his verse turns to the imperial theme in a series of "navigation" poems. Located for the most part in the *Calíope* section of the *Las tres últimas musas castellanas*, the 1670 addition to the also posthumously published *El Parnaso español* (1649), these poems supplement the moral, largely Neo-Stoic concerns that dominate the *Polimnia* section of the collected verse. Refashioning Horatian and Senecan commonplaces associated with the seafarer's audacity,

Quevedo employs hyperbole to marshal allegory, prosopopoeia, and apostrophe to interrogate sailors, ships, and sails, with the recurring query: why risk
life and virtue for the unmeasured pursuit of evanescent riches?[43] Thoroughly
informed by Neo-Stoic *sumpatheia*, these poems movingly express geographical space as an extension of individual, ethical space.

In a late sonnet González de Salas titles simply "Don Francisco de
Quevedo" [#134], the poet presents a transparent allegory of his financial
need and bleak prospects at court. The second quatrain reads:

> ¡Malhaya el que, forzado de dinero,
> el nunca arado mar surcó, de suerte
> que en sepultura natural convierte
> el imperio cerúleo, húmedo y fiero!

Damn him who, short on money, tilled the never-plowed sea, such that
the fierce, wet, cerulean empire changes into a natural sepulchre.

While the hyperbole of the sea become a "sepulchre" recalls the poem on
Columbus [#236], the catachrestic verb *surcar* suggests the moral that it
would have been better for humans to have busied themselves cultivating their
gardens than foolishly plowing the sea. As Voltaire concludes in *Candide*,
Quevedo wants his readers to spurn global ambitions and realize: ". . . il faut
cultiver notre jardin." And in conflating the personal and imperial in this
way, a moribund Quevedo shows himself deeply affected by Spain's fluctuating fortunes at home and overseas, yet also inspired by the Stoic allegory of the
soul seeking its eternal port and release from bodily desires.

In one of his very last poems, "El escarmiento" [#12], an embittered
Quevedo, belittling the body as "ambiciosa ceniza" [*ambitious ash*], makes his
extreme "desengaños" into "jueces" [*judges*]. Cataloguing the "lamentable despojos, / desprecio del naufragio de mis ojos" [*lamentable spoils, shipwreck's scorn
in my eyes*] hanging on his walls, he implicitly answers, with a pessimism born
from personal and national experience, Herrera's famous call decades earlier
in the *Anotaciones* for Spanish poets to appropriate the "despojos" of the classical and Petrarchan traditions to achieve poetic glory ("hiziera mi lengua co-
piosa i rica de aquellos admirables despojos" [*that I might make my language
abundant and rich from those admirable spoils*]).[44] Herrera's martial metaphorics are
further subverted when later in the poem Quevedo returns to the ship allegory:

No solicito el mar con remo y vela,
ni temo al Turco la ambición armada;
no en larga centinela
al sueño inobediente, con pagada
sangre y salud vendida,
soy, por un pobre sueldo, mi homicida;
ni a Fortuna me entrego,
con la codicia y la esperanza ciego,
por cavar, diligente,
los peligros precisos del Oriente;
no de mi gula amenazada vive
la fénix en Arabia, temerosa,
ni a ultraje de mis leños apercibe
el mar su inobediencia peligrosa:
vivo como hombre que viviendo muero,
por desembarazar el dia postrero. (81–96)

I do not court the sea with oar and sail, nor do I fear the Turk's armed ambition; I am not — in the long night's vigil, disloyal to sleep, with blood bought and health sold — for a meager wage, my own homicide; nor do I deliver myself to Fortune, with greed and blind hope, to excavate diligently the certain dangers of the East. Unthreatened by my belly, the Arabian phoenix does not live fearfully; nor does the sea's dangerous disobedience warn of the shipwreck of my planks: I live like a man, for I die living to get rid of the last day.

Though being one's own murderer is a familiar conceit in Quevedo's *obra* — Hieronymus Bosch, whose paintings are known to have influenced Quevedo, was also fascinated by the theme — here it is given new *energeia* against the background of the "ambición armada," "ultraje," and "codicia" he associates with the history of Spanish navigation. Myth ("la fénix") and contemporary history ("al Turco") furnish the metaphoric field for the poet to cultivate his volatile subjectivity and to rethink recent poetic tradition. Meanwhile, the extended *omissio*, fueled by anaphora, emphasizes the speaker's despair, as does the decidedly non-*culto* "gula" ('esophogus' but more abstractly, 'gluttony').

If these poems reveal the ethical and subjective impetus behind Quevedo's navigation theme, elsewhere he points to a broader, cosmological basis for his hyperbolism. In the *silva* González de Salas aptly entitles "Sermón estoico de censura moral" [#145], "la gula" disastrously transforms nature's fabric.[45] Desire for material excess becomes a debased form of the once laudable desire for rhetorical *copia*:

> Ni la pluma a las aves,
> ni la garra a las fieras,
> ni en los golfos del mar, ni en las riberas
> el callado nadar del pez de plata,
> les puede defender del apetito;
> y el orbe, que infinito
> a la navegación nos parecía,
> es ya corto distrito
> para las diligencias de la gula,
> pues de esotros sentidos acumula
> el vasallaje, y ella se levanta
> con cuanto patrimonio
> tienen, y los confunde en la garganta.
> Y antes que las desórdenes del vientre
> satisfagan sus ímpetus violentos,
> yermos han de quedar los elementos,
> para que el orbe en sus angustias entre. (21–37)

Not the birds' feathers, not the beasts' claws, not the silent swimming of silver fish in the sea's depths or in the shallows, can defend them from (human) appetite; and the Earth's orb, which seemed infinite to us to navigate, now is a tiny region for the belly's business, and it amasses the fealty of those other senses, and it elevates itself atop whatever patrimony they have, and it mixes them up in the throat. And before the stomach's disorders can satisfy its violent impetuses, the elements (of the earth) must be stripped bare, so that the earth's orb in its agony can enter (the body).

An outraged Quevedo urges readers here to rethink and thereby moralize the nature of physical space. Methodically shrinking "infinito" space to a "corto distrito," the "gula" violently "confunde" the proper order of the elements. And as the cosmos ("el orbe") is reduced to the belly's province, hyperbole becomes more discursive than metaphoric, more proper to the process of invention than to the realm of *elocutio*. Poetic overreaching, in other words, should be read here with and against nautical overreaching. The extreme image of "los elementos" as "yermos" [*desolated*] — the physical, topographical complement to Góngora's subjective *soledad* — as they vainly try to satisfy the belly's "angustias," rather than merely ornamenting his moral ideas, is a necessary but extreme consequence of them. Radical metonymic transformation proves the rule where Stoic *sumpatheia* reigns. And while this version of the microcosmic-macrocosmic analogy enables Quevedo to salvage some manner of metaphorical solace in his love poetry — think of his celebrated "polvo enamorado" [#472] — here it creates an irredeemable sense of dislocation and disproportion. We are not at home in the world intimates Quevedo with his gloomy versions of the Stoic allegory of the soul seeking its eternal port and thus release from bodily desires.[46] Moreover, on a metapoetic level, his hyperboles against navigation raise again the question: if it is possible to go too far on the sea, is there not a *Nec plus ultra* for language as well? Although I would of course want to distinguish Quevedo's notion of an aggrieved nature with Quintilian's idea of nature as the measure of true eloquence ("Naturam intueamur, hanc sequamur"), it does seem relevant here to recall the exception that Quintilian makes for hyperbole: "Tum est hyperbole virtus, cum res ipsa, de qua loquendum est, naturalem modum excessit."

From beginning to end of this remarkable 389-line *silva*, nature is repeatedly and variously deformed by humanity's unnatural cupidity. With a grave, unequivocal tone as befits a "Stoic Sermon," Quevedo, borrowing again from Horace's *Ode* 1.3,[47] transforms "el callado nadar del pez de plata" into a colonial *aex triplex* dedicated to the "despojo precioso de occidente" [*the precious spoils of the West*] (90), the pillage of Potosí and Lima (125), but also to the ruthless violation of nature by "el hombre":

> por saber los secretos
> de la primera madre
> que nos sustenta y cría,
> de ella hizo miserable anatomía.
> Despedazóla el pecho,
> rompióle las entrañas,
> desangróle las venas,
> que de estimado horror estaban llenas . . . (108–115)

to know the secrets of the primal mother, which sustains and nourishes us, he made her a miserable object of anatomy. He ripped apart the chest, tore open the entrails, bled the veins, which were full of righteous horror . . .

In this graphic but metrically refined manner, the mines' gold and silver become a metonymic "horror," while Quevedo transforms himself into a purveyor of "doctos desengaños" (279). In this way, he also transforms Horace's poem dedicated to Virgil into a contemporary history of "ultraje" [*outrage*] (52), into a mere "teatro de espumas" [*theater of foam*] where "feathers" foolishly try to "navigate" (58), but also where the Neo-Gongorist conceit joining the "magnet" and "lover" is deliberately stripped of all "éxtasis" [*ecstasy*] (72–79).

Quevedo has no intention of eroticizing empire and the precious metals it may yield, metals that for him, as for many of his contemporaries, are a particularly strong source of alienation. As Greenblatt observes: "The *unnaturalness* of the desire for gold is one of the great themes of the fifteenth and sixteenth centuries, a theme tirelessly rehearsed by poets, playwrights, and moralists and frequently illustrated by tales of European behavior in the New World. One of the most famous images of the Spanish in America depicts a group of Indians punishing a conquistador for insatiable thirst for gold by pouring the molten metal down his throat."[48] Offering an extended lyric commentary on this image, Quevedo in several poems devotes himself to excoriating the Spanish lust for precious metals. A sonnet addressed to Nebuchadnezzar [#127] warns "[e]s la soberbia artífice engañoso" [*pride is the deceitful artifice*] that constructs a statue whose head is made "del metal precioso" [*of precious metal*], neck and chest of "plata y bronce" [*silver and bronze*] but whose feet consist only of "barro temoroso" [*frightful mud*].[49] In a silva, "A una mina" [#136],[50] Quevedo decries the naive audacity of seafaring: "Diste crédito a un pino / a quien del ocio dura avara mano / trajo del monte al agua peregrino . . ." [*You entrusted a pine tree to a slothful, harsh, greedy hand, which hauled it from the mountains to the peregrine sea*]. Then he wonders, addressing an aristocratic explorer whom Quevedo knew, why one would trade the sea's tyranny only to find oneself debased on land as well:

> Mucho te debe el oro
> si, después que saliste,
> pobre reliquia, del naufragio triste,

en vez de descansar del mar seguro,
a tu codicia hidrópica obediente,
con villano azadón, del cerro duro
sangras las venas del metal luciente.
¿Por qué permites que trabajo infame
sudor tuyo derrame?
Deja oficio bestial que inclina al suelo
ojos nacidos para ver el cielo. (22–32)

Gold, poor relic, owes you a great deal if, after escaping the sorrowful shipwreck, instead of resting safely from the sea, you, obedient to your hydropic greed, with huge, lowly shovels, bleed shining metals from the mountain's veins. Why do you allow vile work to spill your sweat? Quit the bestial office that turns earthward eyes born to sea the sky.

Infecting the earth with his "codicia hidrópica," fallen man, as the play of up and down emphasizes, continues to ignore his true nature. In marked contrast, say, with Pico della Mirandola, who famously dubs man a "chameleon," or Thomas Browne, who calls him a "great and true amphibian," Quevedo insists that *homo volens* has a static, unchanging, and ultimately bestial nature. To this end, he deftly employs later in the poem various figures to create the rhetorical *copia* needed to condemn the desire for material *copia*. In doing so, he wittily proves the folly of pursuing earthly riches:

Rico, dime si acaso,
en tus montones de oro
tropezará la muerte o tendrá el paso;
si añadirá a tu vida tu tesoro
un año, un mes, un día, un hora, un punto.
No es poderoso a tanto el mundo junto.

. . .

Sacas, ¡ay!, un tirano de tu sueño;
un polvo que después será tu dueño,
y en cada grano sacas dos millones
de envidiosos, cuidados y ladrones. (68–73; 80–83)

Rich man, tell me by chance, will death trip or lose a step on your mountains of gold? Will your treasure add to your life a year, a month, a day, an hour, an instant. There's not world enough for that . . . Oh, you extract a tyrant from your dreams, a piece of dust that later will be your master, and in each grain you extract two million envious, careworn men and thieves.

Hyperbolizing the biblical commonplace of man as dust in the light of what Eduardo Galeano in the 1960s called, still implicitly relying on the micro-cosmic-macrocosmic conceit, "las venas abiertas" [*the open veins*] of Latin America, Quevedo resembles Milton, who in *Paradise Lost* also treats the sub-terranean search for minerals as essentially diabolic: "Deep under ground, materials dark and crude, / Of spiritous and fiery spume . . . / These in their dark nativity the deep / Shall yield us, pregnant with infernal flame, / Which into hollow engines long and round . . ." (6.478–485). And as in Milton's portrayal of that ur-overreacher, Satan, Quevedo makes pride (*soberbia*) the greatest obstacle to the reason and rhetoric that would dispell such illusions.

Another *silva*, which González de Salas titles simply "La soberbia" [#135], insists upon the "tanta desdicha y tanta afrenta" [*great misfortune and great affront*] of those whose hubris incites them to scale "la cumbre" [*the sum-mit*] of power; then it conveys this dire warning:

> Vosotros, ambiciosos pretensores,
> vulgo de la ignorancia y del engaño,
> sedientos de la muerte todo el año,
> polvo, ruido y afán de los señores,
>   ¿con qué esperanza ciega y porfiada
> no dais crédito a tantos escarmientos?
> ¿Por qué no recatáis los pensamientos
> de fiera hasta en los ángeles cebada?
>   Disponed medios a mejores fines,
> dad crédito a tan altos testimonios,
> que quien hizo de arcángeles demonios,
> mal hará de demonios serafines.[51] (53–64)

You, ambitious pretenders, vulgar in your ignorance and illusion, thirsty for death all the year, (and for) dust, noise, and zeal of the mighty, on account of what blind, stubborn hope do you refuse to believe so many warnings? Why do you not suppress bestial thoughts fattened even on angels? Find the means for better ends, give credit to such lofty testimonies, for who made demons of archangels, will fail to make seraphim of demons.

By focusing so skeptically on the sin of excessive pride, these concluding lines, as well as allegorizing and ironizing the fate of ambitious courtiers (*arcángeles* were also coins), target all post-lapsarian humanity. And by alluding to the *exemplum* of Icarus earlier in the poem, Quevedo catachrestically raises pride to illusory, celestial heights and proportions in order then to lower man's pretensions:

> Es [la soberbia] un cielo mentido
> a las inadvertencias del sentido;
> y aunque de estrellas coronada viene,
> las que ella derribó son las que tiene.
> Ésta, en el reino de la paz eterno,
> con máquinas de viento, con escalas,
> fue el primer tropezón de plumas y alas,
> primera fundadora del Infierno.
> En ella resbalaron
> los que por más dolor mejor volaron
> y, a fuerza de traiciones,
> de los rayos del sol hizo carbones. (15–26)

Pride is a deceptive heaven for the incautious senses; and though it comes crowned with stars, those whom it overthrows are those which it possesses. Pride, in the eternal kingdom of peace, with devices for (riding) the wind, with ladders, was the first stumbling block for feathers and wings, the first founder of Hell. In pride those slipped who flew to their greater sorrow and, by betrayals, were carbonized by the sun's rays.

What a far cry Quevedo's carbonized, diminished man is from Pico's seraphic vision of *humanitas*, a vision that may well be said to inaugurate Renaissance humanism. Pico's *Oration on the Dignity of Man* (1486) urges a stirring species of "holy ambition" [*sacra . . . ambitio*]: "If unoccupied by deeds, we pass our time in the leisure of contemplation, considering the Creator in the creature and the creature in the Creator, we shall be ablaze with Cherubic light. If we long with love for the Creator himself alone, we shall speedily flame up with His consuming fire into a Seraphic likeness."[52] But if to juxtapose Pico and

Quevedo ignores too much the chronological gap between them, recall how Gracián, writing in 1648, three years after Quevedo's death, praises man and his native *agudeza* with an equally expansive hyperbole of ascent: "Si el percibir la agudeza acredita el águila, el producirla empeñará el ángel: empleo de querubines y elevación de hombres que nos remonta a extravagante jerarquia."⁵³ By making such illumination and ascent essential aspects of man's being, Gracián like Pico, insists that human *oratio* can begin to approximate the divine *ratio* that is its beginning and end. For the ingenious poet of "La soberbia," on the contrary, *ratio* all too often produces only infernal machines. *Ingenium* can still express the tenuous links between heaven and earth, but it no longer makes credible ontological claims.

Clearly, though, Quevedo derives enormous aesthetic pleasure in crafting his scourges of Spanish greed, pride, and vanity. The following sonnet, which González de Salas helpfully entitles, *Comprehende la obediencia del mar, y la inobediencia del codicioso en sus afectos*, allegorizes "Codicia" in a manner that would produce admiration as well as disdain:

> La voluntad de Dios por grillos tienes,
> y ley de arena tu coraje humilla,
> y, por besarla, llegas a la orilla,
> mar obediente, a fuerza de vaivenes.
> Con tu soberbia undosa te detienes
> en la humildad, bastante a resistilla;
> a tu saña tu cárcel maravilla,
> rica, por nuestro mal, de nuestros bienes.
> ¿Quién dio al robre y a l'haya atrevimiento
> de nadar, selva errante deslizada,
> y al lino de impedir el paso al viento?
> Codicia, más que el Ponto desfrenada,
> persuadió que, en el mar, el avariento
> fuese inventor de muerte no esperada.⁵⁴ [#107]

God's will is your manacles, and the law of sand humiliates your courage, and, in order to kiss it, you, obedient sea, arrive at the shore, because of the wave's comings and goings. With your undulating pride, you pause in humility, enough to resist pride; for your brutality you have a marvelous prison, to our grief one rich with our goods. Who gave the oak and beech, a wandering slippery forest, the audacity to swim? And (who gave the audacity) to the sail to impede the wind's passage? Greed, more than the unchecked sea, persuaded (them), that, in the sea, the avaricious man was the inventor of unexpected death.

Beginning with the startling meiosis in which "God's will" reduces the sea to a humiliated prisoner, Quevedo methodically amplifies the notion of moral and physical limits. But all of this is turned on its head in the last tercet where "Greed" outbids the sea's "soberbia undosa." As such, the sonnet seems to revel in its own masterful invention as it presents avarice as the "inventor de muerte no esperada." Like the peregrinations of Birnam wood in *Macbeth*, or Góngora's "selvas inconstantes," Quevedo's "selva errante deslizada" is an impossibility, an *adunaton*, a hyperbolic sign of the world upside down.[55] It also seems to be a response and, perhaps, a furtive homage to the opening lines of the *Soledad primera* ("Pasos de un peregrino son errante . . ."). Here though the hyperbole depends upon the *ethos* of outrage and confusion as much as it leans on the poet's ingenious ability to amplify, *ponderar* as Gracián terms it, an insight. Incredulous at nautical "atrevimiento," Quevedo blames "Codicia" in the same breath as he makes it (and by implication himself) a master of persuasion, greater than the "unstoppable sea." In short, in this sonnet and elsewhere, such rhetorical *atrevimiento*, unlike its nautical cousin, is not perceived as being unnatural but rather as a necessary, elevated form of understanding. As literary and ethical *suppléments*, Quevedo's sonnets and *silvas* on the audacity of seafaring succeed in giving shocking dialectical energy and meaning to the catastrophes of history and empire.

Nonetheless, Quevedo is not immune to the kind of ambivalence we saw in Góngora's navigation digression. Whether from real conviction or political necessity, he also sometimes vehemently brings the tools of epideixis to praise Spanish imperialism. In *España defendida*, he embraces providential language to argue that God ordains conquest and conversion. Playing upon the Biblical account of Joshua praying for the sun and moon to stop in their courses so that he might slaughter his enemies (Joshua 10:12–14), Quevedo appropriates the rhetoric of miracles for the sake of imperial orthodoxy:

La diestra de Dios venció en el Cid, y la misma tomó a Gama y a Pacheco y a Alburquerque por instrumento en las Indias orientales para quitar la paz a los ídolos. ¿Quién sino Dios, cuya mano es miedo sobre todas las cosas, amparó a Cortés para que lograrse dichosos atrevimientos, cuyo premio fué todo un Nuevo Mundo? Voz fué de Dios, la cual halla obediencia en todas las cosas, aquélla con que Ximénez de Cisneros de, tuvo el día en la batalla de Orán, donde un cordón fué por todas las ar, mas del mundo.[56]

The right hand of God triumphed in the *Cid*, and the same used da Gama, Pachecho, and Alburquerque as an instrument to destroy the reign of idols in the eastern Indies. Who but God, whose hand strikes fear in all things, protected Cortés to enable such felicitous daring, whose prize was a completely New World? It was God's voice, which finds obedience in all things, with which Ximénez de Cisneros detained the day in the Battle of Oran, where a belt equaled all the arms of the world.

Because his motive is religious conversion rather than territorial gain or eco, nomic rapine, a mere "cordón" can become a hyperbolic synecdoche of "to, das las armas del mundo" in Cisneros' hands.[57] Likewise, Quevedo's praise of the "dichosos atrevimientos" of Pacheco, Alburquerque, and Cortés is ultimately more theological (and nostalgic) than epic. With this said, ab, sent from this orthodox stance is any meaningful trace either of the epistemo, logical wonder or heroic mentality informing and shaping the *relaciones* themselves. The contrast of Quevedo's *laudes* with Cortés's earnest, if still calculating hyperbolism upon first seeing Tenochtitlán is striking:

Porque para dar cuenta, muy poderoso señor, a vuestra real excelencia, de la grandeza, extrañas y maravillosas cosas de esta gran ciudad de Temixtilán [Tenochtitlán] . . . sería menester mucho tiempo, y ser mu, chos relatores y muy expertos; no podré yo decir de cien partes una, de las que de ellas se podrían decir, mas como pudiere diré algunas cosas de las que vi, que aunque mal dichas, bien sé que serán de tanta admiración que no se podrán creer, porque los que acá con nuestros propios ojos las vemos, no las podemos con el entendimiento comprender.[58]

Because to give account, most powerful Sir, to your Excellency, of the greatness, and the strange and marvelous things of this great city of Tenochtitlán . . . much time would be needed, and for there to be many, extremely expert narrators; I will not be able to say one part in a hundred of the things that could be said about them. But as I might be able to tell some of things that I saw, which although badly said, I know well that it will provoke such great admiration that they will not be believed, since those of us here who saw these things with our own eyes, cannot com⁄prehend them with the understanding.

In this wider context, Quevedo's exaggerated poetics of disillusion has not the first nor should have the last word. For in the seventeenth century's waning decades, in the city built atop the ruins of Tenochtitlán, a nun will dream she is the Phaeton of the mind and marvel at her flight and her fall.

Chapter Seven

Exorbitant Desires: Sor Juana's *Sueño*

> Cae sin vértigo
> A través de todos los espacios y todas las edades
> A través de todas las almas de todos los anhelos
> y todos los naufragios
>
> — Vicente Huidobro, *Altazor*

AN "INFELIZ ALTURA"

Well after the Baroque style in Spain had begun to degenerate into contests of slavish imitation among Góngora's epigones, an epyllion penned by a Mexican, Hieronymite nun in 1691 defends poetic "daring" (*atrevimiento*) with inordinate, contradictory energy. A belated poem at the end of an epoch narcissistically aware of its belatedness, Sor Juana Inés de la Cruz's *Primero sueño* at once defies and exploits its historical position.[1] Inheriting the Gongorist stylistic tradition from across the sea, Sor Juana infuses it with remarkable philosophic rigor, scientific precision, and psychological realism. The *silvas* of the *Sueño* map the *chiaroscuro* contours of the poet's insights and aporias as they sometimes blatantly, sometimes subtly, strain the boundaries of linguistic expression. In the course of this mapping, hyperbole — as metaphor, *concepto*, and amplification — becomes the test vehicle for a sustained, metapoetic experiment. Like Descartes, who hits upon his method of hyperbolic doubt closeted in his wintertime *poêle*, Sor Juana in her convent cell (*celda*) carefully explores the rhetorical and epistemological potential of hyperbole as she seeks scientific certainty (*scientia*) and self-knowledge (*sapientia*). But unlike Descartes, she relies on hyperbole to demarcate the cognitive limits of such a search. In this recognition of limits, she also effectively refashions Bacon's metaphorics heralding scientific progress by transforming herself into a mythic, emblematic figure to whom the contingent world of things warns: *Nec plus ultra*.

The *Primero sueño* has been called many things: the first great poem of the Americas, the last great poem of the Spanish Baroque, a Cartesian reverie, a hermetic vision, a Goyan nightmare, and a feminist broadside. José Pascual Buxó interprets Sor Juana's *silva* as an unrivaled synthesis of humanist thought and culture, one that fuses various philosophical traditions, emblematics, and the legacy of Gongorism for aesthetic, subjective, and epistemological ends.[2] Karl Vossler reads it as a "belated and premature" masterpiece marrying Baroque stylistics with Enlightenment rigor even as it synthesizes Greek, Egyptian, and Aztec mythologies.[3] Octavio Paz, in his critical biography of Sor Juana, sees the poem as a testament of "absoluta orginalidad" that prophetically captures the contours of modern(ist) poetic subjectivity: "... it is the revelation of the fact that we are alone and that the world of the supernatural has dissipated. In one way or another, all modern poets have lived, relived, and re-created the double negation of *First Dream*, the silence of space, and the vision of nonvision."[4] Paz looks forward to European high modernism to situate this "double negation" (he compares the *Sueño* to Mallarmé's "Un coup de dés n'abolira le hasard"). For my part, I adopt in this and the next chapter a more formalist approach to read the poem as exemplary of Baroque tensions between epistemology and rhetoric. The manner in which Sor Juana makes herself a lyric *exemplum* of what occurs when the desire for philosophic knowledge runs up against the limits of linguistic expression is above all a textual event requiring a hermeneutic grounded in close readings. A savvy hyperbolist exploring irreconcilable cognitive ambitions and abilities, ostentatiously displaying a mastery of the literary and classical traditions, Sor Juana fills the *Sueño* with copious, but contradictory content. At once empirically rooted, philosophically abstract, and redolent of the riches of Renaissance humanism, this content protects poet and poem from the commonplace critique of *culteranismo* which asserts that behind the bizarre façade of words and ornament of the *culto* poets, there is no *res*, no matter worthy of an epic style. In equivocally enacting, praising, and condemning "insolente exceso" [*insolent excess*], Sor Juana's rhetoric proves acutely self-conscious, especially in regard to the many scientific, hermetic, and neo-Platonic ideas tested in the course of her oneiromantic vision.[5]

Beneath the flanks of the volcanoes the Aztecs named Popocatéptl and

Iztaccíhuatl, the "Smoking Mountain" and the "White Lady," in a Hieronymite convent on the outskirts of colonial Mexico City, Sor Juana composes the *Sueño*. Her only known comments concerning the poem appear in
an epistle, *Respuesta a sor Filotea*, also written in 1691: ". . . nunca he escrito
cosa alguna por mi voluntad, sino por ruegos y preceptos ajenos; de tal manera que no me acuerdo haber escrito por mi gusto sino el papelillo que llaman
El Sueño" [*I have never written anything of my own volition, but rather following the requests and commands of others. So it is that I cannot remember having written anything for
my pleasure except a trifle called* The Dream].[6] If this invites us to read her epic
"papelillo" as the inscription of subjective desires, her contemporaries immediately sought to situate the poem and her poetic *obra* in a more historical context. The engraved frontispiece to her *Fama y obras posthumas* (1700) depicts Sor
Juana both as the culmination of Petrarchism and as the ultimate glory of the
voyages of discovery and conquest. Her portrait, accompanied by the motto
"Gemino petit aethera colle" [*twin peaks court the ether*] occupies the engraving's
center and is surrounded by a circle of laurel perched above two mountains —
one of fire, the other of ice. These presumably are the two volcanoes near her
convent, but they surely also represent that Petrarchan commonplace concerning the lover's *furor* and the beloved's disdain. Flanking Sor Juana are
two columns, the Pillars of Hercules, upon which stand the figures of "Europa" and "America." At the base of one of the columns is inscribed the word
"PLUS," on the other "ULTRA." But lest all this be taken as simply reworking Charles V's emblem, on the top of the columns, forming a kind of
scroll arching across the page, is emblazoned: "Mulierem forte q[u]is inveniet
Procul & de ultimis finib[u]s?" [*Who will discover the courageous woman at the
earth's farthest boundaries?*]. In this way, Sor Juana becomes an unexpected
synecdoche for the Conquest; poetry replaces the sword, a nun eclipses
Cortés, and space is refigured to render her center and circumference of a different sort of agonistic struggle. Thus Lisa Rabin sees Sor Juana as transformed here into the avatar of Mexican Petrarchism whereby her civilizing
influence refines the Spanish lust for glory and gold into nobler desires propagated by the muses.[7] Or as Gordon Braden comments: "Sor Juana's *obra*
gives Renaissance Petrarchism an appropriately liminal case: both poetically
and . . . geographically."[8] To this I would add that the frontispiece with its
enigmatic question also challenges the reader to invent ("q[u]is inveniet . . .")
Sor Juana, to apply that supreme faculty of *ingenio* to the interpretation of her

verse and subjectivity. For as Gracián insists, to discover and understand a poet's *agudeza* demands nearly as much *ingenio* and invention as it does to pro-duce it. It also demands a great deal of erudition. The phrase, for example, linking the two mountains, "Gemino petit aethera colle," is borrowed from Lucan's *De bello civili* (5.72) where it describes the twin-peaks of Parnassus, which form part of Thessaly's hyperbolic topography where the ideals of the Roman republic will perish in civil war. Thus even as it belongs to the com-monplace, paratextual rhetoric and imagery used to frame (and sell) a poet's work, it emblemizes Sor Juana's poetic and cosmographical striving, striving cast in terms borrowed from literary tradition but now infused with novel cul-tural and conceptual force.[9]

At the end of chapter four, I briefly discussed one of Sor Juana's occa-sional poems, a panegyric to the Marquesa de la Laguna, María Luisa de Gonzaga. Given the precarious circumstances in which Sor Juana attended to her muse — largely in defiance of ecclesiastical authorities, but with the enthusiastic albeit contingent support of the viceroy and his wife — such epideixis may be read as expressing real gratitude rather than as merely an exercise in flattery. Since nearly half of her *obra* consists of occasional verse, the poetry of praise inevitably serves a principal field of invention. While her occasional verse has all the typically mannered traits that the epoch demanded, González Boixo notes: "Sor Juana customarily adds personal references, cre-ating a tone of familiarity which serves as a counterpoint to the unmeasured panegyrics that she lavishes on her subjects."[10]

Supplementing such contrapuntality, her various epideictic discourses frequently attempt to express rather abstract if not hermetic intuitions and ideas. Exemplary of this balancing act is *Neptuno alegórico* (1680), a complex treatise written to accompany the triumphal arch she designed to welcome the new viceroy to Mexico. Here the *virrey* is cast as an "allegorical Neptune" who through a series of visual "hieroglyphs" is transformed into Isis, the Egyptian virgin-goddess. Interpreting Sor Juana's labyrinthine, etymological conceits, Paz argues that ultimately they figure the author herself as Isis, "knowledge," and the "universal mother."[11] Magnificent *bricolages* of Baroque rhetorical and visual artifice, the arch and accompanying treatise constitute a public profession of her peculiar mixture of mannerist poetics and hermetic learning. More to the point, at the outset of the treatise, Sor Juana visits the in-expressibility *topos* to explain the didactic and spiritual need for symbolic *enargeia.* After quoting from Piero Valeriano's *Hierogliphica, sive de sacris Aegyp-tiorum* (1556), which relates how the Egyptians use the circle and the hiero-glyphic "Eneph" to represent God, she comments on their motives:

> No porque juzgasen que la deidad siendo infinita pudiera estrecharse a la figura y término de cuantidad limitada, sino porque, como eran cosas que carecían de toda forma visible y por consiguiente imposibles de mostrarse a los ojos de los hombres . . . fue necesario buscarles hiero-glíficos que por similitud, ya que no por perfecta imagen, las represen-tasen. Y esto hicieron no sólo con las deidades, pero con todas las cosas invisibles, cuales eran los días, meses y semanas, etc. Y también con las de quienes era la copia difícil o no muy agradable, como la de los elemen-tos, entendiendo por Vulcano, el fuego; por Juno, el aire . . . Hiciéronlo no sólo por atraer a los hombres al culto divino con más agradables atractivos, sino también por reverencia de las deidades, por no vulgarizar sus misterios a la gente común e ignorante.[12]

> Not because they judged that the divinity, being infinite, could be con-tained in the figure and expression of a limited quantity, but because, as they were things that lacked all visible form and consequently impossible to be shown to human eyes . . . it was necessary to find them hiero-glyphs, which by similitude, and not by a perfect image, could represent them. And this they did not only with the deities, but with all invisible things, which were the days, months, weeks, etc. They also did so with things whose *copia* was difficult or not very pleasant, such as that of the elements; understanding thereby Vulcan for fire, or Juno for air . . . They did this not only to attract men to divine worship with pleasant in-ducements, but also in reverence for the deities and so not to vulgarize their mysteries for the common and ignorant people.

In this manner, the urgent need for a rhetoric that can explain and obscure "cosas invisibles" is heralded, even as possible motives for the copious use of hyperbole in the *Sueño* begin to be discerned. Confirming Sor Juana's debts to the Neo-Platonic, hermetic tradition, this passage also points to the Augus-tinian doctrine of promoting difficulty and obscurity for spiritual reasons. The "copia difícil o no muy agradable" is the *copia* of the mutable world that the poet must translate with the help of figures and hieroglyphs into copious, ele-gant language.

To better navigate Sor Juana's hermetic rhetoric, the repressive if eclectic intellectual atmosphere in colonial Mexico should also be recalled. Paz notes that this elaborately artificial culture was held together by all the bonds of or/ thodoxy, an orthodoxy that prompted the aspiring poet to take the habit at the age of sixteen in order to perserve a modicum of intellectual freedom. Yet Sor Juana was clearly conversant with realities beyond the convent. Not only was the Hieronymite regimen relatively lax, but as her considerable output of neo-Petrarchan lyrics attests, she spent three years attending and observing the Mexican court. Her numerous *villancicos* and *romances* with their idiomatic diction and quotidian subject matter also indicate that she was no stranger to the lives of the lower classes.[13] That several *villancicos* were composed fully or partially in Nahuatl also confirms her familiarity with Mexico's indigenous culture.[14]

Generally speaking, however, her intellectual formation and culture were rather bookish: "... proseguí, digo, a la estudiosa tarea ... de leer y más leer, de estudiar y más estudiar, sin más maestro que los mismos libros" [*I continued, I say, with my scholarly task ... to read and to read more, to study and to study more, with-out any teacher but the books themselves*].[15] Given her inability to obtain a formal education, these books (that literally frame her in each of her six, surviving portraits) provided the primary intellectual and stylistic bases for her idiosyn-cratic reworking of Gongorism.[16] As Abréu Gómez details, she possessed a formidable library by any standards in colonial Mexico. Dominated by Greek and Latin literature and philosophy, with a particularly strong emphasis on silver Latin poetry, it also contained numerous volumes of scholastic and Neo-Platonic philosophy, a great deal of contemporary religious and secu-lar Spanish prose and poetry, as well as a smattering of contemporary, non-Hispanic works, including, Abreu Gómez surmises, Descartes and Tesauro.

One person with whom Sor Juana would probably have discussed such books was the polymath, Carlos Sigüenza y Góngora. A distant relative of the Cordoban poet, Sigüenza y Góngora was, if not a friend, then certainly Sor Juana's close intellectual peer. He read deeply in all the hermetic sciences, undertook various astronomical, ethnographic, and historiographic investi-gations, as well as writing what is considered to be the first Mexican novel. And while his *Libra astronómica y filosófica* (1690) adopts a strong empirical, materialist approach, many of his texts rely on the kind of hermetic and highly allusive rhetoric we glimpsed in Sor Juana's *Neptuno alégorico*.[17] Briefly put, Sigüenza's views on theology, colonialism, and indigenous culture were far more unorthodox than anything surviving from Sor Juana's pen. Like Sor Juana he was invited to design a triumphal arch for the new viceroy's arrival in 1680, but his accompanying treatise strikingly depicts Huitzilpochtli, the Aztecs' sanguinary warrior god, as a model for the new governors to imi-tate. Thus although Paz regards Sor Juana and Sigüenza as "doubly isolated from the world by orthodoxy and geographical distance," both writers find novel ways to defy their isolation.[18] And both respond sympathetically to the European Baroque aesthetic. As Marie-Cécile Bénassy-Berling writes of late seventeenth-century Mexican culture: ". . . l'on est plus Gongoriste que Gón-gora, plus baroque que l'Europe."[19]

One is also more Kircherian than in Europe. The *Neptuno alegórico* takes its chief inspiration from Athanasius Kircher's *Oedipus aegyptiacus* (1654), a nearly two thousand-page, encyclopedic study in which the German Jesuit traces central aspects of Greek, Roman, and Hebrew thought and culture (as well as aspects of Chinese, South Asian, Mesoamerican, and other non-European civilizations) back to ancient Egyptian origins and hieroglyphs in order to find *prisca sapientia* and thus the means of creating unity out of multi-plicity.[20] Such a project and the copious erudition supporting it — the book's paratexts include dedicatory poems in twenty-seven languages including Greek and Latin, most of the European vernaculars, as well as Hebrew, Arabic, Ethiopean, Chinese, Coptic, and of course Kircher's inventive (if utterly mistaken) version of Egytpian hieroglyphics — clearly appealed to Sor Juana's own hermetic and syncretic tendencies. More to the point, Kircher also proves to be a decisive influence on the *Sueño*. Vossler, Paz, and others detail how his voluminous writings provided her with convincing ac-counts of astronomy, human physiology, optics, magnetism, as well as more recondite subjects such as Egyptian mythology.[21] Alternately, his *Iter exsta-ticum coeleste* (1671) furnished an important formal and thematic model for the *Sueño*.[22] In this elaborate dream-allegory describing a cosmic flight, Teodi-dacto (a thinly veiled stand-in for Kircher) is at first overwhelmed by the heav-enly spheres' incomparable harmonies, but then God's minister, Cosmiel, appears as a guide to instruct him in celestial mechanics. Leaning on Tycho Brahe's cosmology (which is largely adopted in the *Sueño* as well), Cosmiel then adumbrates various mystical truths. Yet notwithstanding these important similarities with the *Sueño*, I would caution that while Kircher's dream ends on an ecstatic note, Sor Juana never achieves *exstasis* in her epyllion. In brief, one must not ascribe to the *Sueño* the same degree of mystic enthusiasm that fills the pages of the *Iter exstaticum*. To anticipate my argument below, unlike Kircher's protagonist Sor Juana's poetic persona is content to be without any-one to guide her past epistemological and spiritual obstacles. Her journey, even as it extravagantly plays upon numerous literary, mythic, and hermetic precedents, remains essentially a solitary one. Conversely, that it ends with her awake, *desengañada* in dawn's sober light, endows her exorbitant rhetoric with enormous *ethos*. Even at her most hyperbolic, Sor Juana never permits the es-sential, if sometimes highly tenuous link between *res et verba* to be eclipsed, de-spite her palpable yearning for transcendence.

Such reluctance becomes more understandable in the light of her *Res-puesta*, her most sustained effort at self-fashioning. This epistle passionately but rigorously describes the compulsive nature of Sor Juana's muse in the course of eloquently defending her right as a woman to pursue intellectual matters. It recounts first how she has avoided divine subjects in her writing from a "sobra de temor y reverencia debida a aquellas Sagradas Letras, para cuya inteligencia yo me conozco tan incapaz y para cuyo manejo soy tan in-digna" [*excess of fear and reverence due to those Sacred Letters, by whose spiritual sub-stance I know myself so incapable and for the mastery of which I am so unworthy*]. The strategic quality of such hyperbole vanishes, however, when she plainly as-cribes her "grandísimo amor a la verdad" [*enormous love of the truth*] to a "nat-ural impulso que Dios puso en mí" [*the natural impulse God placed in me*]. Since this love is divinely sanctioned, she should not be blamed for her *atrevimiento* of wanting to be educated as a little girl, or for becoming a nun to secure "la libertad de mi estudio" [*the freedom to study*] and "el sosegado silencio de mis li-bros" [*the calm silence of my books*]. Such study must be diverse and exhaustive, if she is "subir por las escalones de las ciencias y artes humanas" [*to climb by the rungs of the liberal sciences and arts*]. Celebrating the "cadena universal" [*univer-sal chain*] linking all forms of knowledge, she then cites Kircher's *De magnete* to adduce this geometric-hermetic truth: "Todas las cosas salen de Dios, que es el centro a un tiempo y la circunferencia de donde salen y donde paran todas las líneas criadas" [*All things proceed from God, who is at once the center and the cir-cumference from where all created lines emerge and end*]. In rehearsing this venerable, hermetic hyperbole, Sor Juana confirms that geometry is not merely a source of poetic ornament; instead, it is innate to her way of seeing the world. In-deed, in one of the letter's most striking moments, she tells how once when watching children playing with a top, she was so struck, "con esta mi locura" [*with this mania I have*], by the question of whether its movements described perfect circles, that she tried to devise an experiment to test her hypothesis.[23] (The *Sueño*, I shall argue below, is also a kind of thought experiment.)

But for all its moments of detached introspection, the *Respuesta* also paints a dramatic picture of an agonized soul. Reacting to those who attack her for daring as a woman to write and publish, she ironically declares: "Rara especie de martirio donde yo era el mártir y me era el verdugo!" [*Strange kind of martyrdom in which I am the martyr and my own executioner!*].[24] Insisting that any talented individual will always be despised, she boldly compares her predicament to Christ's. Then she turns to another allegory to figure her plight:

> Suelen en la eminencia de los templos colocarse por adorno unas figuras de los Vientos y de la Fama, y por defenderlas de las aves, las llenan todas de púas; defensa parece y no es sino propiedad forzosa: no puede estar sin púas que la puncen quien está en alto. Allí está la ojeriza del aire; allí es el rigor de los elementos; allí despican la cólera los rayos; allí es el blanco de piedras y flechas. ¡Oh infeliz altura, expuesta a tantos riesgos! ¡Oh signo que te ponen por blanco de la envidia y por objeto de la contradicción! Cualquiera eminencia, ya sea de dignidad, ya de nobleza, ya de riqueza, ya de hermosura, ya de ciencia, padece esta pensión; pero la que con más rigor la experimenta es la del entendimiento.[25]

> On the highest point of temples typically some figures of the Winds and of Fame are placed as ornaments; and to protect them from birds, they are all covered with barbs. This seems like a defense, but it is rather a necessary property: whoever is up high cannot but feel barbs that puncture her: up there is the air's resentment, and the rigors of the elements; up there lightning bolts hate; there is the target for rocks and arrows. Oh, unhappy height, exposed to so many risks! Oh sign that they make you a target of envy and an object of contradiction! Whatever eminence, be it in dignity, nobility, wealth, beauty, or knowledge, suffers this pain; but what experiences it with more severity is the eminence of the understanding.

This image of Sor Juana as an "infeliz altura," as a gargoylelike figure willing to become an "objeto de la contradicción" for the sake of knowledge, neatly emblemizes the most subjective desires fueling the *Sueño*.[26] Never without her "barbs," Sor Juana is willing to weather "tantos riesgos" to experience "la eminencia" that, above all, the "entendimiento" affords. Pointedly playing with the notions of ornamentation and signification ("¡Oh signo que te ponen por blanco . . ."), she sets herself here atop "los templos," as if she were a cere⁄monial sacrifice, to suffer the rigors of an idea.

IMPOSSIBLE MEASURES

In the barest of terms, the *Sueño* argues that the understanding (*entendimiento*) cannot match the power and scope of the imagination (*fantasía*). The under⁄standing fails literally and figuratively to follow the imagination's trajectory. In this sense, the imagination would trace a hyperbolic arc, while the under⁄standing, like a rocket defeated by gravity, must follow a parabolic one. But again, that Sor Juana exemplifies this parabolic course by depicting her own understanding and imagination tempers her theme's more abstract aspects with enormous pathos. In formal terms, the poem triumphantly succeeds in dressing philosophic and scientific ideas in elaborate lyric garb. Yet rather than being a panegyric to that ancient dream of attaining divine knowledge, or becoming what Bacon dubs a "progress," the *Sueño* offers a kind of *Traumdeutung* of the limits of Renaissance philosophy. Ingeniously portraying the understanding's attempts, with its faculties of intuition and deduction, to reach the desired epistemological heights, the exorbitant if equivocal language of her dream doggedly strains credulity as she struggles to win knowledge of God, wrest knowledge from the world, and, ultimately, to heed the Socratic command to know the self.

At the same time, the *Sueño* audaciously puts Góngora's *culto* tools of hyperbaton and hyperbole to heuristic uses.[27] In navigating the poem's laby⁄rinthine syntax, the reader may well decide that hyperbaton is its most dra⁄matic figure, yet its hyperboles, with their rich, daring intertextual gestures, their insistent but increasingly ineffable dialectic of quantity and quality, and their enormous conceptual demands on the understanding, prove to be its most elusive objects of interpretation. Like Donne in the *Anniversaries*, Sor Juana uses hyperbole to reach new metaphysical heights and, like Pascal in the *Pensées*, she employs it as if it were a bathysphere to plunge her to barely imag⁄inable depths. But if I, too, abuse here the metaphorics of ascent and descent in describing her hyperbolism, then the poem's metaphorics leaves one little choice. Gaston Bachelard writes in *Air and Dreams*: ". . . of all metaphors, metaphors of height, elevation, depth, sinking and the fall are the axiomatic

metaphors par excellence. Nothing explains them, and they explain everything."[28] Bachelard's phenomenological, psychological approach to the poetics
of verticality provides a particularly apt conceptual framework in which to
view Sor Juana's poem:

> Going beyond thought is the very law of poetic expression. Of course,
> this transcendence often appears to be crude, artificial or flawed. Some-
> times, it happens too quickly and becomes illusory, impermanent, and
> diffused . . . Poets, then, can be classified by their response to the ques-
> tion: 'Tell me which infinity attracts you, and I will know the mean-
> ing of your world . . .' Language, conditioned by forms, is not readily
> capable of making dynamic images of height picturesque. Nevertheless,
> these images have amazing power: they govern the dialectic of enthusi-
> asm and anguish. Vertical valorization is so essential, so sure — its su-
> periority is so indisputable — that the mind cannot turn away from it
> once it has recognized its immediate and direct meaning. It is impossible
> to express moral values without reference to the vertical axis. When we
> better understand the importance of a physics of poetry and a physics of
> ethics, then we will be closer to the conviction that every valorization is
> a verticalization.[29]

As strong an argument as any against tying the poetics of hyperbole to the creation of *enargeia*, here Bachelard also underscores why such extreme vertical
metaphors may be catachrestic expressions of both subjective truths and ethical values. Or as Hans Blumenberg affirms, certain metaphors — he calls
them "absolute metaphors" — can neither be paraphrased nor reduced to logical formulations even though they serve essential philosophic and heuristic
functions.[30] Sor Juana's famous "mental pirámide," we shall see, functions
as an absolute metaphor in that it belongs to a rich, complicated history of
metaphors expressing degrees of enlightenment in terms of height. Yet such
metaphors still manage to defy paraphrase or the stringencies of logic. To this
I would add that her constant amplification of such metaphors verges, in both
senses of the word, on catachresis. On the one hand, her play of high and low
is so dependent upon her Gongorist diction and imagery that words like "despeñada" [*precipitously fallen*] or "altiva" [*haughty*] are at once dead metaphors
and signs to be reanimated in the topography of her soul's infinite striving.[31]

They function, as Gracián puts it, as the rhetorical "fundamento," the linguistic foundations, upon which her most pointed poetic conceits are built.
On the other hand, her exaggerated metaphorics of ascent and descent is often catachrestic in that catachresis is synonymous with a far-fetched metaphor,
with metaphor that uses and abuses the reader's credulity at decorum's expense but for the sake of winning new imaginative heights.[32]

As Nietzsche in "Truth and Lies in an Extra-Moral Sense" and later
Derrida in "White Mythology" have shown, the limits and aporias inherent
in any theory of metaphor are partially due to the manner in which all
metaphor is catachrestic. The critic examining Sor Juana's use of hyperbole
might thus naturally choose the more direct road of analyzing the poem's exaggerated metaphorics by pursuing a *Begriffsgeschichte* in the manner of
Georgina Sabat de Rivers who eruditely traces how the topical tradition informs invention in the *Sueño*. Such an approach would emphasize the diachronic aspects of her hyperboles. Yet if one wishes to interrogate their
synchronic or heuristic value, it is important to recognize at the outset, as Derrida argues in his reading of metaphor as a philosopheme, the limits or even
the "condition d'impossibilité" of such a project. A metapoetical analysis, in
other words, is unable to do without metaphor or reduce its subject matter to
the bare exigencies of logical representation: ". . . une métaphore, au moins,
resterait toujours exclue, hors du système: celle au moins, sans laquelle ne se
serait pas construit le concept de métaphore ou, pour syncoper toute une
chaîne, la métaphore du métaphore."[33] When one considers the spatial
metaphors already lurking in the words "metaphor" and "hyperbole," and if
Dumarsais' notion, a notion championed by Derrida, that catachresis is the
essential force driving language itself is accepted, it becomes evident that any
attempt to say what might be the philosophical value of a text's hyperbolic
metaphors will inevitably become an investigation into our inability to think
without confusing the literal and figurative. It will become an inquiry into
language's paucity and, in particular, poetry's struggle to give voice to the most
abstract ideas. As Lucretius observes in *De rerum natura*, the poet often faces a
double bind, "egestatem linguae et rerum novitatem" [*the poverty of language
and novelty of things*] (1.139), when doing natural philosophy. Faced with an
analogous dilemma as she seeks to express her scientific ideas and oneiric vision, Sor Juana self-consciously measures the limits of thought and signification with catachrestic hyperbole. In doing so, she maps out the different

realms native to the "fantasía" and reason, and shows, or rather enacts, how the former is sometimes inaccessible to the latter's demands. In this sense, Sabat de Rivers's study of the *Sueño* remains exemplary, for it demonstrates that any formal analysis of the poem's hyperboles must be supplemented by an historical inquiry into their origins.

Such supplementarity is integral to late Renaissance poetics as well. Not only does poetic *imitatio* dictate that *copia* beget yet more *copia*, but the genre of the poetic commentary, which in Spain begins in earnest with Herrera's treatment of Garcilaso, requires that poetic *copia* be met with critical *copia*. Still, Herrera's *Anotaciones* also illustrate how difficult it is to distinguish between the imitation native to creative and critical literature. Herrera's own sonnets (some of which he interpolates into the *Anotaciones*) rethink Garcilaso's just as Góngora's *Soledades* comment on Garcilaso's *Églogas*. And if the *Anotaciones* seem to transform Garcilaso into a kind of Plinian encyclopedist, Sor Juana's *Sueño*, coming after the commentaries of Salcedo Coronel and Pellicer, has the effect of crystallizing Gongorist *copia* into its most rigorous, philosophically luminous form. With the *Polifemo* and *Soledades* as her diachronic models, Sor Juana uses her epyllion to reopen the questions concerning meaning and interpretation that I raised earlier reading Góngora and his critics. Analogously, her first important commentator, Pedro Álvarez de Lugo Usodemar, in his *Ilustración al Sueño* (1705), consciously mimics Sor Juana's audacity as he lavishly glosses her verse.[34] After unabashedly comparing himself to Argos for his keen powers of observation, he boasts:

> Tenerme yo la osadía de haber sido riesgo pesado, y que puede infamarme de ligero . . . Pero en el seguro riesgo de tropezar en tan oscura noche tengo también el seguro de las glorias de osado, por más que quede vencido. Que es también vanidad el atreverse alguno a lo más dificultoso, y gloria de la caída el ser muy digno de gloria el esfuerzo del héroe que consiguió el triunfo del que le arrostró atrevido.[35]

> I have the daring to have taken a heavy risk, and one that can easily cause me infamy . . . But given the certain risk of stumbling in such an obscure night I have also the surety of the glories belonging to the audacious, even more so if I remain defeated. For it is also vanity for someone to have dared the most difficult thing, and it is the glory of the fall very worthy of the glory of the hero's effort that achieves triumph over what is boldly confronted.

Echoing Herrera's "el osado español," Álvarez de Lugo remakes the *armas y letras* theme by fancying himself a hermeneutic "héroe" for having dared tackle Sor Juana's difficulty. For critical "gloria," as the legion of commenta-tors on Góngora also prove, lies not only in the difficulty of the object of crit-icism, but also in the critic's ability to create fame or infamy, like an aura, around the critical object. Just as poetic glory in the Renaissance resides more in outbidding predecessors than inventing *ab ovo* subject matter or themes, the commentator's "osadía" is more supplemental than original.

DREAMING WITHOUT A NET

Sabat de Rivers usefully divides the *Sueño* into three sections: *The Prologue: Night and Dream of the Cosmos*, *The Intellectual Dream of Man*, and *The Epi-logue: Triumph of the Day*.[36] Two stages comprise in turn the dream proper: the poet's efforts to use "neo-Platonic intuition" (151-485) and "neo-Aristotelian ratiocination" (486–886) to perfect her knowledge. My main focus will be on these central, epistemological sections, though I shall also consider the framing sections since their imagery and metaphors, which eventually reach hyperbolic proportions at the poem's two central apexes, begin and end in its margins.

The *Sueño* commences with an ominous image worthy of di Chirico:

> Piramidal, funesta, de la tierra
> nacida sombra, al cielo encaminaba
> de vanos obeliscos punta altiva,
> escalar pretendiendo las estrellas . . . (1–4)

A pyramidal, funereal shadow, born from the earth, aimed toward Heaven the haughty tops of vain obelisks striving to scale the stars . . .

Outbidding line 13 of the *Soledad segunda* where the pilgrim's itinerary is traced ("escalar pretendiendo el monte en vano . . ."), these lines adumbrate death's shadow and the folly of human artifice, which would usurp, as did the Giants and Titans, the terrestrial boundaries set for them. This is to say that Sor Juana's metaphorics of ascent, her "alpinismo," is at once more ambitious and more gnostic than her model's.[37] It is also more precise. Stressing the ex-traordinary physical aspects of this "sombra," Antonio Alatorre notes that it is made from obelisks which, given their shape, must be enormously wide at the base to be so elongated at the top.[38] For his part, Álvarez de Lugo glosses these lines first by insisting on an etymology that has the Greek *pyr* or "fire" as the root of "pyramidal"; he also cites Isidore of Seville (*Etymologiae*, 3.12.6), who notes that the pyramid and flame have a similar shape.[39] Hoping then to lend the lines verisimilitude, he tries a physical justification for the skyscraping shadow. Citing Titelmanus' *De Coelo et mundo* where the Flemish savant argues that the height of the earth's mountains disfigures the planet's round shape, he extends this idea to the shadow's "punta altiva" that would scale the stars. After this pseudo-scientific note he takes a more familiar tack: "Dar acciones de vivientes a lo que carece de alma es tropo elevado, es acumen de alma mucha entre retóricos grandes, como se la da Virgilio, y el poeta Papinio, al río Araxes" [*To ascribe actions of living beings to that which lacks a soul is an elevated trope; it is a mark of wit and much spirit amongst great rhetoricians, such as Virgil and Statius, who ascribe life to the Araxes river*].[40] In other words, as the subsequent examples taken from the *Aeneid* and Statius' *Silvae* confirm, the poem's decorum must be judged in terms of the grand style with its ample metaphoric license. Leaning then on Cipriano Suárez and Francisco de Castro as his authorities, Álvarez de Lugo celebrates Sor Juana's opening "hipérbole" and the manner "finge atreverse la sombra de la noche a escalar las estrellas" [*the nocturnal shadow feigns daring to scale the stars*]. Yet in the same breath, he also warns his readers: "No se pone falta a los hipérboles la sobra de exceso, sí la disproporción" [*hyperboles must not be faulted for too much excess, but rather for disproportion*]. To illustrate such disproportion, he offers an outlandishly recondite analysis of Góngora's hyperboles (lines 409–416) describing Polifemo's size. Repeating the Horatian commonplace — *Aliquando bonus dormitat Homerus* — he blames Góngora for effectively giving the cyclops a height of "cinco mil millas" [*five thousand* (Roman) *miles*]. Hyperbole, he insists, using as his measure Clavius's famous calculation of the number of sand granules (10^{63}) that it would take to fill up the space between the earth and the firmament, must be more scientific than this.[41] It must, like those in Juvenal's satires, have "modo" [*measure*]. Unfortunately, despite his admirable willingness to reconcile literary and scientific discourses via the figure of hyperbole, Álvarez de Lugo never meditates upon the absurdity of such a number in this context. Nor does he ask what hyperbole's decorum should be when poets wish to thematize the very impossibility of measure itself.

At the beginning of the poem, nature establishes an Epicurean "imperio silencioso" [*silent empire*] (20) in which even the atoms in the wind do not move (80–82).[42] The scene is set in the absolutist of terms:

> El sueño todo, en fin, lo poseía;
> todo, en fin, el silencio lo ocupaba:
> aun el ladrón dormía;
> aun el amante no se desvelaba. (147–150)

Sleep, in the end, possessed everything; silence, in the end, controlled everything; even the thief slept; even the lover did not lie awake.

Here Sor Juana adopts an *ethos* of absolute authority — the repetition of "todo" and "aun" leave no room for equivocation.[43] From out of this static back‑ground, however, emerges a parade of Ovidian creatures and myths prefigur‑ing the dreamer's own unrest, unbridled *deseo*, and eventual metamorphoses: Nictimene, the three daughters of Minyas ("aquellas . . . atrevidas hermanas" [*those . . . audacious sisters*]), Alcione, and Actaeon. Meanwhile, the empirical details of her portrait of somnolent nature begin to wrestle with the poetics of Góngora's potent pastoral legacy. Birds are "nocturnas aves, tan obscuras, tan graves" [*nocturnal birds, so dark, so solemn*] (22–23), the mountains are "cóncavos de peñascos mal formados" [*ill‑formed, rocky concaves*], and the vigilant eagle who holds a pebble in its claw so that it will drop and awaken it if it falls asleep is "cuidadosa / de no incurrir de omisa en el exceso" [*careful not to indulge by omis‑sion in the excess* (of rest)] (132–133).[44] Thus at least part of nature — the best part, since the eagle is identified with Jupiter — strives to avoid the grave fault of "exceso" to which those mythological figures already mentioned are prey. The extended description of a sleeping body (151–291) that follows generates a bevy of analogies for the parts of the body, though Sor Juana also betrays a marked cautiousness as she fuses mythic allusions and scientific exactitude:

> está, pues, si no fragua de Vulcano,
> templada hoguera del calor humano . . . (252–253)[45]

the stomach, then, if not Vulcan's forge, mild bonfire of human heat . . .

A retooling of the Gongorist *si . . . no* formula, such hyperbole by *omissio* or preterition injects an element of skepticism into the comparison, even while the mention of Vulcan lends it a certain epic grandeur.

The *Sueño*'s ambivalent narrative of ascent resumes as the stomach, trying to moderate "los atemporados cuatro humores" [*the four tempered humors*], feeds the "fantasía" [*imagination*]. And in shifting its attention from the vegetative faculty to the higher faculty of sense, the poem's rhetoric appropriately becomes more elevated. This double shift takes its most elaborate form in the justly celebrated comparison of the *fantasia* with one of antiquity's Seven Wonders, the mirror of the Lighthouse of Alexandria, which allowed observers to see ships before they crested the horizon. As a mediator between the multiplicity of sensation and the desired singularity of thought, the imagination is figured by means of an extended analogy whereby the silver-coated "moon" of the lighthouse's convex mirror reflects the chaos of the sea into an immaterial order:

> y del modo
> que en tersa superficie, que de faro
> cristalino portento, asilo raro
> fue, en distancia longísima se vían
> (sin que ésta le estorbase)
> del reino casi de Neptuno todo
> las que distantes lo surcaban naves
> — viéndose claramente
> en su azogada luna
> el número, el tamaño y la fortuna
> que en la instable campaña transparente
> arresgadas tenían,
> mientras aguas y vientos dividían
> sus velas leves y sus quillas graves —:
> así ella, sosegada, iba copiando
> las imágenes todas de las cosas,
> y el pincel invisible iba formando
> de mentales, sin luz, siempre vistosas
> colores, las figuras
> no sólo ya de todas las criaturas
> sublunares, mas aun también de aquellas
> que intelectuales claras son estrellas,
> y en el modo posible
> que concebirse puede lo invisible,

> en sí, mañosa, las representaba
> y al alma las mostraba.[46] (266–291)

in the manner that on the smooth surface — crystal marvel and extraordinary protection of Pharos Island — remote ships, which plowed
almost Neptune's entire realm, were seen from the furthest distance,
without this being an obstacle; and the number, size and fortune, which
these bold ships have, were clearly visible in the quicksilver moon, while
their light sails and heavy keels divided the winds and the waves; so the
imagination calmly was copying all the images of things, and the invisible paintbrush was fashioning figures — in mental colors having no
light, but always beautiful — not only of all sublunary creatures, but
also of those that are clear, intellectual stars; and in the manner that it
was possible to conceive of the invisible, it skillfully represented these
things in itself, and showed them to the soul.

The dynamic *enargeia* of this extended simile depends in part on the fact that
it metapoetically describes the image-making faculty itself, the imagination's
"pincel invisible." More than merely ornamenting an idea, the period's first
fourteen, supremely difficult lines are, like the imagination itself, deeply heuristic. The extravagant ("todas de las cosas") but exacting ("no sólo ya") comparison between an ancient, architectural-mechanical wonder and a solitary,
late seventeenth-century mind exploring its limits advances as well as amplifies
the poem's *dianoia*. Pointing to "lo invisible" and "las intellectuales claras . . .
estrellas," the simile figures the limits of sight ("distancia longísima") and
physical space by portentously invoking the specter and spectacle of a shipwreck. In this way, Sor Juana further subjectivizes this *topos* by transforming
Góngora and Quevedo's ethical qualms into what is, at least at this point
in the poem, a purely specular, philosophical dilemma. In the name of intellectual desire, the sea and it ships become allegorical actors in her cognitive
drama. If because of the lighthouse's mirror "el numero, el tamaño y la fortuna / que en la instable compaña transparente / arresgadas tenían . . ." were
clearly seen, this did nothing to cure the folly of navigation itself. In other
words, imagination without action is suspect, even though, like Gracián's *ingenio*, Sor Juana's imagination is "mañosa" and exhaustive.[47] As the mind's
faculty where carnal and spiritual desires roam the most freely, the imagination has no pre-ordained, ethical constraints. As she observes in the *Respuesta*:

". . . ni aun el sueño se libró de esto continuo movimiento de mi imaginativa; antes suele obrar en él más libre y desembarazada, y confirmiendo con mayor claridad y sosiego las especies que ha conservado del día, arguyendo, haciendo versos . . ." [*not even sleep is free from this continual movement of my imagination; indeed, in sleep it is accustomed to work more freely and unconstrainedly, and confirming with greater clarity and calm the images and events that remain from the day, deliberating and making verses out of them*].[48]

Optimally, the poetic imagination discovers the nature of things on behalf of its ambitious "alma." At line 293, the imagination enables the poet to grasp for the first time something of the Platonic forms ("esencia bella") or universals. Through the imagination the soul judges itself to be a "similitud" of the "alto ser" (295–296). And for a time, thanks to the venerable Renaissance idea of the Chain of Being,[49] the immensity of the soul's ambition seems to correspond to cosmic dimensions:

> y juzgándose casi dividida
> de aquella que impedida
> siempre la tiene, corporal cadena,
> que grosera embaraza y torpe impide
> el vuelo intelectual con que ya mide
> la cuantidad inmensa de la esfera . . . (297–302)

and judging itself, moreover, almost unlinked from that corporeal chain, which always frustrates it, and which heavily hampers and sluggishly impedes the intellectual flight by which it measures now the immense quantity of the firmament's sphere . . .

Ingeniously incorporating various elements of Renaissance Neo-Platonism, these lines are also rightly read by Mari-Cécile Bénassy-Berling as being rigorously "épistémologique."[50] Specifically, their rigor hinges on two key notions — both more metaphoric than logical — that will determine the precision of many of the poem's subsequent hyperboles: the conceit of flight and the idea of measure.

As we saw earlier, Gracián compares the ability to perceive similitudes, especially between mortal and divine objects, to a flight of ascent. Remaking an allegorical tradition that runs unbroken from Plato's *Phaedrus*, Dante's *Paradiso*, Pico's *Oration*, the lyric flights of San Juan de la Cruz, and Kircher's *Iter exstaticum coeleste*, Sor Juana methodically conflates the imagery of height

and flight with the notion of intuition. While Gracián renovates this commonplace at the beginning of his *Agudeza* to introduce his theory of wit, Sor
Juana complicates, hyperbolizes, and abstracts it to the point of paradox and
aporia.[51] Motion through space, especially upward and downward, is never
without conceptual turbulences in the *Sueño*. In the process of celebrating the
soul's ability to participate in the "alto ser" (295) and to gain an "altivo eminencia" (322), Sor Juana struggles to gauge the attempts of "el vuelo intelectual" to separate itself from the body and so measure the celestial sphere from
the predictions of astrology, an "estudio vanamente judicioso" [*a fruitlessly discerning study*] (308), but one that likewise pretends to know celestial things.

Close attention to the poem's diction also shows how fundamental the
idea of measure is to its greatest conceptual ambiguities. Developed partially
through paronomasia or what Gracían would call *agudeza verbal* (in contrast to
agudeza de concepto) and akin to what Curtius dubs "etymology as a category of
thought," the act of measurement for Sor Juana has cardinal importance.[52] In
brief, a "vuelo intelectual" that "mide / la cuantidad inmensa de la esfera" is
an etymological conceit as well as a conceptual paradox. For while the word
"inmensa" comes of course from the Latin *immensa*, *mensa* is a past participle
of *metior*, which means "to measure" and is the root of the Spanish verb *medir*.
Along with an impossible case of measuring an infinite "cuantidad," then,
Sor Juana adduces here an instance of language fighting against itself. Her
"intellectual flight" tries to glimpse not just "mentales . . . colores" but also
measure a "mental pirámide elevada" (424). Her mind, *mens*, seeks correspondences with the *immensa* universe, but *mens*, as she certainly knew, has no semantic kinship with *metior*. Indeed, the subsequent frequency of words in the
poem that in one way or another play upon the idea of measure confirm how
crucial the semantic play with this disjunction is to its poetic logic. Just as the
pyramidal shadow in the poem's first lines inevitably becomes a flame, the
pyramides dominating the poem's center are transformed into pyrrhic measures.
To borrow Frederick Ahl's phrase from his etymological and paronomastic
readings of Roman poetry, verbal "metaformations" riddle the *Sueño*.[53]

The metaphorics of ascent grow more extreme when, in the face of the
soul's audacious ascendancy, another extended simile mines hyperbole's conceptual riches:

> puesta, a su parecer, en la eminente
> cumbre de un monte a quien el mismo Atlante

> que preside gigante
> a los demás, enano obedecía,
> y Olimpo, cuya sosegada frente,
> nunca de aura agitada
> consintió ser violada,
> aun falda suya ser no merecía:
> pues las nubes — que opaca son corona
> de la más elevada corpulencia,
> del volcán más soberbio que en la tierra
> gigante erguido intima al cielo guerra —,
> apenas densa zona
> de su altiva eminencia,
> o a su vasta cintura
> cíngulo tosco son, que — mal ceñido —
> o el viento lo desata sacudido,
> o vecino el calor del sol lo apura. (309–326)

the soul, so it seemed to her, perched on the highest summit of a mountain of which Mount Atlas, presiding as a giant over all others, obeyed
as a dwarf, and which Mount Olympus, whose tranquil brow never
consented to be violated by agitated winds, did not merit even to be its
lower flank; for the clouds, which are the obscure crown of the highest
body, of the proudest volcano, upraised giant that on the earth threatens
the sky with war, hardly form a tangible zone on its great heights, or a
crude belt on its vast waist, which, poorly tightened, either comes untied
in the turbulent wind or, as a neighbor to the sun's heat, hurries away.

This is the poem's most visually daring use of hyperbole to express inexpressible height. Like Donne's "Tenarife" in the *First Anniversarie*, Sor Juana's
"monte" signals nature's limits even as the mountain is invidiously compared
to the limitlessness of the mind's intuitive reach. More remarkably still, like the
object it describes, the simile knows no limits. Although the period begins
with "apenas" and then adds "a su parecer" (both of which work as *remedia*),
the string of hyperbolic conceits are hardly made more meek or decorous. Atlas is an obedient "dwarf" compared to this "monte," and Olympus does not
even merit being its flank. Meanwhile, the gigantomachic myth is explicitly
trumped in lines 317–320 where the proudest volcano, presumably Aetna, is
mockingly compared to the intuitive mind's height and presumption. The

volcano's martial threat also recalls the pyramidal shadows and "tenebrosa guerra" in the poem's opening lines — thereby forging an extended gigan- tomachic conceit of some three hundred lines. More generally, these corre- spondences between mountains, giants, and pyramids confirm the integral role hyperbole plays in the poem's larger allegorical structure as the poet fig- ures her own ambivalent rise and fall. By also relying on meiosis ("las nubes . . . cíngulo tosco son"), Sor Juana further enhances the mind's stature by debasing, what Gracián calls the *circunstancias*, here the clouds, attending the terms of comparison.[54] Hyperbole and the related tropes it controls lift the reader past myth and nature into new semantic realms. Yet they also begin to suggest the impossibility of expressing the inexpressible as well as the tragic consequences inevitably accompanying such an effort. The eagle's failure, "pretendiendo / entre sus luces colocar su nido" [*aiming to arrange its nest amidst the sky and sun's lights*] (333–334), prefigures Sor Juana's own failure to main- tain such heights, while the gerund "pretendiendo" again recalls the threaten- ing "sombra . . . escalar pretendiendo las Estrellas" in the opening lines.[55]

Asombro begins to yield to *escarmiento* in earnest, however, only when the pyramidal theme explicitly returns. Exploring in lines 340–411 the extraordi- nary nature of the Egyptian pyramids and poetic genius, the latter as now em- bodied by Homer, Sor Juana traces what Méndez Plancarte dramatically dubs "The Defeat of the Intuition" in lines 412–559. Arguably the richest philosophic moment in Spanish Baroque lyric, these verses marvelously syn- cretize historical, mythic, architectural, geometric, epic, hermetic, and scholas- tic discourses as they try to adumbrate the soul's fervent, but ultimately vain desire for intuitive knowledge of the highest things. Using both space and time as objective measures of the soul's subjective "ambicioso anhelo" [*ambi- tious yearning*] (429), Sor Juana tries to gauge the ethical consequences of her overreaching. In the course of her vertiginous play of high and low, the pyramids become ambivalent monuments to artistic *atrevimiento* and folly. Her Gongorist puns and conceits solicit wonder, incredulity, and eventually "es- panto" [*fright*] at her heroic epistemological efforts. Enacting the conflicted motions of the curious soul in its ascent and fall, the syntax in these lines is marked by extreme hyperbaton, anaphora, and periphrasis.[56] The diction, meanwhile, repeatedly verges on catachresis as the limits of signification and expressibility are explored. By stubbornly emphasizing, if not abusing, the notions of quantity and measure in the description of the soul's efforts, these *silvas* underscore the inability of normal language or even conventional poetic

semantics to serve purely philosophical ends. They also confirm the Aristotelian notion that if a quality, such as color or taste, best represents the
sensual aspects of the world, then quantity, itself already something of an abstraction, more effectively expresses the world's more universal and eternal
aspects.[57]

The upward trajectory of the *Sueño* continues when the pyramids are introduced as "ostentaciones" [*ostentations*] serving as "tumba y bandera" [*tomb
and pennant*] for the deceased Ptolemies. More enduring than "Fama" itself, the
pyramids' height once "publicaba" [*vaunted*] Egypt's deeds to the wind, the
clouds, and the heavens ("si ya también al cielo no decía" [*even if the Heavens
did not admit it*]). Such publication metapoetically suggests the entire section
should be read as a commentary on panegyric, albeit a panegyric that also
rather idiosyncratically praises the powers of the poet's own mind. Likewise,
as architecture's "último esmero" [*ultimate effort*] — architecture being the discipline that gives concrete, material form, even more than geometry, to abstract
ideas — the pyramids ostentatiously rival any human attempt to defy time
and, as the following remarkable parenthesis makes clear, space as well:

> éstas, — que en nivelada simetría
> su estatura crecía
> con tal diminución, con arte tanto,
> que (cuanto más al cielo caminaba)
> a la vista, que lince la miraba,
> entre los vientos se desparecía,
> sin permitir mirar la sutil punta
> que al primer orbe finge que se junta,
> hasta que fatigada del espanto,
> no descendida, sino despeñada
> se hallaba al pie de la espaciosa basa,
> tarde o mal recobrada
> del desvanecimiento
> que pena fue no escasa
> del visual alado atrevimiento —, (354–368)

these pyramids, — whose stature grew in symmetrical levels, with such
diminution, with such art, that (the more it rose toward the sky) it disappeared amidst the winds to the sight, which like a lynx gazed at it,
though without enabling it to see the subtle point that feigns uniting it-

self with the first celestial sphere (the moon); until exhausted from
fright, the gaze, not descended but cast down found itself at the foot of
the spacious base, belatedly or poorly recovered from its fainting and
vanity, which was not a small punishment for its wingéd visual
daring —,

As if one form of rhetoric is exhausted and therefore another becomes necessary to track sight's trajectory, the period begins with the diction of quantity
("tal diminución . . . tanto . . . cuanto más"), resorts next to metaphor and
simile ("lince . . . despeñada . . . visual alado atrevimiento"), and then the
dramatic syncrisis of "no descendida, sino despeñada" paves the way for the
hyperbole, while the litote ("que peña fue no escasa") increases the ambivalence of the exaggeration. Similarly, in terms of content, the period moves
from symmetry to disequilibrium, from sight to invisibility. In this way, the
reader intimates enormous vistas as well as the consequences of the sight's
"desvanecimiento" and "visual alado atrevimiento."[58] Still clinging to the visual paradigm, the dialectic tracing the soul's movement also manages to look
forward to the poet's imminent intellectual fall (or what Walter Benjamin
would call her allegorical *Verfall*), as her dense but agile *silvas* and the vertiginous rhymes that conclude them send the reader careening from one cognitive
extreme to another.

Her absolutist rhetoric takes a different turn when the pyramids, "todo
bañados" [*completely bathed*] by sunlight, are described as fully inimical to human needs and as casting not even a trace of a shadow: "nunca de calorosos
caminantes / al fatigado aliento, a los pies flacos, / ofrecieron alfombra / aun
de pequeña, aun de señal de sombra" [*never to the weary breath of sweltering travelers they offered even the smallest carpet, or sign of a shadow*] (375–378). Cast now
as allegorical ruins, the pyramids are branded as "bárbaros jeroglíficos de
ciego / error, según el Griego / ciego también, dulcísimo poeta" [*barbaric hieroglyphs of blind error, according to the also blind Greek, the sweetest poet*] (381–383).
By apocryphally invoking Homer as the supreme authority on the subject, the
poem momentarily shifts from a panegyric to an epic mode. Homer is so perfect a poet, Sor Juana affirms as she reworks a passage from Macrobius, that it
would be easier to steal a lightning bolt from Jupiter or the "clava" [*club*] from
Hercules than to alter even a "hemistiquio solo" [*single hemistich*] of his.[59] Yet
ironically, such rewriting exactly describes the invention in these lines, as
Homer becomes the *auctoritas* for a late seventeenth-century, Mexican poet's

subjective meditations (an irony further heightened by the fact that in her
Carta atenagórica Sor Juana has a female figure steal Hercules' club).[60]

The ambiguous invocation of Homer is also folded into the poem's
changing stance toward the pyramids. If before they were "elaciones pro-
fanas" [*profane presumptions*] now they hermetically point to God's infinitude:

> según de Homero, digo, la sentencia,
> las Pirámides fueron materiales
> tipos solos, señales exteriores
> de las que, dimensiones interiores,
> especies son del alma intencionales:
> que como sube en piramidal punta
> al cielo la ambiciosa llama ardiente,
> así la humana mente
> su figura trasunta,
> y a la causa primera siempre aspira
> — céntrico punto donde recta tira
> la línea, si no ya circunferencia,
> que contiene, infinita, toda esencia —. (399–411)

according to Homer's maxim, then, the Pyramids were solely material
symbols, external signs, of what are internal dimensions, or purposive images of the soul; for just as the ambitious flame climbs towards heaven in
a pyramidal point, so the human mind reflects this shape, and always aspires to the first cause — which is the center to which all straight lines tend,
if not also being the infinite circumference, which contains all essence —.

To signal the move from "señales exteriores" to "dimensiones interiores," Sor
Juana supplements her pyramid metaphorics with the hermetic simile of the
mind as an "ambiciosa llama ardiente." This additional fold conveys the ambition and, intriguingly, the naturalness of the mind that would sublimate
("su figura trasunta") all material concerns. More subtly still, on top of these
two conceits she places a geometric one that begins with a "piramidal punta"
only to envelop it at the period's end with her curious reworking of the infinite, hermetic circle. She thus suggests at once a geometric transformation of
pyramid into sphere, and point into infinite figure, but also the spiritual transformation of physical matter into "esencia." And if the stylistic remains of
Góngora ("señales . . . si no ya") and Homeric apocrypha are made to serve

the most transcendental aspects of Neo-Platonism and scholasticism, the totalizing diction ("siempre," "toda") and geometric imagery signal the extent
to which the poem now seeks to overstep the limits of *enargeia* in its attempt to
measure the immeasurable. The aim is no longer visualization but rather to
convey the experience of a transcendent intuition. Or as Vossler puts it, the
"Grundmotiv" of the poem is captured by the Greek verb *thaumazein*, which
he glosses as "staunende Verwunderung vor dem göttlichen Naturgeheimnis
der Schöpfung" [*astonished amazement before the divine secret of nature in the
creation*].[61] To create such "Verwunderung" or *asombro*, the poetics of *ut pictura
poesis* no longer suffices.

In terms of *imitatio*, then, Homer becomes the mythic poet to be outbid.
Building upon his apocryphal pyramid lore in the subsequent lines, Sor Juana
compares the artifice of the pyramids to that of "aquella blasfema altiva torre /
de quien hoy dolorosas son señales" [*that blasphemous, lofty tower of which there
are still sorrowful signs*] (414–415). This invocation of the Tower of Babel underscores the theological and so ethical dilemma in wanting to aspire to such
heights, as well as proleptically indicating the poet's own imminent failure to
use language to scale the heavens. It also imports the specter of an angry Old
Testament God, as well as relying on the rich Renaissance tradition of using
Nimrod's folly to emblemize the fruitless desire for universal *mathesis*.[62] Further,
it functions as another in a series of "señales" in her play of high and low. With
this blasphemy in the air, the physical pyramids ("Montes dos artificiales") are
then delicately — "si fueran" (423) serves as yet another *remedium* — compared
to a "mental pirámide elevada" [*elevated mental pyramid*] (424), which leaves its
models "tan atrasados" [*so far behind*]. This mental pyramid's flight defies physical laws:

> . . . que cualquiera
> graduara su cima por esfera:
> pues su ambicioso anhelo,
> haciendo cumbre de su propio vuelo,
> en la más eminente
> la encumbró parte de su propia mente,
> de sí tan remontada, que creía
> que a otra nueva región de sí salía. (428–434)

. . . for anyone would take its peak for a sphere; for its ambitious yearning, making of its own flight a summit, sets her atop the highest point of

her own mind, mounted so high above herself, that she believed she had
left herself for another, new region.

Straining to the point of ecstatic incomprehensibility, these lines reshape the
metaphorics of mountains and flight to map the trajectory of the soul's "am⁄
bicioso anhelo." Transforming "summit" into "sphere," physical space into a
mental experience, such extreme desire ("de sí tan remontada") again defies
visualization. Meanwhile, the repetition of "propio . . . propia," the play on
"cumbre" and "encumbró," the twice⁄repeated, reflexive "sí," and the way
"remontada" neatly refigures "Montes dos artificiales," all reinforce the lin⁄
guistic nature of her experience in this "nueva región." Not only is Sor Juana
commenting on the difficulty of representing such abstruse matters by syntac⁄
tically clotting up her verse, but she also prepares the ground for the extreme
and sudden motions of the next period, where, with inimitable mastery of
rhetorical and psychological detail, she traces the soul's final mystical ascen⁄
dancy toward the "mental" pyramid's summit and its sudden, subsequent
frustration:

> en cuya casi elevación inmensa,
> gozosa mas suspensa,
> suspensa pero ufana,
> y atónita aunque ufana, la suprema
> de lo sublunar reina soberana,
> la vista perspicaz, libre de anteojos,
> de sus intelectuales bellos ojos
> (sin que dictancia tema
> ni de obstáculo opaco se recele,
> de que interpuesto algún objeto cele),
> libre tendió por todo lo criado:
> cuyo inmenso agregado,
> cúmulo incomprehensible,
> aunque a la vista quiso manifiesto
> dar señas de posible,
> a la comprehensión no, que — entorpecida
> con la sobra de objetos, y excedida
> de la grandeza de ellos su potencia —
> retrocedió cobarde. (435–453)

from this almost immeasurable elevation, joyful but uncertain, uncertain but proud, and astonished though proud, the supreme Queen (i.e.,
the soul) of the sublunary, extended freely (without fearing distance or
distrusting that an opaque obstacle could, coming between, hide some
object) the perspicacious sight, free of lenses, of her intellectually beautiful eyes, over all creation: whose immeasurable aggregate, incomprehensible accumulation, being manifest to sight, wanted to give signs that
this was possible; yet it defied the comprehension, which made sluggish
by the excess of objects whose greatness exceeded its power, cowardly retreated.

More discursive than metaphoric, hyperbole here helps conceptualize the
"posible" and the impossible, as the reader is led rung by rung, with the help
of the marvelous diacope in lines 436–438, up a cognitive and ontological
ladder. With the "gozosa más suspensa" soul stuck in self-contradiction, and
with its "casi elevación inmensa" pitting vision against thought, inevitably the
"inmenso agregado, / cúmulo incomprehensible" thwarts its best efforts. This
failure is conveyed most persuasively by the passage's syntax and diction.
When the hiatus in line 450 and its startling "no" are reached, we share in
Sor Juana's aporia and her impending sense of *desengaño*. More dramatically
still, the acrobatic hyperbaton structuring the entire passage deepens this sense
of frustration — for when the semantic resolution is finally reached, the reader
discovers only an ignominious defeat. In terms of the passage's diction, the
repetition of "inmensa . . . inmenso" reinforces the notion that the mind (*mens*)
cannot measure (*metior*) its object. And if "todo lo criado" and "la sobra de
objetos" literally prove excessive for the soul ("excedida / de la grandeza de
ellos su potencia"), then its defeat ("retrocedió cobarde") is linguistic as well
as cognitive. To give this paronomasia still greater rigor, a few lines later, Sor
Juana reports how the "tan asombrado" [*greatly astonished*] understanding
"cedió" [*yielded*] before the "copia puesto" [*abundance before it*] (475–476). Semantically, the antithesis created by the play between *ceder* and *exceder* lends
this dialectic of daring and retreat an air of inevitability. If *ceder* means to cede
or yield a place, *exceder*, like its Latin root, *excedo*, suggests an active transgressing of limits or expectations. The soul's motion thus intrinsically responds to excess by ceding its place. (Like its Greek cousins ὑπερβαλλω (to
overshoot) and ὑπερβαίνω (to overflow), *excedo* may signify unnatural, even
violent movement). There may also be an allusion here to the debates on the

new and old astronomies, as *retroceder* belongs to the Ptolemaic vocabulary used to describe a planet's apparent and seemingly unnatural motion. Conversely, telescopic wit, in the manner of Tesauro, is discounted, as Sor Juana bravely dismisses the need for any "anteojos" to span the "dictancia." In sum, her hyperbolic, etymological wit is less an artifice than a way of being and thinking in response to the empirical perception of the extraordinary nature of things. While the Gongorist *señas* littering these lines serve to dramatize that perception.

As for the geometry of these mental pyramids, Vossler and Paz have shown that it must be read in terms of the poem's foreboding first lines and Kircher's symbolic geometry.[63] Vossler, moreover, suggests that the choice of double pyramids was influenced by the proximity to her convent of the Sun and Moon pyramids at Teotihuacan.[64] Whether she also saw these pyramids through the encyclopedic prism of Kircher's *Oedipus aegyptiacus*, which includes an allegorical engraving of the Teotihuacan pyramids in its discussion of how they are not "dissimilar" to the "temples of the Egyptians," remains unclear.[65] Manifest, however, is the extreme skepticism she ultimately betrays in regard to the audacity of those who would scale such heights. In other words, the pyramids loom so large because they serve as exemplary human measures of the immeasurable divine.[66] Their historical and symbolic presence measures the continuity of human ambition and folly from the Egyptians and Aztecs up to Sor Juana herself. But they also serve as etymological guideposts to help the reader navigate the poem's difficult rhetoric and imagery.

In the final section on the intuition's flight (454–494), Sor Juana compares the soul, "arrepentida" [*repentant*] of its "descomedida ... alarde" [*daring display*] of trying to match its "rayos" with the sun's, to Icarus whose "propio llanto / lo anegó enternecido" [*own tender weeping drowned him*]. While the Petrarchan hyperbole of drowning in one's own tears nicely reconceptualizes the mythic consequences of Icarus' "necia experiencia" [*foolish experiment*] the experimental consequences of this "llorado ensayo" [*tear-worthy attempt*] are far more cosmic: "... el entendimiento, aquí vencido / no menos de la inmensa muchedumbre / de tanta maquinosa pesadumbre ... cedió" [*the understanding, here defeated no less by the immense multitude of such great, cunning grief ... yielded*].[67] Such stubborn reliance on quantitative adjectives ("immensa ... tanta") confirms how in their most abstract, hyperbolic incarnations the ideas of height, weight, and luminosity refuse to be sublimated into qualitative notions. Like the pyramids themselves, such adjectives are necessary but insufficient measures. When the universe, "la máquina voluble de la esfera" [*the sphere's voluble mechanism*] is perceived as a whole, the mind loses itself "en tanta, tan difusa / incomprehensible especie" [*in so diffuse, such an incomprehensible image*]. A "mar de asombros" [*sea of marvels*], melancholy waves, and nothingness are the fruits of its effort, as the intuition is rendered unable to perceive the harmonious proportion between "partes," between the many and the one.[68] In sum, as we reach the end of the poem's first half, the creation and experience of disproportion has become the poem's theme if not its method — exactly what Álvarez de Lugo warns against.

Chapter Eight

A Dream Deferred:
The Overreacher's Conscience

But the Quincunx of Heaven runs low, and 'tis time
to close the five ports of knowledge; We are unwilling
to spin out our awaking thoughts into the phantasmes
of sleep, which to often continueth praecogitations;
making Cables of Cobwebbes and Wildernesses of
Handsome Groves. Beside *Hippocrates* hath spoke so little
and the Oneirocriticall Masters, have left such frigid
Interpretations from plants, that there is little
encouragement to dream of Paradise it self.

— Thomas Browne, *The Garden of Cyrus*

METHODICAL OVERREACHING

Having dramatically failed to reach any certainty with her intuition in the first half of the *Sueño*, in the second half Sor Juana finds other means to pursue "the phantasmes of sleep." Like Thomas Browne, she too dares not "dream of Paradise it self," but like Browne's countryman, John Bunyan, she also refuses to remain in the Slough of Despond. Attempting to recover from its *Icarean* fall, her soul briefly seeks "la obscuridad" as a remedy for "la sobra de la luz" [*the excess of light*] (495–496). There, in what could serve as a gloss on the Baroque penchant for remaking *coincidentia oppositorum*, Sor Juana pauses to meditate on the nature of "excess": ". . . el exceso contrarios hace efectos / en la torpe potencia . . ." [*excess produces contrary effects in the sluggish faculty*] (500–501).[1] Excess riddles Sor Juana's poetics, her phenomenology, and, as we shall see, her Neo-Platonic theology. More urgently still, it creates the cognitive, creative spur for the poet to continue dreaming.

The elaborate simile running from lines 495 to 510 compares the effects felt by someone suddenly thrust into daylight after having been deprived of all color by darkness with the plight of the poet's soul. Merging seamlessly with Sor Juana's main argument, this *chiaroscuro* episode is no mere mannerist exercise; instead, it neatly if gnostically emblemizes the poet's difficult search for illumination. Indeed, her confused soul then turns to its own "innata ciencia / que confirmada ya de la experiencia, / maestro quizá mudo, / retórico ejemplar" [*innate science, which is confirmed by experience, perhaps a silent teacher, a rhetorical exemplum*] (516–519) for assistance. This dual appeal to experience and rhetoric I take as indicating the necessity of discovering some contingent form of mediation between the subjective mind's extremes and the external, physical universe. In this sense, it recalls how orators use a shared language (with all its traditions and commonplaces) to persuade an audience of a proposition however outlandish or subjective. But it also recalls seventeenth-century developments in the scientific method in which the results of individual experiments begin to mediate the abstract claims of Aristotelian logic.

Again, Sor Juana's adaptation of the diverse strands scientific thought available to her is highly syncretic. Incorporating potentially conflicting aspects of Galenic physiology, medieval physics, the hermetic sciences, and the new philosophy, such syncretism, while clearly endemic to the motions of the aspiring soul fueling the *Sueño*, proves finally an unreliable means of reaching metaphysical truths. As Sabat de Rivers, Elías Trabulse, and Ruth Hill have variously shown, there are many potential sources for the poem's scientific content.[2] Most recently, Hill reads the *Sueño* through the lens of Pierre Gassendi's attempt to mediate between scholasticism and Cartesianism.[3] Yet it is Galen, not Gassendi, whom Sor Juana cites in line 520 when she asserts that, just as darkness is recommended to heal the excessive light of revelation, the antidote to a poison is that same poison given in small, incremental doses. The nature of this physical cure prompts her to ponder the dramatic, metaphysical effects of the soul's first defeat after it has encountered "diversidad tanta," which:

> permitiéndole apenas
> de un concepto confuso
> el informe embrión que, mal formado,
> inordinado caos retrataba
> de confusas especies que abrazaba
> — sin orden avenidas,

> sin orden separadas,
> que cuanto más se implican combinadas
> tanto más se disuelvan desunidas,
> de diversidad llenas —,
> ciñendo con violencia lo difuso
> de objeto tanto, a tan pequeño vaso
> (aun al más bajo, aun al menor, escaso). (547–559)

permitting the soul barely a shapeless embryo of a confused concept, poorly formed, which traced inordinate chaos from confused images that it embraced — without synthetic order, without analytic order — which the more they suggest combinations, the more they dissolve disunited, from diversity overwhelmed —, violently circumscribing so many diffuse objects, into such a small vessel, insufficient even for the basest, most minute object.

To mediate this "caos" depends on Sor Juana's ability to amplify, retrospectively, a "concepto confuso." The extended apostrophe ("sin orden . . ."), the hyperbaton ending with "escaso," the diction of quantity ("cuanto más . . . tanto más . . . objeto tanto . . . tan pequeño"), and the constant anaphora that increases the sense of inevitability of her *salida*, all work to depict the "violencia" the mind experiences trying to circumscribe ("ciñendo") so many things in so small a space. Size still matters, but now it is the extremes of multiplicity and diversity that overwhelm. Having just scaled an invisible pyramid's invisible summit, the confused mind, in what is perhaps the poem's most striking *peripeteia*, now cannot even grasp the "más bajo" of things. Thus, as we shall see with Pascal who hyperbolizes physical space to help prove his skeptical epistemology, Sor Juana uses the witty rhetoric about the largest and smallest of quantities to undermine the claims of reason.

Further meditating on the process of deduction, she then ominously reworks the navigation *topos* and the poem's earlier maritime metaphorics to portray the ship of her "desatento" [*distracted*] soul, with sails furled and trusting in the "triador . . . mar" [*traitor . . . sea*], as it founders:

> mal le hizo de su grado
> en la mental orilla
> dar fondo, destrozado,
> al timón roto, a la quebrada entena,

> besando arena a arena,
> de la playa el bajel, astilla a astilla . . . (565–570)

against her will the wind made her, wrecked, founder on the mental shore, with the rudder broken, with the yard snapped, and each splinter from the ship kissing a grain of sand.

The hyperbole of having each splinter kiss a grain of sand directly imitates the *Soledad primera* where "la menor onda chupa al menor hilo" [*where the least wave sucks the least thread* (of the pilgrim's clothes)] (41); but unlike Góngora, Sor Juana employs such exaggerated correspondences to pursue specific philosophic as well as aesthetic ends.[4] Here she depicts the ponderous, methodical motion of deductive reasoning. I would note, however, that this meticulous hyperbole would have been inappropriate in the wild tumult of the section on intuition, whereas here it nicely illustrates the "ciencia a formar de los universales" [*science of forming universals*] according to Aristotle's ten logical categories. Such an unwieldy discursive task excuses the rather abstract and slightly repetitive amplification of the process by which the mind tries to organize its thoughts.[5]

Further confirming the linguistic quality of Sor Juana's desire is how the representation of the methodical workings of the deductive mind relies on conceited wordplay. Recalling her description of Olympus (". . . o a su vasta cintura / cíngulo tosco son, que — mal ceñido —") and the intuitive mind's vain efforts (". . . ciñendo con violencia lo difuso / de objeto tanto, a tan pequeño vaso"), she now adopts the same conceit to describe the smaller compass of the deductive mind, which seeks to discuss things one by one so that: ". . . las cosas / que vienen a ceñirse en las . . . categorías" [*things that appear can be contained in the (ten Aristotelian) categories*] (579–581). This effort, however, also proves futile. Not only does her deductive approach soon founder, but by the poem's end the usurping night is described as "negro laurel de sombras mil ceñía" [*crowned with black laurel of a thousand shadows*] (913). In short, the polyptoton with the verb *ceñir* becomes more than a figure of speech; it functions as a crucial element in a larger discourse of circumscription, praise, and measure. Whereas Quevedo's "cordón" helps to hyperbolize terrestrial conquest, Sor Juana's "cíngulo tosco" and its variations help hyperbolize the attempt at self-conquest.

Moreover, in these sections Sor Juana no longer is describing a depersonalized soul. For if she gave us "el Alma" at line 540, now she confesses: "mi entendimiento / el método quería" [*my understanding wanted the method*] (617–618). While this is the first time a first person pronoun appears in the poem, the search for the proper method has undoubtedly been the poet's singular task from the opening line. Indeed, as I shall argue in the chapters on Descartes, the early modern search for a proper method often is an immanently personal, even solipsistic task. A word derived from the Greek *hodos* meaning "road" or "path," *método* is itself a conceit (or at least an easily resurrected dead metaphor) with potentially enormous personal and theological resonances. Journeying through an interiorized, hyperbolic topography, Sor Juana searches for that singular *via* that will not force her to admit: "cobarde el discurso se desvía" [*the cowardly discourse turned aside*] (760). In this, her tropological "alpinismo" recalls the Pauline-Augustinian allegory of the *via*, an allegory refashioned for Renaissance humanists by Petrarch's "Ascent of Mont Ventoux," which likewise masterfully combines the two metaphors to paint the birth of a troubled subjectivity. It is worth noting, though, that Petrarch's brother accompanies him up the mountain part of the way, and that St. Augustine, allegorically at least, is there on the summit to give him comfort and direction. While for her part, Sor Juana's solitude is complete from beginning to end, bottom to top.[6]

Another point of comparison worth considering is with the young Descartes, who in his dream narrative, the *Olympica*, hopes to "perceive Olympian things" by teaching his reason to emulate the imagination's ability to mediate between matter and spirit.[7] In this bizarre, oneirocritical text, Descartes describes a series of three dreams that occured on a November night in 1619. After encountering a series of phantasmic obstacles, the dreaming Descartes finally succeeds in finding his "way" by eluding an "evil spirit," after which he plants "seeds" of wisdom with the divine assistance of the "Spirit of Truth." Ultimately, he ascends to Olympian heights where he glimpses the possibility of a clear and universal science. With their Rosicrucian, Hermetic elements, on the one hand, and with their integral connection to the genesis of his own philosophy, on the other, Descartes' dreams, like Sor Juana's *Sueño*, speak to the great epistemological issues of the Baroque: the sky-scaling desire for knowledge and certainty, the dubious value of Neo-Platonic, Scholastic, Neo-Stoic, and Neo-Sceptic approaches to knowledge, and the role that rhetoric and poetry, and in particular metaphor, play in heurisis and the constitution of self-knowledge. Yet whereas Descartes quickly turns his back on the dream narrative, or rather transforms it in the *First Meditation* into a heuristic device that eventually becomes the hypothesis of the "evil genius," Sor Juana persists in her deductive oneiromancy.

The desire for a valid method leads her to reconsider human physiology and so investigate the process of digestion, "cuatro adornada operaciones / de contrarias acciones" [*ornamented by four operations of contrary actions*] (634–635). With this she can, among other things, "lo superfluo expele, y de la copia / la substancia más útil hace propia" [*expell the superfluous, and from abundance appropriate the most useful substance*] (637–638).[8] But while one of the principal obstacles in the traditional pursuit of deductive knowledge is "lo superfluo" (thus Spinoza casts his *Ethics* in geometric, deductive form to avoid discursive superfluity and the burden of *auctorita*), for Sor Juana the excess and "copia" native to Baroque poetics are anything but superfluous. Instead, mythic allusions and daring amplifications fuel here the poem's heurisis. Emphasizing the vegetable aspect of her soul, she compares herself to Thetis, with "sus fértiles pechos maternales" [*her fertile, maternal breasts*] (628). This surprising image then precipitates several others as she associates herself in rapid, protean succession with the myths of Arethusa, Persephone, Atlas, Hercules, and finally Phaeton. She shares, if you will, Pico's "holy ambition," and so is willing to play the "chameleon."[9] Ventriloquizing God, Pico addresses humanity in his famous *Oration*: "You, confined by no limits, on account of your free will, in whose hand I have placed you, you shall yourself prescribe [*your nature*]."[10] Like Pico (and Pascal), Sor Juana lauds the advantage any living being has over every object in nature without consciousness; indeed the former

> . . . justa puede ocasionar querella
> — cuando afrenta no sea —
> de la que más lucida centellea
> inanimada estrella,
> bien que soberbios brille resplandores
> — que hasta a los astros puede superiores,
> aun la menor criatura, aun la más baja,
> ocasionar envidia, hacer ventaja —; (645–651)

may justly provoke a quarrel, if not cause affront, with the inanimate star that sparkles most luminously, no matter how proudly, resplendently it shines; for even the least creature, even the vilest, may cause the envy of and show its advantage over the loftiest stars.

Even as the auxesis at the end of this passage recalls the drama of line 559, the stakes of the comparison here are carefully increased with another *remedium* ("cuando afrenta no sea"). More generally, these lines strongly exemplify the manner in which her poetics, instead of obfuscating her thought, affords it a metaphoric *energeia*, an emotional veracity, and, strangely enough, an intellec-tual honesty that critics of Baroque rhetoric such as Bacon, Descartes, Hobbes, and their epigones dismiss as implausible because of the poet's putative di-vorce of words and things. Poetic and philosophic discourses converge here as she exploits the topical tradition in late Renaissance poetry to infuse it with new *energeia* born from the same epistemological desires that Bacon and Descartes trumpet as their own. Earlier she visits the epic *topos* of outbidding the stars, but here the "proud" stars momentarily give way to the Juanista-self in much the same manner that the mutable world yields to the Archimidean-self in Descartes' *Meditations*.

THE BROKEN CHAIN

Swiftly passing through the mineral, vegetable, and animal realms, Sor Juana pauses as she discovers her place, our place, in the hierarchy of being:

> y de este corporal conocimiento
> haciendo, bien que escaso, fundamento,
> al supremo pasar maravilloso
> compuesto triplicado,
> de tres acordes líneas ordenado
> y de las formas todas inferiores
> compendio misterioso:
> bisagra engazadora
> de la que más se eleva entronizada
> naturaleza pura
> y de la que, criatura
> menos noble, se ve más abatida . . . (652–663)

and making from this knowledge of the body, though it is scant, a foun-dation, to turn then to the supreme, marvelous, triple composite, the mysterious compendium, which in an orderly fashion unites three as-pects (the vegetative, sensitive, and rational) and all the inferior forms; the linking hinge between pure Nature which is enthroned most high (the angels) and the least noble, most debased created thing . . .

Meditating on that paradoxical link, the "bisagra engazadora," between high and low, she now makes "el hombre" (690) her sole meditative object. Her diction literally and figuratively tries to take his measure, for, despite his in-famy, man is the "última perfección" of the "circúlo que cierra / la esfera con la tierra" [*circle that joins the earth with the celestial sphere*] (671–672). Other her-metic echoes resonate when man's place in the world is contemplated. Epideixis becomes theological as this lowly "compendio misterioso" is ambiguously compared to the angel of the apocalypse:

> fábrica portentosa
> que, cuanto más altiva al cielo toca,
> sella el polvo la boca
> — de quien ser pudo imagen misteriosa
> la que águila evangélica, sagrada
> visión en Patmos vio, que las estrellas
> midió y el suelo con iguales huellas, (677–683)

portentous construction that, the higher to Heaven it strives, seals it mouth with dust; whose mysterious image may be the sacred vision that the evangelic eagle (St. John) saw in Patmos, a vision which trod the stars and earth with equal steps . . .

But this redemptive "visión" is also infused with the same skeptical strains we heard in Quevedo's moral poetry:

> o la estatua eminente
> que del metal mostraba más preciado
> la rica altiva frente,
> y en el más desechado
> material, flaco fundamento hacía
> con que a leve vaivén se deshacía —: (684–689)

or the lofty statue, which displayed a haughty, sumptuous brow of the most precious metal, and who had a flimsy foundation made of the most abject material, which a light rocking undoes . . .

Rewriting the description of the statue in Nebuchadnezzar's dream from the *Book of Daniel* (2:34–35), Sor Juana further contemplates the notion of mea-sure ("midió"), the semantics of ascent, and the navigation *topos* ("a leve vaivén se deshacía").[11] Now it is no longer a question of sheer quantity, whether of height or distance, but rather of quality — the statue's feet are made of clay, and neither deductive reason nor poetic rhetoric can pierce revealed truth's "imagen misteriosa." Thus only after the search for abstract truth irrevocably fails do sensual realities and the rhetoric of quality fully reemerge. Only then do hyperbolic quantities yield to the naked paradoxes of man's condition, to his "altiva bajeza" [*haughty baseness*] (695).

Possessing the mystic overreacher's will, but evincing also the metaphysician's rigor, Sor Juana stays any *ecstasis* as she realizes the contingent nature of her ambition. The head ("rica altiva frente") is willing, but the body ("flaco fundamento") is weak. At once narrative, heuristic, and empirical, this realization is rooted in the dynamics of *imitatio* as well. The *copia* that proved so aesthetically pleasing, so conceptually and ethically complex in Góngora and Quevedo's hands, proves insufficient for Sor Juana's desires. At the same time, the literary and humanist legacies that so richly garb her vision are what allow her to glimpse that vision in the first place. This familiar double bind is why Paz's absolute dichotomy should be refused: "The language of Góngora is aesthetic; that of Sor Juana intellectual."[12] It should be refused not only because it seems to strip the former of all its *conceptista* force, but also because it tends to separate form from content in the latter. For her part, Hill devalues the poem's Gongorist aspects in order to emphasize another species of materialism, namely Gassendi's.[13] And whether or not one is willing to join her in making Sor Juana a devoted reader of Gassendi, Hill certainly is right to argue that Sor Juana's Gongorist language and *conceptos* need the assistance of the poem's syncretic assemblage of scientific and philosophic doctrines to furnish matter (*res*) substantive enough that the poet might have the material and phenomenological bases to deconstruct her own beliefs, ambitions, and perceptions of the imperceptible. Put another way, Sor Juana perceives the existence of the divine union and of the microcosmic-macrocosmic "link," but her conscience (be it poetic, intellectual, Christian, or otherwise) seems to intervene. This despite the fact that the now mythic, now scholastic, now Galenic, now Platonic vision of nature adumbrated throughout the *Sueño* is largely in sympathy with her mystic ambitions. In the *Respuesta*, she expresses the hope "saber todo lo que en esta vida se puede alcanzar, por medios naturales, de los divinos misterios" [*to know all that can be attained in this life, by natural means, of the divine mysteries*]. She describes how, "dirigiendo siempre . . . los pasos de mi estudio a la cumbre de la Sagrada Teología" [*directing always . . . the steps of my study to the summit of Sacred Theology*], she feels it necessary "subir por los escalones de las ciencias y artes humanas" [*to climb the rungs of the human arts and sciences*].[14] But in the heuristic rough and tumble of the *Sueño* itself, the study of "lógica . . . retórica . . . física" eventually prove to be inadequate steps, if not *pasos perdidos*. No kindly, learned Virgil emerges to be her guide. And without such divine intercession, she is left to fall back on herself.

Given this fundamental impasse, the poem's next section (704–780) strikes a decidedly pessimistic tone. Here — in another parallel with Donne's *Anniversaries* — the folly of the empirical sciences is described. Condemn‑ ing the "excesivo . . . atrevimiento el discurrirlo todo" [*excessive . . . audacity of discoursing about everything*], Sor Juana explains how the understanding can‑ not even comprehend a single isolated object, such as an underground stream or "la breve flor" [*the ephemeral flower*]. But then, continuing her strategy of self‑mythologization, she obliquely alludes to the tragic, feminine figures, Arethusa and Persephone, as she amplifies her encounter with these objects (712–729). For instance, an allusion to the "tornasol" [*sunflower*] precipitates a brief polemic against cosmetic beauty (749–756). All this suggests that rather than being an exercise in superficial heliotropism, this section of the poem allegorizes her suffering at the unforgiving hands of unbridled episte‑ mological desire. The flower discourse, for example, underscores the vanity of seeking knowledge of and through earthly things — even things that pro‑ duce beauty. Finally, at line 770, the incomprehensibility and thus inexpress‑ ibility of the world are poetically adduced by appealing to those newly renovated hyperbolic *topoi* concerning Hercules and Atlas.[15] While the value of knowledge reigns supreme, her own thought ("tímido . . . pensamiento"), Sor Juana tries to persuade herself, cannot share this greatness. For if reason, "el discurso,"

> . . . rehúsa
> acometer valiente,
> porque teme — cobarde —
> comprehenderlo o mal, o nunca, o tarde,
> ¿cómo en tan espantosa
> máquina inmensa discurrir pudiera,
> cuyo terrible incomportable peso
> — si ya en su centro mismo no estribara —
> de Atlante a las espaldas agobiara,

de Alcides a las fuerzas excediera;
y el que fue de la esfera
bastante contrapeso,
pesada menos, menos ponderosa
su máquina juzgara, que la empresa
de investigar a la naturaleza? (766–780)

refuses to attack valiantly, because it fears, coward, to comprehend (even an isolated object) badly, or belatedly, or never, how could she discourse on such an immense, frightening cosmos, whose terrible, unbearable weight — if it were not supported in its very center (by God) — would oppress the back of Atlas, would exceed the strength of Hercules? And he who was sufficient counterweight to the celestial sphere, would he not judge this mass less heavy, less ponderous than the task of investigating nature?

Similar to the concluding gesture in *De rerum natura*, Sor Juana invests the investigation of nature with mythic terror.[16] By invidiously invoking Hercules and Atlas, she also implies that such an investigation is an impossibility, if not a monstrosity. The adjectives ("tan espantosa . . . immensa") surrounding the "máquina" semantically dwarf it. In the end, geometry and weight can only be approximate, insufficient frameworks, as the universe's *inmensidad* becomes, as with Pascal, a source of fear and terror rather than wonder.[17] Yet because such spiritual, epistemological obstacles must be confronted, Sor Juana persists in representing her microcosmic attempt at understanding as more heroic than the macrocosmic, merely physical efforts of Atlas and Hercules. In this the *Sueño* darkly resembles Bacon's reworking of the same myths to furnish an ideology for the new science. But it also relies on the Renaissance tradition that casts the aging Hercules as a master of eloquence. Having abandoned his sword and shield, the hero, as Alciato vividly depicts him in the emblem *Eloquentia fortitiudine praestantior*, now leads men by a chain running from his tongue to their ears.

Méndez Plancarte titles the poem's last section concerning deductive reason (781–826), "The Uncurbed Thirst for Knowledge," though a more fitting title might be: *The Ambivalent Desire for Fame*, since by this late point in the poem the desire for knowledge has largely waned and been replaced by another hope. Phaeton is invoked to warn against overreaching — he is dubbed an "ejemplo osado" [*daring example*] and an "ejemplar pernicioso" [*pernicious exemplum*]. Even so, his desires are nearly indistinguishable from Sor Juana's.[18] Just as she still longs for the "lauro" (783) despite the two falls she has already taken, Phaeton will not be dissuaded from taking "abiertas sendas al atre- vimiento" [*open paths towards audacity*] (792) and thereby trying "su nombre eternizar en su rüina" [*to make eternal his name through his ruin*] (802).[19] Like Phaeton, Sor Juana ruinously strives to write her own panegyric. Having re- placed scientific inquiry with epideixis, and conflating now her poetic ambi- tions with his, she makes Phaeton's hyperbolic fate ("las glorias deletrea / entre los caracteres del estrago" [*spell glorious things amidst the letters of destruction*]) into an allegory describing the trajectory of her poem's letters and words:

> — auriga altivo del ardiente carro —,
> y el, si infeliz, bizarro
> alto impulso, el espíritu encendía . . . (787–789)

haughty charioteer of the burning car, and he, though miserable, with his noble, brave impulse, sparked the spirit . . .

Height via the polyptoton of "altivo" and "alto" dominates this image, as Phaeton's *furor* mirrors her own "bizarro" [*brave*] but unhappy passion. Whether or not she is also motivated by *fama* — the section quoted above from the *Respuesta* suggests that at least she is not adverse to it — certainly his am- bition and curiosity belong to her as well, or at least to her rhetoric. Still more strikingly, in order that he have no imitators, Sor Juana urges that his deeds be met either with a "pólitico silencio" [*politic silence*] or a "fingida ignorancia" [*feigned ignorance*] or that "con secreta pena castigara / el insolente exceso" [*with hidden pain insolent excess be castigated*].

That Sor Juana effectively exempts herself from her own advice against "insolente exceso" confirms how integral such excess is to her poetic and self- invention. Alatorre's comments on Sor Juana's conflicted use of the Phaeton myth speak directly to the psychological tensions lodging in such excess:

> Quien ambiciona conocerlo todo fracasará ineluctablemente, sí, pero ese fracaso será su gloria. La reflexión sobre el *nocivo* del ejemplo de los dos arriesgados mancebos no puede aplicarse al anhelo de saber, pues entonces Sor Juana no habría escrito el *Sueño*, su poema predilecto; se habría quedado callada para que el "mal ejemplo" no cundiera. El

Primero Sueño es una entusiasta proclamación de este anhelo. Sor Juana dice "Soñé que quería saberlo todo, y no pude", pero *todo el tiempo*, desde el primer verso, con su explicación cosmográfica del fenómeno llamado noche, está exhibiendo — ¡y qué gozosamente¡ — las muchas cosas que sí ha podido saber.[20]

Whoever hopes to know everything will ineluctably fail; yes, but this failure will be her glory. The reflection on the *harmful* example of the two daring young men cannot be applied to the yearning for knowledge, for then Sor Juana would not have written the *Sueño*, her favorite poem. She would have remained quiet so that the "bad example" would not be diffused. The *Primero Sueño* is an enthusiast proclamation of this yearning. Sor Juana says, I dreamt that I wanted to know all, and I could not," but *all the time*, from the first verse, with her cosmographic explanation of the phenomenon called night, she is exhibiting — and how joyfully! — the many things that, yes, she has been able to know.

Pointing to the central paradox of the poem, Alatorre stops short though of analyzing the deeper implications it might have on Sor Juana's rhetoric and epistemology. Like Giordano Bruno, whose enthusiastic sonnet on Icarus Méndez Plancarte recalls in his notes to lines 805–810, Sor Juana flirts with unmeasured rhetorical excess to express the pathos of seeking knowledge in a world hostile to such pursuits.[21] And yet the Mexican nun also knows a certain humility — a character trait that could never be ascribed to Bruno. Unafraid to thematize her own confusion, she begins the next section of the poem (827–886) by figuring her will, her "confusa la elección" [*confused choice*], as a vessel that foundered by "sirtes tocando de imposibles" [*touching the shoals of impossibilities*]. Faced with the impossible again, she begins to awake, which means she also begins to conclude the poem. Another ascent is described, but now it concerns only a literal, material process as the stomach begins to rumble and the body, subject now to "ascendiendo / soporíferos, húmedos vapores" [*ascending, soporific, humid vapors*], commences to stir. Her visions dissipating from her brain, she reflects about the value of "la docta perspectiva" [*the learned perspective*] via a simile comparing what the awaking brain sees to the projections in a magic lantern show.[22] Neither anamorphotic nor exaggerated in any way, these new images are perfectly mimetic and, she adds, perfectly unworthy of further exploration. Like a Platonic shadow on a cave wall or a Freudian screen memory, they are illusory objects of desire: "la sombra fugitiva . . . cuerpo finge formado, / de todas dimensiones adornado, / cuando aun ser superficie no merece" [*the fugitive shadow . . . feigns a body's shape, adorned with every dimension, though it cannot even be called a surface*] (882–886).

The next section (887–916), the beginning of the poem's conclusion, recounts a virtual *cosmomachy*. A recasting of the classical gigantomachy, it partially depends on Sor Juana's idiosyncratic version of the Ptolemaic cosmos for its content and characters. Here, as with Plato, not to mention Lucan and Donne, the limits of reason give myth new urgency. Depicting the epic struggle between day and night, between "el Padre de la Luz," who is "tropas reclutando" [*recruiting troops*], and night with his "negro escaudrones" [*black squadrons*], Sor Juana sends us back to the poem's opening lines where the earth's shadows threaten the sky. And with the example of Phaeton still resonating, she complicates further her syncretic, self-mythologization by tracing now the figure of dawn or Aurora:

> y del viejo Tithón la bella esposa
> — amazona de luces mil vestida,
> contra la noche armada,
> hermosa si atrevida,
> valiente aunque llorosa . . .[23] (898–902)

and the beautiful spouse of old Tithonus — amazon attired with a thousand lights, armed against the night, beautiful if daring, valiant though tearful . . .

Thematizing the equivocal nature of *atrevimiento* one last time by visiting the innumerability *topos* ("luces mil"), Sor Juana stresses the tragic *affectus* ("llorosa") experienced by this vicarious figure ("hermosa si atrevida"). A similar ambivalence occurs a few lines later when night amazes herself with her own majesty:

> . . . tirana usurpadora
> del imperio del día,
> negro laurel de sombras mil ceñía
> y con nocturno cetro pavoroso
> las sombras gobernaba,
> de quien aun ella misma se espantaba. (911–916)

tyrannical usurper of day's empire, crowned with black laurel of a thousand shadows, and with a terrifying, nocturnal scepter, governed the
shadows, of which even she herself is frightened.

Not only does Night imitate Sor Juana's own audacity, but it alone commands the Petrarchan "laurel" that all poets desire. By identifying herself so
closely with Night, the poet also indicates that this *cosmomachy* occurs entirely
within her own dream space. And by internalizing the gnostic symbolism of
light and darkness, she reverses the poem's earlier movement in which the external struggles of nature eventually infected the sleeping self. Now the self
contaminates nature, even as the vivid *chiaroscuro* play here repeats the poem's
larger dialectic of knowledge and ignorance.

As the poem concludes, the lines separating self and nature become so
exaggerated as to be indistinguishable. The lines demarcating the powers
of poetry and nature (seen through the lens of Tycho Brahe's astronomy) become blurred as well, as the sun assumes the role of the hyperbolic poet-
sculptor-geometer-arithmetician:

> Llegó, en efecto, el sol cerrando el giro
> que esculpió de oro sobre azul zafiro:
> de mil multiplicados
> mil veces puntos, flujos mil dorados
> — líneas, digo, de luz clara — salían
> de su circunferencia luminosa,
> pautando al cielo la cerúlea plana . . . (943–949)

The sun, that is, arrived, completing the circuit that it carved in gold on
the sapphire blue: a thousand times a thousand points, a thousand
golden torrents — lines, I mean, of clear light — emerge from its luminous circumference, providing rules for the cerulean plane of heaven.

The sun achieves what the poet could not — circumscription and completion. Night too, even in defeat, can claim a kind of victory: ". . . en su mismo
despeño recobrada / esforzando el aliento en la ruina" [*recovered from her own
precipitous fall, straining her breath amidst the ruin*] (961–962). Night's stubborn
courage, meanwhile, recalls Phaeton's determination "su nombre eternizar en
su ruina." Its determination to play the "rebelde" [*rebel*] a "segunda vez" [*second time*] (965), moreover, may well refer to Sor Juana's own lifelong refusal to

bow before ecclesiastical and patriarchal antipathy to her intellectual and poetic vocations. Indeed, night — and so also doubt, dream, and her epistemological ambition — are not really vanquished in the concluding lines, rather they have retreated to the other, sleeping half of the globe. In this way, the *orbis terrarum* reemerges as the only true measure for her exorbitant philosophic and aesthetic strivings. Or as Sor Juana's near contemporary, Thomas Browne intimates in the concluding paragraph of *The Garden of Cyrus*, the search for knowledge knows no resting place: "The Huntsman are up in *America*, and they are already past their first sleep in *Persia*."[24]

Browne's cosmographic wake-up call is matched by Sor Juana who ends the *Sueño* with a series of images adumbrating illumination. With the sun's return, she solicits closure: ". . . quedando a luz más cierta / el mundo iluminado, y yo despierta" [*with the light remaining more certain, the world illuminated, and me awakened*]. Nonetheless, despite the waning of physical darkness and the change in her physiological state, it remains unclear given the poem's downward thematic trajectory whether she considers herself to be permanently *iluminada* or merely momentarily *desengañada*. There is little hint of a skeptical epiphany, but nor does the marvelously precise Gongorist description in lines 944–946 of the sun's artistry ("que esculpió de oro sobre azul zafiro / de mil multiplicados / mil veces puntos, flujos mil dorados . . .") seem to transfer to the poet's simple self-conceit ("y yo despierta"). In other words, the possibility suggested by Sabat de Rivers that these last lines should be read ironically ought to be seriously entertained.[25] For they recall the illusions encountered in the dream even as they push the reader out of the poem's fictional frame and into the infinite, material world again; they signal, that is, an irreparable disjunction between the dream's copious, hyperbolic language and a nascent rhetoric of irony where the individual knowingly speaks to, and from within, an unknowable cosmos. Or, as Friedrich Schlegel neatly phrases it: "Ironie ist gleichsam die *epideixis* der Unendlichkeit" [*Irony is as it were the* epideixis *of infinity*].[26]

A lyric *Wunderkammer*, the *Primero Sueño* is rightly considered one of Baroque's poetry's greatest repositories of learning. But it should also be viewed as the site of one of its grandest epistemological defeats. Sor Juana's epic representation of the failure to intuit or deduce epistemological certainty, and thus win what would be its attendant spiritual rewards, reworks the hyperbolics of *desengaño* beloved by earlier Spanish Baroque poets to lend it a philosophical weight and rigor which Góngora never sought and which Quevedo achieves only vicariously through his Neo-Stoicism. A late incarnation of the same skeptical humanism that fuels Sánchez's *Quod nihil scitur*, Montaigne's *Essais*, and Pascal's *Pensées*, the *Sueño* demands to be read as an urgent, humanistic counterpoint to the triumphant history of Cartesianism.[27] For like its prose counterparts, the poem makes no pretensions at system-building, nor does it apologize for its reliance on the legacy of humanist learning whose methods of argument and attaining eloquence had already begun to fall into disfavor in Europe. Instead, Sor Juana's sometimes exuberant, sometimes ironic stance toward modernity's novel epistemological enterprise depends on precisely those species of rhetorical exaggeration and artifice that Descartes, Bacon, and Hobbes sought to discredit.

While both Sor Juana and Descartes adapt the hermetic-dream allegory to pursue decidedly "modern" aims, their respective dreams also represent the forking-paths of the early modern sensibility. Descartes inherits the dream of universal knowledge as propagated by Agrippa, Bruno, and Kepler. As such he is the overreaching thinker piggybacking on the hermetic sciences he will later discredit. And if he sublimates the poetic *furor*, inspired *sententiae*, and subjective idealism of the *Olympica* in his later writings into the largely dis-cursive metaphors of wax, machines, and Archimedean points, then at least in the *Olympica* we see what Cartesian rationalism might owe to Baroque tastes for the incredible and supernatural. Still, as I shall argue later, only the first step in the mature Descartes' method is truly hyperbolic, while Sor Juana's entire *hodos*, the sum of her metaphors and amplifications, are sus-tained by hyperbole. By taking the Gongorist style, overloading it with classi-cal allusion and myth, and then riddling it with the ironies of epistemological uncertainty, Sor Juana lends language an opacity that works mimetically, per-formatively, to represent the struggles of the philosophically ambitious soul. In both their dreams, and here I mean dream in the largest sense of the word, Descartes and Sor Juana seek clarity beyond physical experience. But whereas Descartes has a hermeneutic ready to disperse the "spectres" of his "evil ge-nius," a hermeneutic he claims is guaranteed him by the Christian God, Sor Juana, the nun, never appeals to a Christian *deus ex machina*.

Admittedly, these observations ignore somewhat the contingencies of his-tory and biography, as well as eliding differences of temperament. Descartes is free to gallivant about the territories ravaged by the Thirty Year's War. His wintertime stay in the *poêle* where his method is born, is but a point, albeit a decisive, Archimedean point, in his itinerant biography. For Sor Juana, on the contrary, her monastic cell is a fixed sphere in a collapsing universe. Three years after the composition of the *Sueño*, with food riots by *indios* and *mestizos* raging throughout Mexico, and with the departure of her patrons, Sor Juana renounces poetry, sells her books to feed the poor, declares herself "yo peor del mundo" [*I, the worst in the world*], and takes a vow of silence that is capped soon afterward by a premature death. Her liberating dream of knowledge is thwarted, even as the *Sueño* succeeds in monumentalizing the epistemological potential and limits of lyric poetry. If for her Descartes' dream (or nightmare) never truly crosses the Atlantic, then in her *celda* we glimpse that other, skeptical strain of modern subjectivity whose legacy begins in antiquity but is enriched by Sánchez, Montaigne, and Pascal — Pascal who ascribes all man's ills to his inability to remain contentedly in his room. Cut off from many of the latest intellectual developments of seventeenth-century Europe, Sor Juana's room seems more expansive and inviting than Descartes' hermetically sealed *poêle*; perhaps, because there is still space there for doubt and the aesthetic ornaments of desire. For all its dependence on difficult, obscure *conceptos* and the other trappings of the Baroque style, Sor Juana's *celda* is ultimately more transparent, more open to human(ist) contingency and concerns, than Descartes' chamber of certainty. This is not to say, however, that she lacks all Cartesian hubris. Responding in a letter to the priest who challenged her intellectual vocation, Sor Juana defiantly affirms:

Yo tengo este genio. Si es malo, yo me hice. Nací con él y con él he de morir. V. R. quiere que por fuerza me salve ignorando. Pues, amado padre mío, ¿no puede esto hacerse sabiendo, que al fin es camino para mí más suave? Pues ¿por qué para salvarse ha de ir por el camino de la ignorancia si es repugnante a su natural? ¿no es Dios, como suma Bondad, suma sabiduría?[28]

I have this genius. If it is bad, I am responsible. I was born with it and I must die with it. Your Reverence forcefully endeavors to save me when I am ignorant. Well, my beloved father, can this not be done when I have knowledge, which in the end is for me a gentler road? For why in order to save someone must the road of ignorance be taken, which is repugnant to my nature? Is not God, as the culmination of goodness, the culmination of knowledge?

BACON'S PROGRESS

In *The Advancement of Learning* (1605), Francis Bacon likewise vehemently defends the thirst for knowledge as what is most proper to humanity and as what
honors most God's nature and providence: "... let no man ... think or
maintain that a man can search too far or be too well studied in the book of
God's word or in the book of God's works; divinity or philosophy; but rather
let men endeavour an endless progress or proficience in both."[29] In the same
breath, Bacon's theology is nothing if not pragmatic. Branding as mere "wonder, which is broken knowledge," the kind of metaphysical knowledge desired by Sor Juana, and warning against the "swelling" and "presumption"
of those whose learning is without "use" or "charity," he masterfully borrows
from Scripture and theological rhetoric to promote his epistemological revolution.[30] Moreover, Bacon's rhetoric championing natural philosophy also
borrows directly from Spanish imperial, epideictic rhetoric, as he transforms
the ideology of *Plus ultra* into a call to arms on behalf of the new scientific
method. He conflates, that is, the early modern rhetoric of *translatio imperii*
with his own complicated rejection of Renaissance humanism's *translatio stu-
diorum*.[31] For all its optimism, then, Bacon's epideixis of scientific progress
contains elements that bring his epistemological project much closer to Sor
Juana's than one would expect.

Part of the pessimism of early modern Spain and its poets was due to external factors: the rise of France, the Netherlands, and England served as a
constant, distressing reminder that the ideology of *Plus ultra* was not limited to
Spain. One instrument of that ideology was cartography, which adeptly
served imperial needs even as it became a dynamic discursive site where scientific and aesthetic interests could converge. Indeed, with certain technical advances and the increasingly detailed knowledge provided by the voyages of
discovery, cartography and geography were, along with astronomy, those early
modern branches of learning that most dramatically had been improved
upon from the ancients.[32] Considering also that the greatest obstacle to scientific "progress" was inordinate reverence for antiquity and authority, it seems
altogether fitting that an inventive stylist like Bacon should mine the rhetoric
of geography and empire to promote the new experimental philosophy.[33] In
the dedication to King James of Book Two of *The Advancement of Learning*,
Bacon asks: "... why should a few received authors stand up like Hercules'
Columns, beyond which there should be no sailing or discovering, since we

have so bright and benign a star as your majesty to conduct and prosper us?"[34] While the star reference is a classical commonplace, Bacon is also slyly usurping here royal prerogative even as he pays it lip service. Jonathan Goldberg notes that Bacon's immediate source may have been a wellknown postArmada engraving in which Queen Elizabeth is portrayed as standing between the columns.[35] Here, though, Bacon the experimental philosopher, and not the sovereign, points the way. Conversely, in so far as the passing of the columns is made an emblem of scientific exploration, Bacon is preceded by Samuel Daniel who exhorts the learned in his 1601 poem, "Musophilus," to ". . . set their bolde *Plus ultra* farre without / The Pillers of those Axioms Age propounds: / Discou'ring daily more and more about, / In that immense and boundlesse Ocean / Of Nature's riches, never yet found out, / Nor foreclos'd, with the wit of any man."[36] But it was Bacon who was largely responsible for the phrase's popularity in seventeenthcentury English scientific discourse.[37] If so, surely Simon van de Pass's striking frontispiece for the 1620 *Great Instauration*, which depicts not one, but two ships passing beyond the Pillars, contributed to its diffusion. Accompanied by a motto adapted from the *Book of Daniel* which translates as: "Many shall pass to and fro and knowledge shall be increased," the engraving is the visual antithesis of the many contemporary maps which represent the margins of knowledge as threatening, monstrous locales, or simply as potential sources of lucre.[38]

A more extensive refashioning of the *Plus ultratopos* occurs in the second book of *The Advancement*. There Bacon affirms "the history of cosmography," which "being compounded of natural history" and "mathematics," is the "part of learning of all others in this latter time [that] hath obtained most proficience." By "proficience" he means progress beyond the knowledge of the ancients; he continues, accordingly, with this explicit outbidding of classical authority:

For it may be truly affirmed to the honor of these times, and in a vertuous emulation with Antiquitie, that this great Building of the world, had never *through lights* made in it, till the age of us and our fathers: For although they had knowledge of the *Antipodes*:

Nosque ubi primus equis Oriens afflavit anhelis:
Illic sera rubens accendit lumina vesper. [*Georgics*, 1.250–251]
[*. . . and where the rising sun, with panting horses, first breathed on us: there luminous Vesper kindles its crimson rays.*]

yet that mought be by demonstration, and not in fact; and if by travaile, it requireth the voiage but of halfe the Globe.[39]

In the passage from which these lines are taken Virgil is contemplating whether the inhabitants of the antipodes experience a sunrise at the same time as "us" or rather "the silence in the dead of night" [*intempesta silet nox*].[40] And though he seems to get it right, in Bacon's view Virgil deserves blame as a natural scientist for his overly abstract method of "demonstration." By contrast, Bacon would have his readers follow the example of the planets and stars, Magellan and Drake, in order to undertake unprecedented journeys:

> But to circle the Earth, as the heavenly bodies doe, was not done, nor enterprised, till these latter times: And therefore these times may iustly beare in their word, not onely *plus ultrà*, in precedence of the ancient *Non ultrà*, and *Imitabile fulmen*, in precedence of the ancient: *Non imitabile fulmen*,
>
> Demens qui nimbos et non imitabile fulmen; etc. [*Aen.*, 6.590]
> [*Madman! to mimic the clouds and the inimitable thunder . . .*]
>
> But likewise, *Imitabile cœlum*: in respect of the many memorable voyages after the manner of heaven, about the globe of the earth.[41]

The *Aeneid* citation comes from the description of Aeneas' descent to the Underworld where he witnesses the Giants being punished for their attempt to overthrow the Olympian gods. While this is not the place to consider the many semantic, agonistic echoes of the gigantomachy in Bacon's project, I do wish to underline how he boldly strips away all the moral implications in Virgil's lines. Bacon would outbid his literary predecessors, but not because he would wrestle, like Sor Juana, with the history of literary *imitatio*. Instead, he would improve upon his literary model by giving "precedence" to the experience of mariners and astronomers. Elsewhere he urges "natural and experimental history be collected and completed, true and rigorous, free of anything philological," that is, tied not to *auctoritas*, but solely to "experience."[42] It is all the more intriguing, then, that his *Non ultra* may have, as Michael Kiernan notes, a classical source, albeit one mediated by translation: namely, Holland's 1601 translation of Pliny's *Natural History*, where Holland writes of "Hercules pillers *non ultra*."[43] If this is the case, then Bacon's idea of progress is certainly more "philological," more intertextual, than he is willing to admit.

Not content just to outbid Virgil or Pliny, or to limit his notion of discovery to geography, Bacon concludes this passage from the *Advancement* by
throwing Augustinian caution to the wind. Deftly invoking Biblical authority, he calls for an epistemological and methodological revolution:

> And this proficience in navigation and discoveries may plant also an ex-
> pectation of the further proficience and augmentation of all sciences; be-
> cause it may seem they are ordained by God to be coevals, that is, to meet
> in one age. For so the prophet Daniel, speaking of the latter times, fore-
> telleth PLURIMI PERTRANSIBUNT, ET MULTIPLEX ERIT
> SCIENTIA; as if the openness and thorough passage of the world and
> the increase of knowledge were appointed to be in the same ages; as we
> see it is already performed in great part . . .

Just as the discoveries in the New World are providential, so, Bacon's analogy
goes, is the "proficience" of science. *Plus ultra* in this way is transformed into
the hyperbolic paradigm for the epistemological and spiritual passage from
"darkness" to "light" — Bacon's recurrent "absolute metaphor" for the advancement of knowledge.[44] To combat the widely prevalent feeling in the late
Renaissance that nature itself, to say nothing of the human sciences, has inex-
orably decayed since antiquity, Bacon avails himself of other rhetorical strategies as well. He uses paradox to turn the common conception of history
upside-down: "*Antiquitas saeculi, juventus mundi . . .* These times are the ancient
times." And to combat despair in the face of the great task of piercing nature's secrets, Bacon lets modesty's veil fall and makes himself an *exemplum*:
"If there be any that despond, let them look at me."[45]

It is all the more telling, then, how in *The Great Instauration* Bacon combats the inevitable charge that his project entails a kind of Herculean hubris
by appealing to his theory of gradualism. He aims, he writes, to "bring about
a complete *Instauration* of the arts and sciences, and all the learning of mankind, raised upon proper foundations. And while at the beginning this might
appear infinite and beyond mortal capacity, once in train it will be found reasonable and sober, more so in fact than those things that have been done hitherto."[46] The phrase "in train" points to how crucial the metaphors of the
"path" and "progress" — the latter also signifying a royal procession — are
for an understanding of Bacon's conception of *Plus ultra*.[47] Insisting that "discovery" is common to the voyages of exploration and the "progress" of the

natural sciences, he likens the overestimation of the arts we already possess and the underestimation of our innate strengths to "the pillars of fate in the path of the sciences, since men have neither desire nor hope to encourage them to explore beyond." Such hortatory rhetoric is clearly self-reflexive as well, for on the same page he signals that the pillars also stand on the "threshold of my work."[48]

No wonder Bacon needs to confront the moral and theological implications of his enormous ambitions. He would have the sciences be "democratic" and so freed from the "virtual dictatorship" of Time. In this way, he tries to strip *Plus ultra* of the aristocratic connotations it acquires via Charles's motto. By urging attention to "the things themselves," Bacon can insist upon his own "humility" and also underscore the unreliability of words.[49] Touching all too swiftly on the theological implications of such inquiry, he prays that "we may give to faith, that which is faith's." Yet in the next breath he hopes "that with knowledge rid of the poison instilled by the serpent, whereby the human mind becomes swollen and puffed up, we may not reach too high nor too far in our wisdom, but may seek the truth in Christian love."[50] The "true ends" of knowledge are Augustinian; we must "direct and bring it to perfection in charity, for the benefit and use of life. For the angels fell through hunger for power; men through hunger for knowledge. But of love and charity there can be no excess." Here again, the specters of "excess" and overreaching raise their hydra heads. In contrast to Donne, Milton, and Sor Juana, however, Bacon does not ultimately desire self-knowledge or divine knowledge; instead, he "seeks knowledge, not arrogantly in little recesses of human ingenuity, but humbly in the wider world."[51] Self-knowledge is thus divorced from knowledge of the world — a historical and epistemological break of enormous proportions, a break, arguably, enabled by his somewhat disingenuous reliance on the metaphorics of space. (Curiously, as we shall see, Pascal institutes the very same break, although he brands as folly the desire for empirical knowledge of the infinite universe. For Pascal, the "little recesses" of the human soul prove to be more than enough.)

In the *Advancement*, Bacon warns that "an affectionate studie of eloquence, and copie of speech" may grow "speedily to an excesse."[52] An apt diagnosis of the humanist legacy, this warning does not address, however, whether such "excesse" might retain any heuristic or epistemological value. Also, does such "excesse" betray a more congenital "distemper" than Bacon is willing or able to admit? Comparing the orator's preference for words over matter to "*Pig-*

malians frenzie," Bacon permits rhetoric to serve as the philosopher and legis-lator's handmaiden, even as he accuses it of causing several, fatal cognitive mistakes:

> [Rhetoric] is a thing not hastily to be condemned, to cloath and adorne the obscuritie, even of Philosophie it selfe, with sensible and plausible elocution . . . For surely, to the severe inquisition of truth, and the deep progresse into Philosophie, it is some hindrance; because it is too early satisfactorie to the minde of man, and quencheth the desire of further search, before we come to a just periode. But then if a man be to have any use of such knowledge in civile occasions . . . Then shall he finde it pre-pared to his hands in those Authors, which write in that manner. But the excesse of this is so justly contemptible, that as *Hercules*, when hee saw the Image of *Adonis*, *Venus Mignon* in a Temple, sayd in disdaine, *Nil sacri es*. So there is none of *Hercules* followers in learning, that is, the more severe, and laborious sort of Enquirers into truth, but will despise those delicacies and affectations, as indeede incapable of no divineness.[53]

Rhetoric must be ornamental and hortatory; but when it comes to "to the severe inquisition of truth," its heuristic value is minimal. Still, as Bacon's own ambivalent syntax suggests — note the two antitheses beginning with "But" — rhetoric remains indispensable for the expression of ambivalent, complex thoughts. It also continues to lend authority to any discourse, even one that would condemn its own excesses. Thus in pursuit of a fitting simile to ornament his views, Bacon makes that Ur-overreacher, Hercules (and his labors), an emblem of the new science. He would persuade us by granting "contemptible" authors who prize words over matter, absolutely no quarter, even as he renovates hyperbolic commonplaces for his own ends. Given this startling ambiguity, and given the uses and abuses of antiquity that I high-lighted earlier, Bacon's rhetoric, to steal a phrase from Levin's study of Marlowe and hyperbole, may well be said to inaugurate the age of "science without conscience."[54]

Bacon refashions *Plus ultra* to serve as a call to arms to promote his exper-imental natural philosophy. Promising a "triumph over nature," he insists that real epistemological and historical limits separate antiquity and the Middle Ages from his own self-conscious modernity. Yet by adopting *Plus ultra* with all its religious, imperial, and antiquarian weight, Bacon actually increases rather than diminishes his own authority — something he frequently claims not to want. By contrast, Sor Juana refuses to limit the claims of rhetorical subjectivity and contingency in the name of scientific progress. Her epyllion in *silvas* implicitly challenges the epistemology of the author of the *Sylva Sylvarum* (1631) by insisting on the most material and indeterminate aspect of thought: namely, the dependence of the *ingenium* on language for its expressive means. Such witty language for all its extravagant reach and acute insight is not to be made commensurate with the world. It exceeds the world but falls short of God. And in the process, hyperbole as a mode of thought begins to cede to the more inscrutable claims of irony. As Sor Juana writes in the *Respuesta*:

> . . . como dijo doctamente Gracían, las ventajas en entendimiento lo son en el ser. No por otra razón es el ángel más que el hombre que porque entiende más; no es otro exceso que el hombre hace al bruto, sino sólo entender; y así como ninguno quiere ser menos que otro, así ninguno confiesa que otro entiende más, porque es consequencia del ser más. Sufirirá uno y confesará que otro es más noble que él, que es más rico, que es más hermoso y aun que es más docto; pero que es más entendido apenas habrá quien lo confiese: *Rarus est, qui velit cedere ingenio.*[55]

> . . . as Gracián learnedly said, the advantages of understanding come from one's being. For no other reason is the angel more than man than because he understands more; the only way man exceeds beasts is by understanding. And thus since nobody wants to be less than another, thus nobody will confess that another understands more, because this follows from superiority of being. A person will allow and confess that another is nobler than he, that the other is richer, that the other is more handsome, and even that the other is more learned, but that another has more understanding there is hardly anybody who will confess it: *Rare is he willing to yield to another in intelligence.*

For the rare *ingenio* that pens the *Sueño*, to reason about God or the world, or to analyze the mind's inductive and deductive powers, is not to use language as a means to an end, but rather to explore the hyperbolic limits, the "insolente exceso" of linguistic expression. That ultimately Sor Juana denies herself the glory of achieving a philosophical *Plus ultra* may well be fodder for psychoanalytical readings, or it may be read as symptomatic of larger cultural and historical forces shaping the Mexican Baroque. The text itself, however, asks a very simple question of reason and language: "¿cómo en tan espantosa / máquina inmensa discurrir pudiera . . . ?" In the course of 975 lines of lyric poetry readers experience the discovery that such a discourse is impossible. Granted, Sor Juana's poetry posthumously wins her a place on the summits of Parnassus (at least in the eyes of her publishers); yet as her skillful exhaus-tion of the hyperbolics of ascent and descent in the *Sueño* makes abundantly clear, she intends to improve upon the "necia experiencia" of Icarus. Her aim is the godlike perspective Dante wins in the *Paradiso*, even if she ends up sound-ing more like Ulysses, who having failed to reach the Mountain of Purgatory, teaches us to savor instead the "esperïenza" of his marvelous "folle volo."

Chapter Nine

Staging Hyperbole, Skepticism, and Stoicism

> The question for the theater, then, is to create a metaphysics
> of speech, gesture, and expression, in order to rescue it from
> its psychological and human stagnation. But all this can be
> of use only if there is behind such an effort a kind of real
> metaphysical temptation, an appeal to certain unusual
> ideas which by their very nature cannot be limited, or even
> formally defined. These ideas, which have to do with
> Creation, with Becoming, with Chaos, and are all of a
> cosmic order, provide an elementary notion of a realm
> from which the theater has become totally estranged.
>
> — Antonin Artaud, "The Theater of Cruelty
> (First Manifesto)"

CAVELL, SHAKESPEARE, AND "HYPERBOLIC SEPARATENESS"

Rather than sharing Artaud's seminal vision, and viewing the theater as a place to "create a metaphysics," Stanley Cavell cultivates the other extreme. In his essays on Shakespearean tragedy, collected in *Disowning Knowledge: In Seven Plays of Shakespeare*, Cavell makes the theater the place where Artaud's boundless "ideas" are dramatically upstaged by "psychological and human stagnation." This upstaging and the related notion that Shakespearean drama may be the most urgent if improper response to Cartesian skepticism precipitate and ultimately frame my readings of hyperbole in Baroque drama and philosophy. Why this should be the case needs some explaining.

In the Introduction to *Disowning Knowledge*, Cavell observes:

> . . . Othello's jealousy itself is an unstable, turned concept. He seeks a possession that is not in opposition to another's claim or desire but one that establishes an absolute or inalienable bond to himself, to which no claim or desire *could* be opposed, could conceivably count; as if the jealousy is directed to the sheer existence of the other, its separateness from him. It is against the (fantasied) possibility of overcoming this hyperbolic separateness that the skeptic's (disappointed, intellectualized, impossible, imperative, hyperbolic) demand makes sense.[1]

If the word "hyperbolic" here acquires almost a tautological force, this is not accidental. Characteristically, Cavell would challenge the hermeticism and inaccessibility of thinking that uses language in absolute, solipsistic, or "turned" ways. As Timothy Gould puts it in a recent paper, Cavell questions the philosopher's "false" or "enforced literality" that fuels skeptical claims about the world, claims that undermine the demands of situated human voices and their contingent needs and experiences.[2] Inspired by Wittgenstein's model of philosophy as therapy, Cavell in his thinking and writing would make us responsive to and responsible for "ordinary language" and "the phenomenon of ordinary language philosophy."[3] Put another way, Cavell first attends to texts and kinds of discourse and then only reluctantly to those abstractions, concepts that shape Western philosophy from Plato to Descartes and beyond. Thus, when he reflects that his own rhetoric sometimes verges on the "immodest and melodramatic," that it can be "exaggerated, melodramatically excessive," Cavell's readers are invited to consider what hyperbolic criticism of philosophic and dramatic hyperbole might mean.[4]

Reading Shakespearean tragedy, Cavell discovers in the jealousy of Othello and Leontes, Coriolanus's disdain, Hamlet's "desire never to have succeeded, or acceded, to existence,"[5] and Lear's extravagant pride and suffering, not only psychologically realistic beings whose motives can be dissected but also the philosophical implications of such "hyperbolic separateness." Briefly put, these Shakespearean characters help him "make sense" of Descartes' skeptical, isolated, hyperbolic *cogito* — the motives for and the precipitousness of its deduction. For if dramatic hyperbole is the vehicle of self-consciousness of, as well as extreme skepticism toward, the motives and even "existence" of other people, this recalls Descartes' experience in the stove-heated room in Germany where he intuits the possibility of philosophic certainty at the expense of what Cavell, Austin, and others have championed as ordinary language. Leaning throughout on "ordinary language philosophy," that is, the attempt to make philosophy responsive to how meaning and truth are produced by acknowledgment as much as by knowledge, Cavell presents his essays on Shakespeare as an intuitive, admittedly anachronistic, response to Cartesian skepticism. He warns from the outset that his "epistemological reading of Shakespearean tragedy" offers no "stable solution" to skepticism. Instead, he sees in *King Lear* and *Antony and Cleopatra* a "response to skepticism," one contemplating the "denial" of what we already know about ourselves and others, and therefore also "the self-consuming disappointment that seeks world-consuming revenge." Such feelings find expression, for example, in Lear's imperious rage at the daughter who loves him most or in Antony and Cleopatra's "eroticization" and "theatricalization of the world," which is precipitated by the way they lose political mastery over it.[6]

For my part, in this book's remaining chapters, I would trace how the hyperbolist in Baroque drama and philosophy often acts to deny the stringencies of circumstance, how he refuses to recognize faults, aporias, and limits, and yet sometimes how he is also able to express what is most transcendent, outrageous, or sublime in the human condition. I aim, that is, to discover how ordinary language might be extraordinary — without surrendering contingency, psychological verisimilitude, and the commonsensical that Cavell prizes. And if and when that surrender is made, either by the dramatist self-consciously plumbing a character's depths or a metaphysician measuring his understanding of the divine, then what understanding, what bargain is made with the audience or reader so that hyperbole's semantic or conceptual violence is accepted, excused, or simply ignored? When Cavell, in *The Claim of Reason*, ponders "the fierce ambiguity of ordinary language" he opens the door to the possibility that such language may be used in uncanny, sublime, and mysterious ways.[7] He invites the reasonable inference that ordinary language is sometimes necessarily hyperbolic, even as it remains to be seen how such hyperbole might differ from that species of expression which he and Wittgenstein regard as corrupting philosophy.

Cavell's various perspectives on hyperbole illuminate the ever-shifting, always porous lines between art and life. In a sense, he refashions Wordsworth's desire in the *Preface to Lyrical Ballads* (1800) to promote the "language really

used by men" over the "extravagant and absurd language" used by poets imitating other poets. Yet he also expands his vision of quotidian language to include philosophy and literature, such that these discourses, at their liveliest,
are responsive to the way people talk and live. Put another way, what Jakobson calls the "poetic function" is not limited to literature nor is it excluded
from philosophy. Thus Cavell insists that the extraordinary theatricality he
discovers in *King Lear* is akin to our own culture's denial of death, that is, our
loss of "presentness" — though with the chilling difference that the trajectory
traced by *Lear* passes through love, whereas our culture (intellectual and otherwise) often bypasses love altogether.[8]

For the purposes of my analysis, then, Cavell's approach to literary criticism via "ordinary language philosophy" helps to narrow the gap between
how an orator (Quintilian) would use hyperbole, how different dramatists
(Shakespeare and Seneca) employ it, and how and why certain philosophers
(Descartes and Pascal) rely on it. The rub, as Cavell insists in *Disowning
Knowledge*, is to distinguish between what a person (be it a character in a play,
or a philosopher pretending to live in a cave) says and what she means. To accomplish this one must attend to and imagine how "human beings in particular circumstances" speak and how their words may or may not express what
they mean; or, that "for various reasons they may not know what they mean,
and that when they are forced to recognize this they feel that they do not, and
perhaps cannot, mean anything, and they are struck dumb."[9] The psychological implications of this aside — Cavell's later work (including his essay on
The Winter's Tale) will increasingly focus on these — such an approach may
reveal how characters in a drama like *Lear* experience inexpressibility. Or
such an approach may explain the motives behind certain strains of analytical
philosophy. In brief, Shakespeare and Wittgenstein are intent on exploring the
space — often the abyss — between saying and meaning, or to put it in more
familiar rhetorical terms, between literal and figurative language. Indeed,
Shakespeare and Wittgenstein prove to be immensely self-conscious of how
hyperbole can create hermeneutic difficulties and affective pathos. "What shall
Cordelia say? Love and be silent" and "Wovon man nicht sprechen kann,
darüber muß man schweigen" [*Whereof one cannot speak, thereof one must be silent*],
turn out to be starting rather than end points.[10] Both utterances exemplify
what it means to be struck dumb by the difference between saying and meaning, or between asserting and knowing, and in doing so they narrow the gap
between poetry and philosophy. They also open the door to those primarily

theological discourses such as apophasis and cataphasis, which are precipitated by the perception of the "Unaussprechliches" [*the inexpressible*] and "das
Mystische" [*the mystical*].[11]

Because it erases artificial discursive barriers and invites self-reflection
about the nature of language, the circulation between philosophy, literature,
and literary criticism has long occupied Cavell. This circulation and the attendant possibility of disorientation, inexpressiveness, error, and faith for the
subjective critic place a great cognitive burden on the reader: "The problem of
the critic, as of the artist, is not to discount his subjectivity but to include it;
not to overcome it in agreement, but to master it in exemplary ways."[12] Such
subjectivity precipitates the first section of "The Avoidance of Love: A Reading of *King Lear*," which concentrates on offering solutions to the tragedy's traditional cruxes.[13] In the second section, Cavell metarhetorically reflects on the
"immodest and melodramatic quality of the claims" he makes about the play
and asks why, if his thesis of "avoidance" is so "obvious," other critics have
not hit upon it.[14] Rather than directly answering this question, though, he diagnoses the audience's fundamental "complicity" in the tragedy and its various language games.[15] The gist of his argument is that skepticism, like Lear,
makes impossible, hyperbolic demands on the world. Seizing upon Lear's
declaration to Cordelia: "Better thou hadst not been born than not to have
pleased me better" (1.225), Cavell perceives that Lear, like the skeptical epis-
temologist, does not really seek certainty. Instead, both want to avoid acknowledging the world and truths they already know.[16]

Cavell concedes in the first paragraph of *Disowning Knowledge* that he
fears readers may misunderstand his "project as the application of some philosophically independent problematic of skepticism to a fragmentary parade of
Shakespearean texts."[17] Indeed, when it comes to hyperbole, I do wonder
sometimes how Cavell's lifelong philosophical preoccupations mark his reading of dramatic hyperbole. For Cavell discovers in Shakespearean tragedy
an allegory of a phenomenon whose origins are first found in philosophy:
namely, skepticism about the possibility of knowledge regarding objects serves
as his model:

> Here one would one day have to look at the philosopher's extraordinary
> treatment of objects, as in Descartes's wax that is melting, in Price's
> tomato with nothing but its visual front aspect remaining, in Moore's

raised moving hands, in Heidegger's blooming tree, to explore the sense of hyperbolic, unprecedented attention in play . . . The philosopher is as it were looking for a *response* from the object, perhaps a shining. And of course one may not sense this; the skeptic exactly would not. It is in tak- ing tragedy as the display of skepticism with respect to other minds as allegorical of skepticism in respect to material objects that in my experi- ence the treatment of the object forces its attention upon us.[18]

While I will address the question of critical allegories when I discuss below Benjamin's approach to the Baroque *Trauerspiel* and how it might illuminate *Lear*, here I want to raise a red flag: for just as we are alerted to the "hyperbolic, unprecedented attention in play" that shrinks, mutes, and reifies the world, the pale abstractions of allegory seem antithetical to the dialogic, contingent responses to skepticism that preoccupy Cavell. Cavell clips the wings of cer- tain transcendental albatrosses even, perhaps, as he launches his own critical allegory.

But in so far as such hyperbolic demands are felt in tragedy, Cavell's car- dinal insight in *The Claim of Reason* should be recalled: "In making knowl- edge of others a metaphysical difficulty, philosophers deny how real the practical difficulty is of coming to know another person, and how little we can reveal of ourselves to another's gaze, or bear of it."[19] Likewise, as he ar- gues in his interpretation of Othello's motives, Shakespearean tragedy stages the problem of skepticism, "the conversion of metaphysical finitude into in- tellectual lack," by showing us, readers and audience members, "the conse- quences, or price," of philosophy's insistence on denying our contingency and dependence on other humans in its search for certainty. Othello "cannot for- give Desdemona for existing, for being separate from him, outside, beyond command, commanding, her captain's captain."[20] Caught between a desire for self-certainty and autonomy, on the one hand, and our need for others, on the other, we waver between the "*avoidance* (of others, of the common, of what is common with others in oneself because these things are decayed, vulgar- ized, inhibiting, and empty) and *acknowledgement* (of others, of the common, of what is common with others in oneself which brings thought, recovery, conversation, and restoration)."[21] Thus Cavell proposes that in *Lear* skepti- cism takes the form of a tragic refusal to be known by other minds. The epis- temological consequences of such tragedy concern, then, not the failure of knowledge, but rather why Lear's avoidance of anagnorisis — "he hath ever but slenderly known himself" (1.282) — can only be shaken by language's aesthetic and rhetorical "superflux" (11.33).

For Cavell, Lear's "avoidance of love" is always specific, not only because the form and language of Shakespearean tragedy are unsurpassed, but also because he does frequently treat Shakespeare's characters as if they have motives beyond those expressed on the stage. Yet he also attends closely to the ways such motives are staged, just as he is inordinately moved by the ways Wittgenstein stages philosophy's pathos on the page. Cavell asks us to acknowledge Othello's ridiculous doubts and Lear's histrionic avoidance as our own; he asks us to measure them by and against how we ordinarily speak about our world and ourselves. He asks us, in short, to make their hyperbole our hyperbole, and then to consider the consequences.

SENECA, STOICISM, AND DRAMATIC RHETORIC

Cavell's scant engagement with late Renaissance forms of skepticism, and his neglect of the historical forms of Stoicism or Epicureanism ought to give any reader of Renaissance or Baroque tragedy pause.[22] While he points briefly to Montaigne and his influence via Florio on Shakespeare, the skepticism of the *Essais* is dismissed as not being refined or radical enough for his purposes.[23] Conspicuously avoided is any sustained consideration of the philosophic influences (be they Stoic, Epicurean, or Fideist), the dynamics of literary imitation, or the cultural conditions that may have helped Shakespeare produce his art. Cavell's formalism is at once textual and synchronic. With its untraditional emphasis on character over action, and its insistence that heuristic fictions, such as Descartes in his *poêle*, are as common to philosophy as literature, he gives the problem of skepticism a new cast and urgency. Ahistoricist and deeply interdisciplinary, Cavell's essays in *Disowning Knowledge*, Anthony Cascardi observes, can seem "mannered" for the way that they discover "recherché" motives and thoughts in Shakespeare's characters. Critic and characters converge, making it difficult to distinguish "mannerism from self-reflection, or extravagant speculation from the extremes of consciousness that expose themselves under the dire conditions of tragedy."[24]

Cavell does briefly suggest that his interpretations of dramaturgical motive and language are more attentive to Renaissance Epicureanism than that other current of classical philosophy dominating the Elizabethan stage: the Stoicism of Seneca, Lipsius, and their epigones. Yet I would show that his

readings of Shakespearean tragedy become still more complex and persuasive if the influence of Senecan drama and Stoic thought on English Renaissance drama is pondered. To prepare properly the ground for a rhetorical and
epistemological (re)reading of dramatic hyperbole in *King Lear* (written probably in 1605; First Quarto, 1608), I first want to consider, then, how Senecan
thought and drama may inform Shakespeare's responses to the "problem of
skepticism."

While a full defense of Senecan drama from the damning verdicts of neoclassical tastes is beyond this chapter's brief, suffice it to say that scholarship
over the last hundred years has largely obviated the traditional calumnies that
this drama is indecorous, bombastic, *schwülstig*, jejune, and even unstageable —
that, in a word, it is too hyperbolic. As for the reception history of Senecan
tragedy, after reviewing the previous three hundred years of *Senecarezeption*,
Otto Regenbogen in 1930 defiantly asserts that Seneca's influence on Renaissance drama is "a historical fact, having such force and stability, that it cannot
be dismissed through any kind of judgment of taste by individuals or whole
periods of time."[25] This underscores the obvious; for Renaissance tragedy begins with Albertino Mussato's *Ecerinis* (1315), which makes Seneca its model
in theme, style, and prosody. And even as cinquecento critics debated the
value of Aristotelian unities, in practice Seneca rather than the Greek dramatists provided the chief paradigm for late Renaissance tragedy. Cinthio's
Orbecche (1541), Kyd's *The Spanish Tragedy* (printed 1592), Shakespeare's
Titus Andronicus (~1590), Optiz's *Trojanerinnen* (1625), Calderón's *El médico
de su honra* (1635), Corneille's *Médée* (1635), and Racine's *Phèdre* (1677) exemplify how throughout Europe dramatists borrowed heavily from Seneca for
their *imitatio*. Yet just as classicists today often still find it necessary to defend
Seneca and "silver" Latin verse from judgments of taste, scholarship on the
influence of Senecan drama in the Renaissance and Baroque continues the
task of reconciling its extravagant style with its severe ethical and cosmological vision.[26]

In this last respect, T. S. Eliot's criticism marks the decisive turn.[27] Reacting to the myriad versions of Shakespeare that Edwardian England produced
("there is the fatigued Shakespeare . . . the messianic Shakespeare . . . a Papist
Shakespeare . . ."), Eliot in his 1927 essay, "Shakespeare and the Stoicism of
Seneca," begins with coy modesty: "I wish merely to disinfect the Senecan
Shakespeare before he appears. My ambitions would be realized if I could
prevent him, in so doing, from appearing at all."[28] As fate would have it, his

essay, together with his 1927 Introduction to a reprint of the Tudor translations of Seneca, had just the opposite effect. And while this may have been
partially a result of Eliot's fame, surely it was also his ability to look beyond the
question of taste that guaranteed the *aperçu* of Seneca's influence on Shakespeare became a critical commonplace.

Eliot allows for the influence of Seneca's Stoicism but not Seneca's
tragedies themselves on Shakespeare.[29] Shakespeare, that is, was probably affected more by his contemporaries, the Senecan Kyd, Marston, Chapman,
and Peele, than a direct reading of Seneca's dramas. As for why Stoicism had
such a strong philosophical effect on Elizabethan thought and drama, Eliot,
with a curious mixture of common sense and historical sensitivity, observes:

> . . . Seneca is the *literary* representation of Roman stoicism, and . . . Ro-
> man stoicism is an important ingredient in Elizabethan drama. It was
> natural that in a time like that of Elizabeth stoicism should appear . . .
> Stoicism is the refuge for the individual in an indifferent or hostile world
> too big for him . . . [Elizabethan England] was a period of dissolution
> and chaos; and in such a period any emotional attitude which seems to
> give a man something firm, even if it be only the attitude of "I am my-
> self alone," is eagerly taken up.[30]

In this way what is now conceived as early modern subjectivity or self-
fashioning fuels Eliot's reading of the Elizabethan Senecans and their response to
a sense of cultural and spiritual crisis. In brief, the "attitude of self-dramatization
assumed by some of Shakespeare's heroes at moments of tragic intensity" may
be attributed to Seneca and his Stoicism.[31]

Taking a still more direct tack, Eliot's 1927 Introduction begins by confronting the petty tyrannies of taste.[32] Noting that contemporary Italian drama
helped nurture an English predilection for the grotesque, Eliot offers this eloquent apology for Senecan "bombast" in Elizabethan drama:

> Certainly, Elizabethan bombast can be traced to Seneca; Elizabethans
> themselves ridiculed the Senecan imitation. But if we reflect, not on the
> more grotesque exaggerations, but on the dramatic poetry of the first
> half of the period, as a whole, we see that Seneca had as much to do
> with its merits and its progress as with its faults and its delays. Certainly,
> it is all "rhetorical," but if it had not been rhetorical would it have been

anything? . . . Without bombast, we should not have had *King Lear*. The art of dramatic language, we must remember, is as near to oratory as to ordinary speech or to other poetry. On the stage, M. Jean Cocteau re-minds us, we must weave a pattern of coarse rope that can be appre-hended from the back of the pit, not a pattern of lace that can only be apprehended from the printed page. We are not entitled to try fine effects unless we achieve the coarse ones. If the Elizabethans distorted and trav-estied Seneca in some ways, if they learned from him tricks and devices which they applied with inexpert hands, they also learned from him the essentials of declaimed verse. Their subsequent progress is a process of splitting up the primitive rhetoric, developing out of it subtler poetry and subtler tones of conversation, eventually mingling, as no other school of dramatists has done, the oratorical, the conversational, the elaborate and the simple, the direct and the indirect; so that they were able to write plays which can still be viewed as plays, with any plays, and which can still be read as poetry, with any poetry.[33]

While my reading of *Lear* will challenge the distinction between dra-maturgy's "coarse rope" and "the pattern of lace" on the "printed page," Eliot's evolutionary account of the salutary effects of rhetorical bombast on English drama deserves to be quoted at length because he ascribes real dialec-tical force to such "padding." Moreover, by the end of the passage he nuances his claims on behalf of theatrical bombast with a historicist perspective on the unique "progress" achieved by the Elizabethan stage as it refines the Senecan legacy. In mediating between "the oratorical" and "the conversational," be-tween "poetry" and "ordinary speech," Eliot provides an early version of what Cavell casts as the tension between absolutism and complicity in Shake-spearean tragedy.

To historicize further Eliot's critique, I would recast his most striking claim: the increasing subtleties of "Elizabethan bombast" that culminate in *Lear* respond to how late Renaissance readers reconciled the conflicting claims made by Seneca's drama and philosophy. Beginning with Regenbogen, schol-ars have generally taken more comparatist, interdisciplinary approaches to the question of Senecan influence on European Renaissance drama.[34] But also, spurred by the bloodbaths of the two world wars, the grim realities of totali-tarianism, and the threat of nuclear annihilation, scholars came to reevaluate the relative gruesomeness and propriety of Senecan themes and rhetoric.[35] As is the case with Cavell's reading of *Lear* that responds, in part, to the Vietnam War, readers of Seneca found that the distance between *res* and *verba* in the dramas much smaller than their predecessors had claimed. Alternately, the advent of Expressionist drama and later Brecht's formal and ideological in-novations made Seneca's aesthetics seem less alien.

Embodying this changed perspective, Gordon Braden's *Anger's Privilege: Renaissance Tragedy and the Senecan Tradition* amplifies Regenbogen's insight that Senecan tragedy marks "a new and important interest in the subjectivity of consciousness."[36] In tracking the role that Stoic philosophy — with its em-phasis on *voluntas* — plays in Senecan drama, Braden also engages the prob-lem of hyperbole.[37] To justify Senecan hyperbole and its crimes against taste he promises to find its "primary topic." Discussing *Medea*, he tries to reconcile its bombast and other rhetorical extravagances with the detachment stressed by Seneca's philosophy: ". . . Stoic detachment is continuous and deeply in-volved with the most paralytic kind of anger. The real common ground be-tween Seneca's plays and his philosophy is on this level . . . The madmen and his victim, in dark complicity, split the world between them."[38] This dialogic "dark complicity" between characters complements Cavell's notion of the "complicity" between Shakespearean tragedy and its audience. That is, Seneca and the best of his early modern imitators, such as Marlowe, Shakespeare, Corneille, and Racine, incorporate the possibility of countering the hyper-bolic within their dramas via conflicting characters, dramatic ironies, and rhetorical *heteroglossia*, even as they task the audience with placing the hyper-bolic claims from the stage in their proper dramatic and psychological con-text.[39] Such mediation hardly diminishes, though, the almost Nietzschean will to power that Braden discovers in the dramatic representations of Senecan wrath. Regarding the chief protagonists of *Medea* and *Thyestes*, Braden com-ments: "They strain to take a fantasy of individual autonomy beyond almost any kind of limit."[40] The *affectus* (passions) that accompany such straining and that precipitate such hyperbolic, cosmological effects give Senecan tragedy its unique force. Again, the difference is between what happens on the stage and the philosophical page. C. A. J. Littlewood comments: "Seneca's Sto-icism is habitually conducted *in extremis* and in isolation."[41] But in the dramas Seneca tries to figure out how extreme emotions and events affect other people and the fabric of nature.

This focus on self and cosmos dominates Thomas Rosenmeyer's *Sene-can Drama and Stoic Cosmology*.[42] Initially justifying the "spectacle," "extrava-

gance," and hyperbole in plays like *Hercules furens* and *Othello* as essential vehicles of "self-dramatization" and self-consciousness, Rosenmeyer ranges beyond purely dramaturgical and ethical (in the moral as well as Aristotelian
sense of a character's *ethos*) explanations to detail the intimate correspondences between different spheres of activity.[43] Focusing on the cardinal Stoic
concept of *pneuma* (breath, air, spirit), which intrinsically links the ethical and
cosmological realms, he insists that "an examination of moral action cannot
be conducted without a full accounting of the various biological and envi-
ronmental factors that enter into it."[44] Stoicism reveals urgent ontological and
rhetorical analogues between two realms conventionally viewed as distinct:
namely, the impassioned, extravagant world of Senecan drama and the ac-
uleate vision of *apatheia* and restraint promoted by Seneca's version of Stoic
wisdom.

The problem, in other words, is to reconcile the bleak pessimism of
Seneca's plays with the relative optimism of his philosophy. Justus Lipsius
(1547–1606), the most influential advocate and translator of Stoic philosophy
in late Renaissance Europe, largely disposed of the problem by refusing to
acknowledge Seneca's authorship of the tragedies.[45] William Cornwallis's
Discourses upon Seneca the Tragedian (1601), the first important English commentary on Senecan drama, focuses on eleven *sententiae* derived from Senecan
Stoicism rather than considering the drama's formal or rhetorical aspects
per se, or trying to synthesize the two discourses. Nearly four centuries later,
Rosenmeyer charts the gulf between the aphoristic quality of many of the
speeches Seneca gives to his characters and the chaos and tragedy they are
made to experience, only to conclude that the "mannerism" of the former have
little relevance to the staging of catastrophe.[46]

But must we concede the irrelevance of Seneca's philosophical "mannerism" for his drama so quickly? Senecan moral philosophy makes control of *affectus* its chief concern. An idea of Seneca's curt, aphoristic style in moral
philosophy may be gleaned from his ninety-second epistle to Lucilius. Here he
examines what can be attained by someone who follows a "perfecta ratio"
rather than the soul's irrational parts, that is, by someone who masters his passions and pleasures and refuses to submit to fortune's whims. First he pithily
places the Stoic sage beyond all contingency: "Is est, inquam, beatus quem
nulla res minorem facit; tenet summa, et ne ulli quidem nisi sibi innixus.
Nam qui aliquo auxilio sustinetur, potest cadere" [*He is, I say, blessed who does
not bother with any trifle. He sticks to the heights; he leans on himself and nobody else. For*

he who is supported by any help may fall].[47] Then he describes to his young friend the positive aspects of the Stoic ideal:

> Quid est beata vita? Securitas et perpetua tranquillitas. Hanc dabit animi magnitudo, dabit constantia bene iudicati tenax. Ad haec quomodo pervenitur? Si veritas tota perspecta est; si servatus est in rebus agendis ordus, modus, decor, innoxia voluntas ac benigna, intenta rationi nec umquam ab illa recedens, amabilis simul mirabilisque. Denique ut breviter tibi formulam scribam, talis animus esse sapientis viri debet, qualis deum deceat. (92.3)

> What is a happy life? Security and perpetual tranquility. This will be gained by greatness of soul and firm constancy in judging well. But in what way are these things reached? If truth is regarded in its entirety, if in the things to be done is kept order, moderation, decorum, a good and innocuous will, intentions that are reasonable and never wavering, and which seem loving and admirable. Indeed, if I might write a brief rule for you, the wise man's soul must be such that would be fitting for a god.

As Seneca zeroes in on the cardinal Stoic virtue of the great-souled man, that *constantia* which offers a godlike perspective on the *beata vita*, parallelism, ellipses, antitheses, and sententiae convey supreme self-confidence. For all its sky-scraping idealism, his rhetoric is as orderly and decorous as he would have the Stoic sage be. His diction ("ordus, modus, decor . . . deceat") further insists upon such decorum. Quintilian's *vir bonus dicendi peritus*, in effect, pursues the "mean" [*modum*] that conforms with reason (92.12).

Seneca's imagination, meanwhile, returns again and again to the natural world to supply the material for his analogies. Stoic virtue, for example, is as immune to adversity as the sun remains undamaged by passing clouds (92.18). Similarly, he describes the paradox of the happy man beset by misery and physical afflictions with this spatial image: "Quae res illum non patitur ad imum devolvi, retinet in summo" [*Whatever doesn't suffer him to hit bottom, keeps him on top*] (92.23). The metaphorics of high and low is retooled, though, to describe the virtuous man's ambition to be like the gods: "Nemo improbe eo conatur ascendere, unde descenderat" [*Nobody is wicked who tries to ascend to the place from where he descended*] (92.30). Finally, urging us to ignore all bodily cares and pleasures, Seneca ends the letter by painting a picture of an elevated soul immune from catastrophe and contingency.[48]

We thus glimpse the potential relevance of Seneca's Stoicism for under-standing his dramatic rhetoric. Not only is the convergence of ethics, physics, and rhetoric cultivated in the Stoic cosmovision, but the cardinal notions of *krasis, contagio, tonos,* and *sumpatheia* variously explain why events (and the lan-guage used to describe them) that occur either in the microcosmic or macro-cosmic realms are cognitively seen as belonging to a single continuum. Put another way, this qualitative sameness tends to distort conventional distinc-tions of quantity — a small ethical fault can cause earthquakes. And, as will become clearer through a closer consideration of Seneca's dramatic rhetoric, an important analogy links the *tonos,* the dynamic tension, of the ethical and physical realms with the dramatic tension unique to Senecan drama.

By adopting Rosenmeyer's compelling if somewhat unorthodox view concerning the lack of a distinction between an ordered and chaotic universe, we immediately see important consequences for dramatic hyperbole. "The Stoic moralist knows that there is no such thing as a limited or moderate flaw. The most negligible frailty is inevitably transformed into gross peccability . . . The grounding in *sumpatheia* further makes for an automatic surge of expo-nentiality."[49] But how is such "exponentiality" represented in dramatic verse? More generally, how does Seneca represent in his dramas the Stoic theory of the passions? And what happens on stage when the passions overcome the claims of reason, a condition minutely explored in treatises like *De ira* but also in Cavell's readings of Shakespearean tragedy?

THE POETICS OF WRATH

Seneca adopts various rhetorical strategies, such as auxesis, anaphora, con-geries, the device of the catalogue, and, most obviously, the *Schreirede* (tirade, rant, screed), to achieve his hyperbolic aim of portraying the triumph of *affec-tus* over *ratio.* Conversely, mannerist use of paradox, ellipsis, omissio, and, more generally, the (in)famous concision of his periods and reliance on *senten-tiae* lend his diction and syntax an intensity that creates a centripetal effect balancing the centrifugal force of his sympathetic thought. Thus C. J. Her-ington, quoting Seneca's *Epistle* 6.5, "Longum iter est per praecepta, breve et efficax per exempla," argues that the plays are "extended, fantastic *exempla* in verse" of Stoic *praecepta.*[50] What, though, is the *res,* the idea or matter, that in-forms these exemplary tragedies? In a passage from *De Beneficiis,* which we al-ready saw Erasmus and Scaliger paraphrase, Seneca offers his most explicit ethical and psychological justification for the hyperbolist's fabrications:

In hoc omnis hyperbole extenditur, ut ad verum mendacio veniat. Itaque ille, cum dixit: *Qui candore nives anteirent, cursibus auras* [*Aen.*, 12.84], quod non poterat fieri, dixit, ut crederetur, quantum plurimum posset. Et qui dixit: *His inmobilior scopulis, violentior amne* [*Met.*, 13.801], ne hoc quidem se persuasurum putavit aliquem tam immobilem esse quam scopulum. Numquam tantum sperat hyperbole, quantum audet, sed incredibilia adfirmat, ut ad credibilia perveniat.[51] (7.23.1–2)

The set purpose of all hyperbole is to arrive at the truth by falsehood. And so when the poet said: *Whose whiteness shamed the snow, their speeds the winds*, he stated what could not possibly be true in order to give credence to all that could be true. And the other who said: *Firmer than a rock, more headlong than the stream*, did not suppose that he could convince anyone by this that any person was as immovable as a rock. Hyperbole never expects to attain all that it ventures, but asserts the incredible in order to arrive at the credible.

Rhetorical excess and deceit are advocated in the name of the complex dynamics of human credulity and incredulity. In the larger pursuit of "truth," hyperbole's provisional violence against belief and reason becomes necessary and fitting. Likewise, Seneca's hyperbolic tragedies are incredulous confrontations with the enormous "truth" of metaphysical and human evil. The obsession with this primeval conflict requires hyperbole because it is grounded in a phenomenological perception of the world. As Herrington puts it: "People speak much of what they call Seneca's rhetorical exaggeration, when phenomena occur such as the ghost of Tantalus or the Senecan Oedipus . . . They might equally well use the same language of Van Gogh's *The Starry Night* . . . Stars aren't like that, like great Catherine wheels; but that is what they feel like. A Senecan tragedy, by similar means, tells what evil feels like to an acutely sensitive mind under abnormally evil conditions."[52] While ultimately sharing Herington's basic insight here, Bernd Seidensticker focuses first on the formal, quantitative dynamics of Seneca's mannerism: "The author and his creations are always searching for the unusual (*insolitum*), the not yet dared (*inausum*), on the hunt for something that oversteps everything that has been there before, for the *maius aliquid*, the grander, more violent, more terrible, more gruesome. The Senecan comparative, as one might label this phenomenon with a concept, plays in all the dramas a more or less meaningful role."[53] In terms of the history of rhetoric, this "senecanische Komparativ" recalls the dynamic of

ultra fidem and *ultra modum* in Quintilian's discussion of hyperbole.[54] It also reveals how Seneca's perception of the extraordinary becomes the driving
cognitive force, as well as the formal principle of excess, for the literary genre
that will yield *King Lear*. Tragedy, as Harry Levin reasons in his study of Marlowe, structurally resembles the overreaching of hyperbole. The tragic protagonist is trapped in a vicious circle of invidious comparisons.

Exemplifying this circle is *Thyestes*, the play Seidensticker calls the
"senecanischste der senecanischen Tragödien."[55] Its monomaniacal theme is
furor, and its protagonist, Atreus, is moved by an "insano . . . tumultu" (85–
86) to avenge the treachery of his brother Thyestes, who has seduced his wife
and stolen the gold-fleeced ram, which confers the right to rule. The Prologue,
a dialogue between Tantalus' ghost and a *furia* who sparks "furorem" (101),
jumpstarts the revenge mechanism. (I use engine metaphorics here with a nod
to Jean Cocteau's description of tragedy as "la machine infernale," a phrase
that perfectly applies to the way Seneca lets the *machina* of his plot bulldoze any
human attempt to deviate from fate's decrees.) And yet Seneca does provide
the dramatic-rhetorical space for his characters to protest; Atreus is given this
self-conscious auxesis early in the play:

> Nil quod doloris capiat assueti modus;
> nullum relinquam facinus et nullum est satis. (255–256)

> Not such a one as may the meane of woonted griefe abide.
> No guilt will I forbeare, nor none may be enough despight.[56]

This is a fine instance of Seidensticker's *maius aliquid* — epitomized by the
phrase, "nullum est satis" — while the curt phrases also starkly depict the psychological consequences of wrestling with so much emotion. Likewise, the
play's opening lines, spoken by the *Tantali umbra*, set the stage, with a series of
anaphoric questions, for the process of *Überbietung* that Atreus (and Seneca)
will pursue to such immoral, stylistic extremes. Already imbued with the
trepidation (*metus*) that dominates the play's mood, Atreus adumbrates the fatal logic of revenge, even as he expresses astonishment at his plight:

> Quis inferorum sede ab infausta extrahit
> avido fugaces ore captantem cibos,
> quis male deorum Tantalo vivas domos

ostendit iterum? peius inventum est siti
arente in undis aliquid et peius fame
hiante semper?[57] (1–6)

What furye fell enforceth mee to fle, th'unhappy seat,
That gape and gaspe with greedye jawe, the fleeyng food to eate
What God to Tantalus the bowres wher breathing bodyes dwel
Doth shew agayne? is ought found worse, then burning thyrst of hel
In lakes alow? or yet worse plague then hunger is there one,
In vayne that ever gapes for foode?

Seneca's self-appointed dramatic task is to find (in the sense of *invenire* as an
act of *ingenium*) "peius . . . aliquid." As Tantalus predicts a few lines later:
"iam nostra subit / e stirpe turba quae suum vincat genus / ac me innocentem
faciat et inausa audeat" [*Io now there doth aryse / My broode that shal in mischiefe
farre the grandsyers gilt out goe, / And gyltles make: that first shall dare unventred ils to
do*] (18–20).[58]

While this challenge participates in the dynamics of literary imitation
such that Tantalus-Seneca must outbid their predecessors, it is also grounded
in Stoic philosophy and cosmology. For readers remaining within the confines
of the conceptual frameworks described by Ruskin's pathetic fallacy, Love-
joy's *great chain of being*, or Tillyard's "Elizabethan world-picture," it may be
difficult to perceive the degree to which Senecan tragedy is permeated by the
culturally and historically specific notion of the Stoic dynamic continuum.[59]
A further abstraction of *pneuma* (breath, spirit), the concept of *sumpatheia* pervades Seneca's tragedies, his ethical treatises, as well as the *Naturales quaestiones*.
While his preoccupation with Stoic ethics dominates his portrayal in *Hercules
furens* of an agonized hero who must judge his own monstrous but unknowing actions, or in *Phaedra* of a self-conscious heroine whose measureless passion leads her to overstep all law and reason, Seneca also places his characters
before cosmic backdrops borrowed directly from his natural philosophy. The
drama's extreme rhetoric, rhetoric representing characters' dire psychological
plights as well as nature's cataclysmic gyrations, paints a cosmos inimical to
the attainment of the Stoic *apatheia*. In this respect, then, Seneca strays from
Stoic doctrine. By depicting his protagonists' colossal failures to secure the bless-
ings of reason (*ratio*), not only must the cosmos (*mundus*) be disordered but rhetoric (*oratio*), too, must be correspondingly exaggerated. Form self-consciously

follows content in a kind of hyperbolic mimeticism. If a Stoic poet, like his characters, feels great outrage, nature will necessarily be depicted as greatly outraged. Inversely, if nature is perceived as greatly animated or grandiose, then the poet and his protagonists will be forced to adopt a corresponding magniloquence. And while Ruskin will later dub this correspondence the "pathetic fallacy," it makes more historical sense to stress here the subjective pathos felt by the poet rather than to question whether his sentiments are objectively veracious or not.[60] Thus Timothy Reiss writes in his interpretation of Senecan subjectivity or "who-ness": "Seneca experienced person (soul, mind, being) as webbed in crowded surroundings: divine and universal . . ." Reiss reminds us that the Senecan self, bound by innumerable social "enlacements," is more not less human. Ideally, a balance between the personal and social may be achieved, and "the identity of *ratio* and *oratio*" glimpsed, but when this balance and these networks are disrupted, the ethical, epistemological, and rhetorical consequences are wide ranging and historically specific.[61]

Nowhere are these monumental consequences more vividly experienced than in Senecan tragedy. For, notwithstanding its Stoic foundation, the shocking manner in which Senecan drama plumbs this "total interconnectedness" and its characters desperate, all-too-human efforts to deny it, often strains credulity. In *Thyestes*, the horrors of unwittingly dining on one's children is (re)figured by the eclipse of the sun at midday. This sympathetic astronomical phenomenon, and the human acts that precipitate it are first reported by a horrified but verbose messenger, and then commented on by the confused Chorus, which pathetically exclaims:

> Sed quidquid id est, utinam nox sit!
> trepidant, trepidant pectora magno
> percussa metu:
> ne fatali cuncta ruina
> quassata labent iterumque deos
> hominesque premat deforme chaos,
> iterum terras et mare cingens
> et vaga picti sidera mundi
> natura tegat . . .
> . . . ibit in unum
> congesta sinum turba deorum. (827–835, 842–843)

What so it be, God graunt it be the night.
Our hartes do quake with feare oppressed gret,
And dreadfull are least heaven and earth and all
With fatall ruine shaken shall decay:
And least on Gods agayne, and men shall fall
Disfigurde Chaos: and the land away
The Seas, and Fyres, and of the glorious Skise
The wandring lampes, least nature yet shal hide . . .

. . . . .

The Gods on heaps shal out of order fall,
And each with other mingled be in place.

Such are the exaggerated consequences, conceptual and syntactical — the in-
terlocked word order mimics the conceptual chaos — of Atreus' crime.[62]
These lines also pave the way for the catastrophe (*ekpyrosis*) to come. Indeed,
the elliptical grandeur ("pectora magno / percussa metu") and pathos ("trepidant, trepidant") of the passage, and its intimation of absolute *copia* ("cuncta
ruina") — in sum, its extravagant "congesta . . . turba deorum" — appear
less fantastically, less capriciously hyperbolic, if as Herington urges, we consider them in light of Seneca's attempt to create "a truly religious drama."
Propelled by a "terrible moral sensitivity" born from the "monstrous" political situation and horrors he witnessed in Neronian Rome, Seneca necessarily,
catachrestically, turns to the bolder rhetorical figures.[63]

Another species of physical-rhetorical extremity manifests itself in *Hercules furens*, where "the ponderous carapace of stoicism" is not enough to protect humanity from divine malignity.[64] Here Hercules is that *Ur-*overreacher
whose blurring of the lines between the mortal and the immortal leads him to
extremities of word and deed. His sense of his own *granditas* infects the universe. When Juno's madness comes upon him, he first hallucinates an eclipse,
and then perceives the constellations to be at war.[65] Finally, he conceives another Titanomachy with himself taking the lead:

. . . astra promittit pater.
quid si negaret? non capit terra Herculem
tandemque superis reddit . . .
. . . bella Titanes parent,
me duce furentes; saxa cum silvis feram
rapiamque dextra plena Centauris iuga.[66]

iam monte gemino limitem ad superos agam;
videat sub Ossa Pelion Chiron suum,
in caelum Olympus tertio positus gradu
perveniet aut mittetur. (959–961, 967–973)

... my father doth me promise starres t'obtayne.
What if he it denyde? all th'earth can Hercles not contayne,
And geeves at length to gods ...
... Let Titans now prepare agayne their fight
With me theyr captaine raging: stones with woods I will down smight
And hye hilles tops with Centaures full in right hande will I take.
With double mountayne now I will a stayre to Gods up make.
Let Chyron under Ossa see his Pelion mountayne gret:
Olympus up to heaven above in thyrd degree then set
Shall come it selfe, or ells be cast.[67]

This time, though, he is not destined to outbid the gods; instead of fulfill-
ing his boasts, Hercules turns his wrath upon his wife and children. With
such exacting ("in caelum Olympus tertio positus gradu") semantic and syntactic play of high and low ("superis ... ad superos / videat sub Ossa"),
space itself becomes too small to contain the hero's anger and pride (*superbia*).

Like Virgil's portrayal of Rumor in the *Aeneid*, the only real greatness
Seneca permits Hercules is his infamy. By the play's end, Hercules' guilt and
suffering appear to transcend the moral order and achieve cosmic significance.
They would outstrip all terrestrial space and reorder the celestial-divine one:

Quem locum profugus petam?
ubi me recondam quave tellure obruar?
quis Tanais aut quis Nilus aut quis Persica
violentus unda Tigris aut Rhenus ferox
Tagusve Hibera turbidus gaza fluens
abluere dextram poterit? arctoum licet
Maeotis in me gelida transfundat mare
et tota Tethys per meas currat manus,
haerebit altum facinus. in quas impius
terras recedes? ortum an occasum petes?
ubique notus perdidi exilio locum.
me refugit orbis, astra transversos agunt

> obliqua cursus, ipse Titan Cerberum
> meliore vultu vidit . . . (1321–1334)

What place shall I seeke ronnagate for rest?
Where shall I hyde my selfe? or in what land my selfe engrave?
What Tanais, or what Nilus els, or with his Persyan wave
What Tygris violent of streame, or what fierce Rhenus flood,
Or Tagus troublesome that flowes with Ibers treasures good
May my ryght hand yow wash from gylt? Although Maeoris cold
The waves of all the Northen sea on me shed out now wolde,
And al the water ther of shoulde now pas by my two handes,
Yet wil the mischiefe deepe remayne, alas into what landes
Wilt thou O wicked man resort? to East or westerne costs?
Ech where wel knowen, all place I have of banishment quight loste
From me the worlde doth flee a back, the starres that sydelyng rone
Do backwarde dryve their turned course, even Cerberus the sone
With better count'naunce did behold . . .[68]

Infused with Seneca's idiosyncratic brand of Stoicism, Hercules' pathos demands the *ultra fidem* content and *ultra modum* form of these lines. Seneca,
though, adds characteristic geographical and mythological *copia*, and so discursively grounds his hyperboles in natural history. Furthermore, if his dual
tendency toward excess and brevity, his predilection for irony and paradox,
and his penchant for the monstrous and pathetic, point to a particular aesthetic, to a mannerism which begs to be contrasted with Virgil's putative classicism, this is due, as Erich Burck has argued, as much to the themes (*res*) he
chooses as to the reigning tastes of his age.[69]

   Likewise, Braden's initial reading of Stoic *furor* — a notion only superficially oxymoronic — is informed by the history and politics of Imperial
Rome. With free speech severely limited, a process of interiorization occurs in
which private concerns and the contours of the individual soul replaced those
of the polis. Stoicism thus becomes a "philosophy of the will."[70] Alternately,
with regard to Senecan drama, Braden argues that the political and physical
worlds are metaphorically and cognitively transformed into stage and spectacle.
The Stoic apocalypse is reduced to a theatrical trope, or convention, in which,
however, human agents find new voices as actors. But humans are not the only
beings susceptible to political or cosmic *tumultus*; the gods, their scope, and
powers are also transformed. In *De beneficiis*, for example, in order to persuade

his interlocutor of the necessity of *sumpatheia*, Seneca offers this vivid, apoca-
lyptic vision:

> Omnia ista ingentibus intervallis diducta et in custodiam universi dis-
> posita stationes suas deserant; subita confusione rerum sidera sideribus
> incurrant, et rupta rerum concordia in ruinam divina labantur, contex-
> tusque velocitatis citatissimae in tot saecula promissas vices in medio
> itinere destituat, et, quae nunc alternis eunt redeuntque opportunis li-
> bramentis mundum ex aequo temperantia, repentino concrementur in-
> cendio, et ex tanta varietate solvantur atque eant in unum omnia; ignis
> cuncta possideat, quem deinde pigra nox occupet, et profunda vorago
> tot deos sorbeat. (6.22)

> Let all the heavenly bodies, separated as they are by vast distances and
> appointed to the task of guarding the universe, leave their posts; let sud-
> den confusion arise, let stars clash with stars, let the world's harmony be
> destroyed, and the divine creations totter to destruction; let the heavenly
> mechanism, moving as it does with the swiftest speed, abandon in the
> midst of its course the progressions that had been promised for so many
> ages, and let the heavenly bodies that now, as they alternately advance
> and retreat, by a timely balancing keep the world at an equable temper-
> ature be suddenly consumed by flames, and, with their infinite variations
> broken up, let them all pass into one condition; let fire claim all things,
> then let sluggish darkness take its place, and let these many gods be swal-
> lowed up in the bottomless abyss.

The fact that this violent cosmovision also riddles the tragedies suggests that
they may be read as imaginative exercises in contrafactual morality. The plan-
etary gods will be destroyed, but only if humanity makes the inconceivable
choice to usurp their place and prerogatives. In this sense, the traditional deities
in Senecan tragedy appear to have lost much of their agency.[71] In early imperial
Rome, that is, the traditional deities are anachronisms; they are dramatic
stand-ins for the causal network of fate, necessity, fortune, and will promoted
by Stoic philosophy. Conversely, as the study of the heavens is shrunk and
shifted to fit the confines of the stage, the gods and cosmic forces are replaced
with more dramatically effective demons or ghosts.

More needs to be said, though, about the imaginative if at times absolutist
manner in which Seneca transforms Stoic science. For instance, the energy of

anaphora and other figures that in the dramas fuel amplification and propel
the rhetoric of the catalogue is an aspect of the Stoic scientific legacy derived
from Chrysippus and Posidonius. But if Pliny also exploits it, so does Lucan's
De bello civili, whose catalogues display the poet's erudition, expand his scope
of reference, and make his rhetoric seem universal and credible. And while
such rehearsals may indecorously disrupt Seneca's dramatic momentum, they
also serve an urgent thematic function.[72] The most extraordinary instances of
this occur in *Medea*, whose protagonist's occult knowledge perceives cosmic
correspondences and analogues even in those moments when her passions
threaten to overwhelm her (and us). Exemplary is Medea's soliloquy, spoken just
before Jason first enters. Contemplating extremes of love (*amor*), hate (*odium*),
and madness (*furor*), she opens up vast but detailed cosmic and mythic vistas,[73] vistas blithely padded by John Studley's alliterative, creaking translation:

> Si quaeris odio, misera, quem statuas modum,
> imitare amorem. regias egone ut faces
> inulta patiar? segnis hic ibit dies,
> tanto petitus ambitu, tanto datus?
> dum terra caelum media libratum feret
> nitidusque certas mundus evolvet vices
> numerusque harenis derit et solem dies,
> noctem sequentur astra, dum siccas polus
> versabit Arctos, flumina in pontum cadent,
> numquam meus cessabit in poenas furor
> crescetque semper. quae ferarum immanitas,
> quae Scylla, quae Charybdis Ausonium mare
> Siculumque sorbens quaeve anhelantem premens
> Titana tantis Aetna fervebit minis?
> non rapidus amnis, non procellosum mare
> Pontusve Coro saevus aut vis ignium
> adiuta flatu possit imitari impetum
> irasque nostras; sternam et evertam omnia. (397–414)

> > O wretch if thou desire,
> What measure ought to payse thy wrath then learne by Cupids fire
> To hate as sore as thou didst love, shall I not them anoy
> That doe unite in spousall bed, theyr wanton lust t'enjoy?
> Shall Phoebus fiery footed horse goe lodge in western wave

The drowping day, that late I did with humble crowching crave,
And with such ernest busie suite so hardly graunted was?
Shall it depart ere I can bring my devylish dryst to passe?
Whyle hovering heaven doth counterpaysed hang with egall space,
Amid the marble Hemispheares, whyle rounde with stinted race,
The gorgeous Sky above the Earth doth spinning roll about,
Whyles that the number of the sandes, lyes hid unserched out,
While dawning day doth keepe his course with Phoebus blase so bright,
While twinkling starres in golden traynes doe garde the slumbry nyght,
While Isle under propping poale with whyrling swying so swift,
The shyning Beares unbathde about the frosen Sky doe lift,
While flushing floudes the frothy streames to rustling Seas doe send,
To gird them gript with plonging pangues my rage shall never end.
With greater heate it shall reboyle, lyke as the brutishe beast,
Whose tyranny most horrible, exceedeth all the rest,
What greedy gaping whyrle poole wide what parlous gulp unmilde,
What Sylla coucht in roring Rockes, or what Charybdes wylde,
(That Sicill, and Ionium Sea by frothy waves doth sup)
What Aetna bolking stifling flames, and dusky vapours up,
(Whose heavy payse with stewing heate doth smoldring crush beneath
Encelades, that fiery flakes from choked throte doth breath)
Can with such dreadfull menaces in sweeting fury fry?
No ryver swift no troubled surge of stormy Sea so hye,
Nor sturdy seas (whom ruffling winds with raging force to rore)
Nor puissaunt flash of fyre, whose might by boystrous blast is more,
May byde my angers violence: my fury shall it foyle:
His court Ile over hourle, and lay it leavell with the soyle.

Here Medea eloquently explores the limit ("modum") of her rhetorical art even as she details the extent to which nature may share her outrage.[74] She begins by asking whether her "hate" can "imitate [her] love" only to end by affirming that nature's most powerful forces cannot "imitate" her wrath. But to reach this conclusion she must mediate her doubt concerning her fate with her recondite knowledge of the cosmic stage on which she stands. That anaphora propels both her doubt ("quae . . . quae . . . quae") and her *scientia* ("dum . . . dum . . . non . . . non") further confirms how indistinguishable these two modes of perception have become for her.

The Chorus in *Medea* avails itself of an equally discursive and only

slightly less subjective species of hyperbole. Its second major speech (301–
379), digressively and derivatively — the audience surely is meant to hear
echoes of Horace and Lucretius — recounts the perils of navigation ("Audax
nimium qui freta primus / rate tam fragili perfida rupit . . .") and the Argo-
nauts' voyage, only to close with this stunning prophecy:

> quaelibet altum cumba pererrat.
> terminus omnis motus et urbes
> muros terra posuere nova,
> nil qua fuerat sede reliquit
> pervius orbis:
> Indus gelidum potat Araxen,
> Albin Persae Rhenumque bibunt.
> venient annis saecula seris,
> quibus Oceanus vincula rerum
> laxet et ingens pateat tellus
> Tethysque novos detegat orbes
> nec sit terris ultima Thule. (368–379)

Eche whirry boate now scuddes aboute the deepe,
All stynts and warres are taken cleane away,
The Cities frame new walles themselves to keepe,
The open worlde lettes nought rest where it lay:
The Hoyes of Ind Arexis lukewarme leake,
The Perseans stout in Rhene and Albis streame
Doth bath their Barkes, time shall in fine out breake
When Ocean wave shall open every Realme.
The wandering World at will shall open lye.
And Typhis will some newe founde Land survay,
Some travelers shall the Countreys farre escrye,
Beyonde small Thule, knowen furthest at this day.

As many readers will recognize, the imaginative pull that this passage
achieves with early modern cosmographers cannot be overestimated.[75] Moreover, this catalogue of geographic names also nicely exemplifies what Lausberg calls the *Steigerung der evidentia* native to hyperbole. Seneca imagines here
what might happen when "terminus omnis [est] motus" on the Earth's surface.[76] Such an event serves as both a cataclysmic consequence to and a dra-

matic analogue with Medea's unbridled passion, which would dispense with all *modus*. It also intertwines the individual's fate with cosmological and historical phenomena: here the migrations of nations and conquest of new worlds. One should not be surprised then to find the Chorus returning to the navigation theme in lines 579–669, where a magnificent, if dramatically awkward, catalogue of mythic death at sea is recited just before the nurse enters to declare: "Pavet animus, horret, magna pernicies adest" [*My soul fears, is horrified; some great calamity is near*] (670). On closer consideration, though, such bombast becomes dialectical, as it ironically rejects the Chorus's momentary sense that rhetorical and ethical limits have been crossed: "iam satis, divi, mare vindicastis; / parcite iusso" [*enough already, gods, you have avenged the sea; spare him* (Jason) *who was following orders*] (668–669).

At first glance, the tirades littering Senecan tragedy might be seen as sophisticated versions of the school exercises in early imperial *paideia*. But while we should not ignore that Seneca's father taught and wrote about declamatory rhetoric, far from being set pieces or "empty rhetoric," the tirades infusing these dramas with their characteristic *energeia* are vehicles for vital elements of the playwright's eclectic ethical, cosmological, and rhetorical vision. In them we discover the language of passionate characters — perhaps one of the literary origins of what Cavell will call "passionate utterance" — and a world reduced to a "hugy heapye of Chaos."[77] Thus Rosenmeyer reads the *Schreirede* as "the dramatized interaction of the struggling or decomposing self and the living cosmos," the latter an externalization, a theatrical response to the kind of internalization or interiorization that he and Braden celebrate.[78] As we saw with Góngora and Sor Juana, instead of discounting reality, or weaving a network of illusions, extreme *copia* can increase one's self-consciousness and skepticism.

With this said, the degree of self-consciousness won by Seneca's characters and their exorbitant rhetoric often remains ambiguous. Turning back to *Thyestes*, we watch as an "iratus Atreus" (180) maps the extent of his hatred for his brother, even as he commands himself to undertake excessively cruel deeds:

> tota sub nostro sonet
> Argolica tellus equite; non silvae tegant
> hostem nec altis montium structae iugis
> arces; relicitis bellicum totus canat
> populus Mycenis, quisquis invisum caput

tegit ac tuetur, clade funesta occidat.
haec ipsa pollens incliti Pelopis domus
ruat vel in me, dummodo in fratrem ruat.
age, anime, fac quod nulla posteritas probet,
sed nulla taceat. aliquod audendum est nefas
atrox, cruentum, tale quod frater meus
suum esse mallet. scelera non ulcisceris,
nisi vincis. et quid esse tam saevum potest
quod superet illum? (184–197)

                       all under foote of horse let every syde
Of Argos lande resound: and let the woundes not serve to hyde
Our foes, nor yet in haughty top of hilles and mountaynes hye,
The builded towers. The people all let them to battel crye
And clere forsake Myceneas towne who so his hateful head
Hides and defendes, with slaughter dire let bloud of him be shed.
This princely Pelops palace proude, and bowres of high renowne,
On mee so on my brother to let them be beaten downe,
Go to, do that which never shall no after age allow,
Nor none it whisht: some mischefe greate ther must be ventred now,
Both fierce and bloudy: such as woulde my brother rather long
To have bene his. Thou never dost enough revenge the wronge,
Except thou passe. And feercer fact what may be done so dyre,
That his exceedes?

Here we witness all at once Seneca's infamous talent for *sententiae* ("scelera non ulcisceris, nisi vincis"); the subtleties of the imperative voice ("age" wonderfully rendered by Heywood as "Go to"), which are increased further when they merge with the subjunctive ("ulcisceris," "superet"); the accumulation of external, hyperbolic correspondences to measure the scope of internal passions ("nec altis montium structae iugis arces"); and, most dramatically, the speaker's battle to outbid all predecessors (and imagined successors) in word and deed. In the same breath, though, the syntax suggests that Atreus has a vibrant, immediate sense of self, however conflicted it might be; for the sudden prospect of posterity's silence ("sed nulla taceat") — paradoxical though it may seem given the very public form of the drama itself — betrays a poignant, individual awareness of being dwarfed by time.[79]

    Given this beginning, it is little wonder that when Atreus' insatiable *ira* pushes the action to its gruesome climax, it also propels the *Schreirede* to new extremes and complexities. Beset by melancholy (938–956) and anxiety (957–969), Thyestes, the failed usurper, now plays the victim. His imprecations (1006–1021, 1069–1096) demonstrate just how far he has fallen, or been pushed, from the Stoic ideal that, however imperfectly, he represented at the outset. After he is shown his sons' dismembered bodies, but before he realizes his own cannibalism, his prayer to *Tellus* (1012–1021) literally and figuratively — such as the paronomastic play on *supra* and *superi* — maps his physical and ethical downward trajectory with remarkable spatial exactitude. While he ap-pears to realize, at his plea's conclusion, his inability *movere* (the "Gods are fled" and already in sympathetic outrage at Atreus' crimes), Thyestes has not yet exhausted rhetoric's arsenal. Language is too intrinsically related to his moral outrage and amazed perception that the fabric of the universe has changed to be traded for silence, even though the understated, elliptical "fugere superi" (1021) momentarily approaches sublime resignation.

Instead, he now appeals in a magnificent *imprecatio* to the mightiest of the absent gods for vengeance:

> tu, summe caeli rector, aetheriae potens
> dominator aulae, nubibus totum horridis
> convolve mundum, bella ventorum undique
> committe et omni parte violentum intona,
> manuque non qua tecta et immeritas domos
> telo petis minore, sed qua montium
> tergemina moles cecidit et qui montibus
> stabant pares Gigantes, — haec arma expedi
> ignesque torque. vindica amissum diem,
> iaculare flammas, lumen ereptum polo
> fulminibus exple. (1077–1087)

Thou guyder great of skyes above, and prince of highest might,
Of heavenly place now all with cloudes ful horrible to sight,
Enwrap the worlde, and let the wyndes on every syde breake out:
And send the dredfull thunderclap through al the world about
Not with what hand thou gyltles house and undeserved wall
With lesser bolt are wonte to beate, but with the which did fall
The three unheaped mountaynes once and which to hils in height
Stoode equall up, the gyantes huge: throuw out such weapons streight,

And flyng thy fires: and therwithall revenge the drowned day.
Let flee thy flames, the light thus lost and hid from heaven away,
With flashes fyll . . .

Despite the strangely deflated, inconclusive, final lines of the play ("Vindices
aderunt dei . . ."), this appeal to the mythic paradigm of the gigantomachy is
doubly futile considering Atreus' gloating and Thyestes' already defeated position.[80] Like the "gyantes huge" who engage the Olympian gods, Thyestes
with his invocation of the *superi* not only forgets the Stoic doctrine of *apatheia*
but also that of *providentia*. His tragedy has been a necessary, purely human,
thoroughly linguistic, embodiment of the larger laws of fate that are beyond
both his and the gods' control.

Finally, looking forward to *Lear*, I would broach again the question of
anagnorisis. What do Atreus and Thyestes learn about themselves as they re-
cite Seneca's dense, startling verses? To what extent is the poet interested in
representing self-knowledge in a tragedy so invested in remaking Stoic philosophy and science, to say nothing of mythic precedents?

Two moments of particularly intense solipsism — early and late in
Thyestes — contain some clues as to how these queries might be answered.
Prompted by his attendant (*satelles*), Atreus tries to understand, to measure,
"the reache" of his anger and *Rachelust*:

> Nescio quid animo maius et solito amplius
> supraque fines moris humani tumet
> instatque pigris manibus — haud quid sit scio,
> sed grande quiddam est. ita sit. hoc, anime, occupa.
> dignum est Thyeste facinus et dignum Atreo;
> uterque faciat. (267–272)

A bove the reache that men are woont to worke, begins to swell:
And stayth with slouthfull hands. What thinge it is I cannot tell:
But great it is. Bee'te so, my mynde now in this feate proceede,
For Atreus and Thyestes bothe, it were a worthy deede.
Let eche of us the crime commit.

As the fitful motion from "Nescio" to "faciat" and, ultimately, seven tumes-
cent lines later, to the self-satisfied conclusion of "bene est, abunde est. hic
placet poenae modus" indicates, the potential for action, however gruesome,

is for Atreus the same as that of knowing himself. He cannot, moreover, conceive of himself without comparing himself to his brother or, as the subsequent lines confirm, to the macabre figures that myth provides. Though initially unsure of his exact intentions, his insistence on being extraordinary and achieving *megethos* never wavers. And while his curt, elliptical syntax in lines 269–270 reads compellingly like someone talking to himself, here and later in the same speech he already is detached enough from his deed to refer to himself in the third person. And, as if his motive were fame as much as revenge, he compares himself to the mythic Procne who avenges Tereus' betrayal and violation of her sister Philomela by having him unwittingly dine on their son. The opportunity for anagnorisis is peremptorily cut short by his haughty invocation of myth.[81]

In the end, the immense *voluntas* of both Medea and Atreus proves to be criminal — directed toward others more than themselves. Overweening *superbia* and *ira* eclipse any sense of interiority previously won by Atreus:

> Aequalis astris gradior et cunctos super
> altum superbo vertice attingens polum.
> nunc decora regni teneo, nunc solium patris.
> dimitto superos; summa votorum attigi.
> bene est, abunde est, iam sat est etiam mihi.
> sed cur satis sit? pergam et impleto patre
> funere suorum. ne quid obstaret pudor,
> dies recessit. perge dum caelum vacat. (885–892)

Nowe equall with the Starres I goe, beyond each other wight,
With haughty heade the heavens above, and highest Poale I smite.
The kingdome nowe, and seate I holde, where once my father raynd:
I now lette goe the gods: for all my wil I have obtaynde
Enoughe and well, ye even enough for me I am acquit
But why enough? I wil procede and fyl the father yet
With bloud of his least any shame should me restrayne at all,
The day is gone, go to therfore whyle thee the heaven doth call.

Here, if for a moment translation might serve as hermeneutic, Heywood superbly transforms Seneca's dense wordplay ("superbo . . . superos" and "pergam . . . perge") with alliteration ("haughty heade the heavens above, and highest"), rhyme ("wight . . . smite" and the internal rhyme "shame . . .

restrayne" that picks up on the end rhyme "rayned . . . obtayne"), and symploce ("goe . . . goe . . . gone, go") to emphasize how the great compass of Atreus' thought is fused with enormous (e)motion. But the speech's most vivid and emblematic moment is how, via the figures of erotesis and diacope, it plumbs the depths of Atreus' desire for revenge.[82] When is "enough" "enough"? What words and deeds will satiate his "wil"? The gruesome rhyme ("I wil procede and fyl . . .") immediately provides the answer but it also, if we pick up "all my wil" from two lines above, makes the agent nothing more than its action. And while his point of comparison is the celestial gods, his realm of action remains decidedly chthonic. It is important to note, then, that Heywood's translation loses the dramatic shift from satisfaction to sudden doubt that Seneca achieves by following the string of indicative forms of *esse* with the sudden subjunctive of "sed cur satis sit?" This question, the last great variation on Seidensticker's *maius aliquid* formula, suggests at once the insatiability of Atreus' desire, but it also confirms the limits of Seneca's dramatic form. There will always, it seems, be yet another victim, another corpse to be counted, while there remains precious little conceptual, rhetorical, or dialogic space for the kind of boundless rumination characteristic of a Macbeth, Hamlet, or Lear. And while my intention is not to construct an invidious comparison of Seneca with Shakespeare, still, it does seem that hyperbole ends up becoming something of a conceptual straitjacket for Seneca, rather than the potential means for exploring the possibility of self-knowledge, especially as such knowledge concerns excessive desire, extravagant doubt, and what Cavell reads as the quite ordinary need for acknowledgment from others, no matter how extreme circumstances might be. Put another way, the question with which Cavell ends *The Claim of Reason* remains open: ". . . can philosophy become literature and still know itself?"[83]

Chapter Ten

Going Baroque in Shakespearean Drama

> Look in your glass, and there appears a face
> That overgoes my blunt invention quite,
> Dulling my lines, and doing me disgrace.
> — William Shakespeare, Sonnet 103

SURPASSING SENECA

As Senecan excess is translated throughout the Renaissance, a pattern emerges: just as the Senecan hero has insatiable ambitions, the Senecan dramatist tries to outdo previous dramatists. The dynamics of *imitatio* in Renaissance tragedy follow largely Senecan lines, even as these merge and conflict with Christian theology and medieval forms (especially the "Herod" drama). But rather than try to recover historical ground deftly mapped elsewhere, I want first to consider Gordon Braden's compelling insight on the conceptual aspects of the imitation and outbidding of Senecan tragedy. Leaning on Hegel's twin dialectic of self- and historical becoming, Braden writes:

> Seneca bequeaths to later times some extraordinary standards for the self's ambitions and some ways of realizing those ambitions dramatically, in a rhetoric of psychic aggression that seemingly allows a character to make himself and his world up out of his own words. Yet it is a heritage that does not forestall but invites a countervailing astringency — a more sophisticated awareness of the relations between the self's ambition and its grounds, between the speaker and the audience to whom he will always be beholden. Watching that awareness grow around Seneca's heritage, we watch Seneca's own dead end become the starting

point for a distinct and important line in dramatic history than can be seriously and usefully spoken of as the Senecan tradition.[1]

By stressing the degree to which *imitatio* in the Senecan tradition was self-aware and dialectical, Braden offers a cogent historical reason why English drama-tists began to represent within their plays the limitations inherent in the tradi-tion of Senecan *Überbietung*. The dialectical, but still historicist manner that Braden interprets Shakespeare's versions of Senecan poetic ambition thus sig-nificantly differs from Cavell's "ordinary language" interpretation of Shake-spearean tragedy's ahistoricist, dialogic response to hyperbolic skepticism. Sketching a broad historical perspective, Braden portrays a neo-Stoic, neo-Senecan Shakespeare who subtly remakes and rejects these legacies in response to other historical influences such as Christianity, medieval drama, Italian Senecanism, the rhetorical revival, and contemporary Elizabethan drama, es-pecially that of Chapman, Marlowe, and Kyd. Shakespeare thus transfigures the "Senecan world of the closed self" in plays like *Lear* with its "expansive vehemence" to reveal also "a sense of the abyss" looming behind the actors' words.[2] My aim in this and the next chapter, however, is to show how what Braden calls the "countervailing astringency" of English Senecanism also oc-curs within the plays themselves. In this sense, Cavell's largely ahistoricist reading of Shakespearean tragedy is true, despite itself, to the historical dy-namics of Shakespeare's restless invention. For Braden Senecan drama is where Stoic philosophy is made to answer the complicated realities of power and the passions, while for Cavell tragedy is the place where philosophic skep-ticism is made to answer the claims of ordinary language.

Notwithstanding the appealing symmetry of these hermeneutics, the lit-erary history of late Renaissance Senecanism may also be interpreted as the struggle to answer Atreus' question: "sed cur satis sit?" Specifically, for much of the period, the cosmological aspects of Seneca's Stoicism were simply treated as *de trop*. With their focus on the emotional, moral, and spiritual life of the in-dividual, most versions of Renaissance neo-Stoicism either ignore the natural philosophy component of Seneca's writings or use it mainly to adorn their rhetoric with certain venerable but unexamined ideas such as the *theatrum mundi* or *navigatio vitae*. Erasmus, who edits and anthologizes Seneca's writings, and who limns his own writings such as the *Colloquia familiaria* (1518) and the *Colloquium senile* (1533) with Stoic wisdom even as he critiques the Stoic eth-ical ideal as too narrow, is exemplary in this regard.[3] Aiming to reconcile

Stoic precepts with Christian theology, Erasmus — like Petrarch before him, and Montaigne, Quevedo, Lipsius, Dolet, Plantin, du Vair, Gryphius, Huygens, and Corneille after him — treads a fine syncretic line. He responds to orthodox concerns about salvation and provides a practical philosophy that would help the individual endure a foolish, mutable world. Accordingly, as sixteenth-century religious turmoil gives way to the political, epistemological, and spiritual crises of the seventeenth century, the Stoic doctrine of *non moveri* becomes a central, even commonplace theme. Embodying this ideal and hubristically echoing Seneca's tragic heroes is Shakespeare's Julius Caesar when he declaims:

> I could be well moved if I were as you.
> If I could pray to move, prayers would move me.
> But I am constant as the Northern Star,
> Of whose true fixed and resting quality
> There is no fellow in the firmament.
> The skies are painted with unnumbered sparks;
> They are all fire, and every one doth shine;
> But there's but one in all doth hold his place.
> So in the world: 'tis furnished well with men,
> And men are flesh and blood, and apprehensive;
> Yet in that number I do know but one
> That unassailable holds on his rank,
> Unshaked of motion; and that I am he . . .[4] (3.1.58–70)

To move and not to be moved; such is the paradoxical, potentially impossible *propositio* for the Stoic tragic hero on the Baroque stage.[5] Caesar's elaborate analogy in which the constancy of the "Northern Star" outdoes that of the "unnumbered sparks," just as he, "in the world," is more "constant" than "that number" of men (a set that includes all men), seems to promise exactly this impossibility. He aims to move the audience and thereby accomplish that ancient Ciceronian rhetorical ideal, which in the Baroque period increasingly became an aesthetic one as well. Yet given the play's dramatic contingencies, Caesar also strives not be moved by events and emotions ("Unshaked of motion"), so that he alone ("I do know but one") might achieve *apatheia* in a not very "constant," hostile world. Of this latter aim, Lessing in *Laokoon* later offers this damning verdict:

Alles Stoische ist untheatralisch; und unser Mitleiden ist allezeit dem Leiden gleichmäßig, welches der interessierende Gegenstand äußert. Sieht man ihn sein Elend mit großer Seele ertragen, so wird diese große Seele zwar unsere Bewunderung erwecken, aber die Bewun-derung ist ein kalter Affekt, dessen untätiges Staunen jede andere wärmere Leidenschaft, sowie jede andere deutliche Vorstellung aus-schließet.[6]

Everything Stoic is untheatrical; and our pity is always indifferent to suf-fering, which the theme at hand expresses. When one sees him bear his misery with greatness of soul, then this great soul indeed awakes our ad-miration. But admiration is a cold emotion, whose idle astonishment excludes every other, warmer passion, as well as every other clearer con-ception.

As if prophetically confirming Lessing's insight, Caesar, unable to contem-plate mercy for the banished Cimber, hyperbolically strains to "show" why he is above such an act.[7] And while his magnificent, extended stellar analogy confirms Stoic *sumpatheia*, its occurrence just before the speaker is stabbed proves its untenability, as does the way Shakespeare henceforth focuses on Brutus' "große Seele" rather than Caesar's.

A quick look at Montaigne reveals another version of this rich ambivalence toward the Stoic legacy. Imbued with strong but shifting strains of Epicureanism, Pyhronnic skepticism, Fideism, and occasional dashes of Neo-Platonism, the *Essais* directly engage central Stoic ethical concerns about the passions and death.[8] Ultimately, as Montaigne argues most extensively in the "Apology for Raymond Sebond," the ideal of *apatheia* is rejected as un-workable and inhuman, for the changeable passions are indispensable for achieving "the finest actions of the soul."[9] Thus after quoting Petrarch's *Against the Stoics* and chiding Lucretius and his praise of Epicurean serenity, Mon-taigne insists:

Ceci est aussi de Seneque: que la sage a la fortitude pareille à Dieu, mais en l'humaine foiblesse; par où il le surmonte. Il n'est rien si ordinaire que de rencontrer des traicts de pareille temerité. Il n'y a aucun de nous qui s'offence tant de se voir apparier à Dieu, comme il faict de se voir de-primir au reng des autres animaux: tant nous sommes plus jaloux de nostre interest que de celuy de nostre createur.

This also is Senecaes, that the wise man hath a fortitude like unto Gods; but in [humane] weaknesse, wherein he excelleth him. There is nothing more common, than to meet with such passages of temeritie: There is not any of us that will be so much offended to see himselfe compared to God, as he will deeme himselfe wronged to be depressed in the ranke of other creatures. So much are we more jealous of our owne interest, than of our Creators.[10]

Montaigne's self-appointed task is to deflate, hyperbolically, man's presumption and to teach him thereby the difference between Christian "sapience" and Stoic doctrine or "science":

Le moyen que je prens pour rabatre cette frenaisie et qui me semble le plus propre, c'est de froisser et fouler aux pieds l'orgueil et humaine fierté; leur faire sentir l'inanité, la vanité et deneantise de l'homme; leur arracher des points les chetives armes de leur raison; leur faire baisser la teste et mordre la terre soubs l'authorité et reverance de la majesté divine. C'est à elle seule qu'apartient la science et la sapience . . .

The meanes I use to suppresse this frenzy, and which seemeth the fittest for my purpose, is to crush, and trample this humane pride and fierce-ness under foot, to make them feele the emptinesse, vacuitie, and no worth of man: and violently to pull out of their hands, the silly weapons of their reason; to make them stoope, and bite and snarle at the ground, under the authority and reverence of Gods Majesty. Onely to her be-longeth science and wisdome . . .[11]

No wonder Jill Kraye calls Montaigne "[o]ne of the most persuasive Renais-sance opponents of the Stoic theory of the emotions."[12] Nonetheless, the force and *copia* ("froisser et fouler") of his Pyrrhonnic eloquence suggest just how entrenched his adversary is. Further, as the final paragraphs of the "Apology" indicate, Montaigne's earlier attraction to Stoic prescriptions for self-mastery is not easily dissolved. There he quotes from the preface of the *Quaestiones nat-urales* ("Oh, what a vile and abject thing is man, if he does not rise above hu-manity"), only to conclude:

Voylà un bon mot et un utile desir, mais pareillement absurde. Car de faire la poignée plus grand que le poing . . . cela est impossible et monstrueux . . . Il s'eslevera si Dieu lui preste extraordinairement la main; il s'eslevera, abandonnant et renonçant à ses propres moyens, et se laissant hausser et soubslever par les moyens purement celestes. C'est à nostre foy Chrestienne, non à sa vertu Stoïque de pretendre à cette divine et miraculeuse metamorphose.

Observe here a notable speech, and a profitable desire; but likewise absurd. For to make the handfull greater then the hand . . . is impossible and monstrous . . . He shall raise himself up, if it please God to lend him his helping hand. He may elevate himselfe by forsaking and renouncing his own meanes, and suffering himselfe to be elevated and raised by meere heavenly meanes. It is for our Christian faith, not for his Stoicke vertue to pretend or aspire to this divine Metamorphosis, or miraculous transmutation.[13]

While John Florio's florid translation of Montaigne's *Essayes* was known to Shakespeare, the most influential and accessible account of Stoic philosophy available to him and his contemporaries was John Stradling's 1595 translation of Justus Lipsius' *De constantia libri duo* (1584).[14] *Two Bookes of Constancie* consists of a lively, fictional dialogue between a younger Lipsius who wishes to flee the Belgian wars and an older Charles Langius who embodies Stoic teachings. Set initially on the requisite "portch," Stradling's translation is a crucial step in the English staging of Stoicism. Littered with metaphors of all stripes, the *Two Bookes of Constancie* recasts the canonical Stoic metaphorics of sea, storm, and tranquility ("I lie at rest amid the waves") with real dramatic and subjective force.[15] Likewise, the analogy of world and theater is repeatedly, often poignantly, invoked: "You play a Comedy, & under the person of your country, you bewail with tears your private miseries. One saith *The whol world is a stage-play*. Trulie in this case it is so."[16] Still, "this huge Theater of the worlde" demands explication as well as performance; and so Lipsius distinguishes at length between fortune, fate, necessity, and providence — the first now imbued with sufficient Christian orthodoxy to protect him from charges of blasphemy.[17] In particular, his argument against fortune is directed at would-be Epicureans, then often synonymous with atheists.[18] While the numerous, subtle distinctions he makes between fate, destiny, necessity, and providence (necessity and providence are "neere kinne") are beyond this book's scope, Lipsius' version of Homer's "golden chaine" deserves attention as it translates the notion of *sumpatheia* into late Renaissance cultural and political contexts, even as it uncannily prefigures the melancholic rhetoric of Hamlet and Lear:

> ... for as Pindarus saith well, The *dispensers and doers of all things are in heaven.* And there is let downe from hence a golden chaine (as *Homer* ex⁄ presseth by a figment) whereto all the inferior things are fast linked ... Therefore *Euripides* sayd wel and wisely, *that all calamities came from God.* The ebbing and flowing of all human affaires dependeth on that Moone ... Thou therefore in loosing the raynes thus to thy sorrowe, and grudging that thy countrey is so turned and over⁄turned, considereth not what thou art, and against whome thou complainest. What art thou? A man, a shadowe, dust: Against whom doest thou fret? I feare to speak it, even against GOD.
>
> The Auncientes have fayned that Gyantes advaunced themselves against God, to pull him out of his throne. Let us omitte these fables: In very trueth you querulous and murmuring men be these Gyantes ... O blind mortality: The Sun, the Moon, Stars, Elements, and all creatures els in the world, doe willingly obey that supreme lawe. Onely MAN, the most excellent of all Gods workes lifteth up his heele, and spurneth against his maker. If thou hoiste thy sayles to the windes, thou must fol⁄ low whither they will force thee, not whither thy will leadeth thee. And in this greate Ocean sea of our life wilt thou refuse to follow that breath⁄ ing spirite which governeth the whole worlde? Yet thou strivest in vaine."[19]

That this remarkable passage is then framed by a "golden sentence" from Seneca concerning the wisdom of accepting things we cannot change, ap⁄ pears further to devalue the power of "libertas" to alter the decrees of divine providence, which one necessarily remains ignorant of before they are insti⁄ tuted in the world. Thus Lipsius, preparing the way for Shakespeare's Gloucester, observes: "For this greate Master⁄builder pulleth downe, setteth up, and (if I may so lawfully speake) maketh a sporte of humaine affaires."[20]

Whatever the cause of such fatalism — the Wars of Religion that raged on the continent, or the same skeptical spirit that leads Montaigne to his idio⁄ syncratic fideism — Lipsius' treatise would also create real pathos: "Thus spoke *Langius,* and with his talke caused the teares to trickle down my cheekes."[21] Conversely, he presents Stoic doctrine, despite its pagan flaws, as offering phi⁄ losophy's most persuasive consolations:

> I come to the Stoics my friendes (for I professe to hold that sect in esti-
> mation and account) who were the authours of VIOLENT FATE,
> which with *Seneca* I define to be, *A necessitie of all thinges and actions, which
> no force can withstand or breake.* And with *Crissipus, A spirituall power, gov-
> erning orderly the whole world.*[22]

In short, though Lipsius expresses his wariness regarding Stoic materialism
and pantheism, clearly the explanatory power of Stoic physics had great conceptual appeal for him. This, despite the fact that for many of his readers, such
a physics and the moral philosophy that accompanies it shockingly lack any
mention of salvation.[23]

Likewise, when it came to Seneca the dramatist, Lipsuis' ambivalence is
instructive. "Justus Lipsius," Robert Miola notes, "admired Seneca's *sonus*
and *granditas*, while questioning his affectation and bombast (*adfectatio* and *tu-
mor*)."[24] For his part, Lipsius' frequent opponent, J. C. Scaliger, was busy
hyping the style of Senecan drama:

> . . . Seneca . . . quem nullo Graecorum majestate inferiorem existimo,
> culto vero ac nitore etiam Euripide maiorem. Inventiones sane illorum
> sunt, maiestas carminus, sonus spiritus ipsius. In quibus Sophoclis se
> esse voluit similiorem, frustra fuit.[25]

> . . . Seneca . . . whom I judge not to be inferior to any of the Greeks in
> grandeur; and likewise greater than Euripides in polish and luster. The
> plots are indeed from the Greeks, though the poetic loftiness, sound, and
> spirit are his own. But in those things that he would have emulated
> Sophocles, he was thwarted.

Rivaling, even outstripping the Greeks in style, Seneca still falls short in poetic invention, and thus, Scaliger implies, should not serve as a model for imitation. Finally, in his dedicatory letter to the influential 1581 volume of
Seneca's plays he helped edit and translate, Thomas Newton justifies the
translations and thus the Senecan style more generally on account of their
rhetorical and so ethical efficacy:

> And whereas it is by some squeymish Areopagites surmyzed, that the
> reading of these Tragedies . . . cannot be digested without great daunger
> of infection; to omit all other reasons, if it might please them with no

forestalled judgment, to mark and consider the circumstances, why, where, and by what manner of persons such sentences are pronounced, they cannot in any equity otherwise choose, but find good cause ynough to leade them to a more favourable and milde resolution. For it may not at any hand be thought and deemed the direct meaning of Seneca himselfe, whose whole wrytinges [penned with peerelesse sublimity and loftinesse of Style], are so farre from countenauncing vice, that I doubt whether there bee any amonge all the Catalogue of Heathen wryters, that with more gravity of Philosophical sentences, more waightynes of sappy words, or greater authority of sound matter beateth down sinne, loose lyfe, dissolute dealinge, and unbrydled sensuality: or that more sensibly, pithily, and bytingly layeth downe the guedon of filthy lust, cloaked dis-simulation and odious treachery: which is the dryft, whereunto he lev-eleth the whole yssue of ech one of his Tragedies.[26]

Reworking the rhetorical technique of *stasis*, Newton's "why, where, and by what manner of persons" marks the plays as rhetorical discourses dependent on context and contingency for their ultimate meaning. Confronting also the perceived disjunction between Seneca's philosophy and drama, Newton em-phasizes how Seneca's style in the plays ("gravity . . . waightynes of sappy words . . . sensibly, pithily, and bytingly") not only immunizes them from moral condemnation, but ensures that the "whole yssue of ech" play will be read with the proper *ethos*. In short, Newton ensures that Senecan hyperbole will receive a fair and a decidedly rhetorical hearing in subsequent decades.

SHAKESPEARE AND "'ERC'LES' VEIN"

For all the hermeneutic hay to be made from the insights of Newton, Scaliger, Lipsius, and Montaigne, judging the exact influence or confluence of Sto-icism and Senecanism in particular Shakespearean plays remains a vexing task. How much of these intellectual currents had become commonplace and part of the period's conceptual sea, and how much was direct imitation has long proved a byzantine debate. Fortunately, the debate is already comically inscribed in Bottom's first long speech in *A Midsummer Night's Dream* (ca. 1596), a speech rightly read as spoofing the Senecan manner.[27] Confused, seemingly, by the oxymoronic title of the play, *The Most Lamentable Comedy and Most Cruel Death of Pyramus and Thisbe*, which he and his fellow "mechanicals" will perform for the Duke's wedding, Bottom is initially uncertain whether

Pyramus is a "lover or a tyrant." Told then that he will be playing a lover who takes his own life, he responds with the knowing enthusiasm of someone who has seen too many Senecan tragedies:

> That will ask some tears in the true performing of it. If I do it, let the au-
> dience look to their eyes. I will move stones.[28] I will condole, in some
> measure. To the rest. — Yet my chief humour is for a tyrant. I could
> play 'erc'les rarely, or a part to tear a cat in, to make all split.
>
> > The raging rocks
> > And shivering shocks
> > Shall break the locks
> > Of prison gates,
> > And Phibus' car
> > Shall shine from far
> > And make and mar
> > The foolish Fates.
>
> This was lofty. Now, name the rest of the players. — This is 'erc'les'
> vein, a tyrant's vein. A lover is more condoling. (1.2.21–35)

Bottom deflates his own bombast with solecisms, awkward rhymes, and lack of *gravitas*, but also, and more subtly, via the way Shakespeare makes him mock the very dramatic conventions employed in *Titus Andronicus* (ca. 1594), the conventions which Marlowe used to reinvent blank verse and give voice to his overreachers, and which lesser hands unwittingly transformed into clichés.[29] A. J. Boyle, for instance, observes that "[b]ombast can be overdone," as in this "hyper-Senecan conceit" in Tourneur's *The Atheist's Tragedy*: "Drop out | Mine eye-balls, and let envious Fortune play | At tennis with 'em" (2.4.27–29).[30] Such remarkable infelicities aside, the blinkered self-consciousness that emerges from Bottom's lines — he knows what he likes and what "humor" moves him and yet he cannot know how swiftly and completely this brief speech endears him to the audience as the object of its laughter — proves how the fragments of the Senecan legacy can be reassembled for ironic ends; "'erc'les' vein," the *Schreirede*, still has some life in it. Just as the Petrarchan vein occa-sionally became a satiric vehicle for Sidney, Donne, Daniel, and Shakespeare himself, so the Senecan is here mined to highlight the distance between words and reality, literary tradition and ordinary speech.[31] Furthermore, the ridicu-lous, yet somehow edifying manner in which the everyday language of Shakespeare's rude mechanicals is made to seem especially lunatic in its Senecan straightjacket also speaks to Cavell's concern for the fate of ordinary language in tragedy.

Similarly, right before the newly crowned Hal enters to pronounce: "I know thee not, old man . . ." to Falstaff, the gap between saying and meaning is made ludic in a different manner when Pistol, in the closing scene of *2 Henry IV* (1600), plays the Senecan *satelles* who incites the fat knight to revenge:

> My knight, I will inflame thy noble liver,
> And make thee rage.
> Thy Doll, and Helen of thy noble thoughts,
> Is in base durance and contagious prison,
> Haled thither
> By most mechanical and dirty hand.
> Rouse up Revenge from ebon den with fell Alecto's snake,
> For Doll is in. Pistol speaks naught but truth. (5.5.29–36)

Pistol's uneven rhetoric and prosody, borrowed in part from the plays we imagine him to have seen in the London theaters, prove as ineffective in terms of dramatic action as they are effective from the perspective of Shakespeare's comedic ends — the comparison of the whore Doll Tearsheet to the woman whose face "launched a thousand ships" is utterly incongruous but somehow apt given the two worlds that Hal travels between. Likewise, earlier in the play (2.4.140–146) Pistol consciously if ineptly imitates "the expansive, hyperbolic rhetoric" of Marlowe's Tamburlaine in a manner that provides aesthetic pleasure to an audience even if all of his mangled references cannot be deciphered.[32]

What results, however, when Shakespeare makes a tragic protagonist both perpetrator and judge of Senecan hyperbole? His use of the figure in *Hamlet* exemplifies the dramatic ambiguity of such a ploy; indeed, his young prince embodies the promise and not a little of the risk native to every early modern hyperbolist. When the players arrive at Elsinore, Hamlet offers this invidious comparison between his own ability to express woe and that of the player who has just recited a set speech:

> O, what a rogue and peasant slave am I!
> Is it not monstrous that this player here,

> But in a fiction, in a dream of passion,
> Could force his soul so to his own conceit
> That from her working all his visage wanned,
> Tears in his eyes, distraction in 's aspect,
> A broken voice, and his whole function suiting
> With forms to his conceit? And all for nothing,
> For Hecuba!
> What's Hecuba to him, or he to Hecuba,
> That he should weep for her? What would he do
> Had he the motive and the cue for passion
> That I have? He would drown the stage with tears,
> And cleave the general ear with horrid speech,
> Make mad the guilty and appal the free,
> Confound the ignorant, and amaze indeed
> The very faculty of eyes and ears. (2.2.527–543)

The Baroque *mise-en-abîme* of having the actor who plays Hamlet envying the ability of an actor playing an actor to make his "conceit" a moving piece of theater out of "nothing" emblemizes the sophistication with which Shakespeare interpolates his metapoetic thoughts on the nature of dramaturgical exaggeration. The player is able to "drown the stage with tears" and cause madness, atonement, and amazement, but as of yet Hamlet is unskilled in the fine art of hyperbole. Yet when Hamlet momentarily plays the drama critic, he critiques a well-known species of dramatic hyperbole:

> O, it offends me to the soul to hear a robustious, periwig-pated fellow tear a passion to tatters, to very rags, to split the ears of the groundlings, who for the most part are capable of nothing but inexplicable dumb shows and noise. I would have such a fellow whipped for o'erding Termagant. It out-Herods Herod (3.2.7–13).[33]

If these lines recall Bottom's hope for "a part to tear a cat in," they also suggest a distinction between popular Senecan "o'erding" and the refined, witty hyperbole that wins theatrical fame for Hamlet himself. Not long before this scene, the sensitive Dane, embodying Aristotle's dictum that hyperbole is for the young, proves himself master of such "o'erdoing" and "dumb shows."

Heeding the Ghost's summons in Act I, Hamlet earnestly refashions that ancient Herculean, hyperbolic *topos*, by boldly declaring: "My fate cries out, / And makes each petty artere in this body / As hardy as the Nemean lion's nerve" (1.4.58–60). In another vein altogether, he waxes extravagantly philosophical before the befuddled Rosencrantz and Guildenstern:

> . . . it goes so heavily with my disposition that this goodly frame, the earth, seems to me a sterile promontory. This most excellent canopy the air, look you, this brave o'erhanging firmament, this majestical roof fretted with golden fire — why, it appears no other thing to me than a foul and pestilent congregation of vapours. What a piece of work is a man! How noble in reason, how infinite in faculty, in form and moving how express and admirable, in action how like an angel, in apprehension how like a god — the beauty of the world, the paragon of animals! And yet to me what is this quintessence of dust? (2.2.288–297)

While this two-edged panegyric explores the two extremes of Renaissance humanism, as marked, say, by the optimism of Pico's *De hominis dignitate* and the pessimism of Montaigne's adaptation of maxims from *Quaestiones naturales*, its pathos-laden, hyperbolic logic also furthers the dramatic action.

For, as in all things, Hamlet's hyperbole is powered by the extreme self-consciousness of his unenviable (dramatic) situation, a situation where *non moveri* is no longer an option. In the last Act, as if wanting both to literalize and further hyperbolize his vision of man as a "quintessence of dust," Hamlet, following Laertes, leaps into Ophelia's grave and declares:

> 'Swounds, show me what thou'lt do.
> Woot weep, woot fight, woot fast, woot tear thyself,
> Woot drink up eisel, eat a crocodile?
> I'll do't. Dost thou come here to whine,
> To outface me with leaping in the grave?
> Be buried quick with her, and so will I.
> And if thou prate of mountains, let them throw
> Millions of acres on us, till our ground,
> Singeing his pate against the burning zone,
> Make Ossa like a wart. Nay, an thou'lt mouth,
> I'll rant as well as thou. (5.1.259–269)

Goaded into playing the hyperbolist yet again, Hamlet manages, even as he reduces the gigantomachic Ossa to a "wart," to express and put into action, at least partially, the immanent depth of his suffering. That such pathos can be produced by such disproportionate rhetoric, exemplifies the complexity of Shakespearean dramatic hyperbole.[34] For when Claudius hears these lines and thinks "madness," perhaps, despite his ignorance about their real cause, he is not so far from the mark.

SAYING THE "MOST" IN *LEAR*

If the ill-fitting discourse of the Senecan stage ultimately obtains various levels of meaning for Bottom and his fellows, then even greater mutability occurs in Lear's Neo-Senecan rhetoric: from the tempestuous extravagance of the early scenes (in which he but slenderly knows himself), through the mad, cosmographic *copia* of the middle scenes (in which the microcosmos and macrocosmos prove out of joint), to the condensed pathos and sublime inexpressibility of the last scenes (in which the *nescio quid* is no longer a passing moment but the ironic closing of a fatal circle). The language of *King Lear* (ca. 1604) runs the gamut of possible styles and ideologies: echoes of Erasmus cheek by jowl with the obscene ditties of the Elizabethan balladeers in the Fool's lines; the Harsnett-inspired *copia* and gibberish of Poor Tom; the debased Machiavellianism and Petrarchism of Edmund, Gonoril, and Regan; the lofty, neo-Stoic self-fashioning and maxims of Kent, Albany, Edgar, and Cordelia. All of which contends, much as Lear contends with the thunder, with Lear's cosmic, Senecan hyperbole, hyperbole that, in turn, vainly battles with a species of skepticism worthy of Montaigne. Put another way, the play's language, the soliloquies and asides included, is highly dialogic — ever responsive to the dynamics of deceit, wit, eloquence, imprecation, and silence. When Lear mourns Cordelia at the end of the play ("Her voice was ever soft, / Gentle, and low . . .") (24.268–269), we do not so much forget the drama's other voices, but begin to see what was vital and superfluous about them.

Hyperbole in *King Lear* proves structural as well as discursive and metaphoric. It deeply informs, that is, the *inventio* and *elocutio* that Shakespeare cultivates to create the play's metaphysical pathos and what Wilson Knight dubs its "cosmic mockery."[35] For in addition to giving Lear his most characteristic voice, it structures the incongruities, impossibilities, and grotesqueries of the tragedy's excessive, double narrative of woe. From the opening scene of

failed flattery, to the Fool's choric, contrapuntal humor, to the radical perspectivism of the Dover Cliffs scene, to the final spectacle of death, hyperbole
forces us to ask, to quote Gonoril and Albany, when is "so much" (1.55,
24.321) too much? If man is a beast, fate a wheel, and the gods apathetic, then
hyperbole helps us to make sense of these bitter insights, as it tries the impossible task of explaining why these truths are at once immanent yet insufficient.
In the light of the palpable inadequacy of Stoic philosophy and Christian
revelation to explain or justify Lear's fate, Shakespeare reshapes the boundaries of inexpressibility *topoi*. And yet given that the play is also replete with
many moments of quiet pathos and self-deprecating wit, one wonders how to
gauge the decorum of such hyperbole. Further, in what sense and in what circumstances does hyperbole prove to be dialogic? How, finally, do we judge to
what degree hyperbole is heuristic for Shakespeare the thinker? In so far as *Lear*
explores the theater's discursive and imaginative limits and thereby humanity's marginal place in the *theatrum mundi*, how does Shakespeare the hyperbolist betray the kind of self-consciousness Cavell ascribes to Shakespeare the
playwright wrestling with skepticism?

In the play's opening scene Lear's extreme, and extremely perverse gambit unfolds and unravels, a gambit upon which all the subsequent dramatic
action hangs. Blithely, blindly, inviting his daughters to hyperbolize, Lear
transforms himself into a blinkered, wrathful Senecan caricature. The scene
begs to be read as a failed exercise in courtly rhetoric wherein a desire for epideixis precipitates servile flattery and self-condemning imprecation.[36] It begins wih a bizarre calculus:

> Tell me, my daughters,
> Which of you shall we say doth love us most,
> That we our largest bounty may extend
> Where merit doth most challenge it? (1.44–47)

Staking his love, generosity, and vanity on his daughters' ability to hyperbolize, Lear makes the fatal mistake of imperiously wanting to exchange their
language for his power and property. He would quantify love and "merit"
through the repetition (*conduplicatio*) of the superlative "most"; a mode of being is thus reduced to a mode of speech. With kingdoms as their reward, he
would have his daughters rhetorically map their love. As Lear shifts back and
forth from his daughter's telling to his own saying, their "most" reciprocally

becomes "our largest." Thus William Elton observes: "His initial question, 'How much?' throws upon the tragedy the ironical consequences of posing quantitative human measurements against the cosmos."[37] This is to say that the way Cavell reads Lear's behavior as an extreme "attempt to avoid recognition, the shame of exposure, the threat of self-revelation," need not preclude the kind of external, cosmic consequences described by Elton.[38] For, as Seneca insists, such boundless *superbia* is by definition cosmic. Alternately, it might simply be that like all humans, Lear has a natural and so excusable desire for hyperbole's *ultra fidem*.

Gonoril proves a willing, albeit facile hyperbolist. Too quickly to be credible save to Lear's deficient ears, she gestures immediately at inexpressibility:

> Sir, I do love you more than words can wield the matter;
> Dearer than eyesight, space, or liberty;
> Beyond what can be valued, rich or rare;
> No less than life; with grace, health, beauty, honour;
> As much as child e'er loved, or father, friend;
> A love that makes breath poor and speech unable.
> Beyond all manner of so much I love you. (1.49–55)

Her love, she claims, is "beyond all" quantification ("so much"). And her insistent use of invidious comparison self-consciously points to her ability to convert "matter" into "manner." But as his response confirms, Lear hears her speech as convertible into a quantifiable "bounds." One wonders, however, why Lear, after so many decades on the throne, proves such a poor interpreter of hyperbole. Why does he seem so unable to perceive the gulf between figurative and literal meaning? Or has he in his senescence become such a creature of courtly flattery and panegyric that he has confused his roles of father and king? Cavell offers plausible answers to these questions, answers rooted in his insights on how people use words to say and not to say what they mean. But if Lear's tragedy is that of someone who refuses to acknowledge his own and others' humanity, then in this he resembles the Senecan tyrant.[39] Unable to "know himself," as Gonoril will later observe, Lear seems to subsist on self-conceit and the *inflatus* of others.

The opening scene presents another epistemological enigma, one made acutely urgent by Shakespeare's dramatic techniques. Cordelia's first spoken words occur immediately after Gonoril's speech in the form of an aside: "What shall Cordelia do? Love and be silent." Made vertiginously privy to her private world, the audience hears this curt, interior dialogue with admiration for and trepidation at her refusal to play the shallow, if traditional language game required of her.[40] Her silence, in light of things to come, is deafening. It is also, in a certain sense, inexcusable since she has told us — but not Lear — that she loves him. Why, then, must she be silent? Why is she unable to humor the old man? Is it a question of taste? Is Gonoril's speech too fawningly preposterous to deserve a reply? Or is it, perhaps, an ethical or cognitive refusal to name the unnamable? Furthermore, how does Shakespeare exploit this refusal for rhetorical, dramatic, or even metaphysical ends?

It is critical commonplace that Cordelia's character is, like her sisters', more symbolic than realized. Cavell's nuanced interpretation of her motivations in this scene, though, stresses just how "impossible" Lear's desire for flattery from her is and how fraught with ordinary, psychological complexities such impossibility is.[41] Yet in regard to the effect that this impossibility will have on subsequent dramatic action, Shakespeare seems to be asking what dramaturgical price is to be paid because a would-be Stoic saint refuses or is unable to play a certain language game. Even if her stance and her character here are archetypically Stoic, there is also a pressing philosophic issue at stake here that outstrips the purview of any particular school of thought. Cordelia's inability to equate love with words, an ineffable *res* with the *verba* at her disposal, suggests a larger crisis in representation. The task early modern theologians call accommodation is at risk. True, Kent, France, and her sisters variously understand her meaning; but that such silence appears amidst such dubious eloquence creates a conceptual tension, one that needs to be read against a broader philosophical background than Stoicism and Skepticism provide. Cordelia's tragedy is a liminal one. Sharing that cardinal Baconian and Cartesian desire to make words commensurate with things, she lives (and dies) in a Baroque world of signification where rhetorical excess is symptomatic of the untenability of that desire. One also thinks of Wittgenstein, who takes the Cordelian position in the concluding sentence of the *Tractatus*, but who also explicitly abandons such silence in the subsequent *Philosophical Investigations* thereby reopening the door to ineffability and tragedy, and to what Cavell regards as his philosophy's peculiar "pathos."

Likewise, much of the pathos in *Lear* is caused by hyperbole's myriad roles in ordinary and extraordinary ways of speaking and thinking. When her turn comes, Regan swiftly, sophistically, solipsistically, outdoes Gonoril:

> In my true heart
> I find she names my very deed of love —
> Only she came short, that I profess
> Myself an enemy to all other joys
> Which the most precious square of sense possesses,
> And I find I am alone felicitate
> In your dear highness' love. (1.63–69)

Substituting "name" for "deed," Regan's *inventio* on paternal "love" is curiously self-involved. Discounting "all other joys," she claims to discover a unique, superlative place ("I find I am alone") in Lear's affections. Though not quite an invidious comparison, the speech does prefigure the rivalry between the sisters for power and Edmund's affections, a rivalry that will end not in words but in poison and suicide. In this sense, Gonoril does get the last word, albeit only for a moment.

In response, Cordelia, in her second aside, reminds herself (and us) that Regan's speech is just that: "Then poor Cordelia — / And yet not so, since I am sure my love's / More richer than my tongue" (1.70–72). Insisting in this way on Cordelia's self-contained anguish, Shakespeare devalues the courtly ornamentation of the elder sisters' sycophantic speeches. Yet when Lear expectantly turns to his youngest to hear her requisite response, Cordelia shocks with a different kind of hyperbole, one that Lear hears as a stingy litote, but Cordelia intends as an ironic paradox:

> *Lear*: What can you say to win a third more opulent
> Than your sisters?
> *Cordelia*: Nothing, my lord. (1.78–80)

With this bald, absolute reply, the play's dialectic of being, seeming, and annihilation — an extreme variation on Shakespeare's more familiar dialectic of being and seeming — commences. "Nothing can come of nothing.[42] Speak again," Lear demands, but at this juncture Cordelia can only point to her inability to express her feelings ("Unhappy that I am, I cannot heave / My heart into my mouth") and her moral duty ("I love your majesty / According to my bond, nor more nor less") (1.81–84). This latter attempt to quantify her inexplicable "bond" of love points to the still compelling classical ideal of the mean, the *via media*, which Joshua Scodel reminds us is so very central to the period's literary representations, to say nothing of its political, moral, and religious thinking.[43] And yet the structure and contingencies of the drama in which Cordelia finds herself will not allow for the tranquil pursuit of *mediocritas*. She is instead asked to flatter in order that she may then marry — two acts that by definition complicate her ideal. Marriage, she realizes, will subtract from her love for her father, and so she reproaches Gonoril and Regan: "Why have my sisters husbands if they say / They love you all?" (1.90–91). As for herself, she concludes: "Sure, I shall never marry like my sisters, / To love my father all" (1.94–95). To put it another way, her conception of the mean in love is thoroughly, paradoxically, hyperbolic. It precludes all false rhetoric and compromising actions, and its unworldliness will precipitate barely human consequences. Conversely, Shakespeare echoes the criticism of the Stoic ideal as lacking charity and *affectus*. Cordelia is "true," she tells her father, but mere "truth," Lear replies, does not suffice (1.99–100).

If the rapid manner in which Lear quotes Cordelia's words back to her suggests that, however deaf he is to his own feelings, he is able to grasp literal meanings, then the *imprecatio* against Cordelia indicates that he has heard and inverted his eldest daughters' epideixis. The opening scene now careens from praise to blame:

> For by the sacred radiance of the sun,
> The mysteries of Hecate and the night,
> By all the operations of the orbs
> From whom we do exist and cease to be,
> Here I disclaim all my paternal care,
> Propinquity, and property of blood,
> And as a stranger to my heart and me
> Hold thee from this for ever. The barbarous Scythian,
> Or he that makes his generation
> Messes to gorge his appetite,
> Shall be as well neighboured, pitied, and relieved
> As thou, my sometime daughter. (1.101–112)

Lear's tirade plumbs the depths of cosmic space ("sun . . . night . . . orbs") and mythic time ("for ever"), even as it denies kinship's elemental bonds by insisting that the strangest, most unsympathetic humans, the "barbarous Scythian" and the cannibal, are more deserving than Cordelia. This preposterous hyperbole seems not meant to persuade but rather to wound Cordelia and, perhaps, convince Lear himself that such injury is necessary. It becomes performative, analogous to what Cavell calls "passionate utterance"; it is an exemplary, invidious comparison that, like many of Shakespeare's eloquent invectives, endows language with an incantatory, contagious power infecting both addressee and speaker.[44] Lear becomes a domestic Tamburlaine, or, as he dubs himself, a "dragon" (1.113) who, unable to bear his daughter's "pride" or "plainness," would obliterate her memory.

However — and it is not the case generally with Marlowe's overreachers and their "high astounding terms" (*Tamburlaine, Part I*, Pr.5) — Lear and his hyperboles find an interlocutor who immediately deflates their pretensions and redirects their barbs.[45] Advocating Stoic equanimity, Kent interposes himself as the target of Lear's Senecan wrath and "hideous rashness."[46] Heedless of personal risks, he vainly reminds Lear of the emptiness of courtly rhetoric ("Think'st thou that duty shall have dread to speak / When power to flattery bows?") (1.138–139), and then reproves the duplicity of the elder daughters ("And your large speeches may your deeds approve") (1.173). His task is to teach Lear the difference between speaking and being. Telling the absolutist Lear, who invokes "Jupiter" — in the first of several instances — to sanction his folly, that he does "evil," Kent, with his caution and moderation, serves as the urgent, if premature and ineffectual, counterpoint to his master's hyperbole, to say nothing of Gonoril and Regan's hyperbolics. Likewise, after Kent's banishment, France and then Cordelia herself offer similar, if less direct, challenges to Lear's rhetorical absolutism and the sycophantic epideixis he seems to require. Reacting to Lear's precipitous rhetorical transformation of Cordelia into a "little seeming substance . . . Covered with our curse and strangered with our oath" (1.187; 193), France expresses the play's deepest psychological mystery:

> This is most strange, that she that even but now
> Was your best object, the argument of your praise,
> Balm of your age, most best, most dearest,
> Should in this trice of time commit a thing
> So monstrous to dismantle
> So many folds of favour. (1.203–208)

That the attempt to understand the "strange" nature of Cordelia's fall from "praise" relies on a string of superlative adjectives ("most . . . best . . . most best, most dearest"), and then the anaphoric "So monstrous . . . So many," confirms how integral the rhetoric of extreme quantities will be also for those reacting to the chain of events Lear precipitates. A response to Lear's emotional and geographical calculations, as well as to his attempts to annihilate his daughter via the maniacal repetition of "nothing" and other forms of extreme negation ("for we / Have no such daughter, nor shall ever see / That face of hers again") (1.252–253), the rhetoric of extremes becomes congruent with the sublime quality of the play's pathos.[47] It should be distinguished, then, from "that glib and oily art / To speak and purpose not" (1.215–216), which Cordelia lacks. Quantitative rhetoric is the earnest, even if ultimately insufficient vehicle for those who would gauge and so comprehend, or "compass" — to borrow Henry Peacham's term — the tragic trajectory of the play's events.[48] Or, as Cavell puts it in a recent essay, the "question of true praise" is double, "as if praise within the text and praise of the text are issues forming allegories of each other."[49]

Before Cordelia leaves with France, Shakespeare has her refashion France's sartorial-metaphor from lines 1.207–208, such that now she metapoetically declares to her sisters: "Time shall unfold what pleated cunning hides" (1.270). And while there is not time and space enough for me to unfold these myriad complications, one that needs mention is the theme of "[u]naccommodated man" championed explicitly by Lear and implicitly by Edgar. This theme speaks to Seneca and Lipsius' ethical polemics contra superfluous material goods and pleasures. It also informs my own focus on the self-conscious indecorousness of excessive figuration. Not only are the play's imagery, dramatic logic, and metaphysics related to this theme, but this zero-sum game also provides the empirical, objective basis for Shakespeare's poetics of extremes.

In the middle of the storm scene, Lear encounters Edgar disguised as a "*Bedlam beggar.*" His first reaction is to think that, like himself, Mad Tom has been brought to his lowly state by his daughters' perfidy ("Couldst thou save nothing? Didst thou give them all?") (11.57). Soon, though, owing to the combined effect of Edgar's wise nonsense, their common sufferings in the storm, Lear declares to the feigning madman: ". . . thou art the thing itself. Unaccommodated man is no more but such a poor, bare, forked animal as thou art" (11.96–97). With this realization, Lear moves to imitate Edgar, whom he calls a little further on a "[n]oble philosopher," by stripping off his

own clothes. But what prompts Lear to traverse these quantitative and qualitative extremes, to move from bathetic self-pity to philosophical curiosity, or
from interested to disinterested knowledge? And what prompts him to shift
just as suddenly back to his solipsistic universe, in the "trial" scene, where he
would *in absentia* prosecute and punish his daughters ("To have a thousand /
With red burning spits come hissing in upon them!") (13.11–12)?

Several signposts indicate just how central hyperbole is to the ability of
characters to speak about and so know something about themselves and others. Concluding his first great soliloquy that announces his transformation
into Poor Tom — "That's something yet. Edgar I nothing am" (7.186) —
Edgar remakes the rhetoric of annihilation such that it now riddles the subplot as well as the main plot. Earlier, Edmund blames his father for ascribing
"the surfeit of our own behaviour" (2.111) to astrological causes.[50] But he also
confuses matters (and Edgar) with his slippery wit: "I am no honest man if
there be any good meaning towards you. I have told you what I have seen and
heard but faintly, nothing like the image and horror of it" (2.155–158). Such
paradoxical phrasings are only to be resolved by the action of the play, by the
proof or disproof of deeds to come.

Scene 7 begins with Kent's withering invective against Oswald (". . . art
nothing but the composition of a knave, beggar, coward, pander, and the son
and hier of a mongrel bitch . . ." (7.13–22). Oswald does not "know" how
to answer such extravagant ontological debasement, save to call Kent and his
rhetoric "monstrous" (7.23). For his part, Lear continues his variations on the
themes of quantification and annihilation when he declares to Regan apropos
of Gonoril, "Thy sister is naught" (7.295). The pun on "naughty" and nothingness signals a moral twist, as it is precipitated by Lear's outrage at being
treated like a number.[51] Having sought "[a] little to disquantity" (4.240) Lear's
retinue, Gonoril first becomes "[m]ore hideous . . . [t]han the sea-monster,"
then a "detested kite" (4.252–253), and then a possessor of a "wolvish visage"
(4.299), before she is reduced to nothing in Scene 7 in response to her efforts
at subtraction. The rhetoric contra superfluity is thus intrinsically related to
the rhetoric of plenitude and dearth — a way of seeing and valuing the world
which is literalized and ultimately mocked in the back and forth over the
number of attending knights Lear will be allowed to keep. Informed with the
ideology of Renaissance social hierarchies, hyperbole powers his precipitous
arithmetic and helps him translate quantities into notions of quality: "Return

to her, and fifty men dismissed? . . . I could as well be brought / To knee his throne and, squire-like, pension beg / To keep base life afoot" (7.364, 370–372). But then the angry Lear, commencing the imagery of "disease" (7.378) and lechery that will culminate in Scene 20, briefly turns to tapinosis to "chide" his daughter: "Thou art a boil, / A plague-sore, an embossèd carbuncle / In my corrupted blood" (7.380–382). Lear, though, is not yet ready to rely solely on judgments of quality; reviving his attempts to calculate moral worth through external appurtenances, he declares:

> Those wicked creatures yet do seem well favoured
> When others are more wicked. Not being the worst
> Stands in some rank of praise. (*To Gonoril*) I'll go with thee.
> Thy fifty yet double five-and-twenty,
> And thou are twice her love. (7.414–418)

His use of comparative and superlative adverbs and adjectives here shows just how oblivious he is to his daughters' zero-sum game, which would relieve him of all his knights ("What needs one?") (7.421). For according to their Machiavellian mathematics to stand in "some rank of praise" is already a function tending towards zero.

Lear's magnificent speech in reply — "O, reason not the need . . ." (7.422–444) — for all its psychological realism in portraying a man wracked by doubt and anger, initially seems to ignore that the "sisters' motive is not service but the new *appetitus divitiarum infinitus*."[52] Lear would still make quantitative distinctions the basis for the qualitative distinction between human and animal life. For to say that

> Our basest beggars
> Are in the poorest thing superfluous.
> Allow not nature more than nature needs,
> Man's life is cheap as beast's . . . (7.422–425)

is still to value human life in material terms. By then having the King point to Regan's "gorgeous" clothes as proof of her humanity, Shakespeare ironically prepares the way for his revelations in the storm ("Off, off, you lendings!"). And if Lear does not yet realize that in his daughters' eyes he himself is

"superfluous" as his clothes, the speech with its semantic stress on "need" signals a crucial shift in his thinking. Abandoning all attempts to persuade Regan, the old king addresses the gods: "But for true need — / You heavens, give
me that patience, patience I need" (7.428–429). That the "heavens" (directed
by Shakespeare) does not intend to grant Lear this Stoic virtue only increases,
I think, the prayer's importance for an interpretation of the play's subsequent
hyperbolics. For if hyperbole is to be prized for marking the disproportionality between language and the world, then Lear's prayers for patience, his plea
for "noble anger" (7.434), and finally his aborted promise of revenge that
closes the speech all ingeniously mark the tragic gulf separating subjective intention, however confused or solipsistic, and the way things are.

Put another way, Lear's *ira* would imitate a Senecan tragic hero's rather
than be taught and so tamed by Stoic philosophy:

> No, you unnatural hags,
> I will have such revenges on you both
> That all the world shall — I will do such things —
> What they are, yet I know not; but they shall be
> The terrors of the earth . . . (7.436–440)

Shakespeare's vivid use of *dubitatio* here opens an ancient window upon Lear's
inner tumult. Commenting on these lines, Braden observes: "No Renaissance
playwright is more adept at inducing a sense of the nothingness opening behind so many powerful words."[53] In comparison with Atreus' ephemeral gesture of ignorance ("Nescio quid animus . . ."), Lear's speech "acquires a new
and frightening poignance: we see, almost as Lear sees, that he genuinely does
not know what he is going to do."[54] This is partially, I will argue in the next
chapter, because the storm has yet to teach him the larger lessons of *sumpatheia* —
thus the ominous, cosmological irony of the stage direction embedded within
this heart-wrenching hyperbole:

> No, I'll not weep.
> [*Storm within*]
> I have full cause of weeping, but this heart
> Shall break into a hundred thousand flaws
> Or ere I'll weep. — O fool, I shall go mad! (7.441–444)

"No," but nature will weep for him. Such sympathy, I think, buttresses Miola's rejection of readings of this scene, such as Wilson Knight and Brower's,
that finds Shakespeare's *imitatio* to verge on parody of the Senecan or Marlovian manner. The quantitative hyperbole here of "a hundred thousand flaws"
is not spoken by a Bottom or Pistol, but by a kingly man whose sufferings are
teaching him, and will continue to teach him in subsequent scenes, the folly
of counting.

Chapter Eleven

Saying the "worst" in *Lear*

Methode ist Umweg.

— Walter Benjamin, *Ursprung des deutschen Trauerspiels*

STORM WITHIN AND WITHOUT

In the wake of models offered by Virgil, Lucan, and Seneca, and inspired by contemporary histories written to chronicle, defend, and advertise the voyages of discovery and conquest, the storm at sea *topos* beckons, Siren-like, to early modern imitators.[1] Shakespeare's great innovation in *King Lear* is to set this storm on land rather than on the "wild waters," as he calls them, some six years later in *The Tempest*.[2] The extent to which "this dreadful pother" owes stylistic and conceptual debts to Senecan representations of anger and the apocalypse (*ekpyrosis*) is also complicated by how Shakespeare puts these extremes in dialogue with anti-Senecan voices and themes.[3] In other words, the storm on the heath also quickly becomes what Lear refers to as "[t]his tempest in my mind" (11.12).[4] The hyperbolic storm rages within and without. To express such exorbitant "weather" (8.1–2) and extraordinary emotion, and to figure the unstable boundaries of self and cosmos, Shakespeare leans on the unique *energeia* of hyperbole. Yet as these extremes converge to precipitate a state bordering on madness and catastrophe, he also makes hyperbole interrogate the immanence of superfluity and monstrosity.

To begin with, the play establishes an objective basis for Lear's stubbornly subjective perception of the storm. Responding to Kent's query, "Where's the King?" the First Gentleman, in his first timely appearance, vividly depicts Lear's experience of the storm. This description, in addition to helping overcome the scenographic difficulties of trying to represent the storm, brims over with classical and biblical *topoi*.[5] Lear, he tells us, is

> Contending with the fretful element;
> Bids the wind blow the earth into the sea
> Or swell the curlèd waters 'bove the main,
> That things might change or cease; tears his white hair,
> Which the impetuous blasts, with eyeless rage,
> Catch in their fury and make nothing of;
> Strives in his little world of man to outscorn
> The to-and-fro conflicting wind and rain. (8.3–10)

Since the storm occurs within the analogical frame of microcosm and macro-cosm, if Lear is "[c]ontending," then the "wind and rain" are "conflicting." Likewise, Kent, the Fool, and Gloucester all perceive this "naughty night" (11.99), this "tyrannous night" (11.136), to herald an exceptional state of be-ing threatening not just human safety but also sanity and morality. With his "traitorous" daughters pretending to fear his "desperate train" (7.461), and so declaring what Agamben theorizes as a "state of exception" to shut him out in the storm, Lear, "minded like the weather" (8.2), hopes that nature, and the "great gods" that orchestrate its "affliction" and "force," will rain down universal "justice" (9.49–53). But even as he hints at the primeval chaos (". . . and make nothing of") associated with the Stoic *ekpyrosis* or the Chris-tian apocalypse and refashions the epic commonplace of the world upside down, Shakespeare mocks Lear's grandiosity by having the Fool interject am-biguous quips like: "Marry, here's grace and a codpiece — that's a wise man and a fool" (9.40–41). Indeed, given the Fool's song just before (9.27–34), such wit begs to be read as a satiric hyperbole belittling the King's fallen status.

When Lipsius writes: "All things run into this fatall whirle poole or ebbing and flowing," he paints the philosophic backdrop for Shakespeare's drama-tizing of the Stoic notion of *contagio* between self and cosmos.[6] As Gloucester's analogy will confirm moments before his eyes are plucked out, there is real, phe-nomenal sympathy between the storm's magnitude and Lear's wrath:

> The sea, with such a storm as his bowed head
> In hell-black night endured, would have buoyed up

And quenched the stellèd fires. Yet, poor old heart,
He helped the heavens to rage. (14.56–59)

These lines — which Miola reads as directly echoing Seneca — indicate that
Lear's anger is not only mimetically mirrored in the "rage," "the eyeless rage"
of the elements, as the First Gentleman intimates, but that his *ira* animates and
heightens it as well.[7]

Yet this hyperbolic wrath is helpless to cure the wrongs Lear's "poor old
heart" so keenly feels. Unlike the Senecan tyrant, Lear immediately becomes
the victim of his own wrath rather than exacting revenge on others. Just as
grievously, his words on the heath, like the words of his eldest daughters in
Scene 1, neglect obvious human realities. Ignoring at first the Fool, who wants
him seek shelter, Lear addresses instead the storm directly.[8] Part anatomy,
prosopopeia, prayer, incantation, and curse, his eloquent rant (*Schreirede*)
would alter the course of cosmic and human justice:

> Blow, wind, and crack your cheeks! Rage, blow,
> You cataracts and hurricanoes, spout
> Till you have drenched the steeples, drowned the cocks!
> You sulphurous and thought-executing fires,
> Vaunt-couriers to oak-cleaving thunderbolts,
> Singe my white head; and thou all-shaking thunder,
> Smite flat the thick rotundity of the world,
> Crack nature's mould, all germens spill at once
> That make ungrateful man.[9] (9.1–9)

Air, water, fire, and earth — "all" are ingeniously prompted to exceed their
natural limits (or in the Earth's case to suffer its limits to be exceeded). The an-
thropomorphized wind gods (who marked the limits of knowledge on the
edges of Renaissance maps), exotic "hurricanoes" drowning churches, and
Jupiter himself are urged to take up Lear's cause and ruin human generation.
Given, moreover, the furious rhythm of this imprecation and the thundering
ethos fueling it, I suspect that the anachronisms of church "steeples" and
"[weather]cocks" amidst the raging rhetorical tempest of Lear's "affliction"
(9.49) would have made the experience of the storm more vivid, not more preposterous, for a Jacobean playgoer. As Longinus asserts, exaggeration will be
forgiven when emotions run high. The remarkable imperative "force" (9.49)

of his speech ("Blow ... Rage, blow ... Singe ... Smite ... Crack ... spill") is heightened by the antithetical puniness of the target, "ungrateful man," a target filling not even a pentameter. Instead, Shakespeare semantically overwhelms "man" with the phrase "all germens spill at once," a phrase encompassing both matter and time.[10] His initial invocation of Jupiter "allshaking thunder" recalls his imprecations against his elder daughters, while, intertextually, it echoes Lucan's NeoStoic *Pharsalia* where the providential bolt of *fatum* destroys the oaklike Caesar.[11] But as readers of the entire play, we learn to be skeptical of any hint of providence that might accompany such wonders. For the "great gods, that keep this dreadful pother o'er our heads" (9.49–50) will of course ignore Lear's solipsistic verdict on his fate ("I am a man more sinned against than sinning") (9.60), as well as his call for divine, providential justice ("caitiff, in pieces shake ...") (9.55). Musing on the diverse roles that Shakespeare may have assigned the thunder (and synecdochally, the storm), Elton thus imitates his mentor William Empson when he observes: "Probably, as in the tenet *ex nihilo* and in other analogous instances, Shakespeare seized on an ambiguous idea which could be exploited in both directions for the complex ends of his multiply significant tragedy."[12] That these "ends" may be philosophical or conceptual as well as theatrical further underscores the rich ambiguity of Shakespearean hyperbole.

As for the Fool, he hears and responds to Lear's hyperboles with common sense ("Good nuncle, in ...") and the mocking advice that it would be better to "court holy water" (i.e., flattery) indoors than to seek nature's sympathy (9.10–13). His aqueous pun also suggests an analogy between the microcosmic, Christian "holy water" and the macrocosmic, pagan "cataracts and hurricanoes." In brief, the Fool would deflate Lear's hyperboles with the familiar and the human. His song early in the scene aims to turn Lear's attention back to domestic, corporeal concerns. In this respect, his role is somewhat reversed from that in scenes 4 and 5 where he mockingly reminds Lear of his political folly. But in general, the Fool in this dialogic role "continually functions as an antiSenecan figure, as one whose very presence mocks the Senecan obsession with wrath, personal identity and selfcreation."[13] This is not to say that Shakespeare has abandoned his own dialogue with the Stoic precepts as championed by Lipsius and others. Instead, Lear, albeit for a very brief moment, becomes the storm's eye and so uncannily imitates his youngest daughter's Stoicism: "No, I will be the pattern of all patience ... I will say nothing" (9.37–38). What he does not seem to realize, however, is that the "pattern" he now confronts is cosmic, his interlocutors are no longer human, and his cares no longer kingly. Lacking such realizations, he verges toward dramaturgical bathos rather than Stoic *apatheia*: "Here I stand your slave, / A poor, infirm, weak and despised old man . . ." (9.19–20).[14] While the Fool's banter and song are initially directed more toward the audience than toward Lear, they effectively undercut Lear's solipsistic rhetoric with the attendant ironies of his master's fall. Indeed, by the end of Scene 9, when Lear's "wit begins to turn" and he finally attends to Kent's and the Fool's pleas to go inside, the Fool becomes an object of sympathy, rather than a source of satire. The effect, though, is the same as if Lear had heard and understood the Fool's *deflatus* — Lear begins to admit contingency, qualification, and responsibility into his world.

Pulling Lear back from the brink of madness, Shakespeare has him momentarily eschew his agonistic struggle to attend to others, to the Fool and presently to Edgar. That Lear comes to prefer human voices rather than the storm's bombast suggests both the complexity of his internal dialogue and his potential for anagnorisis. Yet as Cavell observes, Lear still hopes here to avoid the Fool's keener truths concerning guilt and responsibility.[15] Such avoidance helps explain his shift in attention from the Fool to Mad Tom, who seems to symbolize and give voice to more general truths concerning the human condition. But if Lear is not yet ready to answer his own questions or respond directly to the Fool's wit, as was also the case earlier when he asks, "Who is it that can tell me who I am? / Lear's shadow?" (4.222–223), he proves eager to pursue other aspects of *sapientia*. Even as the Fool's ironic, self-deprecating wit cuts too near the truth in one still searching for scapegoats, Lear still needs to see himself rhetorically reflected and refracted within the larger perspective of human justice and natural history.[16]

SHAKING "THE SUPERFLUX"

Meanwhile, the perspective afforded by the play's dramatic action and characters broadens and becomes still more Baroque with Edgar's feigned madness. At the outset of Scene 11, a more judicious, self-conscious Lear explains to Kent the calculus of his suffering: he weighs "filial ingratitude" (11.14) against the "contentious storm" (11.6), as he discovers that ". . . where the greater malady is fixed, / The lesser is scarce felt" (11.8–9). Subsequent events, though, will prove such aphoristic ethics radically insufficient, if not simply false. The same holds for Edgar's similarly Stoic maxims at 14.95–100 and 15.1–6, as well as for Albany's bromides in the final scene. Characters who try to step outside the flow and contingency of dramatic action to estab, lish an absolute scale of good and evil dramatically fail to gain pragmatic knowledge.

Belatedly, if only momentarily, realizing his moralistic follies, Lear's thoughts turn to a form of justice far removed from his desire to revenge his daughters' treachery:

> O, I have ta'en
> Too little care of this. Take physic, pomp,
> Expose thyself to feel what wretches feel,
> That thou mayst shake the superflux to them
> And show the heavens more just. (11.29–33)

In wanting to cure courtly "pomp," Lear does not abandon the hyperbolic mode; his desires are still Promethean. But in wanting "to feel what wretches feel" he discovers, or at least learns to imagine, a less solipsistic way of re, sponding to the "pitiless night" (11.26; "pitiless storm" in the Folio). In brief, Lear has begun the fitful process of turning away from his microcosmic con, cerns to attend to macrocosmic ones. This complicated conversion includes what Elton calls Lear's increasingly "materialist" discussions with his natural "philosopher," Edgar, which ultimately result in the trial scene, where the "[o]ppressèd" (13.90) Lear rejects all Stoic *apatheia* to slake his thirst for aveng, ing justice: "To have a thousand / With red burning spits come hissing in upon them" (13.11–12). This pathetic scene yields Edgar's moralizing solilo, quy and soon,to,be,proven false hopes (13.95–108). More prescient is Lear's insight: ". . . let them anatomize Regan; see what breeds about her heart. Is there any cause in nature that makes this hardness?" (13.70–72).[17] That Lear himself answers this query in the tragedy's last scene, with his final, agonistic reproach of the Stoic ideal: "O, you are men of stones" (24.253), confirms just how inadequate a skeptical Shakespeare finds the anatomy theater, the courtroom, and, above all, Stoic philosophy to dissect human motives. In this way, as Richard Strier notes, *Lear* participates "in the humanist and Reforma, tion critiques of being 'unmoved.'"[18] Though also, *pace* Lessing, there might well have been a dramaturgical objection to having a Stoic hero prevail.

Hyperbole becomes increasingly dialogic and qualitative as the play pro, gresses. The stark antithesis between the "[t]oo little care" Lear had given to suffering other than his own and "the superflux" that he would now "shake" to the poor ("wretches") indicates that Lear hears the excess, literally the bombast, of his previous rhetoric. The notion of "superflux" is also central to the role that Edgar, disguised as Poor Tom, plays in Lear's self-conception. While Edgar's mad *copia* offers a more diffuse, even more fantastic version of rhetorical excess than Lear's, his miserable appearance argues in Lear's mind for the universal truth of his own fate: "Couldst thou save nothing? Didst thou give them all? . . . Nothing could have subdued nature / To such lowness but his unkind daughters" (11.56; 11.63–64). Lear's monomania aside, his drastic reasoning quickly becomes circular; for if Edgar is imitating his peculiar woe, then Lear, inspired also by his experience in the storm, imitates Edgar's misery. Prompted by Edgar's lowly example, he rhetorically and sartorially shakes the "superflux" from him:

> Why, thou wert better in thy grave than to answer with thy uncovered body this extremity of the skies. Is man no more but this? Consider him well. Thou owest the worm no silk, the beast no hide, the sheep no wool, the cat no perfume. Here's three on's are sophisticated; thou art the thing itself. Unaccommodated man is no more but such a poor, bare, forked animal as thou art. Off, off, you lendings! Come on, be true.
> (11.91–98)

Edgar's pretendings must be outdone by the still overreaching Lear. Just as Hamlet is spurred by Laertes's display of grief at Ophelia's grave to greater histrionics, Lear to be "true" to himself and his sense of injustice would strip away with exorbitant deeds and words all the bombast that separates men from beasts.[19] This profoundly skeptical, anti-humanist gesture demands to be read with and against the myriad metaphoric transformations throughout the tragedy of men and women into beasts — from Gonoril as a "detested kite" to Lear and Cordelia as "birds i'th' cage." It also echoes Montaigne's skepticism in the "Apologie pour Raymond Sebond" where moral and conceptual boundaries between the human and bestial are blurred throughout. Finally, the phrase "this extremity of the skies," with its physical and scenographic connotations, anticipates Edgar's later realization of rhetorical, emotional, and conceptual limits: "To amplify, too much would make much more, / And top extremity" (24.203–204).[20]

Indeed, the subplot offers another version of "extremity." When blind

Gloucester gives the disguised Edgar the contents of his purse as payment for being lead to Dover, his rationale invites scrutiny:

> That I am wretched
> Makes thee the happier. Heavens deal so still.
> Let the superfluous and lust-dieted man
> That stands your ordinance, that will not see
> Because he does not feel, feel your power quickly.
> So distribution should undo excess,
> And each man have enough. (15.63–69).

This concern with "excess" supplements Lear's rhetoric against superfluity. Still, there is little reason to conclude that the play espouses a Pauline or proto-Marxist vision of economic justice. Its effect is far more subjective than ideological. In one of the play's cruelest ironies, the blinded Gloucester, who would here have the "superfluous" rich "feel" the "power" that the poor already "feel," can only "see" the world "feelingly" (20.144). The dramatic irony of having the guilt-ridden father unknowingly give his "humbled" (15.63) son his remaining wealth is further heightened by the fact that such charity ("distribution") is an act of despair in the face of implacable fate ("Heavens deal so still"), an act that serves as a prelude to Gloucester's intended suicide.

Shakespeare's double-plot increasingly becomes a form of architectonic excess, as the extraordinary degrees of perfidy, perversity, and suffering contained in the subplot push the audience to the harrowing conclusion that rather than being caused solely by Lear's solipsism or his daughters' evil, tragedy is in fact universal, cosmic, or, as Albany puts it in the final scene, an expression of "general woe" (24.314). The two plots supplement each other and thereby create an irreducible reflexivity in which Lear and Cordelia's suffering mirrors and augments Gloucester and Edgar's. At the same time, such supplementarity only emphasizes the lack of any stable, unitary metaphysical ground for such universal "woe." It was Shakespeare's peculiar innovation to add the Gloucester plot to the King's travails as first described in the anonymous play he used as his main source, *The True Chronicle History of King Leir and his three daughters, Gonorill, Ragan, and Cordella*. But the Baroque mirroring effect, the *mise-en-abîme*, produced by this innovation, like the play within a play in *Hamlet*, or, say, the various narrative and authorial frames that Cervantes constructs in *Don Quijote*, increases the sense that the tragedy is at once contrived and yet somehow as inevitable as a natural catastrophe. Such structural hyperbolism marks the kind of extreme artistic ambition and self-consciousness that Benjamin, Rousset, Buci-Glucksmann, and others have made defining traits of Baroque literature and thought. Or, as G. Wilson Knight observes: "The Gloucester-theme throughout reflects and emphasizes and exaggerates all the percurrent qualities of the Lear-theme. Here the incongruous and fantastic element of the Lear-theme is boldly reflected into the tragically absurd. The stroke is audacious, unashamed, and magical of effect."[21]

As for specific effects (or affects), after Edgar usurps the role previously played by the Fool, in a metapoetic aside ("My tears begin to take his part so much / They'll mar my counterfeiting") (13.55–56) and in a choral soliloquy he teaches the audience what to feel about Lear's "sufferance." Stepping out of his Tom O'Bedlam character, Edgar muses:

> When we our betters see bearing our woes,
> We scarcely think our miseries our foes,
> Who alone suffers, suffers most i'th' mind,
> Leaving free things and happy shows behind.
> But then the mind much sufferance doth o'erskip
> When grief hath mates, and bearing fellowship.
> How light and portable my pain seems now,
> When that which makes me bend, makes the King bow.
> He childed as I fathered. (13.95–102)

Drawing upon his own recent experience as well as the commonplaces of neo-Stoic moral philosophy, Edgar's insights into human nature and the differing degrees of "sufferance," "grief," and "pain" are the closest the play comes to articulating a response to the various brands of skepticism, if not nihilism, that can be heard in the lines of Edmund, Lear's elder daughters, and, at times, the Fool. But close is not enough. Edgar's emergent hope and relative tranquility find an implacable antagonist in the play's own bleak, dramatic logic. The structural web of characters and deeds Shakespeare spins acquires a tragic, fatal complexity that makes any attempt at ethical mediation seem facile and, ultimately, false. Edgar's Neo-Stoic platitudes concerning the benefit we derive from seeing "our betters . . . bearing our woes" echo Aristotelian ideas explaining why an audience may take pleasure in watching tragedy as well as Christian theology explicating Christ's sacrifice for humanity. But with his father about to be blinded, and Lear and Cordelia still to be mur/ dered, their promise is deaf to the extreme, savage contingencies often lurking in human events: "What will hap more tonight, safe scape the King! / Lurk, lurk" (13.107–108).

Violating all classical decorum, the blinding of Gloucester, this obscene deed mise/en/scène, is the tragic equivalent of the comic, grotesque excess cul/ tivated by Rabelais. As in Bakhtin's reading of the Rabelesian grotesque, it marks a "downward trajectory" away from transcendence and towards the in/ fernal and bodily. Coleridge, always eager to cultivate the imagined over the real, recoiled from the scene: "I will not disguise my conviction, that in this one point the tragic in the play has been urged beyond the outermost mark and *ne plus ultra* of the dramatic."[22] An act belying Gloucester's improbable invo/ cation of the "[k]ind gods" (14.32) soon afterwards, his blinding gains sym/ bolic, ironic force in Scene 15 as he, having met his disguised son, ruminates on the perversion of divine justice: "As flies to wanton boys are we to th' gods; / They kill us for their sport" (15.35–36). This witty analogy, which is set up by the radical meiosis of reducing humans to "flies" and "gods" to "wanton boys," has often been read as expressing the play's bleakest outlook, even though it still promises some measure of correspondence, however cruel, be/ tween the human and divine. But rather than confirming the designs of a malign deity or a *deus absconditus*, the remainder of the play reveals the impos/ sibility of even this far/fetched correspondence. The still direr prospect of divine indifference — or what may be yet worse for a Baroque dramatist — the failure of analogy itself looms.

For his part, Edgar is dramaturgically shown the folly of his Stoic *dicta*. Even as he meditates

> To be worst,
> The low'st and most dejected thing of fortune,
> Stands still in esperance, lives not in fear.
> The lamentable change is from the best;
> The worst returns to laughter. (15.2–6)

his blinded father is led on stage before him. Such "strange mutations" (15.8) prompt Edgar to muse upon language's inability to express the depths of the human condition, which always seem able to go deeper:

> O gods! Who is't can say 'I am at the worst'?
> I am worse than e'er I was . . .
> And worse I may be yet. The worst is not
> As long as we can say, "This is the worst." (15.23–26)

The superlative (an echo of the Senecan *pessimus*) progressively loses its meaning in these four lines as it succumbs first to the horror produced by dramatic reversal, and then to the paradoxical realization that "the worst," death itself, is the true superlative condition but one that can yield only silence. A new frame of judgment is needed, a frame that will be provided by the idea of monstrosity.

MONSTROUS AND VERTIGINOUS SPEECH

Like Edward Topsell's *The historie of foure-footed beastes* (1607) or Ambroise Paré's *Des monstres et prodiges* (1573), Shakespeare's tragedy plumbs in its later scenes the extremities of what it means to be human and animal. It does this by triangulating these with a third term, the monstrous. As Rosenmeyer notes, *monster* has a distinctly Senecan and dramaturgical heritage: "The distinction between *monstrum* and *scelus* is moot, because *monstrum* is merely a cosmic augmentation of *scelus* . . ."[23] But as Daston, Park, Greenblatt, and Céard have shown, the rhetoric of monstrosity, for all its roots in classical, medieval, and early Renaissance natural philosophy, also marks specific epistemological tensions that accompany the arrival of the new sciences.[24] To cultivate monstrosity fosters *curiositas* and *admiratio*, which in turn can be exploited to persuade readers and viewers of the truth of new ideas and perspectives.[25] Copernicus, for example, in the Preface to *De revolutionibus* compares the Ptolemaic system to a woman whose bottom half is a fish. And though the idea of a *monster*, as its etymology suggests, usually relies on visual imagery for its rhetorical force, frequently in the Baroque, as in Racine's portrayal of the sea monster in *Phèdre*, it outstrips the resources of *enargeia* and related figures.

In *Lear* admiration at the monstrous belongs to the characters as well as the audience. As his lines slide along the scale of creation, the incredulous Albany asks his wife:

> What have you done?
> Tigers, not daughters, what have you performed?
> . . . .

> If that the heavens do not their visible spirits
> Send quickly down to tame these vile offences,
> It will come,
> Humanity must perforce prey on itself,
> Like monsters of the deep. (16.38–39; 45–49)

As the "daughters" are transformed by their crimes into "[t]igers," their potential punishers are seen as avenging "spirits" or, if they fail to come, "monsters of the deep." Compassing high and low, angels and leviathans, Albany's hyperbole briefly makes "visible" the diverging paths the play might follow: divine justice or the proto-Darwinian, cannibalistic prospect of endless revenge. But if his logic seems extreme, he soon eschews completely hope for divine justice. Albany, whom his wife calls a "moral fool," would name the extreme evil he confronts with these invidious comparisons: "See thyself, devil. / Proper deformity shows not in the fiend / So horrid as in a woman . . . Bemonster not thy feature . . . thou art a fiend, / A woman's shape doth shield thee" (16.58–66).[26] Such vituperation, however, raises an intriguing possibility. Even without taking into account the play's denouement where fiendish monstrosity proves the rule rather than the exception, given what he knows about his wife, Albany's rhetoric manages to name being over seeming, to identify essence out of the swirl of the play's events. Lear failed to see the evil in his daughters, nor did Gloucester detect it in his monstrous son (thus those productions that cast the usurpers as lacking physical beauty miss a crucial crux). But Albany discerningly invites us to allegorize the characters as latter-day players in a medieval morality play, and to treat the play's chiaroscuro themes in gnostic terms. To call Gonoril a "monster," in other words, may be the most decorous response to such a being, even if Shakespeare's tragedy only flirts with allegory in order to subvert it. Benjamin, as I shall discuss below, insists in his *Trauerspiel* study that the "drastic externality" furnished by allegory, bombast, and other forms of rhetorical excess is the most fitting formal response to the specters of tyranny and ruin.[27] But Shakespeare insists on "drastic" internality as well.

Gloucester's extreme despair is externalized topographically in Scene 20 at Dover Cliffs. More generally, the dramaturgical subtleties of this scene raise fundamental questions concerning mimesis, performativity, visual perspective, and the viability of certain theoretical or "speculative" reactions to Shakespearean drama.[28] Following Stephen Orgel's insight that "we know from the

very beginning of the scene that we are being lied to, and that we are accom-
plices in the lies,"[29] I see Edgar's exaggerated, deceitful "conceit" as playing
on early modern notions of perspective. But his perspectivism also cognitively
functions in a way that recalls Quintilian's account of the dynamics of making and understanding hyperbole. The descriptions, narration, and interpretations Edgar offers to his father are, if you will, lies told without mendacity
to express an extraordinary truth.

Circumspect, if not incredulous, Gloucester is led by Edgar to "th'extreme verge" (20.26), where the latter offers this masterpiece of *enargeia*:

> Come on, sir, here's the place. Stand still. How fearful
> And dizzy 'tis to cast one's eyes so low!
> The crows and choughs that wing the midway air
> Show scarce so gross as beetles. Halfway down
> Hangs one that gathers samphire, dreadful trade!
> Methinks he seems no bigger than his head.
> The fishermen that walks upon the beach
> Appear like mice, and yon tall anchoring barque
> Diminished to her cock, her cock a buoy
> Almost too small for sight. The murmuring surge
> That on the unnumbered idle pebbles chafes
> Cannot be heard, it's so high. I'll look no more,
> Let my brain turn and the deficient sight
> Topple down headlong. (20.11–24)

Edgar's various ingenious appeals to the senses in this vertiginous description
marvelously obscure the central fact (one often forgotten when reading) that
solely his imagination and memory, and not his "eyes" or ears, create belief in
his father and in the audience.[30] Since Gloucester has already decided on suicide, Edgar's rhetorical *propositio* consists solely in creating sufficient *enargeia*;
though with the catch that his addressee is blind and his audience knows that
they are in a theater, not hundreds of feet above a "beach." Undertaking
a tour de force manipulation of "the techniques of illusion — verbal and
pictorial — upon which Shakespearean theater depends," Edgar spurns the
kind of anamorphotic technique seen in *Richard II* (2.2.14–27) in favor of an
Albertian exercise in perspective, replete with a vanishing point at infinity
("Diminished to a cock . . . almost too small for sight"), by which Glouces-

ter is deceived and the audience agrees to be deceived.[31] If nature feels immense ("it's so high") and contains infinities ("the unnumbered idle pebbles"), careful, verisimilar attempts to measure it ("so low . . . midway . . . Halfway down . . . so gross . . . no bigger . . . too small") temper these gestures of in, expressibility. Likewise, self-consciously employing synecdoche ("Methinks he seems no bigger than his head") and simile ("fishermen . . . [a]ppear like mice") helps ensure the *ethos* of Edgar's vision of shrunken humanity. In other words, even as he captures the psychological effects of standing on such heights, Shakespeare offers a veritable natural history of the cliff. As with mad Tom's motley language, successfully playing here his father's eyes par, tially depends on an ability to furnish a cornucopia of words and things. The "fishermen" and the euphuistic "crows and choughs" add objectivity and dis, interestedness to Edgar's rhetoric. Still, the *pathos* of the situation is never eclipsed: the exclamation, "How fearful / And dizzy 'tis to cast one's eyes so low!", and the parenthetical "dreadful trade!" instruct us how to experience the scene. Indeed, by the end of his description, Edgar — as Cicero pre, scribes for an orator who would stir feelings in others — has begun himself to feel the vertigo, the *affectus*, that he would convey to his father and Shake, speare's audience.

As the Dover Cliffs episode further unfolds, the manner in which Edgar would "trifle"[32] with and so "cure" his father's "despair" (20.33–34) — and thereby prevent a Stoic suicide and, temporarily, at least a triumph of skepti, cism — veers between hilarious farce and solemn mystery play.[33] Here again Cavell's relatively scant engagement with the dynamics of plot or action — imagined though it is in this scene — needs to be amended given how Gloucester so precipitously moves (and is moved) from skeptical despon, dency to credulous admiration by the "miracle" about to happen. Events con, stitute Shakespearean tragedy as well as characters. Before Gloucester undergoes his spiritual transformation, the supernatural is extravagantly in, scribed into the event that Gloucester thinks he has directed. First, Edgar re, counts his father's fall:

> Hadst thou been aught but goss'mer, feathers, air,
> So many fathom down precipitating
> Thou hadst shivered like an egg. But thou dost breathe,
> Hast heavy substance, bleed'st not, speak'st, art sound.
> Ten masts a-length make not the altitude

Which thou hast perpendicularly fell.
Thy life's a miracle. (20.49–55)

Producer and now narrator of this decidedly Christian "miracle," Edgar hyperbolizes the material and spatial aspects of Gloucester's plunge. Transformed not into an "egg" that might shatter but rather into "goss'mer,
feathers, air," Gloucester falls "[s]o many fathom," a distance reimagined just
three lines later with the litote "Ten masts a-length make not . . ." The heuristic if hazy quality of these and earlier measures aids Edgar to blur and therefore cross the temporal and spiritual divides between the before and after of the
(non)event. Likewise, his parataxis creates psychological verisimilitude, as if
words were hurrying to catch up with astonishment. Having exhausted spatial quantities and confounded the contraries of high and low, levity and gravity, spirit and body, and, most urgently, life and death, Edgar saves the most
extreme, paradoxical hyperbole for last. He transforms with four words his father's earthly misery into a spiritual boon: "Thy life's a miracle."

As for the still-seeing audience, the tension between literal and figurative
is of a slightly different order. In his note to the stage direction, "*Gloucester falls
forward*," Stanley Wells stresses "the discrepancy between Gloucester's and the
audience's point of view."[34] Though accustomed to the suspension of disbelief, the audience still inevitably shares something of Gloucester's incredulity.
At best — depending on the production — we see him fall but a few feet.
Thus when he asks, "But have I fallen, or no?" (20.56), common sense sec-
onds his doubt, even if our sense of wonder and thirst for spectacle eagerly anticipate Edgar's response:

From the dread summit of this chalky bourn.
Look up a-height. The shrill-gorged lark so far
Cannot be seen or heard. Do but look up. (20.57–59)

The insistent deixis ("this chalky bourn"), and the layered ironies of twice
asking a blind man to "look up" at something that flies so high even the
sighted cannot see it, is truly, as Gloucester presently comments, "above all
strangeness" (20.66).

We are asked, though, to believe in more than physical paradoxes. Edgar
must account for his own transformation. He does this by folding himself into a
Manichean battle between a surreal, hyperbolic demon and providential "gods":

As I stood here below, methoughts his eyes
Were two full moons. A had a thousand noses,
Horns whelked and wavèd like the enridgèd sea.
It was some fiend. Therefore, thou happy father,
Think that the clearest gods, who made their honours
Of men's impossibilities, have preserved thee. (20.69–74)

The qualitative ("his eyes / Were two full moons") and quantitative ("a thou-sand noses") hyperboles find their ultimate justification in theology. Menaced by "some fiend," Gloucester escapes infernal powers by virtue of the "clearest gods." Yet these are no pagan deities; as Wells and others have noted, "impos-sibilities" has a decidedly New Testament ring: "With men this is impossible, but with God all things are possible" (Matthew 19:26); "The things which are unpossible with men are possible with God" (Luke 18:27).[35] Likewise, in a marginal gloss to *Two Bookes of Constancie*, Stradling writes as a Christian apologist: "Manie of the Stoicks paradoxes are no impossibilities."[36] Edgar's lines thus persuade Gloucester to reject the "fiend" urging suicide and, in-stead, in the best Christian Stoic mode, to prompt him to declare: "Hence-forth I'll bear / Affliction till it do cry out itself / 'Enough, enough,' and die" (20.75–77). Responding explicitly to the Senecan "Sed cur satis est?," Shake-speare offers here his most powerful answer — albeit one that remains all-too-vulnerable to dramatic contingencies.

Demetrius and John Hoskins insist that hyperbole is essential in the task of representing the impossible (*to adunaton*);[37] but Shakespeare teaches his au-dience a more audacious lesson: the theater is capable of producing rhetorical circumstances where no epistemological or phenomenological claim is too ex-travagant for belief. Defying the dichotomy between the literal and figurative, Scene 20, arguably more than any other in Shakespearean drama, tests the limits of dramatic representation.[38] Exemplary of this is how Edgar casts himself in the dual role of the tempting "fiend" and the vicar of the "clearest gods" (20.72–73). Both roles rely solely on verbal wit and invention. They de-mand enormous subtlety from Edgar's hyperboles, which must provoke at once sufficient *admiratio* and be verisimilar enough to satisfy Gloucester's skep-tical ears. Precipitated by another kind of extremity, Gloucester's onstage blinding, the theatrical trajectory of events momentarily halts before the inef-fable. And while Senecan drama implicitly rejects the impossible as being outside the causality of *sumpatheia*,[39] this is no longer the case with the more syncretic Shakespeare. His dramaturgical imagination is alchemical: he takes the residue of Senecan dramatic conventions and sublimates it to produce a blind "miracle" of Christian revelation.

Yet Shakespeare characteristically permits Gloucester only the briefest anagnorisis. In the same scene, immediately after the epiphany at Dover Cliffs, Lear at his maddest, "*crowned with weeds and flowers*," interrupts Gloucester's "free and patient thoughts" (20.80). This startling conjunction appears to verge on the allegorical. If Lear personifies anger and Gloucester lust, then, as Elton neatly puts it: "According to the traditional irascible-concupiscible distinction, Lear's intellectual error of anger receives the conventional punishment of madness (*ira furor brevis*), and Gloucester's physical sin of lechery the conventional retribution of blindness."[40] Alternately, as Edgar's aside suggests at 20.163–164, in Shakespearean *furor* the full range of "Reason" and unreason is discovered: "O, matter and impertinency mixed — / Reason in madness." This is to say that to account for the scope of Lear's rhetoric in this scene would require a small monograph. At times he sounds like the Fool, other times like Poor Tom; but more relevant for us, his rhetoric mockingly reshapes the grand homiletic style ("I will preach to thee . . . When we are born, we cry that we are come / To this great stage of fools") (20.164; 171–172), by infusing it with confessional, physical directness that, in the face of his immense pathos, strips away any pretense of decorum and undermines any eschatology.[41] Not only is "the worst" yet to come, but the various moments of recognition here bring little psychic relief to the tormented figures on the stage. Whatever wisdom is wrenched from pathos is belied by a seeming awareness, especially on Lear's part, of humanity's fundamental folly and powerlessness. This enormous gap between maxim and action thus veers away from allegory and toward irony — at least for the reader-audience. One moment we hear Lear's carefully balanced: "If thou wilt weep my fortune, take my eyes . . . Thou must be patient. We came crying hither . . ." (20.165, 167), and almost in his next breath: "kill, kill, kill, kill, kill" (20.175).

True, Lear shows here — finally! — a keen self-consciousness of how he has been buffeted and deceived by rhetorical bluster and bombast:

> Ha, Gonoril! Ha, Regan! They flattered me like a dog, and told me I
> had white hairs in my beard ere the black ones were there. To say "ay"

and "no" to everything I said "ay" and "no" to was no good divinity. When the rain came to wet me once, and the wind to make me chatter, when the thunder would not peace at my bidding, there I found them, there I smelt them out. Go to, they are not men of their words. They told me I was everything; 'tis a lie, I am not ague-proof. (20.95–103)

These lines capture the acme of Lear's self-knowledge. Parsing the gnostic logic of *omnis et nihil*, he charts here his rhetorical career: from having courted flattery's bestial, even sacrilegious debasement, through his fruitless, if extravagant, invocations of nature on the heath, to the humble realization that he is less than "everything," that he is, in short, mortal. And yet Gloucester, as if to discount the neatness of any such narrative, insists on recasting Lear's fate as a part in some immanent catastrophe:

> O ruined piece of nature! This great world
> Should so wear out to naught. (20.129–130)

With this, Gloucester's recently won equanimity lies annihilated between the cosmic extremities ("[t]his great world" and "naught") that he perceives ruining Lear. No wonder he later welcomes Oswald's threat of murder (20.222–223) and later still (20.271–276) seems to court madness himself, as Lear, somewhere off-stage, absurdly plays tag with those who would rescue him from his "pitiful" (20.193) state.

GROUND ZERO

The critical history of *King Lear* runs the gamut of responses to the spectacular tragic excess produced by the play's last four scenes. From Samuel Johnson's reluctance to "read again the last scenes of the play" and so endure Cordelia's death, to Swinburne's acceptance of the play's "fatalism" ("Requital, redemption, amends, equity, explanation, pity and mercy, are words without meaning here . . ."), to Wilson Knight's warning against "sentimentalizing the cosmic mockery of the play," to Cavell's "immodest and melodramatic" claims, and beyond, the ending of *Lear* has become an intellectual and cultural barometer of the shifting status yet constant allure of tragic hyperbole. From revisionist neoclassicism to Lacanian analysis, every conceivable hermeneutic approach has tried to explicate the "general woe" closing the

play. In brief, the suffering of Lear, Cordelia, and Gloucester, to say nothing
of the nasty fates Shakespeare prescribes for the play's unsavory characters,
have produced at once a surplus and dearth of interpretive meaning. As we
saw with Góngora's lyric excesses, Shakespeare's theatrical extremity has long
generated a peculiar species of critical excess, one that would remedy the perceived lack of decorum and meaning. In the light of this critical history, my
reading of the ending of *Lear* would supplement Shakespeare's hyperbole by
tracing the final arc of certain lexical, rhetorical, and structural elements that
runs throughout the play, culminates in the final scenes, but balks at providing the reader with any measure of closure. For like a hyperbola, while this arc
may be doubled, it remains asymptotic.

To begin with, Edgar's gnomic maxim, "Ripeness is all" (23.11), sounds
less authoritative when read within its dramatic context and against other examples of the play's rhetorical absolutism — be it the two sisters' speeches in
the first act ("Beyond all manner of so much I love you"), Lear's imprecation
("By all the operations of the orbs"), or Kent's claim made to Cordelia before
the battle that: "All my reports go with modest truth. / Nor more, nor clipped,
but so" (21.5–6). For all such assertions attempting to define the mean and
the extreme have thus far proven ineffectual or deceptive. More to the point,
they have yet to be measured against the words and deeds in the play's final careening scenes. Yes, Edgar would cheer his despondent father with his assertions of Stoic self-sufficiency and endurance, but these relatively optimistic
notes sound just before the bloody *dégringolade* of the last scene, whose moral
is expressed best by the broken Kent: "All's cheerless, dark, and deadly"
(24.285).

To extend the music metaphor, the bleak coda gains more power by
Shakespeare's contrapuntal play of light and dark tones preceding it. For instance, Cordelia's muted outrage at the way her father has been treated ("Was
this a face / To be exposed against the warring winds . . .") (21.29–30) is converted into measured, wary tenderness when Lear awakes.[42] But then Lear's
response to her kindness vividly paints the spiritual gulf separating him from
his daughter:

> You do me wrong to take me out o'th' grave.
> Thou art a soul in bliss, but I am bound
> Upon a wheel of fire, that mine own tears
> Do scald like molten lead. (21.43–46)

Yet even as the classical allusion to Ixion's fate and the hyperbolic simile of "tears" as "molten lead" vividly epitomize Lear's suffering, Shakespeare refuses to let Lear's pathos stray into bathos. Instead, he explores the depth of Lear's confusion in another take on the Senecan *nescio quid*: "Where have I been? Where am I? . . . I know not what to say . . . Methinks I should know you, and know this man; Yet I am doubtful . . ." But then, further altering the Senecan tradition, he also grants Lear an unprecedented degree of ironic, self-knowledge: "I am a very foolish, fond old man" (21.58) — ironic because the Fool had told him this from the outset and because events have yet to prove the real depth of his folly. From a metapoetic perspective, such self-nomination (repeated at 21.83) also risks inviting a premature sense of closure. The battle between France's forces and Albany and Cornwall's is still imminent; nor have Edmund, the two elder daughters, or for that matter, Edgar, finished plotting. While Lear would escape with Cordelia into some imagined, marginal refuge where they would be like "birds i'th' cage" (24.9), or, more precariously still, hunted "foxes" (24.23), Shakespeare concurrently casts Edmund and his captain as determined to explore the more monstrous aspects of being human ("If it be man's work, I'll do it . . .") (24.38). In this sense, the latter pair more closely embody the skeptical pessimism promoted by the play's subsequent action, while Lear, though "cured" of his "great rage," and despite his and Cordelia's tears, still ignorantly places his hopes in providence and divine justice ("Upon such sacrifices, my Cordelia, / The gods themselves throw incense") (24.20–21). As Cavell puts it, "in the end he still avoids Cordelia," that is, he still puts his "need, or his interpretation of his need" over any understanding of what Cordelia's need, or, more importantly, her love might be.[43]

The undeniable pathos of Lear's reaction to Cordelia's death partly results from his failure to know the object of his desire, or for that matter who his friends are.[44] Kent's genuflecting commiseration is initially dismissed: "A plague upon you, murderous traitors all" (24.265); and though this is understandable given Lear's grief, it signals his refusal to relinquish hyperbole as his chief mode of seeing, feeling, and being in the world. At the verge of death, Lear is still learning to qualify.[45]

But, of course, Kent is right: the play's world is literally "murderous." With the defeat of the forces championing Lear and Cordelia's cause comes Edgar's challenge to Edmund, and here hyperbole, given its target and occasion, becomes nearly verisimilar. "[T]hou art a traitor," he tells his brother,

> And from th' extremest upward of thy head
> To the descent and dust beneath thy feet
> A most toad-spotted traitor. (24.133–135)

Edgar, moreover, is willing to back his words with deeds ("this sword") —
a desire for correspondence sorely lacking in his adversary. Meanwhile, Edmund can only gesture at the quantity of his crimes: "that I have done, / And
more, much more." Perhaps this is because his treason surpasses any individual's agency, however bestial s/he may be. What Lear calls "this great stage of
fools" is too overrun with evil and treachery for any one character to explain
and thereby begin to master it — neither the aphoristic Edgar and Albany,
nor the empathetic Gloucester, who cannot bear to hear the tale of Edgar's
"pilgrimage":

> . . . but his flawed heart —
> Alack, too weak the conflict to support —
> 'Twixt two extremes of passion, joy and grief,
> Burst smilingly. (24.193–196)

Only in death are "extremes" resolvable, for Gloucester finds no way to bridge
the antithesis of "joy and grief." Nor does Shakespeare find a way to stage
these irreconcilable "extremes," even though earlier he staged Gloucester's
blinding. In contrast to Sophocles and Seneca, who refuse to stage the most
gruesome physical deeds, the ineffable "worst" for Shakespeare consists more
in interior or subjective events than in exterior ones. To obviate any doubt as
to how we should hear these lines, Shakespeare offers the dying Edmund's reaction ("This speech of yours hath moved me") (24.196) and the decidedly
un-Stoic sentiments of the "ready to dissolve" (24.200) Albany. Edmund and
Albany thus unwittingly give voice to the tragic law of excess fueling the
play's rhetoric and action. "But speak you on — / You look as you had something more to say," Edmund urges. To which Albany ineffectually counters:
"If there be more, more woeful, hold it in" (24.197–199).

This concurrent desire for and fear of verbal excess or extremity creates
fearful symmetry with the play's opening scene where the three daughters
wrestle with another ineffable *res* and where quantity ("Beyond all manner of
so much I love you . . .") wins out over silence. But now the question unambiguously concerns language's insufficiency rather than its insincerity. The

characters confront a profusion of awe-inspiring dramatic ironies rather than the insidious consequences of verbal irony. Thus, amazingly, Edgar has "more to say" (24.198). He immediately outbids — the Baroque web of Shakespeare's double plot makes this possible — the story of his father's death, with the story of Kent, who tells his own story:

> This would have seemed a period
> To such as love not sorrow; but another
> To amplify, too much would make much more,
> And top extremity. (24.201–204)[46]

Seeing the father and son, Kent "bellowed out / As he'd burst heaven" (24.209–210). But then, adding woe to woe, he tells to Edgar "the most piteous tale of Lear and him / That ever ear received" (24.210–211). Hyperconscious how his own words "amplify" and "top extremity," Edgar becomes Shakespeare's metapoetic mouthpiece. Following the "too weak" he uses to describe Gloucester's condition, now the "too much" describing Kent's suffering confirms that Edgar-Shakespeare has found no satisfactory way to calculate the worth of deeds with words. It is not then "too much" to say that Shakespeare strains the Senecan legacy to its breaking point, to where verbal and structural ironies riddle all hyperbole. Edgar is his mouthpiece but also his dupe, for "the most piteous tale" is about to be made more piteous still by what transpires on the stage before him and us.

   Non satis est. Albany has yet to mutter emptily, hearing Cordelia's death sentence: "The gods defend her!" (24.252) — an irony heightened by the fact that Albany now inhabits the rank in the political-theological hierarchy that would place him closest to the "gods." Nor has Lear yet to enter, "*with Queen Cordelia in his arms,*" to mark the expressive limits of language:

> Howl, howl, howl, howl! O, you are men of stones.
> Had I your tongue and eyes, I would use them so
> That heaven's vault should crack. (24.253–255)

The play's final and most powerful expression of the inexpressibility *topos*, it also looks beyond the play's tragic rhetoric to the Petrarchism of the Sonnets: "For we, which now behold these present days, / Have eyes to wonder, but lack tongues to praise" (#106).[47] And for his part, Kent has yet to gesture numbly at "the promised end" — here much more the Stoic apocalypse than a New Testament Day of Judgment, since no saving angels are at hand. Nor has Albany offered yet his most monumental, Polonian platitude, the one mocking all other absolute judgments made in the play:

> All friends shall taste
> The wages of their virtue, and all foes
> The cup of their deservings. — O see, see! (24.297–299)

With its shocking inaccuracy, Albany's moralizing underscores language's paucity in the face of radical dramatic ironies and exigencies. His blunt imperative (or is it an entreaty?) to "see" functions disjunctively. It marks a break from aphoristic detachment, even as it unintentionally recharges the wordplay on sight and insight, blindness and ignorance, dominating the play.

What, though, do we "see" as the tragedy's last 22 lines (24.300–321) are spoken and acted? Most crucially, we see the King die a pathetic death holding Cordelia's corpse in his arms. We see the uncertainty (which varies depending on whether we are watching-reading the First Quarto or First Folio) in Lear's mind whether or not she still clings to life. But aside from these Senecan passions and gestures ("vex not his ghost"), other species of extremity should be pondered here, especially aural, conceptual, and even typographic excess. The last two passages quoted contain several internal rhymes on the phoneme *o*. That these rhymes proliferate wildly in the last 22 lines suggests several things. First, such rhyming creates a kind of music or echolia that takes up where language fails — Lear's agonistic "No, no . . . no . . . O . . . o, o, o, o!" (24.300–304) is echoed and amplified by Kent's "O, let him pass," Edgar's "O, he is gone indeed," Kent's ominous final couplet suggesting a Stoic suicide, "I have a journey, sir, shortly to go: / My master calls, and I must not say no," and Albany's, "We that are young / Shall never see so much, nor live so long." Further, like Lear's last absolute epizeuxis, "Never, never, never," these repetitions create an aural solidity where emotionally and conceptually there is only an abyss.[48] Likewise, Albany's "so much" and "so long" in the play's final line repeats with an ironic difference Kent's observation: "The wonder is he hath endured so long." And while there is a choral quality to the conflation of these individual voices, the effect is less a harmony of thought than the discordant convergence of overwhelming sorrows.

Secondly, such rhyming pushes the attempt to use the rhetoric of quantity to express ineffable qualities to its breaking point.[49] The "somuch" that Albany and the others witness has its ironic origins in Gonoril's first speech ("Beyond all manner of so much I love you . . ."). But it also originates in Lear's initial, flawed attempt to exchange flattery for territory:

> *Lear*: So young and so untender?
> *Cordelia*: So young, my lord, and true.
> *Lear*: Well, let it be so. (1.98–100)

But then, in the middle of the play, another ploce anticipates the "o, o, o, o!" of Lear's final agony, when the mad King lies down to sleep and implores:

> Make no noise, make no noise. Draw the curtains.
> So, so, so. We'll go to supper i'th' morning. So, so, so. (13.77–78)

In short, Shakespeare's lexical and aural play asks us to measure, respectively, the depths of human evil and of ignorance. For a time, nature embodied by the Stoic storm serves as a hyperbolic analogue for human anguish and anger, but ultimately nature proves inadequate to satisfy Lear when he angrily veers towards madness and "woe."[50] Likewise, the extreme perspectivism of the Dover Cliffs scene creates a new coordinate system on which to plot natural and supernatural limits. Such a grid works for a time to ameliorate Gloucester's agony. But then Ixion's wheel continues to spin and the momentum of the dual plots overwhelms Shakespeare's all-too-human, never sufficiently allegorical characters. Edgar's cryptic lines ("but another / To amplify, too much would make much more / And top extremity") apply just as well to Shakespeare's own dramatic rhetoric.

Thirdly, a final possibility is that the letter *o* should also be read, or heard, as a cipher, a grapheme for nothingness. This interpretation, buttressed by the typography of the 1608 Quarto page layout, hears in Lear's line, "And my poor fool is hanged," a memory of the disappeared Fool and his witty, chiasmic harangue:

> Now thou art an O without a figure. I am better than thou art, now. I am a fool; thou art nothing. [*To Gonoril*] Yes, forsooth, I will hold my tongue; so your face bids me, though you say nothing. (4.184–187)

In the light of the Fool's existential, mathematical verdict, Lear's penultimate words, or sounds — "O, o, o, o!" — become less a death rattle than a conceited cry summing up the rhetoric of annihilation running throughout the tragedy. They serve as his own *Leichrede*. Typographically, these bared letters mimic Lear's ontological disappearance. Of course, they literally mark a groan of woe, but even as such, like hyperbole, they function on the margins of expressibility.

Lear's audible woe thus points in two conceptual directions: first, toward the ineffability of the experience of death, but, secondly, toward silence. Thus we return to Cordelia's "Love and be silent," that self-imperative whose apparent Stoic simplicity has been undercut by all the linguistic and rhetorical *copia* it has precipitated, to say nothing of the unredeemed, unavenged tragic excess that finds its most palpable expression in the overwhelming specter of death at the play's end. Cordelia's four words are matched now by Lear's four sounds. The former, as an aside, seemed private, whereas the latter now culminate a public spectacle. Yet the audience hearing this in a theater called The Globe is privy to both, and only it can appreciate how Edmund's, "The wheel has come full circle," transcends any Stoic or Epicurean reference to Fortune's power. Shakespeare's play has made a cipher of all fortune; its "wheel," its *orbis theatrum*, has reduced the real or allegorical claims of the supernatural to zero by placing the entire ethical, epistemological, and dramaturgical onus on human actors.[51]

BENJAMIN, HYPERBOLE, AND ALLEGORY

How is allegory a response to hyperbole's semantic and logical violence against literal meaning? Conversely, what conceptual value does hyperbole have on the Baroque stage? In his wide-ranging chapter dedicated to dramaturgical "extremity" in *Lear*, Richard Fly skillfully mediates the play's myriad extremes by seizing upon Shakespeare's allegorization of character.[52] I wonder, though, whether a play's characters can be allegorical without its plot and themes participating in the allegory? Put another way, what, if any, didactic claims does *Lear* make? And can hyperbole, without approaching the totality of allegory, produce meaning from a (theatrical) world in crisis? Finally, given my interpretation of the play, how does Cavell's allegorization of Shakespearean tragedy as a response to hyperbolic skepticism now read?

In his study of German Baroque drama, *Ursprung des deutschen Trauerspiels* (1928), Walter Benjamin discovers in the *schwülstig* "mourning plays" of Lohenstein, Gryphius, Hallmann, and Opitz a drama of ideas and a "philoso-phy of art" fueled by rhetorical and conceptual extremity.[53] The plays and his method of interpreting them are thoroughly excessive — they exceed reason in that the former defy all decorum and the latter makes "inferior" works the objective vehicle for escaping subjectivity, history, and death, thereby allowing the apprehension of the origin and existence of timeless ideas.[54] Benjamin traces the many ways the *Trauerspiele* break with neoclassical aesthetics and Aristotelian prescriptions. But he does not stop there. Syncretizing aspects of Renaissance Neo-Platonism, German Romanticism, Nietzsche's *The Birth of Tragedy*, scholarship by Burckhardt, Saxl, Panofsky, and Warburg, literary criticism about the newly-discovered (or invented) *Barock*, as well as early twentieth-century literary Expressionism, he proves that a study of a single poetic genre can reveal literature's universal epistemological value. Such epis-temology, moreover, is inseparable from Benjamin's metaphysics, though whether this metaphysics is kabbalistic, Neo-Platonic, or a kind of ontology of lack, I cannot resolve here. More important for my purposes is how, as Cavell puts it, "Benjamin enacts, more or less blatantly, a contesting of the philosophical with the literary, or of what remains of each . . ."[55]

A crucial if often oblique part of this contest is the claim that dramatic bombast is essential to allegory's redemptive powers. Emphasizing the "un-remitting artistic will" [*unablenkbaren Kunstwollens*] that spurs the Baroque style, Benjamin sees in the didacticism and obscurity of Baroque allegory a poor substitute for the sublime silences of classical tragedy.[56] "With every idea the moment of expression coincides with a veritable eruption of images, which gives rise to a chaotic mass of metaphors. This is how the sublime is presented in this style."[57] Spurring this excessive metaphoricity is the general atmosphere of mourning and melancholy that pervades the spirit of the age.[58] The "violent distortion of history" gives rise to "the stylistic law of bombast" and a certain ubiquitous species of "theological hyperbole" in German Baroque drama.[59] Benjamin then explicates this correspondence within an allegorical frame that views the emblematic figure of the monarch-tyrant-martyr as more Senecan than Christian, more melancholic than trium-phant.[60] And while this melancholic type has a specific historical basis in the catastrophe of the Thirty Years War, Benjamin would also show that melancholic excess is symptomatic of larger shifts in late Renaissance con-sciousness. If history provides the characteristic content of the *Trauerspiel*, "[m]elancholy," he observes, "betrays the world for the sake of knowledge" [*um des Wissens willen*].[61] From a physiological perspective melancholy is caused by excessive black bile, while from an artistic one, given its traditional associations with the *ingenium*, melancholy generates extraordinary forms of rhetorical and visual representations.[62]

But since "the only pleasure the melancholic permits himself, and it is a powerful one, is allegory," no wonder Benjamin's discussion of allegory becomes itself at times allegorical, if not hyperbolic, in its praise of this figure.[63] All other rhetorical tropes and figures — such as anaphora, apostrophe, zeugma, metaphor, and, yes, hyperbole — are subsumed and sublimated by allegory, for allegory is effectively made equivalent with writing itself. Baroque allegory is a form of expression or externality, but it also functions as a mode of intuition (*Anschauung*) whereby the extremity of phenomena yields concepts that, in turn, can yield a "timeless constellation" of ideas possessing the being "of truth." While this sounds rather Platonic, Benjamin largely treats these ideas as lacking real presence and thus needing literary representation. "The idea is something linguistic," and it lodges in the symbolic aspects of the word. This explains why the "form" or "genre" of the *Trauerspiel* is the "idea" that Benjamin most closely scrutinizes.[64] To make this idea seem immanent, paradoxically, Baroque allegory in these plays destroys the world and then tries to redeem it. As such it is an experience, an intuition, of absence as much as presence.[65] "For a critical understanding of the *Trauerspiel*, in its extreme, allegorical form, is possible only from the higher domain of theology; so long as the approach is an aesthetic one, paradox must have the last word."[66]

Ultimately, the *Trauerspiel* demands the abandonment of the microcosmic-macrocosmic notion of *sumpatheia* in favor of Christian eschatology and causality riddled by the miraculous and the mystical.[67] Thus Benjamin treats the subjectivity that Eliot, Regenbogen, Braden, Rosenmeyer, and, in his own manner, Cavell, locate at the heart of Neo-Senecan, late Renaissance tragedy as merely a part of a totalizing allegorical economy. Nonetheless, allegoresis does have hermeneutic limits. These are encountered in the allegorist's contemplation of what Benjamin dubs "the empty abyss of evil," that is, in the extreme, melancholy attempts of the Baroque theater to represent and so know the fallen world, and thereby also "to make sure of infinity." The dramatist's "fall" is arrested not by some new knowledge of the world but by the awareness of an epistemological "limit" and the concomitant turn to the redemptive "allegory of resurrection."[68] Benjamin's allegorical dramatist, in short, resembles Edgar stage managing his father's despair on the (false) cliff in hopes of producing a "miracle."[69] But the dialectic of extremes traced by Benjamin and Shakespeare produces neither lasting knowledge nor the avoidance of it; rather it marks an excess of "data" and language that can only gesture at but never represent the absolute.[70]

Given that allegory for Benjamin marks more a failure of signification than its fulfillment, the most characteristic from of excess in the *Trauerspiel* is found in the flight from the real and the literal:

> Any adequate masking of content is absent from the typical works of the baroque. The extent of their claims, even in the minor forms, is breathtaking. And they lack any feeling for the intimate, the mysterious. They attempt, extravagantly and vainly, to replace it with the enigmatic and the concealed.[71]

Unwilling or unable to linger with the quotidian, the Baroque dramatist turns to allegory to transform the world into a ruin. By analogy, then, any critique of this Baroque drama will to some extent be allegorical: "Criticism means the mortification of the works."[72] Not that this necessarily makes every critic (critics of hyperbole included) into a *de facto* melancholic or allegorist; nor does it necessarily justify (*pace* Cavell) making Shakespeare answer for Descartes' abuse of hyperbole. But Benjamin does remind us how any reading of a literary text reifies some of its elements only to obscure or ignore other ones. Indeed, if at times in my reading of Shakespearean hyperbole form has followed content, and if Cavell qualifies his own approach to Shakespearean tragedy as sometimes "melodramatic and "excessive," Benjamin is even more forthright about his cultivation of a certain species of critical excess. In his infamously knotty *Erkenntniskritische Vorrede*, he summarizes his method: "Vom Extremen geht der Begriff aus" [*From extremity the concept emerges*].[73] He elaborates on this maxim in the first section of the treatise proper, *Trauerspiel and Tragedy*:

> The necessary tendency towards the extreme, which in philosophical investigations, constitutes the norm in the formation of concepts, means two things as far as the representation of the origin of German baroque *Trauerspiel* is concerned. Firstly it serves as a reminder that the whole range of subject matter should be disinterestedly observed . . . Secondly the study of extremes means taking account of the baroque theory of drama.[74]

Thus his "method" will be syncretic and dialectical rather than literary/critical. And in order to obviate the dictates of taste that traditionally dismissed this drama as just so much bombast, he will focus on poetics and questions of form (even with its "eccentric features" as found in the works of "lesser writers") over considerations of content.[75] This focus explains why, though he repeatedly asserts that the *Trauerspiel* is inferior aesthetically to the drama of Shakespeare and Calderón, he chooses this (then nearly) ignored genre as his critical object. And while Benjamin's dialectical focus on "extremes" signals his affinities with Hegel and the hermeneutics of Husserl and Gadamer, significantly, he also seems to find the roots of his critical approach in these obscure seventeenth/century texts themselves: "[T]he baroque apotheosis is a dialectical one. It is accomplished in the movement between extremes."[76] Likewise, he is moved in part to compare the "endeavours of the baroque" with the expressionist drama of his own day, because "[e]xaggeration is characteristic of both."[77]

How does all this help us understand the dynamics of dramatic hyperbole in *King Lear*? Although Benjamin comments on *Hamlet* several times, curiously, given his focus on kingship, tyranny, melancholy, astrology, and spectacle, he never mentions *Lear*. He does, however, call *Hamlet* one of the "great *Trauerspiele*" for the "death of Hamlet . . . is in its drastic externality characteristic of the *Trauerspiel*."[78] The reverse implication, though, is that Shakespearean tragedy also undertakes the kind of drastic internality nowhere seen in the *Trauerspiele*. This becomes more evident when Hamlet's melancholy and mourning are discussed as the acme of Baroque self/consciousness and syncretism:

> [Hamlet's] life, the exemplary object of his mourning, points, before its extinction, to the Christian providence in whose bosom his mournful images are transformed into blessed existence. Only in a princely life such as this is melancholy redeemed, by being confronted with itself. The rest is silence . . . Only Shakespeare was capable of striking Christian sparks from the baroque rigidity of the melancholic, un/stoic as it is un/Christian, pseudo/antique as it is pseudo/pietistic . . . It is only in this prince that melancholy self/absorption attains to Christianity. The German *Trauerspiel* was never able to inspire itself to new life; it was never able to awaken within the clear light of self awareness.[79]

While I am not suggesting that "king" be substituted for "prince," nor *furor* for melancholy, Benjamin's insights on the way Shakespeare's formal mastery pushes tragedy away from Stoic doctrine and toward "silence" and a self-conscious accommodation to Christian theology, powerfully illuminate *King Lear* as well. Cordelia's actions acquire a different valance when Benjamin insists: "The tragic hero has only one language that is completely proper to him: silence."[80] Still, a Christian interpretation of the suffering represented in *King Lear*, an allegorical interpretation that Cavell himself entertains for several pages, feels insufficient if not impossible given the way the play undermines the ideas of grace, providence, and, most importantly, forgiveness.[81] For Shakespeare in *Lear* provides no theology, no deus ex machina, and not even a hint of Christ's sacrifice to balance the image of the death's head, the *memento mori*, that haunts the Baroque allegorist. Then again, Benjamin's chief lesson is ultimately formal not thematic: it is *Hamlet*'s form, and not its ideology or main character, that causes "the clear light of self awareness" to appear. This is why he juxtaposes Shakespearean tragedy with the *Trauerspiele*, for "what is most characteristic of Shakespeare" is the "essential" and so aesthetically successful manner in which he fuses the elemental and the allegorical: "Every elemental utterance of the creature acquires significance from its allegorical existence, and everything allegorical acquires emphasis from the elemental aspect of the world of the senses."[82]

Undoubtedly, the characters in *Lear* experience "the elemental aspect of the world," but does the reader experience them as allegorical figures? My short response to this inevitably subjective question is that they may be experienced as failed allegories, as allegories too riddled with the enigmatic abundance of words and the ruined world to afford transcendence, as figures given too much ironic self-awareness to be captured by an ethical abstraction, a providential design, or a single hermeneutic. Edmund's Machiavellianism and Lear's "pelican daughters" give birth neither to a medieval morality play nor to a Benjaminian *Trauerspiel* wherein death, history, and mystery are allegory's ostentatious offspring, but rather to a tragedy in which the pedestrian thirst for power joined with an old king's vanity, caprice, and ignorance, together with a young woman's inexplicable silence, create a form of hyperbolism that resists transcendence. In this respect, the exchange between Albany and Edgar, commenting on Lear who has carried his daughter's corpse onto the stage (a Shakespearean *memento mori*), should be our guide:

> *Albany*: He knows not what he sees; and vain it is
>   That we present us to him.
> *Edgar*:   Very bootless. (24.288–289)

Such a failure of presentation I read as the purposeful failure of allegory and the representation (*Darstellung*) of ideas. It is precipitated by the incommensurability of the self and the world, between the self and others, an incommensurability produced, from the opening to the closing scenes of the play, by hyperbole. Dramatic hyperbole in *Lear* results in ignorance of self and the world ("He knows not . . ."). And the immense, immanent pathos elicited by this ignorance remains unredeemed by ideas.

Yet, as I have argued, the key to *King Lear*'s aesthetic, emotional, and conceptual force is the miraculous, theatrical manner in which Shakespeare makes hyperbole dialogic. Hyperbole acquires immense dramaturgical subtlety from the context in which it is spoken, from the *ethos* of those who speak it, and from the way it is heard by others. If this drama still moves us and deserves our reflection — and many have argued that it does so more than any other in the Western canon — then it is because we are still made incredulous by its rhetorical and dramaturgical extremities. If this tragedy's insistent, pervasive hyperbolism remains unredeemed by allegory, then it is because it works toward something more immanent, more inscrutable than a mere idea. What this might be or mean, I cannot say. *Lear* defies the "capture" of hermeneutics, for Shakespeare refuses to mortify, to commit allegorical violence against his own drama.[83] Hermes himself could not limn the breach, the "abyss," the play precipitates. The critic is tempted to respond to the rhetorical and conceptual violence of hyperbole with the metaphysics of allegory, but hyperbole in *Lear* proves such efforts "bootless."

Chapter Twelve

Fabulous Discourse: Descartes and Hyperbole

> He is a brittle crazie glasse . . .
> — George Herbert, "The Windows"

EXAGGERO, ERGO SUM

At the end of "The Avoidance of Love," Stanley Cavell pivots again from literature to philosophy. Wondering what lessons the fates of Lear and Gloucester have for us, he concludes: "The cause of tragedy is that we would rather murder the world than permit it to expose us to change."[1] Thus implicated, we turn back to the problem of skepticism, which for Cavell is a metaphysical problem as well. It is not only that philosophers such as Descartes tend to interpret "metaphysical finitude as an intellectual lack" and therefore seek extreme remedies, or that more humanist, syncretic thinkers, such as Montaigne (a sceptic of another stripe) calls for philosophical "moderation" in those who would "escape human nature," but that this late Renaissance debate has baroquely become our debate as well. In the wake of Kant's three critiques, Nietzsche's death of God, Wittgenstein's attempts to strip the sublime from the philosopher's docket, Heidegger's onto-theology, and waves upon waves of structuralist and post-structuralist theory, Descartes still provides one of the most powerful narratives of how metaphysics (*prima philosophia*) might solve the skeptical conundrum.[2] More to the point, in casting his own reading of Shakespearean tragedy as an anachronistic "response" to Descartes' hyperbolic skepticism, Cavell invites us, as we saw in chapter nine, "to look at the philosopher's extraordinary treatment of objects" and "to explore the sense of hyperbolic, unprecedented attention in play" in philosophy. In this chapter and the next I accept this invitation by scrutinizing the rhetorical, epistemological, and ethical aspects of Descartes' hyperbolism. Descartes' reliance on hyperbole, I shall argue, is both heuristic and structural. But as Gassendi already objected when the *Meditations* circulated in manuscript, Descartes also exploits the resources of hyperbole in less than "good faith" [*bona fide*]. Descartes hyperbolizes with the imaginative force of a Baroque poet, but he does so in part to limit the harmful effects of rhetoric and the imagination on his philosophical "fable."

Largely ignoring the potential pitfalls of using the most unbelievable trope to establish absolute certainty, Descartes' accelerated use of hyperbole as a vehicle for doubt proves spectacular in its heuristic power. To arrive at the paradox of the *cogito*, at what Jean-Luc Nancy dubs "*extremity* itself" and "the *extreme curtailment*," the philosophical hyperbolist wagers the world and his own enormous ambitions.[3] Or at least he appears to do so. An artifice as mannered as the most extravagant poetic conceit, Cartesian hyperbolic doubt self-consciously outbids itself until the desired philosophic *pointe* is reached — and then it melts into thin air. As with the other hyperbolic overreachers contemplated in this book, and, I might add, as with du Bartas, Sponde, d'Aubigné, Saint Amant, and those humanists whose artful rhetoric he turns his back on in Part I of the *Discourse on Method* (1637), Descartes knows he is straining the truth and he knows, or at least hopes, that his sophisticated readers, in the first instance the Faculty of Theology at the Sorbonne — whom he praises in the *Meditations on First Philosophy* (1641) as having "intelligence and learning," but who "are few and far between"[4] — know he is doing so. To adapt Quintilian's prescription, the reader is persuaded to assume that Descartes' "lies" are told without mendacity, and that behind them lurk truths that can only be attained in an *ultra modum* manner. For, as is decidedly not the case with the deceptive wit of the "evil genius," Descartes characterizes his own *ingenium* as having a degree of "franchise" [*candor*] that readers of good will ought to embrace. Yet despite the fictive extremes to which such forthrightness leads, Descartes is extremely careful to limit the scope of his ingenious hyperbolic doubt to the world of ideas — thereby leaving untouched the realms of action and moral choice. In short, because his doubt is so incredible and artificial, we learn to regard it as a rhetorical artifice and a heuristic tool. Cartesian doubt, as Martial Gueroult demonstrates, is "methodological . . . universal . . . and radical," but also "provisional."[5] Fueled by a species of hyperbole stripped of any ontological contingency (though retaining some narrative contingency), and answering only to the demands of analysis and the a priori desire for epistemological certainty, doubt becomes for Descartes a world-destroying, God-debunking, logic-annihilating specter that astonishingly is vanquished, or vanquishes itself, at the exact moment when the solidity of the *cogito* is intuited.

I hyperbolize, therefore I am. And from this swiftly follows, Ferdinand Alquié notes, *dubito, ergo Deus est.*[6] A singular, instrumental act, hyperbolic doubt is precipitous, violent, and a smashing metaphysical success. Yet notwithstanding the monumental expression of will involved in such hyperbolic doubt, it is only meant, Janet Broughton observes, to be a one-time restructuring of "our basic picture of the world and our own faculties for understanding it."[7] It functions as an indirect, "strategic" way of securing the epistemological ground for defending physical theories that had already earned the more direct Galileo a papal condemnation.[8] In short, as soon as God's existence, his perfection, and thus also the epistemological objective basis for truth are deduced, Descartes discards hyperbole like a person sloughing off the fading memory of a nightmare in the clear light of the morning sun.[9] Further, if Cartesian hyperbole is provisional, it is not so in the same sense of the *morale par provision*; the former is provisional in a strictly notional manner, whereas the latter is designed to protect Descartes from acting immorally in the world while he deconstructs and reconstructs his "opinions" and ideas.

Unlike the Neo-Stoics, Descartes makes his moral condition merely a propaedeutic to and not an integral factor in his metaphysical speculations — it informs his *morale par provision* but not his epistemology. Alternately, as contemporaries and more recent critics have argued, Skepticism, both in its Pyrrhonian and Academic varieties, is the philosophic tradition that most engages Descartes.[10] His engagement, however, is generally at once reactionary and utilitarian. There are biographical as well as formal reasons indicating that Descartes was affected deeply by the *crise pyrrhonienne* precipitated by renewed interest in the writing of Sextus Empiricus, and the refashioning of the skeptical tradition by Heinrich Cornelius Agrippa, Montaigne, Pierre Charron, Francisco Sánchez, and others.[11] Remarkably though, Descartes responds to this tradition by outdoing the Pyrrhonians. He rewrites the skeptical position such that the epistemological potential for doubt is exhausted and the cognitive and psychological ground prepared for philosophic certainty to be pursued once again.

To measure the success of these efforts depends largely on one's perspective, that is, whether one interprets Descartes' hyperbole from the retrospective, universalist vantage point achieved by the *cogito* or whether one adopts the pro-leptic, contingent, and ultimately aberrant vantage point of the extravagant "fable" that leads to the *cogito*. As Jacques Lezra remarks in his subtle reading of events and examples in Descartes' texts, this perspectival difference is be-tween thinking and reading, between following reason's path and being tempted by the lure of the aesthetic.[12] Viewed from the former, Descartes' own perspective, he succeeds beyond all expectation in finding the limits of skepticism and thereby distinguishing uncertainty from certainty, falsehood from truth. Viewed, though, from the perspective of many Counter Refor-mation theologians and Neo-Aristotelians, his hyperbolic doubt destroys all criteria for truth in a manner such that when he offers his proof of God and other positive assertions of knowledge, these claims are infected by the very skepticism that he himself had cultivated in order to negate skepticism. Like-wise, those thinkers who considered themselves inheritors of the skeptical tradi-tion, such as Gassendi, Huet, Bayle, and Hume, read Descartes' triumphant conclusions concerning God's perfection and thus the correspondence of his subjective perceptions with objective reality, skeptically, that is, as failing to ap-ply the same skepticism that produced the *cogito* in the first place.

That Descartes' intentions in refashioning the Pyrrhonian method of skeptical doubt were misconstrued by readers with agendas different than his should not surprise. More strikingly, and what I wish to explore in the follow-ing pages, is how the hyperbole that informs not only his method, but also his diction and the conceits used to describe his philosophical ambitions, carries with it rhetorical and hermeneutic risks that Descartes appears to have ig-nored or discarded as inconsequential. Briefly put, what are we to think when late in the Sixth Meditation Descartes concludes that "the exaggerated doubts of the last few days should be dismissed as laughable" [*sed hyperbolicae super-iorum dierum dubitationes, ut risu dignae, sunt explodenae*]?[13] Does Descartes' a pos-teriori condemnation of his instrumental use of hyperbole excuse it as the necessary means to a powerful end? What, if any, are the negative conse-quences of such ridiculous overreaching? How does Descartes immunize himself from the specters of madness, hubris, aporia, and silence that haunt other hyperbolists? And if these consequences are curtailed in the works them-selves are they, perhaps, to be felt in their reception, and, more generally, in the subsequent genealogy of Western philosophy?

Like Leibniz and John Wilkins after him, Descartes expresses the desire to rescue philosophical language both from the wrangling of Scholastics and

Humanists, and from the contingency and errors inherent in all things human. In a letter to his long-time friend and interlocutor, Marin Mersenne, he hopes for a "universal language . . . which would help judgment, repre senting all things to it so distinctly that it would be almost impossible for it to be deceived."[14] Although he realizes that such a universal, ordinary language, "by means of which peasants would better be able to judge of the truth of things than philosophers are able to now," is but a Utopian dream, proper only to a "pays des romans," it still stubbornly serves as Descartes' ideal in his later pursuit of philosophical clarity.[15] Or as Timothy Reiss neatly phrases it, "language reveals thought" for Descartes.[16] Similarly, Derrida comments: "Descartes never confronts the question of his own language."[17] His lan guage, that is, even in its most figurative aspects, is presented as a transparent medium, an efficient vehicle, for a metaphysical tenor. Ambitious to resolve the *crise pyrrhonienne* and thereby to set the sciences on firm ontological and epistemological footing, neither the *Discourse* nor the *Meditations* spare much room for reflection on the nature of signification. What few observations are offered on this matter pale in comparison, for example, to the many pages Montaigne, one of the proponents of this *crise*, devotes to examining his own rhetoric. But surely this is symptomatic of larger issues; for if Montaigne ar rives at his skeptical stance by adducing and producing all manner of rhetor ical *copia*, then Descartes' efforts to combat skepticism proceed by his making his prose bear the enormous weight of excessive doubt until he and, he trusts, his readers (perhaps after several readings) see clearly and distinctly a way out of the skeptical dilemma.[18] Thus his rhetoric still risks being misunderstood (by us) not because it is elliptical, diffuse, obscure, pointed, or paradoxical, nor for the most part because of any historical distance from the culture that informs it, but because relatively unadorned, ordinary language is made to bear hyperbolic thoughts without the former ever acknowledging the burden of the latter. Descartes wagers that such a burden will go unnoticed, which is all the more remarkable as he is self-consciously inaugurating a revolution in self-consciousness.

Although it is puzzling how one can be exemplary and at the same time not want to persuade others, Descartes should be taken at his word when he writes in the *Discourse*, Part I: "My present aim, then, is not to teach the method which everyone must follow in order to direct his reason correctly, but only to reveal how I have tried to direct my own."[19] Ambivalently straddling a desire to persuade a small, but learned audience and a more solipsistic desire to represent himself to himself in a consistent manner, he ultimately aims to describe an essentially interior experience.[20] Easy credulity is attacked throughout the *Discourse*; he initially likens his text ("cet écrit") to an exemplary "fable" that he would have his readers find useful but never noxious.[21] But if this would seem to precipitate the question of his rhetoric's believability or verisimilitude, Descartes effectively postpones the issue by insisting first on his own "franchise" and then by offering a *petite histoire* concerning his education which, among other things, allows him to praise "eloquence" and "poésie" while indicating their limited methodological value.[22] Then he critiques other "fables" as making one "imagine many events possible which in reality are not so." On the one hand, he distances himself from "even the most accurate histories" [*les histoires plus fidèles*], which "while not altering or exaggerating the importance of matters" [*ne changent ni n'augmentent la valeur des choses*], still err by omitting "baser and less notable events."[23] On the other, he condemns the imitative excess in those histories that represent such fables as verisimilar: " . . . as a result, the other events appear in a false light, and those who regulate their conduct by examples drawn from these works are liable to fall into the excesses of the knights-errant in our novels of chivalry, and conceive plans beyond their powers" [*d'où vient que le reste ne paraît pas tel qu'il est, et que ceux qui règlent leurs mœurs par les exemples qu'ils en tirent, sont sujets à tomber dans les extravagances des paladins de nos romans, et à concevoir des desseins qui passent leurs forces*].[24] Echoing the morale that Cervantes announces in the Prologue *Don Quixote*, Descartes condemns the hyperbolism of novels as threatening the subject with a fall ("sont sujets à tomber"). Yet to curtail this threat Descartes will offer another kind of hyperbolism. And what he omits in his hyperbolic "fable," and when and why he decides to stop exaggerating, will prove constitutive not only of his method but also of his truth claims.[25]

"[E]xcess being usually bad,"[26] Descartes hopes to obviate it with his *morale par provision*, the first maxim of which is to obey the laws and customs of one's country (he is then living in exile in Holland). In the third maxim, as he reminds himself to strive for self-mastery and "to make virtue out of a necessity," he notes that such moderation is grounded in the exemplary stance of Stoic philosophers

> qui ont pu autrefois se soustraire de l'empire de la fortune et, malgré les douleurs et la pauvreté, disputer de la félicité avec leurs dieux. Car, s'occupant sans cesse à considérer les bornes qui leur étaient prescrites par la

nature, il se persuadaient si parfaitement que rien n'était en leur pouvoir que leurs pensées, que cela seul était suffisant pour les empêcher d'avoir aucune affection pour d'autres choses; et ils disposaient d'elles si absolu‑ ment, qu'ils avaient en cela quelque raison de s'estimer plus riches, et plus puissants, et plus libres, et plus heureux, qu'aucun des autres hommes qui, n'ayant point cette philosophie, tant favorisés de la nature et de la fortune qu'ils puissent être, ne disposent jamais ainsi de tout ce qu'ils veulent.

who in earlier times were able to escape from the dominion of fortune and, despite suffering and poverty, rival their gods in happiness. Through constant reflection on the limits prescribed for them by nature, they became perfectly convinced that nothing was in their power but their thoughts, and this alone was sufficient to prevent them from being attracted to other things. Their mastery over their thoughts was so ab‑ solute that they had reason to count themselves richer, more powerful, freer and happier than other men who, because they lack this philoso‑ phy, never achieve such mastery over all their desires, however favoured by nature and fortune they may be.[27]

Three aspects of Descartes' reformulation of this ancient ideal are crucial for a reading of his hyperbolism: first, it allows for a relatively objective, passion‑ less state in which the body's demands are minimal, as is the effect of external, public opinion; second, by making the Stoics a model for at least part of his method, Descartes engages, imitates, and idiosyncratically outdoes one of the major philosophical traditions — just as he will presently do with skepti‑ cism; third, it marks, as distinct from Seneca and the Neo‑Senecans, the sep‑ aration of the ethical and moral spheres. Yet if I might divorce form from content for a moment, Descartes' diction and syntax here also reveal a great deal about the extravagant quality of his thought. The passage is littered with adjectival and adverbial phrases that strive to portray the Stoic enterprise in the absolutest terms: "sans cesse . . . si parfaitement que rien . . . aucune affec‑ tion . . . si absolument . . . plus riches, et plus puissants, et plus libres, et plus heureux, qu'aucun des autres hommes." All of this culminates in the final dependent clause which subtly balances "point . . . tant . . . jamais . . . tout" to insist at once on the Stoics' incomparable victory over "l'empire de la for‑ tune" and, conversely, the heavy loss of those who fail to follow their example. A kind of auxesis, the passage persuades us of Descartes' admiration for the

Stoic ideal of self-sufficiency even as its rhythm projects complete self-assurance precluding any doubt — thereby providing a rhetorical model for the up-coming intuition of the *cogito*.

Generally speaking, then, absolutist diction, together with associated fig-ures of thought such as antithesis, parataxis, anaphora, and auxesis, are the principle rhetorical means by which Descartes lends his methodological hy-perbole its air of verisimilitude and necessity. Another means of persuasion is Descartes' beloved metaphorics of architecture and the path to describe his project and aims. But while such metaphors are certainly instrumental and of-ten verge on a kind of stylistic mannerism, they rarely are particularly daring or original.[28] Rather it is by careful attention to his diction that one learns to appreciate the extent to which Descartes relies on discursive hyperbole to gen-erate the logic of the *cogito*, a logic that simultaneously allows him to realize that clarity and distinctness — and not the intuitions produced by willed, imagined hyperbole — are the criteria by which his "natural light of reason" discovers truth. Even more than in the passage concerning the Stoics quoted above, the diction in the following, most pondered passage of Cartesian phi-losophy is riddled with superlatives and antitheses:

> J'avais dès longtemps remarqué que, pour les mœurs, il est besoin quelquefois de suivre des opinions qu'on sait être fort incertaines, tout de même que si elles étaient indubitables, ainsi qu'il a été dit ci-dessus; mais, parce qu'alors je désirais vaquer seulement à la recherche de la vérité, je pensai qu'il fallait que je fisse tout le contraire, et que je reje-tasse, comme absolument faux, tout ce en quoi je pourrais imaginer le moindre doute, afin de voir s'il ne resterait point, après cela, quelque chose en ma créance, qui fût entièrement indubitable ... jugeant que j'étais sujet à faillir, autant qu'aucun autre, je rejetai comme fausse toutes les raisons que j'avais prises auparavant pour démonstrations. Et enfin, considérant que toutes les mêmes pensées, que nous avons étant éveillés, nous pouvent aussi venir, quand nous dormons, sans qu'il y en ait au-cune, pour lors, qui soit vraie, je me résolus de feindre que toutes les choses qui m'étaient jamais entrées en l'esprit n'étaient non plus vraies que les illusions de mes songes. Mais, aussitôt après, je pris garde que, pendant que je voulais ainsi penser que tout était faux, il fallait néces-sairement que moi, qui le pensais, fusse quelque chose. Et remarquant que cette vérité: *je pense, donc je suis*, était si ferme et si assurée, que toutes

les plus extravagantes suppositions des sceptiques n'étaient pas capables de l'ébranler, je jugeai que je pouvais la recevoir, sans scrupule, pour le premier principe de la philosophie que je cherchais.

For a long time I had observed, in regard to morals, that in practical life it is sometimes necessary to act upon opinions which one knows to be quite uncertain, just as if they were indubitable. But since I now wished to devote myself solely to the search for truth, I thought it necessary to do the very opposite and reject as if absolutely false everything in which I could imagine the least doubt, in order to see if I was left believing any, thing that was entirely indubitable . . . and because I judged that I was as prone to error as anyone else, I rejected as unsound all the arguments I had previously taken as demonstrative proofs. Lastly, considering that the very thoughts we have while awake may also occur while we sleep without any of them being at that time true, I resolved to pretend that all the things that had ever entered into my mind were no more true than the illusions of my dreams. But immediately I noticed that while I was try, ing thus to think everything false, it was necessary that I, who was think, ing this, was something. And observing that this truth "I am thinking, therefore I exist" was so firm and sure that all the most extravagant sup, positions of the sceptics were incapable of shaking it, I decided that I could accept it without scruple as the first principle of the philosophy I was seeking.[29]

Despite the initial reliance on the kind of the confessional rhetoric that domi, nates the opening of the *Discourse*, this passage signals the flight from what Cavell calls "the common" or "the ordinary."[30] In other words, the disjunctive force of the "mais" is enormous; it signals an irrevocable break with ordinary reality in the light of urgent philosophical desires. Here Descartes at once an, ticipates and would help precipitate the "grands changements en l'ordre des choses" that, as he describes it in his letter to Mersenne quoted above, would accompany the institution of a "langue universelle" fit for science and hitherto only imagined in "pays des romans." He performs this feat by privileging his own absolute fiction over the "extravagantes suppositions des sceptiques." Meanwhile, his insistence on a first person, narrative perspective — heightened by the mannered repetition of *je* — tends to protect his *ethos* by conveying the sense, or the illusion, that his doubt is a lived experience by someone in a partic, ular place and time (notwithstanding that such doubt will be later be represented as a necessary consequence of pure deductive reason). The Cartesian self thus becomes a spectacular event and the sympathetic reader who has become curious about its vertiginous fortunes tends to be distracted from the Baroque manner in which the diction of this passage, with its numerous absolutes ("toutes les mêmes pensées . . . sans qu'il y en ait aucune . . . tout était faux"), intensifications ("si ferme et si assurée"), superlatives ("toutes les plus extravagantes suppositions"), allied with a particularly uncompromising antithesis ("je rejetasse, comme absolument faux, tout ce en quoi je pourrais imaginer le moindre doute, afin de voir s'il ne resterait point"), work to astonish and persuade. More generously, Descartes' hyperbolic diction — despite the momentary ambivalence of *fusse quelque chose* — may be read as heuristically advancing the intuition of the *cogito*. Adjectives like *tout* and *sans*, adverbs such as *entièrement* and *absolument*, and the sudden shift from *je* to *nous* and back to *je* again, may be less rhetorical tricks to force consent than indicative of a faith in language to serve as the neutral means to reach philosophical goals. Descartes rescues the notion of certainty from "all the most extravagant suppositions of the sceptics" by, paradoxically, adopting an even more radically skeptical position than they do and presenting his narrator's stance as fictional ("je me résolus de feindre que toutes les choses qui m'étaient jamais entrée en l'esprit . . ."). Having abandoned the *morale par provision* that allowed him formerly to succeed in geometrical reasoning, he presents here an amoral fiction, whose form turns out to be shaped as much by the extreme rhythms of hyperbole as is its content.

But then his novel fiction abruptly stops. And when it does, the paratactic progression of hyperbole is swiftly transformed into a logical proposition:

> Puis, examinant avec attention ce que j'étais, et voyant que je pouvais feindre que je n'avais aucun corps, et qu'il n'y avait aucun monde, ni aucun lieu où je fusse; mais que je ne pouvais feindre, pour cela, que je n'étais point . . .

> Next I examined attentively what I was. I saw that while I could pretend that I had no body and that there was no world and no place for me to be in; I could not for all that pretend that I did not exist.[31]

Does the deflating "mais que" signal a new intuition? Is it meant to recall the disjunctive "mais" in the previous passage? More importantly, does it mark a failure of Descartes' imagination? And if so, is it a necessary (logical) or a feigned (rhetorical) failure? Or has Descartes' expository, narrative voice, adopting now the stance of deductive reason, rather than seeing the problem from the in-the-trenches perspective of the intuition, perceived the sought-for clarity and distinctness, and so willingly yielded to the claims of logic? Peter Markie notes just how muddled the causality is here: "Descartes intuits the self-evident proposition that he thinks and simultaneously infers that he exists."[32] By conflating intuition, inference, and being so precipitously Descartes elides, or even ignores, numerous issues concerning context and logic,[33] his relation to his own thoughts,[34] and, as Bertrand Russell sees it, his thinking to his language.[35] But these are issues that have long occupied commentators. To try yet again to find a hard and fast distinction between an *ordo cognoscendi* and an *ordo essendi*, an order of cognition and an order of being, in Descartes' thought is not my aim. My focus in the following pages is instead more pointedly concerned with the relationship between words and things. In particular, what is the model for this relationship if the geometric model on which Descartes pins his epistemological hopes has not yet proven its efficacy? And if the model up until the point, the *punctum*, of the *cogito* is radically hyperbolic, then how does Descartes set, proleptically or retrospectively, rhetorical and aesthetic limits for his hyperbolic fiction?

FEIGNING HYPERBOLE

Unlike the geometer, the philosopher who would publish and defend his ideas needs to appeal to his reader's will as well as reason. While early in the *Discourse* Descartes discounts the study, his study, of rhetoric as inimical to his scientific and metaphysical projects, undoubtedly he depends on important aspects of *inventio, elocutio, dispositio*, and *memoria* for his philosophic narrative to succeed. The *Discourse* is cast in the past tense, carefully arranged in sequential sections, and filled with metaphor, figures of thought, and idiomatic diction. Above all, it is a tale of discovery (*heurisis*). His choice of the vernacular over Latin, as he observes in the treatise's penultimate paragraph, is made so that he can appeal to his readers' "natural reason" and thereby circumvent ancient authority. The *Discourse* courts readers whose reason has been ruined, not by other philosophies or any moral defects, but simply by the accumulation of worldly experience. Before he commences his metaphysical doubts, therefore, Descartes fashions an *ethos* steeped in commonsense yet one also possessing an extraordinary will to power:

My second maxim was to be as firm and decisive in my actions as I could [*d'être le plus ferme et le plus résolu en mes actions que je pourrais*], and to follow even the most doubtful opinions, once I had adopted them, with no less constancy than if they had been quite certain. In this respect I would be imitating a traveler who, upon finding himself lost in a wood, should not wander about turning this way and that, and still less stay in one place, but should keep walking as straight as he can in one direction, never changing it for slight reasons even if mere chance made him choose it in the first place; for in this way, even if he does not go exactly where he wishes, he will at least end up in a place where he is likely [*à la fin quelque part, où vraisemblablement*] to be better off than in the middle of a forest.[36]

The narrator acts as an exemplary guide hoping to lead his reader out of the dark wood by means of "probable opinions." Like those of his Tuscan predecessor, Descartes' metaphorics of the sylvan path reflects on his art as well as his ideas. For despite the last sentence's apparent ambivalence, a singularly determined Descartes is not content to end up just anywhere. In both the *Discourse* and the *Meditations*, the probable inevitably but "vraisemblablement" gives way to the absolutely certain. Must the reader, then, as L. Aryeh Kosman incisively does in an essay on the formal, thematic, and stylistic aspects of Descartes' appropriation of the religious genre of meditation, always distinguish between the narrator dallying with probability and the author fixed on certainty? And is this a distinction that Descartes himself would care to admit?

In his unfinished dialogue, *Recherche de la vérité*, Descartes momentarily concedes that his journey might alarm readers who adhere to other schools of thought. Here Epistemon, who gives voice to Scholastic thought, fears that methodical doubt "would lead us straight into the ignorance of Socrates or the uncertainty of the Pyrrhonists. These are deep waters, where I think we may lose our footing" [*c'est une eau profonde, où il ne me semble pas qu'on puisse trouver pied*].[37] But Eudoxus, Descartes' mouthpiece, responds by assuring him that he will be rewarded for having strengthened his will:

I confess that it would be dangerous for someone who does not know a ford [*gué*] to venture across it without a guide [*de s'y hasarder sans conduite*], and many have lost their lives in doing so. But you have nothing to fear if you follow me [*mais vous ne devés pas craindre d'y passer appres moy*]. In-

deed, just such fears have prevented men of letters from acquiring a body
of knowledge which was firm and certain enough to deserve the name
'science'. Supposing that there was no firmer basis for their opinions
other than the things perceivable by the senses, they have built upon sand
instead of digging further down to find rock or clay . . . But in case you
should now lack the courage to proceed any further, I would advise you
that these doubts, which alarmed you at the start, are like phantoms and
empty images which appear at night in the uncertain glimmer of a weak
light: if you flee from them, your fear will follow you, but if you approach as if to touch them, you will find nothing but air and shadow
and you will be more confident the next time such an encounter may
occur. [*Mais, afin que vous ne refusiés pas de passer outre avec plus de courage, je
vous advertis que ces doutes, qui vous ont fait peur à l'abord, sont comme de fantosmes
& vaines images, qui paroissent la nuit à la faveur d'une lumiere debile & incer-
taine: si vous les fuyés, vostre crainte vous suivra; mais si vous approchés comme
pour les toucher, vous decouvrirés que ce n'est rien, que de l'air & de l'ombre, & en
s[f]erés à l'advenir plus assuré en pareille rencontre.*][38]

After neatly remaking the familiar allegories of the path and the architect,
Descartes offers a thoroughly Baroque simile comparing hyperbolic doubt to
an *ignis fatuus*. In terms of the rhetoric of *desengaño*, this recalls Prospero's
speech to Ferdinand meant to disabuse him of his fears: "You do look, my
son, in a moved sort, / As if you were dismayed. Be cheerful, sir. / Our revels
are now ended. These our actors, / As I foretold you, were all spirits, and /
Are melted into air, into thin air . . ." (4.1.146–150). More ominously, it also
echoes Andreas Gryphius's comparison in "Menschliches Elend" — a poem
prompted by the same Thirty Year's War witnessed by Descartes — of humanity to "ein Irrlicht dieser Zeit." Descartes' remedy for such "phantoms,"
however, is not magical, dramaturgical, or theological. It is thoroughly empirical, but also proleptic of the unimpeachable metaphorics of light that he,
with his invocation of the *lumen naturale* as the final arbiter of epistemological
questions, will deny in his Replies to Hobbes is a metaphorics at all. Moreover, in contrast to the subtler *Discourse* and *Meditations*, here Descartes unabashedly anoints himself as the guide to the unenlightened. If his followers
have enough "courage," then his method of doubt will dissipate the lesser,
spectral doubts enveloping those who dally with skepticism. Still, the unfinished (and undated) *Recherche* only adumbrates such a method, whereas the

Discourse and *Meditations* offer a progressively fuller experience of hyperbolic doubt.[39] Picking up the image above of the "ford," one might say that the *Discourse* offers shallower waters than the *Meditations*. As Descartes pointedly tells Mersenne in a letter, he hoped "que les femmes mêmes pussent entendre quelque chose" when they read the *Discourse*.[40] Conversely, the dangers and obscurities are greater in the *Meditations* because of the hypothesis of the *malin génie* but also because of the scanter use of narrative and autobiographical rhetoric.[41] In this sense, Descartes offers a meta-narrative of outbidding (himself). These three texts trace, then, his fitful efforts to find the best rhetorical means — whether dialogue, autobiography, or meditation — to represent his thoughts and method.

But again, if and how these efforts succeed depend on the angle of one's hermeneutic perspective. Written just before the structuralist turn in France, Henri Gouhier's *La pensée métaphysique de Descartes* offers a comprehensive analysis of the role that rhetoric, especially invention and arrangement, plays in the exposition of Descartes' thinking. Less interested in specific questions concerning *elocutio* than he is in the relation Descartes would establish with his readers in order to persuade them of his revolutionary metaphysics, Gouhier proves a bold theorist of Descartes' intentions and a subtle, patient reader of individual texts and passages. In his ironically titled chapter, "La résistance au vrai dans une philosophie sans rhétorique," he argues that though Descartes would completely subordinate *persuasio* to *scientia* (thereby replacing *doxa* with *epistêmê*), one still discovers a vital "drame" wherein the philosopher risks being misunderstood in order to communicate his novel ideas: "Sûr de sa raison, Descartes doute de sa parole."[42] Leaning on Chaim Perelman's *Rhétorique et philosophie*, Gouhier notes that the criteria of clear and distinct evidence would seem to preclude a role for rhetoric. Yet to reform metaphysics, and thereby save it from Scholasticism and Skepticism, Descartes must, like Plato before him, make some kind of truce with rhetoric, the linguistic art, Gouhier reminds us, that Aristotle identifies with the probable.

The extent to which this undeclared truce operates in the stages of hyperbolic doubt can be felt in Pierre Gassendi's objection, in the Fifth Set of Objections, where he compares the fictional method of doubt in the First Meditation to "an ingenious device" [*machinam*]. Gassendi does not object to the doubt itself, but rather to the devious, verbose ways Descartes conceives it:

Would it not have been more in accord with philosophical honesty and the love of truth [*philosophico candore et veritatis amore dignum*] simply to state the facts candidly [*bona fide*] and straightforwardly, rather than, as some critics might put it, to resort to artifice, sleight of hand and cir-cumlocution [*recurre ad machinam, captare praestigias, sectari ambages*]?[43]

Sounding as if he were upbraiding a young, mannerist poet for his exces-sive attachment to abstruse figures of rhetoric, Gassendi, as other passages in the Fifth Set of Objections confirm, believes Descartes abuses his readers' credulity with the dream hypothesis and the evil genius (a *machina* often signi-fied in the Baroque a rhetorical artifice or device, such as a elaborate plot or a conceit).[44]

Less skeptically, Gouhier stresses the advantages Descartes seeks by fol-lowing an analytic rather than a synthetic order in his exposition. Descartes composes his metaphysical texts in a manner that the reader's memory and habit can be affected, cleansed, and improved. The order of his exposition at-tempts to keep in mind "à la fois de la logique des idées et de la psychologie de cet 'autre' [the reader]."[45] Descartes assumes a reader of good will will be ea-ger to follow Descartes' own path toward knowledge. But this path is largely catachrestic; that it does not in fact initially follow the *more geometrico*, which Descartes insists is the trustworthiest method for arriving at clear and distinct ideas, calls for some explanation.[46] And answering Mersenne, in the Second Set of Replies, Descartes offers exactly this. Two methods of demonstration are outlined: "analysis" [*l'analyse ou résolution*] and "synthesis" [*la synthèse ou composition*].[47] By analysis is meant the solution or explication of a complex problem through the discovery and understanding of its simplest compo-nents. Inevitably, though, one also hears in his reply connotations associated with the will; for, as we saw above in that passage where the *cogito* is first named ("je me résolus de feindre que toutes les choses qui m'étaient non plus vraies que les illusions de mes songes . . ."), the resolution to "feign" is voluntary. Analysis persuades the reader to make the philosopher's will his own:

Analysis shows the true way by means of which the thing in question was discovered methodically and as it were a priori, so that if the reader is willing to follow it and give sufficient attention to all points, he will make the thing his own and understand it just as perfectly as if he had discovered it for himself [*quam si ipsemet illam invenisset*].[48]

By transferring his experience of invention (heurisis) to the reader, Descartes places extraordinary responsibility and faith in the latter's imagination. He assumes that invention will lead to understanding and that, in a strong sense, it will enable each reader to become a hyperbolic author (or as Lezra comments, become a fellow traveler on Descartes' "novelistic" path). Conversely, in the next paragraph he asserts that a synthetic approach — such as the one Spinoza will adopt — will compel even the most "argumentative or stubborn." But again, this "method is not as satisfying as the method of analysis, nor does it engage the minds of those who are eager to learn, since it does not show how the thing in question was discovered" [*quia modum quo res fuit inventa non docet*].[49]

By conflating analysis, invention, and hyperbole, Descartes underscores the extent to which the last is able *move* and *teach* those "minds" [*animos*] thirsting for knowledge.[50] Hyperbole serves an essential psychological and narrative purpose — through it readers are urged to slake their own epistemological desire. Further, the narrative experience of invention goes a long way to explaining, in cognitive terms, Descartes' inordinate attachment to the metaphorics of the path ("la vraie voie"). It also recalls the experience of puzzling over a difficult poetic conceit and, as I shall argue below, of arriving at a witty *pointe*. For once the path's destination is reached, analysis can immediately cease and synthesis can begin its drier, more logical operations. The synthetic geometer need not be concerned with persuading anyone of his first principles or axioms; they are simply adduced at the outset and then referred to when necessary in the course of proving particular propositions.[51] By contrast, as Gouhier notes, analysis is "historical" — it creates a chronology in which effects are meticulously traced back to their causes — whereas the synthetic method practiced by geometers (and metaphysicians like Spinoza, who offers definitions and axioms before *demonstrata*) operates in the timeless realm of pure logic, *sub specie aeternitatis*. Thus when hyperbole disappears, narrative and history vanish along with it.

In sum, a prodigious conceptual tension exists between the universal aims of Descartes' philosophy and the fact that he writes and is read in a historical moment. Disdaining almost completely any appeal to *auctoritas* in the exposition of his ideas, Descartes prefers autobiography and self-analysis to tracing the possible lineage — whether it runs through Plato, Sextus, Augustine, Aquinus, or more contemporaneously through Montaigne, Sánchez, or Charron — of his own thought and language. He also has little overt use for philological or etymological concerns, or for the other discursive habits of traditional hu-

manism.[52] Like Bacon, Descartes insists that obscurity of thought often results from an equivocal use of language, equivocation that inevitably results
from the accumulation of culture and history.[53] Summarizing Descartes' position, Gouhier writes: "La pensée est donc par nature et doit rester relative-
ment indépendante des signes qui la signifient. Le langage est un instrument
et à la limite, semble-t-il, tous les instruments sont bons, serait-ce une langue
non culturelle comme le bas-breton: au philosophe d'en faire un instrument
de précision."[54] But if Gouhier sees Descartes as largely rejecting the linguistic and rhetorical legacy of Renaissance humanists to achieve this aim, can a
present day reader, encountering Descartes after Foucault and other strains of
post-structuralism, regard this putative rupture with such assurance? In other
words, even if Descartes spurns, for example, the rabid intertextuality of
Montaigne, can he so easily dispose of the "Que sçais je?" of Montaigne? Is
not his *Je* somehow still redolent of Montaigne's? Gouhier demonstrates that
Descartes often adopts the stance of *l'ingenu*: "Sous la plume de Descartes, in-
génuité signifie surtout franchise, l'évidence doit être sans fard puisqu'elle
est sans arrière-pensée."[55] Yet it is clear from Part I of the *Discourse*, where
Descartes offer "ma franchise" as one reason why his reader might be pleased
by his text, that the *ethos* of a plain spoken man is as much a construction as
any role written for the stage. If nothing else, his thought's complexity and
novelty belie such a rhetorical stance. Descartes is like the disguised Kent who
"doth affect a saucy roughness." Descartes' readers, in turn, may well agree
with Cornwall: "These kind of knaves I know, which in this plainness / Har-
bour more craft and more corrupter ends / Than twenty silly-ducking obser-
vants / That stretch their duties nicely" (7.91–92, 96–99).

MEDITATION AND DOUBT

In the *Meditations*, Descartes methodically ponders the faculty of the imagination, its functions, powers, and limits. Here the crucial links between the
imagination and hyperbolic doubt become more transparent, if also more
strained. Unlike in the *Discourse*, the beginning of the *Meditations* devotes little
narrative time setting the stage for a philosophical *via*. We learn only that
Descartes feels himself mature enough and in favorable circumstances to proceed with his destruction of received opinions. The text then charts a swift
progression: the First Meditation explores the intuitive consequences of hyperbolic doubt; the Second seizes upon the certainty of the thought "I exist";
in the Third, relying on the axiom that effects cannot be greater than their

causes, and the related axiom that if an idea can be thought (such as the notion of perfection) then it must have some basis in existence (i.e., *ex nihil, nihil fit*), Descartes concludes that since he has an idea of perfection, and that perfection must include ontological existence, then God must exist; in the Fourth, he finds that God's existence a posteriori confirms the truth of clear and distinct ideas; in the Fifth and Sixth, he likewise resurrects his certainty of mathematical ideas and establishes as probable some of his beliefs regarding material things on the basis also of the distinction between mind and body.

This famous last distinction necessarily factors in any analysis of Cartesian hyperbole, as the mind-body split is based in part on the argument that epistemological error results from the imagination's dependence on the body. In other words, if the causal reach of the body-imagination can be compassed, so can the limits of epistemological doubt. Such causality will eventually explain why Descartes is able at the end of the *Meditations* to dismiss his hyperbole as ridiculous. Hyperbole as a form of intuition is necessary, but *superiectio* from a deductive standpoint, after the certainties of the self as a *res cogitans* and of God as the source of our idea of perfection are established, becomes mere superfluity. In part this is due, as commentators beginning with Mersenne and Arnauld have stressed, with the necessity of bridging the individual, subjective perception of the *cogito* with more objective criteria that could guarantee that Descartes' certainty of having attained an unimpeachable truth can be sustained over time (be repeatable if necessary and so always be valid) and be valid for other minds as well. This urgent task is accomplished by leaning on several axioms, but principally the one asserting that a thought perceived clearly and distinctly by the *lumen naturale* must be true — an axiom that Descartes announces in his reply to Hobbes need not be subject to hyperbolic doubt.[56] Such immunity has provoked critics, beginning again with Mersenne (AT 7.124–125) and Arnauld (AT 7.214), to charge that his reasoning is circular (thus the so-called "Cartesian circle"). Put another way, Descartes needs to prove God's existence to guarantee that the certainty produced by clear and distinct ideas is not the effect of a deceiver, but in order to prove God's existence clear and distinct ideas are needed.[57]

Descartes (in letters and in the full set of seven *Objections and Replies* appended to all editions of the *Meditations* after the first) and his apologists have offered various ways out of this circle, exits that usually require various degrees of sophisticated (if sometimes sophistic) logic-chopping as to the nature of clear and distinct ideas, the Cartesian self, God, or the method itself. But a more (im)proper response, my response, to the Cartesian circle is to view it as resulting from Descartes' failure to be hyperbolic enough. By this I mean he pays a dear price for curtailing the trajectory of his intuitions where he converts it, immediately after the attainment of the *cogito*, into deductive logic, once the engine of scholasticism, but now to be retuned as the motor of the new sciences. As Gadamer argues in his reading of Nicholas of Cusa's *complicatio*, or how human language by embracing its contingency, historicity, and fundamentally metaphoric nature is able to intuit, albeit inexactly, something of the divine *explicatio*, philosophy depends, especially in the finding of first principles and concept formation, on the "genius of verbal consciousness" that can find similarities in diverse, often wildly diverse things.[58] By suddenly privileging the "ideal of logical proof" over the weird logic of his hyperbole, Descartes short-circuits his own intuitions. Indeed, it would not be outlandish to claim that the extreme claims that yield the *cogito* might have yielded still larger truths such as Spinoza discovers regarding the infinite qualities of substance in Part One of the *Ethics* or concerning the "third kind of knowledge" where one sees particular things (modes) *sub specie aeternitatis*. And while it would be silly to blame Descartes for not being Spinoza, still, if the former had not abandoned the claims of the imagination so precipitously in his thirst for the clear and distinct, the circle might have become large enough not only to prevent the synthetic, invidious comparison between the *cogito* and God's infinity, but also for thinking and being to correspond with one another in a manner more expressive than logical.[59] But by impeaching his hyperbolic doubts as absurd after they have catapulted him to his goal, Descartes undermines the very faculty of intuition that allows him to conceive of perfection (and so also God) in the first place. By retrospectively limiting hyperbole to the will and the bodily imagination — both prone to error and solipsism — he deprives his philosophy of the very figure that might have prompted certain skeptical readers to credit and share in his ambition to a greater extent. Or to risk a metaphor: they might have seen a hyperbola yearning for the infinite rather than a circle closed in on itself.

At the outset of the First Meditation, Descartes recalls how he had long wanted to free himself from all his former opinions: "I realized that it was necessary, once in the course of my life, to demolish [*esse evertenda*] everything completely and start again right from the foundations if I wanted to establish anything at all in the sciences that was stable and likely to last" [*si quid aliquando firmum & mansurum cupiam in scientiis stabilire].*[60] The six Meditations that follow aim to accomplish this "huge task" [*ingens opus*]. Each contains a *post-facto* account of what transpired on a different day, thus providing a blueprint for a new philosophic edifice. And though this blueprint is sometimes quite detailed, other times it is sketchy at best. (Further details are later provided in the *Objections and Replies*.) But perhaps this is to be expected; to reject centuries of scholastic quibbling while fending off the threat of skepticism, as embodied by the likes of Montaigne and Sánchez, requires radical measures. To give the sciences the firm ontological and epistemological grounding they so urgently need to be able to know particular things with certainty, Descartes takes the swiftest route imaginable.

Such celerity, however, makes it difficult to distinguish between invention meant for others and the heuristic tools of analysis. Expressing inordinate faith that his own language, which he would strip of all traces of scholastic jargon, can serve as a reliable instrument for his intuition, he swiftly, synecdochally, discards common experiences and "opinions." His method is ruthless, as if from the very first day of his six days of meditation he anticipates a day, the seventh, when he can rest from hyperbole:

> . . . to accomplish this, it will not be necessary for me to show that all my opinions are false, which is something I could perhaps never manage. Reason now leads me to think that I should hold back my assent from opinions which are not completely certain and indubitable just as carefully as I do from those that are patently false. So, for the purpose of rejecting all my opinions, it will be enough if I find in each of them at least some reason for doubt. And to do this I will not need to run through them all individually, which would be an endless task [*quod operis esset infiniti*]. Once the foundations of a building are undermined [*sed quia, suffossis fundamentis*], anything built on them collapses of its own accord; so I will go straight to the basic principles on which all my former beliefs rested.[61]

What he calls "reason" here is synonymous with the intuition, which has been prompted by, but now is divorced from, the imagination.[62] To sidestep the abyss of infinite quibbling, Descartes, inductively taking the mast for the ship, the sword for the man, the part for "the whole," declares he will not deductively consider each aspect of the matter at hand. He will instead hyperbolize

each doubt, however fantastic or improbable, that it may serve the same purpose as would an exhaustive argument. In this sense the entire, so-called hyperbolic reduction may perhaps also be seen as a form of "enumeration," as
Descartes describes it in Rule 7 of of the *Regulae*: "*In order to make our knowledge* [scientia] *complete, every single thing relating to our understanding must be surveyed
in a continuous and wholly uninterrupted sweep of thought, and be included in a sufficient
and well-ordered enumeration.*"[63] Notwithstanding the scope of such *scientia*,
Descartes permits no contingency or qualifications as he progresses to the desired point of certainty. His hyperbole has no rhetorical *kairos* save for his ambition's needs. And yet in the passage above his reasoning also seems
intrinsically linked to the thoroughgoing analogy between philosophy and architecture. Thus if the "quia" is granted a logical, causal force, and not just an
ornamental function, the analogy would persuade the reader as well as play a
heuristic role for Descartes. Metaphor here is a necessary adjunct to hyperbolic doubt — it makes Descartes' otherworldly project, like medieval memory theaters, seem more worldly, contingent, and thus attainable by virtue of
its invocation of the familiar activity of building (or demolishing) an edifice.

   In the Seventh Set of Objections and Replies, responding to the florid, if
acerbic Pierre Bourdin, Descartes offers another extraordinary simile, one
that would bolster his claim that hyperbolic doubt is itself commonsensical:

> . . . any true opinions which we have before we begin to philosophize se-
> riously are mixed up with many others that either are false or at least
> doubtful. And hence, in order to separate out the true ones, it is best to
> begin by rejecting all our opinions and renouncing every single one [*op-
> timum sit omnes initio rejicere, sive nihil plane ex iis non abdicare*]; this will make
> it easier, afterwards, to recognize those which were true (or discover new
> truths), so that we end up by admitting only what is true. Now this is
> just the same as if I had said that if we have a basket or tub full of apples
> and want to make sure that there are no rotten ones, we should first tip
> them all out, leaving none at all inside [*omnia esse effundenda, nihilque pror-
> sus in eo relinquendum*], and then pick up again (or get from elsewhere)
> only those apples in which no flaw [*nullum vitium*] can be detected.[64]

As refreshing as this quotidian image is, and as striking as the appearance of
the ancient formula of *omnia et nihil* may be, Gouhier is right to insist "les com-
paraisons pittoresques ont une limite."[65] Opinions tested over a lifetime are

not "just the same" as mere objects eyed for the first time in a market. The former contain a much stronger claim to empirical truth by virtue of having been
repeatedly tested. Thus the bushel of apples simile helps only partially explain
what I mean by synecdochal or inductive reasoning. A more exact analogy
would be that if it were suspected (but not confirmed) that even one bad ap-
ple is contained in the bushel, then the whole bushel would be thrown away
for good, and not just *du commencement*, and this because, the extreme logic
goes, if even only one were found to be hypothetically rotten, then any number of them, if not all of them, might also be rotten. And while he might
starve in the meantime, at least the zealous philosopher would have the absolute conviction that his stomach was pure.

Perhaps though it is less a question of zeal for Descartes than creating the
proper heuristic conditions for gaining assent. Kosman argues that in formal
terms the meditation is peculiarly suited for this. As a spiritual exercise — the
Latin title is *Renati Descartes Meditationes de Prima Philosophia in qua Dei existen-
tia et animae immortalitas demonstratur* — the *Meditations* are presented as belonging to a genre that is "about reflexive awareness, about self-consciousness and
self-examination."[66] As a literary, narrative representation of this exercise involving the reader in the meditator's fictive (but not fallacious) experience of
the world, the meditation becomes a complex discursive form and frame in
which the tensions between the evolving, analytic claims of the meditator-
narrator are balanced against synoptic claims made when the deductive perspective has already been won, for example, in the paratexts (the *Epistola*,
Praefatio, and *Synopsis*), the Sixth Meditation, and the *Objections and Replies*.
More specifically, a narratological approach to the *Meditations* requires that one
always ask which "I" is speaking, which "I" is hyperbolizing, and which "I"
is branding hyperbole as silly. Kosman rightly observes that the reader knows
how the story will turn out before reading the first word in the First Meditation and thus is always able to look to some extent beyond the narrator's doubt
toward Descartes' primary task of doing natural philosophy. Yet we also must
be able to believe the narrator's plight. If we are incredulous, then Descartes'
pedagogic and expository intentions have utterly failed. Ironically, then, given
his disdain for the excesses of rhetoric, this places enormous weight on the
written word and, alternately, great responsibility on the reader who must decide whether to accept the different stances of the analytic narrator and synthetic philosopher.

Reading the *Meditations*, we watch as hyperbolic doubt assumes monstrous proportions. Descartes commences by examining the various data that his senses give him. His first concern is knowledge of his own body. His examples ingeniously, fantastically, dismiss the possibility of certainty in this regard, even as he self-consciously flirts with the specter of madness. Momentarily relying on the Renaissance theory of humors, he imagines himself to be like one of those "madmen, whose brains are so damaged by the persistent vapours of melancholia." After then considering the possibility that his hands may not belong to him or that he is "made of glass" — an imaginative possibility wonderfully realized in Cervantes's *novela*, "El licenciado vidriera" — he quickly concludes with this self-admonition: "But such people are insane, and I would be thought equally mad if I took anything from them as a model for myself." (The Latin paronomastically plays with "mens": *sed amentes sunt isti, nec minus ipse demens viderer, si quod ab iis exemplum ad me transferrem.* The French is sharply idiomatic: *Mais quoi? ce sont des fous, et je ne serais pas moins extravagant, si je me réglais sur leurs exemples.*)[67] That a hyperbolist briefly flirts with madness should come as no surprise, given what we saw in Senecan and Shakespearean drama. The improbability, on the contrary, lies in the swift, apparently off-handed way it is dismissed as untenable in this context. But perhaps the need to buttress his reader's credulity for more radical forms of doubt makes a digression into or exploration of madness too risky for his *ethos*. Or, perhaps, as Derrida argues in a text I will consider presently, Descartes' overall pursuit of certainty is more *demens* than he is willing to admit here and thus madness is implicitly folded back into his project before and after it is explicitly denied.

Descartes' next and more fully considered step in his hyperbolic progress is to consider whether he can distinguish between dreaming and waking. After expressing bewilderment at this dilemma, he observes that painters who "try to create sirens and satyrs with the most extraordinary bodies" cannot create creatures that are "new in all respects," and thus even if a painter's "imagination is extravagant enough" to create something "completely fictitious and unreal," the colors given to these creatures must be familiar.[68] Furthermore, by analogy, even if we were to dream that we had no hands or eyes, we still would have to admit the existence of objects "more simple" such as extension, magnitude, number, place, and time. While this certainly is a curious way of pointing to what Kant will call the Transcendental Aesthetic, Descartes' aim here is not rigor per se, but rather to persuade his readers (and himself) that doubt has not yet become exhaustive. In this sense, his reliance on hyperbole's extravagance to accomplish this exhaustion is partially justified by his observation in *The Passions of the Soul* concerning the primacy of wonder as both a feeling and as a impetus to do philosophy:

> *Wonder* [*L'Admiration*]. When our first encounter with some object [*objet*] surprises us and we find it novel, or very different from what we formerly knew or what we supposed it ought to be, this causes us to wonder and to be astonished [*estonnez*] at it. Since all this may happen before we know whether or not the object is beneficial to us, I regard wonder as the first of all the passions. It has no opposite, for, if the object before us has no characteristics that surprise us, we are not moved by it at all and we consider it without passion.[69]

Descartes in the *Meditations* astonishes himself with the swift extravagance of his doubt concerning the familiar object called the body, but he also would sway the reader (and perhaps himself) with the marvelous nature of his perspective into not demanding that the train of his argument slow down, for wonder "may happen before we in any way know whether this object is agreeable to us or is not so." A more charitable solution, though, is hinted at by Lorraine Daston and Katherine Park, who show how wonder is an emotion whose worth for Descartes (and Bacon) is realized only if and when it leads to productive, attentive curiosity.[70]

However they may be interpreted, the reader's wonder and attention are further increased in the third and most violent stage of hyperbolic doubt where even geometric and arithmetic knowledge are undermined. Now Descartes asks whether it is possible that in the simplest thoughts, such as adding two plus three, or numbering the sides of a square, he may be deceiving himself.[71] Yet while he doubts that anything simpler could be imagined ("vel si quid aliud facilius fingi potest") than these simple mental operations, he then immediately imagines another possibility: the hypothesis — he calls it a "fiction" [*fictitium*] — that if God did not exist, then we would be susceptible to error in all things.[72] Moreover, "this is not a flippant or ill-considered conclusion, but is based on powerful and well thought-out reasons [*rationes*]."[73] What these "rationes" are he touches upon directly in the next paragraph, which traces the Herculean act of will involved in such hyperbole:

... non male agam, si, voluntate plane in contrarium versâ, me ipsum fallam, illasque aliquandiu omnino falsas imaginariasque esse fingam, donec, tandem, velut aequatis utrimque praejudiciorum ponderibus, nulla amplius prava consuetudo judicium meum a rectâ rerum percep⁄ tione detorqueat.

... I think it will be a good plan to turn my will in completely the op⁄ posite direction and deceive myself, by pretending for a time that these former opinions are utterly false and imaginary. I shall do this until the weight of the preconceived opinions is counterbalanced and the distort⁄ ing influence of habit no longer prevents my judgment from perceiving things correctly.[74]

Hyperbolic skepticism thus fully assumes the form of an imaginative fiction to balance out — the scale metaphor, with its connotations of both objective jus⁄ tice and science, works to mask the arbitrariness inherent in this proposition — the weight of error accumulated by a lifetime spent feeling and thinking in the world. It is a willed, artificial, absolutist stance taken only for a "certain time" [*aliquandiu*], for it looks forward to another time when his judgment and deductive powers will work correctly and no longer anamorphotically ("*detorqueat*"). It builds on the "fiction" of God's nonexistence to portray the philosopher as a passive victim of his own imagination. But this "fiction," as the friendly Arnauld observes in *The Fourth Set of Objections*, may well be "dangerous for those of only moderate intelligence."[75] In response, Descartes makes a slight concession, but then defends his strategy with a pointed metaphor: "Although fire and knives [*ignis & ferrum*] cannot be safely handled by careless people or children [*imprudentibus aut pueris*], no one thinks that this is a reason for doing without them altogether, since they are so useful for hu⁄ man life."[76] Hence either we assent to his method or we risk being branded children and fools playing with "fire and knives." Refusing to keep his hyper⁄ bolic sword, his methodical doubt, in his scabbard, Descartes boldly praises himself and wounds his detractors.

Yet as Janet Broughton sees it, by availing himself of the fiction of God's nonexistence in order to achieve his larger philosophic ambitions, the medi⁄ tator irrevocably turns his back on positions that still may be ascribed to commonsense: "I think the 'I' of the *Meditations* does not have a set of episte⁄ mological beliefs and goals that we can see as fully rational . . . [N]o ordinary person, untutored in Cartesian metaphysics, would ever have a good reason for suspending judgment about something simply by considering the radical grounds for doubt. This is a serious internal flaw in Descartes' representation of the method of doubt, one that I think he does not recognize."[77] Whether or not Descartes produces unintended consequences with his hyperbole — a question addressed in the next chapter — I agree with Broughton that Cartesian doubt "is strategic in character."[78] Yet the "flaw" results only if one applies "fully rational" criteria to Descartes' philosophic narratives. Other criteria may redeem, if only provisionally, the route Descartes takes. Like the conceits of the Baroque and metaphysical poets, Cartesian doubt is directed at a sophisticated audience already accustomed to suspending judgment long enough to let the author develop his thoughts with the freest license (*franchise*). But Descartes has no interest in imitating the endless, *chiaroscuro* folds inherent in the aesthetic play of Shakespeare, Góngora, and their ilk. Instead, he claims an immediacy and transparency for his account of his experience of doubt that he would have every intelligent reader of good will, every *honnête homme*, accept as "clear and distinct," and therefore also as true.

Chapter Thirteen

Hyperbole and Descartes' Will to Reason

> Meanwhile the mind, from pleasures less,
> Withdraws into its happiness:
> The mind, that ocean where each kind
> Does straight its own resemblance find,
> Yet it creates, transcending these,
> Far other worlds, and other seas,
> Annihilating all that's made
> To a green thought in a green shade.
> — Andrew Marvell, from "The Garden"

GREAT EXPECTATIONS

Never does Descartes demand more credulity than when he looses his "evil genius" upon readers.[1] Having learned to trust his *ethos* and neo-geometric method, we suspend disbelief at this specter in the light of the philosopher's epistemological aims and in the face of the specter's rhetorical *enargeia* and *energeia*. But surely we also experience the satisfaction proffered by any compelling narrative as Descartes amplifies his willingness to doubt into its most monstrous forms:

> I will suppose therefore that not God, who is supremely good and the source of truth, but some malicious demon [*genium aliquem malignum (un certain mauvais génie)*] of the utmost power and cunning has employed all his energies to deceive me. I shall think that the sky, the air, the earth, colours, shapes, sounds and all external things are merely the delusions of dreams which he has devised to ensnare my judgement [*quibus insidias*

credulitati meae tetendit]. I shall consider myself as not having hands or eyes, or flesh, or blood or senses, but as falsely believing that I have all these things. I shall stubbornly and firmly persist in this meditation; and, even if it is not in my power to know any truth, I shall at least do what is in my power, that is, resolutely guard against assenting to any false-hoods, so that the deceiver [*iste deceptor (ce grand trompeur)*], however pow-erful and cunning [*quantumvis potens, quantumvis callidus*] he may be, will be unable to impose on me in the slightest degree.[2]

While there is an undeniable drama in the conflict between this "grand trompeur" — a phantasmagoric refashioning of the Christian devil — and the ambitious philosopher, still greater pathos lodges in the paratactic account of how the macrocosmic and microcosmic worlds have become realms of deceit. Now Descartes' cherished reason has joined sensation as a source of error. As Gouhier dramatically puts it: "Sous le soleil de ce Satan épistémolo-gique, toutes les vérités se flétrissent . . ."[3] This is Descartes' *noche oscura* — the moment when all his former convictions seem lost and no sign of salvation ap-pears imminent. At the end of the meditation, feeling (or feigning) despair, he even compares himself to a prisoner who would prefer to remain in captivity than face "the excessive darkness" [*inextricabiles . . . tenebras*] produced by con-templating such deceit.[4]

Feeling as if he had "fallen unexpectedly into a deep whirlpool," Descartes begins the Second Meditation by recreating the pathos and confu-sion caused by the *mauvais génie*. Supplementing this striking image of the meditator as a drowning man is a comparison that conveys another mood al-together:

> Nihil nisi punctum petebat Archimedes, quod esset firmum & immo-bile, ut integram terram loco dimoveret magna, ut integram terram loco dimoveret; magna quoque speranda sunt, si vel minimum quid inven-ero quod certum sit & inconcussum.

> Archimedes used to demand just one firm and immovable point in or-der to shift the entire earth; so I too can hope for great things if I manage to find just one thing, however slight, that is certain and unshakeable.[5]

While implying that his philosophy progresses *more geometrico*, this epic com-parison also reveals a great deal about Descartes' inveterate *superbia*. Just when he has hyperbolically reduced all that can be thought with certainty to apparent nothingness, he metaphorically transforms himself — a narrator ambiguously bridging antiquity and some ahistorical, fictive, present tense — into a proleptic "punctum" that will, Archimedes-like, move the world. Hence while his provisional, hyperbolic use of doubt promises to be an instrumental response to skepticism, here we see that his philosophic ambitions, his great expectations ("magna . . . speranda sunt"), are not to be dashed by any physical impediments. Moreover, if we recall that the evil genius has just denied the possibility of mathematical knowledge, then it becomes clear it is not Archimedes' mathematics, but rather his ambition that, properly speaking, serves as Descartes' model. And though he will now quickly move to reformulate and amplify the crucial *cogito ergo sum* sections of the *Discourse*, the pathos of his rhetoric suggests that even after the desired Archimedean point of certainty is reached, it may be difficult to erase the memory of the vertiginous, hyperbolic trajectory that the *cogito* has traveled.

Because the imagination has been the primary vehicle by which he arrives at his one certain thought, after clinching the ontological argument and establishing himself as a *res cogitans*, Descartes still must distinguish between the claims of reason and those of the imagination. Treating the "least doubt" the same as complete doubt has raised, a posteriori, the question of what it means to say (only): "I am still something [*ego aliquid sum*]."[6] The overreaching philosopher, who still has nothing but this "aliquid," needs and wants more:

> I will use my imagination [*imaginabor*] (to see if I am not something more).[7] I am not that structure of limbs which is called a human body. I am not even some thin vapour which permeates the limbs — not a wind, fire, air, breath, or whatever I depict in my imagination [*non ventus, non ignis, non vapor, non halitus, non quidquid mihi fingo*]; for these are things which I have supposed to be nothing.[8]

In what sense does he now exercise his imagination? Sobered by previous intuitions, such as the specter of the evil genius and the mad vision of his body made of glass, the imagination at this point in the *Meditations* has limited possibilities. Hence triumphant reason, now fortified by the experience of having thought with clarity and distinctness, usurps the role the imagination played in the progress toward the truth of the *cogito*:

... I can make judgements only about things which are known to me. I know that I exist; the question is, what is this "I" that I know? If the "I" is understood strictly as we have been taking it, then it is quite certain that knowledge of it does not depend on things of whose existence I am as yet unaware, so it cannot depend on any of the things which I invent in my imagination. And this very word "invent" [*effingo*] shows me my mistake. It would indeed be a case of fictitious invention if I used my imagination to establish that I was something or other; for imagining is simply contemplating the shape or image of a corporeal thing. Yet now I know for certain both that I exist and at the same time that all such images and, in general, everything relating to the nature of body, could be mere dreams <and chimeras> [*nihil sunt praeter insomnia*].[9]

The rub, then, is that after the *cogito* has been secured, such "insomnia" no longer have heuristic value. Extravagance in all its forms must now be purged as dangerously inaccurate. When Descartes contemplates what it means to be a *res cogitans* only to hit on a string of participial verbs — "dubitans, intelligens, affirmans, negans, volens, nolens, imaginans quoque, & sentiens"[10] — he indicates that his rhetoric has outstripped his analysis of how we can know what these various faculties are. It is in this context of needing to cure his mind ("gaudet aberrare mens mea"), but especially his imagination, of obscurity and inaccuracy that the celebrated example of "this piece of wax" is offered.

By deictically inviting us to consider a particular, commonplace object as if it were present at hand, Descartes initially puts little strain on the imagination. The image of the wax, and thus also its attendant qualities like smell, color, etc. are readily available to every reader. But then, like a cinematographer, Descartes sets the image in motion. Asking us first to imagine that the wax is melting, he then inquires whether, after observing its various mutations, we really knew its essence beforehand. Answering this negatively, he concludes that at best one can know with certainty only that the wax is a thing with extension. But it also turns out such knowledge is not produced by the imagination at all, for "the infinitude" of the wax's possible shapes outstrips the capacity of any of our senses. Only the mind (*mens*) in the form of the intuition (*inspectio*) can have a "clear and distinct" perception of the wax. Significantly, it is here that Descartes critiques "common sense" (*sensus communis*) and takes a swipe at "ordinary language." Words, he notes, often impair judgment as we often name things, such as wax or men, without judging their internal, unchanging, and therefore essential qualities. By the same token, he warns: " . . . one who wants to achieve knowledge above the ordinary level should feel ashamed at having taken ordinary ways of talking as a basis for doubt."[11] Such shame depends on a bias against those who would quibble, etymologize, or, more generally, take the word for the thing. Seen from another perspective, it warns readers that his own words here and throughout the *Meditations* are abstracted from ordinary usage and contingency. They are addressed, as the *Preface to the Reader* suggests, to the few rather than the many. For the few are supposed to be savvy enough to treat Descartes' language as instrumental rather than as an object of study in itself.

That Descartes goes on to use the knowledge of the wax as a secondary proof of the self's existence and then to show how the self's idea of perfection necessitates God's existence confirms the ontological preoccupations of the treatise, but also its essential solipsism, a structural solipsism tinged by the philosopher's *superbia* or what Valéry calls his "will to power."[12] Truth and falsity find their final criteria in the self's existence, in its understanding and *voluntas*. As Descartes observes in the Fourth Meditation:

> . . . when I look more closely at myself and inquire into the nature of my errors . . . I notice that they depend on two concurrent causes, namely on the faculty of knowledge [*facultate cognoscendi*] which is in me, and on the faculty of choice or freedom of the will [*facultate eligendi*]; that is, they depend on both the intellect and the will [*voluntate*] simultaneously . . . Indeed, I think it is very noteworthy that there is nothing else in me which is so perfect and so great that the possibility of a further increase in its perfection or greatness is beyond my understanding. If, for example, I consider the faculty of understanding [*facultatem intelligendi*], I immediately recognize that in my case it is extremely slight and very finite, and I at once form the idea of an understanding which is much greater — indeed supremely great and infinite [*multo majoris, imo maximae atque infinitae*]; and from the very fact that I can form an idea of it, I perceive that it belongs to the nature of God. Similarly, if I examine the faculties of memory or imagination, or any others, I discover that in my case each of these faculties is weak and limited [*tenuem & circumscriptam*], while in the case of God it is immeasurable [*immensam*]. It is only the will, or freedom of choice [*Sola est voluntas, sive arbitrii libertas*] which

I experience in me to be so great that the idea of any faculty is beyond my grasp [*ut nullius majoris ideam apprehendam*]; so much so that it is above all in virtue of the will that I understand myself to bear in some way the image and likeness [*similitudinem*] of God.[13]

In its capacity for error and, remarkably, its participation in the divine, the will outstrips reason and the imagination.[14] The way Descartes maps the limits of these faculties even as he gestures at inexpressibility ("ut nullius majoris ideam apprehendam") seems almost to parody medieval and Renaissance attempts at accommodation. Informed by emerging Counter Reformation notions of the individual conscience, his ambivalent epideixis of the *voluntas* is central to the larger structural task in the text's second half of reordering knowledge of ourselves and the world on the basis of the certainty provided by God's existence.[15] Having audaciously cast the *cogito* as a "similitudinem Dei," Descartes bridges the gap between the "very weak and limited" nature of the individual mind and the nature of God which he conceives of as "immense, incomprehensible and infinite."[16] Once secured, the metaphysical knowledge of God hinted at here will help secure the reach of human knowledge. It will also drastically limit the meditator's rhetorical fancy.

How, then, does Descartes' devaluation of the will and imagination affect an overall understanding of the role of hyperbole in the *Meditations*? Gueroult's invaluable "objective analysis" of the *Meditations* describes the "architectonic" that brings Descartes' philosophic discourse closer to works of art as well as his "attempts to compel the intelligence of the subject to a judgment ratifying the truth of doctrinal teaching."[17] More to the point, Gueroult incisively describes the dynamics of Cartesian hyperbole. He sees hyperbolic doubt in the *Meditations* as being more methodological, if no less "universal" or "radical" than in the *Discourse*. It is methodological since it assists the exposition if not also the construction of the text; it is, I would add, also a "path" [*hodos*] to an end. It is also methodological since after each of the first two stages of doubt, one type of knowledge remains unimpeached only to have that type assailed in the next stage (though in the third and most radical stage the *cogito* alone remains). It is universal since it treats as absolute what may only be relative and so takes what may be a minor, transitory doubt and transforms it into an all-encompassing, non-contingent conclusion. It is "radical" as it is fictive, willed, and ultimately depends on the extreme hypothesis of a transcendent evil genius. Not only does Descartes doubt the external world's reality, but he also, through what Gueroult calls "the intervention of [the] free will ... which is infinite relative to our understanding and capable of making an attempt against nature," doubts those mathematical and so metaphysical notions that in the first stages of doubt furnished knowledge about simple and general things.[18]

Gueroult is also that rare commentator to acknowledge the proper rhetorical heritage of Cartesian hyperbole:

> Methodological and systematic doubt, which is fictive and proceeds not from things but from the resolution to doubt, differs from true doubt which results from the nature of things and can engender skepticism. It is because of this systematic and generalized character that it deserves the name *hyperbolic*, in accordance with its etymology: from *hyperbole*, excess; in rhetoric it designates a figure by which one gives the object in consideration a higher degree of something, whether positive or negative, it does not possess in actuality. Similarly, there is a twofold principle of this doubt: treat as *absolutely false* what is merely *doubtful*, reject *universally*, as *always* deceptive what could have deceived me *sometimes*; this responds perfectly to the meaning of the world hyperbolic, by accomplishing the hyperbolic leap in two different senses.[19]

To amplify: the first sense refers to hyperbolic doubt based on "natural reasons to doubt" in which empirical data is skeptically, methodically, interrogated for whatever "simple" object — be it color, extension, or fundamental mathematical properties — that can survive the natural errors of the senses or the extreme fictions forged by madness and dream. The second sense refers to hyperbolic doubt based on the "metaphysical opinion" in the form of the evil genius. This is the "most hyperbolic doubt of all ... because, being absolutely universal, it attacks what the dream argument could not have attacked, namely, the intrinsic objective validity of clear and distinct ideas." In so doing, "this voluntary fiction" is an "action of the infinite will" that defies ordinary understanding to deny the "simple" and hitherto certain objects of daily experience.[20] But again, the willed actions of someone lacking certainty differs from those of someone with epistemological certainty and thus (as we saw in the discussion of the piece of wax) aware of his powers and limitations. For this reason, Gueroult regards Cartesian hyperbole as both a subjective and objective "tool":

The voluntary and methodological character of this fiction is high-
lighted by its dual quality as problem-solving device and as a psychological tool: in making possible an operation of the will that must be
carried out against the habits and temptations of the probable, it is a
psychological tool; as giving shape to the principle that ordains the
treatment of the doubtful as false, it is the analogue of these fictive constructions of geometry and astronomy that allow one to accomplish calculations and demonstrations, and to exclude doubtful notions for the
benefit of certain notions.[21]

The "fiction" of doubt, in other words, is an analytic one. Of a different kind
than the fictive details concerning the *poêle* in the *Discourse*, or those the narrator employs to describe the temporal succession of his meditative practice in
the *Meditations*, the fictive or literary elements constituting Descartes' pseudo-
via negativa largely eschew verisimilitude in the face of cognitive demands
made by the intuition itself. As in the thought experiment involving a piece of
wax placed before a fire, the mimetic elements matter to the philosophical hyperbolist only in so far as they do not provoke incredulity. What the evil genius
might look like is irrelevant; it matters only that the cognitive process it represents be credible long enough for the reader to want to take the next step.

Furthermore, this hyperbolic "fiction" differs starkly from the discursive
practices of thinkers like Montaigne or Cavell, who make historical and material contingency constantly felt, or who foreground the presence of other, often dissenting voices. Another point of comparison is offered by Cervantes,
who likewise employs an ingenious "psychological tool" to explore the shifting frontiers between madness, reason, doubt, and certainty. While Descartes
early in the *Discourse* dismisses "les extravagances des paladins de nos romans," his use of hyperbole, like Quixote's, is also "voluntary" ("je me résolus de feindre"). It, too, institutes a powerful dialectic of *engaño* and *desengaño*
that has epic consequences for the project of modernity. Yet the hermeneutic
demands that Cervantes makes on his reader are of a different order, not only
because as we read *Don Quixote* his hero's hyperbole becomes increasingly
contagious, dialogic, and pathetic, but also because as the novel progresses its
satiric force becomes radically diffuse and self-reflexive. Furthermore,
Descartes' hyperbole relies on an anatomy of the imagination far removed
from the Huarte-inspired vision of ingenuity, madness, and melancholy that
Cervantes has his hero explore on the plains of La Mancha. And yet this

most "Cartesian of novels" also provokes readers to rethink early modern methods of producing knowledge.[22]

In a very early work, *Cogitationes privatae* (which includes the *Olympica*), Descartes defends the poetic imagination's heuristic powers in a way that briefly brings him closer to more traditional if also hermetic ideas concerning the muses and divine inspiration:

> It may seem surprising to find weighty judgments [*graves sententiae*] in the writings of the poets rather than the philosophers. The reason is that the poets were driven to write by enthusiasm and the force of the imagina-tion. We have within us the sparks of knowledge [*semina scientiae*], as in flint: philosophers extract them through reason, but poets force them out through the sharp blows of the imagination, so that they shine more brightly.[23]

While Norman Kemp Smith finds "little trace" of this "inspired" species of the imagination in Descartes' later writings, surely, given this defense and the metaphorics informing it, the more fantastic, fictive aspects of the heuristic rhetoric in the *Discourse* and *Meditations* cannot all be ascribed to the "action of reason."[24] In other words, to what extent does Descartes hear or permit to be heard the commonsensical reactions that one would expect his hyperbolic fic-tion to provoke? The *Meditations* only really begins to become dialogic, I think, when the *Objections and Replies* — the first six of which Descartes included in the first edition, with the seventh added in the second edition — are consid-ered. Roger Ariew, Jean-Luc Marion, and Jean-Marie Beyssade have variously made the case that Descartes used the *Objections and Replies* to supplement and correct the doctrine of the *Meditations*.[25] Still, with the exception of the in-stance I cited in the last chapter involving Arnauld and the "fiction" of God, these changes do not seem to have appreciably altered the skeptical, hyperbolic trajectory that results in the *cogito*. Indeed, even if one finds that in Caterus, Mersenne, Hobbes, Arnauld, Gassendi, Bourdin, and Dinet, Descartes found viable interlocutors, they seemed to have caused him, as Popkin and others have argued, to fall defensively back on the essential subjectivity of the *cogito*.[26] The objective concerns of others are barely heard. On the stark, meta-physical stage of the *Meditations*, no mocking Fool or Sancho Panza causes the hero to reconsider the motives for or veracity of his exaggeration; no implaca-ble beloved refuses his overreaching desires; no intransigent windmill refuses to be renamed. In short, hyperbole, which was supposed to open up the objective possibilities of knowledge and then disappear, continues, *malgré lui*, to define his vision's contours. Timothy Reiss argues that the discourse of Cartesian subjectivity is ultimately imbricated with "issues of history and memory"; further, his reading of the subject as a "passage technique" is a persuasive, necessary corrective to the commonplace interpretation of the *cogito* as signaling the sudden advent of "the modern, western, self-possessive, centered and willful subject."[27] Still, Cartesian hyperbole seems particularly immune to the claims of history, memory, or for that matter dialogue. To extend the concept of a "passage technique" to hyperbole, to see it chiefly as provisional, instrumental, or as a concept separate from the conclusions to which it leads, leaves its stubborn absolutism and solipsism untouched. Put another way, the fallibility of memory, as Descartes describes it in the *Regulae*, may be said to precipitate the heuristic device of the Evil Genius in the *Meditations*, where Cartesian hyperbolism reaches its apex and where temporality itself is denied: "I will believe that my memory tells me lies, and that none of the things that it reports ever happened."[28]

HYPERBOLE/A

The question remains whether Descartes' hyperbolic method can be reconciled with his avowed ideal of philosophy based on principles borrowed from geometric and other "pure" mathematical reasoning. Is his use of hyperbole to discover that first certain and distinct idea akin to the search for axioms in geometry? Does it depend on unspoken axioms that will only be annunciated after the fact? Geometrical reasoning as embodied, say, by an Euclidean proposition, proceeds by deduction or synthetic logic. The hypothesis of Proposition 1.6 ("if in a triangle two angles be equal to one another, the sides which subtend the equal angles will also be equal to one another"), is stated at the beginning, and then methodical, logically consistent steps are taken to prove the hypothesis true — thus the Latin phrase that, as tradition has it, concludes many propositions: *Quod erat demonstrandum*. But Euclidean geometry, as well as so-called Non-Euclidean geometries, to say nothing of Descartes' own algebraic geometry (which is expounded in one of the three *Essais* appended to the *Discourse* to demonstrate the fruits of his method), are all initially constructed on a set of nominally self-evident axioms that once accepted admit no revision. In comparison, the method of hyperbolic doubt is initially predicated upon no discernible axioms save perhaps the unexamined

but axiomatic structures of grammar (for example, that every predicative sentence needs a subject and verb).[29] Yet by the time the *cogito* is perceived, the veracity of the *lumen naturale* has also proven axiomatic. Descartes never states it
forthrightly (though he does imply it in his replies to Hobbes), but the existence of a single clear and distinct idea is the *propositio* that fuels his invention.
This goal is reached not by consistent, geometric logic — such as two right
angles must always be equal to one another — but by the extreme logic of the
synecdoche, that is, if any part of a proposition admits doubt then the whole
proposition must be doubted. Geometric *ratio* becomes exemplary only after
oratio runs its intuitive course.

In the Fifth Meditation, the Cartesian subject discovers that it can conceive clearly and distinctly the non-material truths of geometry and arithmetic. It then argues by analogy — or, as some have insisted, by circular
logic — that "existence can no more be separated from the essence of God
than the fact that its three angles equal two right angles can be separated from
the essence of a triangle, or than the idea of a mountain can be separated from
the idea of a valley."[30] When Gueroult thus compares the method of hyperbolic doubt to the "fictive constructions of geometry . . . that allow one to accomplish . . . demonstrations, and to exclude doubtful notions for the benefit
of certain notions," he may be taken to mean that Cartesian doubt proceeds
by intuitive reasoning that is hypothetical much in the same analytic, synthetic, and self-consistent manner that Wesley Trimpi argues that literary discourse can be.[31] It is not hypothetical in the sense of Copernicus's heliocentric
theory. Copernicus — especially if Osiander's preface is ignored — assumed
that the world was made in such a way that humanity could and should be
able to comprehend it, and thus that the criteria of truth are to be found
first in the world and not in ourselves. The proof of his hypothesis, unlike
Descartes', could therefore be empirically discovered. Hans Blumenberg thus
concludes that for Descartes "the rational construction of the system is independent of the real structure of the world; the ideas of Creation are inaccessible, and the *ens perfectissimum* owes man nothing beyond not allowing the
world to become the great deception of his cognitive faculty."[32]

More surprising than the fact that Descartes belatedly turns to the abstractions of geometry to shore up his epistemological paradigm is that hyperbole becomes hypothesis just when he and his contemporaries, such as
Barrozi, Desargues, and Pascal, are making the geometry of conic sections
and specifically of the hyperbola exemplary of the epistemological method he

would use in his metaphysics.[33] But if such treatises seem remote from the issue at hand, I would observe, first, that they all explore the possibility of representing and reasoning about figures that involve infinity. Second, given the
functions generating these different conic sections, the hyperbola is effectively
an exaggerated ellipse, which, in turn, is an exaggerated circle. Like Cartesian hyperbole, therefore, the geometer's hyperbola may be said to bend reason
to its breaking point in order to reconfigure reason's domain.[34] Third, at least
one thinker close to Descartes encourages the hyperbola/e analogy as well.
Mersenne writes in his *Harmonie universelle* (1627):

> One can be ignited in divine love by the comparison to coals heated by
> parallel rays at the focus of the parabola, hyperbola or ellipse . . . And if,
> rather than God complaining about his people when he says, *Factus sum
> illis in parabolam,* we take it in another sense, understanding a reference to
> the conic parabola, it is a parable that will inflame our hearts with his
> love, and a hyperbole that gathers and unites our distracted thoughts,
> *Dispersiones Israel congregibit,* and directs it to a single point, of which it is
> said, *Porro unum est necessarium* . . . and we will . . . even be able to ap-
> propriate the light of science and the fire that results . . . by imitating the
> convex hyperbola that gathers at the exterior focus that which is derived
> from the interior focus.[35]

While Mersenne's witty use of the conic sections as metaphors for spiritual
states starkly contrasts with Descartes' disdain for the humanist practice of
treating a word's material, etymological aspects as a source of truth, nonetheless, it is consonant with his friend's belief that geometry can be exemplary for
metaphysical speculation.[36]

For all this, Descartes is keen to show that "first philosophy" does not
ignore the world and the body, especially since his natural philosophy needs
an objective ontological basis.[37] Accordingly, in the Sixth and final Meditation, he considers the existence of material things. Here he addresses from an
ontological perspective the epistemological question that precipitated the initial step of hyperbolic doubt in the First Meditation. He analyzes, that is, the
faculty whereby we think we know the nature of material objects: the "imagination . . . seems to be nothing else but an application of the cognitive faculty
of knowledge to a body that is intimately present to it, and which therefore exists."[38] But because he has by now already established that God cannot be a

deceiver, and thus that error cannot have a metaphysical cause, the imagination now becomes the passive faculty that perceives error through its perception of corporeal things. In short, the imagination may lead to certain
ontological insights, but given its relation to the body it is also necessarily imprecise and unreliable as a source of knowledge. It may well be asked therefore
whether the methodological use of the imagination hyperbolically depicted in
Part IV of the *Discourse* (". . . et que je rejetasse, comme absolument faux,
tout ce en quoi je pourrais imaginer le moindre doute, afin de voir s'il ne
resterait point, après cela, quelque chose en ma créance, qui fût entièrement indubitable") or in The First Meditation (". . . non male agam, si, voluntate
plane in contrarium versâ, me ipsum fallam, illasque aliquandiu omnino falsas imaginariasque esse fingam") is the same faculty being dissected here, or
whether it is what Descartes synthetically examines in the Second Meditation
after the *cogito* has been established.[39] In the first two passages, the imagination
is synonymous with his ability to will the process of intuition; but now that
the will's object has been attained, the imagination, along with its beloved hyperbole, has lost all legitimacy. Now Descartes would distinguish between
imagination and what he calls "puram intellectionem."[40] A triangle can be
imagined, but a chiliagon cannot, because with its thousand sides the latter shape exceeds the visual imagination's abilities; instead, it can only be
conceived of by reason in its purest, non-aesthetic form. The imagination is
where aesthetic perception and the will to pursue intuition first join forces; but
reason demands their assent and subservience on its own abstract, absolutist
terms.[41]

In narrative terms, the questions raised in the Sixth Meditation are presented as belated acts of "memory." Taking an essentially a posteriori or deductive approach, this last Meditation reads almost like a postscript. From the
cogito's secure vantage point, Descartes examines: first, those matters that he
formerly held to be true; second, the grounds why he doubted these "truths";
third, which of these truths he "must now believe." As for his first concern,
he concludes that "nature" — which consists of our experience of space and
time, our mental habits, and instincts — had led him to believe certain ambiguous things. And while his second concern is not so much addressed as de-
flected (he effectively summarizes the first two Meditations), his third concern
makes explicit the new path of deduction I outlined above. Since he now has
self-knowledge and knowledge of God, and since deception in thought cannot come from God, he concludes that the act of imagination, which may or

may not produce error, must be in some manner corporeal. In this way he reverses the normal order of intuition (i.e., from the physical to the metaphysical) by placing what Hegel calls "sense-certainty" last. Further, the manner in
which he represents nature here signals the impossibility of establishing any
kind of certain causal or epistemic links between his mind and the world.
The microcosmic-macrocosmic analogy has been shattered, or at the very
least, shunted off, like a doddering grandmother, to some dark corner in the
house. Human nature no longer is linked analogically, sympathetically, to the
divine; for when it comes to nature, Descartes insists: "My sole concern . . . is
with what God has bestowed on me as a combination of mind and body."
But he hastens to add, human nature "is not omniscient. And this is not surprising, since man is a limited thing, and so it is only fitting that his perfection should be limited" [*quod non mirum, quia, cum homo sit res limitata, non alia
illi competit quam limitatae perfectionis*].[42] With these two tenets in place, the self
is atomized and irrevocably separated from the epistemological-metaphoric
structure that allowed earlier Renaissance thinkers such as Pico, Paracelsus,
and Kepler to understand the "little world of man" as ontologically and epistemologically linked to the greater world of creatures.[43]

Tellingly, when Descartes later in the same *Meditation* offers his comparison of the "nature" of the human body to the "nature" of a machine (specifically, a man sick with dropsy to a badly constructed clock) he is careful to treat
the word "nature" as a purely verbal characterization, which is "quite extraneous to the things to which it is applied" [*rebusque de quibus dicitur extrinseca*].[44]
This is because such a word ignores the fact that human "nature" derives from
the "composite" of body and mind. From a rhetorical perspective, then, this
deconstruction of his own analogy suggests that he considers his ubiquitous
architectural and path metaphorics in both the *Discourse* and the *Meditations* to
be similarly "extrinsic." It also indicates that the discursive elements in his "fable," neo-Augustinian confession, or Loyolan meditation, which fitfully an-
chor his rhetoric in the particularity and contingency of the world, are merely
ornamental or at best pedagogic. Yet if analogy and metaphor have no intrinsic cognitive function, why is Descartes willing to ascribe hyperbole such a
fundamental epistemological role? Why was the epistemic distinction between
words and things not invoked earlier? Is his hyperbolic fiction merely a tool to
be discarded as soon as the light of reason shines brightly enough? Or is it, in
fact, a rhetorical *machina* — notwithstanding his reply to Gassendi quoted earlier? As wisdom grows, Quixote renounces knight errantry, Pantagruel spurns

Panurge, and Prince Hal outgrows Falstaff, so why should not Descartes turn his back on the evil genius?

It is only in the final paragraph of the *Meditations* that the reformed fabu⁄list, ready to travel pragmatically on the road of science, reveals the degree of artifice and barely suppressed violence involved in his initial intuitions, which were still dependent on the imagination:

> For I know that in matters regarding the well⁄being of the body, all my senses report the truth much more frequently than not. Also, I can al⁄most always make use of more than one sense to investigate the same thing; and in addition, I can use both my memory, which connects pres⁄ent experiences with preceding ones, and my intellect, which has by now examined all the causes of error. Accordingly, I should not have any further fears about the falsity of what my senses tell me every day; on the contrary, the exaggerated doubts of the last few days should be dis⁄missed as laughable [*sed hyperbolicae superiorum dierum dubitationes, ut risu dignae, sunt explodendae* (*Et je dois rejeter les doutes de ce jours passées, comme hy⁄perboliques et ridicules*)]. This applies especially to the principal reason for doubt, namely my inability to distinguish between sleeping and being awake.[45]

The way his diction admits of qualification ("almost always . . . more than one") and contingency ("what my senses tell me every day") was entirely ab⁄sent when hyperbole reigned supreme. But lest we forget, in "these last few days" he has successfully proved the existence of the self, God, and now also material things including the human body. That Descartes, as a parting ges⁄ture to his *culto* readers, rejects his hyperbolic doubts as "risu dignae" belatedly confirms an awareness of hyperbole's risks. Sensitive now to the dangers to his *ethos*, all hyperboles are exiled ("sunt explodendae") as creatures too ridicu⁄lous for philosophic consideration. After hyperbole's extreme peaks and val⁄leys, its dialectic of doubt and certainty, another kind of *apatheia* returns to replace what was established initially by the *morale par provision*; though now the self⁄assured mind is poised to do science rather than metaphysics. More generally though, by so utterly rejecting his narrator's hyperbole and the "common uncertainty respecting sleep," and by insisting now on an exact, "clear and distinct" correspondence between mind (language) and world, Descartes exposes himself to a posteriori charges of rhetorical overreaching and deception. Indeed, it appears from the vantage point of pure reason that there never was a cause, a *res*, to justify such exaggeration. (Wanting to remove such misunderstandings, Spinoza gives the *Ethics* a synthetic structure.)

When Descartes characterizes his doubts as "metaphysical," he tells us that this is the same as saying they are provisional and hyperbolic.[46] As for their ridiculousness, in the Seventh Set of Objections with Replies, he suggests that truly ridiculous is the misunderstanding of those who refuse to credit his doubt with producing certainty. Responding to Pierre Bourdin's Baroque use and abuse of the architectural metaphor to critique the possibility of any knowledge at all emerging from his hyperbolic doubt, Descartes replies: "Here none of the bricklayer's complaints against the architect are more ridiculous [*magis ridicule*] than the complaints which my critic has devised against me. In rejecting what is doubtful I no more cut myself off from knowledge of the truth than the architect's excavation precluded the subsequent building of the chapel . . ."[47] Likewise, he rejects the charge that his discourse suffers from the sins of "excess."[48] He insists that he has adopted this "manner" to combat the Skeptics, not to become one himself, as Bourdin charges. Bourdin, he continues, neither realizes that truth is "indivisible" and so immune to all skeptical doubts, nor that the sect of the Skeptics is a clear and present danger. In other words, any philosophy that fails to establish absolutely God's existence and the soul's immortality is worthless. The *Meditations*, Descartes boasts, achieves these goals in a manner that outstrips all previous attempts. And given its epistemological success, it can never be accused of "the one error which is the hallmark of the sceptics, namely excessive doubt [*nimiam dubitationem*]."[49] The end justifies the means. Indeed, it is Bourdin's text, "si pleine de paroles et si vide de raisons," that deserves blame.

"POUR BRANLER TOUT LE MONDE"

Descartes' conception of the philosopher's will powered by hyperbole begs to be compared with representations of extreme *voluntas* by Petrarch, Donne, Shakespeare, and other Renaissance and Baroque writers. The most obvious difference is that Descartes' will operates only in the notional realm; it does not work in a world where other people act or react. There are no motives, agents, revenge plots, or storms linked to his hyperbole, other than those related to his desire for self-mastery and truth. However vivid his *poêle* or piece of wax may be as fictions — a vividness recently heightened by Durs Grünbein's long narrative poem, *Vom Schnee* — they cannot respond with their own voices to contest Descartes' remaking of reality.

Such deaf ambition recalls the increasingly Baroque desires of the Petrarchist lover who no longer expects any response from the frigid beloved, and who has retreated into a linguistic labyrinth of self-reflection and refraction. If this seems far-fetched, consider the uncannily exact echo of Cartesian hyperbolic rhetoric and diction in this sonnet by Jean de Sponde (1557–1595):

> Tu disais, Archimède, ainsi qu'on nous rapporte,
> Qu'on te donnât un point pour bien te soutenir,
> Tu branlerais le monde, et le ferais venir,
> Comme un faix plus léger de lieu en lieu s'emporte.
> Puisque ton art si beau, ta main était si forte,
> Si tu pouvais encore au monde revenir,
> Dans l'amour que mon cœur s'efforce à retenir,
> Tu trouverais ton point peut-être en quelque sorte.
> Pourrait-on voir jamais plus de solidité
> Qu'en ce qui branle moins plus il est agité
> Et prend son assurance en l'inconstance même:
> Il est sûr, Archimède, et je n'en doute point:
> Pour branler tout le Monde et s'assurer d'un point,
> Il te fallait aimer aussi ferme que j'aime.[50]

You said, Archimedes, so the story goes, that if one gave you a point to stand on, you would shake the world, and cause it, like a deed of no weight, to move from place to place. Since your art is so beautiful, your hand so strong, if you could return to the world again, in the Love that my heart struggles to retain, you would perhaps find your point in some way. Will one ever see more solidity then in that which the more it's agitated the less it shakes and which finds comfort in inconstancy itself: It is certain, Archimedes, and I don't doubt it the least bit, to shake the whole earth and to secure a point you need to love as fixedly as I love.

Seamlessly fusing the rhetorics of science and Petrarchism, Sponde's sonnet eventually yields, in its punning *pointe*, a vision of the self eclipsing all other realities and discourses. The beloved exists only as an absent point of reference, and the conceit constructed on Archimedes' paradigm succeeds (or fails) on the strength of "mon cœur," that is, on the self who is a stranger to doubt ("je n'en doute point"). In short, Archimedes' geometric-physical "art" is made equivalent to Sponde's — the conceit on the physical "point" and lexical "point" guarantees this. And if this bizarrely, if superficially, parallels the Cartesian insistence that philosophic reasoning mimic geometric reasoning, then Descartes, who probably was not familiar with Sponde's poetry, shares with the poet the commonplace, but still extravagant ambition to be an Archimedean overreacher. In the *Discourse*, Descartes cast his will to knowledge as exempt from the kind of rhetoric Sponde employs to represent his will to love, and yet his hyperbolic doubt shares the same hot and cold fervor (*furor*) of the poet-lover. It, too, is fickle in its object of desire. At the outset ruthlessly skeptical, once it achieves its longed for success and begins operating in the theological realm, it recalls the best sky-scraping idealism of Renaissance Neo-Platonism. And as for the comparison between Descartes and the lyric poet, I would invoke Cavell who reads Descartes' narrative in the *Meditations* as not being about any particular, contingent person, and thus essentially removed from the life-world, for "its motive, like the motive of a lyric poem, is absolute veracity."[51] This striking assertion is supplemented by the related claim that "the idea of the fanaticism of unconditioned or hyperbolic love [is] a contrary face of the skepticism of unconditioned or hyperbolic doubt — skepticism under a reverse sign . . ."[52] Such a double bind, I would add, is the same Baroque dynamic that fuels Donne's *Anniversaries* and the belated Petrarchism of Quevedo.

The Sponde-Descartes parallel also reanimates Genette's question in "Hyperboles" where the matter at hand is Sponde's sonnets: "Ce mode hyperbolique de l'esprit n'a-t-il pas ses raisons — que le bon sens ignore, et que la raison veut connaître?" Descartes' "bons sens," we know from the first sentence of the *Discourse*, is the first thing he discards in order to put his "raison" on firmer footing. But as with Sponde, surely one of his "raisons" for the hyperbolic is to will the reader into adopting his cognitive stance. That he fails in this in the eyes of many of his earliest readers is due, he tells them, to their misunderstanding his intentions. For example, the Dutch philosopher, Gysbert Voetius, accuses Descartes of denying the Aristotelian substantial forms, an accusation that caused the faculty of the University of Utrecht to condemn Cartesian philosophy in 1642.[53] Of course, as Descartes himself was keenly aware, there were political and theological differences that caused some readers to read him suspiciously. What he does not consider, though, or seems unwilling to admit, is that a mere rhetorical figure may pose far greater risks. For hyperbole, like irony, depends inordinately on the hermeneutic ingenuity, goodwill, and the cultural and practical experience of those who interpret its radical deformations of literal meaning. Thus there is a touch of pathos, if not tragic *hubris* in the account Popkin gives of Descartes' defense of his method:

> Descartes protested that his sceptical phase was only feigned, that he never had the doubts of the First Meditation, and that no serious, attentive, unprejudiced person could have them, as long as he was aware of some clear and distinct ideas. The doubts, he said, were put forth for therapeutic and dramatic effect, to make the reader see first the weakness of what he now believed, and then the strength of Descartes' principles. He had no attention of inculcating scepticism, but was feigning the disease in order to show more forcefully what the cure was.[54]

To adapt Hamlet's phrase, he is hyperbolic but "northnorthwest," for "when the wind is southerly . . ." The savvy audience, in other words, should be able to see behind his mask. But of course this has not always been the case. What Descartes envisions as a philosophical comedy, by the end of which mind and world are harmoniously married, is transformed by the subsequent history of philosophy — or, at the very least, that history which runs through Gassendi, Pascal, Spinoza, Hume, Rousseau, Nietzsche, Wittgenstein, and Cavell, into the enduring "tragedy" of skepticism.[55] To return to where I began in the previous chapter, if a thinker as penetrating as Cavell refuses to see behind the mask of philosophical skepticism when considering Descartes' legacy of the *cogito*, then, perhaps, this is because the mask, the persona, adopted is more opaque than its maker intended. Alternating in his doubt between a commonsensical stance and a willed, artificial one, Descartes confuses the issue of how we should read the simplest of his words — what for instance does "je" signify in the First Meditation? Is it the confused thinker searching for one certain truth, the sage metaphysician recalling his past folly, or, as I hope I have shown, a chiaroscuro amalgamation of both? While, on the other extreme of the linguistic spectrum, how are we to understand the word "raison" when it itself is the object of his inquiry?

Jacques Derrida's 1963 essay (published 1967), "Cogito and the History of Madness," offers a powerful defense of Cartesian hyperbole in the face of

Descartes' own metaphysics and stance toward language.[56] An early, seminal attempt to move thinking and writing (*écriture*) away from the metaphysics of presence, the essay argues that madness and its primary vehicle, hyperbole, have vital and not just nominal roles in the history of Western philosophy. Put another way, how Cartesian philosophy as an exemplary moment in this history confronts the specter of madness is critical to any understanding of the limits of reason and language. This confrontation, Shoshana Felman observes, is also integral to comprehending our own, post-Nietzschean, post-structuralist tendency to blur the discursive borders between philosophy, literature, and madness.[57]

The first section of Derrida's essay examines a few pages from Michel Foucault's *Folie et déraison: Histoire de la folie à l'âge classique* where Descartes' flirtation with the mask of the madman in the *Meditations* is treated as symptomatic of the "internment" of madness by Enlightenment reason.[58] Here Derrida critiques Foucault's tendency to structure reason and madness as a binary pair, in part by challenging from a linguistic and historical perspective Foucault's interpretation of the Greek *logos*.[59] The essay's second section then attempts to "naïvely reread" sections of Descartes' *Meditations*, thereby setting the stage for a comparison with Foucault's reading of the same passages. Stressing "the rhetorical and pedagogical" nature of hyperbolic doubt, Derrida argues contra Foucault that Descartes does not expel or intern madness until after the *cogito* is intuited and philosophy begins its deductive and metaphysical tasks. Specifically, he traces how threats against reason embodied by madness are not dismissed by Descartes with the sentence: "But they are mad, and I should not be any less insane were I to follow examples so extravagant." Adumbrating how hyperbole supplements hyperbole, Derrida reads Descartes as a thinker who only "feigns" dismissing madness; first through "the hyperbolical exasperation of the hypothesis of madness" in the dream scenario, and second through *"the absolutely hyperbolical moment* which gets us out of natural doubt and leads to the hypothesis of the evil genius."[60] The *telos* of all this hyperbole is of course the *cogito* and the metaphysical riches that follow from it. Mapping the forking paths taken by Foucault and Derrida, Felman comments: "For Foucault, the fictions of madness undermine, *disorient* thought. For Derrida, on the contrary, at least in the case of Descartes, the fiction of madness has as its end to *orient* philosophy."[61] In other words, for Derrida philosophy sublimates madness via hyperbole and then, as we have seen, sublimates hyperbole via the *lumen naturale*. To "orient philosophy" is both to give rise (*orior*) to it and determine what its speculative concerns will and will not be.

This subtle phrase also suggestively links "Cogito and the History of Madness" with Derrida's 1971 essay "White Mythology: Metaphor in the Text of Philosophy." For the way that Derrida in the earlier text traces Descartes' feigned dismissal of madness and hyperbole resembles how he explicates in the latter the failed attempts of Western metaphysics to dismiss "negativity," "polysemia," and "the sensory" in favor of the "intelligible sun and the visible sun" of truth and presence.[62] The philosophical hyperbolist and metaphorist are driven by the same unspoken motive: the denial of *différance* in the pursuit of the absolute. Philosophy's heliotropism denies the *mise-en-abîme* of its own metaphorics; indeed, if I might conflate the two essays, this denial of the "abyss" can be regarded as the founding, hyperbolic gesture of Western philosophy.[63] No wonder, then, the specter of Descartes appears at the end of "White Mythology": " . . . if we put ourselves at the most properly Cartesian point of the critical procedure, at the point of hyperbolic doubt and the hypothesis of the evil genius . . . we know that what permits the discourse to be picked up again and to be pursued, its ultimate resource, is designated as *lumen naturale* . . . everything is illuminated by this system's sun, the sun of absence and presence, blinding and luminous, dazzling."[64] Such extravagant light also blinds, just as the sight-light of God is said to blind. Both lights blind us to the logic of the *supplément*, namely, that nothing, no excess, is ever enough. No metaphor, no hyperbole suffices to translate language into pure presence. Tropes always leave us wanting more.[65]

Seen in this way, it becomes more understandable why, in "Cogito and the History of Madness," the Cartesian *cogito* functions as a "sign" in the larger structure of philosophical discourse and the history of thought.[66] Derrida recounts how Descartes incrementally increases his hyperbole until "everything that was previously set aside as insanity is now welcomed into the most essential interiority of thought."[67] But this simultaneous (re)incorporation of madness into the Cartesian text and self also provokes him to reconsider Foucault's "fundamental motif" in *Histoire de la folie*: "Madness is the absence of the work."[68] Madness, Derrida continues, is to be equated with silence, but a silence that marks the historical limit out of which language and discourse emerge. Thus "[l]ike nonmeaning, silence is the work's limit and profound resource."[69] In the face of this silence, Foucault tries to (re)inscribe madness, an effort that provokes Derrida's most damning verdict: " . . . I

would be tempted to consider Foucault's book a powerful gesture of protection and internment. A Cartesian gesture for the twentieth century. A reap-
propriation of negativity."[70] As for Descartes, he rejects silence in favor of
hyperbole (both of which, I would add, looking back to *Lear* and forward to
Wittgenstein, also mark limits of signification). But after the *cogito* is attained
and hyperbole rejected, madness too must be silenced — for hyperbole and
madness are both obstacles to reason's progress, and both are vehicles of skepticism.[71] Here, then, is where Derrida (really) parts company with Descartes.
Here is where he would read, palimpsestically, the hyperbole that still speaks
(at least to him):

> The hyperbolical audacity of the Cartesian Cogito, its mad audacity,
> which we perhaps no longer perceive as such because, unlike Descartes's
> contemporary, we are too well assured of ourselves and too well accus-
> tomed to the framework of the Cogito, rather than the critical experi-
> ence of it — its mad audacity would consist in a return to an original
> point which no longer belongs either to *determined* reason or a *determined*
> unreason, no longer belongs to them as opposition or alternative."[72]

Like Sponde's "point," this "point," the *cogito*, is a "zero point" because it
contains the possibility of resolving all logical contradictions, because it is "the
impenetrable point of certainty" out of which, among other thoughts, historical structures claiming totality emerge, including, significantly, that structure
proposed by Foucault's book. From *pointe* to *totalité*, this is the arc or, if you
will, the hyperbola that Derrida describes. It is as if the violent motion inherent in βολή ("a throw, stroke, the wound of a missile"; figuratively, "a
glance")[73] cannot be contained; having passed through madness, dream, and a
kingdom where a deceptive demon reigns to arrive at self-certainty, Descartes
would rest and serenely exercise his reason. But Derrida will not let him.
Hyperbole's "violence" is too excessive for that, and, conversely, readers of hyperbole should be wary of "doing violence" in trying to contain it. Rather
than structuring hyperbole, as he accuses Foucault of doing, Derrida analyzes
its trajectory:

> The extent to which doubt and the Cartesian Cogito are *punctuated*
> by this project of a singular and unprecedented excess — an excess in
> the direction of the non-determined, Nothingness or Infinity, an excess

which overflows the totality of all that which can be thought, the totality of beings and determined meanings, the totality of factual history —
is also the extent to which any effort to reduce this project, to enclose it
within a determined historical structure, however comprehensive, risks
missing the essential, risks dulling the *point* itself.[74]

This "*point*" is more than the Archimedean point of which Descartes dreams,
it is also the inhuman, "metaphysical and demonic" hope that "exceeds all
that is real, factual, and existent."[75] It is read by Derrida as the point of madness, a form of excess inscribed at the origins of Western metaphysics:

> The project of exceeding the totality of the world . . . is no more reas-
> suring than the dialectic of Socrates when it, too, overflows the totality
> of beings, planting us in the light of a hidden sun which is *epeikeina tes
> ousias.* And Glaucon was not mistaken when he cried out: "Lord! What
> demonic hyperbole? *daimonias hyperboles*" [*Rep.* 509b].[76]

If Derrida is subtler than Glaucon this is partly due to his awareness of the
many ways he is bound by the history and language of Western metaphysics.
Mimicking Descartes' most famous syntactical construction, he concludes:
"I think, therefore, that (in Descartes) everything can be reduced to a determined historical totality except the hyperbolical project [*Je crois donc qu'on peut
tout réduire à une totalité historique déterminé (chez Descartes) sauf le projet hyperbolique*]."[77] This is to say: nothing can be reduced.

To my mind, then, Derrida's exceptionalism when it comes to hyperbole
seems more faithful to Descartes' method than Descartes is himself. Seizing
upon the "la *différance* de l'excès absolu" produced by Descartes' gesture of
hyperbolic doubt Derrida declares:

> Définir la philosophie comme vouloir-dire-l'hyperbole, c'est avouer —
> et la philosophie est peut-être ce gigantesque aveu — que dans le dit his-
> torique en lequel la philosophie se rassérène et exclut la folie, elle se trahit
> elle-même (ou elle se trahit comme pensée), elle entre dans une crise et
> en un oubli de soi qui sont une période essentielle et nécessaire de son
> mouvement.

> To define philosophy as the attempt-to-say-the-hyperbole is to confess —
> and philosophy is perhaps this gigantic confession — that by virtue of

the historical enunciation through which philosophy tranquilizes itself and excludes madness, philosophy also betrays itself (or betrays itself as thought), enters into a crisis and a forgetting of itself that are an essential and necessary period of its movement.[78]

As philosophy's "gigantic" confessor, Derrida hears the sins of excess in metaphysics, but he does not forgive them, nor does he silently pass over them. Instead, he skeptically shares its secrets with his readers in the hope that "demonic hyperbole" and its "terror" will give way to less absolute, more mediated forms of hyperbole.[79] Perhaps this is why, in what I take to be a not so hermetic allusion to *King Lear*, Derrida points us back to the literary where the thinker's *pathos* becomes more worldly, if no less pathological:

> . . . one could say that the reign of finite thought can be established only on the basis of the more or less disguised internment, humiliation, fettering and mockery of the madman within us, of the madman who can only be the fool of a logos which is father, master, and king. But that is another discourse and another story.[80]

Chapter Fourteen

Between Rhetoric and Geometry: Pascal's Negative Hyperbolics

*Il a exagéré affreusement, grossièrement, l'opposition
de la connaissance et du salut, puisqu'on voyait, dans le
même siècle, de savantes personnes qui ne faisaient pas
moins leur salut, je pense, que lui le sien, mais
qui n'en faisaient point souffrir les sciences.*

— Paul Valéry, "Variation sur une pensée"

APOLOGY AND BLAME

If for Cavell Shakespearean tragedy offers the most urgent response to the persistent threat of Descartes' hyperbolic skepticism, and if for Derrida Descartes' metaphysics exemplify the "vouloir-dire-l'hyperbole" of Western philosophy, then how should the infamous hyperbolism of Descartes' young contemporary and sometime acolyte, Blaise Pascal, be interpreted? To what extent does Pascal in the *Pensées* emulate or reject Descartes in this respect? Conversely, what might be Pascal's debts, implicit or explicit, to the mystical tradition of negative theology where language so dramatically strains but fails to surpass itself? Or, perhaps, as Valéry suggests, Pascalian hyperbole is a phenomenon sui generis.

There is no lack of blame when it comes to Pascal's reliance on hyperbole in the *Pensées* (1658–1662).[1] Exemplifying this is Patricia Topliss's study, which, despite its keen, wide-ranging appreciation of the rhetorical enterprise, treats hyperbole disdainfully. While hyperbole is the "master figure" in the *Pensées*, "it epitomizes all that is intellectually most questionable in the Apology ... The reader who refuses to be stunned and bewildered by Pascal's bludgeoning may well find it paradoxical that, seeking to establish what was for him the supreme Truth, he should resort so insistently to the most obviously mendacious of rhetorical devices."[2] Topliss's verdict may be appealed on two counts: first, I would object, *pace* Quintilian, that the proper use of hyperbole is not mendacious; second, her condemnation of Pascalian hyperbole on the basis of what she imagines the experience of generic reader to be begs the question of what kind of hermeneutic such a reader adopts. If clarity and distinctiveness are not the primary aims, if the reader's horizon of expectation is shaped by the incredible, then her hermeneutic is liable to differ radically from that of Descartes' commonsensical reader. Still, as we shall see, Topliss is certainly correct in asserting the discursive, often nonmetaphoric character of Pascalian hyperbole. She rightly notes that such hyperbole often derives from the use of "the superlative of common adjectives and adverbs, simple words like *plein, seul, unique, nul, aucun, rien, personne, partout, toujours, jamais*, and especially *ne . . . que* and *tout, tous, toutes*."[3] Inexplicably, though, her notions of rhetorical circumstance and decorum exclude Pascalian hyperbole from participating in the sometimes cognitive, often mystical, but always urgent task of persuading readers of a reality incommensurable with our limited being. "Denoting absolute comprehensiveness or absolute exclusion, these are the terms that do most obvious damage to Pascal's arguments, rashly generalizing against the manifest evidence of exceptions, affirming extreme positions that lie far beyond commonplace truth."[4] But again, what does "commonplace truth" mean in the context of a Christian apologetic text?

In this and the next chapter, I shall consider the uncommon causes and effects of Pascal's rhetorical absolutism. Adapting Philippe Sellier's insight that Pascal employs rhetoric in the *Pensées* not to please (*delectare*), nor primarily to teach (*docere*), but rather to accomplish a version of another Ciceronian task, namely, to bend (*flectere*), I read hyperbole as the chief means of such *force majeure*.[5] Pascal uses hyperbole to strain the imagination's limits, to disabuse readers of belief in reason's power, and to point them, force them onto the road of faith. As Stéphane Natan shows in his recent, encyclopedic study of the rhetoric and poetics of the *Pensées*, hyperbole proves crucial to Pascal's unyielding, Jansenist efforts to destroy his reader's pride and epistemological presumptions in order to vaunt the necessity of divine grace.[6] In his synchronic roles as moralist, apologist, philosopher, theologian, and mystic, Pascal relies on hyperbole to express the failure of the traditional *analogia entis* and, conversely, his own perception of God's immanence. Given humanity's innate caprice and the limits of geometrical reason, hyperbole becomes the last and best means of persuasion. The hyperbolic apologist creates new, intentionally shocking conceptual spaces for readers to experience.

To begin with, I would immediately distinguish between this office and other tasks Baroque hyperbolists conventionally undertake. A self-proclaimed foe of "beauté poétique" and the rhetoric of the "faux sonnet," Pascal decries the kind of hyperbolic, belated Petrarchism that dominated early seventeenth-century French poetry. Such poetic language lacks all verisimilitude and produces no useful knowledge:

> . . . on ne sait pas en quoi consiste l'agrément, qui est l'objet de la poésie. On ne sait ce que c'est que ce modèle naturel qu'il faut imiter, et à faute de cette connaissance on a inventé de certains termes bizarres: 'siècle d'or,' 'merveille de nos jours,' 'fatal,' etc. Et on appelle ce jargon beauté poétique.
>
> Mais qui s'imaginera une femme sur ce modèle-là, qui consiste à dire de petites choses avec de grand mots, verra une jolie damoiselle toute pleine de miroirs et de chaînes, dont il rira, parce qu'on sait mieux en quoi consiste l'agrément d'une femme que l'agrément des vers. Mais ceux qui ne s'y connaîtraient pas l'admireraient en cet équipage, et il y a bien des villages où on la prendrait pour la reine. Et c'est pourquoi nous appelons les sonnets faits sur ce modèle-là les reines de village.[7] (#486)

> But we do not know in what consists attractiveness, which is the object of poetry. We do not know the natural model we should imitate, and lacking this knowledge we have invented some bizarre terms: "golden age," "wonder of our times," "fatal," etc. And we call this jargon poetic beauty.
>
> But whoever would imagine a woman on this model, which consists of saying trivial things with big words, will see a pretty young lady loaded with mirrors and chains, which will make him laugh, because we know more about the nature of a woman's attractiveness than that of verse. But those who do not know such things would admire her in this getup, and there are many villages where she would be taken for the queen. This is why we call sonnets based on this model "village queens."

Pascal's witty polemic against poetic diction and the "pleasure" it produces suggests real familiarity with verse such as Tristan's or Théophile's, French avatars of Baroque Petrarchism; but it also suggests his determination not to be conventionally hyperbolic, "to say little things with big words."[8] Alternately, Pascal's own writing aims to (re)create an extreme cognitive rather than aesthetic experience. While such an experience has certain similarities with the meditative path Descartes constructs, Pascal's *hodos* discovers no resting point, no station of contemplation, save in God himself who necessarily escapes our limited capacity to ascribe ideas (or limits) to him. In this sense, the physical connotations of the word *flectere* (to bend, to curve something; sometimes said of a route) indicate also a metaphysical experience in which readers faced with perdition are forced to lose faith in reason and confidence in the imagination by Pascal's dizzying rhetoric of faith.

A bove all, Pascal would affect his reader's will, pride, and understanding:

> S'il se vante, je l'abaisse
> S'il s'abaisse, je le vante
> Et le contredis toujours
> Jusqu'à ce qu'il comprenne
> Qu'il est un monstre incompréhensible. (#163)

If he exalts himself, I humble him. If he humbles himself, I exalt him. And I continue to contradict him until he comprehends that he is an incomprehensible monster.

The hyperbolism of this *quintain*, with its mannerist reliance on antithesis and paradox, epitomizes the extreme heuristic experience Pascal envisions his writings precipitating. As the object of praise and blame, the reader is subjected to the pathos of trying to comprehend the "incompréhensible." But rather than celebrating this dialectic as leading to potential wisdom, Pascal astonishes us with our own monstrosity. We are meant to be shocked, even offended. The celebratory, high Renaissance humanism of Pico, Ficino, and Valla has become chimerical: "Quelle chimère est-ce donc que l'homme, quelle nouveauté, quelle monstre, quel chaos, quel sujet de contradiction, quel prodige, juge de toutes choses, imbécile ver de terre, dépositaire du vrai, cloaque d'incertitude et d'erreur, gloire et rebut de l'univers" [*What a chimera then is man! What a surprise, what a monster, what chaos, what a subject of contradictions, what a prodigy! Judge of all things, weak earthworm; repository of truth, cesspool of uncertainty and error; glory and garbage of the universe*] (#164).[9] Hyperbole, in the service of *l'esprit*, instead of lifting "man" towards the stars now hurls him satirically downward, toward the grotesque, albeit without the slightest trace of Rabelais's humanist laughter.

Pascal the hyperbolist plays other self-appointed roles whose main effect is to astonish us into rethinking conventional truths. Pascal the epigrammist, aiming to change minds about love and self-love, pens this *pointe*: "Le nez de Cléopâtre s'il eût été plus court toute la face de la terre aurait changé" [*Cleopatra's nose: had it been shorter, the whole face of the earth would have been changed*] (#32).[10] Pascal the apologist, hoping to evoke disdain for worldly attachments, exclaims: "Hors du lui il n'y a que vice, misère, erreur, ténèbres, mort, désespoir" [*Apart from [Christ], there is only vice, wretchedness, error, darkness, death, despair*] (#35). Pascal the student of language enigmatically warns: "La vrai éloquence se moque d'éloquence" [*True eloquence makes light of eloquence*] (#671), such that the adjective "vrai" conveys absolute, transcendent value.[11] In brief, such extravagant rhetorical appeals are necessitated by a metaphysical *res* that defies all verisimilitude. As Sellier observes: "L'hyperbole pascalienne est sous-tendue par une pensée forte, si forte même que certains énoncés des *Pensées*, qui ont été pris pour des hyperboles, révèlent à l'analyse une stricte adéquation du contenu et de l'expression. Rien du commun avec . . . la raréfaction du sens dans les pétrarquistes ou précieuses!"[12] However, my own contention in the following pages is, given Pascal's notion of humanity's fallen language, that such "stricte adéquation" is impossible. Pascal the hyperbolist consistently, self-consciously underscores language's conceptual inadequacy, even as his negative theology leaves him little choice but to hyperbolize. He could of course have chosen to remain silent, as Wittgenstein at the end of the *Tractatus* urges when faced with the ineffable. Or he might have sought to create what de Certeau, reading Renaissance mystics, describes as a "mystic fable."[13] But such solutions would have been ill suited for a Christian apologist aiming to sway Catholics, skeptics, and *libertines*. Given his *propositio*, Pascal's *via negativa* actually becomes a *via media*, as he carefully mediates between his own *nuit de feu* and his readers' incredulity.[14] Ironically then, his constant recourse to hyperbole may be read as a form of compromise — a rhetorical mediation between subjective *ecstasis* (interiority) and objective contingency and circumstance (exteriority). Such recourse, I shall argue, is as much apophatic as cataphatic; that is, cataphasis for Pascal extravagantly indicates the way to apophatic silence. Aside from these theological modes, though, Pascalian hyperbole also functions cognitively and epistemologically. Closely allied with paradox, hyperbole helps Pascal chart the limits of language and reason, a process cultivating astonishment and aporia in his readers, and, ultimately, he hopes, the recognition of faith's necessity.

THE GEOMETRY OF PERSUASION

Pascal's early treatise *De l'esprit géométrique* (ca. 1655) investigates the convergence of rhetoric and geometry in so far as both disciplines are able to convey knowledge.[15] Aiming mainly to explain how to demonstrate truth to others if one already possesses it, Pascal begins by expressing real Cartesian optimism concerning geometry's ability to provide "démonstrations . . . méthodiques et parfaites." However, in the course of the treatise he admits that geometry depends on "nominal definitions" [*définitions de nom* or *mots primitifs*], which must be intuited and so cannot be reduced to linguistic or logical formulas. Thus even as geometry is presented as the paradigmatic form of reasoning, it is grounded upon what in the *Pensées* are called the "reasons of the heart." In this sense, such *noms* as "movement," "number," and "space" already point to the limits of analytical reasoning and language, thus moving Pascal away from the Cartesian stance and towards a more nominalist, Hobbsean view of the matter. While geometry remains the most reliable means of attaining knowledge, because human understanding is limited, the geometer cannot demonstrate the truth of "premières vérités" even though they are perceived by the "lumière naturelle." Citing the commonplace derived from the Book of Wisdom (11:20), which ornaments and inspires much of late Renaissance cosmography — *Deus fecit omnia in pondere, in numero, et mensura* — Pascal converts it into a cause for wonder. Asserting that the "plus grands merveilles de la nature" are "les deux infinités" of largeness and smallness discoverable in all things, but especially in time and space, Pascal, prefiguring the cognitive strategy of the *Pensées*, transforms aporia into thaumaturgy.[16]

Concerned that certain "esprits excellents" will find these double infinities shocking, he then tries to methodically describe the infinite divisibility of space. This eventually leads to a discussion of indivisibles whose relation to divisibles, he urges, is comparable to that of zero with numbers. Yet for all these logical distinctions and the various empirical demonstrations he adduces, Pascal concludes that "les deux merveilleuses infinités . . . non pas à concevoir, mais à admirer." He then peremptorily declares that whoever is not convinced by "ces raisons" will never accept geometric reasoning. But those who do accept his reasoning will admire humanity's precarious place suspended between two infinities. More to the point, such acceptance explains Pascal's oblique declaration at the treatise's beginning: "[C]e qui passe la géométrie nous surpasse."[17] Geometry yields to metaphysics; it accomplishes here what his cataphatic rhetoric will in the *Pensées*.

In the treatise's second part, entitled *De l'art de persuader*, two means of persuasion are described: either through the understanding (*entendement*) or the will (*volonté*).[18] Initially, any appeal to the will is dubbed "base, unworthy, and inappropriate" [*basse, indigne et étrangère*]; but after decrying the public's caprices and thirst for delight (*volupté*), Pascal admits that to persuade well one must have knowledge of one's audience: "il faut connaître l'esprit et le cœur."[19] While certain truths, such as those concerning number, space, and movement, appeal only to the understanding, most thoughts are "introduites en foule par les caprices téméraires de la volonté."[20] Curiously though, when Pascal pauses to consider the two means of persuasion, "l'une de convaincre, l'autre d'agréer [*to please*]," only the former is seen as practical as it is based on logical, universal truths. Concerning the latter, he asserts:

> . . . la manière d'agréer est bien sans comparaison plus difficile, plus subtile et plus admirable; aussi, si je n'en traite pas, c'est parce que je n'en suis pas capable; et je m'y sens tellement disproportionné, que je crois la chose absolument impossible.[21]
>
> . . . the manner of pleasing is easily without comparison the most difficult, most subtle and most admirable. Thus, if I do not treat it here, it is because I am incapable of it and I feel myself entirely unequal to the task, such that I believe it to be absolutely impossible.

Rather than regarding Pascal's high praise of this form of persuasion ("bien sans comparaison") and complete disavowal of his own talents ("tellement disproportionné") as disingenuous, I read this passage as a moment when a brilliant young mathematician with a spiritual vocation is still debating the role that traditional rhetoric should play in an epoch in which the truth claims of the empirical sciences are increasingly vital and ubiquitous.[22] That such disproportion will later, in the "Disproportion de l'homme," be terrifyingly transferred to the world itself suggests that even if it proves true that Pascal will continue to find the task of pleasing his readers "absolument impossible" —

his hyperboles describing the world will have a psychological as well as empirical basis.

Conversely, Pascal explicitly claims not to be concerned with religious rhetoric:

> Je ne parle pas ici des vérités divines, que je n'aurais garde de faire tomber sous l'art de persuader, car elles sont infiniment au-dessus de la Nature: Dieu seul peut les mettre dans l'âme, et par la manière qu'il lui plaît.[23]

> I do not speak here of divine truths, which I take care not to let fall under the art of persuasion, because these are infinitely above Nature: God alone can place them in the soul, and in the manner that pleases him.

Infinity, here in a cognitive not material sense, is again the lynchpin, the *res*, grounding his discussion of geometric reasoning and, ultimately, an understanding of what rhetoric can and cannot accomplish. What Pascal idiosyncratically calls the "art of persuasion" — an art that does not know how to please or appeal to people's emotions or opinions — aspires to "methodical, perfect proofs" [*preuves méthodiques parfaites*].[24] His conflation of geometry and rhetoric depends on their shared inability to meet the formal necessity of representing the infinite. A hyperbolic, impossible conflation, Paul de Man reads it as essentially chiasmic. He argues that Pascal is unable to separate logic (epistemology) from persuasion (rhetoric), and that this inability inscribes figurative language at the heart of logical discourse.[25] Given this furtive inscription, Pascal radically circumscribes rhetoric's traditional compass:

> Voilà en quoi consiste cet art de persuader, qui se renferme dans ces deux règles: définir tous les noms qu'on impose; prouver tout, en substituant mentalement les définitions à la place des définis.[26]

> Behold in what this art of persuasion consists, which is contained in these two rules: define all the names that one uses; prove everything by mentally substituting definitions for things to be defined.

If these rules are followed, persuasion acquires an absolute ("tous . . . tout") and "invincible force."[27] Pascal thus appears to share here the Cartesian conviction that clear and distinct ideas persuade of themselves. (The treatise ultimately adduces eight rules for the geometrization of rhetoric, rules based on

notions of clarity and the intuitive acceptance of the truth of nominal definitions.)

Crucially though, in terms of his hermeneutics, Pascal emphasizes how
different readers will reach different understandings of words and texts. The
caprice he ascribes to potential readers thus effectively impeaches the faith
Descartes places in his own "franchise" and the linguistic transparency of his
arguments to persuade. In fact, Pascal cites Descartes' "Je pense, donc je suis"
to show that though Descartes may be the "véritable auteur" of this already famous thought, he cannot prevent some readers (such as Arnauld and, perhaps, Pascal himself) from hearing Augustinian echoes in the phrase — this
despite the fact that the phrase was not written "à la aventure" and that one
may perceive "une suite admirable de conséquences" from the deduction of
the *cogito*.[28] Their many affinities aside, Pascal suggests that Descartes is mistaken when he assumes that metaphysical truths can be accurately represented
by imperfect, contingent language.

Remarkably, the analogy between rhetoric and geometry does obtain in
one instance. Geometry provides an analogical model for interpreting scripture; since in these two discourses alone are clarity and perfection possible. In
both discourse "names" are intuitively understood and a perfect Author guarantees meaning. Both also try to represent the infinite: rhetoric would represent
the divine infinite, geometry the spatial one. Both discourses thus rely on "figures" and "names" (*définitions de nom*), which are immediately perceived as true
by the *cœur*, or intuition. Nonetheless, geometric truths are less contingent on
circumstance and caprice than rhetorical truths. What Philip Sidney dubs the
"infected will" prevents us from embracing via rhetoric what our "erected
wit" via geometry may understand.[29] Yet geometry, too, though it increases a
capacity for wonder, remains a human art that cannot measure or gauge the divine and its infinite, inexpressible essence.

This last realization helps explain Pascal's subsequent decision largely to
abandon the pursuit of the empirical and mathematical sciences in favor of
the theological reasoning that dominates the *Lettres provinciales* and the *Pensées*.
But in so far as his Jansenism relies on hyperbole, the latter differs from the
kind of excessive rhetoric that Pascal condemns at the very end of *De l'esprit
géométrique* in his polemic against "inflated words":

> Rien n'est plus commun que les bonnes choses: il n'est question que de
> les discerner . . . Ce n'est pas dans les choses extraordinaires et bizarres

que se trouve l'excellence de quelque genre que ce soit. On s'élève pour
y arriver, et on s'en éloigne: il faut le plus souvent s'abaisser . . . Il ne faut
pas guinder l'esprit; les manières tendues et pénibles le remplissent d'une
sotte présomption par une élévation étrangère et par une enflure vaine
et ridicule au lieu d'une nourriture solide et vigoureuse. Et l'une des
raisons principales qui éloignent autant ceux qui entrent dans ces
connaissances du véritable chemin qu'ils doivent suivre, est l'imagination qu'on prend d'abord que les bonnes choses sont inaccessibles, en
leur donnant le nom de grandes, hautes, élevées, sublimes. Cela perd
tout. Je voudrais les nommer basses, communes, familières: ces noms-là
leur conviennent mieux; je hais ces mots d'enflure . . .[30]

Nothing is more common than good things; it is only a question of discerning them . . . It is not in extraordinary and bizarre things, in whatever genus, that excellence is found. When one ascends to arrive at
excellence, one goes astray: more often it is necessary to abase oneself . . .
It is not necessary to trick the mind; strained and labored manners of
reasoning fill it with foolish presumption caused by strange elevations
and vain, ridiculous pomposity instead of with vigorous, solid nourishment. And one of the principal reasons why those who begin with these
subjects stray so far from the true path they should follow is that the
imagination, which assumes at first that good things are inaccessible,
gives them great, haughty, elevated, sublime names. This ruins everything. I would like to name these things lowly, common, familiar. These
names are more suitable to such things. I hate these pompous words.

And here the treatise breaks off — just where Pascal sounds the first notes
("Je voudrais les nommer basses, communes, familières") of what Cavell via
Austin dubs ordinary language philosophy. Yet in rejecting the still popular
scholastic modes of argument ("les manières tendues et pénibles"), Pascal
also opens the door to his own peculiar brand of metaphysics ("véritable
chemin"), which teaches that the road to heaven heads downward first.[31] If
the potential hyperbolist is to have any efficacy, if he is to follow the "véritable
chemin," he must deflate not inflate the meaning of words — thus the simple
but extreme phrase, "Cela perd tout," which strips skyscraping rhetoric of
all ambition and hubris. Hyperbole should be neither ornamental nor lexical,
rather, as exemplified in this passage, it should function discursively and cognitively. Hyperbole should also deconstruct the hyperbole of others. In part

this is because "les bonnes choses," like the concepts of space and number, are truths open to the heart [*le cœur*], but not to the analytic understanding, nor, in the end, to the imagination.

Nevertheless, the absolutist ("Rien n'est plus commun . . ."), scornful ("d'une sotte présomption . . .") tone adopted by Pascal suggests that the assertion, "Il ne faut pas guinder l'esprit," may already be at odds with his *ethos* adopted here, to say nothing of that of the apologist in the *Pensées* who avails himself of all rhetoric's persuasive force to bring readers to their knees. Considerable caution therefore must be exercised in applying directly the ideas from *De l'esprit géométrique* to the *Pensées*, texts written in distinct periods of Pascal's life and each with a radically different *propositio* and style. Nicholas Hammond argues that the former is essentially Cartesian and the latter thoroughly Augustinian.[32] While Thomas Carr warns: "Pascal's premature death left to scholars the task of harmonizing the theory found in *De l'esprit géométrique*, which explicitly does not apply to religious questions, with the conversion-oriented rhetoric of the *Pensées*. The first, as the title suggests, requires univocal definitions as the basis of tightly reasoned proofs, while the second allows for paradox, digression, and figures of speech."[33] And yet, to complicate matters further, Pascal's sister, Gilberte Périer, recalls how well Pascal, as a child, learned the "rules" of rhetoric and how skillfully he was later able to hide the lessons that allowed him to write in a manner at once "naïve et forte."[34]

PRIDE AND THE PARADOXICAL MEAN

The Baroque's most eloquent apologist for the *via negativa*, Pascal dramatizes the Derridean claim that Western philosophical reason depends on the paradoxical logic of the *supplément*. Armed with diverse species of hyperbole, Pascal attacks the *superbia* of Descartes' metaphysics and his ideal of linguistic transparency. And whereas *De l'esprit géométrique* appears to deny any rational basis for the use of hyperbole, the *Pensées* gives Baroque hyperbole its most forceful but rigorous incarnation.[35]

Within the fragmentary textual spaces of the *Pensées* Pascal employs hyperbole with an apologist's fervor, a mathematician's exactitude, and frequently with a poet's ingenuity ("Notre propre intérêt est encore un merveilleux instrument pour nous crever les yeux agréablement" (#78)). But in so doing he also variously reminds his readers that relying on such extreme rhetoric is to acknowledge humanity's fallen moral and epistemological state. As Sara

Melzer argues, the *Pensées* at once assert and perform language's insufficiency to represent divine truths; in this way alone is the text able to indicate a realm of meaning and being beyond signification, though not intuition. "Language not only points to the debasement of its representative capacity; it also suggests something other than its codes and structures, something that they exclude. Pascal wagers that the otherness within language itself figures God's Otherness, which is outside of language."[36] Given this "double-bind" or *epoché*, the *Pensées* are shot through with disjunctions and silences in the face of the impossible task of representing the divine. Its "figures" are for the fallen and hence necessarily obscure.[37] From a phenomenological perspective, Pascal's now cataphatic, now apophatic, rhetoric responds primarily to the infinite, silent universe that stands in for the divine. But it also responds to the challenge of explaining his intuition of God's immanence and grace. In fragment #756, for instance, he offers this analogy:

> Le moindre mouvement importe à toute la nature: la mer entière change pour un pierre. Ainsi dans la grâce la moindre action importe pour ses suites à tout, donc tout est important.

> The least movement affects all of nature: the whole sea changes because of a rock. Thus, in grace, the least action affects everything by its consequences; therefore everything is important.

Twice moving swiftly from "moindre" to "tout," this analogy linking the physical and theological realms retains a trace of the epistemological optimism of the *analogia entis* promoted by Aquinas and others. Or to risk my own analogy: Pascal the theological hyperbolist yearns for his object much like the branch of a hyperbola approaches but never reaches its neighboring asymptote.

  From the perspective of classical and neoclassical rhetorical theory, his constant recourse to hyperbole is an ostentatious affront to decorum and the precepts that would guarantee it. Yet it is worth recalling that when Aristotle, Cicero, and Quintilian do loosen these precepts, they suppose extraordinary circumstances and an audience that is able to sympathize with the speaker's plight and character. How, then, do we understand the *ethos* Pascal adopts in the *Pensées*? Who is the author, the self, or persona that writes with such urgent, self-conscious eloquence and conviction? And how might his *ethos*, in turn, render the text's insistent hyperbole more palatable or believable? Finally, how would such an *ethos* respond to the charge made by Topliss that Pascal's rhetoric is mendacious?

In his early thirties at the time of its composition, the author of the *Pensées* could no longer count on Aristotle's allowance for hyperbole in the young. Adopting sometimes an Augustianian, confessional stance, but more frequently that of a scriptural hermeneut and moral scold, Pascal frustrates any attempt to ascribe a single mood or character to his fragmentary, unfinished text. Furthermore, the arrangement or *dispositio* of the fragments — which given the state of the manuscripts and the *liasses* continues to be debated — provides conflicting indications as to whether certain *pensées* should be regarded as *exordia* or perorations and thus granted more rhetorical license.[38] As a more traditional apologist, Pascal had already published the *Lettres provinciales*. But since their publication in 1656–1657 until his death in 1662, the period during which he composed most of the *Pensées*, he suffered increasingly from physical maladies, not to mention from attacks on the Jansenists by ecclesiastic authorities in Rome.[39] Thus one certainly could take a psychoanalytic route to diagnose Pascal's *ethos*. Or one could try to improve on Nietzsche's already extravagant verdict in *Ecce Homo*: " . . . Dass ich Pascal nicht lese, sondern *liebe*, als das lehrreichste Opfer des Christenthums, langsam hingemordet, erst lieblich, dann psychologisch, die ganze Logik dieser schauderhaftesten Form unmenschlicher Grausamkeit."[40] But Valéry, I think, has already succeeded in this regard.[41]

For my part, I would lean on Pascal's own thoughts on character and motive to interpret his *ethos* as hyperbolist. To begin with, mining again the connotations of the verb *abaisser*, he contends that our corrupted will (*volonté*) is a form of *superbia*: "Dieu veut plus disposer la volonté que l'esprit. La clarté parfaite servirait à l'esprit et nuirait à la volonté. Abaisser la superbe" [*God wants to dispose the will more than the mind. Perfect clarity would serve the mind and harm the will. Humble your pride*] (#266). A similar diagnosis occurs in this *Prosopopée*: "Vos maladies principales sont l'orgueil, qui vous soustrait de Dieu, [et] la concupiscence, qui vous attache à la terre, et ils n'ont fait autre chose qu'entretenir au moins l'une de ces maladies. S'ils vous ont donné Dieu pour objet, ce n'a été que pour exercer votre superbe" [*Your main maladies are the pride that takes you away from God and the concupiscence that binds you to the earth; and they* (i.e., the philosophers) *have done nothing but entertain at least one of these maladies.*

If they gave you God as an end, it was only to cater to your pride] (#182). Pride ("la superbe") is "la plus radicale" of the various perversions of the will that the Augustinian Pascal combats.[42] When he, accordingly, undertakes the will's purification, pride ranks as the most pernicious spot. One of his chief rhetorical tasks, therefore, is to tame this *superbia* by constant application of *superiectio* and related figures in order that the reader may realize a properly humble relation with God.[43] That Pascal assigns himself this enormous task suggests remarkable *hubris*, even a touch of messianism. And though it is important to remember that, unlike Descartes, he first moves to abase (*abaisser*) his own pride, still, the contradictions involved in maintaining his *ethos* as both scourge and mystic are immense. As Cavell observes: "The arrogance of philosophy is not one of its best kept secrets. It forever toys with worlds, and when its discoveries humble human pride, like Kant's in proving the necessary limitation of human knowledge, or Nietzsche's in interpreting our resentments, it finds itself exorbitantly superb."[44]

Paradoxically then, the attainment of *mediocritas* or the mean is a principal target of Pascal's rhetorical and spiritual overreaching. First, there is this reminder of what he wishes to avoid: "Deux excès. Exclure la raison, n'admettre que la raison" [*Two excesses. Excluding reason, admitting only reason*] (#214). And then from an ethical perspective, he confesses:

> Je n'admire point l'excès d'une vertu, comme de la valeur, si je ne vois en même temps l'excès de la vertu opposée . . . Car autrement ce n'est pas monter, c'est tomber. On ne montre pas sa grandeur pour être à une extrémité, mais bien en touchant les deux à la fois et remplissant tout l'entre-deux. Mais peut-être que ce n'est qu'un soudain mouvement de l'âme de l'un à l'autre de ces extrêmes et qu'elle n'est jamais en effet qu'en un point, comme le tison de feu. Soit, mais au moins cela marque l'agilité de l'âme, si cela n'en marque l'étendue. (#560)

> I do not admire the excess of a virtue like valor, unless I see at the same time an excess of the opposite virtue . . . For otherwise it is not rising but falling. We do not show greatness by being at one extreme, but by touching both at the same time and filling everything in between. But perhaps it is only a sudden movement of the soul from one extreme to the other, and it is never in fact but at one point, as in the case of a fire ember. So be it, but at least this indicates the agility of the soul, if it does not indicate its range.

The hermetic idea informing this *pensée* is that two extremities must meet at some transcendent "point" where they will resolve themselves into a mediated third term. Unwilling to allow such ethical "extremes" to remain unmediated, Pascal reaches for a mystical solution.[45] His complex spatial metaphorics, crowned by the subtle simile contrasting the way the "soudain mouvement de l'âme" can mediate ethical extremities to the way a "fire ember" concentrates a fire's strength at one point, tries to reconcile ethics, physics, and metaphysics. Yet the subsequent fragment, titled "Mouvement infini," reveals why this "ember," this "point," is also an impossibility: "Le mouvement infini, le point qui remplit tout, le mouvement en repos, infini sans quantité, indivisible et infini" [*Infinite motion, the point that fills everything, motion at rest, infinite without quantity, indivisible and infinite*] (#561). Like Leibniz's vision of the monad as a "mirror" of God, Pascal's gnomic adumbration of the soul (as a point) and God (as infinity) would account for our place in the infinite. And while savoring more of paradox and tautology than hyperbole, these two *pensées* furnish Pascal with the chief impetus for his constant hyperbolism. In sum, his reliance on hyperbole is empirical as well as conceptual; it depends on the experience of an ineffable, arduous spiritual state and the mystical intuition of the infinite author of infinity. Like these "extrêmes," his hyperbole must be read dialectically, or at the very least, as inviting the reader to begin the process of mediating extremes whether or not any lasting, logical synthesis is attainable.

As a dialectician of extremes and philosopher of the "heart," Pascal rejects the absolute claims made by contemporary skeptics and dogmatists.[46] In #164, after rehearsing the Pyrrhonian position, he halts precisely where Descartes once paused and asks: "Doutera-t-il de tout? . . . Doutera-t-il s'il doute? Doutera-t-il s'il est? On n'en peut venir là . . . La nature soutient la raison impuissante et l'empêche d'extravaguer jusqu'à ce point" [*Shall he doubt everything? . . . Doubt whether he doubts? Doubt whether he exists? We cannot go that far . . . Nature sustains our feeble reason and prevents it from ranting so wildly*].[47] This decidedly non-Cartesian "point" — a geometric metaphor for the *lumière naturelle* — freezes the skeptic's extravagant rant ("extravaguer") and his infinitely regressing doubt. No longer the author of *De l'esprit géométrique*, Pascal now undermines even the claims of natural reason or intuition. What results is an epistemological "embrouillement," which Pascal will not so much unravel ("demêlera") as embrace. Such a "muddle" or "confusion"

... passe le dogmatisme et le pyrrhonisme et toute la philosophie humaine. L'homme passe l'homme. Qu'on accorde donc aux pyrrhoniens
ce qu'ils ont tant crié, que la vérité n'est pas de notre portée ni de notre
gibier, qu'elle ne demeure pas en terre, qu'elle est domestique du ciel,
qu'elle loge dans le sein de Dieu et que l'on ne la peut connaître qu'à
mesure qu'il lui plaît de la révéler. (#164)

... this transcends dogmatism and skepticism and all of human philosophy. Man transcends man. Let us grant the skeptics what they have so
often proclaimed: that truth is neither our quarry nor within our grasp;
that it does not reside on earth but is at home in heaven, in God's bosom;
and that we can know it only to the extent that is pleases him to reveal it.

Confronted with this paradox of false transcendence ("L'homme passe
l'homme . . ."), the reader is commanded, in a series of shrill imperatives, to
follow Pascal's directions:

Connaissez donc, superbe, quel paradoxe vous êtes à vous-même!
Humiliez-vous, raison impuissante! Taisez-vous, nature imbécile! Ap-
prenez que l'homme passe infiniment l'homme et entendez de votre
Maître votre condition véritable que vous ignorez.
    Écoutez Dieu.

Know then, proud man, what a paradox you are to yourself. Humble
yourself, powerless reason; be silent, dumb nature; learn that man infinitely transcends man, and hear from your Master your true condition,
of which you are ignorant.
    Listen to God.

Outdoing the hyperboles of skeptics and dogmatists with imprecation, invidious comparison ("nature imbécile"), and "paradoxe," Pascal aims his excess
at the reader who, like Baudelaire's "hypocrite lecteur," is mocked, solicited,
and commanded in the same breath.[48] The pride of the "superbe" reader in
tatters, he is now buffeted, now cajoled toward the end of the *pensée* where he
is urged to accept both the consequences of original sin ("cet abîme") and the
promise of grace he has not yet learned to hear. Hyperbolic invective yields to
apophasis ("Taisez-vous") in which God's ineffable voice silences our own.

REASONS OF THE HEART

Informing all the *Pensées* is Pascal's vision of the "three orders" wherein he distinguishes reasons (*raisons*) of the body (*corps*), mind (*esprit*), and faith (*foi*). The last of these involves what he usually dubs "reasons of the heart," which are sometimes equated with the more traditional notion of charity (*charité*). How these three orders function and interact is a fundamental concern for Pascal, and yet, given the nonsystematic form of the *Pensées* and the nature of the orders themselves, one that resists any single schema. Perhaps the most lucid sketch of them occurs in #339 — Sellier dubs it a "poème" — which begins with another invocation of infinity to mediate and limit his thinking: "La distance infinie des corps aux esprits, figure la distance infiniment plus infinie des esprits à la charité, car elle est surnaturelle" [*The infinite distance between bodies and minds is a figure of the infinitely more infinite distance between minds and charity, for charity is supernatural*]. By equating the heart with the supernatural, and thereby infinitely distancing it from mind and body, Pascal gestures at a way out of aporia.[49] The third order is where God's grace and human intuition are able to meet; this order furnishes, Melzer urges, an "absolute perspective." (It also enables the acceptance of miracles.) As Pascal unequivocally asserts at the end of the *pensée*: "Tous les corps, le firmament, les étoiles, la terre et ses royaumes, ne valent pas le moindre des esprits. Car il connaît tout cela, et soi, et les corps rien" [*All bodies, the firmament, the stars, the earth and its kingdoms, are not worth the least of minds. For mind knows all these, and itself, and bodies know nothing*]. But then he ups the ante again: "Tous les corps ensemble et tous les esprits ensemble et toutes leurs productions ne valent pas le moindre mouvement de charité. Cela est d'un ordre infiniment plus élevé" [*All bodies together and all minds together and all their productions are not worth the least impulse of charity. This belongs to an infinitely higher order*]. Finally though, he softens and justifies the hyperbole by revealing that this hierarchy of orders is one of kind not of degree: "De tous les corps ensemble on ne saurait en faire réussir une petite pensée, cela est impossible et d'un autre ordre. De tous les corps et esprits on n'en saurait tirer un mouvement de vrai charité, cela est impossible et d'un autre ordre, surnaturel" [*From all bodies together we cannot succeed in obtaining a single small thought; this is impossible and of a different order. From all bodies and minds we cannot derive a single impulse of true charity; this is impossible and of a different order*]. While the infinite partakes of all three orders, ultimately if it is to have any human meaning, it must find a home in the third order where its outstripping of the imagination (*corps*) and defiance of reason (*esprit*) will no longer disturb.

Despite this radically disjunctive hierarchy, it remains the apologist's task to appeal to the unbeliever's reason, and if that fails, to his emotions, will, and imagination. Yet if reason, as we have seen, is riddled with infinity's para-doxes, and the will infected by the still-unredeemed Fall, then the imagina-tion, "cette suberbe puissance," is also highly suspect. Prey to the mutable lures of the senses — especially those of sight — the imagination is a thor-oughly unreliable though undeniably potent means of persuasion:

> C'est cette partie dominante dans l'homme, cette maîtresse d'erreur et de fausseté, et d'autant plus fourbe qu'elle ne l'est pas toujours, car elle serait règle infaillible de vérité si elle l'était du mensonge. Mais étant le plus souvent fausse, elle ne donne aucune marque de sa qualité, marquant du même caractère le vrai et le faux. (#78)

> In man it is that dominant part, that master of error and falsity, and all the more deceptive because it is not always so; for it would be an infalli-ble rule of truth, if it were an infallible one of falsehood. But being more often false, it gives no indication of its quality, impressing the same mark on the true and the false.

A "cheat," the imagination hinders self-knowledge and the heart's motions that might lead to faith. As the same *pensée* asserts with chagrin: "L'imagina-tion dispose de tout. Elle fait la beauté, la justice et le bonheur qui est le tout du monde" [*The imagination disposes of everything. It creates beauty, justice, and hap-piness, which are the whole of the world*]. While in epistemological terms, Pascal's striking metaphors argue that the imagination is a tool that fits poorly the task at hand: "La justice et la vérité sont deux pointes si subtiles que nos instru-ments sont trop mousses pour y toucher exactement. S'ils y arrivent, ils en écachent la pointe et appuient tout autour plus sur le faux que sur la vrai" [*Jus-tice and truth are two points so fine that our tools are too blunt to touch them exactly. If they get at it, they either crush the point or press in all around, more on the false than on the true*]. The bleak conclusion drawn from such incommensurability appears to condemn utterly the imagination: "L'homme n'est qu'un sujet plein d'erreur naturelle et ineffaçable sans la grâce. [Rien ne] lui montre la vérité. Tout l'abuse" [*Man is but a subject full of natural error that cannot be eradicated without grace. [Nothing] shows him the truth. Everything deceives him*]. In sum, in so far as the imagination belongs to the first two orders, the body and the mind, it is cast as an absolute obstacle to, not a vehicle for, his apology.

And yet even in these passages, to say nothing of the rest of this celebrated *pensée* with its philosopher on a plank and judges in sumptuous robes, Pascal relies heavily on vivid visual and tactile imagery to make his case. More generally still, the *Pensées* are littered with images of mites, worms, planets, prisons, towers, boats, soldiers, and kings, as well as all manner of Biblical, scientific, and spatial imagery. In sum, Pascal's imagery can often be quite copious and his imagery startlingly vivid, even while, as we saw in his polemic against extravagant poetic diction and "mots d'enflure," his stated antipathy to rhetorical ornament knows no bounds. Less a disjunction between *res et verba*, than one between practice and theory, this tension speaks to the apologist's pressing need to appeal to his readers' imagination.

Much more than is the case with Descartes, Pascal requires us to experience the imagination's allure and force for ourselves in order that we may eventually realize its deceptive nature and so look elsewhere for illumination. The imagery of the *Pensées* works to achieve a kind of chiaroscuro, almost gnostic effect in which quotidian objects and experiences are infused with such obscurity and mutability that faith's distant rewards appear more compelling. Just as someone looking at a Caravaggio painting is directed by the play of light and shadows to a boy's smile, a clenched fist, or a hidden passion, the mind's eye in the *Pensées* is repeatedly led through a valley of shadows, past the stink of the "cloaque," as it is guided by images which, though still inmates in the prison house of the bodily imagination and language, seek to awaken the intuition of a more lasting and luminous reality.[50]

Accordingly, in their study of the imagination in the *Pensées*, Gérard Bras and Jean-Pierre Cléro refuse to take Pascal at his word in #78; instead, they consider how, as Pascal pursues his syncretic but fragmentary apology, the imagination rather than being limited to the *ordre du corps* necessarily participates in the orders of reason and faith.[51] When reason seems to have hit a wall, Pascal perceives the reach of infinity through the "symbols" of the imagination. Through the use of figures, culled largely from the Bible, faith is able to apprehend a hidden God. Most importantly, Bras and Cléro demonstrate through close readings of Pascal's metaphorics of the center, as well as his play with perspective and point of view, that the imagination permits the reader to realize his own subjective reality, which is the necessary basis for perceiving "un réel incompréhensible" that still escapes him.[52] In this sense, when the imagination, like its beloved hyperbole, engages the other two orders, it be-comes self-aware, dialectical, and, to a certain extent, objective.

As for *l'ordre d'esprit* or the faculty of reason, Pascal's antipathy to *philosophes* in the *Pensées* can be largely traced to his self-nominated rôle as apologist and theologian. Such antipathy marks also a decisive rhetorical and epistemological break from the stance taken in *De l'esprit géométrique*. Now he distinguishes between *l'esprit de finesse*, which is able to reason intuitively and deeply from only a few principles, and *l'esprit de géométrie*, which is able to comprehend a great number of principles and so reason deductively.[53] Ulti-mately *l'esprit de finesse* is preferred, as the principles of geometry are

> tellement délicates, et si nombreuses, qu'il faut un sens bien délicat et bien net pour les sentir, et juger droit et juste selon ce sentiment, sans pouvoir le plus sentiment le démontrer par ordre comme en géométrie, parce qu'on n'en possède pas ainsi les principes, et que ce serait une chose infinie de l'entreprendre. Il faut tout d'un coup voir la chose d'un seul regard, et non pas par progrès de raisonnement, au moins jusqu'à un certain degré. Et ainsi il est rare que les géomètres soient fins, et que les fins géomètres, à cause que les géomètres veulent traiter géométrique-ment ces choses fines, et se rendent ridicules . . .[54] (#670)

> . . . so delicate and numerous that a very delicate and clear sense is needed to apprehend them, and to judge rightly and correctly according to this feeling, without most often being able to demonstrate them as in geometry; because the principles are not known to us in this way, and be-cause it would be an endless task to undertake it. We must see the matter at once, at a glance, and not by a process of reasoning, at least up to a point. And thus it is rare for geometers to be intuitive and for intuitive people to be geometers, because geometers want to treat matters of intu-ition geometrically and make themselves ridiculous . . .

With this indirect critique of how Descartes treats metaphysical truth, Pascal champions a form of intuition ("Il faut tout d'un coup voir la chose d'un seul regard . . .") that more nearly resembles a poetic or mystic approach to meta-physics than one that aims at logical rigor. Pascal finds virtues in both forms of *esprit*, for both are superior to "les esprits faux"; but he also denies the Cartesian hope that language can be a clear and distinct medium for thought. Instead, as he insistently reminds us, humanity and its language are fallen in

myriad ways.[55] This explains his ambiguous assessment of figurative language: "Figure porte absence et présence, plaisir et déplaisir. Chiffre a double
sens. Un clair et où il est dit que le sens est caché" [*A figure carries absence and
presence, pleasure and displeasure. A cipher has a double meaning, one clear and one about
which it is the meaning is hidden*] (#296). Rhetorical obscurity may well find its
spiritual justification in Augustine's *De doctrina Christiana*, but for Pascal it is
also a reaction to the Cartesian insistence on "clarity and distinctiveness."[56]
Conversely, Pascal, like Augustine feels compelled to negotiate the mystic's
temptation to embrace silence. As a fellow apologist, Augustine describes
their common bind:

> Have we spoken or announced anything worthy of God? Rather I feel
> that I have done nothing but wish to speak: if I have spoken, I have not
> said what I wished to say. Whence do I know this, except because God
> is ineffable? If what I said were ineffable, it would not be said. And for
> this reason God should not be said to be ineffable, for when this is said,
> something is said. And a contradiction in terms is created, since if that
> is ineffable which cannot be spoken, then that is not ineffable which can
> be called ineffable. This contradiction is to be passed over in silence
> rather than resolved verbally.[57]

This "contradiction" forms the fulcrum of the Western tradition of negative
theology. And yet Augustine, with his enormous textual legacy, fluid eloquence, and genius for metaphor and other rhetorical strategies for representing the divine, also balks at embracing it. Once adumbrated, the aporia for
him is boldly, silently left behind — and confession and apology proceed con-
fidently and volubly.

Concerning Pascal's views on figurative language in Scripture and elsewhere much more could and should be said.[58] While Pascal nowhere discusses hyperbole *per se*, he does offer a consistent hermeneutic for figurative
language. *Pensées* #268, #270, #278–307 confirm his debts to Moses Mai-
monides, the Kabbala, and especially *De doctrina Christiana* where the spiritual
value of the labor needed to interpret difficult and obscure biblical figures and
parables is stressed. Augustine recommends that the exegete exercise *caritas*, or
what Pascal calls "reason of the heart," when choosing what meaning to ascribe figures, for such charity reflects Christ's own. Characteristically, Pascal
casts this in absolute terms: "L'unique objet de l'Écriture est la charité. Tout

ce qui ne va point à l'unique bien en est la figure" [*The sole object of Scripture is charity. Everything that does not lead to the sole end is a figure of it*] (#301). That such an "objet" remains inaccessible to human understanding underscores at once the ubiquitous necessity of figures in human discourse and, paradoxically, the built-in momentum, thanks to Christ's sacrifice, for every figure to reveal itself as unvarnished, absolute truth. It is in this context that he again reconfigures his ideal of mediating extremes: "Deux erreurs: 1. Prendre tout littéralement. 2. Prendre tout spirituellement" [*Two errors: 1. Taking everything literally. 2. Taking everything spiritually*] (#284). Only in so far as charity and holiness are complete — an impossibility for fallen humanity — will all figuration and so all enigma be abolished. Hermeneutic understanding, in short, depends on the mediation of grace: "Jésus Christ leur ouvrit l'esprit pour entendre les Écritures" [*Jesus Christ opened their minds to understand the Scriptures*] (#285).

Now in as much as this scriptural-hermeneutic model justifies the enigmas of *l'écriture pascalienne*, we learn to treat it as an invitation to a performance, or better yet *une répétition* (rehearsal) of the fall and ascent of linguistic meaning through and beyond language. Such an undulation necessarily traverses the three orders. Indeed, the order — or nonorder — that structures the *Pensées* may itself be said to follow the "order of the heart":

> J'écrirai ici mes pensées sans ordre et non pas peut-être dans une confusion sans dessein. C'est le véritable ordre, et qui marquera toujours mon objet par le désordre même.
>
> Je ferais trop d'honneur à mon sujet si je le traitais avec ordre, puisque je veux montrer qu'il en est incapable. (#457)

> I will write my thoughts here without order, but not perhaps in unplanned confusion. This is true order, and it will always indicate my aim by its very disorder.
>
> I would be honoring my subject too much if I treated it with order, since I want to show that it is incapable of it.

Pascal's chaotic "véritable ordre" enacts and repeats the gap between discourse and the divine. The enormity of this gap for Pascal presents itself as a psychological as well as a spiritual truth. Thus while sometimes pointing at the divine, his hyperboles frequently verge grotesquely on self-hate: "Que le cœur de l'homme est creux et plein d'ordure" [*How hollow and full of garbage is the heart of man*] (#171).[59]

NEGATIVE THEOLOGY

Like his spiritual predecessors, Pseudo-Dionysius the Areopagite, Meister Eckhart, and Nicholas of Cusa, Pascal voices an essentially negative theol-ogy.[60] God is perceived at once as the fundamental ontological and phenome-nological reality, but one that is too sublime, too ineffable to be expressible in fallen, human language. Save for what Scripture imparts, one is able instead only to say, apophatically, what the hidden God (*deus absconditus*) is not.[61] Yet like Heidegger, Pascal insists on meditating on non-being as he explores the cognitive limits of thought:

> En écrivant ma pensée, elle m'échappe quelquefois, mais cela me fait souvenir de ma faiblesse, que j'oublie à toute heure. Ce qui m'instruit autant que ma pensée oubliée, car je ne tiens qu'a connaître mon néant. (#540)

> When writing down my thought, it sometimes escapes me, but this makes me remember my weakness, which I am constantly forgetting. This is instructive to me as my forgotten thought, for I care only to know my nothingness.

That the act of writing becomes uncontrollable or indecorous ("elle m'échappe") for Pascal as it plunges him toward nonbeing is remarkable — especially in the light of Descartes' refusal to assign his writing any meta-rhetorical value. More remarkable still is the way his writing would precipitate the same experience in the reader. Reading Pascal, one negotiates not only labyrinths of hyperbole, paradox, and ellipsis, but also the figurative silences between his fragmentary *pensées* that point to a kind of textual "néant," an absence, or a forgetting ("ma pensée oubliée") that frustrates any easy hermeneutic. Epitomizing this aporia is this passage in "Le pari," also known as *Le discours de la machine*, where Pascal infamously considers the question of God's existence according to natural reason (*les lumières naturelles*):

> S'il y a un Dieu, il est infiniment incompréhensible, puisque, n'ayant ni parties ni bornes, il n'a nul rapport à nous. Nous sommes donc inca-pables de connaître ni ce qu'il est, ni s'il est. Cela étant, qui osera entre-prendre de résoudre cette question? Ce n'est pas nous, qui n'avons aucun rapport à lui. (#680)

If there is a God, he is infinitely incomprehensible, since, having neither
parts nor limits, he bears no relation to us. We are therefore incapable of
knowing either what he is or whether he is. This being so, who will dare
undertake to resolve this question? Not we, who bear no relation to him.

Reason and its principal instrument, language, cannot ascertain the ontological status of the divine. But they can negatively express the conceptual and ontological distance separating us from God. They can express, as Hélène
Michon has convincingly argued, Pascal's conviction that any proportion,
any Aquinian *analogia entis*, between the human and divine is untenable.[62]
And if the Senecan brevity and ellipticality of these sentences yields the impression of unvarnished, improvised thought, the precision of their hyperbole
("infiniment incompréhensible," "nul rapport," "aucun rapport") leaves little
doubt that for the author an apophatic experience of the divine or the *via negativa* is the only credible one.

The motive for such apophasis can be gleaned from the maxim: "Tout
ce qui est incompréhensible ne laisse pas d'être" [*Not all that is incomprehensible
fails to exist*] (#262).[63] This conundrum is obviously not original to Pascal;
as Dawn Ludwin argues in a slender but acute book comparing Pseudo-
Dionysius and Pascal, Dionysius' theological writings pervade the early modern mystical tradition even if they were not always known at first hand.
Paraphrasing Dionysius, Ludwin observes that "[t]he God of apophatic theology is eminently a God-beyond-being, a 'hyper-essentiality' (*hyperousia*)."[64]
Divine being, in other words, can be intuited but never represented. The apprehension of this *hyperousia* depends, though, on having had the experience
of attempting to circumscribe God's essence with the resources of language.
In occidental negative theology, to call God "light," "wisdom," "love," etc.,
or to apply to Him any name, image, or metaphor, or better yet to exhaust all
names, images, and metaphors, is to become all too aware of God's unrepre-
sentability and thus incomprehensibility. Such exhaustion, or cataphasis, is
the positive, predicative, often metaphoric, thoroughly hyperbolic, and so futile attempt to reconcile the believer's intuition of divinity with the desire to
represent fully and truly in language that intuition. As Denys Turner, in *The
Darkness of God*, glosses it:

> The cataphatic is . . . the verbose element in theology, it is the Christian
> mind deploying all the resources of language in the effort to express

something about God, and in that straining to speak, theology uses as many voices as it can. It is the cataphatic in theology which causes its metaphor-ridden character, causes it to borrow vocabularies by analogy from many another discourse, whether of science, literature, art, sex, politics, the law, the economy, family life, warfare, play, teaching, physiology, or whatever. It is the cataphatic tendencies which account for the sheer *heaviness* of theological language, its character of being linguistically *overburdened*; it is the cataphatic which accounts for that fine *nimietas* of image which we may observe in the best theologies, for example in Julian of Norwich or Bernard of Clairvaux. For in its cataphatic mode, theology is, we might say, a kind of verbal riot, and anarchy of discourse in which anything goes.[65]

Cataphatic abundance also precipitates the same kind of cognitive recognition of God's inexpressibility that apophasis accomplishes. To write of God's "madness" as Dionysius does, or to ascribe to the divine hands and feet forces the issue. The cataphatic is a kind of baroque crucible or gauntlet through which all mystic theology must pass. Rather than contradicting the apophatic trajectory toward silence, cataphasis provides the experiential basis for it. Further, as with the dialectic precipitated by poetic hyperbole and *copia*, "the basic law of cataphatic language," as Turner defines it, is to heighten our self-consciousness of language's limits: "No partial, restricted vocabulary is adequate to express the inadequacy of theological language; only language under the requirement to say everything possible can do this. It is in the profusion of our affirmations that we encounter the limits of language, and then break through them into the dark silence of the transcendent."[66] Thus the pathos of cataphasis derives from the second-order realization of the irreconcilable gap between the *copia* of insufficient, all too human signifiers and the single, infinite, eternal, immovable, and all knowing signified. Dionysius explains in *The Divine Names* how we must accept that

> ... with regard to the supra-essential being of God — transcendent goodness transcendentally there — no lover of truth which is above all truth will seek to praise it as word or power of mind or life or being. No. It is at a total remove from every condition, movement, life, imagination, conjecture, name, discourse, thought, conception, being, rest, dwelling, unity, limit, infinity, the totality of existence.[67]

Given this realization two discursive strategies are cultivated to speak of the divine: "theologians praise it by every name — and as the Nameless One." As for the second, apophatic strategy, Dionysius cites Judges 13:17, where God refuses to name himself.[68] But it is the first, cataphatic impulse that interests Dionysius here:

> And yet on the other hand, [the theologians] give it many names, such as "I am being," "life," "light," "God," the "truth." These same wise writers, when praising the Cause of everything that is, use names drawn from all the things caused: good, beautiful, wise, beloved, God of gods, Lord of Lords, Holy of Holies, eternal, existent, Cause of the ages. They call him source of life, wisdom, mind, word, knower, possessor beforehand of all the treasures of knowledge, power, powerful, and King of Kings, ancient of days, the unaging and unchanging, salvation, righteousness and sanctification, redemption, greatest of all and yet the one in the still breeze. They say he is in our minds, in our souls, and in heaven and on earth, that while remaining ever within himself he is also in and around and above the world, that he is above heaven and above all being, that he is sun, star, and fire, water, wind, and dew, cloud, archetypal stone, and rock, that he is all, that he is no thing.[69]

With this intertextual profusion of nominal definitions (almost all originate in Scriptural passages), Dionysius enacts and describes cataphasis. As his treatise goes on to demonstrate, it is not that individual names are hyperbolic — they should, arguably, be read as litotes given how the divine outstrips them — but rather it is the always futile accumulation of names in the attempt to represent and so understand the divine that is properly hyperbolic. Excess of signification, or discursive *copia*, points both to His superabundance and our own linguistic and conceptual lack.[70]

Pascalian cataphasis, it is true, sometimes takes the more traditional form of nominalism wherein each *mot primitif*, be it *grace*, *charity*, or *God*, reads as a litote containing this self-awareness — an awareness that often verges on irony given the word's radical insufficiency. In this sense, no single name is hyperbolic when applied to God. But conversely, as I shall endeavor to demonstrate in the next chapter with a close reading of "Disproportion de l'homme," Pascal no longer accepts other "definitions de nom," such as *man* and *space*, as universally available to human intuition. Instead the world and the words used to describe things in the world are regarded as motives for hyperbole, as confirmation of the essential disjunction between our capacities for perception and meaning, on the one hand, and the ultimate, infinite reality, on the other. Citing #99, Ludwin thus asserts that every word, every *mot primitif*, contains a potential infinity of names: "Like the hyperessential God, the simple terms circumscribe the very limits of language."[71] To paraphrase Pascal: because words can be endlessly anatomized for the potentially infinite meanings that they contain, the "sciences" are doomed alongside philosophy to the neverending task of interpretation.

From a more general, conceptual perspective, the negativity cultivated by Dionysius and Pascal should be regarded as a form of excess and "[e]xcess, or in [Nicholas of] Cusa's language a 'superlative,' overcomes oppositional thinking."[72] Such excess, I would add, must be strictly distinguished from the excessive doubt that powers Cartesian skepticism. For cataphatic excess leads the reader away from reason via a "cognitive dissonance"[73] and toward transcendence. It is self-consciously, metapoetically, performative rather than claiming to state how things are in the world, in the mind, or with God. It also appeals to Pascal's "raisons de la cœur," thereby escaping the condemnation he reserves for "excés" in the moral sphere. As with Heidegger's multifarious, verbose refusals to offer a definition of *Dasein*, Pascal's explication of these "raisons" eschews mimetic and discursive logic and avails itself instead of hyperbole, meiosis, paradox, ellipsis, and silence to map and perform the contours of his impossible task.[74]

In order to further delineate the labor(s) of hyperbole in this theological context, and to distinguish better between hyperbole and paradox, I wish to turn to two recent interpretations of Dionysius' negative theology. Jacques Derrida and Jean-Luc Marion engage in a long-running, sometimes pointed, but always subtle debate on the meaning and implications of negative theology.[75] The crux of their disagreements, as I see it, is hyperbole or, properly speaking, the hyperbolic. In two essays, "How to Avoid Speaking: Denials" and "Post Scriptum: Aporias, Ways and Voices," Derrida confronts and typically sublimates the long-standing imputation that deconstruction is but a belated form of negative theology. Responding to this charge, he first addresses the common perception that both forms of discourse are propelled by "negativity" and thus are conflatable. This kind of critique, he insists, would convert the deconstructionist into a closet metaphysician:

> Every time I say: X is neither this nor that, neither the contrary of this nor of that, neither the simple neutralization of this nor of that with which it *has nothing in common*, being absolutely heterogeneous to or incommensurable with them, I would start to speak of God, under this name or another. God's name would then be the hyperbolic effect of that negativity or all negativity that is consistent in its discourse. God's name would suit everything that may not be broached, approached, or designated, except in an indirect and negative manner.[76]

But such a "hyperbolic effect" is far too broad and imprecise; it threatens to turn all negative discourse into theological discourse. Derrida states flatly: "No, what I write is not 'negative theology,'" for negative theology, as opposed to deconstruction, "seems to reserve . . . some hyperessentiality."[77] By contrast, Dionysius, Meister Eckhart, and other negative theologians (Pascal is conspicuous by his absence here) make a "ontological wager" and thus are effectively classed as what Derrida calls, in other contexts, metaphysicians of presence.[78]

This conclusion, however, does not prevent Derrida from appreciating the complexities of Dionysius' texts (one might say that after first distancing his own project from negative theology, he draws the latter closer to himself again). Tracing the increasing concision and "rarefaction of signs" in, respectively, Dionysius' three main works, *Symbolic Theology*, *Mystical Theology*, and *Divine Names*, Derrida discovers a progress or "elevation" toward silence, a movement from metonymy and verbosity to a wordless, mystic union. He then quotes those seminal propositions that conclude Wittgenstein's *Tractatus*, in order to mark the fact that for Wittgenstein, as for Dionysius, the "inexpressible [*Unaussprechliches*] . . . exists," but also to distance the "thinking of *différance*" from them both. Promising to meditate on Wittgenstein's "man muß" [*il faut*] later in the essay, for the time being he observes that despite its "injunction to silence" it leaves a "trace."[79] By insisting on this trace Derrida implies, wrongly I think, that Wittgenstein too remains a metaphysician of presence.

Why I disagree with Derrida on this point will become clearer below, but for now I would note how his focus in his reading of Dionysius on the linguistic and conceptual place where apophasis occurs underscores the ambiguity in the Greek *hyper*:

As for the beyond (*hyper*) of that which is beyond being (*hyperousias*), it has the double and ambiguous meaning or what is above in a hierarchy, thus both beyond and more. God (is) beyond Being but as such is more (being) than Being: *no more being* and *being more than Being*; being more. The French expression *plus d'etre* (more being, no more being) formulates this equivocation in a fairly economical manner.[80]

Derrida thus slyly (re)inscribes the logic of the *supplément* into Christian apophasis. But he also discovers the same lack and excess in another text that he sees as anticipating the *via negativa*. Seizing upon Plato's argument in the *Republic* (509b) that "the idea of the Good has it place beyond Being or essence," Derrida muses:

> . . . whatever may be the discontinuity marked by this beyond . . . in relation to Being, in relation to the Being of beings or beingness . . . , this singular limit does not give place to simply neutral or negative determinations, but to a *hyperbolism* of that, beyond which the Good gives rise to thinking, to knowing, and to Being. Negativity serves the *hyper* movement that produces, attracts, or guides it . . . [T]his negative form is not neutral. It does not oscillate between the *ni ceci—ni cela*. It first of all obeys a logic of the *sur*, of the *hyper*, over and beyond, which heralds all the hyperessentialisms of Christian apophases and all the debates that develop around them . . .[81]

If hyperbolism "heralds . . . hyperessentialisms" it does so here without betraying any consciousness of a semantic or ontological gap between saying and knowing. In effect, Derrida invokes in addition to the logic of hyperbole that of metaphor, with its play of the familiar and the strange, to explain how the limit between the here and the beyond can be both transcended and maintained:

> This maintains a sufficiently homogeneous, homologous, or analogous relationship between Being and (what is) beyond Being, in order that what exceeds the border may be compared to Being; albeit through the figure of hyperbole; but most of all, in order that what is or is known may *owe* its being and its beingknown to this Good. This analogical

continuity allows for the translation, and for the comparison of the
Good to the intelligible sun, and of the latter to the perceptible sun.[82]

This refashions the central argument in "White Mythology" concerning the
heliotropics of Western metaphysics such that hyperbole now explicitly powers the "analogical continuity" that may yield transcendence (whereas in most
of "White Mythology" metaphor fuels this ascending motion). Curiously, in
both texts Derrida cites the same passage from the *Republic* where Socrates reveals the presence of being and Glaucon exclaims: "Oh Apollo, what divine
hyperboles [*daimones hyperboles*]!" However, here Derrida labels the latter utterance "theatrical" and views it as a parodic version of prayer. Yet despite this
difference, both negative theology and metaphysics cultivate and suffer from
the "hyperbolic effect." Only deconstructionist philosophy, as Marion will
bitingly observe, appears immune from such an effect.

For his part, Derrida would exclude one form of speech from this circle.
Distinguishing first between prayer and encomium, he notes that though both
are performative, the latter seeks to predicate of God, whereas the former addresses Him. Prayer is therefore the species of discourse that separates Greek
from Christian thought, and that allows apophasis to come closer to Hyper-
essentiality: "Between the theological movement that speaks and is inspired by
the Good beyond Being or by light and the apophatic path that exceeds the
Good, there is necessarily a passage, a transfer, a translation."[83] Prayer is
rhetorical not only in its performativity, but also because it assumes an audience. It prevents apophatic hyperbole from becoming what Wittgenstein
would call a private language, for it locates speech in place and time. As
Dionysius employs it at the end of the *Divine Names*, it also helps determine
and form the proper reader, the future reader of good faith (as opposed to
Pascal's reader who is left alone to discover grace by any means possible). But
Derrida also compares prayer to "apostrophe" and to a "supplement."[84] In
this sense, the differences between Derrida's own approach and negative theology's are further narrowed. Not that Derrida prays in the essay; no, he coyly
avoids that, preferring to note the absence of prayer (and addressee) in "Heidegger's rhetoric." He ends instead with a series of unanswered or unanswer-
able questions, almost as if he were performing in another manner the aporia
that he will not, cannot surpass. The essay, based on a lecture that he gave
in Jerusalem in 1986, becomes preoccupied with the question of address.
How does one address being and nonbeing? How does one address *khora*

(Plato's receptacle for being)? With what kind of language? With or without metaphor? How is address here different from prayer? Does such an address preclude the possibility of an answer? What emerges from this litany of questions is the impression, my impression, that Derrida's voluble avoidance of "speaking" and "prayer" throughout an essay of nearly seventy pages is much more cataphatic than apophatic. Derrida's avoidance of prayer resembles Cavell's thick description of Lear's "avoidance of love" — in both instances skepticism becomes cataphatic, but discontentedly so.

A Wittgensteinian dialogue with himself about negative theology, Derrida's "Post-Scriptum" amplifies this discontent. Using the German Baroque poet Angelus Silesius as the dialogue's touchstone — though without exploring how Silesius's historical and cultural context might inform his poetics — Derrida defines *post-scriptum* as the writing that follows the apophatic experience. (That it comes at the end of the volume only further sharpens the obvious question: does "How to Avoid Speaking: Denials" describe/ perform an actual apophatic/cataphatic experience or only mimic one in order to deconstruct it?) Promising through a reading of Silesius' impassioned, cryptic verses to explore the tension between negative theology's tendency to exceed language and the obvious fact that there is a long textual tradition of negative theology, Derrida stresses the "analytic exhaustion" and "impoverishment" occasioned by negative theology. He quotes, for example, this hyperbole from Silesius: "Stop, my *Augustine*; before you have penetrated God to the bottom [*ergründen*], one will find the entire sea in a small pit [*Grüblein*]." And while he ignores Silesius' wonderful hyperbole here in favor of the more pervasive metaphor of the desert that he finds elsewhere in the poet's verses, Derrida later reanimates the image of descent — an image that often accompanies cataphasis — as he ponders the hyperbolic more generally: "'God' is the name of this bottomless collapse, of this endless desertification of language."[85] Such "desertification" or impoverishment is conventionally schematized as the first cataphatic step in which the mystic exhausts language's resources and thus the possibility of reference only then to embrace the negations and paradoxes of apophasis proper. Or as Denys Turner puts it: "We can only know the inadequacy of our language from within it. It is for this reason that the proper route to the apophatic is . . . through the dialects of the cataphatic."[86] In cognitive and figurative terms, the *via negativa* ascends such that "inadequacy" and "impoverishment" yield to an intuition of overwhelming sublimity. The poem that begins *The Mystical Theology*, for instance, epitomizes this ascent: "Trinity!! Higher than any being, / any divinity, any goodness! / Guide of Christians / in the wisdom of heaven! / Lead us up beyond unknowing and light, / up to the farthest, highest peak / of mystic scripture . . ."[87]

For his part, Derrida chooses Silesius' more Baroque version of the same transcendent theme: "*Das überunmöglichste ist möglich. / Du kannst mit deinem Pfeil die Sonne nicht erreichen, / Ich kan mit meinem wol die ewge Sonn bestreichen.*"[88] Yet his gloss emphasizes the hyperbolic over the sublime:

> . . . in the cultural or historical zone in which the expression 'negative theology' appears as a sort of domestic and controlled appellation . . . the apophatic has always represented a sort of paradoxical hyperbole . . . This hyperbole *announces*. It announces in a double sense: it signals an open possibility, but it also provokes thereby the opening of the possibility. Its event is at once revealing and producing, *post-scriptum* and inaugural writing. Its event announces what comes and makes come what will come from now on in all the movements in *hyper, ultra, au-delà, beyond, über*, which will precipitate discourse or first of all existence . . . Now the hyperbolic movements in the Platonic, Plotinian, or Neoplatonic style will not only precipitate beyond being of God as he is (the supreme being), but beyond God even as name, as naming, named, or nameable, as reference is made there to some thing.[89]

Hyperbole is the *beta* and *psi* of the apophatic experience.[90] Hyperbole is heuristic in that it "provokes . . . the opening of the possibility" and it is rhetorical in that it freezes, reifies, that experience long enough for it to be translated into a "reference . . . to some thing." While the negativity of apophasis may resemble the claims of skepticism and the phenomenological reduction, hyperbole in eschewing silence always already "announces" *hyperousia* as the way out of and up from the abyss of nonsense and disbelief. Put another way, aporia and the *via negativa* are mutually constitutive because of the way hyperbole transgresses linguistic and conceptual boundaries.[91]

The third leg in Jean-Luc Marion's phenomenological trilogy, *In Excess: Studies of Saturated Phenomena*, investigates those phenomena, "paradoxes," that "appear thanks to (or in spite of) an irreducible excess of intuition over all concepts and all the significations one would assign them."[92] Careful to divorce this interpretation of "givenness" (he is thinking in part of Heidegger's "Es gibt," though he might have also turned to Wittgenstein's "Es gibt allerd‑ings Unaussprechliches") from a thirst for transcendence, Marion reads this "donation" through Kantian categories (categories we will reencounter below in Kant's discussion of the sublime). His book describes an arc: "Marion con‑siders in each chapter . . . the saturated phenomena of the event (which saturates according to quantity, being unable to be accounted for), the idol (which satu‑rates according to quality, being unable to be accounted for), flesh (which sat‑urates according to relation, being absolute), the icon (which saturates according to modality, being unable to be looked at), and Revelation (which saturates according to all four categories at once) . . ."[93] This progression is neither prop‑erly apophatic nor cataphatic in that its object is not immediately the divine. Instead, by structuring his entire analysis with what he calls the "first princi‑ple of phenomenology: 'As much reduction, as much givenness,'" Marion "eliminates all transcendence" and leaves his readers simply with the intuition of excess itself.[94] But in order to give voice to the excess (*le surcroît, l'excès*) that he discovers in saturated phenomena, and as an aspect of his refusal to repre‑sent it as any kind of essence, he cultivates the kind of linguistic self‑awareness and attention to the materiality of the signifier one finds in the most rigorous philological studies and in the deconstructive readings practiced by Derrida.[95]

It is all the more striking, then, that in the last turn taken in their debate about negative theology, Marion, when he considers the intuition of the satu‑rated phenomenon he calls Revelation, utterly rejects Derrida's claim that "the apophatic has always represented a sort of paradoxical hyperbole."[96] Using Dionysius as his textual and spiritual guide, Marion instead affirms a "third‑way" beyond both "affirmation" (cataphasis) and "negation" (apophasis), one that is not ultimately hyperbolic, but rather "pragmatic."[97] This "third‑way" he dubs *dénomination* (a jab, surely, at Derrida's *dénégation*):

> It is no longer a question of naming, nor by contrast of not naming, but of de‑nominating God‑in the twofold sense that this term can have: to name (to name in view of . . . , to nominate), but with something close to a negation, and consequently also to undo from all nomination, to release and deliver God from it, thwarting it. In its ambiguity, de‑nomination bears the twofold function of saying (affirming negatively) and undoing this saying of the name. It concerns a form of speech that

no longer says something about something (or a name of someone) but which denies all relevance to predication, rejects the nominative function of names, and suspends the rule of truth's two values.[98]

Denomination thus "aims" at God, but does not represent God; on the contrary, it is an attempt to respond to, to move toward God's "demand" [*aitia*]. More specifically, it is partly through his close analysis of how the adverb or prefix "hyper" has been used by Dionysius that Marion challenges Derrida's reading of negative theology as "paradoxical affirmation." Leaning on Kevin Hart's *The Trespass of the Sign: Deconstruction, Theology and Philosophy*, as well as passages from Dionysius and John Scotus Eriugena, Marion shows that *hyper* "reestablishes neither essence nor knowledge but rather transgresses them both in view of praising what precedes and makes possible all essence."[99]

In sum, when Dionysius writes that God is super-essence (*hyperousia*), Marion reads this superlative as more of a negation than an affirmation. Thus in Marion's view Derrida would "stigmatize" negative theology by making it rely on the same kind of hyperbole that we saw Derrida critique in "White Mythology" and "Cogito and the History of Madness."[100] Derrida does this, Marion argues, because he would protect deconstruction from any pretenders to the throne; for if negative theology did not ultimately depend of the "metaphysics of presence" then the "originality" and "preeminence" of deconstruction would be challenged by the long tradition of negative theology.[101] While I hesitate to interpolate myself further into this critical gigantomachy, I would add that in the four texts of Derrida's that I have considered here, hyperbole is largely treated as lacking the madness, indeterminacy, and irony, or, if you will, the logic of the *supplément*, that might have prevented it from becoming in his eyes a discourse of "présence." In short, it remains a symptom of logocentrism rather than a remedy for it, notwithstanding that fact that its semantic violence always seem poised to exceed the boundaries of the discourse — be it literary, philosophical, or theological — in which it occurs.

Finally, I find it curious that neither Marion nor Derrida focus on the βολή in negative theology's hyperbole. Who throws, and who is thrown, and how does the agency implicit in such motion speak to the subjectivity of this verbal, cognitive act? To pass through aporia as Derrida would have it neglects the rhetorical violence and caprice that we discover reading Pascal; Derrida turns vicariously, ambivalently, to prayer for a more humane, controlled, means of passage or translation. Conversely, Marion's *dénomination* defangs the figurative force of the hyperbolic *énonce*; it rashly (hyperbolically!) strips Dionysius' rhetoric of its full imaginative effect. Is it not extravagant to claim, for instance, that the poem opening *The Mystical Theology* "denies all relevance to predication"?[102] Likewise, in this emblematic passage from the *Divine Names*, even if we grant that Dionysius will ultimately "de-nominate" its terms and claims, the mystic's verbal and conceptual *copia* is surely extravagant to the point of *hubris*:

> And we may be so bold as to claim also that the Cause of all things loves all things in the superabundance of his goodness, that because of his goodness he makes all things, brings all things to perfection, holds all things together, returns all things. The divine longing is Good seeking good for the sake of the Good. The yearning which creates all the good-ness of the world preexisted superabundantly within the Good and did not allow it to remain without issue. It stirred him to use the abundance of his powers in the production of the world.[103]

Through this "production" the possibility of an apprehension of the Good, however cataphatic or apophatic it may be, is also precipitated in humanity. In this way, Dionysian hyperbole fits perfectly into the hermeneutic circle, even if this traditional figuration effectively leaves, as I will try to show in the next chapter, Pascal out of the loop.

Chapter Fifteen

Disproportion and Taste: Measuring the "little cell"

His greatness takes in all space, surpasses all number,
moves far beyond infinity in its abundance . . .
— Dionysius the Areopagite, *Divine Names*

DISPROPORTIONS

As we learned reading *Lear*, silence can be extravagant. Both Derrida and Marion dramatically avoid speaking of Pascal's hyperbolism in the service of negative theology.[1] Their reticence is especially startling since Pascal too discovers "absence" haunting his language and is likewise determined to express the impossible experience of the divine. But perhaps the historical specificity of Pascal's project dissuades them. Pascal's silences are most resonant when he tries to measure the newly discovered spaces of the Copernican universe. Writing soon after Pascal's death, Leibniz eagerly appropriates Pascal's most celebrated *pensée*, "Disproportion de l'homme" (#230): "Ce qu'il vient de dire de la double infinité n'est qu'une entrée dans mon système."[2] Here Leibniz signals the extent to which Pascal's hyperbolic wrestling match with infinity provides him with the epistemic break needed to conceive or, at the very least, to introduce his theories of the monad and pre-established harmony. Not that Pascal's use of hyperbole in this *pensée* is itself systematic; instead, as I shall argue in this chapter, its discursive, imaginative force annihilates the claims of reason even as it fulfills the epistemological promise of hyperbole as an immanent way of knowing the world and oneself. In this sense, it also violently marks a break, a "rupture" Foucault would say, between an early modern analogical worldview wherein language is still material, still a medium for being and non-being, and the dawning Enlightenment view, heralded by Descartes, wherein language is cast as a transparent medium without "reasons" of its own. Finally, lingering on the discursive and rhetorical features of this vertig-inous *pensée* will deepen some of the questions concerning taste, the sublime, and inexpressibility that run throughout this book and that become central in post-Baroque thought. This, in turn, will precipitate a broader consideration in my last chapter of the philosophical risks and rewards of hyperbole.[3]

My reading of hyperbole in "Disproportion de l'homme" hinges on four main points: First, seeing that neither physical nor metaphysical manifesta-tions of infinity can be adequately thought, Pascal relies on hyperbole to dis-cover dramatic epistemological and spiritual consequences of this cognitive impasse. Hyperbole helps him plumb the failure of *analogia entis*.[4] Second, through *superiectio* and the corresponding abasement of man Pascal defini-tively rejects the *superbia* inherent in Cartesian metaphysics. Third, the use of superlatives in his diction, especially variations on *tout* and *rien*, proves essen-tial, not ornamental, when it comes to realizing his cognitive and theological aims. Fourth, the ironic aspects of his hyperbole deprive him and his readers any fixed vantage point, and so render impossible the adoption of any single hermeneutic stance. In short, the *pensée* performs and repeats the scriptural Fall. Via hyperbole it forces the reader to experience the insufficiency of empirical knowledge, the consequences of philosophical hubris, and — perhaps most grievously — it turns wonder and curiosity into enemies of faith.

"Disproportion de l'homme" appears in the section of the *Pensées* entitled "Transition de la connaissance de l'homme à Dieu" according to the so-called *liasse-table* of June 1658. It is positioned, accordingly, not to increase a sense of misery or ennui — there are other sections for that — but to commence the vertiginous cognitive and spiritual motion (*transition*) toward God. Such mo-tion also inverts traditional ideas concerning decorum. If the orthodox Ci-ceronian derives decorum from a perception of nature's order, then Pascal, given that *disproportion* is his subject, riddles his rhetoric with disproportional-ity (or makes it proportionate to the degree of disproportion he perceives be-tween human thought and divine truths). Aimed at the disjunctive "orders" of body and mind, Pascal's *propositio* is to condemn the folly of pursuing the "natural sciences" given the astonishing disproportionality between our lim-ited knowledge and the objects (chiefly, ourselves and nature) that we seek to know:

Voilà où nous mènent les connaissances naturelles. Si celles‑là ne sont véritables, il n'y a point de vérité dans l'homme, et si elles le sont, il y trouve un grand sujet d'humiliation, forcé à s'abaisser d'une ou d'autre manière.

Et puisqu'il ne peut subsister sans les croire, je souhaite avant que d'entrer dans de plus grandes recherches de la nature, qu'il la considère une fois sérieusement et à loisir, qu'il se regarde aussi soi‑même et juge s'il a quelque proportion avec elle, par la comparaison qu'il fera de ces deux objets.

Here is where natural knowledge leads us: if it is not true, there is no truth in man; and if it is true, he finds in it a great source of humiliation, forced to humble himself one way or another.

And since he cannot subsist without believing this knowledge, be‑ fore entering into greater explorations of nature, I want him to consider nature both seriously and at leisure just once, and also to reflect upon himself and to judge, in a comparison of these two objects, whether any proportion holds between them.

Beginning *in medias res*, the first paragraph with its first‑person, plural pro‑ noun immediately implicates the reader in Pascal's plight, which, in a taste of things to come, is cast in a spatial metaphor ("où nous mènent"), which though seemingly moribund, will soon be given new, astonishing *energeia*. Likewise, the two subsequent conditional phrases create two drastic impasses: either man is incapable of attaining scientific truth, or, possessing such truth, it humiliates him. Then, after positing another conundrum, the second para‑ graph switches to the first person as Pascal reveals his authorial desire ("je souhaite"). He wants his reader to undertake an act of will, to "observe" him‑ self and "judge" himself in relation to nature. Implying that he has already made this "comparison," Pascal makes the act of reading an experience anal‑ ogous to what Descartes demands of readers of the *Meditations*. Like Descartes' swift inducement of hyperbolic doubt, to abase oneself ("s'abaisser") need only be experienced once ("qu'il la considère une fois sérieusement et à loisir"); for, in both cases, the epistemological consequences are presumed lasting. But that Pascal's invitation to contemplate humanity's place in the universe will tend to annul not only the possibility of what Descartes calls "first truths," but more radically still the objective basis for the *cogito* as well, confirms just how irredeemable such consequences can be.

As for style, the enormous distance that Pascal would put between him and his predecessor quickly becomes manifest. The Senecan anaphora and isocolon inaugurating the *pensée* proper swiftly propels us from the contemplation of immediate surroundings to the admiration of the entire visible universe:

> Que l'homme contemple donc la nature entière dans sa haute et pleine majesté, qu'il éloigne sa vue des objets bas qui l'environnent, qu'il regarde cette éclatante lumière mise comme une lampe éternelle pour éclairer l'univers, que la terre lui paraisse comme un point au prix du vaste tour que cet astre décrit, et qu'il s'étonne de ce que ce vaste tour lui-même n'est qu'une pointe très délicate à l'égard de celui que ces astres qui roulent dans le firmament embrassent.

> Let man then contemplate the whole of nature in its lofty and full majesty, and let him avert his view from the lowly objects around him. Let him behold that brilliant light set like an eternal lamp to illuminate the universe. Let the earth seem to him like a point in comparison with the vast orbit described by that star. And let him be amazed that this vast orbit is itself but a very small point in comparison with the one described by the stars rolling around the firmament.

The liberal use of adjectives ("haute et pleine"), simile ("comme une lampe éternelle"), metaphor ("ces astres qui roulent"), and sundry figures of repetition marks Pascal's prose as thoroughly mannerist. Such mannerism, though, casts itself as a means rather than an end. Rather than wanting to draw attention to his rhetoric per se, Pascal, with his constant resort to indirect injunction ("Que l'homme contemple"; "qu'il éloigne"; "qu'il regarde"; "que la terre lui paraisse"), commands his reader's admiration ("qu'il s'étonne") of humanity's incommensurability with the cosmos.[5] But not content with mere admiration, his desire to stretch his spatial vision beyond these two *pointes* fuels the same dynamic of an initial hyperbole begetting further hyperbole(s) that is native to Senecan drama and, ironically (given the antipathy we saw above), Petrarchism:

> Mais si notre vue s'arrête là, que l'imagination passe outre. Elle se lassera plus tôt de concevoir que la nature de fournir. Tout ce monde visible n'est qu'un trait imperceptible dans l'ample sein de la nature, nulle idée

n'en approche. Nous avons beau enfler nos conceptions au-delà des espaces imaginables, nous n'enfantons que des atomes au prix de la réalité
des choses. C'est une sphère infinie dont le centre est partout, la circon-
férence nulle part. Enfin c'est le plus grand [des] caractères sensibles de
la toute-puissance de Dieu que notre imagination se perde dans cette
pensée.

But if our gaze stops here, let our imagination pass beyond. It will
sooner tire of conceiving things than nature of producing them. This
whole visible world is only an imperceptible trace in the amplitude of
nature. No idea approaches it. However much we may inflate our conceptions beyond these imaginable spaces, we give birth only to atoms
with respect to the reality of things. It is an infinite sphere whose center
is everywhere and circumference nowhere. In the end, the greatest perceptible sign of God's omnipotence is that our imagination loses itself in
this thought.

Imagination here means not only going beyond ("passe outre," "au-delà")
what can be seen but also what other thinkers have thought and written. Such
overreaching is made palatable by the period's improvisatory Atticism: the illusion of balance fostered by the second sentence dissipates in the semantic absolutism of the third where "Tout" yields to "n'est qu'un," which then gives
way to the summary verdict: "nulle idée n'en approche."[6] Likewise, the notion one might have any control over this process is shattered as Pascal satirically folds time ("plus tôt") and becoming ("nous n'enfantons que") into his
argument. Recalling Pascal's youthful distaste for *mots d'enflure*, the presumption of our swollen "conceptions" ("Nous avons beau enfler nos conceptions . . .") finds its initial cure by being hyperbolically figured as the smallest
possible particles, Lucretian "atomes," in the face of "réalité des choses."
This "reality" is then paradoxically figured in a reworking of the hermetic
commonplace of the infinite sphere. As Borges observes in "Pascal's Sphere,"
Pascal is by no means the first to contemplate an infinite universe with a "center everywhere" and a "circumference nowhere," but he is the first to imbue
fully this paradoxical space with the all-too-human feeling of infinite insufficiency — a feeling, Borges and Valéry insist, deeply tinged with his own misery.[7] More audaciously, in attempting to represent nature's infinity, Pascal, like
Bruno before him, subverts this venerable conceit by replacing God with nature. Unlike the Nolan, though, Pascal finds no metaphysical solace in na-

ture's infinity. Glimpsing in the next sentence the "toute-puissance de Dieu" beyond this infinite sphere," Pascal makes "cette pensée" overwhelm our imagination and threaten our perdition.

But then, leaving aside the impossibility of a non-contradictory represen-tation of God's infinity, Pascal makes it clear that his more urgent challenge is to express our relation to this purely ontological infinity. He thus resumes his initial anaphora, setting the stage for the remainder of the *pensée*:

> Que l'homme étant revenu à soi considère ce qu'il est au prix de ce qui est, qu'il se regarde comme égaré dans ce canton détourné de la na-ture, et que de ce petit cachot où il se trouve logé, j'entends l'univers, il apprenne à estimer la terre, les royaumes, les villes et soi-même, son juste prix.
>
> Qu'est-ce qu'un homme, dans l'infini?

> Let man, returning to himself, consider what he is with respect to what exists. Let him regard himself as lost in this remote corner of na-ture, and from the little cell in which he finds himself lodged, I mean the universe, let him learn to estimate the just value of the earth, kingdoms, cities, and himself.
>
> What is a man in the infinite?

The drastic auxesis in which the universe is progressively reduced to a "can-ton," then to a "petit cachot," dramatizes the extent to which Pascal's episte-mological inquiry has immense ontological stakes as well.[8] In Heideggerean terms, Pascal juxtaposes human *Dasein* with material *Existenz*; we are "lost," lodging somewhere between being and non-being, where Nature refuses any anthropomorphic care (*Sorge*). At once general and specific (as signaled dra-matically by the comma), the question posed here goes far beyond the compass of natural science — the answer has immediate moral significance. Like Au-gustine's struggle with concupiscence, Pascal's heroic efforts to understand the newly enlarged universe's dimensions spur his willingness to accept the tenets of Scripture as truth's final arbiter. Not that Scripture figures directly in the logic of the *pensée*. Though he briefly quotes the Book of Wisdom and Augustine, Pascal carefully couches his main arguments to appeal primarily to our profane imagination and reason. The more positive aspects of his Jansenism, especially its doctrine of grace, will be expounded elsewhere in the *Pensées*. Here his task is to force his fallen readers to experience vicariously their condition. In so doing, he outdoes Pyrrhonian and Cartesian skepticism by exclaiming the complete incommensurability of our faculties with knowl-edge of physical reality.

"What is a man, in the infinite?" Pascal responds to this ancient query by cataphatically rehearsing the infinity of nature — an ambiguous metonym for God. In the course of this elaborate *amplificatio*, his invention achieves its greatest novelty:

> Mais pour lui présenter un autre prodige aussi étonnant, qu'il recherche dans ce qu'il connaît les choses les plus délicates, qu'un ciron lui offre dans la petitesse de son corps des parties incomparablement plus petites, des jambes avec des jointures, des veines dans ses jambes, du sang dans ses veines, des humeurs dans ce sang, des gouttes dans ses humeurs, des vapeurs dans ces gouttes, que divisant encore ces dernières choses il épuise ses forces en ces conceptions, et que le dernier objet où il peut arriver soit maintenant celui de notre discours. Il pensera peut-être que c'est là l'extrême petitesse de la nature.
>
> Je veux lui faire voir là-dedans un abîme nouveau, je lui veux pein-dre non seulement l'univers visible, mais l'immensité qu'on peut con-cevoir de la nature dans l'enceinte de ce raccourci d'atome. Qu'il y voie une infinité d'univers, dont chacun a son firmament, ses planètes, sa terre, en la même proportion que le monde visible, dans cette terre des animaux, et enfins des cirons, dans lesquels il retrouvera ce que les pre-miers ont donné, et trouvant encore dans les autres la même chose sans fin et sans repos, qu'il se perde dans ces merveilles aussi étonnantes dans leur petitesse, que les autres par leur étendue! Car qui n'admirera que notre corps, qui tantôt n'était pas perceptible dans l'univers impercepti-ble lui-même dans le sein du tout, soit à présent un colosse, un monde ou plutôt un tout à l'égard du néant où l'on ne peut arriver?

> But to present him with another equally astonishing prodigy, let him examine the most delicate things he knows. A mite with its minis-cule body shows him incomparably more minute parts, legs with joints, veins in its legs, blood in its veins, humors in this blood, drops in the hu-mors, vapors in these drops. Let him divide these last things again until he exhausts his powers of conception, and let the final object to which he can now arrive be the object of our discourse. Perhaps he will think that this is nature's extremity of smallness.

> I want to make him see a new abyss in there. I want to depict for him not just the visible universe, but the immensity of nature we can conceive inside the boundaries of this compact atom. Let him see there an infinity of universes, each with its firmament, its planets, its earth, in the same proportion as in the visible world; and on this earth animals, and finally mites, where he will find again what he saw before, and find still in the others the same thing without end and without cessation. Let him lose himself in wonders as astonishing in their minuteness as the others are in their extent! For who will not marvel that our body, imperceptible a little while ago in the universe, itself imperceptible inside the totality, should now be a colossus, a world, or rather a whole, with respect to the nothingness beyond our reach?

Hijacking the rhetoric of wonder that characterizes so much cosmographic writing in the sixteenth and seventeenth centuries, Pascal creates a perspectival "prodige" whose aim, his diction signals ("étonnant," "étonnantes," "n'admirera que"), is to cultivate *admiratio*. His periods rely on those same stylistic features that Morris Croll, reading Pascal alongside Seneca, Montaigne, Browne, and Lipsius dubs "loose," "Attic," and "Baroque."[9] By leaning, that is, on antithesis, anaphora, parataxis, ellipsis, and asyndeton, Pascal rejects Ciceronian symmetry to pursue extreme concinnity. The effect is to convey the undulating experience of discovering the cosmological contours of this "prodige" and "abîme nouveau." Still, the prose rhythm ultimately feels more ineluctable than improvisatory: spiraling vertiginously down the scale of creation the period arrives precisely where Pascal aims, at the "parties incomparablement plus petites." And, in a moment of chilling self-reflexivity, these prove inseparable from the object "de notre discours." The discursive search for the smallest quantity thus proves as subjective as it is objective. Pascal's will appeals to the reader's will: "Je veux lui faire voir là-dedans un abîme nouveau, je lui veux peindre . . ." Such "an abyss" is willed not because it is capricious but because a thinker intends to follow the rhythm of a thought to its abyssal limit. Pascalian hyperbole is discursive in the manner of Burton and Rabelais, who also depend inordinately on parataxis and figures of *amplificatio* to elicit simultaneously the world's excessive *copia* and urgent proofs of self-consciousness. But it is also convincingly anchored (see his "proof" below) in empirical, physical reality, such that startling phrases like "cette terre des animaux, et enfins des cirons" are at once verisimilar and hyperbolic. Seen through a microscope — invented in 1618 — a mite becomes more than an imagined world.[10] It now belongs to the set of *realia* poised to overpower readers.

Theological verities also animate this perspectivism. One hears in phrases like "le sein du tout" the Greek *to pan*, or in "colosse" a Goliath about to be slain. Likewise, the pointed antithesis of "un tout à l'égard du néant" begins to savor of the gnosticism that Augustine struggles with in the *Confessions*. Spiritual truths require hyperbole, but they also demand the will and learning to pursue anagogic interpretation. Without such anagogy the reader would be in an untenable spiritual condition ("sans fin et sans repos, qu'il se perde dans ces merveilles"), in a recurring aporia more perilous than epistemic doubt. But if Augustine has his garden, Pascal contemplates his condition in the cold of interstellar space and in the atomized wonders of the mite. To contemplate fully such places, which still lack all proportion with God, is to join fear with admiration:

> Qui se considérera de la sorte s'effraiera de soi-même et se considérant soutenu dans la masse que la nature lui a donnée entre ces deux abîmes de l'infini et du néant, il tremblera dans la vue des ses merveilles, et je crois que sa curiosité se changeant en admiration, il sera plus disposé à les contempler en silence qu'à les rechercher avec présomption. Car enfin qu'est-ce que l'homme dans la nature? Un néant à l'égard de l'infini, un tout à l'égard du néant, un milieu entre rien et tout, infiniment éloigné de comprendre les extrêmes, la fin des choses et leur principe sont pour lui invinciblement cachés dans un secret impénétrable (*que pourra-t-il donc concevoir? il est*) également incapable de voir le néant d'où il est tiré et l'infini, où il est englouti.

Whoever considers himself in this way will be afraid of himself, and, seeing himself supported by the size nature has given him between these two abysses of the infinite and nothingness, he will tremble at these marvels. I believe that, as his curiosity changes into admiration, he will be more disposed to contemplate them in silence than to examine them with presumption. For, in the end, what is man in nature? A nothing compared to the infinite, an everything compared to the nothing, a midpoint between nothing and everything, infinitely removed from understanding the extremes: the end of things and their principle are hopelessly hidden from him in an impenetrable secret. What will he be able to conceive? He is equally incapable of seeing the nothingness from which he derives and the infinite in which he is engulfed.

Taking a quick, mocking shot at Descartes' *cogito* ("*il est*"), Pascal proves the promise of his own version of totalizing, hyperbolic doubt. Beyond the mere fact of existence, no essence — such as calling him a *res cogitans* — can be ascribed to man; instead, depending on the perspective adopted, he is "un néant," "un tout," or an unstable "milieu." Rather than inventing an evil genius, Pascal insists on the conceptual and psychological consequences of being caught between two empirical "abysses." He forces us to contemplate these deeply and fearfully enough that when we avert our eyes "silence" seems preferable to science. That Pascal, like Augustine, rejects (momentarily at least) the mystic's silence in favor of a voluble apologetics, suggests that he would teach us how to mediate between the extremes of the void and infinity. Alternately, Pascal's lyrical contemplation of what Kant will critique as the mathematical sublime rejects any teleology of reason. To draw such a consequence from the experience of reading this *pensée* would be, in Pascal's eyes, foolishly to presume that the "order" of reason remains viable, not yet annihilated, after wrestling with the infinite.

Having responded to the query that precipitated the *pensée*, Pascal now surveys the desperate topography facing man:

> Que fera-t-il donc sinon d'apercevoir [quelque] apparence du milieu des choses, dans un désespoir éternel de connaître ni leur principe ni leur fin? Toutes choses sont sorties du néant et portées jusqu'à l'infini. Qui suivra ces étonnantes démarches? L'auteur de ces merveilles les comprend. Tout autre ne le peut faire.
>
> What will he do then, but perceive [some] appearance from the middle of things, in an eternal despair at knowing neither their principle nor their end? All things come from nothingness and are swept away toward the infinite. Who will follow these astonishing proceedings? The author of these wonders understands them. No one else can.

If Pascal exaggerates by making human despair "eternal," this is done to cure it. First though, he would save us from the illusion that he himself once possessed: namely, that lasting empirical knowledge may be won. As the ploce of "Toutes . . . Tout" argues, God alone can "follow" the progress of things. Bacon's "advancement of learning" effectively becomes a march of folly as Pascal lambastes the temerity and *superbia* of those who "ont voulu comprendre les principes des choses, et de là arriver jusqu'à connaître tout, par une présomption aussi infinie que leur objet." Not only does "presque toutes [choses]" in nature participate in this double infinity, but "toutes les sciences sont infinies en l'étendue de leur recherches."[11] Pascal thus improves on the First Meditation's synecdochic logic by making his expressions of infinity reason enough to view all science as folly. Geometry, for example, is capable of generating "une infinité d'infinites de propositions," so Pascal now rejects it implicitly along with the *définitions du nom* that previously enabled him to embrace geometric reasoning without confronting a conceptual abyss with each axiom and definition.

Having supplemented, then, the two spatial infinities with the methodological infinity characterizing the epistemology of the new sciences, Pascal pauses to mock the vanity and presumption of those thinkers — he cites titles by Descartes, Democritus, Scotus, and Pico — who have sought "connaître toutes choses."[12] While such blame is but part of his larger moral aim to debase man's sense of grandeur and emphasize his native misery, remarkable still is how the concept of infinity serves as the pivot on which the *pensée* shifts away from infinity per se and toward that other cataphatic term in his initial query: "man."[13] To amplify the dangers of philosophic presumption, the paradoxes and metaphorics associated with infinity are now redeployed to emphasize just how incommensurable the desire for knowledge is with actual human capabilities:

> On se croit naturellement bien plus capable d'arriver au centre des choses que d'embrasser leur circonférence, et l'étendue visible du monde nous surpasse visiblement. Mais comme c'est nous qui surpassons les petites choses, nous nous croyons plus capables de les posséder, et cependant il ne faut pas moins de capacité pour aller jusqu'au néant que jusqu'au tout. Il la faut infinie pour l'un et l'autre. Et il me semble que qui aurait compris les derniers principes des choses pourrait aussi arriver jusqu'à connaître l'infini. L'un dépend de l'autre, et l'un conduit à l'autre. Ces extrémités se touchent et se réunissent à force de s'être éloignées, et se retrouvent en Dieu, et en Dieu seulement.

We naturally believe we are far more capable of reaching the center of things than of embracing their circumference. The visible extent of the world visibly surpasses us. But since we surpass the small things, we believe we are more capable of possessing them, and yet it takes no less capacity to reach nothingness than totality. Infinite capacity is required for both. It seems to me that whoever had understood the ultimate principles of things could also have reached knowledge of the infinite. The one depends on the other, and one leads to the other. These extremities touch and reunite by dint of their separation from one another, and find each other in God and God alone.

Neatly transforming his hyperboles measuring the macrocosmic and microcosmic universes into ones mapping cognitive limits, Pascal depends on what Lakoff and Johnson call the basic cognitive metaphors of *knowledge as a journey* ("pour aller . . . arriver") and *knowledge as a possession* ("de les posséder") to plot epistemological difficulty.[14] Even his diction — such as the repeatedly-used verb *surpasser* — participates in spatial and quantitative metaphorics. Meanwhile, the spatialized antithesis between knowledge of first principles and the infinite eventually yields hermetic insight into God's unity, here figured as a closed circle. Indeed, the way that this circle recalls the paradoxical, infinite sphere invoked earlier confirms just how sophisticated Pascal's "manière d'agréer" has become. Still, as dazzling as these hermetic images are, it is crucial to remember that even if all difference and "extrémités" dissolve in God's absolute nature ("en Dieu seulement"), then this dissolution depends on the thinker's own conceptual ability ("il me semble") to exploit and surpass language's logical limits.

Similarly, after neatly summarizing the disproportionalities already explored ("Notre intelligence tient dans l'ordre des choses intelligibles le même rang que notre corps dans l'étendue de la nature"), Pascal charts the limits of "toutes nos puissances." To put us in our proper place, he overwhelms with extreme quantities:

Nos sens n'aperçoivent rien d'extrême. Trop de bruit nous assourdit, trop de lumière éblouit, trop de distance et trop de proximité empêche la vue. Trop de longeur et trop de brièveté de discours l'obscurcit, trop de vérité nous étonne.

Our senses perceive nothing extreme. Too much noise deafens us; too much light dazzles, too great a distance or proximity hinders our view. A great length or great brevity obscures discourse; too much truth confounds us.

That this paratactic, anaphoric play on *trop* continues for several sentences more underscores the extent to which the movement of Pascal's own "discours" works to astonish just as much, if not more, as the excess of truth ("trop de vérité") adumbrated by it. Pascal has myriad predecessors in the blaming of extremes — as his interpolation of a moralistic quote from Tacitus and the echoing of Montaigne's *Essais* signal. Yet because his "heightening of *evidentia*" (Lausberg) relies heavily on insights culled from the new sciences, he can paradoxically ground his critique in the same quantitative epistemology he eventually rejects. Interrupting his litany above, he offers this acute analogy and maxim: "J'en sais qui ne peuvent comprendre que qui de zéro ôte quatre reste zéro. Les premiers principes ont trop d'évidence pour nous" [*I know people who cannot understand that four from zero leaves zero. First principles are too self-evident for us*]. De Man, we saw in the previous chapter, argues that Pascal's zero is "heterogeneous" and "nameless"; but here the same obtains for "first principles" and all quantitative reason. Instead of charting a *via media* or a mean proportion as a remedy, Pascal adds, via ellipsis and analogy, yet more phenomenal and ontological extremes:

> ... les qualités excessives nous sont ennemies et non pas sensibles ... Trop de jeunesse et trop de vieillesse empêche l'esprit, trop et trop peu d'instruction. Enfin les choses extrêmes sont pour nous comme si elles n'étaient point, et nous ne sommes point à leur égard, elles nous échappent ou nous à elles.

> Qualities in excess are harmful to us and cannot be perceived ... Extreme youth and extreme ages disturb the mind, as do too much and too little learning. In short, extremes are for us as though they did not exist, nor we for them. They escape us, or we them.

That these "choses extrêmes" cause him now to doubt humanity's relation to what Husserl calls the foundational, pre-rational *Lebenswelt* dramatizes just how radical Pascal's skeptical critique threatens to become.[15]

Hearkening back to the *pensée*'s opening "Voilà," his peroration further sharpens this critique:

> Voilà notre état véritable. C'est ce qui nous rend incapables de savoir certainement et d'ignorer absolument. Nous voguons sur un milieu vaste, toujours incertains et flottants, poussés d'un bout vers l'autre. Quelque terme où nous pensions nous attacher et nous affermir, il branle et nous quitte. Et si nous le suivons, il échappe à nos prises, il glisse et fuit d'une fuite éternelle. Rien ne s'arrête pour nous, c'est l'état qui nous est naturel et toutefois le plus contraire à notre inclination. Nous brûlons du désir de trouver une assiette ferme, et une dernière base constante pour édifier une tour qui s'élève à l'infini, mais tout notre fondement craque et la terre s'ouvre jusqu'aux abîmes.

> This is our true state. It is what makes us incapable of certain knowledge or absolute ignorance. We float on a vast ocean, ever uncertain and adrift, blown this way or that. Whenever we think we have some point to which we can cling and fasten ourselves, it shakes free and leaves us behind. And if we follow it, it eludes our grasp, slides away, and escapes forever. Nothing stays still for us. This is our natural condition and yet one farthest from our inclination. We burn with desire to find firm ground and an ultimate secure base on which to build a tower reaching up to the infinite. But our whole foundation cracks, and the earth opens up into abysses.

Conflating the Lucretian shipwreck metaphor with the figure of the Tower of Babel, Pascal's truth claim ("Voilà notre état véritable") rests on two unstable foci: the extreme desire for knowledge and the extreme reluctance of the world to yield any "terme" that might aid this desire.[16] As such we — with the help of the insistent repetition of "nous" and "notre" — are implicated in our own perdition and fall. Caught between two absolute epistemological conditions, we witness a "tour" become "tout" only to be transformed into "abîmes." Reading, we become philosophic Tantaluses ("il glisse et fuit d'une fuite éternelle"). The omnipotent but elusive "terme" exercises the greatest agency. A synecdoche for all philosophic abstractions and so for philosophy itself, this "terme" is figured as a raging sea, even as it is ingeniously endowed with the simple, material quality of water slipping between one's fingers.

Shifting from shipwreck to tower, Pascal varies the basic spatial metaphor of *knowledge is space* (i.e., a person's knowledge *extends* to the smallest detail) to describe the wavering between certainty and ignorance. Symptomatic of the Baroque preoccupation with human inconstancy, Pascal's dashed desire for "une assiette ferme" inverts Descartes' hope of finding an epistemological, Archimedean point.[17] Instead of a "point," Pascal repeatedly, exultantly, discovers "rien." Implicitly responding to the Third and Fourth Meditations, the entire passage creates irrevocable disjunctions between mind and world. The macrocosmos is actively hostile to all microcosmic desire for knowledge. Yet the notion that such hostility might be due to an ontological link between man and the cosmos is destroyed by the violent imagery of disruption ("il branle et nous quitte," "tout notre fondement craque") and dislocation ("Nous voguons sur un milieu vaste . . ."). In sum, just as Pascal builds a rhetorical Tower of Babel with hyperbole, he demonstrates how the Tower's destruction is an act of self-consciousness and not a consequence of some divine edict. The hyperbolist's task is again *desengaño* rather than *engaño*; the apologist's *superiectio* would slay the *superbia* of the natural philosopher and metaphysician. Like Lear in the storm, Pascal abnegates then annihilates his own subjectivity by subjectively hyperbolizing the cosmic forces arrayed against him.

Standing back from his crumbling rhetorical edifice, Pascal finally discerns the *morale* of his *pensée*: "Cela étant bien compris, je crois qu'on se tiendra en repos, chacun dans l'état où la nature l'a placé" [*Once this is well understood, I think we will remain at rest, each of us in a state where nature has placed us*]. Such *ataraxia*, though, proves premature; instead of allowing us "repos," Pascal immediately adduces further epistemological and psychological consequences from his perception of the infinite:

> Dans la vue de ces infinis tous les finis sont égaux, et je ne vois pas pourquoi asseoir son imagination plutôt sur un que sur l'autre. La seule comparaison que nous faisons de nous au fini nous fait peine.
>
> From the perspective of these infinites, all finites are equal, and I see no reason for fixing our imagination on one rather than on another. The only comparison we make of ourselves to the finite is painful to us.

Hyperbole becomes here pure, invidious comparison.[18] To hyperbolize produces pain; but not to hyperbolize is to ignore our true, immanent condition.

The imaginative act of comparing ourselves to the infinite irredeemably infects even the most familiar, seemingly innocuous ways we measure our lives and ourselves. The quantities we use to calculate time's passage lack all proportionality and therefore all meaning because, Pascal passionately if sophistically argues, knowledge of the infinite whole ("le tout") to which they logically belong is impossible. Such extreme disproportionality is ontological as well as epistemological; ultimately, it points to God, who authors another kind of circle:

> Donc toutes choses étant causées et causantes, aidées et aidantes, médiatement et immédiatement, et toutes s'entretenant par un lien naturel et insensible qui lie les plus éloignées et les plus différentes, je tiens impossible de connaître les parties sans connaître le tout, non plus que de connaître le tout sans connaître particulièrement les parties.

> All things, then, are caused and causing, supporting and dependent, mediate and immediate; and all support one another in a natural, though imperceptible chain linking together things most distant and different. So, I hold it is as impossible to know the parts without knowing the whole as to know the whole without knowing the particular parts.

While this aporia strongly prefigures the phenomenologist's hermeneutic circle, one essential difference emerges: namely, that for Pascal this circularity may also be ascribed to our fallen condition as spiritual beings trapped in material bodies. Thus the *pensée* concludes by insisting, via Augustine, on the impossibility of knowing with any certainty the nature of the ontological links between body and spirit.[19] To say that a body fears the void or that a soul occupies a place is to confuse corporeal and spiritual attributes. Reasoning by analogy can only go so far until it also becomes aporetic. Indeed, as one of the parenthetical asides following this last quote confirms, the entire *pensée* aims to create a cognitive, disjunctive "effet." Pascal hopes, literally and figuratively, to debase his skeptical reader, to strip him of epistemological, Cartesian illusions, and thereby prepare him for spiritual salvation. Only God via his grace offers a way out of the circle.[20]

SILENCE AND THE VOID

It seems that the nominal confusion Pascal ascribes to "tous les philosophes" is intentionally cultivated by his own *pensée*, which also moves from corporeal to spiritual things and back again. (Such confusion may go by the name of metaphor or what Ryle calls a "category mistake."[21]) In other words, I take Pascal's concluding hyperbole to apply to him as well as to "man" in general:

> L'homme est à lui-même le plus prodigieux objet de la nature, car il ne peut concevoir ce que c'est que corps, et encore moins ce que c'est qu'esprit, et moins qu'aucune chose comment un corps peut être uni avec un esprit.[22]

> Man is to himself the most prodigious object of nature, for he cannot conceive what body is, still less what mind is, and least of all how a body can be united to a mind.

Made increasingly ironic by the increasingly small ("ce que . . . moins ce que . . . moins qu'aucune") amount of certainty available to humanity, this period, with its initial superlative qualification of praise ("le plus prodigieux"), also recalls the "prodige" of microscopic infinity that astonished earlier. But here, inverting Pico's optimism, Pascal marvels how limited the scope of our syncreticism is.

The *pensée* ends by indicating four subsequent "considerations" in the "preuve de notre faiblesse."[23] Its final sentence gestures contradictorily at logical closure and how Pascal's fragmentary form of proof must be open-ended if it is to remain true to his teleology of faith over reason and the cardinal insight that the divine and its manifestations defy all resources of our fallen language. But then, after contemplating the empty, silent space on the page, the reader turns to *pensée* #231 only to discover that in fact a certain paradoxical species of *superbia* has survived, even thrived, in the crucible of #230:

> L'homme n'est qu'un roseau, le plus faible de la nature, mais c'est un roseau pensant. Il ne faut pas que l'univers entier s'arme pour l'écraser, une vapeur, une goutte d'eau suffit pour le tuer. Mais quand l'univers l'écraserait, l'homme serait encore plus noble que ce qui le tue, puisqu'il sait qu'il meurt et l'avantage que l'univers a sur lui. L'univers n'en sait rien.

> Man is only a reed, the weakest thing in nature, but he is a thinking reed. The whole universe does not need to take up arms to crush him; a vapor, a drop of water, is enough to kill him. But if the universe were to

crush him, man would still be nobler than what killed him, because he knows that he is dying and the advantage the universe has over him. The universe knows nothing of this.

The suddenness with which the progressive hyperbolic diminuition of man is stopped by a mere conjunction has epochal importance; the "mais" harmo-nizes the initially discordant metaphor of man as a reed so that "l'homme" may now see himself as both a material ("roseau") and spiritual ("pensant") being. Pascal then amplifies this hyperbole from another direction by person-ifying the "universe" — a personification made jarringly vivid by the twice-repeated verb *écraser* — and its tiny forces ("une vapeur, une goutte d'eau") as killers. Just as the juxtaposition of "l'univers" and "rien" in the last sentence sharpens the conceit by exaggerating the impossibility of knowledge, Pascal audaciously remakes Descartes' *cogito* by assigning moral worth, because of his self-consciousness, to the victim of this potential homicide. But now the *res cogitans* possesses an ethical and spiritual value rather than an epistemological one. The "thinking reed" about to be murdered can be folded into the larger metaphoric, theological narrative of a "Word made flesh," a *logos* or *verbum* then voluntarily sacrificed to redeem disproportionate man's sins. Put another way, Pascal confuses the corporeal and spiritual, not as a *philosophe*, but as a Christian hyperbolist.

The second *pensée* supplementing "Disproportion de l'homme" reads:

> Toute notre dignité consiste donc en la pensée. C'est de là qu'il faut nous relever, et non de l'espace et de la durée, que nous ne saurions remplir.
>
> Travaillons donc à bien penser. Violà le principe de la morale.

> All our dignity consists, then, in thought. It is from this that we must raise ourselves, and not from space and duration, which we could not fill.
>
> Let us labor, then, to think well. This is the principle of morality.

Pascal makes credible this absolute claim ("Toute") on behalf of the value of moral and religious thought (as opposed to empirical, mathematical, or philo-sophic thought) in two ways. First, he draws on the cataphatic and apophatic experience of reading #230: the sublime phrase, "que nous ne saurions remplir," conjures up vast vistas, multiplicity without end, and an epistemo-logical impasse that only can be resolved by taking the transcendent ("morale") bridge of grace over the sublime, but negative abysses of physical space. Prefiguring Kant's moralization of the dynamical sublime, this tran-scendence confirms the epistemological conundrum posed by such enormous quantities, or what Kant will call the mathematical sublime. (Though, as I will argue below, the different solutions offered by Pascal and Kant to these difficulties derive from radically divergent notions concerning the ultimate value of rational or philosophic thought.) Second, the "Voilà" creates clo-sure; it circles back to the "Voilà" commencing #230, and thus marks the "moral principle" as the unique remedy for epistemological "weakness." The basic metaphor of ascent as knowledge and salvation acquires a powerful specificity, as Pascal's *relève* is explicitly divorced from its source domains of time and space and our corresponding limitations in these realms. In this way, elevation discards all quantitative connotations and becomes fully metaphysi-cal. It becomes an experience vouchsafed for the few willing and able to fol-low Pascal's hyperbolic ascent.[24]

The third supplementing *pensée*, however, topples the entire rhetorical, re-ligious, sky-scraping edifice in one fell swoop. It reads simply, shockingly: "Le silence éternel de ces espaces infinis m'effraie" [*The eternal silence of these infinite spaces frightens me*] (#233). Arguably, one could ascribe this terrifying "Poème"[25] to Pascal's evil genius, to a provisional character determined to mine the most nihilistic consequences from a thought. Indeed, the objective genitive signals that this "silence" is always already infused with the vertigi-nous conceptual and psychological momentum that Pascal discovers in the macrocosmic and microcosmic infinities. And yet the new cosmological logic of infinity, as Bruno exuberantly demonstrates in *On the Infinite Universe and Worlds* (1584), need generate neither fear nor incredulity. In the infinite spaces of his syncretic cosmos, Bruno sees a plurality of Lucretian worlds and hears the divine, now Pythagorean, now Platonic music of the spheres.[26] But for the more melancholic Pascal, his earlier "désespoir éternel" finds here its macro-cosmic, metaphysical correspondence in "le silence éternel." With one sub-lime *aperçu*, infinite subjectivity becomes infinite objectivity. But such fearful symmetry cannot hold. To loose mere terror upon the centerless self would be to create a Pyrrhonian abyss exactly where Pascal would discover the non-subjective means to mediate infinity.

Why, then, does Pascal adopt this new persona exactly here? Has the value of "thinking well," which he has just embraced at the cost of the world, been vitiated by this "eternal silence"? I am reluctant to read the *pensée*, as many superb twentieth-century readers have, as marking a fatal, existential impasse that will make Pascal's subsequent recourse to God's grace seem al-most an act in bad faith. In other words, is the most authentic response to this *pensée*, "The Wager" (#681) in which self-interest and sterile reason try to hoodwink the soul into belief? Or, conversely, is #233 a final apophatic turn or detour on the *via negativa* before arriving at Paradise? It is true that in #234, the last supplementing *pensée*, Pascal offers a measure of consolation. But such comfort appears to emerge from the very same infinite, silent, eternal spaces filling Pascal with dread. How then does Pascal get from here to there, from, if you will, the negative to the positive sublime?

In my view the answer lies in the way that discussions about the plenum and void inform Pascal's one-line poem. Whereas Bruno, manneristically re-making the Lucretian void, sees an infinite, animist Plenum, Pascal's theo-logical cosmos is riven with the consequences of the Fall. These include the possibility that God will abandon man, with his boundless presumption but limited knowledge and power, in his impossible attempt to compass the void. Early in his career, in the wake of Torricelli's experiments with the barometer, Pascal dedicated several scientific texts to investigating the properties of the void or vacuum.[27] In the *Pensées*, however, empirical knowledge is repeatedly dismissed or converted into moral and metaphysical speculation. In particu-lar, *pensée* #181 complements the bleak, apophatic gesture of #233, by trans-forming the void into a site of cataphasis.[28] Ostensibly dedicated to describing the extent of the folly of the faithless man who still seeks happiness, virtue, and justice, it paints the grimmest of pictures of the human condition by re-fusing to exclude any place, time, or rank: "Tous se plaignent, princes, sujets, nobles, roturiers, vieux, jeunes, forts, faibles, savants, ignorants, sains, malades, de tous pays, de tous les temps, de tous âges et de toutes conditions" [*All com-plain: princes, subjects, nobles, commoners, old, young, strong, weak, learned, ignorant, healthy, sick, from all countries, all times, all ages, and all conditions*]. But then Pascal offers a theological explication for these perpetually unfulfilled desires:

> Qu'est-ce donc que nous crie cette avidité et cette impuissance, sinon qu'il y a eu autrefois dans l'homme un véritable bonheur, dont il ne lui reste maintenant que la marque et la trace toute vide, et qu'il essaie inutilement de remplir de tout ce qu'il environne, recherchant des choses

absentes le secours qu'il n'obtient pas des présentes, mais qui en sont toutes incapables, parce que ce gouffre infini ne peut être rempli que par un objet infini et immuable, c'est-à-dire que par Dieu même.

What then does this craving and inability cry to us, if not that there once was a true happiness in man, of which there now remains only the mark and the empty trace? He tries vainly to fill it with everything around him, seeking from things absent the help he does not receive from things present. But they are all inadequate, because only an infinite and immutable object — that is, God himself — can fill this infinite abyss.

Further interiorizing his vision of infinite space, Pascal here precariously bal-ances hope with fear, "Dieu même" with "la trace toute vide." Now the pos-sibility that a benevolent "objet infini et immuable" might fill "ce gouffre infini" is pondered. Yet even this glimpse of grace does nothing to remedy the lack, the "absence," inherent in all human discourse. In the next paragraph, "ce gouffre infini" proves more far more cataphatic than apophatic:

Lui seul est son véritable bien. Et depuis qu'il l'a quitté, c'est une chose étrange qu'il n'y a rien dans la nature qui n'ait été capable de lui en tenir la place: astres, ciel, terre, éléments, plantes, choux, poireaux, ani-maux, insectes, veaux, serpents, fièvre, peste, guerre, famine, vices, adultère, inceste.

He alone is man's true good. And since man has forsaken him, it is strange that nothing in nature has been capable of taking his place: stars, heavens, earth, elements, plants, cabbages, leeks, animals, insects, calves, serpents, fever, pestilence, war, famine, vices, adultery, incest.

Like Quirinus Kuhlmann's paratactic poetry, Pascal's discursive *copia*, "cab-bage" and all, ennumerates the world in order to sublimate it.[29] Such ennu-meration temporarily fills the nothingness left by the perception of a hidden God. Then its place is taken by the objective "eternal silence" of Copernican space, a silence that evokes the *affectus*, the fear, which finally permits an inef-fable *logos* to be heard. All of which is to say that the line drawn by Pascal be-tween hyperbole and silence is as inscrutable and fluid as the lines between vanity, fear, and faith. According to his negative theological logic, eternal si-lence is a hyperbolic metonym for a spiritual void, a void emerging from the

realization that the physical and mathematical sciences leave us only with un/
translatable ("n'ait été capable de lui en tenir la place") infinity and nullity
(*néant*).[30] The void is Pascal's zero, the Fool's "naught"; it requires hyperbole
because it is literally beyond belief. It is *ultra fidem*; but then again so is faith. As
Pascal exclaims in #182: "Incroyable que Dieu s'unisse à nous" [*Incredible that
God should unite himself to us*].

PASCAL'S READERS

As hyperbole becomes truly heuristic, the active reader necessarily becomes
something of a hyperbolist as well. Echoing the structuralist analyses of Gans
and Perrin linking hyperbole and irony, Sellier observes that the hyperbolist
requires "une certaine complicité intellectuelle du lecteur." Without such
complicity, "se multiplient les controverses, sur la base d'objections fallaci/
euses."[31] This also resembles Cavell's claim that Shakespearean tragedy re/
quires the audience's "complicity," as well as Descartes' assumption that his
readers accept at face value his "franchise." In short, the hyperbolist depends
inordinately on readerly sympathy for his motives and aims. Pascal expects,
even demands, such sympathy and complicity. For again, if we are not able to
share to a significant extent the hyperbolist's project — be it poetic, philo/
sophic, political, or religious — then his figure is likely to seem merely men/
dacious or sophistic. When such complicity disappears, so does the means for
deriving value from hyperbole.

In regard to Pascal's contemporaries, the most lethal cause for their loss of
complicity and hence vehement objections to his hyperbole are the mutable,
often inchoate dictates of taste. The increasingly rancorous debate in the latter
half of the seventeenth century on the nature of *bienséance* and *le bon goût*
and whether taste should be treated as a moral, aesthetic, or social phenome/
non claims hyperbole as one of its principal victims. In order to engage this
debate and to historicize further Pascal's hyperbole, then, I wish briefly to
consider Arnauld and Nicole's *La logique ou l'art de penser* (1662), the Abbé
de Villars' *Traité de la délicatesse* (1671), Bouhours' *La Manière de bien penser
dans les ouvrages d'esprit* (1688), and Dumarsais' treatise *Les Tropes* (1729) —
especially as the latter also incorporates some of Boileau's thoughts on poetic
"excès."[32]

In *La logique ou l'art de penser* (also known as *La logique de Port/Royal*), An/
toine Arnauld and Pierre Nicole take a largely skeptical view of hyperbole.
Tolling another death/knell for the *ars retorica* as it was generally practiced

throughout the Renaissance and Baroque, they present themselves as avatars of neo-classical restraint. Rhetoric, they urge, should be grounded in nature and custom rather than in the study of traditional models or in the cultivation of figures and *copia*. Rhetoric is thus relegated to being an "aesthetic supple-ment" to logical discourse, such that its figures are granted only expressive or affective value.[33] Thinking logically is encumbered rather than enabled by ex-cessive attention to language and its material aspects:

> On a consideré . . . en ce qui regarde la Rhetorique, que le secours qu'on en pouvoit tirer pour trouver des pensées, des expressions, & des embellissemens, n'etoit pas si considerable. L'esprit fournit assez de pen-sées, l'usage donne les expressions; & pour les figures & les ornemens, on n'en a toûjours que trop. Ainsi tout consiste presque à s'éloigner de cer-taines mauvaises manieres d'écrire & de parler, & sur-tout d'un stile ar-tificiel & rethoricien composé de pensées fausses & hyperboliques & de figures forcées, qui est le plus grand de tous les vices.[34]

> . . . we thought that rhetoric is not very helpful for finding thoughts, ex-pressions, and embellishments. The mind furnishes enough thoughts, and usage provides the expressions. And usually there are too many metaphors and figures of speech. So the main idea is to avoid certain bad styles of writing and speaking, and above all the artificial rhetorical style made up of false and exaggerated thoughts and forced metaphors, which is the worst vice.

By way of contrast, they assure readers that their own book contains numer-ous "choses utiles" to help one avoid such "pensées fausses & hyperboliques." Rhetorical excess ("on n'en a toûjours que trop") has no heuristic or logical value. Instead, a reader-listener is often seduced by what Cicero (and later, Augustine) calls the husk of words rather than the seed of meaning:

> Entre les causes qui nous engagent dans l'erreur par un faux éclat qui nous empêche de la reconnoître, on peut mettre avec raison une certaine éloquence pompeuse & magnifique, que Ciceron appelle *abundantem so-nantibus verbis uberibusque sententiis*. Car il est étrange, combien un faux raisonnement se coule doucement dans la suite d'une periode qui remplit bien l'oreille, ou d'une figure qui nous surprend, & qui nous amuse à la

regarder . . . Combien le desir de faire une pointe a⸝t⸝il fait produire de fausses pensées? Combien la rime a⸝t⸝elle engagé de gens à mentir.[35]

Among the causes that lead us into error by a false brilliance that pre⸝ vents us from recognizing it, we ought to put a certain pompous and magnificent eloquence, which Cicero calls *abundantem sonantibus verbis uberibusque sententiis*. For it is strange how a fallacious inference can slide gently by us following a phrase that is pleasing to the ear of a figure that is startling and delightful to consider . . . How many false thoughts have been produced from the desire to make a point? How often has rhyme tempted us to lie?

Here the baby, or a large portion of the practice and values associated with hu⸝ manist eloquence, is thrown out with the bathwater in the name of logical clarity and aesthetic taste. The conceited style, the Petrarchan manner, and, more generally, the writer's desire to produce novelty, surprise, and brilliance are all blamed. Condemning as jejune those who still call a "Damoiselle" a "Vestale," Arnauld and Nicole pummel this easy target to shift their critique further away from what constitutes a proper style to the more Cartesian con⸝ cern of establishing rules for the proper mode of reasoning:

> Les faux raisonnemens de cette sorte, que l'on rencontre si souvent dans les écrits de ceux qui affectent le plus d'être éloquens, font voir combien la plûpart des personnes qui parlent, ou qui écrivent, auroient besoin d'être bien persuadés de cette excellente regle. Qu'il n'y a rien de beau que ce qui est vrai: ce qui retrancheroit des discours une infinité de vains ornemens, & des pensées fausses. Il est vrai que cette exactitude rend le stile plus sec & moins pompeux; mais elle le rend aussi plus vif, plus se⸝ rieux, plus clair, & plus digne d'un honnête homme . . .[36]

Fallacious arguments of this sort, which are so often encountered in the writings of those who affect the most eloquence, show how most people who speak or write need to be thoroughly convinced of this excellent rule: Nothing is more beautiful than the truth. This would remove countless useless flourishes and false thoughts from their speech. Now it is true that precision makes the style drier and less pompous. But it also makes it livelier, more serious, clearer and more worthy of an honest person.

Reminiscent of those Samuel Johnson will offer in "Cowley" concerning the neoclassical ideal, these dictates are based, like Johnson's, on an ethical critique ("plus digne d'un honnête homme") that excludes the kind of cognitive and so theological effects pursued by Pascal. Put another way, subtraction ("re-trancheroit") rather than addition ("une infinité de vains ornemens, & des pensées fausses") characterizes Arnauld and Nicole's proleptic take on the logic of the *supplément*.

It is in this context that the oft-quoted phrase, "Feu Monsieur Pascal qui savait autant de véritable rhétorique que personne n'en ait jamais su," a phrase that appears unambiguously to praise Pascal's rhetorical skills, should be con-sidered. It occurs where Arnauld and Nicole are arguing that self-love leads to "l'esprit de contradiction." They then cast Pascal as someone who carefully uses language to preclude this tendency:

> Feu Monsieur Pascal qui savait autant de véritable rhétorique que per-sonne n'en ait jamais su, portoit cette regle jusques à prétendre, qu'un honnête homme devoit éviter de se nommer, & même de se servir de mots de *je*, & *moy*, & il avoit accoûtumé de dire sur ce sujet, que la piété chré-tienne aneantit le *moy* humain, & que la civilité humaine le cache & le supprime.[37]

> The late M. Pascal, who knew as much about true rhetoric as anyone has ever known, carried this rule as far as to claim that honest peo-ple ought to avoid referring to themselves, and even using words like "I" and "me." On this subject he was accustomed to saying that Chris-tian piety nullifies the human "me" and human civility hides and sup-presses it.

The recently deceased Pascal is portrayed as a virtuous extremist who, with great rhetorical skill, eschewed personal vanity for the sake of truth. A "hon-nête homme," Pascal earns the praise but avoids the blame that we saw in the discussion of "faux raisonnemens" just above. Intriguingly, he is also posi-tively compared to Montaigne whose *libertinage* and extreme subjectivity are re-proached as tasteless and ethically suspect:

> C'est ce qui fait voir qu'un des caracteres des plus indignes d'un hon-nête homme, est celui que Montaigne a affecté, de n'entretenir ses lecteurs, que de ses humeurs, de ses inclinations, de ses phantasies, de ses

maladies, de ses vertus & de ses vices; & qu'il ne naît que d'un defaut de jugement aussi bien que d'un violent amour de soi-même.[38]

This shows that one of the most ignoble traits of an honest person is the one Montaigne affected, of entertaining his readers with all his moods, inclinations, fancies, maladies, virtues, and vices. This arises from a lack of judgment as well as an extreme love for oneself.

Pascal possesses the "jugement" and decorum that the affected Montaigne lacks. But even if we grant this dubious proposition, why do Arnauld and Nicole ignore Pascal's frequent and often startling use of the first person in the *Pensées*?[39] Also, on what basis do they distinguish Pascal's "véritable rhé-torique" from "éloquence pompeuse & magnifique" or a "stile artificiel & rethoricien composé de pensées fausses & hyperboliques & de figures forcées"?

Answers to these questions surely lie in the Cartesian insistence that lan-guage should serve only as a cognitive instrument for thinking well (where thinking well is synonymous with thinking clearly and distinctly). Their gen-eral praise of Pascal's rhetoric notwithstanding, Arnauld and Nicole's subse-quent discussion of how best to represent infinity confirms that their fellow Jansenist's "raisons" for deploying the most extreme figures are foreign to their own project. If we compare their treatment of the idea of infinity to how in-finity is represented in the *Pensées*, we see that their chief objection is grounded on an unwillingness to apply the logic of infinity to metaphysical questions:

Le plus grand abrègement que l'on puisse trouver dans l'étendue des sci-ences, est de ne s'appliquer jamais à la recherche de tout ce qui est au-dessus de nous, & que nous ne pouvons esperer raisonnablement de pouvoir comprendre. De ce genre sont toutes les questions qui regardent la puissance de Dieu, qu'il est ridicule de vouloir renfermer dans les bornes étroites de notre esprit, & generalement tout ce qui tient de l'in-fini; car notre esprit étant fini, il se perd & s'éboulit dans l'infinité, & de-meure accablé sous la multitude des pensées contraires qu'elle fournit.[40]

The best way to limit the scope of the sciences is never to inquire about anything beyond us, which we cannot reasonably hope to be able to un-derstand. Of this type are all questions concerning God's power, which it is ridiculous to try to confine within the narrow limits of the mind, and generally anything having to do with infinity. Because the mind is finite, it gets lost and is dazzled by infinity, and remains overwhelmed by the multitude of contrary thoughts that infinity furnishes us.

With his "misère" and his "esprit . . . fini," Pascal haunts this passage (though Arnauld and Nicole also may be responding to the debate between Descartes and Gassendi on the difference between the infinite and indefinite). Seeking to demarcate the proper "bornes" of logical discourse, they condemn the inquiry into the nature of infinity as "ridicule." A logical as well as an aesthetic mistake, such an inquiry creates only Baroque *copia*, a "multitude des pensées contraires." Dedicating themselves instead to the progress of the "sciences," they judge the most perilous kind of "pensées fausses & hyperboliques" to be metaphysical.

Anticipating Voltaire, the Abbé de Villars blames Pascal's hyperbole for the way that its rhetorical brilliance blind readers into adopting a single point of view.[41] In his *Traité de la délicatesse*, a largely hostile treatise in the form of a dialogue, the Abbé casts a certain Paschase to play an absolute, unforgiving, and so easily mocked Pascal. For his part, Aliton, the Abbé's mouthpiece, regrets Pascal's lack of subtlety in the *Pensées*. Explicitly attacking *pensées* #230–234, Aliton observes:

> Je me mets en la place d'un de ces hommes que vous voulez persuader: quelque odieuse que soit cette supposition. Penseriez-vous me bien *effrayer* . . . quand dans cette plaisante anatomie du ciron que vous nous avez faite, vous entreprendriez de me faire voir dans la plus petite vapeur qui sort de la plus petite goutte du sang qui est dans les veines d'un ciron; tout l'Univers visible; et ensuite une infinité de mondes, dont chacun a son firmament, son Soleil, ses Planettes? Estes-vous asseuré quand vous me faites ces propositions, que je ne vous prendray pas pour visionnaire? et qu'au lieu de *m'effrayer* de cela je n'en riray point; ou de moins que mon esprit n'essayera pas de secouër le joug de la Philosophie, sur les principes de laquelle vous faites ces bizarres demonstrations.[42]

> I put myself in the shoes of one of those men whom you want to persuade — however odious this supposition be. Do you think that you will *frighten* me . . . when, during this charming anatomy of the mite that you made, you undertake to make me see in the tiniest vapor that comes from the smallest drop of blood, which is in the veins of a mite,

the whole visible universe, and then an infinity of worlds, each of which with its firmament, sun, and planets? Are you confident when you make these propositions to me that I won't take you for a seer? And that, instead of *frightening me* with this, that I won't laugh more than a little? Or at least that my mind will not attempt to throw off the yoke of philosophy, upon whose principles you make these bizarre demonstrations.

The Abbé's emphasis on exploiting the reader's psychology underscores again how risky the use of hyperbole is. Without sympathy for the rhetorical task of "Disproportion de l'homme," or for that matter, Pascal's larger apologetic project, the Abbé only perceives two consequences of "ces bizarres demonstrations": laughter and despair. That neither of these aims corresponds to Pascal intentions confirms just how vulnerable the hyperbolist is to a reader who refuses to labor hermeneutically with the requisite Augustinian *caritas*. Lacking such charity, the Abbé mocks Pacal's *ethos* and taste. Thus when Aliton calls Paschase a "visionnaire," this has heterodox, enthusiast, and decidedly non-philosophical connotations.

To this (and much more) Paschase replies: "Je ne voulois pas parler en cet endroit des espaces imaginaires; tout ce que j'ay dit lá n'estoit qu'une figure un peu embellie pour discourir agreablement de la grandeur de la Nature" [*I did not wish to speak in this place of imaginary spaces; all that I have said there was merely a figure a little embellished in order to offer a pleasant discourse on Nature's grandeur*]. Made to reduce his vertiginous, metaphysical hyperboles into mere *plaisantries*, Paschase-Pascal becomes the weakest apologist imaginable for his own rhetoric. But even this does not placate Aliton-Abbé: "Sçachez, Paschase, que quand on veut prouver les veritez divines, on ne peut pas faire de plus grand faute que d'employer la figure et l'hiperbole. On s'ôte par là toute creance. Une pure et simple sincerité est la plus riche figure de l'eloquence Chrestienne" [*You should know, Paschase, that when one wants to prove divine truths, a greater mistake cannot be made than to employ figures and hyperbole. All belief is destroyed in this way. A pure and simple sincerity is the richest figure of Christian eloquence*]. Ignoring both the cataphatic and apophatic aspects of Pascal's attempt to "prove divine verities," the Abbé strips hyperbole of all its heuristic force and casts it instead as the enemy of a "pure et simple sincerité." Rather than regarding the acceptance of hyperbole as a propaedeutic, or as a necessary cognitive experience for the acceptance of Christian faith, the Abbé chooses to excommunicate it.

Taste becomes the explicit criterion of judgment in Dominique Bouhours' *La Manière de bien penser dans les ouvrages d'esprit*. That such taste is decidedly anti-Baroque makes it all the more significant that Bouhours would rescue hyperbole's vanishing legitimacy by folding it into the putatively more subtle workings of irony. In his *Avertissement*, Bouhours distances his treatise from what he perceives to be the narrowly Aristotelian and Cartesian project of Arnauld and Nicole in *La logique*. He offers instead "une Logique sans épines, qui n'est ni seché ni abstraite; mais une Rhétorique courte & facile, qui instruit plus par les éxemples que par les préceptes . . ." [*A logic without thorns, which is neither dry nor abstract; but a brief and easy rhetoric, which instructs more by examples than precepts . . .*].[43] His subject matter is "les ouvrages d'esprit . . . les histoires; les poëmes; les piéces d'éloquence, comme les harangues, les panégyriques, les oraisons funébres; enfin tout ce qui s'écrit avec soin, & où il faut une certaine justesse qui va encore plus aux choses qu'aux paroles" [*The works of the mind . . . histories, poems, pieces of eloquence, such as polemics, panegyrics, funeral orations, and finally all that is written with care and where is necessary a certain accuracy that concerns far more things than words*].[44] Bouhours thrice quotes approvingly the *Pensées* (he also calls Pascal "un des bons esprits de notre siècle"),[45] though he unfortunately does not analyze their "éloquence." Still, he does offer an acute perspective on the late seventeenth-century debate on the relative values of *res et verba* in so far as it concerns hyperbole.

Bouhours' two interlocutors are Eudoxe and Philanthe. The former has decidedly neoclassical tastes, the latter prefers a more Baroque canon:

> Eudoxe a le goust trés bon, & rien ne luy plaist dans les ouvrages ingénieux qui ne soit raisonnable & naturel. Il aime fort les Anciens, sur tout les Auteurs du siècle d'Auguste, qui selon luy est le siècle du bon sens . . . Pour Philanthe, tout ce qui est fleuri, tout ce qui brille, le charme. Les Grecs & les Romains ne valent pas à son gré les Espagnols & les Italiens. Il admire entre autres Lope de Vegue & le Tasse . . .[46]

> Eudoxe has very fine taste, and nothing pleases him in ingenious works that is not reasonable and natural. He loves very much the Ancients, above all the authors of the Augustan century, which according to him is the century of common sense . . . For Philanthe, all that is florid, all that is brilliant, charms him. To his taste, the Greeks and Romans are not worth what the Spanish and Italians are. He admires among others Lope de Vega and Tasso. . . .

An offshoot of *La querelle des anciens et des modernes* which was raging at the time, this stark division of tastes suggests why difficulty and hyperbole were becoming antithetical. Tellingly, along with "les Espagnols & les Italiens," Philanthe cites Macrobius and Seneca as exemplary wits. Likewise, he celebrates *vivezze d'ingegno* and *agudezas* as well as Aristotle's praise of metaphor and Tesauro's recommendation that the enthymeme be used as a basis for the *concetto*.[47] Such pursuit of ingenuity, however, sits poorly with the more pragmatic, Cartesian Eudoxe. After disputing the truthvalue of the pun or *equivoque*, the interlocutors commence an extended discussion of hyperbole in which Eudoxe asserts:

> L'origine seule du mot . . . décide la chose en général. Tout ce qui est excessif est vicieux, jusqu'à la vertu, qui cesse d'estre vertu dés qu'elle va aux extrémitez, & qu'elle ne garde point de mesures. Ainsi les pensées qui roulent sur l'hyperbole sont toutes fausses d'elles mesmes, & ne méritent point d'avoir place dans un ouvrage raisonnable, à moins que l'hyperbole ne soit d'une espece particuliére, ou qu'on y mette des adoucissemens qui en tempérent l'excés; car il y a des hyperboles moins hardies, & qui ne vont pas audelá des bornes, bien qu'elles soient au dessus de la créance commune. Il y en a que l'usage a naturalisées, pour ainsi dire, & qui sont si établies qu'elles n'ont rien qui choque.[48]

> The origin alone of the word . . . decides the matter in general. All that is excessive is vicious, including virtue, which ceases to be virtue as it goes to extremes, and as it fails to keep moderation. Thus the thoughts that are borne atop hyperbole are all false in themselves, and they do not merit a place in a reasonable work. This is the case in so far as the hyperbole is not of a particular kind, namely, when one applies blandishments that temper their excess. For there are less bold hyperboles, which do not want to go beyond bounds, even if they are above common belief. There are some that usage have naturalized, if you will, and which are so established that they no longer shock.

Only when hyperbole is tamed by *remedia* ("adoucissemens") or becomes a commonplace can it be called a "vertu." Offering as a marginal gloss Quintilian's "Ultra fidem, non ultra modum," Bouhours focuses solely on the latter half of this formula. More concerned with formal simplicity and maintaining decorum than giving the hyperbolist the license to respond to an extraordinary subject or occasion, he ignores Quintilian's most important caveat: "Tum est hyperbole virtus, cum res ipsa, de qua loquendum est, naturalem modum excessit."[49]

For his part, Eudoxe exemplifies what he means by decorous hyperbole when he notes how Homer, to prepare the way for the extravagant image of Polyphemus tearing off a mountaintop to hurl at Odysseus' ship, methodically amplifyies the stature of the cyclops before the hyperbole proper. Given such preparation, "on ne trouve point son action trop étrange."[50] Although this effectively makes hyperbole discursive as well as metaphoric, it also tends to diffuse the figure's force. After citing Quintilian's by then commonplace example from the *Aeneid* ("Pelago credas innare revulsas Cyclades"), Eudoxe argues that you can soften hyperbole's impact by giving it an "air de vraysemblance" and having the speaker acknowledge that it requires a certain credulity on the audience's part (i.e., "credas"). The latter "précaution sert comme de passeport à l'hyperbole."[51] Likewise, after citing a letter by one Madame de Saintot, which imitates the hyperbolic description of Angela in a French translation of *Orlando Furioso*, Eudoxe praises the way she qualifies her exaggerations.[52]

The striking metaphor of enabling hyperbole *to pass* muster (or censor) is refashioned again when Bouhours-Eudoxe considers how the addition of irony may mitigate or alter its impact: "L'ironie me semble encore toute propre à faire passer l'hyperbole."[53] Praising the coterie poet Vincent Voiture's "ton railleur" when exaggerating, Eudoxe cites as a counter example a hyperbole favored by Tesauro in *Il Cannocchiale aristotelico*. Tesauro's hyperbole about fireworks ("par che Sagliano ad infiammar la sfera del fuoco; à fulminare i fulmini, & a gridar allarme contra le stelle" [*because they ascend to ignite the sphere of fire, strike with lightning the lightning, and alarm the stars*]),[54] Eudoxe suggests, is naïve in its audacity and thus abuses the truth:

S'il badinoit comme Voiture, on luy passeroit ses pensées toutes hardies, toutes fausses qu'elles sont; car je le répéte, on peut tout dire en riant, & mesme si vous y prenez garde, le faux devient vray à la faveur de l'ironie: c'est elle qui a introduit ce que nous appellons *contrevéritez*, & qui fait que quand on dit d'une femme libertine & scandaleuse, que c'est une trés-honneste personne; tout le monde entend ce qu'on dit, ou plûtost ce qu'on ne dit pas.[55]

If he bantered like Voiture, one would overlook his thoughts, for all their boldness and falsity; for, I repeat, one can say anything in jest, and even, if you take care, the false can become true with the aid of irony. It is irony that has introduced what we call *contrevéritez*, and which makes it possible, when one says of a loose, scandalous woman that she is a very honest person, that the whole world understands what one says, or rather what one does not say.

This is symptomatic of an important historical shift in hyperbole's reception. It is as if Bouhours is at once looking backward to Rabelais, closing his eyes to Sponde, d'Aubigné, Pascal, and the rhetoric of the marvelous (*meraviglia*) promoted by Tesauro, even as he looks forward to the cynical mythopoesis practiced in Louis XIV's court and the world-weary style of La Rochfoucauld and Voltaire. Reduced to a *badin*, to someone "qui aime à rire, a plaisanter," the hyperbolist becomes a sly mannerist who loses all philosophical and theological authority. His play with truth and falsity, his *badinage*, needs never to be taken too seriously, mainly because it no longer participates in the aesthetics of difficulty. Hyperbolic wit must be transparent or not at all.

Finally, Dumarsais' influential *Les Tropes* represents the culmination, at least in France, of the Ramist tendency to relegate *inventio* to other disciplines and so reduce rhetoric merely to the study of tropes and figures of speech. With this noted, his largely hostile treatment of hyperbole is striking for its initial insistence that hyperbole has an important heuristic function.[56] To hyperbolize is almost to calculate:

Lorsque nous sommes vivement frappés de quelque idée que nous voulons représenter, et que les termes ordinaires nous paroissent trop foibles pour exprimer ce que nous voulons dire, nous nous servons de mots, qui, à les prendre à la lettre, vont au-delà de la vérité, et représentent le plus ou le moins pour faire entendre quelque excès en grand ou petit. Ceux qui nous entendent rabatent de notre expression ce qu'il en faut rabatre, et il se forme dans leur esprit une idée plus conforme à celle que nous voulons y exciter, que si nous nous étions servis de mots propres: par exemple, si nous voulons faire comprendre la légèreté d'un cheval qui court extrêmement vîte, nous disons qu'*il va plus vîte que le vent*. Cette figure s'apèle *hyperbole*, mot grec qui signifie *excès*.[57]

When we are forcefully struck by some idea that we want to represent, and when ordinary terms seem to us too weak to express what we way to say, we avail ourselves of words, which, taken literally, go beyond the truth, and represent more or less in order to make understood some ex-cess in greatness of smallness. Those who hear us tone down our ex-pression in that which it is necessary to tone down, and there forms in their mind an idea that conforms more with what we want to call forth there than if we had used proper words. For example, if we want to make comprehensible the light-footedness of a horse that gallops ex-tremely swiftly, we say that *he moves more swiftly than the wind*. This figure is called *hyperbole*, a Greek word signifying *excess*.

To exemplify this "excès," Dumarsais cites Virgil's *Aeneid* (8.808), *Exodus* (5:17), and then the *Gospel according to John* where the apostle proclaims (21:25): "But there are also many other things which Jesus did; were every one of them to be written, I suppose that the world itself could not contain the books that would be written."[58] Like Henry Peacham before him, Dumarsais thus partially protects the hyperbolist's *ethos* by invoking the authority of Scripture. In the next breath, however, he dismissively comments: "L'hyper-bole est ordinaire aux Orientaux."[59] He then pointedly, improbably, disavows hyperbole on behalf of classicist France by asserting: "Excepté quelques façons de parler comunes et proverbiales, nous usons trés-rarement d'hyper-boles en français."[60]

As if to confirm this, Dumarsais then approvingly quotes a short treatise by Pierre Nicole that banishes hyperbole to less decorous times, cultures, and social strata:

> Les Grecs avoient une grande passion pour l'hyperbole, comme on le peut voir dans leur Anthologie, qui en est tout remplie. Cette figure est la ressource des petits esprits qui écrivent pour les bas peuple.
>   Juvénal élevé dans les cris de l'école,
>   Poussa jusqu'à l'excès sa mordante hyperbole.
>   [*Boileau, L'art poétique* (chant 2)]
> Mais quand on a du génie et de l'usage du monde, on ne se sent guère de goût pour ces sortes de pensées fausses et outrées.[61]

The Greeks had a great passion for hyperbole, as one can see in their Anthology, which is filled with it. This figure is the recourse of small minds who write for the mob. *Juvenal, exalted by the clamor of the school, pushed to excess his mordant hyperbole.* But when one has genius and worldly experience, one hardly has a taste for these kinds of false and extravagant thoughts.

Besides its haughty disdain for those "small minds" (does this include Virgil, St. John, or Pascal?) and the less sophisticated (whom Quintilian more generously calls "rusticos"), this intertextual condemnation of hyperbole is particularly provocative for its insistence that genius and experience ought to preclude a "goût" for "pensées fausses et outrées." Dumarsais cunningly perverts the hyperbolist's greatest ambition: namely, to produce true thoughts through *outrée* language.[62] By piggybacking on Boileau, Arnauld, and Nicole, he avails himself of the rigor of *La logique* and the laureate authority of one of his day's leading poets. Indeed, throughout *L'art poétique* (1672) Boileau scathingly rebukes the kind of mannerist excess that characterizes much of the poetry and prose in early seventeenth-century France. As he urges in the *Chant premier*:

> Aimez donc la raison. Que toujours vos écrits
> Empruntent d'elle seule et leur lustre et leur prix.
>   La pluspart, emportez d'une fougue insensée,
> Toujours loin du droit sens vont chercher leur pensée:
> S'ils pensaient ce qu'un autre a pu penser comme eux.
> Evitons ces excès. Laissons à l'Italie
> De tous ces faux brillans l'éclatante folie.
> . . . .
> Fuyez de ces Auteurs l'abondance sterile,
> Et ne vous chargez point d'un détail inutile.[63]

By rejecting poetic furor ("d'une fougue insensée") as a motive for hyperbole, Boileau saves reason ("raison," "droit sens") from the taint of madness ("l'eclatante folie") and worthless *copia* ("l'abondance sterile"). His series of neat, spatial metaphors imperiously distance the French from the marvelous but illusory kingdom of rhetorical excess. Perhaps this is because the specter of mannerist rhetoric still looms too large for Boileau and Dumarsais to acknowledge hyperbole as a native phenomenon. For as with Quintilian, who discusses hyperbole in the shadow of the declaimers and Seneca, they treat hy-

perbolic excess after the protean excesses of the French Baroque. They in-
stinctively seem to realize how the hyperbolic threatens any attempt to objectify
"le bon goût." And so, as Freud might say, hyperbole is "displaced" [*verstellt*]
and "repressed" [*verdrängt*].

Yet hyperbole will not be so easily denied. Despite insisting that
the French generally eschew hyperbole, that it is the province of "petits esprits," and the joy only of the "bas peuple," in the treatise's next entry, "L'Hy-
potypose" [*an image, tableau*], Dumarsais enthusiastically quotes one of the
most famously hyperbolic passages in French literature, the "recit de
Théramène," from the penultimate scene of Racine's *Phèdre* (1677). The lines
he cites describe how the innocent Hippolyte is killed by a "montagne hu-
mide," a sea monster who stands in for fate:

> Cependent sur le dos de la plaine liquide,
> S'élève à gros bouillons une montagne humide;
> L'onde approche, se brise, et vomit à nos yeux,
> Parmi des flots d'écume, un monstre furieux;
> Son front large est armé de cornes menaçantes,
> Tout son corps est couvert d'écailles jaunissantes;
> Indomptable taureau, dragon impétueux,
> Sa croupe se recourbe en replis tortueux;
> Ses longs mugissemens font trembler le rivage;
> Le ciel avec horreur voit ce monstre sauvage,
> La terre s'en émeut, l'air en est infecté;
> Le flot qui l'aporta, recule épouvanté.[64] (1513–1524).

By making these lines exemplary, Dumarsais adds his voice to the contentious
débat, which raged from when the play was first performed until well into the
eighteenth century, on the relative propriety, verisimilitude, and sublimity of
the *récit*.[65] Reanimated by Leo Spitzer and others in the mid-twentieth century, this *débat* still marks faultlines between partisans of the stylistic ideals of
French classicism and proponents of the kind of subtle *excès* that would legit-
imize a French Baroque. Like Boileau, Houdart de la Motte, and others,
Spitzer seizes on the Alexandrine, "Le flot qui l'aporta, recule épouvanté," as
especially emblematic of Racine's affronts against "nature" and a natural
style. But he does so to argue for *Phèdre* as "the ideal type of a baroque tragedy,
not only by its style, but by its basic conception."[66] In terms of style, however,

I would argue that this alexandrine is more a hyperbole in the mode of Virgil, Góngora, and Pascal than a "paradox."[67] Informed by Senecan *sumpatheia* — Racine's chief literary model is Seneca's *Phaedra* — the "terrified" wave "re-coils" because the cosmos is polarized, riven by extremes, and, as Spitzer con-tends, because the gods and nature have repudiated humanity, thereby denying the reader or the characters within the play any soothing conceptual or spiri-tual mediation. The reader may well search for such mediation; Spitzer him-self, even in championing Racine's "demoniac" Baroque, goes to detailed lengths to discover throughout the *récit* and the play as a whole myriad, so-phisticated efforts at "klassische Dämpfung [*classical damping*]."[68] In making Théramène a stand-in for Racine, and perhaps, as Amy Wygant suggests, a stand-in for himself as well, Spitzer grants the most authoritative perspective to this "compassionate and detached philosopher."[69] This is to say that ulti-mately, despite positively comparing Racine's *Weltanschauung* several times to Pascal's, Spitzer too would defang the hyperbolic; not because it offends his tastes, but because he regards the author of a "great masterpiece" as always in control of his language and the conceptions that inform it.[70] Reading the sub-sequent lines describing Neptune's disguised, monstrous attack on Hip-polyte's horse ("On dit qu'on a vu même, en ce désordre affreux, / Un dieu qui d'aiguillons pressait leur flanc poudreux."), Spitzer inexplicably insists: ". . . simply by the act of calling something 'extreme,' we liberate ourselves from its impact; the impression of disorder or disharmony is not allowed to dominate the scene; on the contrary, the scene is gauged and defined for us."[71] But for my part, I would contend that however metrically or even syntactically measured Théramène's ornate alexandrines are, the *récit* itself remains, like the dead Hippolyte, "un corps défiguré" (1568). In the middle of his speech, Théramène begs forgiveness for his stylistic sins: "Excusez ma douleur. Cette image cruelle / Sera pour moi de pleurs une source éternelle" (1545–1546). Indeed, Racine's "cruel" *hypotypose* is an "eternal source" of hyperbole, one that brings home the tragedy of fate to Hippolyte's father, Thésée, and which eventually provokes Phèdre "rompre un injuste silence" (1617). Just as Hip-polyte cannot tame the earthshaking fury of nature and the gods, Dumarsais cannot put the hyperbolic genie back in the bottle. Anxious to restrict the power and allure of Racine's "monstre sauvage" — close kin to Pascal's "monstre incompréhénsible" — Dumarsais places it *au delá*, in the beyond, in the margins, much like Renaissance cartographers placed monstrous figures in the blank spaces, the *terrae incognitae*, yet to be explored and measured.

Chapter Sixteen

Critique of Hyperbolic Reason

> The road of excess leads to the palace of wisdom . . . You
> never know what is enough unless you know what is more
> than enough . . . Enough! or Too much.
> — William Blake, *The Marriage of Heaven and Hell*

KANT AND THE "GREAT CHASM"

While the taste for Pascal's Baroque brand of hyperbole, with its use and abuse of reason, markedly dissipated in the period bookmarked by the *esprit* of La Rochefoucauld and the *Witz* of German Romanticism, the rhetorical and epistemological questions raised by "Disproportion de l'homme" remained unresolved. They are, I think, still unresolved. Interpreting the exorbitant, inventive *métis* (cunning) of Odysseus in his encounter with Polyphemus as a form of "classifying reason" that seeks to destroy myth, Horkheimer and Adorno make this primal scene an emblem of the "dialectic of enlightenment."[1] Another act in this dialectic, I contend in this final chapter, is when that emblematic Enlightenment philosopher, Immanuel Kant, slyly makes hyperbole an object of practical reason (*praktische Vernunft*). Specifically, Kant's treatment of the infinite and sublime in the *Critique of the Power of Judgment* (1790, 1793) inordinately depends on the language and experience of hyperbole. Even as he affirms a lack of "any respect" for rhetoric (*ars oratoria*), a "deceitful art" [*hinterlistigen Kunst*] that "understands how to move people, like machines, to a judgment in important matters which must lose all weight for them in calm reflection," Kant's timely use of hyperbole serves crucial cognitive and teleological ends.[2] For at the heart of Kant's project lurks a "great chasm" between the imagination and reason, which he would persuade read-

ers can only be bridged by aesthetic judgments. Two readers famously not persuaded, however, are Stanley Cavell and Ludwig Wittgenstein. Their aver-
sion to Kant's frozen abysses and their respective explorations of the limits of
philosophical language to describe how we secure measures of truth and
meaning provide the foundation for what I would like to call a critique of hyperbolic reason.

In what sense does Kant makes hyperbole a philosopheme? When it
comes to the task of rescuing hyperbole from epistemological scorn and capricious judgments of taste, the third *Critique*, I wish to contend, succeeds despite
itself. Maintaining throughout that there can be no "determinate" judgments
of taste, Kant goes to extravagant lengths to demonstrate that even when confronted with the most incommensurable, displeasing objects in nature, the
mind may discover the comforts of reason.[3] In ultimately nominating the reasonable mind "sublime," as opposed to the scenes and objects it previously
imagined without the beneficial, morally-uplifting perspective characterized
by "free play," and in making the experience of the sublime "purposive" for
reason and stripping "purposiveness" from nature (if only provisionally),
Kant leaves a residue, a remainder, an object, whose "limitlessness" is wholly
hyperbolic.[4]

But before I flesh out this admittedly unorthodox reading of the third
Critique, we might recall how Pascal in *De l'esprit géométrique* conflates the sublime and the hyperbolic in order to condemn both on epistemological
grounds:

> It is not necessary to trick the mind; strained and labored manners of
> reasoning fill it with silly presumption caused by strange elevations and
> vain, ridiculous pomposity instead of with vigorous, solid nourishment.
> And one of the principal reasons why those who begin with these sub-
> jects stray so far from the true path they should follow is that the imagi-
> nation, which assumes at first that good things are inaccessible, gives
> them great, haughty, elevated, sublime names. This ruins everything. I
> would like to name these things lowly, common, familiar. These names
> are more suitable to such things. I hate these pompous words [*je hais ces
> mots d'enflure*].

In practice, however, Pascal in the *Pensées* hyperbolically inflates and deflates
words like "ciron" and "homme" to create what might, anachronistically, be

called an imaginative experience of the negative sublime, an experience that would compel readers to embrace faith or "reasons of the heart."

Kant does not name hyperbole in the *Critique of the Power of Judgment*, nor, again, is the role he assigns rhetoric very promising. As he describes it, rhetoric, the "art of persuasion," is a deceptive "dialectic" that would "win minds over to the advantage of the speaker before they can judge and . . . rob them of their freedom."[5] Yet, after proceeding to ban the *ars oratoria* from the "courtroom" and "pulpit," Kant cites approvingly, if circumspectly, an ancient, familiar ideal:

> He who has at his command [*in seiner Gewalt*], along with clear insight into the facts, language in all its richness and purity, and who, along with a fruitful imagination capable of presenting his ideas, feels a lively sympathy for the true good, is the *vir bonus dicendi peritus*, the speaker without art [*ohne Kunst*] but full of vigor, as Cicero would have him, though he did not himself always remain true to this ideal.[6]

It is in this sense that I read the language of the third *Critique* as rhetorical. Armed with Cicero's (and Quintilian's) ethical "ideal," his own "facts," pure and copious "language," and a "fruitful imagination," Kant would authoritatively, forcefully ("in seiner Gewalt"), persuade us of his "ideas." Specifically, in explaining the mathematical sublime and how it yields to the dynamical sublime, Kant leans heavily upon the quantitative rhetoric of hyperbole to describe how the imagination's pyrrhic encounter with the infinite is consonant with triumphant reason. Thus even as Pascal and Kant consider the same aporetic, infinite object of knowledge, Kant dramatically inverts the epistemological lessons of "Disproportion de l'homme." Moreover, the implicit and explicit ways by which Kant tries to exempt his own rhetoric from any taint of artifice or falsity again highlights the need to make the hyperbolic and its sublimation an object and event to be scrutinized, instead of a fact to be swiftly, silently assumed. In this sense, I read Kantian hyperbole as an essential element in what de Man calls the unacknowledged "materiality" of the philosopher's language, one that helps ensure the success of Kant's critical narrative or "allegorical tale" that would demonstrate the harmony between the mind's three higher faculties: understanding, reason, and judgment — faculties that in the course of the three *Critiques* are recast as the "capacities" of cognition, desire, and feeling pleasure and displeasure.[7] In writing the third

Critique, Kant would reconcile what he discovers about "theoretical reason" in the first *Critique* with the chief lesson learned in the second *Critique*, namely, that "[r]eason legislates *a priori* for freedom and its own causality."[8] In brief, the "great chasm" [*große Kluft*] that separates the supersensible from appearances" needs a "bridge," and it is the "power of judgment" that "provides the mediating concept between the concepts of nature and the concept of freedom."[9]

Now judgments of beauty are best suited for this task, but Kant, seemingly bewitched by this "chasm" of his own invention, or less dramatically, because he feels obliged to answer the theories of Burke and Addison, devotes §§23–29 of the third *Critique* to analyzing judgments of the sublime. Hyperbole is used in these sections to help construct a schematic, invidious comparison whereby in the encounter with the sublime Kant belittles and renders helpless the imagination in order that the mind realize the superiority of the ideas of practical reason and eventually experience the moral feelings of "intellectual satisfaction" and "respect."[10] Such invidiousness emerges at the outset of Kant's treatment of the sublime when he defines it with the formalist language of disproportionate comparisons:

> *That is sublime in comparison with which everything else is small . . . That is sublime which even to be able to think of demonstrates a faculty of the mind* [ein Vermögen des Gemüts] *that surpasses* [übertrifft] *every measure of the senses.*[11]

Thinking the sublime strains the limits of the purely aesthetic. It also frustrates language's ability to name or compass. The very act of comparison, whether rhetorical or cognitive, verges on the nonsensical in the face of the sublime. Nevertheless, Kant's subsequent discussion goes to great, often byzantine lengths to apply to judgments of the sublime the same four moments or logical categories of judgment — quantity, quality, relation, and modality — that he applies earlier to judgments of taste.[12] (The first two moments correspond to what he calls the mathematical sublime, the latter two to the dynamical sublime.) Why he insists on this parallelism, despite the "serious strain on the reader,"[13] lies beyond this chapter's scope. What I would emphasize, though, is that the harmony between humanity and nature, as well as the harmony between the faculties, two *desiderata* undergirding Kant's critical project, and which depend upon the mind's ability to accommodate the conceptual motion and violence (*Gewalt*) inherent in the experience and description of the sublime.[14]

Nowhere is this accommodation given more vivid expression than in this celebrated passage from §28, which Kant titles *On nature as a power*:

> Bold, overhanging, as it were threatening cliffs, thunder clouds tower-
> ing up into the heavens [*Kühne überhangende gleichsam drohenede Felsen, am
> Himmel sich auftürmende Donnerwolken*], bringing with them flashes of
> lightning and crashes of thunder, volcanoes with their all-destroying
> violence [*in ihrer ganzen zerstörenden Gewalt*], hurricanes with the devas-
> tation they leave behind, the boundless ocean set into a rage, a lofty
> waterfall on a mighty river, etc., make our capacity to resist into an
> insignificant trifle [*zur unbedeutenden Kleinigkeit*] in comparison with their
> power. But the sight of them only becomes all the more attractive the
> more fearful it is, as long as we find ourselves in safety, and we gladly call
> these objects sublime because they elevate [*erhöhen*] the strength of our
> soul above its usual level, and allow us to discover within ourselves a ca-
> pacity for resistance of quite another kind, which gives us the courage to
> measure ourselves against the apparent all-powerfulness of nature [*uns
> mit der scheinbaren Allgewalt der Natur messen zu können*].[15]

In this compelling if abbreviated narrative of the imagination's experience we first feel our powers reduced "zur unbedeutenden Kleinigkeit" in the face of the enormous dimensions offered by these exorbitant landscapes, but then, persisting, we learn to overcome the fear they provoke to "measure" ourselves more detachedly vis-à-vis nature. Seeking "safety" from nature's "all-destroying violence," the imagination turns inward and yields to reason; a conversion that enables us to apprehend calmly the "infinite, which for sensibility is an abyss [*Abgrund*]."[16] And though the psychological implications of this con-version story are potentially enormous, no gloss better epitomizes them, I think, than Brecht's pragmatic motto in *Die Dreigroschenoper*: "Erst kommt das Fressen, dann kommt die Moral" [*First comes eating* (like an animal)*, then comes morality*]. As long as the imagination (and its corporeal lodging) feels threatened, reason (and Kantian morality) in unable to spread its wings. Moreover, all this occurs on "negative" ground for the imagination, since it "*feels* the sacrifice or deprivation and at the same time the cause to which it is subjected."[17]

Yet for Kant to achieve his schematic end of uniting the sensible and supersensible, the ephemeral excess of an intuition can and must become a constant cognition; apprehension must give way to comprehension. In this transformation, language has an essential, if unacknowledged rôle in first presenting but then representing the "negative" feelings associated with the sublime.[18] These feelings consists of "terror . . . horror . . . the awesome shud⁄ der . . . melancholy reflection" because the imagination remains unaided when confronted with the kind of landscapes and natural phenomena we saw in the passage above. But if one strives for the "noble" state of mind — Kant calls it "*apatheia*" — that aims not to cultivate "astonishment [*Verwunderung*] (an af⁄ fect in the representation of novelty that exceeds expectation)," but rather "ad⁄ miration [*Bewunderung*] (an astonishment that does not cease when the novelty is lost)," the same scenes may foster the growth of "pure reason."[19] And while I would note that these two words do indicate different cognitive stances, de Man argues that the entire distinction may also turn on a mere, but momen⁄ tous interchange of prefixes: "Be⁄" for "Ver⁄".[20] In de Man's exposition of such "disarticulation," this metonymy points to a larger, conceptual shift marking the transition from the mathematical to the dynamical sublime. What I am calling the immanent, hyperbolic strain of naming then compass⁄ ing the sublime object, de Man describes (reading closely the stress Kant puts on the verb *denken*) as a dual but disjunctive task for the imagination, which first uses apprehension (*Auffassung*) but then comprehension (*Zusammenfas⁄ sung*) to make sense of the infinite. The former mimics a "syntagmatic, con⁄ secutive motion along an axis" and so "can proceed ad infinitum without difficulty," while the latter, to move beyond the "system of number⁄extension" (which de Man sees as the essence of the mathematical sublime), offers a per⁄ formative, synthetic, and ultimately aporetic solution to the paradoxes of the sublime. Apprehension of the sublime — or what amounts to the same thing here for Kant, the infinite — is based therefore on "the model of discourse as a tropological system," whereas comprehension necessitates "an extension of the linguistic model beyond its definition as a system of tropes."[21] By contrast, Pascal's "Disproportion de l'homme" exemplifies the necessity of moving from an empirical model to a linguistic or tropological one in the task of rep⁄ resenting the infinite, a difference that also highlights the divergent teleologies of Kant and Pascal.[22] In sum, a kind of *fiat* or illocutionary speech act by Kant decrees that reason alone can conceive of the infinite per se.

Kant conceives of admiration as what "happens when ideas in their pres⁄ entation unintentionally and without artifice [*ohne Kunst*] agree with aesthetic satisfaction."[23] This emphasis on the lack of "purposiveness" in objects to be judged as sublime echoes the caveat made several times in the *Analytic of the Sublime* that he is largely uninterested in discussing the sublime in art for there "a human end determines the form as well as the magnitude."[24] In artistic creations concepts limit both form and magnitude, hence they do not offer a sufficient *gradus ad Parnassum* for the comprehension of the idea of the infinite, or the supersensible. This begins to explain why we are urged, in the "General Remark on the Exposition of Aesthetic Reflective Judgments" (where Kant makes the distinction between astonishment and admiration), to regard the "ocean merely as poets do."[25] The poetic perspective for Kant is synonymous with the transcendental aesthetic of the power of judgment, that is, it attends to appearances only and not ends, thus allowing the "free play" that the mind needs to escape the thrall of the imagination and be reminded of the "moral respect" associated with practical reason. How, though, does Kant persuade us to see the ocean or, for that matter, "the starry heavens"[26] in this way? Why should we no longer attend to the "recit de Théramène" when we think of the ocean, or Pascal's "Disproportion de l'homme" when we contemplate the cosmos?

Kant's thoughts on rhetoric and poetry in the third *Critique* are, like his observations on music and the visual and plastic arts, shaped by the book's schematism. They also reflect the ignominy that rhetoric suffered in the Enlightenment *episteme*, to say nothing of the neoclassical tastes characteristic of the period:

> *Rhetoric* is the art of conducting the business of the understanding as a free play of the imagination; *poetry* that of carrying out a free play of the imagination as a business of the understanding.
>
> The *orator* thus announces a matter of business and carries it out as if it were merely a *play* with ideas in order to entertain the audience. The *poet* announces merely an entertaining *play* [*ein unterhaltendes* Spiel] with ideas, and yet as much results for the understanding as if he had merely the intention of carrying on its business. The combination and harmony of the two cognitive faculties, the sensibility and the understanding . . . must seem to be unintentional and to happen on their own; otherwise it is not *beautiful* art. Hence everything contrived and laborious [*Gesuchte und Peinliche*] must be avoided . . .[27]

Chiasmically divorced from rhetoric, poetry is imaginative "*Spiel*" that may serve both sensibility and the understanding and thus help produce those prized judgments of beauty, which are at once subjective and universal; whereas rhetoric's relationship with the understanding is "merely" mercenary and frivolous. Therefore, it is a poet who eschews all "mannerism," who tries to make his art not "singular" but "adequate to an idea,"[28] a poet whose rhet/ oric pretends to do the "business" of philosophy, that Kant lauds:

> . . . man muß den Ozean bloß, wie die Dichter es tun, nach dem, was der Augenschein zeigt, etwa, wenn er in Ruhe betrachtet wird, als einen klaren Wasserspiegel, der bloß vom Himmel begrenzt ist, aber ist er un/ ruhig, wie einen alles zu verschlingen drohenden Abgrund, dennoch erhaben finden können.

> . . . one must consider the ocean merely as the poets do, in accordance with what its appearance shows, for instance, when it is considered in periods of calm, as a clear watery mirror bounded only by the heavens, but also when it is turbulent, an abyss threatening to devour everything, and yet still be able to find it sublime.[29]

Faced with shifting appearances — now a serene, heavenly calm, now an ominous "Abgrund" — the poet, momentarily standing in for the philoso/ pher, knows how to moderate sensuous extremes and thereby defy imaginative limits through the timely use of simile ("als einen," "wie einen"). Such simile is clearly related to Kant's own use of invidious comparison in his initial defi/ nition of the sublime; for the poet, too, possesses the self/assurance that the feeling of disproportion can be sublimated into an idea, an idea that is "pure" and "immune" from mutability. Tellingly, a few paragraphs later Kant sug/ gests an analogous sublimation. Warning that many people delude themselves that they are edified by watching a "tragedy" [*Trauerspiel*], he insists that if the playgoer is to extract more from the work than mere relief from boredom, then he must have "a relation to the manner of thinking" by which "the ideas of reason" prove "superior to sensibility."[30] In this way, Kant urges the philo/ sophical spectator to appropriate, even to author the artwork. How one moves from "so much" (*King Lear*) to "relation" or "complicity" (Cavell) propels Kant's theory of the sublime.

BEYOND THE "ABSOLUTELY GREAT"

To make this progress more transparent, Kant's terms and concepts require closer inspection. The feeling of the sublime is divided into mathematical and

dynamical kinds: the former appeals to the faculty of cognition (understand‚
ing, pure reason), the latter to the faculty of desire (morality, practical rea‚
son).[31] More to the point, Kant's definition of the mathematical sublime, like
Longinus' vision of *to hypsos*, relies catachrestically on hyperbole:

> We call *sublime* that which is *absolutely great* [*was* schlechthin groß *ist*].
> However to be great [*Groß‚sein*] and to be a magnitude [*Größe*] are quite
> different concepts (*magnitudo* and *quantitas*). Likewise, *simply* (*simpliciter*)
> *to say* that something is great is also something entirely different from say‚
> ing that it is *absolutely* great (*absolute, non comparative magnum*). The latter
> is that *which is great beyond all comparison*.[32]

Magnitude denotes an objective, universal judgment ("The board is two feet
long."), while the "great" [*Groß*] is a subjective but universal judgment
("What a great Redwood!"). But the absolutely great, "a mere judgment
about [the object's] representation," is an "intuition" ("Nature is infinite")
that says more about the mind than the object itself.[33] For in this last judgment,
no objective measure, "quantum," or number can serve as a criterion; instead,
one undertakes an "effort at comprehension which exceeds the capacity of
the imagination to comprehend."[34] In short, one can no longer speak of
quantity when terms of comparison do not obtain. Such a comparison would
be more than invidious; it would be nonsensical. Arriving at what Kant calls
"[d]as Überschwengliche" [*the excessive*], a point past all quantification,
where extension outflanks number, the "greatest point beyond which [the
comprehension] cannot go," an "emotion" — sometimes positive, sometimes
negative — is experienced that signals the imagination's surrender in the face
of reason's superior power to comprehend the supersensible whole in one fell
swoop.[35]

    To exemplify how we experience the sublime, Kant first turns to human
artifacts. Gazing at the Egyptian pyramids or the interior of St. Peter's Cathe‚
dral in Rome may, after an initial "bewilderment or sort of embarrassment,"
produce "an emotionally moving satisfaction."[36] But such a feeling proves in‚
sufficiently powerful for his purposes, partly, it seems, because our "astonish‚
ment" [*Verwunderung*] and the notional excess it provokes quickly dissipate.
Nor are the aesthetic emotions accompanying the perception of the monstrous
and colossal — the former overwhelms the "end of the concept" (think of
Goya's monstrous humans as overwhelming the concept of the human), the

latter our senses — sufficiently pure because ultimately such objects, with their manifest and hidden intentionality, disturb reason's ability to contemplate. To ensure, then, that aesthetic judgments are absolutely "pure," Kant locates the sublime in "rohen Natur" where the magnitudes are great enough to advance the imagination toward that "point of excess," and where we need neither fear for our lives nor be distracted by having to consider an artist's intentions. Thus unlike Pascal, whose universe always threatens to annihilate humanity and its reason, Kant carefully avoids the full *affectus* of the experience of disproportionality. For Kant the intuition of the hyperbolic is effectively contained as the monstrous or colossal, which corresponds to an "intuition" [*Anschauung*] that is "almost too great" for "mere presentation" [*bloße Darstellung*] and thus also for our "faculty of apprehension" [*Auffassungsvermögen*].[37] However, the qualifier or *remedium*, "beinahe," speaks to Kant's ambivalent attempt to measure and then limit what counts as the mathematical sublime.[38] For rather than measuring what we already know to be immeasurable, or trying to give a "representation" of what is "mere presentation," he prefers to provide a transition to the dynamical sublime where the potentially endless outbidding native to hyperbole is replaced by the single, totalizing "comprehension" of the idea of the infinite. Thus Kant, Andrzej Warminski asserts, proposes a purely formal solution, one that disjunctively steps out of the very tropological system permitting the initial intuition.[39] Put another way, to escape the unfortunate position of having to rely on invidious comparison, and to solve the problem of the imagination when confronted with the infinite, Kant progressively abandons the realm of sensibility for the purer arena of ideas.

"Nature is thus sublime in those of its appearances the intuition of which brings with them the idea of its infinity."[40] Outdoing Longinus who only requires *megethos* for the sublime to be felt, Kant oversteps here the purely aesthetic realm, as nature and our sensible perception of it are now treated largely as means to an end.[41] Operating alone, the imagination is stymied by paradox when contemplating the infinite ("this basic measure is a self-contradictory concept"), and, consequently, "the mind" (*das Gemüt*) turns to reason (*Vernunft*). Indeed, if the mind's progress seems far less pathetic here than is the case with Pascal, partly this is due to the imminent solace afforded by individual reason. Alternately, it may be because Kant's prose seems less intent on (re)creating an experience of the sublime for the reader. True, he does repeatedly mention the "violence" inherent in the apprehension of enormous spatial quantities; and he does describe "the strength of the soul" and the "courage" needed to resist the fearful aspects of nature's "dominion"; but the reader (at least this reader) never feels that the narration of the mind's struggle threatens to obscure or overwhelm the eventual prospect of engaging the dynamical, "lawful" sublime.[42] Kant, one might say, always already defines the feeling of the sublime not only in terms of *quantity* and *quality*, but also more comfort﹣ingly in terms of *relation* and *modality* of experience.[43]

With this noted, in the following passage, where Kant meditates on the mathematical sublime and the concept of measurement, a heuristic play of extreme quantities is cultivated quite reminiscent of the "Disproportion de l'homme." The result, likewise, is self﹣reflection:

> A tree that we estimate by the height of a man may serve as a standard for a mountain, and, if the latter were, say, a mile high, it could serve as the unit for the number that expresses the diameter of the earth, in order to make the latter intuitable; the diameter of the earth could serve as the unit for the planetary system so far as known to us, this for the Milky Way, and the immeasurable multitude [*der unermeßlichen Menge*] of such Milky Way systems, called nebulae, which presumably constitute such a system among themselves in turn, does not allow us to expect any limits here. Now in the aesthetic judging of such an immeasurable whole [*eines so unermeßlichen Ganzen*], the sublime does not lie as much in the magnitude of the number as in the fact that as we progress we always ar﹣rive at greater units; the systematic division of the structure of the world contributes to this, representing to us all that is great in nature as in its turn small, but actually representing our imagination in all its bound﹣lessness, and with it nature, as paling in insignificance besides the ideas of reason if it is supposed to provide a presentation adequate to them [*wozu die systematische Abteilung des Weltgebäudes beiträgt, die uns alles Größe in der Natur immer wiederum als klein, eigentlich aber unsere Einbildungskraft in ihrer ganzen Grenzlosigkeit, und mit ihr die Natur als gegen die Ideen der Ver﹣nunft, wenn sie eine ihnen angemessene Darstellung verschaffen soll, verschwindend vorstellt*].[44]

As resourceful as the imagination proves here, "the ideas of reason" alone al﹣lows us to comprehend adequately the infinite. To reason about infinity is a su﹣persensible act, as the idea of the infinite outstrips all sensibility and the numerical magnitudes grounded therein. In comparison to reason's objects, the imagination's objects are "tiny" (*verschwindend*). The "use" [*Gebrauch*] of the "power of judgment" in the case of the sublime for the purpose of awak-ening the "supersensible faculty" creates an untenable hyperbole; and only in this manner can the productive paradoxes associated with Kant's notion of aesthetic free play be engaged. (In this sense the logical violence of paradox re-places the "violence" [*Gewalt*] that the intuition of the sublime does to the imagination.) As with Pascal's progressive description of the two infinities, Kant involves the imaginative faculty only to have it participate in its own ver-tiginous sublimation. The apprehension of the sublime creates an invidious comparison that becomes an absolute difference as the transcendental idea of freedom discovered by practical (moral) reason rescues the mind from its con-tingency in the sensible world. Conversely, the cognitive tension in the defini-tion of the sublime is caused by the conflict between language's stringencies and the perception of "that which is great beyond all comparison" and thus momentarily beyond all discursive reach. Kant's hyperbolism consists there-fore in saying something that outstrips the imagination is "absolutely great" and terrifying before that *res* is inverted and made agreeable to reason's sooth-ing claims. In this, it resembles the way a successful hyperbole uses extraordi-nary language to indicate an extraordinary *res* only to have the impatient reader reduce the excess, the gap between figurative and literal meanings. As with the lyric hyperbolist, the producer of sublimity undertakes an impossible act of comparison. Kant first underscores the "subjective" nature of judg-ments of the sublime (by definition all aesthetic judgments are subjective as they are grounded in sensibility and do not appeal to a concept); but then he embraces an objective aim that has increasingly little to do with feelings such as fear or admiration, and everything to do with his larger critical project. In short, the freedom he envisages is alienated from the "freedom" in the "poetic act" that Hölderlin, reacting in part to Kant, celebrates as "the hyperbole of all hyperboles" [*die Hyperbel aller Hyperbeln*], or hyperbole that refuses to be constrained by fixed "procedure" [*Verfahrungsweise*] as the "poetic spirit" tries to "assess" and "supersede" itself.[45]

If at first Kant rhetorically presents "the sublime in objects of nature," quickly the reach of the sublime is limited when we learn that it is incorrect to "call some object of nature sublime." For "what is properly sublime cannot be contained in any sensible form, but . . . concerns only ideas of reason."[46] The mathematical sublime proves literally too much for the senses and therefore eludes the grasp of any aesthetic judgment by the imagination alone. Further, to glimpse greatness beyond any comparison, Kant's theory of the sublime must deny any purposiveness in nature, for purpose would limit the mind's need for saving reason. Accordingly, Kant's description artfully reduces the "great beyond all comparison" to "a purposive use that the imagination makes of its representation," which in turn is discarded as insufficient for his purposes. His exposition of the sublime thus resembles the "subreption" that the mind, aware of its own "rational vocation," is able to offer to the object in nature that allowed it to intuit the sublime in the first place.[47] From the critical vantage point of reason, the initial hyperboles representing the infinitely great are analyzed, but then reduced to meioses by the imagination's defeat and reason's triumph.

Thus in so far as it impacts the thinker's subjectivity, Kant's vision of the sublime recalls more the solipsism of Cartesian hyperbole than the self-destroying, world-destroying trajectory of Pascalian *superiectio*. For Kant, the "subjective purposiveness" of the sublime object is "the enlargement [*Erweiterung*] of the imagination itself."[48] Indeed, the spatial metaphor of "enlargement" nicely maps the expanded rather than the shrunken compass of the Kantian self. But Kant is not interested in metaphor per se, for it would bring his critical philosophy too close to rhetoric. "The orator . . . provides something which he does not promise, namely an entertaining play [*unterhaltendes Spiel*] of the imagination; but he also takes something away from what he does promise, namely the purposive occupation of the understanding [*Verstand*]."[49] That Kant cares little for *Unterhaltung* needs little comment, but that his rhetoric would fulfill the promise of a "purposive occupation of the understanding" seems critical, given how he charges himself with bridging the claims of pure and practical reason. Put another way, he trades rhetorical "play" for the various paradoxes associated with his idea of freedom, the idea riddling the first two *Critiques*, and that decisively reemerges in the last *Critique*: "Aesthetic purposiveness is the lawfulness of the power of judgment in its *freedom*. The satisfaction in the object depends on the relation in which we would place the imagination: namely, that it entertain the mind by itself in free activity."[50] Kant's rhetoric, including his hyperbole, is dedicated to proving the viability of an aesthetics in which the most beautiful thing is thought itself.

Now while the sublime is cast as a universal experience, significantly, not everyone has the "culture" [*Kultur*] to raise it to the level of ideas and hence to the beautiful: "The disposition of the mind to the feeling of the sublime requires its receptivity to ideas."[51] The sublime thus remains an "abyss" if unaccompanied by freedom and the "development of moral ideas," for "the judgment on the sublime in nature requires culture (more so than the beauti-ful) . . ."[52] This culture, however, is decidedly not the early modern culture(s) of Montaigne, Lipsius, and Pascal where rhetorical "play" is inseparable from philosophic content. Nor does Kant, in contrast to many Renaissance and Baroque humanists, depend on an appreciation of the occasion and *ethos* of a discourse to create understanding and assent. Most importantly, unlike Pascal's, his rhetoric ultimately does not try to re-create a full experience of the sublime. Rather than trying to provide a textual, *Ersatz*-sublime, Kant trusts that judgments of the sublime, like judgments of beauty, will allow readers to glimpse a cognitive model for how moral feelings can be cultivated.

In his account of the sublime, Kant assumes that his style does not derail readers from this greater aim by distracting them with his intentions or de-scriptions, his similes or exaggerations. Unconcerned by the terminological labyrinths that his readers must endure, Kant carefully controls the eruption of the sublime in his text. Still, we saw in chapter one with *Peri hypsos*, the line between hyperbole and the sublime can be extremely fine. Exemplary of this is an ineffable footnote placed in *On the Faculties of the Mind that Constitute Genius*:

> Perhaps nothing more sublime has ever been said, or any thought more sublimely expressed, than in the inscription over the temple of *Isis* (Mother *Nature*): "I am all that is, that was, and that will be, and my veil no mortal has removed."[53]

A BAROQUE DIALECTIC

To step back and consider Kant's larger project in the third *Critique* is to dis-cover the fundamental, structural analogy between the aesthetic judgment of the beautiful, which engages the understanding via the faculty of taste, and the aesthetic judgment of the sublime, which involves theoretical reason via the concept of infinity. But as I have indicated above, the sublime briefly plays an asymmetrical, excessive role in that moment of the process of judgment when the mind struggles to put aside its fear in the face of infinitude. Dubbed the dynamical sublime, this moment occurs when the mind learns to adopt a moral stance such that its physical freedom becomes less important than the vivid realization of the superiority of reason over the imagination. Signifi-cantly, this realization of moral agency is *a priori* or *transcendental* since it is based on the supersensible idea that no intuition of an object however large can ever correspond to the totalizing idea of the infinite. With what Hegel will dub the "cunning of reason," Kant thus redefines the sublime; or less generously, it becomes clear why he asks rhetorically: "And who would want to call sublime shapeless mountain masses towering above one another in wild disorder with their pyramids of ice, or the dark and raging sea, etc.?"[54] Such a scene, because it can never transport one to the supersensible, cannot improve the "disposition of the mind." Instead, in the book's greatest *peripeteia*, the disposition of the mind that produces moral feelings vis-à-vis such a scene is now itself nominated the sublime.

Recall Pascal: "Toute notre dignité consiste donc en la pensée. C'est de là qu'il faut nous relever, et non de l'espace et de la durée, que nous ne saurions remplir. Travaillons donc à bien penser. Violà le principe de la morale." Analogously, Kant's encounter with the infinite results in second-order conclusions of an ethical kind. But here the two thinkers also radically diverge. Whereas for Pascal *moralité* serves to prepare the way for reasons of the heart, for Kant the moral feeling is grounded thoroughly in critical reason. Kant's sublimation of the all too human, negative feelings associated with the sublime marks his final and most important divergence from Pascal's abyssal encounter with infinity:

> The feeling of the sublime is thus a feeling of displeasure from the inadequacy [*Unangemessenheit*] of the imagination in the aesthetic estimation of magnitude for the estimation by means of reason, and a pleasure [*Lust*] that is thereby aroused at the same time from the correspondence [*Übereinstimmung*] of this very judgment of the inadequacy of the greatest sensible faculty in comparison with the ideas of reason, insofar as striving for them is nevertheless a law for us.[55]

There is no corresponding "Lust" for the melancholic Pascal contemplating a hostile, infinite universe, unless the skeptical realization of the "dignity" of self-consciousness counts as *Schadenfreude*. For Kant, on the contrary, this "law" compelling us to fold the sublime into the faculty of reason produces immediate moral satisfaction.[56] Thus what began in the third *Critique* as aesthetic pleasure in beauty has become by the end of the *Analytic of the Sublime* pure pleasure in thinking. As he adumbrates it in the *General Remark on the Exposition of Aesthetic Reflective Judgments*, such satisfaction derives from the "modality" created in the dynamical sublime wherein the "disposition of the mind" becomes — via a momentous if largely unanalyzed analogy — "similar to the moral disposition."[57] In other words, by learning the limits of the imagination to represent the totality of nature, we discover in judgments of the sublime the ability "to esteem" something that may even be counter to our "(sensible) interest."[58] This is what Kant idiosyncratically dubs "respect" and "freedom."[59] And while Pascal also strategically forces us to confront the epistemological and moral consequences of contemplating infinity, Kant's teleological reason reconstructs the very claim to self-sufficient reason that Pascal deconstructs in the name of submission to the claims of faith.

Finally, given this book's primary chronological focus, I want to end this section on Kant by considering Paul Crowther's provocative argument that the *Analytic of the Sublime* capriciously relies on the "baroque thesis" that the mind needs the infinite as a measure for vast objects found in nature.[60] Branding it "phenomenologically counter-intuitive and philosophically superfluous," Crowther wonders whether the infinite should be treated as more "symbolic" than necessary. Objects may "seem" infinite but not in fact require the kind of judgment that leads the mind to a measure beyond which nothing is greater, or what Kant calls "the absolutely great."[61] In Kant's defense, Crowther offers three possible explanations why the infinite acquires such prominence: 1) "in order to emphasize the mathematical" and so "bolster his fundamental architectonic distinction between the mathematical and dynamic"; 2) in response to earlier eighteenth-century treatments of the sublime such as Burke and Addison's which rely on the "experience" of infinity; 3) from the "need to stress the imagination's active dimension."[62] Yet I would also note that Kant's first appeal to the infinite occurs in the mathematical sublime where it takes the form of a feeling and not as a concept or a modality, and therefore, at that moment at least, it may not be so "phenomenologically counter-intuitive." As Crowther himself observes, the only thing preventing Kant from following the intuition of William Blake (or Pascal), and discovering "infinity in a grain of sand," is, crudely put, a lack of imagination. As for its philosophical superfluity, the "baroque thesis" concerning infinity and the sublime may indeed be excessive in that the imagination could still have apprehended its own failure and reason could still have comprehended its own necessity without relying on the largest conceivable measures. But this objection undervalues the aesthetic provocation provided by what I am calling the hyperbolic — without Kant's initial invidious comparison and the subsequent chain of reasons leading to the infinite, Bernini's Baroque in the form of St. Peter's might have satisfied readers unwilling to sublimate their aesthetic judgments. But as Kant suggests with his examples of the ocean that mirrors the heavens and the Milky Way that yields to "an immeasurable mul-titude" of other Milky Ways, only the exorbitant presentation (*Darstellung*) of the infinite will serve to fuel "our imagination in all its boundlessness [*in ihrer ganzen Grenzlosigkeit*]."[63]

Moreover, given Kant's teleology the imagination is necessarily prey to the dialectics of excess:

> What is excessive [*Das Überschwengliche*] for the imagination (to which it is driven in the apprehension of the intuition [*Anschauung*]) is as it were an abyss, in which it fears to lose itself, yet for reason's idea of the super-sensible to produce such an effort of the imagination is not excessive [*nicht überschwenglich*] but lawful, hence it is precisely as attractive as it was repulsive for mere sensibility.[64]

The "abyss" Kant saw earlier when looking through the poet's eyes at the ocean, and, more importantly still, the "great chasm" he identified between pure and practical reason in the *Introduction* to the third *Critique* is here defini-tively bridged. And because the faith in individual reason of this *vir bonus di-cendi peritus* is much larger than Pascal's, ultimately he can more neatly contain and transcend the *Überschwengliche*. However displeasing the aesthetic judg-ment of the sublime proves for the imagination, however much excess, im-possibility, or even deceit plays roles here, these are teleologically necessary moments for the establishment of the "lawful" and the teleological, that is, our ability to find "purposiveness" in nature.

Finally, it is intriguing that both Pascal and Kant invoke the telescope and microscope as artificial ways of extending the senses. Such instruments, they agree, are ways of improving the senses so that we may realize, paradoxically, their limits (at least so far as it concerns the apprehension and understanding of the infinite).[65] Apprehension of the infinite is, in short, an epistemological crux for both thinkers. When Pascal conducts his vertiginous thought exper-iment to open up two *abîmes*, these swiftly lead to the surrender of reason. As a result the cognitive, disproportionate effects of the hyperbolic linger on like the feeling in a phantom limb or an image on a closed eyelid. Whereas for Kant, after imagination and sensibility experience fear, his "abyss" [*Abgrund*] becomes "lawful" and "attractive" for reason and thereby made safe. And while many latter-day readings of the Kantian sublime, such as Lyotard's, de Man's, and Derrida's, tend to elevate its negative, incommensurable aspects, the strict, teleological role Kant ultimately assigns the sublime confirms that its minion, the hyperbolic, must not be ascribed excessive powers. Instead, such a teleology mirrors how hyperbole figures in Pascal's absolute apology for religious faith, even if Kant scorns what Pascal calls "reasons of the heart," to buy into a Kingdom of Reason where he, discovering the sublime within his mind, might be his own saving angel.

CAVELL'S MELODRAMA

By way of a closing frame for this book, I wish to consider how two other philosophers engage the dynamics of hyperbole. Stanley Cavell, in *This New Yet Unapproachable America*, contemplates Wittgenstein's late thought and style in ways that have important implications for any analysis of hyperbole as a philosopheme. In the first of the book's two essays, "Declining Decline: Wittgenstein as a Philosopher of Culture," Wittgenstein's objection in the *Philosophical Investigations* to philosophers who try "to sublime the logic of our language" [*die Logik unserer Sprache zu sublimieren*] is considered.[66] In "'leading words home,' back from the sublime into our poverty," Wittgenstein champions not only a philosophic position — one that Cavell himself and Cavell's other favorite thinker, Emerson, share — but he is made to respond to a more general "nomadism of culture" where language has strayed too far from everyday practices and concerns.[67] Unlike, then, the desertification of language Derrida discovers in cataphasis and apophasis, the "poverty" Cavell cultivates here occurs without an obvious hyperbolic signified, divine or phenomenal, as its cause. His stance, as in his essays on Shakespearean tragedy, derives rather from an abiding concern to respond to the temptation of skepticism, which is both "human" and part of "the human drive to transcend itself, make itself inhuman."[68] Remarkably, though, in *This New Yet Unapproachable America*, the purveyor of philosophical absolutism is neither Lear nor Descartes, but Kant whose description of the sublime serves as the occasion for such transcendence.

When Cavell addresses the question of hyperbole and linguistic excess, his comments are fueled by the same concern with the suitability of language to represent contingent truths that we saw provoke Aristotle and Quintilian at the beginning of this book. With this said, his appraisal of "stylistic excess" is also specifically tied to an appreciation for the "intellectual fervor and pathos" of the *Philosophical Investigations*.[69] Significantly, he discovers different ways of interpreting such "fervor":

> Wittgenstein's detractors will respond to his seriousness as a matter of psychology or at best an aesthetic phenomenon, a stylistic excess; his followers are more likely to feel it as an abiding moral or religious demand, an unmarked — perhaps unmarkable abyss.[70]

The challenge, then, is how to distinguish this psychological, "stylistic excess" from Cavell's — as opposed to Pascal's or Kant's — version of the "abyss." This *Abgrund* is "unmarkable" not because it defies commentary, but because "professional philosophy" has largely not known what to do with it. As one of Wittgenstein's "followers,"[71] Cavell responds to a "demand," a call for thinking as Heidegger might put it, that is, potentially endless and unfulfillable. His response, I shall contend below, is only implicitly "religious." Its "moral" force, though, consists mainly in its preoccupation with how a person can truthfully and humanely express meaning and truths to other people. Such a preoccupation deepens, I think, my own inquiry into the nature of the hyperbolist's *ethos*.

Cavell's first response to Wittgenstein is to meditate on and so mediate his own rhetorical "excess." He initially compares Wittgenstein's "many journeys" in the *Philosophical Investigations* to Dante's singular one in the *Commedia* only to conclude abruptly that "the comparison is . . . after all exaggerated, melodramatically excessive."[72] (Similarly, in the beginning of Part II of "The Avoidance of Love," Cavell lavishly contemplates "the immodest and melodramatic quality of [his] claims.")[73] This admission is immediately mediated, though, by the statement: "In a sense, I agree with this and disagree with this." For, on the one hand, Wittgenstein's "spiritual struggle" resembles Descartes' discovery "that to confront the threat of or temptation to skepticism is to risk madness."[74] Wittgenstein flirts with "madness" given the melodramatic "excess" of some of his observations concerning quotidian things and events. But then, with a jab at Descartes, Cavell adds that Wittgenstein never wants to claim "a final philosophical victory over (the temptation to) skepticism, which would mean a victory over the human . . ."[75] Conversely, in comparing his own rhetoric to Wittgenstein's, Cavell asserts: "I also agree with the objection that I exaggerate, because Wittgenstein notably does not sound the note of excess."[76] Here Cavell seems to momentarily suspend or exclude the dissenting voice of the interlocutor(s) that riddle the text of the *Investigations* with its orthodoxies, objections, and outcries. Here he attends not to the "voice of temptation" but to the "voice of correctness."[77] Still, to completely distinguish between the voice of the stubborn, idealistic interlocutor(s) in the *Investigations* — and thus the voice of Western metaphysics — and Wittgenstein's own voices would be to lessen the total dramatic effect of the text's irrepressible dialogism. That Wittgenstein persistently inscribes these now wrong-headed, now naïve, now absolutist perspectives throughout his text argues for their central methodological, if not also epistemological function.[78] As Cavell himself notes, the other's "hyperbolic" expression of what Wittgenstein describes as "THIS pain" is a task for philosophy: "The question is how Wittgenstein's answer admits the expression, answers to it."[79] My own initial "answer" to this "question" is that Wittgenstein hyperbolizes to show the philosophical problems inherent in hyperbole, and that such problems are endemic to philosophy, even his own. By responding to the hyperbolic expression of pain, or the consequences of "Über-Begriffe" [*super-concepts, empty-concepts*], Wittgenstein points to a catharsis and a cure, which may themselves be as illusory as the illness they are meant to remedy.

Imitating and in a sense outbidding Wittgenstein's idiosyncratic, dialogic method, Cavell creates melodrama for the reader in order persuasively to stage his analysis of how the *Investigations* embraces and then rejects the hyperbolic. Such rhetorical excess self-consciously differs from the methodological, teleological hyperbole that precedes Descartes' deduction of the *cogito*. The cultivation of "melodrama" for Cavell mimics instead Wittgenstein's pathos-laden, heuristic method of leading words back home from the empty regions of the frozen sublime. For Cavell, melodrama entails the prospect of other people listening or reading to each other, acknowledging each other, whereas Cartesian hyperbole, at least on first reading, is a private, solipsistic affair — the cardinal figure of the philosopher in the tower.[80]

Put another way, philosophy for Cavell should precipitate what I have called in my readings of Spanish Baroque poetry, Descartes, and Pascal the process of *desengaño*:

The direction out from illusion is not up, at any rate not up to one fixed morning star; but down, at any rate along each chain of a day's denial. Philosophy (as a descent) can thus be said to leave everything as it is because it is a refusal of, say disobedient to, (a false) ascent, or transcen-dence. Philosophy (as ascent) shows the violence that is to be refused (disobeyed), that has left everything not as it is, indifferent to me, as if there are things in themselves. Plato's sun has shown us the fact of our chains; but that sun was produced by these chains.[81]

Whichever way philosophy's metaphorics of ascent and descent leads, "everything" is affected. I wonder, then, why Cavell brands as hyperbolic only the "violence" of climbing the Platonic ladder. Confirmation that the ladder's destruction itself may also require hyperbolic violence is not found here — though I suspect it is implicit, for he explicitly finds it in Shake-spearean tragedy. (Just as we have found it in the poetics of Quevedo and Sor Juana, and the rhetoric of Pascal when he stretches the ladder to untenable ex-tremes, letting philosophy fall into *abîmes* and forcing the reader to leap with his heart.) When, in other words, must ordinary language philosophy (or or-dinary language criticism) become extraordinary?[82] And if it does, is the con-tingency, psychological verisimilitude, and commonsense that Cavell prizes surrendered? Moreover, if and when such a surrender occurs, either by the dramatist self-consciously plumbing a character's depths or a philosopher measuring her understanding of the divine, what bargain is made with the audience or reader so that hyperbole's semantic and conceptual violence can be accepted, excused, ironized, or even allegorized?

The perspective adopted by Cavell's brief essay is at once panoptic and rooted in late twentieth-century concerns about the cultural role of philoso-phy. Its sweep, in short, is as audacious as its critique of Western metaphysics is acute. In a passage of great synthetic power, Cavell compares Kant and Wittgenstein:

> What is this to know? In the previous section, on the Mathematically Sublime, Kant uses a different formula: "The point of excess [*das Über-schwengliche*] for the imagination (toward which it is driven in apprehen-sion of the intuition) is like an abyss in which it fears to lose itself." Kant's conjunction of excess and abyss seems to me to match Wittgen-stein's sense of the hyperbolic (super-connections, super-concepts, etc.) with the groundless as the ideal which philosophy finds at once forbid-ding or terrible, and attractive. (Here is bewitchment. If you say fasci-nation, a psychoanalytic study should seem called for.) But whereas in

Kant the psychic strain is between intellect and sensibility, in Wittgenstein the straining is of language against itself, against the commonality of criteria which are its conditions, turning it as were against its origins. — Thus a derivative romantic aesthetic problematic concerning the sublime moves to the center of the problematic of knowledge, or say the wording of the world; quite as if aesthetics itself claims a new position in the economy of philosophy.[83]

The historical analogy between Kant's embrace of the sublime as a means to an end and Wittgenstein's depiction of philosophy's tendency to hyperbolize the world provokes on a number of levels. First, the analogy is causal; it makes Wittgenstein into a reader of Kant (who is a reader of Descartes, if not of Pascal as well), and thus Wittgenstein's "sense of the hyperbolic . . . with the groundless" responds to Kant's "conjunction of excess and abyss." More colorfully put, Wittgenstein (and so, too, Cavell) plays the skeptic (the Fool) to Kant's queenly ("O royal Lear!") metaphysics. In this way, Cavell's analogy places the dialogism of hyperbole on center stage to be further (*Plus ultra*) theatricalized. Besides, when we read that "the straining is of language against itself" and that this lies at the heart of Wittgenstein's "problematic of knowledge, or say the wording of the world," how can we ignore the "the new rhetoric" associated with the structuralist and post-structuralist revolutions or, more to the point, how can we forget how Derrida epitomizes those revolutions in his deconstructions of Cartesian hyperbole?[84] Second, if I have failed to provide a sustained "psychoanalytic study" in this book, then at least Cavell's account of how a question of aesthetics in the third *Critique* comes to dominate Wittgenstein's investigation into the way philosophers have made language betray its own "origins" parallels my account of how classical treatments of hyperbole and, more generally, the entire rhetorical enterprise inform and deform Baroque literature and philosophy. Baroque writers are bewitched by hyperbole, but so, they assume, are their readers who self-consciously listen to its siren song. In other words, a "derivative romantic aesthetic problematic concerning the sublime" is first a *Baroque rhetorical, aesthetic, and epistemological dynamic*, a dynamic that prevents the hyperbolic from being merely a dalliance with what Cavell and Wittgenstein cast as the frozen sublime. Third, if hyperbole for Wittgenstein is the straining after absolutes and reified words-concepts, is there not in the ordinary, the everyday, or, alternately, in literary or religious discourse, another kind of hyperbole — one that concerns the ineffable, the inexpressible, and the outrageous — that takes the form of self-conscious exaggeration as well as, perhaps, of silence? Determined to mitigate the effects of philosophical skepticism, does Cavell sometimes diminish the potential for hyperbole to be a "form of life," a language game essential to the expression of passion and immanence?[85] Or, to rephrase the question that dominated much of my reading of Pascal: what kind of "grammar" is appropriate to talk about and to God?

WITTGENSTEIN'S UNSAYABLE

While Kant's description of how the imagination experiences the "impossibility of ever attaining to absolute totality through the progression of the measurement of sensible things in the world" may well parallel Wittgenstein's animosity against all manner of philosophical absolutism, the Austrian-English thinker never seeks to transcend (or systematize) this impossibility through the systematic claims of reason.[86] Wittgenstein instead responds to the desire for such absolutism in the *Tractatus Logico-Philosophicus* (1922) with "silence" and then, decades later, in the *Philosophic Investigations*, with a panoply of actual and potential "language games" [*Sprachspiele*]. That these responses are complicated and enriched by concerns that escape the bounds of philosophic logic or linguistics is worth pondering. To begin with, the closing, and to a much smaller extent, the opening, of the *Tractatus* directly engage what Wittgenstein calls "das Mystische" [*the mystical*].[87] Superficially a surprising, even inexplicable coda for a treatise greeted by the so-called Vienna circle as one of the founding documents of logical positivism, upon deeper inspection and with the help of clues left by Russell and Wittgenstein himself, we apprehend that the mystical had been the treatise's central theme all along — in as much as a theme can be defined by an initial presence, a lengthy, determinate absence, and then a stunning return.[88] These are the key propositions forming the arc of Wittgenstein's coda:

> The sense [*Sinn*] of the world must lie outside of the world . . . (6.41)
>
> Hence also there can be no ethical propositions.
> Propositions cannot express anything higher. (6.42)
>
> It is clear that ethics cannot be expressed.
> Ethics is transcendental.
> (Ethics and aesthetics are one.) (6.421)

How the world is, is completely indifferent for what is higher. God does not reveal himself *in* the world. (6.432)

Not *how* the world is, is the mystical, but *that* it is. (6.44)

The contemplation [*Anschauung*] of the world sub specie aeterni is its contemplation as a limited whole.
The feeling of the world as a limited whole is the mystical feeling [*Das Gefühl der Welt als begrenztes Ganzes ist das Mystische*]. (6.45)

There is indeed the inexpressible. This *shows* itself; it is the mystical [*Es gibt allerdings Unaussprechliches. Dies* zeigt *sich, es ist das Mystische*]. (6.522)

With these gnomic assertions we are (suddenly) confronted with a degree of apophasis that makes, all hyperbole aside, Pascal and Dionysius seem moderate in comparison. For now ethics and aesthetics have joined the divine as subjects defying linguistic expression, and therefore as topics that also must be struck from the philosopher's docket. Wittgenstein severely, if subtly, limits the scope of what philosophy can accomplish: "*The limits of my language* mean the limits of my world" [Die Grenzen meiner Sprache *bedeuten die* Grenzen meiner Welt] (5.6). How and why he adopts this limited (or more accurately, limiting) perspective, and how it derives from a fully developed, self-consistent theory of language — language is regarded as a form of picture making that corresponds to a world of simple objects — I must leave to others to unravel.[89] My concern rather is to stress both how Wittgenstein perceives conceptual fields "outside" the world where philosophical language successfully operates, and his insistence that if philosophy tries to offer explanations of these fields it produces only "nonsense." Only in this light can we begin to understand his declarations in the Preface concerning the need to draw "a limit to thinking"[90] — which is similar to marking a limit to language, as language is limited by its ability to say only certain things with clarity — and the book's famous, final *Satz*: "Whereof one cannot speak, thereof one must be silent" [*Wovon man nicht sprechen kann, darüber muß man schweigen*] (7). This last, perfectly apophatic claim epitomizes the entire book's preoccupation with maintaining a rigorous relation between language and the "world."[91] But it also clearly points back to 6.522 and the inexpressible referent. More particularly, much like its cognates *hyper* and *super*, the adverb "darüber" catachrestically gestures toward a place where philosophy's borders might be more fluid and the philosopher more nomadic. What distinguishes Wittgenstein here from theological hyperbolists, though, is that for him the mystical *darüber* should be (almost) left unsaid and unthought, even if it "shows itself."

Wittgenstein himself urges such an interpretation in a letter he writes to a publisher:

> The sense of the book is an ethical one. I once wanted to include in the preface a sentence which actually is not now in it but which I will write out for you here since it will perhaps be a key (to the book) for you. I wanted, then, to write: my work consists of two parts: of that which is under consideration here and of all that I have *not* written. And it is precisely this second part that is the important one . . . I would now recommend you to read the *preface* and the *conclusion*, since these carry the sense to its most immediate expression.[92]

The unwritten book is thus the best expression of his intentions! But since that book, given Wittgenstein's severe criteria, logically remains unwritten, maybe even unthought, he sends us, in a traditional gesture of accommodation, to the apophatic beginning and end of the *Tractatus*. The book in between, Cyril Barrett observes, becomes thereby "nonsensical" in a far profounder sense than it seemed, on face value anyway, were statements about God, beauty, or murder.[93] As Brian Clack asserts: "The *Tractatus* can thus be read as a modern *via negativa*."[94] To which I would add that the majority of it would be cataphatic and only the frames truly apophatic.

What, though, is Wittgenstein's intuition that would be comparable to the traditional mystic apprehension of the *hyperousia*? In 6.44 he affirms that the existence of the world is the "mystical" and then, in 6.45 and 6.46, that this existence may be contemplated "sub specie aeterni," though only when the world shows itself. But what constitutes such a revelation? Notwithstanding the valiant efforts of commentators,[95] these concluding, umbrageous propositions may well find their best gloss in Wittgenstein's "A Lecture on Ethics," a 1929 talk given in English, fittingly, to the Cambridge society known as the Heretics. Here he explains how the idea of "absolute or ethical value" creates a rift between language and a certain kind of "experience":

> I believe the best way of describing [this experience] is to say that when I have it *I wonder at the existence of the world*. And I am inclined to use such

phrases "how extraordinary that anything should exist" or "how extraordinary that the world should exist." I will mention another experience straight away which I also know and which others of you might be acquainted with: it is, what one might call, the experience of feeling *absolutely* safe. I mean the state of mind in which one is inclined to say 'I am safe, nothing can injure me whatever happens. Now let me consider these experiences, for, I believe, they exhibit the very characteristics we try to get clear about. And there the first thing I have to say is, that the verbal expression which we give to this experiences is nonsense! If I say 'I wonder at the existence of the world' I am misusing language.[96]

Intimately familiar to students of hyperbole, such misuse, wonder, and absolutism ("*absolutely* safe" might well be a swipe at Kant's dynamical sublime) are cast in a different light by Wittgenstein at the end of the lecture, where the chagrin, even the melancholy of the philosopher, transfixed by the allure of logic, the danger of "nonsense," and a hunger for the "extraordinary" and "miraculous," becomes most vivid:

> . . . I see now that these non-sensical expressions were not nonsensical because I had not yet found the correct expressions, but that their nonsensicality was their very essence. For all I wanted to do with them was just to go beyond the world and that is to say beyond significant language. My whole tendency and, I believe, the tendency of all men who ever tried to write or talk Ethics or Religion was to run against the boundaries of language. This running against the walls of our cage is perfectly, absolutely hopeless.[97]

Instead of silence, Wittgenstein, pondering the experience of "absolute value" or "the mystical," reluctantly admits that such "nonsensicality" defeats his will. I say reluctantly not only on account of the startling *cage*-metaphor, but also because, as Wittgenstein's examples of ethical and religious speech self-consciously argue, "the desire" to engage in such "nonsensical" speech is well-nigh universal. And while it would be wrong to regard this realization as signaling a decisive break with the *Tractatus*, the phrase "I see now" does suggest the emergence of a new perspective or aspect. Indeed, to anticipate one of the cardinal moments in the *Philosophical Investigations*, it is as if the rabbit's head now has become a duck's head.[98] Following Marcus Hester's work on Wittgenstein and poetic metaphor, and building on Wittgenstein's own claim in the "Lecture" that "in ethical and religious language we seem constantly to be using similes," I read this moving description of our linguistic "cage" as the acceptance that religious, aesthetic, and ethical discourse cannot point to specific "facts" to justify the use of absolute language.[99] As Cavell puts it in "Aesthetic Problems of Modern Philosophy": " . . . to say that Juliet is the sun is not to say something false; it is, at best, wildly false, and that is not being just false. This is part of the fact that if we are to suggest that what metaphor says is true, we shall have to say it is wildly true — mythically or magically or primitively true. (Romeo just may be young enough, or crazed or heretic enough, to have meant his words literally.)"[100] These insights antici-pate Cavell's recent essay on "Performative and Passionate Utterance," as Shakespeare's metaphor is clearly a perlocutionary act, an "improvisation in the disorders of desire," in short, it is, like Wittgenstein's *cage*-metaphor, a wild hyperbole.[101] Indeed, just as metaphor, as Ricoeur puts it, is an "imper-tinent predication" defying logic — Achilles cannot literally be a man and a "lion" at once — Wittgenstein's "wondering at the existence of the world" defies logic because it is based on the unprovable belief that "God had created the world."[102] To anticipate the *Investigations*, such wonder depends on a lan-guage game other than one prescribed by the rules of science.[103] In this sense, "A Lecture on Ethics" is truly a liminal text, one straddling two distinct ways of looking at the world.

Earlier in the "Lecture," after claiming that "[t]here are no propositions which, in any absolute sense, are sublime, important, trivial," Wittgenstein adduces a remarkable sequence of hyperboles to express his frustration with this very claim:

> I can only describe my feelings by the metaphor, that, if a man could write a book on Ethics which really was a book on Ethics, this book would, with an explosion, destroy all the other books in the world. Our words used as we use them in science, are vessels capable only of con-taining and conveying meaning and sense, *natural* meaning and sense. Ethics, if it is anything, is supernatural and our words will only express facts; as a teacup will only hold a teacup full of water and if I were to pour out a gallon over it.[104]

Echoing, intentionally I think, the hyperbole from the end of John 21:25 (which I quoted at the end of the previous chapter in the section on Dumar, sais), Wittgenstein again closes off, though this time cataphatically, the possibility not only of ethical speech, but also of religious and aesthetic discourse. The lack of "facts" facing the believer, aesthetician, or ethicist paradoxically prevents language from becoming "supernatural"; but it also prevents a certain kind of experience from overwhelming the world of ordinary concerns where contingency, sense (*Sinn*), and meaning (*Bedeutung*) are most valued. Not that this narrow definition of value and experience excludes the mystical; no, but it does exclude a philosophy, science, and even a poetics of the mystical or the sublime. As Wittgenstein cryptically observes in *Culture and Value*: "Religious similes can be said to move on the edge of an abyss [*sie bewegen sich am Rande des Abgrundes*]. B(unyan)'s for example . . ."[105]

WITTGENSTEIN'S "ALBUM"

Painstakingly, sometimes playfully unfolding the logic of such similes in the *Philosophical Investigations* (posthumously published, 1953), Wittgenstein makes inclusion rather than exclusion the rule. Conspicuously absent is any mention of the "Unaussprechliches" and the abysses it might occasion. Instead, one finds an "analysis" (§90) of philosophical language at once skeptical of absolute, transcendent claims but also extremely generous when considering the myriad "language games" people ordinarily play to create meaning, express feelings, talk to other people, describe events, etc.: "I shall also call the whole, consisting of language and the actions into which it is woven, the 'language game'" (§7). As he insists earlier in the book: " . . . to imagine a language means to imagine a form of life [*sich eine Lebensform vorstellen*]" (§19). Capacious in its range of subjects and variety of moods, the *Investigations* relies on dialogue, digression, repetition, visual cues, as well as the spaces or silences between *Sätze* to describe these *Lebensformen* and to achieve Wittgenstein's own rhetorical, conceptual, and, as Cavell would have it, confessional ends.[106] These silences, I would add, do not function apophatically, but rather allow for gradations and shades of meaning to accumulate. As we traverse the text's "landscape sketches" (*Preface*), they become themselves stirring objects of philosophic meditation.

To explicate his notion of a *Sprachspiel*, Wittgenstein elicits the enormous range of human grammar. Numerous kinds of "games" are indicated and described, some of which clearly are or could be hyperbolic: "Giving orders . . .

Describing the appearance of an object, or giving its measurements . . . Play-acting [*Theater spielen*] . . . Asking, thanking, cursing, greeting, praying" (§23). And to underscore how this multiplicity differs from his earlier, so-called logical positivism, he offers this self-reproach: "It is interesting to com-pare the multiplicity of the tools in language and of the ways they are used, the multiplicity of kinds of word and sentence, with what logicians have said about the structure of language. (Including the author of the *Tractatus Logico-Philosophicus.*)" With such rhetorical *copia* as his starting point, Wittgenstein proceeds to critique those idealists who insist on the exact correspondence be-tween words and ideas (§§56–57), who think that to say is to know (§78), and who insist that the sublime is available to the logic of language (§89).

While hyperbole is never explicitly discussed in the *Investigations*,[107] the kinds of gaps the savvy hyperbolist self-consciously creates between saying and meaning, between experience and logic, and, conversely the complicity these gaps would create between speaker and hearer are fundamental aspects of many language games. In asserting this, I am acutely aware that I seem to be running counter to most interpretations of Wittgenstein, including Cavell's, and, admittedly, to many of the *Sätze* in the *Investigations* critiquing the philosophic-linguistic drive towards transcendence. It is essential, then, for me to distinguish between Wittgenstein's critique of "*Über-*Begriffe" and my defense of the hyperbolic as literary *Überbietung*, as rhetorical *superiectio*, and as integral to theological cataphasis and apophasis.

Super-concepts are philosophical abstractions and thus denials of daily life, language and practice; they lack all dialogism (save, perhaps, with other philosophers); they may be hyperbolic, but in a Cartesian sense not in the manner that Pascal and other philosophers of *desengaño* would have it. In fact, Wittgenstein's scorn for these super-concepts often betrays this very disillu-sionment. *Überbietung*, on the contrary, is the language game par excellence; it is imitative, dialogic, responsive to history, circumstance, and personality. Quintilian's notion of *superiectio* is likewise alive to the exigencies of circum-stance and audience, even as he would also have the hyperbolist convey the subjective perception of wonder. And for their part, despite their quarrels, Derrida and Marion agree that both cataphatic and apophatic speech are pro-duced by an awareness of limits and contingency rather than a denial of the same. At their most powerful, then, each of these species of hyperbole dram-atizes the failure of concepts to represent the inexpressible, the infinite. While such failure may lead to an ironic self-consciousness, as in the mode finely traced by de Man in "The Rhetoric of Temporality," my concern here is to indicate how it also may point to another kind of speech, one that fulfills what Cavell calls in his reading of Wittgenstein "a moral or religious demand."

First, consider these propositions on the nature of propositions and how Wittgenstein would disabuse us of the notion that a particular form or kind of language should be regarded as "remarkable," "unique," "extraordinary," or especially profound:

> Why do we say a proposition is something remarkable [*etwas Merkwürdiges*]? On the one hand, because of the enormous importance [*ungeheuren Bedeutung*] attaching to it. (And that is correct). On the other hand this, together with a misunderstanding of the logic of language, seduces us into thinking that something extraordinary, something unique [*etwas Außerordentliches, ja Einzigartiges*], must be achieved by propositions. — A *misunderstanding* makes it look to us as if a proposition *did* something queer [*etwas Seltsames*].[108] (§93)

"Meaning" [*Bedeutung*] may well be something "remarkable" [*Merkwürdiges*], but the grammatical-rhetorical vehicle should not be. It is as if the "abyss" charted earlier by religious similes has disappeared:

> 'A proposition is a queer thing [*ein merkwürdiges Ding*]!' Here we have in germ the subliming of our whole account of logic. The tendency to assume a pure intermediary between the propositional *signs* and the facts. Or even to try to purify, to sublime, the signs themselves. — For our forms of expression [*unsere Ausdrucksformen*] prevent us in all sorts of ways from seeing that nothing out of the ordinary is involved, by sending us in pursuit of chimeras. (§94)

While reminiscent of Descartes' warning in the *Meditations* against trusting the images or "chimeras" associated with knowledge about the body, Wittgenstein rejects here Cartesian metaphysical ambitions. Language can never be "cleansed"; it is too imbricated in the here and now:

> Thought is surrounded by a halo . . . We are under the illusion that what is peculiar, profound, essential, in our investigation [*Wir sind in der Täuschung, das Besondere, Tiefe, das uns Wesentliche unserer Untersuchung*],

resides in its trying to grasp the incomparable essence of language. That is, the order existing between the concepts of proposition, word, proof, truth, experience, and so on. This order is a *super*-order [Über-Ordnung] between — so to speak — *super*-concepts [Über-Begriffen]. Whereas, of course, if the words "language," "experience," "world," have a use, it must be as humble a one as that of the words "table," "lamp," "door."[109] (§97)

Wittgenstein is not asserting that a sentence's meaning must be limited; instead, his concern is to abolish any "Täuschung" that the uses of language involved in naming and concept formation are immune from ordinary contingency and relation. Sublimity is equated with the desire for purity, for "ein reines Mittelwesen," and abstraction is made synonymous with a "misunderstanding" of how sentences actually function. Like Pascal's, his skepticism is thus aimed at a kind of idealism that would reify or hierarchize language.[110] Language and grammar — and I read grammar in the *Investigations* as largely synonymous with rhetoric — are not "private" Wittgenstein argues; nor are they separable from those quotidian acts and objects that we share with others and that provide the basis for a mutual understanding of feelings and perceptions. To form any sentence is to invoke all of grammar as a form of life. Similar to the way that the rhetorical enterprise depends for its success on an audience's appreciation of a speaker's *ethos* and the cultural and historical context in which an *oratio* is made, a Wittgensteinian sentence demands complicity and contingency.

"What *we* do is to bring words back from their metaphysical to their everyday use" (§116). Such guidance, however, involves a certain conceptual violence directed at other (rigorously unnamed) philosophers and systems of thought: "What we are destroying is nothing but houses of cards [*Luftgebäude*] and we are clearing up the ground of language on which they stand" (§118). This is to say that the figure that Cavell identifies as Wittgenstein's hyperbolic interlocutor builds idealist Towers of Babel only to have them leveled and then transformed into a myriad *Sprachspiele* by the pathos-laden voice representing Wittgenstein's skeptical point of view (a gesture which incidentally inverts the architectural metaphorics structuring Descartes' *Discourse*).[111] That a similar leveling of philosophical edifices occurs in Pascal's "Disproportion de l'homme" suggests not only the enduring heuristic attraction of certain extreme metaphors, but it also underscores how Wittgenstein's antipathy to the profession of philosophy and its claims of certainty is grounded in a longstanding, anti-Cartesian struggle against the hubris and solipsism of monolithic reason. Preferring always plurality and multiplicity over any single, unitary ideal (§132–133) or Archimidean point, the *Investigations* creates a map, frequently quite a baroque map, of endless expressive and hermeneutic possibilities. In his *Preface*, Wittgenstein describes, with a vivid cartographic metaphor, the genesis of such perspectivism:

> The philosophical remarks in this book are, as it were, a number of sketches or landscapes which were made in the course of these long and involved journeyings.
>
> The same or almost the same points were always being approached afresh from different directions, and new sketches [*Bilder*] made. Very many [*Eine Unzahl*] of these were badly drawn or uncharacteristic, marked by all the defects of a weak draughtsman. And when they were rejected a number [*eine Anzahl*] of tolerable ones were left, which now had to be arranged and sometimes cut down, so that if you looked at them you could get a picture [*Bild*] of the landscape. Thus this book is really only an album.[112]

If only Pascal had left such an account of his "album." The contradictions we discovered in Pascal's *définitions de nom* or *mots primitifs*, whether the term was *nombre*, *l'homme*, or *Dieu*, are reinforced here by the sense that Wittgenstein's text with its gaps and holes is a kind of provisional accommodation with an originary "Unzahl" that defies written expression. In other words, Baroque perspectivism and rhetorical anamorphosis are entirely consonant with Wittgenstein's theory of language: "Die Sprache ist ein Labyrinth von Wegen . . ." [*Language is a labyrinth of paths*] (§203). Describing how to be content in this "labyrinth" is the central aim of the *Investigations*. Thus Wittgenstein famously presents his propositions as "therapies" (§133) for ailing metaphysicians.

Asked what he made of Hegel's philosophy, Wittgenstein replies: "Hegel seems to me to be always wanting to say things which look different are really the same. Whereas my interest is in showing that things which look the same are really different. I was thinking of using as a motto for my book [the *Investigations*] a quotation from *King Lear*: 'I'll teach you differences.'" Then laughing: "The remark 'You'd be surprised' wouldn't be a bad motto either."[113] If there is a defense of hyperbole in the *Investigations*, it is to be found only after the interlocutor's idealism, like Kent, has been put in the stocks and taught "differences." Interrogating the claim that a word's meaning and "use" [*Anwendung*] can be apprehended "in a flash" [*mit einem Schlage*] — one uncannily similar to the claim Pascal makes in *De l'esprit géométrique* — Wittgenstein charges: "You have no model [*Vorbild*] of this superlative [*übermäßigen*] fact, but you are seduced into using a super-expression [*Über-Ausdruck*]. (It might be called a philosophical superlative.)" (§192). This reproach of philosophical superlatives belongs to Wittgenstein's larger refusal to concede that words like "red," "pain," "to read," or "to think" contain a single "essence," or that we can ever abstract a stable "picture" [*Bild*] from the use of such words.[114] Instead, his own nimble, moving, now banal, now clinical, often enigmatic, and frequently witty prose teaches us to recognize "family resemblances" between the ways language is ordinarily used to search for meaning. He does this by valuing description over intention, and by treating each instance of language as a convoluted, involuted "form of life."[115] Pull on a thread, hyperbolic or otherwise, and the whole ball of yarn comes unraveled: "To understand a sentence means to understand a language. To understand a language means to be master of a technique [*eine Technik beherrschen*]" (§199). This "Technik" or *techné* Wittgenstein calls "grammar," but again I am inclined to call it rhetoric, partly because in showing us what can and cannot be known, it frequently fails. Returning, then, to the question of the viability of aesthetic, ethical, and religious discourses, we learn in the *Investigations* to consider each language game according to its own rules, which, though, can never be standardized. Instead, one must examine how the game is played in each instance. Thus, for example, what would be pure "nonsense" to a logician can have subtle significance within a Lewis Carroll poem for a child or literary critic; a description of a storm's fury in the *Aeneid*, which a meteorologist would find absurd, makes perfect cosmological sense for the allegorist ("Geminique minantur / In caelum scopuli . . ."). In sum, a successful literary hyperbole is a "Lebensform" depending on a dynamic network of cultural and intertextual references. And ultimately, to be interpreted, it requires what Umberto Eco calls in his reading of a "good," that is, "open metaphor," an "infinite encyclopedia."[116]

Yet without philosophical superlatives, how does Wittgenstein prescribe that we think and talk about the sublime or the divine? If there are no "super-concepts" how can any language game represent (*darstellen*) the "Unaussprechliches" or *hyperousia*?[117] That Wittgenstein becomes less concerned with logical rigor in the *Investigations* is a critical commonplace, but does this mean that he himself, and not his hyperbolic interlocutor, is more willing to permit statements that would seem to point beyond the world toward the mystical? (I am still responding to Cavell's notion of the "unmarked — perhaps unmark-able abyss" in the *Investigations*.)

In his only mention of theology in the *Investigations*, Wittgenstein writes: "Grammar tells what kind of object anything is. (Theology as grammar.)" (§373). To say, for instance, that "God is everything and nothing," is not a grammatical object subject to scientific, logical investigation. It is, Barrett would argue, an "expression of value" rather than an "expression of fact."[118] A believer and nonbeliever would understand such a proposition differently on account of the distinct language games they perceive it to be playing. How-ever, a believer is not saying the unsayable here — this is still an impossibil-ity — but rather she is enacting, performing it through figures that necessarily have multiple meanings. Barrett thus argues that Wittgenstein's notion of "seeing-as" is more than an instance of visual, cognitive psychology; instead, it allows us to move beyond the strict Tractarian view of language as pictur-ing the way things are in the world towards a richer, more generous, more sub-jective view that allows for, but does not seek to explain, the grammars of aesthetics, ethics, and religion.[119] "It strikes me," Wittgenstein observes in *Culture and Value*, "that a religious belief could only be something like a pas-sionate commitment to a system of references."[120] Such "passionate commit-ment," I take it, may well be hyperbolic.

From the outset of the *Investigations*, the "multiplicity of language games" is treated as "uncountable" [*unzählige*] (§23). While this multiplicity or *copia* never suffices to show (*zeigen*) all that one means — neither to encompass completely what one means by a color nor to express fully the nature of a form (be it a "king" in chess or the act of reading) — it does afford the speaker the pragmatic, successful means to communicate, indicate (*hinweisen*), thoughts, perceptions, and feelings. To illustrate, literally, this modest success of lan-guage, Wittgenstein at one point (§454) draws an arrow on the page and con-structs a dialogue around it:

> . . . How does it come about that this arrow >>>———> *points* [*zeigt*]? Doesn't it seem to carry in it something besides itself? — "No, not the dead line on paper; only the psychical thing, the meaning, can do

that." — That is both true and false. The arrow points only in the application that a living being [*Lebewesen*] makes of it.

This pointing is *not* a hocus-pocus which can be performed only by the soul.

By diminishing the ineffable or magical properties sometimes associated with the linguistic act, Wittgenstein insists that meaning is always a product of someone talking to and being understood by other people. To quote Rosaline again from *Love's Labour's Lost*: "A jest's prosperity lies in the ear / Of him that hears it, never in the tongues / Of him that makes it" (5.2.838–840). And yet this meaning or grammatical "essence" may be "geistig" as well as psychological.[121] That is, it may be spiritual or intellectual as long as it does not busy itself with insoluble philosophic problems, problems that seem always to demand the royal road to truth:

> In the actual use of expressions we make detours, we go by side roads [*machen wir gleichsam Umwege, gehen durch Nebengassen*]. We see the straight highway before us, but of course we cannot use it, because it is permanently closed. (§426)

Such spatial metaphors recall Wittgenstein's topographic description of his text in the Preface, but perhaps they are also meant to recall Augustine's resonant play with the Pauline *via*-metaphor.[122] Conversely, these metaphors contrast positively with Wittgenstein's description of philosophy's permanently aporetic state, namely: "A philosophical problem has the form: 'I don't know my way about [*Ich kenne mich nicht aus*]'" (§123).[123] So when he later observes that his philosophic "goal" is "[t]o show the fly the way out of the fly-bottle" [*[d]er Fliege den Ausweg aus dem Fliegenglas zeigen*] (§309), this indicates less the desire to escape epistemological confusion than to cease philosophizing altogether, in order to turn, perhaps, to more valuable things.

We are now better able to understand why Cavell reads Wittgenstein as cultivating philosophy's impoverishment. Considering the "sense of the loss or exile of words" in the *Investigations* and therefore how Wittgenstein (as well as Nietzsche, Emerson, and Heidegger) would remedy this, Cavell insists that if Wittgenstein is a philosopher of culture, then his book's "Dürftigkeit" [*poverty, need*] responds directly to the dark times ("Finsternis dieser Zeit") in which it was written.[124] Wittgenstein infuses philosophy with this "impoverishment" in order to cure it of its overweening ambitions. And "impoverishment" responds to the skepticism occasioned by philosophy's failure to address or redress historical and cultural decline, as well as the kind of skepticism Descartes embodies for Cavell in his essays on Shakespearean tragedy.

For all this "Dürftigkeit," however, the *Investigations* overflows with voices, moods, examples, allusions, as well as thoughts (*Gedanken*).[125] Aside from the interlocutor's often indignant, incredulous tone, the authorial voice has constant recourse to imperative — the refrain "Denk dir" [*think!*] is sounded throughout as Wittgenstein urges his interlocutors and readers to accept or at least participate in the text's unceasing perspectivism. The rich theatricality of his exposition, with its construction workers, shopkeepers, people reading, people in pain, lions trying to speak, etc. does not so much reject or avoid "lavishness" as invite thinking to respond to it.[126] Most significantly, though Cavell writes of Wittgenstein's "distrust of the need for the profound" and his "relentless project to . . . desublimize thought,"[127] it is not every mode of thought that Wittgenstein would deflate, but specifically "Logik" and the language that claims to be its vehicle.[128] The alternate path for thinking, which treats grammar as a *Lebensform*, often flirts with the cataphatic and apophatic. And if we recognize this tendency of language to verge toward hyperbole and silence, and if we know this as we think, speak, and write, then, as Cavell's masterful readings of the *Investigations* confirm, the sublime can be made more, not less, immanent.

I wonder, then, whether to cultivate impoverishment in this way is to open also the rhetorical space where statements of value can finally be appreciated. After seeing what it means not to do philosophy in a certain way, or, perhaps, not to do philosophy at all, we may be able to begin to respond to Wittgenstein's enigmatic "seriousness," the "seriousness" Cavell glosses as "an abiding moral or religious demand, an unmarked — perhaps unmarkable abyss." This is to say that in the end my aim is to supplement one aspect of Cavell's strong reading of the *Investigations*. Given the overarching concerns and trajectory of this book as it moves from the history of rhetoric to the extravagances of lyric and then through the impossibilities of drama and the aporias of philosophy, I regard Wittgenstein as a therapist for arguably the most abiding species of hyperbole. Wittgenstein charts three possible responses to what he calls "das Mystische": silence in the *Tractatus*, wonder and frustration in the "Letter on Ethics," and play, *copia*, and the dramatic portrayal of "differences" in the *Investigations*. These three stages adumbrate a theory of expression for the mystical hyperbolist.

In *Disowning Knowledge*, Cavell blames that species of hyperbole that serves as a skeptical vehicle for absolute, transcendent, solipsistic claims. His readings of Shakespearean tragedy trace the dire results when the hyperbolist — be it Lear, Pericles, Othello, Hamlet, Macbeth, Leontes, or Cleopatra — interacts with other people. Alternately, his reading in "Declining Decline" of Wittgenstein's critique of philosophy's longing for the frozen sublime instructs us in the human subtleties as well as the conceptual limits of hyperbole. On both the literary and philosophical stage, then, Cavell confirms Quintilian's foundational insight that hyperbole is the riskiest language game, but also, potentially, the one best suited to expressing belief — especially when we lack proof.

Finally, to conflate the concerns of these last chapters, if we, by metonymy, were to read the ineffable, the *Unaussprechliches*, the *hyperousia*, as love instead of God, then we might conclude that Cordelia's silence is apophatic and Lear's outrage and grief cataphatic. In this respect, like the career traced by the *Tractatus* and the *Investigations*, and unlike traditional negative theology, in *Lear* apophasis precedes cataphasis. Cordelia excessively avoids saying what cannot be said, and Lear precipitously declines all that can be said. Neither is permitted any accommodation: their words fail to correspond to the sublimity, positive and negative, of their intuitions. And yet in this failure, within the hyperbolic gap between intention and saying, language and meaning, one discerns not only a spiritual topography of abysses and summits, but more vitally still, the sublimity, absurdity, and power of human speech.

Notes

All unacknowledged translations are mine.

INTRODUCTION

1. Oscar Wilde, "The Decay of Lying," *The Artist as Critic: Critical Writings of Oscar Wilde*, ed. Richard Ellmann (Chicago: University of Chicago Press, 1982), 302.

2. George Puttenham, *The Arte of English Poesie*, ed. Edward Arber (London: Alex. Murray & Son, 1869; reprint AMS Press, 1966), 202.

3. H. G. Liddell and Robert Scott, in *A Greek-English Lexicon* (Oxford: Clarendon Press, 1996), 1861, gloss the noun, ὑπερβολή, which derives from the verb, ὑπερβάλλω, as a *"throwing beyond"*; *"overshooting"*; *"excess"*; (with a preposition in adverbial phrases) *"in excess, exceedingly"*; *"preeminence, perfection* (without any notion of excess)"; *"overstrained phrase"*; *"the superlative degree"*; *"overbid* (at auction)." In the course of this book, we will see nearly all of these meanings come into play. In *A Latin Dictionary* (Oxford: Clarendon Press, 1962), 1807, C. T. Lewis and Charles Short gloss *superiectio* as a *"throwing over or on."* The *Oxford Latin Dictionary*, ed. P. G. W. Glare (Oxford: Clarendon Press, 2004), 1875, derives *superiectio* from the verb, *superiacere*, which can mean: "[t]o throw or scatter on top or over a surface"; "[t]o shoot over the top of a (mark)," as with a "missile"; [t]o travel or throw oneself over the top of (a barrier)" and by transference, "to surpass or transcend." Quintilian (8.6.67) combines both the Greek and Latin terms in his initial comments on hyperbole: "hyperbole audacioris ornatus summo loco posui; est haec decens veri superiectio . . ." See *Institutio oratoria*, 5 vols., ed. and tr. Donald A. Russell (Cambridge: Harvard University Press, 2001). In the *Rhetorica ad Herennium* (4.44) *superlatio* is used. For a neat summary of the figure and its classical pedigree, see Heinrich Lausberg, *Handbook of Literary Rhetoric*, ed. David E. Orton and R. Dean Anderson (Leiden: Brill, 1998), 263–264 (§579).

4. For the sake of economy and given that nearly all the classical and early modern treatises and texts discussed here are written by and addressed to men, I

will employ the pronouns *he* and *his* throughout. The chapters on Sor Juana will, though, provide relief from this unfortunate monotony.

5. Quintilian, 8.6.67–76.

6. For various reasons, which I trust will be justified in due course, I want to have it all three ways. I am also deferring the question of whether the Baroque is a recurring historical phenomenon, and whether our epoch deserves to be called Neo-Baroque. For the "baroque" as describing a literary style and as a period concept see the seminal essay by René Wellek, "The Concept of Baroque in Literary Scholarship," in *Concepts in Criticism* (New Haven: Yale University Press, 1963). Other important discussions of the term "Baroque" and its scholarly, conceptual value include: Leo Spitzer, "The Spanish Baroque" (1943), in *Representative Essays* (Stanford: Stanford University Press, 1988); Jean Rousset, *La littérature de l'âge baroque en France: Circé et le paon* (Paris: José Corti, 1954) and "Adieu au baroque?", in *L'interieur et l'exterieur. Essais sur la poésie et sur le théatre* (Paris: José Corti, 1968); Eugenio d'Ors, *Lo barroco* (Madrid: Aguilar, 1964); José Antonio Maravall, *Culture of the Baroque: Analysis of a Historical Structure*, tr. Terry Cochran (Minneapolis: University of Minnesota Press, 1986); Christine Buci-Glucksmann, *La raison baroque: de Baudelaire à Benjamin* (Paris: Éditions Galilée, 1984); Gilles Deleuze, *The Fold: Leibniz and the Baroque*, tr. Tom Conley (Minneapolis: University of Minnesota Press, 1988); John Beverley, "Going Baroque?" *Boundary 2* 15 (1988): 27–39; José Lezama Lima, "La curiosidad barroca," in *La expresión americana* (Mexico City: Fondo de la cultura económica, 1993); Gisèle Mathieu-Castellani, "Baroque et maniérisme," in *Dictionnaire universel des littératures*, ed. Béatrice Didier (Paris: PUF, 1994), 1:342–345; Gregg Lambert, *The Return of the Baroque in Modern Culture* (London and New York: Continuum, 2004); Walter Moser, "Barock," in *Asthetische Grundbegriffe: historisches Wörterbuch in sieben Bänden*, ed. Karlheinz Barck et al. (Stuttgart: J. B. Metzler, 2000–2005), 1:578–618.

7. Deleuze, *The Fold*, 33.

8. Harold Bloom, in *Map of Misreading* (New York: Oxford University Press, 1975), adds hyperbole and metalepsis to Kenneth Burke's schema of "the Four Master Tropes," which is offered in an appendix to his *A Grammar of Motives* (Berkeley: University of California Press, 1969), 503–517.

9. Gérard Genette, "Hyperboles," in *Figures* (Paris: Éditions du seuil, 1966), 245–252.

10. Genette, 252. An example not cited by Genette is found in Sponde's *Sonnets d'amour*, XXVI: "Les vents grondaient en l'air, les plus sombres nuages / Nous dérobaient le jour pêle-mêle entassés, / Les abîmes d'enfer étaient au ciel poussés, / La mer s'enflait de monts, et le monde d'orages . . ."

11. Quintilian: "... est haec decens veri superiectio" (*Inst.*, 8.6.67). Henry Peacham, *The Garden of Eloquence* (1577, but revised in 1593), ed. Beate-Maria Koll (Frankfurt am Main: Peter Lang, 1996), 40. Peacham emphasizes the spatial nature of hyperbole: "... so high is the reach, and so wide is the compass of this figure, that it mounteth to the highest things, compasseth the widest, and comprehendeth the greatest." Baltasar Gracián, *Agudeza y arte de ingenio* (Madrid: Castalia, 2001), 1:197. The full quote makes explicit the violent idealism of hyperbole: "Poco es ya discurrir lo possible, si no se trasciende a lo impossible. Las démas agudezas dicen lo que es, está lo que pudiera ser; no se contenta con eso, sino que se arroja a lo repugnante."

12. Harry Levin, *The Overreacher: A Study of Christopher Marlowe* (Cambridge: Harvard University Press, 1952); Brian Vickers, "The 'Songs and Sonnets' and the Rhetoric of Hyperbole," in *John Donne: Essays in Celebration*, ed. A. J. Smith (London: Metheun, 1978), 132–174.

13. Stanley Cavell, *Disowning Knowledge in Seven Plays of Shakespeare*, updated ed. (Cambridge: Cambridge University Press, 2003).

14. Joshua Scodel, *Excess and the Mean in Early Modern English Literature* (Princeton: Princeton University Press, 2002).

15. Virgil, *Eclogues, Georgics, Aeneid I–VI*, tr. H. Rushton Fairclough; rev. ed. G. P. Goold (Cambridge: Harvard University Press, 1999).

16. Robert Burton, *The Anatomy of Melancholy* (Oxford: Clarendon Press, 1989), 1:112.

17. Burton, 1:113.

18. Lucretius, *De rerum natura*, 1.968–983.

19. See Desiderius Erasmus, *On Copia of Words and Ideas* [*De utraque verborum ac rerum copia*], tr. D. B. King and H. David Rix (Milwaukee: Marquette University Press, 1963); Terence Cave, *The Cornucopian Text: Problems of Writing in the French Renaissance* (Oxford: Clarendon Press, 1979).

20. Strangely, the *OED* (second edition, 1989) hesitates to derive *hype* from *hyperbole*.

21. César Chesneau Dumarsais-Pierre Fontanier, *Les tropes* [1818], ed. Gérard Genette (Genève: Slatkine Reprints, 1967), 1:147.

22. Sor Juana Inés de la Cruz, "Respuesta a sor Filotea," in *Obras completas de Sor Juana Inés de la Cruz*, ed. Alberto G. Salceda (Mexico City: Fondo de Cultura Económica, 1957), 4:442.

23. See Stanley Cavell, "Performative and Passionate Utterance," in *Philosophy The Day after Tomorrow* (Cambridge: Harvard University Press, 2005).

24. Harry G. Frankfurt, *On Bullshit* (Princeton: Princeton University Press, 2005). Frankfurt's essay nicely complements an earlier essay by Max Black, "The Prevalence of Humbug," in *The Prevalence of Humbug and Other Essays* (Ithaca: Cornell University Press, 1983).

25. Eric Gans, "Hyperbole et ironie," *Poétique* 24 (1975): 488–494. This dichotomy is specifically modeled on Jakobson's distinction between the workings of metaphor and metonymy.

26. Gans, 490.

27. Laurent Perrin, *L'ironie mise en trope: du sens des énoncés hyperboliques et ironiques* (Paris: Kimé, 1996), 49. Perrin's approach is shaped by Sperber and Wilson's work on metaphor.

28. Perrin, 52.

29. Perrin, 102, 67.

30. See Perrin, 197.

31. Perrin, 194.

32. Though Giorgio Agamben's diagnosis, in "The Man of Taste," of the "perversion" inherent in most aesthetic judgment suggests that taste is always tyrannous, no matter the critical object. See *The Man without Content*, tr. Georgia Albert (Stanford: Stanford University Press, 1999), 13–27.

33. Samuel Johnson, "Cowley," in *Selected Poetry and Prose*, ed. Frank Brady and W. K. Wimsatt (Berkeley: University of California Press, 1977), 349.

34. Frank Lestringant, *Mapping the Renaissance World: The Geographical Imagination in the Age of Discovery*, tr. David Fausett (Berkeley: University of California Press, 1994). Describing André Thévet's cosmography, Lestringant writes: "The point of view was elevated, to the point of grasping in a single instant the convexity of the terraqueuous globe. At that imaginary point, the eye of the cosmographer ideally coincided with that of the Creator. Spatial hyperbole allowed this passage from the closeted world of chorography to the plenitude of the universe revealed at last in its totality" (5). This leap "from the qualitative to the quantitative" sees "the cosmographer escaping "the accusation of pride" as he tries to "grasp in his hand the two extremities of the theatre of Nature: the local scale of individual experience, and the universal scale of the divine plan" (5–6).

35. Mikhail Bakhtin, *Rabelais and His World*, tr. Helene Iswolsky (Cambridge: The MIT Press, 1968), 19, 278, 304–307.

36. Bakhtin, 307–308.

37. Bakhtin, 308, 315.

38. Bakhtin, 318, 335–336.

39. Pierre Fontanier, *Les figures de discours*, ed. Gérard Genette (Paris: Flammarion, 1968), 123.

40. Jacques Derrida, *Of Grammatology*, tr. Gayatri Chakravorty Spivak (Baltimore: The Johns Hopkins University Press, 1997), 144.

41. Derrida, 144.

42. Derrida, 144–145.

43. Derrida, 145.

44. Seneca, *Epistles* (Cambridge: Harvard University Press, 1996), writes in the 119th letter: "Numquam parum est quod satis est, et numquam multum est quod satis non est." This maxim is reworked with tragic results in *Thyestes* (256, 290). On p.158 Derrida observes: "... *il n'y a pas de hors-texte.*"

45. Derrida uses the word "exorbitant" to describe his method: "I wished to reach the point of a certain exteriority in relation to the totality of the age of logocentrism. Starting from this point of exteriority, a certain deconstruction of that totality, which is also a traced path, of that orb (*orbis*) which is also orbitary (*orbita*), might be broached." But of course this method proves illusory; there is no point of exteriority; there's only the "abyss" of the "always already." "The supplement itself is quite exorbitant" because it is textual (161–162).

46. Heinrich Wölfflin, *Renaissance and Baroque*, tr. Kathrin Simon (Ithaca: Cornell University Press, 1966), 23. Wölfflin wrongly attributes the quote to Diderot's *Encyclopédie*.

47. Thomas Randolph, *The Poems of Thomas Randolph* (London: Etchells & Macdonald, 1929), 112.

48. "Tum est hyperbole virtus, cum res ipsa, de qua loquendum est, naturalem modum excessit. Conceditur enim amplius dicere, quia dici quantum est, non potest, meliusque ultra quam citra stat oratio" (8.6.76). See Eckhard Kessler and Ian Maclean, eds., *Res et Verba in der Renaissance* (Wiesbaden: Harrassowitz in Kommission, 2002).

49. Michel Foucault, *The Order of Things: An Archaeology of the Human Sciences* (New York: Vintage, 1994).

50. Foucault, 17–44. For a valuable critique of Foucault's history of epistemologies, see Ian Maclean, "Foucault's Renaissance Episteme Reassessed: An Aristotelian Counterblast," *JHI* 59 (1998): 149–166.

51. Foucault, 47.

52. E. R. Curtius, *European Literature and the Latin Middle Ages*, tr. Willard R. Trask (Princeton: Princeton University Press, 1990), 162–166.

CHAPTER ONE: CLASSICAL THEORIES OF HYPERBOLE

1. *De bello civili*, 4.479.

2. Quintilian, *The Orator's Education* [*Institutio oratoria*], 5 vols., tr. Donald A. Russell (Cambridge: Harvard University Press, 2001), 8.Pr.15. All English translations are from this edition. *Ornatus* can mean "well-furnished" or "well-armed," as in Cicero's "scutis telisque ornati" or Caesar's "naves omni genere armorum ornatissimae."

3. Joachim Du Bellay, *La défense et illustration de la langue française*, in *Les regrets* (Paris: Gallimard, 1967), 232–233. The same comparison is used by Juan Luis Vives in Book 4, sec. 4 of *De causis corruptarum artium* (1531).

4. Andrea Alciato, *Emblemata* (Lyon, 1550), ed. and tr. Betty I. Knott (Aldershot: Scolar Press, 1996), 186.

5. John Milton, "On Education," in *Complete Prose Works of John Milton* (New Haven: Yale University Press, 1953–1982), 2:405.

6. George A. Kennedy, *Classical Rhetoric and its Christian and Secular Tradition from Ancient to Modern Times* (Chapel Hill: University of North Carolina Press, 1980), 5. Chapter 6 contains a detailed discussion of *letteraturizzazione*.

7. Seneca, 114th epistle, *17 Letters*, tr. C. D. N. Costa (Warminster: Aris & Phillips Ltd., 1988), 147.

8. See *The Critique of the Power of Judgment*, §§55–60.

9. In *The Rule of Metaphor*, tr. Paul Czerny (Toronto: University of Toronto Press, 1975), Paul Ricoeur demonstrates how the interdependence of these two books often complicates the question of what is the appropriate style for the orator and poet (3–43).

10. *See* J. F. D'Alton, *Roman Literary Theory and Criticism: A Study in Tendencies* (New York: Russell & Russell, 1962), 467.

11. As Quintilian warns: "id quoque vitandum, in quo magna pars errat, ne . . . in illis operibus [of poetry and history] oratores aut declamatores imitandos putemus" (10.2.21). Gorgias, Aristotle observes (*Rhet.* 3.1.9, 3.3.1), teaches a style too "poetic" for oratory.

12. See also *Rhet.* 3.76; Seneca, *Ep.* 114.10.

13. Eduard Norden, in "Die Composition und Literaturgattung der Horazischen Epistula ad Pisones," *Hermes* 40 (1905): 481–528, compares Cicero's "insanus orator" and Horace's "vesanus poeta." The latter lacks art and is ruled by his *ingenium*, while the former has mastered oratorical technique but lacks prudence and ethics.

14. Aristotle (*Rhet.*, 3.7) calls *to prepon* a "mean," a harmonious proportion between what is said and how it is said.

15. See also *De oratore*, 3.52.199–200. See George A. Kennedy, "Theophrastus and Stylistic Distinctions," *Harvard Studies in Classical Philology* 62 (1957): 93–104.

16. Walter Benjamin, *Ursprung des deutschen Trauerspiels* (Frankfurt am Main: Suhrkamp, 1963), 16.

17. "Proportion exists," Aristotle affirms, "if there is neither discussion of weighty matters in a casual way nor shoddy things solemnly . . . [o]therwise the result is comedy" (*Rhet.*, 3.7.2). But as in Homer's mock epic of the battle between mice and frogs, the *Batrachomyomachia*, laughter may be the objective.

18. Cicero, *De oratore*, 2 vols., tr. E. W. Sutton and H. Rackham (Cambridge: Harvard University Press, 2001). He also warns. ". . . it is from knowledge that oratory must derive its beauty and fullness, and unless there is such knowledge, well-grasped and comprehended by the speaker, there must be something empty and almost childish in the utterance [*inanem quamdam habet elocutionem, et paene puerilem*]" (1.20).

19. See Alain Michel, "La rhétorique, sa vocation et ses problèmes: sources antiques et médiévales," *Histoire de la rhétorique dans l'Europe moderne, 1450–1950*, ed. Marc Fumaroli (Paris: PUF, 1999), 17–45.

20. Ernesto Grassi, *Rhetoric as Philosophy: The Humanist Tradition* (University Park: Pennsylvania State University Press, 1980), 10.

21. *De oratore*, 1.83; 3.65; 1.229.

22. *De oratore*, 1.70. Perhaps Sidney had this passage in mind when he paints the poet as "freely ranging within the zodiac of his own wit." Thomas Sébillet refashions Cicero's opinion just in time for the Pléiade, when he writes in his 1548 *Art poétique français*, Bk.1, ch.3: "Et sont l'Orateur et le Poète tant proches et conjoints, que semblables et égaux en plusieurs choses, diffèrent principalement en ce, que l'un est plus contraint de nombres que l'autre."

23. See also *De oratore*, 2.189. Curiously, given Cicero's preference for the grand style, he fails really to discuss how epideictic oratory can best decorously move an audience. Other *doctores* give an almost unlimited license to demonstrative oratory, in which all the ornaments may be used, and where even the euphony-producing, Gorgianic figures are admitted. See, for example, *Rhetorica ad Herennium*, 4.32.

24. See Richard Volkmann, *Die Rhetorik der Griechen und Römer* (Hildesheim: Georg Olms, 1963). Volkmann notes: "Das kakózelon entsteht aus

einer übertriebenen Neigung, den Stil anmuthig und blühend zu machen, wodurch er ins manierte verfället . . . (406)." See also the entry for *affectatio* in *Historisches Wörterbuch der Rhetorik*, ed. Gert Ueding (Tübingen: Max Niemayer, 1992–), 1:209–218. Aristotle in the *Rhetoric* (3.3), discusses "the frigidities" [*ta psykhra*]. There are four types of frigidities, all violations of decorum: unwieldy compounds or coinages, unfamiliar words, inappropriate epithets, and far-fetched metaphors. As Volkmann observes, with their "überflussiger, unpassender und gehäufter Epitheta, übertriebener und zu weit hergeholter Metaphern," the frigidities are largely synonymous with *cacozelia* (406).

25. *Tusc. disp.*, 4.68–71.

26. Cicero, *Topica*, tr. Tobias Reinhardt (Oxford: Oxford University Press, 2003), 138–139.

27. Translation slightly modified. See also *De officiis*, 1.14; *De finibus*, 2.47. Liddell and Scott note that *kosmos* may mean: "order"; "decency"; a "set form or order as provided by a state of government"; the "world or universe" (due to its perfect arrangement).

28. D'Alton sees the contrast between the two terms as a commonplace in Roman criticism (474). *Ingenium* here means natural genius.

29. *De oratore*, 3.156.

30. For overviews of Quintilian's life, work, and influence, see George A. Kennedy, *Quintilian* (New York: Twayne Publishers, 1969), 123–141; Otto Seel, *Quintilian, oder Die Kunst des Redens und Schweigens* (Stuttgart: Klett-Cotta, 1977), 278. The most extensive study of the *Institutio* remains Jean Cousin, *Études sur Quintilian*, 2 vols. (Amsterdam: P. Schippers, 1967). Michael Winterbottom's *Problems in Quintilian* (London: University of London, 1970) clarifies many of the textual problems due to the variety of surviving manuscripts.

31. See John O. Ward, "Cicero and Quintilian," in *Cambridge History of Literary Criticism: The Renaissance*, vol. 3, ed. Glyn P. Norton (Cambridge: Cambridge University Press, 1999), 77–87.

32. For an invaluable collection of essays compassing various aspects of Quintilian's work and influence, see Tomás Albaladejo, Emilio del Río, and José Antonio Caballero, eds., *Quintiliano: Historia y actualidad de la retórica*, 3 vols. (Logroño: Ediciones Instituto de Estudios Riojanos, 1998). For a lively account of the continuing vitality of Quintilian's rhetorical project, see Sarah Spence, *Figuratively Speaking: Rhetoric and Culture from Quintilian to the Twin Towers* (London: Duckworth, 2007).

33. As Tacitus polemicizes in his *Dialogus de oratoribus* (late first century CE),

such devotion to rhetorical artifice and pedantry is symptomatic of the decline in Roman mores.

34. The teaching of the declaimers' brand of rhetoric in the early Empire had already assumed an enormous role in educated Roman circles. As Kennedy (11–54) and Jean Cousin (1.79–99) recount, adolescent boys, after they mastered grammar, practiced declamation, which consisted primarily of *controversiae* (judi- cial declamations), and to a lesser extent the more measured *suasoriae* (deliberative exercises). Despite the putative judicial context of the *controversiae*, students tended to declaim on unconventional, infamous, or recherché subjects — magicians, monsters, plagues, oracles, parricides — and they employed the most "swollen and artificial style" (Kennedy, 51).

35. *Inst.*, 5.17–23. There are two collections of *declamationes* traditionally at- tributed to Quintilian. The *Declamationes maiores* consists of 19 full-scale decla- mations often on rather bizarre subjects. The *Declamationes minores* contain 145 declamations, which are relatively more down to earth. Tellingly, most modern scholars have ceased to attribute either collection to the judicious Quintilian.

36. Probably it was Quintilian's antipathy to the declaimers that prompted him to found a state-sponsored school of rhetoric that taught aristocratic youth his version of the *ars eloquendi*. Seneca the Elder (54 BCE–39 CE), who was also a formidable orator, pithily condemns the sterile, solipsistic school exercises of the declaimers: "In a declamation what is not superfluous, when declamation is itself superfluous?" [*In scolastica quid non supervacuum est, cum ipsa supervacua sit?*]. Seneca the Elder, *Controversiae*, 2 vols., tr. Michael Winterbottom (Cambridge: Harvard University Press, 1974), 3.Pr.12; translation modified. He exemplifies his distaste for the schools' exaggerated rhetoric by pointing to the "insane" outdoing of a certain Dorion who, imitating the *Odyssey* where Homer describes how Cyclops "tore off the top of the mountain" (9.481–482), writes that "mountain is tore from mountain." Seneca the Elder, *Suasoriae*, ed. William A. Edward (Cam- bridge: The University Press, 1928), 1.12.

37. With *De causis* in mind, Kennedy deduces seven causes of corruption from the *Institutio*: license in word choice, childish epigrams, unrestrained pom- posity, empty commonplaces, fragile adornments, extravagance mistaken for sub- limity, and madness mistaken for freedom of speech (24).

38. In the *Controversiae* (1.Pr.7), Seneca the Elder provides a glimpse of what Quintilian's treatise probably contained. He cites three causes for rhetoric's de- cline: luxurious living, lack of incentive either because of imperial oppression or the pursuit of wealth, and, most intriguingly, "fate, whose grim law is universal

and everlasting — things that get to the top sink back to the bottom, faster than they rose." Anticipating later cyclical, metahistorical views of literary history as championed by Vico, Spengler, Wölfflin, D'Ors, and Curtius, Seneca hints here that taste and so also proper *elocutio* change because of the "malign, perpetual" momentum of literary history itself.

39. For Quintilian's place in the history of literary criticism, see Herbert Jaumann, *Critica: Untersuchungen zur Geschichte der Literaturkritik zwischen Quintilian und Thomasius* (Leiden: Brill, 1995).

40. Although Statius is not mentioned by name in the *Institutio*, Kennedy opines that Statius' exaggerated tribute to Lucan in the *Silvae* (2.7) and the "uncontrolled hyperbole" he finds there would have been repellent to Quintilian (27). A significant influence on late medieval and late Renaissance literature, the *Silvae*, a collection of occasional verse, much of it epideictic in nature, long irked neoclassical critics owing to its highly contrived tone, plodding erudition, and abuse of rhetorical figures like hyperbole. Even so, Statius' praise of Lucan, whose fame lifts the author of the *Pharsalia* above Homer, Virgil, and Ovid, and whose meteoric fall earns him a comparison to Alexander the Great, seems heartfelt and may be explained by the real kinship in method and taste between the two poets. Yet such hyperbole might be less objectionable if it were not allied with an almost obsessive predilection for the monstrous, the bizarre, and, in terms of form, for the epigrammatic bordering on obscurity. And while Statius achieves moments of real wit and pathos, his penchant for excessive flattery — perhaps understandable given the political climate in which he wrote — inevitably strikes certain tastes as alien, if not slightly repugnant. For wit, see his prosopopeia "To Sleep" in *Silvae*, 5.4. For pathos, see his praise of Virgil in *Thebiad*, 12.816.

41. Gérard Genette, "La rhétorique restreinte," *Figures III* (Paris: Éditions du Seuil, 1972), 21–40.

42. In terms of the technical aspects of the rhetorical enterprise, Cousin shows that the principal sources in Quintilian's exhaustive treatment are Cicero and the Hellenistic theorists, Celsus, Hermogoras, and Theophrastus.

43. See, for instance, Leonardo Bruni's *De studiis et litteris* (ca. 1424), in *Humanist Educational Treatises*, ed. and tr. Craig Kallendorf (Cambridge: Harvard University Press, 2002).

44. Pliny the Younger's *Panegyric to Trajan*, which will become canonical in the Renaissance, is paradigmatic in this regard.

45. He discusses the last four parts in books 5, 6, and 7; the exordium is treated at 4.1.45–46. In the surviving examples of demonstrative oratory from Quintilian's time, it is in the exordium and peroration where one discovers hyperbole

most frequently. Kennedy notes that Quintilian is unique in having the orator emphasize his own *ethos* in the exordium (64–65). He surmises that Quintilian might not recommend "risky" hyperbole here as it might provoke the audience to suspect the speaker's motives just at the moment when his objective is in sight.

46. For example, casting himself as a champion of both art and nature, Quintilian compares the beauty and utility of fruit trees planted in perfect quincuncial order to how the conflation of *ornatus* and *res*, form and function, exert a stronger aesthetic appeal than if one aspect had been allowed to overwhelm the other (8.3.9). The *decor* of such an orchard is thus related to but not utterly dependent on its *utilitas*. The orchard metaphor also suggests a fundamental relation between geometry and rhetoric. Intriguingly, it will inspire Thomas Browne who, in *The Garden of Cyrus*, cites it as an epigraph and then amplifies it to incredible, metaphysical lengths. Browne, moreover, seems to pun etymologically on Quintilian's notion of "decor" with his own monomaniacal use of "decussation." In addition to perverting Quintilian's aesthetic ideas and notion of taste, Browne's text thus provides an exemplary instance of indecorous, if delightful *translatio*.

47. A trope is initially defined as when "[a] noun or a verb is transferred from the place where it properly belongs to another where there is either no literal term or the transferred is better than the literal" (8.6.5). But earlier he writes: "A Trope is a shift of a word or a phrase from its proper meaning to another, in a way that has positive value" [*Tropos est verbi vel sermonis a propria significatione in aliam cum virtute mutatio*]. Cousin comments: "Dans aucun texte ancien n'existe une définition du trope analogue à celle de Quintilien" (1.437). Though the subsequent distinctions between tropes and figures (9.1.1–22) unnecessarily confuse matters, Quintilian's discussion of the tropes of metaphor, irony, and hyperbole confirm that ornament can affect the meaning as well as the form of language.

48. Patricia Parker, "Metaphor and Catachresis," in *The Ends of Rhetoric: History, Theory, Practice*, ed. John Bender and David E. Wellbery (Stanford: Stanford University Press, 1990), 60–73. Quintilian discusses the relation between *abusio* and metaphor at 8.6.35. The poet is allowed more license with the former, as *abusio* "rarum in prosa est." See also Anselm Haverkamp, "Metaphora Dis/Continua: Base Respects of Thrift But None of Love," *Die Aktualität der Rhetorik*, ed. Heinrich F. Plett (Munich: Wilhelm Fink, 1997), 176–189.

49. Parker, 73.

50. They are: 1) from one animate thing to another 2) from one inanimate thing to another 3) from an inanimate to an animate thing 4) from an animate thing to an inanimate one. See Christine Brooke-Rose, *A Grammar of Metaphor* (London: Seckler & Warburg, 1958), for an inventive analysis of this schema.

51. These examples are taken from *De oratore*.

52. Earlier in the treatise (5.11.22), the invention of similes is discussed in the context of producing proofs. Now, though, we learn that one of the principal virtues of ornament is *enargeia* or "vivid illustration" (8.3.61). Thus simile can either "illuminate" a description or strengthen an argument (8.3.72). Why this dual nature is not ascribed to metaphor is unclear.

53. Presumably, in the case of a hyperbolic simile (see 8.6.71), such remove from the immediate subject at hand would produce an even greater impression of novelty at the expense, perhaps, of lessening the speaker's *enargeia*.

54. See Philip Hardie, *Virgil's* Aeneid: *Cosmos and Imperium* (Oxford: Clarendon Press, 1986), 247. Significantly, the large majority of the literary examples in the *Institutio* are taken from Virgil.

55. *Venus* is a decorous euphemism for *coitus*, but it would be "licentius" in a law court to substitute "Liber" and "Ceres" for "bread" and "wine" (8.6.24).

56. Richard Lanham muses: "Perhaps metonymy has received attention in post-modern critical thinking because it is an affair of scale manipulation, and manipulating scale in time and space undergirds much postmodern art and music." *A Handlist of Rhetorical Terms* (Berkeley: University of California Press, 1991), 102.

57. Allegory or *inversio*, is divided into two species: ". . . aut aliud verbis aliud sensu ostendit aut etiam interim contrarium" (8.6.44). Briefly stated, allegory is meant chiefly to adorn; it should not, Quintilian implies, become itself the principle object of hermeneutics.

58. Irony is "revealed either by delivery, by the character of the speaker, or by the nature of the subject. If any one of these is incompatible with the words, it is clear that the speech intends something totally different [*nam si qua earum verbis dissentit, apparet diversam esse orationi voluntatem*]" (8.6.54–55).

59. Lucan's hyperbolic praise of Nero in *De bello civili* (1.34–66) is an infamous literary example of this.

60. Like the tropes, the figures ". . . vim rebus adiciunt et gratiam praestant" (9.1.2). Figures of thought may, seemingly, work in a manner analogous to forms of proof, for "[figures] lend credibility to our arguments and steal their way secretly into the minds of the judges" (9.1.19). The forceful emotional effect of the figures is also emphasized: "Iam vero adfectus nihil magis ducit" (9.1.21).

61. For concise overviews of classical and Renaissance views on hyperbole, see Volkmann, 439–442; Lausberg §§579, 909; *Historisches Wörterbuch der Rhetorik*, 2:115–122; Katrin Ettenhuber, "Hyperbole: exceeding similitude," in

Renaissance Figures of Speech, ed. Sylvia Adamson, Gavin Alexander, and Katrin Ettenhuber (Cambridge: Cambridge University Press, 2007), 197–216.

62. The adjective *audax* may be translated as "daring" or "bold," although more frequently it means "reckless," "audacious," or "presumptuous."

63. There are both aesthetic and moral connotations in "decens"; it is also etymologically related with the English word, decorum. Thus of crucial importance, potentially, are the variant readings of this passage. Whereas Spalding has "decens," the *Codex Bambergensis* has "decensuris," but the *Codex Ambrosianus* has "demensuris," which appears to be by a hand other than Quintilian's.

The *Rhetorica ad Herennium* prefers *superlatio* to *superiectio* in its definition: "Superlatio est oratio superans veritatem alicuius augendi minuendive causa. Haec sumitur separatim aut cum comparatione. Separatim, sic: 'Quodsi concordiam retinebimus in civitate, imperii magnitudinem solis ortu atque occasu metiemur.' Cum comparatione aut a similitudine aut a praestantia superlatio sumitur. A similitudine, sic: 'Corpore niveum candorem, aspectu igneum ardorem adsequebatur.' A praestantia, hoc modo: 'Cuius ore sermo melle dulcior profluebat.' Ex eodem genere est hoc: 'Tantus erat in armis splendor, ut solis fulgor obscurior videretur.'" [*Hyperbole is a manner of speech exaggerating the truth, whether for the sake of magnifying or minimizing something. This is used independently, or with comparison. Independently, as follows: 'But if we maintain concord in the state, we shall measure the empire's vastness by the rising and setting of the sun.' Hyperbole with comparison is formed from either equivalence or superiority. From equivalence, as follows: 'His body was as white as snow, his face burned like fire.' From superiority as follows: 'From his mouth flowed speech sweeter than honey.' Of the same type is the following: 'So great was his splendour in arms that the sun's brilliance seemed dim by comparison.'*] (4.33.44). *Rhetorica ad Herennium*, tr. Harry Caplan (Cambridge: Harvard University Press, 2004). Caplan's notes indicate possible Homeric sources for these examples.

64. Cicero, *Philippics*, tr. Walter C. A. Ker (Cambridge: Harvard University Press, 1969), 2.63.

65. Fairclough (109) in the Loeb edition of the *Aeneid* identifies this as a much-debated passage.

66. See Michael Putnam, *Virgil's Epic Designs: Ekphrasis in the* Aeneid (New Haven: Yale University Press, 1998), 119–207. I am depending on Quintilian's use of "textus" to refer to something written. But literally it means a "woven cloth," a "texture," or a "web."

67. All English translations are from *The Aeneid*, tr. David West (New York: Penguin, 1990).

68. Lausberg, §404. Erasmus will repeat these examples in *De copia*.

69. Here *plantas* means "the soles of feet" but also may be a pun on the "sprig" of a plant.

70. Cousin observes: "... l'hyperbole par métaphore ... il faut rattacher sans nul doute à la doctrine aristotélicienne ..." (1:449). This refers to Aristotle's insight, which I will discuss below, that the genius of metaphor is to "bring things before the eyes" in a manner that produces novelty, strangeness, and surprise. Kennedy (245) discusses Quintilian's familiarity with the *Rhetoric*.

71. "Überhaupt ist für die Hyperbel charakteristisch, dass sie sich gern durch andere Tropen oder Figuren, wie Metapher, Metonymie, Synekdoche, Antiphrasis, überhaupt Ironie und Ausrufungen zu stützen oder zu verstärken sucht. Man kann auch Hyperbel auf Hyperbel häufen ..." (Volkmann, 440).

72. In his chapter on Virgilian hyperbole (241–292), Hardie writes of internal and external decorum. The former corresponds to generic expectations, the latter to the "content" of the hyperbole.

73. My translation.

74. Unfortunately, Cousin's comments (1:401) on the distinction between how the *urbanus* and *rusticus* receive such ornamental truths does not address the reception of hyperbole.

75. Quintilian revisits this thought-provoking *abusio* when he lauds an *incrementum* of Cicero's: "Sed alius divideret haec et circa singulos gradus moraretur; hic in sublime etiam currit et ad summum non pervenit nisu, sed impetu" (8.4.8). This emphasis on the sublime and speed is amplified, respectively, by Hermogenes and Longinus.

76. Also unable to avoid the metaphorics of ascent/descent, Cousin remarks on *incrementum*: "On peut encore ajouter quelque chose au superlatif absolu ou indiquer d'emblée le point le plus élevé de tout ce qu'on peut concevoir ou y parvenir par une gradation continue et insensible ..." (1:428).

77. "The hyperbole ... is a means of gradual *amplificatio*, and is, as a thought-figure, also a heightening of *evidentia*. Its purpose and limits do not go beyond the creation of momentary poetic *evidentia*. Credibility is relegated to the background in favor of an impressive *evidentia*" (Lausberg, §§909–910).

78. He considers hyperbole at the very end of his discussion of metaphor, which begins in 3.2 of the *Rhetoric* and is picked up again in 3.10–11. See Ricoeur, *The Rule of Metaphor*, 9–43; Richard Moran, "Artifice and Persuasion: The Work of Metaphor in the *Rhetoric*," in *Essays on Aristotle's* Rhetoric, ed. A. O. Rorty (Berkeley: University of California Press, 1996), 385–398; André

Laks, "Substitution et connaissance: une interprétation unitaire (ou presque) de la théorie aristotélicienne de la métaphore," in *Aristotle's* Rhetoric: *Philosophical Essays*, ed. David J. Furley and Alexander Nehemas (Princeton: Princeton University Press, 1994), 283–305; and, in the same volume, Glenn W. Most, "The Uses of *Endoxa*: Philosophy and Rhetoric in the *Rhetoric*," 167–190.

79. English quotations are from *On Rhetoric*, tr. George A. Kennedy (New York: Oxford University Press, 1991). Greek quotations are from *The Rhetoric of Aristotle with a Commentary*, 3 vols., ed. Edward M. Cope, rev. John E. Sandys (Cambridge: Cambridge University Press, 1877).

80. I am condensing the argument in 3.10–11.

81. *Rhetoric* 1405a, 1410b.

82. Moran, 391.

83. See, though, T. H. Irwin, "Ethics in the *Rhetoric* and in the Ethics," in *Essays on Aristotle's* Rhetoric, 142–172. Irwin surmises that the doctrine of the mean is not mentioned in the *Rhetoric* "because a proper understanding and application of it requires us to absorb some of the more complex aspects of Aristotle's theory" (162). Conversely, Kennedy cites Heidegger who calls Book 2 of the *Rhetoric* "the first systematic hermeneutic of everydayness of being with one another" (ix).

84. See also *Rhetoric*, 1405a8–10; *Topica*, 140a8–11 (". . . for a metaphor in a way adds to our knowledge of what is indicated on account of the similarity, for those that use metaphors always do so on account of some similarity.") Aristotle, *Topica*, tr. E. S. Forster (Cambridge: Harvard University Press, 1960). "Metaphor is a movement [*epiphora*] of an alien [*allotriou*] name from either genus to species or from species to genus or from species to species or by analogy" (1457b7).

85. Likewise, the *Poetics* stresses metaphor's ability to incorporate the "alien name" into the proportional "motion" characteristic of rational thought.

86. Aristotle, *On Poetics*, tr. Seth Benardette, Michael Davis (South Bend: St. Augustine's Press, 2002). Benardette and Davis's note on *psuchagōgei* describes the important eschatological connotations of this word. All English translations from the *Poetics* are from this edition; citations from the Greek text are from the *Poetics*, ed. Stephen Halliwell (Cambridge: Harvard University Press, 1995).

87. See David E. Cooper, *Metaphor* (Oxford: Oxford University Press, 1986), 194.

88. This is reminiscent of Quintilian's comments at 8.6.70. E. M. Cope, in *An Introduction to Aristotle's Rhetoric* (London: Macmillan, 1867), notes that

Demetrius makes *ta psykhra* a vice akin to the abuse of *megaloprepeia*. Cope cites Theophrastus who equates the "frigid" with *to uperballōn ten oikeian apaggelian*, which signals an inflated, stilted, bombastic style (286–287).

89. Kennedy points also to 1390a–b, which states flatly: "[t]he young overdo everything."

90. Cope-Sandys observe that "*meirakiodeis* is here meant to convey the fire, vigour, spirit, impetuosity, proneness to passion and excitement; or in general 've-hemence' . . . It is used by Plato (*Rep.* 466b, 498b) in the sense of 'puerile'" (3.143).

91. Homer, *The Iliad*, tr. Richmond Lattimore (Chicago: University of Chicago Press, 1951).

92. The *proemium* would be 308–317, the statement (*prothesis*) 318–343, the argument (*pistis*) 344–420, and the *epilogos* 421–429. See *Rhetoric*, 1414a–b.

93. Cope-Sandys, 3.143.

94. Despite his tendency to brand hyperbole as "frigid," the conservative Demetrius breaks new theoretical ground by dividing hyperbole into three kinds of conceptual "impossibility," and by underscoring its potential emotional effects. By linking hyperbole to the other figures, he also confirms that hyperbole cannot be read in isolation as if it were merely a trope of substitution. Dated to the late second or early first century BCE, *On Style* offers a succinct, Hellenistic, neo-Aristotelian theory of hyperbole. Demetrius makes "hyperbole" [*uperbolē*] the epitome of rhetorical "excess" [*uperballōn*]: "The most frigid of all devices is hyperbole, which is of three kinds. It is expressed either in the form of a likeness, for example 'like the winds in speed' [*Iliad*, 10.437]; or of superiority, for example, 'whiter than snow' [*Iliad*, 10.437]; or of impossibility, for example 'with her head she reached the sky' [*Iliad*, 4.443]. Admittedly every hyperbole is an impossibility. There could be nothing 'whiter than snow,' nothing 'like winds in speed.' But this last kind is especially called impossible. And so the reason why every hyperbole seems particularly frigid is that it suggests something impossible [*adunatos*]. This is also the chief reason why the comic poets use it, since out of the impossible they create laughter, for example when someone said hyperbolically of the voracity of the Persians that 'they excreted entire plains' and that 'they carried oxen in their jaws.' Of the same type are the expressions 'balder than a cloudless sky' and 'healthier than a pumpkin.' Sappho's phrase, 'more golden than gold' is also a form of hyperbole and impossible, but by its very impossibility it is charming, not frigid. Indeed, it is the most marvelous achievement of the divine Sappho that she handled an intrinsically risky and intractable device to create charm [*epicharitos*] (ss.124–127)." As a comparison, comparative, or impossibility, hy-

perbole is portrayed as marshalling other tropes, such as simile, metaphor, and allegory, to achieve its effect. In conceptual terms, by especially emphasizing hyperbole's "impossibility" [*adunaton*], Demetrius blames it for offending propriety and "reason" [*ratio*]. Sappho alone is celebrated here for her ability to use hyperbole in a pleasing aesthetic manner because her hyperbole finds its conceptual justification in her lofty material as well as her subtle style. Still, by approaching hyperbole through examples from epic, lyric, and comic drama, Demetrius confirms its enormous compass and pull on the imagination. His three types of "impossibility" nicely describe how the hyperbolist tends to outdo herself or himself in search for novel effects. See also ss.282–285, where Demetrius concedes that hyperbole can be quite effective when allied with allegory and "innuendo" [*emphasis*]. Thus the figure of *emphasis* (Gr.) or *significatio* (Lat.) may be considered a species of the genus hyperbole. Lanham comments that the "intensification" of emphasis can come through hyperbole when it focuses on a single dramatic image (138). Demetrius, *On Style*, tr. Doreen C. Innes (Cambridge: Harvard University Press, 1995).

95. Halliwell, in a note to this passage, suggests though that Aristotle might have in mind Odysseus' early encounter with Penelope (19.249–250).

96. Ricoeur, 42. In a similar vein, Moran concludes: "Aristotle's ambivalence about metaphor will be . . . explained by the fact that both its value as a vehicle of understanding and the dangers of its rhetorical abuse stem from the same features of its 'live' imagistic power" (396).

97. As an abstract idea, *to hypsos* verges on catachresis. Literally an "elevation," the sublime is figured as the ultimate, nearly inexpressible "height" of linguistic creation.

98. Alexander Pope, *An Essay on Criticism*, in *Pastoral Poetry and An Essay on Criticism*, ed. Émile Audra and Aubrey Williams (London: Metheun & Co. Ltd; New Haven: Yale University Press, 1961), 11.680.

99. Longinus, *On the Sublime*, tr. W. H. Fyfe (Cambridge: Harvard University Press, 1995). All English and Greek quotations are from this text. The numbers in parentheses refer to the sections of the text. Under the rubric of literature I am including here the texts of epideictic orators like Demosthenes and Isocrates since their speeches were committed to writing and they availed themselves of the more difficult and risky figures directed principally at readers. As for the relation between sublimity and the grand style, see *On the Sublime*, ed. and tr. W. Rhys Roberts (Cambridge: The University Press, 1935), 32.

100. See the commentary on 1.2 of D. A. Russell in his edition of Longinus, *On the Sublime* (Oxford: Clarendon Press, 1964), 62.

101. The catachresis of "meteōra" should not go unmentioned. Thus style again takes its paradigms from nature, although here it is nature in its most violent, unordered state.

102. See Robert Lamberton, *Homer the Theologian: Neoplatonist Allegorical Reading and the Growth of the Epic Tradition* (Berkeley: University of California Press, 1986). But as Bacon observes of Homer, in *The Advancement of Learning*: ". . . I should without any difficulty pronounce that his fables had no such inwardness in his own meaning."

103. Anne Carson sees much more here than the rhetorical expression of emotion; for her the poem heuristically represents the "radical constitution of desire." See *Eros the Bittersweet* (Princeton: Princeton University Press, 1985), 16.

104. In this and many other regards, Longinus begs to be compared to Hermogenes' *On Types of Style* (*Peri ideon*). Writing in second century CE Alexandria, Hermogenes offers a unique description of the rhetorical enterprise and a broad defense of stylistic grandeur. Reformulating the concept of the three styles into seven "ideas" — Clarity, Grandeur, Beauty, Rapidity, Character, Sincerity, and Force — Hermogenes considers content (*ennoia*), approach (*methodos*), and form (*lexis*) as inextricable aspects of the same rhetorical enterprise. His treatment of Grandeur (*megethos*) and Force (*deinotes*) are particularly relevant to the study of hyperbole. Moreover, as Cecil Wooten suggests, Hermogenes' view of panegyric at once bridges and blurs the domains of oral rhetoric with those of poetic, philosophical, and historical writing. Hermogenes writes: "Plato is the most beautiful of panegyric styles in prose, and we would recommend this, as the best example to follow, to anyone who is able to construct a panegyric speech. All poetry is panegyric and is in fact, the most panegyric of all literary styles." See Hermogenes, *On Types of Style*, ed. and tr. Cecil W. Wooten (Chapel Hill: University of North Carolina Press, 1987), 389. Annabel Patterson, *Hermogenes and the Renaissance: Seven Ideas of Style* (Princeton: Princeton University Press, 1970). Patterson writes: ". . . there is the direct influence of the Ideas in the criticism of Scaliger, Minturno, and Tasso, or in the religious propaganda of Milton, or in the "flyting" between Thomas Nashe and Gabriel Harvey, or in George Herbert's theory of preaching." She also traces its influence, on a more conceptual level, on Sidney's idea of style in the "Defence."

105. Asyndeton (19–20), hyperbaton (22), and periphrasis (29) are especially recommended, although the last is considered the riskiest as it may become trite very quickly.

106. See Russell's discussion of the three styles and how the sublime may be

achieved in all three since it is more of a "special effect, not a special style" (xxxvii). Thus excess can occur in trying for this effect in any style.

107. Arieti and Crosset note what has been implicit of my discussion throughout: namely, that Longinus uses the term hyperbole in a looser sense than the handbook writers. They also observe that Longinus' definition of hyperbole must have come in the lacuna. See *On the* Sublime, tr. and ed. James A. Arieti and John M. Crossett (New York: The Edwin Mellon Press, 1985), 189–190.

108. Writing in Latin, with his feet firmly planted in the rhetorical tradition, but with ears seemingly deaf to the Schlegelian revolution in criticism, the German classicist, Gottfried Hermann, in *De hyperbole dissertatio* (1829) analyzes hyperbole by expanding and refining the psychological justifications provided by Aristotle and Longinus. See Godofredi Hermanni, *Opuscula* (Leipzig, 1831; reprinted Hildesheim: G. Olms, 1970), 4:284–302. The first modern scholar to devote an entire essay to hyperbole, Hermann applies his theory of hyperbole to close readings of Homeric passages. He effectively reduces hyperbole to a decorous means of expressing "abundance." Nearly all of the Homeric examples he adduces contain either literally or figuratively enormous quantities meant to express some extraordinary quality. This again suggests, the fundamental relation between hyperbole and catachresis. Hermann also distinguishes hyperbole from exaggeration; the former aims to persuade and the latter is content merely to delight. Surprisingly, nowhere does he mention the sublime. Instead, for Hermann, too much or inappropriate overreaching usually results in the monstrous or betrays insincerity, or more radically, insanity. Hermann also writes two related essays: "Quid sit ὑποβολῇ et ὑποβληδην" (5:300–311) and "Defensio dissertationis de ὑποβολή" (7:65–87).

109. Russell concludes: "We can be confident that very little of the book is missing at the end" (193).

CHAPTER TWO: RENAISSANCE THEORIES OF HYPERBOLE

1. Ernst Robert Curtius, *European Literature and the Latin Middle Ages* (*ELLMA*), tr. Willard R. Trask (Princeton: Princeton University Press, 1990), 128. Reappraisals of Curtius's contributions to medievalism and comparative literature include: William Calin, "Ernst Robert Curtius: The Achievement of a Humanist," *Studies of Medievalism* 9 (1997): 218–227; Heinrich Lausberg, *Ernst Robert Curtius (1886–1956)*, ed. Arnold Arens (Stuttgart: Steiner Verlag, 1993); Earl J. Richards, "E. R. Curtius's Vermächtnis an die Literaturwissenschaft: Die Verbindung von Philologie, Literaturgeschichte und Literaturkritik," in

Ernst Robert Curtius: Werk, Wirkung, Zukunftsperspektiven, ed. Walter Berschin and Arnold Rothe (Heidelberg: Carl Winter Universität Verlag, 1989), 249–269. Arthur R. Evans in *On Four Modern Humanists: Hofmannsthal, Gundolf, Curtius, Kantorowicz* (Princeton: Princeton University Press, 1970) offers a general introduction to Curtius's scholarship. For a more recent appraisal, see Hans Ulrich Gumbrecht, *Vom Leben und Sterben der grossen Romanisten: Karl Vossler, Ernst Robert Curtius, Leo Spitzer, Erich Auerbach, Werner Krauss* (München: Carl Hanser Verlag, 2002). In a letter to Curtius after having received *ELLMA*, T. S. Eliot writes: ". . . thank you for your magnificent book. I do not know when I shall ever find time to read the whole of it . . ." (cited in Peter Godman's *Epilogue* to *ELLMA*, 599).

2. *ELLMA*, 145–166. Significantly, chapter 8 is preceded by one on "Metaphorics," where Curtius explores how certain "historical metaphorics" are central to the continuity of the Western literary tradition; it is then followed by two chapters, "Heroes and Rulers" and "The Ideal Landscape," in which he shows how the mannerism associated with what I am reading as hyperbole, not only is required in certain rhetorical occasions but also shapes various literary genres, such as pastoral and epic. Thus hyperbole forms a lynchpin in Curtius's effort to demonstrate how his version of philology must begin with analysis of a multitude of examples or "significant facts" before any synthesis is attempted. See the Epilogue (esp. 380–383) for his illuminating discussion of method.

3. Writing after the initial explosion of literary criticism on the "Baroque," Curtius rejected the term, thinking that it referred too narrowly to only one historical period, whereas he found "Mannerism" in late Antiquity, the thirteenth and seventeenth centuries, and in the Expressionism of his own youth. See the beginning of his chapter on Mannerism (273–274). The best summary of medieval rhetoric remains Richard McKeon, "Rhetoric in the Middle Ages," *Speculum* 17 (1942): 1–32.

4. ". . . the epideictic oration had by far the strongest influence upon medieval poetry" (155). Hermogenes is cited on the same page as defining "poetry as panegyric."

5. *ELLMA*, 157.

6. For Curtius's idea of what constitutes a topic and how it is related to invention and style see chapter five of *ELLMA*, "Topics" (79–105). As Curtius argues in "Topik als Heuristik," in *Toposforschung*, ed. Max Baumer (Darmstadt: Wissenschaftliche Buchgesellschaft, 1973), 19–21, the *topoi* are where the poet begins his invention and so where the reader should begin his discovery of the

poem's meaning and place in the literary tradition (19–21). Some critics have challenged Curtius's use of this term. They charge that he confuses the *loci communes*, general sites of invention, with the more specific notion of the commonplaces. See Edgar Mertner, "Topos und Commonplace," in *Toposforschung*, ed. Peter Jehn (Frankfurt am Main: Athenäum Verlag, 1972), 20–68.

7. For the specific ramifications of these tendencies and numerous examples, see *ELLMA*, 154–165.

8. *ELLMA*, 160–161.

9. *ELLMA*, 162.

10. He traces this concept back to, among other sources, Quintilian's treatment of amplification (7.4.9).

11. *ELLMA*, 164.

12. Curtius quotes Peter's poem, "Against the Slanderers," and then writes: "A poet to be blamed for bestowing praise? Then the most famous poets and doctors are blameworthy. Let us leave the pagans aside. Jerome, Augustine, Ambrose, Cyprian, Sidonius, Fortunatus were masters of the panegyric style" (164).

13. *ELLMA*, 164.

14. Curtius discusses two such formula: *cedat* (let him yield) and *taceat* (let him be silent), the latter in the context of Dante's outdoing of Lucan and Ovid (165).

15. See James J. Murphy, Lawrence D. Green, *Renaissance Rhetoric Short-Title Catalogue 1460–1700*, 2nd ed. (Burlington, VT: Ashgate, 2006). Murphy also traces the transition from medieval to Renaissance rhetoric in *Rhetoric in the Middle Ages: A History of Rhetorical Theory from St. Augustine to the Renaissance* (Berkeley: University of California Press, 1974). See also his *Renaissance Eloquence: Studies in the Theory and Practice of Renaissance Rhetoric* (Berkeley: University of California Press, 1983), a volume that he edited and that I will refer to below. Thomas M. Conley's *Rhetoric in the European Tradition* (Chicago: University of Chicago Press, 1990) provides a succinct yet rigorous overview of rhetoric and Renaissance humanism (109–149). An essential collection of essays on the developments in quattrocento and cinquecento Italy and then in sixteenth-century France is *Poétiques de la Renaissance: Le modèle italien, le monde franco-bourguignon et leur héritage en France au XVIe siècle*, ed. Perrine Galand-Hallyn and Fernand Hallyn (Geneva: Droz, 2001). Kees Meerhoff offers a panoptic but detailed account of the situation in France in *Rhétorique et Poétique au XVIe Siècle en France: Du Bellay, Ramus et les autres* (Leiden: Brill, 1986). For developments in England, see Peter Mack, *Elizabethan Rhetoric: Theory and Practice* (Cambridge: Cambridge

University Press, 2002); Debora K. Shuger, *Sacred Rhetoric: The Christian Grand Style in the English Renaissance* (Princeton: Princeton University Press, 1988); Brian Vickers, *Classical Rhetoric in English Poetry*, with a new preface and annotated bibliography (Carbondale: Southern Illinois University Press, 1986) and *In Defense of Rhetoric* (Oxford: Clarendon Press, 1988), where Vickers observes how ". . . there must have been several million Europeans with a working knowledge of rhetoric [in the period between 1400–1700] . . . The stress on practicality is perhaps the most distinctive feature of the Renaissance rediscovery of classical rhetoric" (270–271). For a broader overview, see Heinrich F. Plett, *Rhetoric and Renaissance Culture* (Berlin: Walter de Gruyter, 2004); also two volumes edited by Plett, *Renaissance-Rhetorik | Renaissance Rhetoric* (Berlin: Walter de Gruyter, 1993) and *Renaissance-Poetik | Renaissance Poetics* (Berlin: Walter de Gruyter, 1994), contain important essays reevaluating the state of research in these respective fields. A similarly valuable collection of essays is: Marjike Spies, *Rhetoric, Rhetoricians, and Poets: Studies in Renaissance Poetry and Poetics*, ed. Henk Duits and Ton van Strien (Amsterdam: Amsterdam University Press, 1999). All these books contain exhaustive bibliographies. For recent work on the intersections of rhetoric and poetics in the early modern period see the *Cambridge History of Literary Criticism The Renaissance*, vol. 3, ed. Glyn P. Norton (Cambridge: Cambridge University Press, 1999).

16. Bernard Weinberg, *A History of Literary Criticism in the Italian Renaissance*, 2 vols. (Chicago: University of Chicago Press, 1961); see also Cesare Vasoli, *La dialettica e la retorica dell'umanesimo* (Milan: Feltrinelli, 1968); John Monfasani, "Humanism and Rhetoric," in *Renaissance Humanism: Foundations, Forms, and Legacy*, ed. Albert Rabil, Jr. (Philadelphia: University of Pennsylvania Press, 1988), 3:171–235.

17. For the history of rhetoric and the influence of Ciceronianism, Seneca, and Erasmus in late sixteenth- and early seventeenth-century France, see Marc Fumaroli, *L'âge de l'éloquence*, esp. 17–109, 279–298. See also the monumental volume edited by Fumaroli, *Histoire de la rhétorique dans l'Europe moderne, 1450–1950* (Paris: PUF, 1999). Wilfried Barner's *Barockrhetorik: Untersuchungen zu ihren geschichtlichen Grundlagen* (Tübingen: Max Niemeyer Verlag, 1970) exhaustively covers developments in Baroque Germany.

18. Walter F. Ong, *Ramus, Method, and the Decay of Dialogue: From the Art of Discourse to the Art of Reason* (Cambridge: Harvard University Press, 1983), 252. The rise and effects of Ramism in England is examined in W. S. Howell, *Logic and Rhetoric in England, 1500–1700* (Princeton: Princeton University Press, 1956) as well as Mack's *Elizabethan Rhetoric*.

19. David Renaker, "Robert Burton and Ramist Method," *Renaissance Quarterly* 24.2 (1971): 210–220.

20. Plett, "Renaissance-Poetik: zwischen Imitation und Innovation," *Renaissance-Poetik / Renaissance Poetics*, 12.

21. See Izora Scott's edition of the *Ciceronianus* in *Controversies over the Imitation of Cicero in the Renaissance* (Davis, CA: Hermagoras Press, 1991). The fundamental study of Erasmian rhetoric remains Jacques Chomarat, *Grammaire et rhétorique chez Erasme*, 2 vols. (Paris: Société d'Édition 'Les Belles Lettres,' 1981).

22. See R. J. Schoeck, "'Going for the Throat': Erasmus' Rhetorical Theory and Practice," *Renaissance-Poetik / Renaissance Poetics*, 43–58.

23. *Ecclesiastes sive de ratione concionandi* (1535), a compendious treatise on homiletics, and his posthumously published *Compendium rhetorices* (1544) offer more detailed versions of his rhetorical vision.

24. "Fondamentalement, Erasme n'est pas un théologien . . . On doit considérer Erasme tout à la fois comme un grammaticus, un rhetor, un orator, c'est-à-dire un spécialiste de la langue et des lettres, un maître dans l'art d'écrire, en prenant le mot 'maitre' dans ses deux acceptions: celui qui possède cet art à fond et celui qui sait l'enseigner" (Chomarat, 1.20–22).

25. For Valla's notes to Book 1 of the *Institutio*, see Lorenzo Valla, *Le postille all'Institutio oratoria di Quintiliano*, ed. L. C. Martinelli and Alessandro Perosa (Padua: Antenore, 1996). Jorge Fernández López, in *Retórica, humanismo y filología: Quintiliano y Lorenzo Valla* (Logroño: Ediciones Instituto de Estudios Riojanos, 1999), recounts the "transmisión, recepción e influencia de Quintiliano y su *Institutio oratoria* en el humanismo italiano" (11). Some of Valla's annotations to Book 1 and part of Book 2 are published in 1494 in Venice albeit in corrupted form. For Valla's use of Quintilian in *Elegantiae linguae latinae*, see Martin L. McLaughlin, *Literary Imitation in the Italian Renaissance: The Theory and Practice of Literary Imitation from Dante to Bembo* (Oxford: Clarendon Press, 1995). For a more general study of Valla's place in the history of Renaissance rhetoric, see Peter Mack, *Renaissance Argument: Valla and Agricola in the Tradition of Rhetoric and Dialectic* (Leiden: E. J. Brill, 1993).

26. Du Bellay, 1.8 (237–238).

27. Cave, *The Cornucopian Text*, 3–77.

28. English citation are from *Copia: Foundations of the Abundant Style*, tr. Betty I. Knott, in *Literary and Educational Writings 2; De Copia / De Ratione Studii*, ed. Craig R. Thompson, *Collected Works of Erasmus*, vol. 24 (Toronto: University of Toronto Press, 1978). All Latin citations are from *De copia verborum ac rerum*, ed. Betty I. Knott, *Opera omnia*, vol. 17 (Amsterdam: North-Holland, 1988). Sec-

tion numbers indicated in the main text correspond to this edition. Both these English and Latin versions are based on the 1534 edition. See also *On Copia of Words and Ideas*, tr. D. B. King and H. David Rix (Milwaukee: Marquette University Press, 1963). The Introduction to this truncated edition describes the text's wide diffusion.

29. See Cave, 18.

30. *De copia*, 24:595. *Locuples* literally means "of landed property"; "rich," "opulent." Already with Cicero *locuples* is used catachrestically to figure eloquence.

31. *De copia*, 24:595, 604.

32. *De copia*, 24:604.

33. For the historical and theological context for Erasmus's efforts, see Jan Rohls, "Schrift, Wort und Sache in der frühen protestantischen Theologie," in *Res et Verba in der Renaissance*, ed. Eckhard Kessler and Ian Maclean (Wiesbaden: Harrassowitz, 2002), 241–272. Brian Vickers's essay in the same volume, "'Words and Things' — 'Words, Concepts, and Things'? Rhetorical and Linguistic Categories in the Renaissance," 287–336, traces the debate's main contours.

34. Ong, 272–291.

35. *Oxford Latin Dictionary* (Oxford: Clarendon Press, 1996), 442. Quintilian describes the *facultas* of producing *copia* as one of the primary "instrumenta" of a successful orator (*Inst.* 12.5.1).

36. For a different, more elaborate version of the myth see Ovid, *Fasti*, 5.115–128.

37. Although given how he viewed the Roman Church's decadence as an obstacle to Christian humanism, Erasmus may have wanted to exclude a certain Popish form of *copia*. See André Chastel, "L'ennemi de la magnificence," in *Dix conférences sur Érasme: Eloges de la folie — Colloques* (Paris: Champion; Geneva: Slatkine, 1986), 163–168.

38. See the entry for *copia* in the *Historisches Wörterbuch der Rhetorik*, 2.386–394.

39. Cave, 8, 19, 23. Compare this with Bacon's adaptation of the Proteus-myth in various texts, for instance *De sapientia veterum*, to represent the transformations of nature.

40. Regarding Erasmus's *Annotations* to the New Testament and his *Ecclesiastes*, Chomarat notes that hyperbole poses a fundamental exegetical challenge: "On peut changer de théologie selon qu'on reconnaît, ou non, la présence d'une hyperbole dans Math. XIX, 24 . . ." (567). See also 647, 675.

41. *De copia*, 24:302, 299, 299; *De Copia*, in *Opera omnia*, 17:30.

42. *De copia*, 24:344. Knott notes that in the *Adages* (Prolegomena, xiii), *saxa clamore rumpit* is given as another example of hyperbole. Erasmus repeats verbatim and amplifies in the *Adages* much of the material on *superlatio* from *De copia*.

43. *De copia*, 24:344.

44. *De copia*, 24:382–395; *De copia*, in *Opera omnia*, 17:100–108. All the following examples are from this chapter. Sources besides Cicero include Ovid, Plautus, Terence, Virgil, Horace, Aristophanes, Pliny, Isidore, Plutarch, and his own *Adages*.

45. Here Erasmus notes: "Per hyperbolen augetur hoc modo: 'mulier plusquam pessima' et 'pessima peior'; homo non loquacissimus, sed 'ipsa loquacitas' et 'ipsa loquacitate loquacior'; 'ipsa Venere venustior' (17:98).

46. Cave argues that Erasmus adds additional chapters to *De copia* because of the "anxiety" that his doctrine is not ample enough (26). Successive editions of the *Adages* and *Colloquia* follow the same pattern of proliferation, while his translation of the New Testament into Latin (1516) undergoes numerous revisions and emendations in the years following its first publication. See Chomarat (2:761–782) on the rhetoric and figures in the *Adages*.

47. *De copia*, 24:388–392.

48. In his discussion of Erasmian amplification in homiletic discourse, Chomarat treats hyperbole and amplification as causing the same tension between "l'exigence de sincérité et celle d'art oratoire" (2:1114). Both have need of *exaggeratio*, Chomart concludes, because the orator's task is more to move than to instruct the audience.

49. They find their latter-day, elegant cousin in Raymond Queneau's 99 variations on a quotidian narrative in *Exercices de style* (1947). Queneau also writes, "Cent mille milliards de poèmes," which consists of a sequence of 10 fourteen-line sonnets. The book is produced in such a way that 100,000,000,000,000 poems can be generated. A note to a recent English translation reads: "Queneau calculated that someone reading the book 24 hours a day would need 190,258,751 years to finish it." Such are the possibilities, real and imaginary, of a certain latter-day species of *copia*.

50. After the last variation in the first set, he pleads: "If anyone thinks that some of these suggestions would hardly be tolerable in prose, he should remember that this exercise is designed for the composition of verse as well" (*De copia*, 24:354). Thus Cave (25) reads 1.33 as a moment where Erasmus abandons *doctrina* for *experientia*, that is, where the reader's experience of pleasure becomes the most forceful means of instruction.

51. *De copia*, 24:349; *De copia*, in *Opera omnia*, 17:78.

52. *De copia*, 24:572; *De copia*, in *Opera omnia*, 17:198. Similarly, the last chapter in Book I is the topic, *Non ultra*.

53. *De copia*, 24:658.

54. *De copia*, *Opera omnia*, 17:204.

55. *De copia*, 24:580–581.

56. Cave, 30–31.

57. "Locupletantur item exempla, si fusius aut latius explicentur, cum exaggerationibus atque amplificationibus" (*De copia*, in *Opera omnia*, 17:234).

58. *De copia*, 24:648.

59. *De copia*, 24:657.

60. *De copia*, 24:648–655.

61. *De copia*, 24:659. Cave concludes that Erasmus ultimately "releases *res* from the constraints of a predetermined *sententiae* so that they may flow with the devious, Protean current of *verba*" (30).

62. Conley, *Rhetoric in the European Tradition*, 120. For a more extended discussion of Erasmian rhetoric in the context of Renaissance skepticism, see Victoria Kahn, *Rhetoric, Prudence, and Skepticism in the Renaissance* (Ithaca: Cornell University Press, 1985).

63. Desiderius Erasmus, *The Praise of Folly and Other Writings*, tr. Robert M. Adams (New York: Norton, 1989), 8; *Moriae encomium id est stultitiae laus*, ed. Clarence H. Miller, in *Opera omnia*, vol. 9 (Amsterdam: North-Holland, 1979), 72.

64. *The Praise of Folly*, 4.

65. Marcel Tetel, "L'éloge de la Folie: Captatio benevolentiae," in *Dix conférences sur Érasme: Eloges de la folie — Colloques*, 23. For Erasmus as commentator and literary critic, see Jean-Claude Margolin, *Erasme: le prix des mots et de l'homme* (London: Variorum Reprints, 1986).

66. Tetel, 29, 31.

67. If M. A. Screech's reading, in *Erasmus: Ecstasy and* The Praise of Folly (Harmondsworth: Penguin, 1988), is adopted of the peroration in praise of Christian ecstasy, which occurs in the 1511 version of the *Moria*, then the ultimate trajectory of Erasmus's hyperboles may be toward a more familiar though no less ineffable signified.

68. Christopher Celenza, *The Lost Italian Renaissance: Humanists, Historians, and Latin's Legacy* (Baltimore: The Johns Hopkins University Press, 2004). Curtius writes: "The culture of the Middle Ages cannot be presented, because its Latin literature has as yet been incompletely studied. In this sense the Middle Ages is still dark today as it — wrongly — appeared to the Italian humanists.

For that very reason a historical consideration of European literature must begin at its darkest point" (13).

69. Celenza, 17.

70. See Julius Caesar Scaliger, *Oratio pro M Tullio Cicerone contra Desiderium Erasmum* (1531); *Adversus Desiderii Erasmi Roterodamensis dialogum Ciceronianum oratio secunda* (1537); *Exotericae exercitationes ad Hieronymum Cardanum* (1557). On the controversy provoked by the last text, Anthony Grafton, in *Cardano's Cosmos: The Worlds and Works of a Renaissance Astrologer* (Cambridge: Harvard University Press, 1999), comments: "Like all good heroes of satirical novels, Cardano paid the price, and more than the price, for his posturing. In 1557 he became the object of the most savage book review in the bitter annals of literary invective. Julius Caesar Scaliger, another vain and articulate natural philosopher of Italian origins, devoted more than nine hundred quarto pages to refuting one of Cardano's books, *On Subtlety* . . ." (4).

71. Luc Dietz, *Einführung* to Julius Caesar Scaliger, *Poetices libri septem / Sieben Bücher über die Dichtkunst*, 5 vols., ed. and tr. Luc Dietz and Gregor Vogt-Spira (Stuttgart-Bad Cannstatt: frommann-holzboog, 1994), 1:xxxiii.

72. See Anthony Grafton, *Joseph Scaliger: A Study in the History of Classical Scholarship*, 2 vols. (New York: Oxford University Press, 1983–1993).

73. Dietz, 1:xxxii.

74. Heinrich F. Plett, "The Place and Function of Style in Renaissance Poetics," *Renaissance Eloquence*, 363.

75. Bernard Weinberg observes of the *Poetices*: "Its first impression . . . is as a work of unlimited erudition. Into this erudition there necessarily enters all the available knowledge on the art that Scaliger is treating. But whereas in Minturno knowledge of other critical systems leads to eclecticism and disorganization, in Scaliger a different result is achieved. For he is basically an orderly thinker, capable of seeing the necessary consequences of his distinctions and of creating a subordination of his ideas to guiding principles" (2:744).

76. As to whether Scaliger's poetics is ultimately a rhetorical or ethical (i.e., philosophic) poetics, Dietz is unequivocal: "Scaligers *Poetik* zeigt deutlicher als andere, daß Dichtungslehre und Rhetorik eng miteinander verzahnt sind und nicht unabhängig voneinander betrachtet werden können" (2:43).

77. Aside from the increasingly popular "defenses of poesy," Weinberg traces the variety of other approaches to poetics. If the theorist were an Aristotelian he would think of poems in terms of the poet-poem-audience relationship; if he were a Ciceronian, then in terms of invention, arrangement, elocution; if he saw poetry as a part of moral philosophy, "his whole theory would be oriented toward

the ability of the poet to produce or the critic to judge the desired ethical effect" (1:2). Scaliger himself takes up the question in a somewhat confusing manner in Bk. 3.1.82a–b. See also Weinberg, "Scaliger versus Aristotle on Poetics," *Modern Philology* 39 (1942): 337–360.

78. Bk. 7.2.347a / 5:494.

79. Dietz, 2:24. See Scaliger's comments on Bk. 3.1.81d / 2.70; also the entire chapter later devoted to *prudentia* (Bk. 3.25).

80. "lyrica, scolia, paenes, elegiae, epigrammata, satyrae, sylvae, epithalamia, hymni, alia in quibus nulla exstat imitatio, sed sola nudaque ἐππαγγέλια, id est enarratio aut explicatio eorum affectuum, qui ex ipso proficiscuntur ingenio canentis, non ex persona picta" (Bk. 7.2.347a–b / 5:494). See Claudie Balavoine, "La *Poétique* de J. C. Scaliger: Pour un *mimèsis* de l'imaginaire," in *La statue et l'empreinte: la poétique di Scaliger*, ed. Claudie Balavoine and Pierre Laurens (Paris: Vrin, 1986), 107–129; also Weinberg, 1:250–296 on the Neo-Platonic defenses of poetry in the Cinquecento. Also relevant is Giraldo Cinthio's *On the Composition of Romances* (1554) where Platonic *furor* is promoted jointly with the pursuit of Aristotelian mimesis. Cinthio praises the poet's pursuit of the marvelous in the making of "fables."

81. Dietz, 2:18.

82. Bk. 3.1.80a–83a / 2:60–79.

83. Bk. 3.1.80a / 2:60; see also Bk. 7.2 for further discussion of *res* and imitation.

84. Anne Moss, "Theories of Poetry: Latin Writers," in *The Cambridge History of Literary Criticism*, 3:103. As David Marsh comments: "Scaliger uses the term *idea* to denote a notion that combines both Platonic paradigm and Aristotelian form and that suggests an ascent from the syllabic and metrical 'matter' discussed in Book 2." David Marsh, "Julius Caesar Scaliger's *Poetics*," *Journal of the History of Ideas* 65.4 (2004): 667–676; 669. Dietz sees this as one Scaliger's most original contributions (2:20).

85. Bk. 3.28.120b / 2:372.

86. Bk. 3.28.120b–121a / 2:372–375.

87. Dietz summarizes Scaliger's sources in his discussion of figures and tropes; these include George of Trebizond, Hermogenes, Quintilian, and the *Rhetorica ad Herennium* (2.35).

88. Bk. 3.31.122a / 2:382; Bk. 3.31.122a / 2:382.

89. Bk. 3.73.135b / 2:502. The *Quaestiones*, better known as the *Problemata*, was incorrectly ascribed to Aristotle. See *Problems*, 2 vols. tr. W. S. Hett (Cambridge: Harvard University Press, 1953–1957), Pr.1.1.859a.

90. Bk. 3.74.135b / 2:504.

91. "Nearly half of this lengthy book [Book 5] consists of a comparison be-tween Homer and Virgil in which Scaliger outdoes even the shrill 'Maronolatry' of the rabid Evangelus in Macrobius. In addition to this late classical source Scaliger also draws on writings by Quattrocento humanists, especially Poliziano's *Silvae* and Pontano's dialogue *Antonius*" (Marsh, 670). See esp. Bk. 5.3, "Homeri et Vergilli loca," which begins: "Homer's epithet are frequently frigid, puerile, or miss their mark" [*Homeri epitheta saepe frigida aut puerilia aut locis inepta*]. Commenting on Book 5, Anne Moss asserts: "Scaliger was the first to make comparison a critical methodology" (104).

92. "Quae ex suo modo finem imponat progressibus nostris" (Bk. 6.7.348b / 5:468).

93. Marsh argues this may involve another type of critical overreaching: "A striking feature of this book is Scaliger's endorsement of *emendatio*, which means proposing stylistic improvements in poetic texts rather than the philological restoration of a corrupt passage" (670–671).

94. Bk. 5.12.266a–268a / 4:470–941. For a reading of this *topos*, see Mark Morford, *The Poet Lucan: A Study in Rhetorical Epic* (Oxford: Basil Blackwell, 1967), 30–31.

95. Bk. 5.12.266b / 5:476.

96. See Dietz, "Zur Wirkungsgeschichte," (1:xxxii–lxiii). Summing up his research, Dietz claims: "... daß die *Poetik* in der Hauptsache punktuell, unkritisch und unsystematisch rezipiert wurde: Die miesten der bedeutenderen Theoretiker scheinen sie bestenfalls angelesen zu haben; synthesiert und in größerem Rahmen in die eigenen Reflexion einbezogen hat sie offenbar niemand" (xxxv).

CHAPTER THREE: BAROQUE THEORIES OF HYPERBOLE

1. Here the Elizabethan use of "conceit" with its wide semantic range — i.e., "idea," "mind," "witticism" — should be recalled. Helen Gardner's gloss nicely captures the cognitive experience that attends it: "A conceit is a comparison whose ingenuity is more striking than its justness, or, at least, is more immediately striking . . . a comparison becomes a conceit when we are made to concede like-ness while being strongly conscious of unlikeness." Introduction to *The Meta-physical Poets* (London: Penguin Books, 1985), 19. See also Alexander Parker, "'Concept' and 'Conceit': An Aspect of Comparative Literary History," *MLR* 77.4 (1982): xxi–xxxv.

2. Baltasar Gracián, *Oráculo manual y arte de prudencia* (Salamanca: Anaya, 1968), 41.

3. A Jesuit, who resided much of his life in the provincial city of Huesca, Gracián also writes *El Héroe* (1637), a book describing the twenty "primores" [*principal skills, excellences; outstanding achievements*] desirable in great men; *El Discreto* (1646), a treatise aimed at a less lofty audience and which rehearses via twenty-five "realces" [*outstanding features*] the ways anyone can refine their judgment and perception; *Oráculo manual y arte de prudencia* (1647), a collection of moral maxims organized under three hundred heading and written in the best laconic, Senecan style; and finally, a satiric, proto-Bildungsroman, *El Criticón* (published in three parts, 1651, 1653, and 1657), which portrays the fate of two allegorical characters representing reason and natural instinct as they make their way through a hostile world only to be disabused by a mercenary court. The last work, translated into English in 1681 as *The Critick*, quickly became a part of *Weltliteratur* — Schopenhauer preferred it to *Don Quixote* and *Gulliver's Travels*, and Nietzsche celebrated it. See Victor Bouillier, *Baltasar Gracián et Nietzsche* (Paris: Honoré Champion, 1926); reprinted and translated along with other essays in Alfonso Moraleja, ed., *Gracián hoy* (Madrid: Cuaderno Gris, 2002).

4. Hans-Georg Gadamer, *Truth and Method*, 2nd rev. ed. (New York: Continuum, 1999), 35–36.

5. Anthony Cascardi, "Gracián and the Authority of Taste," in *Rhetoric and Politics: Baltasar Gracián and the New World Order*, ed. Nicholas Spadaccini and Jenaro Talens (Minneapolis: University of Minnesota Press, 1997), 255–283.

6. Curtius, *ELLMA*, 297–298.

7. Baltasar Gracián, *Agudeza y arte de ingenio* (Madrid: Castalia, 2001), 1:47. While it is certainly true that none of the classical *doctores* devote separate works to what Gracián calls *agudeza*, we saw above how Aristotle and Quintilian address, respectively, the notions of *asteia* and *urbanitas*.

8. Samuel Johnson, "Cowley," in *Selected Poetry and Prose*, ed. Frank Brady and W. K. Wimsatt (Berkeley: University of California Press, 1977), 348.

9. While in Rome, a Polish Jesuit, Mathias Casimirus Sarbievius (or Sarbiewski), also lectured on "De acuto et arguto liber unicus" (1623), but the text was only published in 1958. See Holt Meyer, "Jesuit Concedes Jesuit Conceits: A Hit on Sarbievius' Head," in *Gedächtnis und Phantasma: Festschrift für Renate Lachmann*, ed. Susi K. Frank et al. (Munich: Otto Sanger, 2001), 372–389.

10. Yves Hersant, *La métaphore baroque: D'Aristote à Tesauro. Extraits du Cannochiale aristotelico et autres textes* (Paris: Éditions du Seuil, 2001), 11. See also Pierantonio Frare, *"Per istraforo di perspettiva": il Cannochiale aristotelico e la poesia del Seicento* (Pisa: Instituti editoriali e poligrafici internazionali, 2001).

11. Emanuele Tesauro, *Il Cannocchiale aristotelico* (1670), ed. August Buck (Bad Homburg: Gehlen, 1968). The engraving also has a *subscriptio* that reads: *EGRE-GIO INSPERSOS REPREHENDIT CORPORE NAEVOS Horatius*.

12. Cited in Buck, "Einleitung," vi.

13. Tesauro, 267. The phrase occurs in chapter seven, the *Trattato della metafora*, where Tesauro describes the cognitive effect of hearing a metaphor like *prata rident*.

14. Tesauro, 279.

15. Hersant, 17.

16. "Egli è ver nondimeno che il troppo è troppo. Perché così nelle Metafore, come nelle altre Voci Pellegrine, hassi a guarder la santa legge del *Decoro* . . ." But in almost the next breath, Tesauro advises breaking this "holy law": "Che se al-cun suggetto si deve sterminatamente *esaggerare*, ti fia lecito di vibrar Metaforone rigonfie; ò nella grandezza, come il *BOMBOMACHIDES* di Plauto: overo nel significato iperbolico: come Licofrone di Serse; *Vir MONTIS instar*. Et, *MONTES AVRI polliceri*. Et, *Telis UMBRARE diem*; per significare una folta moltitudine de saette. Et il Barbaro di Seneca: *AEQUALIS ASTRIS gradior* . . . In oltre, quando il Suggetti fia *Ridicolo*, come ne' Comici sali, & ne' faceti rac-conti; il Decoro starà nello scantonatti da' cancelli del Docoro; concertando cose spropositatamente sconcertate . . ." (270–272).

17. Tesauro, 266, 279. In the analysis of these three stages I am indebted to Robert E. Proctor, "Emanuele Tesauro: A Theory of the Conceit," *MLN* 88.1 (1973): 68–94, esp. 75.

18. Tesauro, 82.

19. "Il quarto *Esercitio* [of human subtlety] . . . si pratica per via di uno IN-DICE CATEGORICO. Secreto veramente secreto: nouva, & profonda, & in-efausta Miniera d'infinite Metafore, di Simboli arguti, & di' ngegnosi Concetti. Peroche . . . altro non è l'ingegno, che virtù di penetrar gli obietti altamente api-attati sotto diverse Categoríe; & di riscontrarli fra loro. Laonde gratie infinite si denno al nostro Autore [i.e., Aristotle], primo ad aprir questa Porta secreta à tutte le Scienze; altro non essendo il Filosofare, che volar con la mente per tutte le Cat-egoríe: à ricercar la *Notitie*, ò sia, *Circonstanze*; per trarne Argomenti: & chi più ne comprende, meglio filosofa" (107). See J. W. van Hook, "'Concupiscence of Witt': The Metaphysical Conceit in Baroque Poetics, *Modern Philology* 84.1 (1986): 24–38.

20. Tesauro, 267. The verb *travedere* literally means "to deceive oneself by seeing something that is not there."

21. Eugenio Donato, "Tesauro's Poetics: Through the Looking Glass," *MLN* 78 (1963): 15–30; quotation from 21. To my mind, in arguing against Joseph Mazzeo's claim that Baroque theories of poetic wit still wish to discover objective "correspondences" between mind and world, Donato goes too far to the other extreme. See Joseph Mazzeo, "Metaphysical Poetry and the Poetry of Correspondences," *JHI* 14 (1953): 221–235. For the interpretation of wit as imaginative play, see Guido Morpurgo Tagliabue, "Aristotelismo e barocco," in *Retorica e barocco. Atti del III Congresso internazionale di studi umanistici*, ed. Enrico Castelli (Rome: Fratelli Boca, 1955), 119–195.

22. Proctor, 78–79.

23. Tesauro, 487–489.

24. Tesauro, 490. He also calls these "fallacies," citing the *Rhetoric* (2.25), "Apparentium Enthymematum loci."

25. Quoted in van Hook, 34.

26. Tesauro, 298. He provides brief examples here of these eight species of metaphor. See Donato (20–22) on the primacy of metaphor in Tesauro's theory of the conceit.

27. Tesauro, 426.

28. Tesauro, 288.

29. Tesauro, 289–290.

30. Tesauro, 90. Beyond embracing the Neo-Platonic theories of *furor* and inspiration, Tesauro allows that "madness" [*pazzia*] may, given its proximity to wisdom and since its power to forge surprising connections makes it synonymous with metaphor, produce invaluable wit (93–96).

31. Tesauro, 427–428. Using sensible qualities for spiritual qualities amounts to the same effect, Tesauro claims.

32. Like Gracián's, Tesauro's reliance throughout his treatise on the exemplary Martial is enormous — another confirmation of the cardinal influence of Silver Latin poetry on Baroque aesthetic practice and thought.

33. Tesauro, 430, 431.

34. Tesauro, 288. He cites the *Rhetoric*, 1411b–1413b and *Poetics*, 1460a in support.

35. Tesauro, 433.

36. Tesauro, 487, 522–525, 566–567. This same theme, taken from Martial's *Epigrams* (4.32), is used as the initial example of the conceit (487) and serves as the starting point for the discussion of the other species of paralogic wit (551–569). In this sense, Tesauro's critical wit resembles Erasmus's facility for amplification in *De Copia*.

37. Roland Barthes, "The Old Rhetoric: an aide-mémoire," in *The Semiotic Challenge*, tr. Richard Howard (New York: Hill and Wang, 1988), 60.

38. Quoted in Mario Praz, "The Flaming Heart: Richard Crashaw and the Baroque," in *The Flaming Heart: Essays on Crashaw, Machiavelli, and Other Studies in the Relations between Italian and English Literature from Chaucer to T. S. Eliot* (Garden City, NY: Doubleday, 1958), 206.

39. *Agudeza*, 1:48.

40. Leaning on Quintilian, Aristotle, Horace, and numerous other authorities, Carillo praises the "notable atrevimiento" of poetry, even as he constantly distinguishes it from oratory. See Luis Carillo y Sotomayor's *Libro de la erudición poética*, ed. Manuel Cardenal Iracheta (Madrid: CSIC, 1946), 28. López Pinciano's take on hyperbole emblemizes this generally dismissive treatment: "Y de la hipérbole, el que para engrandecer la grandeza de un aluañil dixo que podía desde el suelo trastexar las más altas torres; y deste género son las me[n]tiras rídiculas, como los que dizen fieros. Esta hipérbole se haze más rídicula quando el que quiere exagerar la cosa, la disminuye, y más, acerca de alguna cosa torpe, como fué la del predicador que en un sermón de la adúltera, afeando el adulterio, dixo que más quisiera pecar con dos vírgenes que con una casada." Alfonso López Pinciano," *Epístola nona. De la comedia*," *Philosophia antigua poética*, ed. Alfredo Carballo Picazo (Madrid: CSIC, 1953), 3:56. For a synopsis of developments in fifteenth and sixteenth-century Spain, see Dietrich Briesemeister, "Rhetorik und Humanismus in Spanien," *Renaissance-Poetik / Renaissance Poetics*, 92–106. A more extensive history is Antonio Vilanueva's "Preceptistas de los siglos XVI y XVII," in *Historia general de las literaturas hispánicas, III Renacimiento y barroco*, ed. Guillermo Díaz-Plaja (Barcelona: Barna, 1953), 567–694. See also Sanford Shepard, *El Pinciano y las teorías literarias del siglo de oro*, 2nd ed. (Madrid: Gredos, 1970). For a comprehensive collection of sixteenth and seventeenth-century Spanish literary criticism, see Alberto Porqueras Mayo, ed., *La teoría poética en el Renacimiento y manierismo españoles* (Barcelona: Puvill, 1986).

41. *Agudeza*, 1:51.

42. "Si frecuento los españoles, es porque la agudeza prevalece en ellos, así como la erudición en los franceses, la eloquencia en los italianos y la invención en los griegos" (1:46).

43. Another approach to Gracián's syncretism is adopted by Aurora Egido in *La rosa de silencio: Estudios sobre Gracían* (Madrid: Alianza, 1996). Egido considers Gracián's mastery of diverse discourses and contrasts it with the hermetic of ideal of silence as wisdom, though she also underscores the influence of Quintilian and other rhetors.

44. *Agudeza*, 1:51.

45. *Agudeza*, 1:49–50.

46. See *Discurso I*. In his exhaustive study of Gracián's theory of wit, *Gracián, Wit, and the Baroque Age* (New York: Peter Lang, 1996), Arturo Zárate Ruiz treats Gracián as a "realist." But this describes only half of his project. The theological, transcendent, universal function of the *ingenio* is also essential as Gracián's many references to Augustine, Anselm, and the Jesuits attest. In this respect, Gracián's determination to give the conceit and thus also metaphor real philosophical currency finds a latter-day cousin in Hans Blumenberg's "Paradigmen zu einer Metaphorologie," *Archiv für Begriffsgeschichte* 6 (1960): 7–142. Blumenberg's phenomenological approach to metaphor, while obviously employing far different critical assumptions and methods, is partially born from Husserl's idea of the inexpressible *Lebenswelt* — a concept Husserl first discovers in seventeenth-century thought.

47. *Agudeza*, 1:204.

48. Covarrubias glosses *esmalte* as: "Cierta labor de diversas colores, que se hace ordinariamente sobre oro, y es obra de mucho primor y su materia tiene principio en el arte de la alquimia."

49. *Agudeza*, 1:55.

50. Zárate Ruiz regards the task of such ingenious thinking as indicative of a "mastery" comparable to that possessed by Quintilian's "vir bonitus" (145–150).

51. Juan de Guzmán, *Primera parte de la Rhetorica*, ed. Blanca Periñan (Pisa: Giardini, 1993), 144. For a fine recent reappraisal of *conceptismo* in Europe, see Florence Vuilleumier, "Les conceptismes," in *Histoire de la rhétorique dans l'Europe moderne*, ed. Marc Fumaroli (Paris: PUF, 1999), 517–537.

52. T. E. May, "An Interpretation of Gracián's *Agudeza y Arte de Ingenio*," "Gracián's Idea of the *concepto*," "Notes on Gracián's 'Agudeza,'" in *Wit of the Golden Age* (Kassel: Reichenberger, 1986).

53. *Agudeza*, 1:54.

54. *Agudeza*, 1:55–56. Correa Calderón notes that in the Millé edition of Góngora's *Obras completas* (Madrid: Aguilar, 1943) this sonnet is only "attributed" to the poet.

55. See May, 271. Zárate Ruiz observes that *exprimir* "denotes the act of squeezing the juice from something, and connotes both the acts of intellectually abstracting and verbally expressing" (188). Given Deleuze's outsized presence in recent scholarship on the Baroque and Neo-Baroque, it would be interesting to compare what Deleuze reads as the philosophy of expression in Spinoza and Leibniz against Gracián's poetics of witty expression.

56. May reads the phrases "todo el artificio" and "artificiosa conexión" as in- dicating a more subjective basis for such correspondences (66–67).

57. See *Discurso II*.

58. *Agudeza*, 1:63.

59. See *Discurso XXXIII*.

60. This species of wit is the concern of Gracián's *El Héroe* and *El Discreto*.

61. Zárate Ruiz, 192.

62. See Zárate Ruiz's discussion, 271–280.

63. "Su mismo nombre de invención, ilustra este modo de agudeza, pues ex- prime novedad artificiosa del ingenio y obra grande de la inventiva. No siempre se queda la sutileza en el concepto, comunícase a las acciones; son muchos y pri- morosos sus asuntos" (*Agudeza*, 2:141).

64. *Agudeza*, 2:141.

65. The examples are mine. For ratiocination see Discourses 36–38 and for invention see Discourses 35 and 45.

66. See Croce's criticism of Gracián's nomenclature and method in "I trat- tatisti italiani del concettismo e Baltasar Gracián," in *Problemi di estetica: e contributi alla storia della estetica italiana* ([first published, 1899] Bari: G. Laterza, 1954). Ed- ward Sarmiento responds to Croce in "On Two Criticisms of Gracián's *Agudeza*," *Hispanic Review* 3.1 (1935): 23–35.

67. May, 19.

68. *Agudeza*, 1:88. Examples of the former are *agudeza por semejanza* and *agudeza por paridad*, while the latter include *agudeza por desemejanza* and *agudeza por disparidad*. But immediately after citing a sonnet by Marino, Gracián asserts that the species of correlation deserving the greatest praise mixes both proportion and disproportion, concord and dissonance.

69. *Agudeza*, 1:66. Gracián comments: "Esto es propriamente conceptear con sutileza, y este modo de concepto se llama proporcional, porque en él se atiende a la correspondencia que hacen los extremos cognoscibles entre sí."

70. "Nace de la proporción la hermosura, no siempre de la improporción en el hecho; pero el notarla en el concepto es perfección" (*Agudeza*, 1:76).

71. *Agudeza*, 1:84. *Repugnancia* means "incompatibilidad de dos atributos o cualidades de una misma cosa" according to Covarrubias.

72. *Agudeza*, 1:76.

73. These are: "*Y mi gozo trocó en pena infinita . . . Hallé por Paraíso cárcel fiera . . . Bebí por agua fresca ardiente fuego.*"

74. May, "Gracián's 'Agudeza y arte de Ingenio,'" 10.

75. According to Covarrubias, *ponderación* means "atención, consideración,

peso y cuidado con que se dice o hace una cosa." But *ponderar* can also be synony‑mous with *pesar, exagerar, encarecer* and *contrapesar*.

76. Thus Zárate Ruiz, seizing on the "juiciosa" in its name, rightly makes the faculty of judgment essential to its success (243).

77. *Agudeza*, 1:197. Perhaps "arroja" is an intralingual pun on *iacere* as in *su‑periectio*. In any case, both words connote unnatural, violent motion.

78. Though he does discuss "decencia" in terms of style in *Discurso XL*, it is no accident that this comes so late in the treatise. Again, the *Oráculo manual y arte de prudencia* is far more concerned with decorous speech and action.

79. *Agudeza*, 1:197. See Seamus Heaney, "Anything Can Happen," *District and Circle* (New York: Farrar, Straus & Giroux, 2006).

80. Gracián's complex appropriation of Horace the poet (for example in the last discourses of the treatise) and theorist throughout the treatise deserves further investigation. The verb *illabor* means "to fall to ruins; slip, glide, or fall into." Nietzsche in his lectures on rhetoric at the University of Basel also cites a verse from Horace to exemplify decorous hyperbole: "sublimi feriam sidera vertice," which is the final line of the dedicatory *Ode*, 1.1.36, to Maecenas: "Quodsi me lyricis vatibus inseres, sublimi feriam sidera vertice." Thus hyperbole assumes its proper place in panegyric, as Nietzsche the hyperbolist and classical philologist surely knew it should. See *Nietzsche on Rhetoric and Language*, ed. and tr. Sander L. Gilman, Carole Blair, David J. Parent (Oxford: Oxford University Press, 1989), 65.

81. Johnson, "Cowley," 349.

82. *Agudeza*, 1:99.

83. *Agudeza*, 1:102.

84. *Agudeza*, 1:197, 1:198.

85. *Agudeza*, 1:197.

86. Mercedes Blanco, *Les rhétoriques de la pointe: Baltasar Gracián et le concep‑tisme en Europe* (Geneva: Éditions Slatkine, 1992), 274–275. Blanco adds, echo‑ing Quintilian, "pour soutenir l'hyperbole . . . les plus mauvaises raisons sont préférables à l'absence de raison."

87. *Agudeza*, 1:198–199.

88. *Agudeza*, 1:199.

89. *Agudeza*, 1:200–201.

90. *Agudeza*, 1:202.

91. Andrea Alciato, *Emblemata* (Lyon, 1550), ed. and tr. Betty I. Knott (Aldershot: Scolar Press, 1996), 194.

92. *Agudeza*, 1:205–206.

93. *Agudeza*, 1:208. The hyperbole seems to be allegorical, that is, based on the literal fact that Christ was already dead, although there have been interpretations of the passage based on the anatomy of the heart that remove any taint of exaggeration. Compare Gracián's gloss with Tesauro's discussion (522–525) of Luke 22:44.

94. *Agudeza*, 1:206. Praising another hyperbole of Martial, Gracián notes: ". . . ayudóse de la fingida circunstancia del sueño."

95. *Agudeza*, 1:213.

96. *Agudeza*, 1:214. Gracián's emphasis.

97. *Agudeza*, 1:215, 210, 215. Gracián writes: "Así el divino Dionisio exprimió la milagrosa belleza y el sobrehumano decoro del sol de los serafines, María, si caben encarecimientos en tanto objeto . . ."

98. *Agudeza*, 1:216.

99. *Agudeza*, 1:217. The poem refers to Caesar in the fourth line, but he is outbid by Felipe II in the next, such that even the moon dares not challenge this new "Sol."

100. *Agudeza*, 1:219.

101. *Agudeza*, 1:220–221.

102. *Agudeza*, 1:223. Gracián's emphasis.

103. Leo Spitzer, "The Spanish Baroque," in *Representative Essays*, ed. Alban K. Forcione, Herbert Lindenberger, and Madeline Sutherland (Stanford: Stanford University Press, 1988), 135.

104. I will discuss specific instances where hyperbole verges on paradox in later chapters. See Rosalie Colie, *Paradoxia Epidemica: The Renaissance Tradition of Paradox* (Princeton: Princeton University Press, 1966).

105. In *Discursos XXIII–XXIV*, *De la agudeza paradoja* and *De los conceptos por una propuesta extravagante, y de la razón que se da de la paradoja*.

106. *Agudeza*, 1:226.

107. *Agudeza*, 1:211. As for witty paradoxes: "Son estos conceptos unos agudísimos sofismas para declarar con una extravagante exageración el sentimiento del alma" (1.238).

108. *Agudeza*, 1:236.

109. *Agudeza*, 1:236. *Autoridades* (1732) glosses *escrupuloso* as "dudoso, temeroso, cuidadoso, lleno de rezélos, especialmente en lo que mira à la conciéncia."

110. Commenting on some verses by the Jesuit, Remondo, in *Discurso XII*, Gracián notes: "La exageración hace muy salida la semejanza y la da mucho vivo

por el desengaño . . ." (1.142). The wit of satirists, we are told in the same *Discurso*, also leads to "desengaño y la moral enseñanza."

CHAPTER FOUR: YONDER: SPANISH BAROQUE HYPERBOLES

1. Dante Alighieri, *Inferno*, tr. John and Jean Hollander (New York: Random House, 2002), 483–485. This is one of the most imitated, analyzed episodes in the *Commedia*. Landmarks include Cristoforo Landino's *Comento sopra la Comedia* (1481), Tennyson's "Ulysses" (1833), Borges's "El último viaje de Ulises" (1982), and John Freccero's "Dante's Ulysses: From Epic to Novel" (1986). For an overview of some of the scholarship, see John A. Scott, "L'Ulisse dantesco," in *Dante magnanimo: studi sulla Commedia* (Florence: L. S. Olschki, 1977). A more recent appraisal is by Karlheinz Stierle, "Odysseus und Aeneas. Eine typologische Konfiguration in der *Commedia*," in his *Das große Meer des Sinns. Hermenautische Erkundungen in Dantes "Commedia"* (Munich: Wilhelm Fink, 2007).

2. *Inferno*, 26.136–138.

3. Hans Blumenberg, *The Legitimacy of the Modern Age*, tr. Robert M. Wallace (Cambridge: The MIT Press, 1983), 340.

4. See Earl Rosenthal, "*Plus Ultra, Non Plus Ultra*, and the Columnar Device of Emperor Charles V," *Journal of the Warburg and Courtauld Institutes* 34 (1971): 204–228; Frances Yates, "Charles Quint et L'idée d'empire," in *Fêtes et cérémonies au temps de Charles Quint*, ed. Jean Jacquot (Paris: CNRS, 1960), 57–97; Marcel Bataillon, "Plus Oultre: La cour découvre le nouveau monde," *Fêtes et cérémonies au temps de Charles Quint*, 13–27. Bataillon's essay details the phrase's use and reception in Spain, while Yates's essay paints a broader, European perspective.

5. See Bataillon, 23.

6. Ruscelli, Rosenthal notes (221), also relates it to Ariosto's *Orlando Furioso* (15.21–25).

7. See Otis Green, *Spain and the Western Tradition* (Madison: University of Wisconsin Press, 1965). His chapter "*Plus Ultra*: Geographical Expansion" (3:27–52) shows how consciousness of the new geographical discoveries slowly shaped Spanish Renaissance writing. Also germane is Anthony Pagden, *Lords of All the World: Ideologies of Empire in Spain, Britain and France, c.1500–c.1850* (New Haven: Yale University Press, 1995), esp. chapter one where Pagden discusses the motto "orbis non sufficet."

8. Ruscelli notes that though a variety of interpretations of the device were already prevalent in 1566, the improper Latin (taken alone it should read *plus ul-*

terius) suggests it was an anachronism. His reading confirms that it does not mean "there is more beyond" but simply "yet farther."

9. See Rosenthal, 206.

10. Francisco Lopéz de Gómara, *Historia general de las Indias* (Madrid: Iberia, 1982), 6.

11. Lopéz de Gómara, 5.

12. Henri Lefebvre, *The Production of Space*, tr. Donald Nicholson-Smith (Oxford: Blackwell Publishing, 1991), 168.

13. Rosenthal, 216.

14. *Opera omnia Desiderii Erasmi*, vol. 2, pt. 5 (Amsterdam-Oxford: North-Holland Publishing Company, 1981), 308–310. For Erasmus's self-reflective interpretation of *Herculei labores*, where he compares the task of adage making and collecting to Hercules' labors, see Margaret Mann Phillips, *The "Adages" of Erasmus: A Study with Translations* (Cambridge: The University Press, 1964), 190–208.

15. *Plus ultra* has also found a new currency in recent scholarship on trans-Atlantic literary relations. It frames Ricardo Padrón's article, "Mapping Plus Ultra: Cartography, Space and Hispanic Modernity," *Representations* 79 (2002): 28–60, and it is the title of Gordon Braden's final chapter on Sor Juana in *Petrarchan Love and the Continental Renaissance* (New Haven: Yale University Press, 1999).

16. M.A. Saint Amant, "Le passage de Gibraltar," in *Anthologie de la poésie française de XVIIe siècle*, ed. Jean Pierre Chauveau (Paris: Gallimard, 1987), 229.

17. Martin González de Cellorigo, *Memorial de la política necessaria y útil restauración a la República de España y estados de ella y del desempeño universal de estos Reinos* (1600), ed. José Luis Pérez de Ayala (Madrid: Instituto de cooperación iberoamericana, 1991), 12. For a more general historical background to the period's *Geist* see J. H. Elliott, "Self-Perception and Decline in Early Seventeenth-Century Spain," *Past and Present* 74 (1977): 41–61.

18. Cellorigo, 89.

19. José Antonio Maravall, *Culture of the Baroque: Analysis of a Historical Structure*, tr. Terry Cochran (Minneapolis: University of Minnesota Press, 1986), 20. Maravall, eschewing a "stylistic or morphological" analysis, calls the "baroque . . . a historical concept," and locates "its center of greater intensity and fuller significance between 1605 and 1650" (4).

20. Maravall, 62.

21. Generally speaking, the ideas of Paracelsus and Vesalius had a warmer reception than did discoveries in physics and astronomy. See J. M. López Piñero,

Ciencia y técnica en la sociedad española de los siglos XVI y XVII (Barcelona: Labor Universitaria, 1979).

22. See Numa Broc, *La géographie de la Renaissance (1420–1620)* (Paris: Bibliothéque Nationale, 1980), esp. 223–239.

23. Covarrubias, in his *Tesoro de la lengua castellana o española* (1611), defines *atrevido* as "[e]l determinado y arrojadizo en acometer una cosa sin considerar primero lo que se podría seguir de hacerla"; *despeñarse* as "[e]s acometer locamente un hecho, en el cual se ha de destruir y perder. Precipitado, el que no toma primero consejo de lo que piensa hacer, si puede correr algún peligro." *Autoridades* (1732) glosses *desaliento* as "quebrantamiento ù descaecimiento del ánimo y esfuerzo."

24. Pedro Calderón de la Barca, *La vida es sueño*, ed. José M. Ruano de la Haza (Madrid: Castalia, 1994).

25. Paul Julian Smith, *Writing in the Margin: Spanish Literature of the Golden Age* (Oxford: Clarendon Press, 1988), 7. But rather than seeking points of comparison, Smith stresses the Spanish difference in this matter: ". . . it should be noted that the problems of clarity and of excess seem to be linked to the peculiar sensitivity of Spanish rhetoricians to the marginal status of their culture" (23).

26. See Smith, 72.

27. Smith, 70. On the first page of his 1636 commentary on the *Soledades*, José García de Salcedo Coronel, leaning on the authority of Scaliger and Quintilian, as well as the example of Statius and some "composiciones" in "nuestro idioma," links the *silva* etymologically with "selva" and "bosque" and observes how fitting the title "Soledades" is, since "que cosa [es] mas solitaria?" See *Soledades de D. Luis de Góngora* (Madrid, 1636), 1r–v.

28. Antonio Carreño, "Of 'Orders' and 'Disorders': Analogy in Spanish Baroque Poetry," in *The Image of the Baroque*, ed. Aldo Scaglione (New York: Peter Lang, 1995), 152.

29. Smith, 66.

30. In his chapter on the lyric, Smith discusses *enargeia, evidentia* and *illustratio*: ". . . enargeia is associated with the demonstrative genre . . . moreover it is always excessive" (45). Yet I wonder if this holds for Alciato's subtle emblems, or the graceful, often understated sonnets of Garcilaso or Góngora. Further, is not Smith himself exaggerating the illumination afforded by the Derridean logic of supplementarity when he uses the excess he perceives in *enargeia* to conclude that "the marginality and deviance of the single figure are thus symptomatic of the more general contradictions implicit in lyric poetry and literary criticism"? (45–46). See my article, "De Doctrina Gongorina: Góngora's Defense of Obscurity," *BHS* 77.1 (2000): 21–46.

31. J. L. Borges, "La metáfora," *Historia de la eternidad* (Madrid: Alianza, 1996), 74, 74, 77. See also "The Metaphor," *This Craft of Verse* (Cambridge: Harvard University Press, 2000), 33; "The Fearful Sphere of Pascal," *Labyrinths* (New York: New Directions, 1964).

32. Borges, "La metáfora," 78.

33. Luis de Góngora, *Soledades*, ed. John Beverley (Madrid: Cátedra, 1995). All quotations from the *Soledades* in the main text are from Beverley's edition.

34. My paraphrases of the *Solidades* and *Polifemo* are at best a crib of only a portion of the semantic possibilities contained in Góngora's verse. Obviously, they are also interpretations. With the help of the Spanish prose translations of Alonso and Jammes, and the English verse translations of Wilson and Dent' Young, I have tried to convey the kernel of Góngora's meaning in a syntax that does not do too much violence to Góngora's, yet avoids the nonsense that would result from a more strictly interlinear approach.

35. José Pellicer de Salas y Tovar, *Lecciones solemnes a las obras de Don Luis de Gongora y Argote* (Hildesheim: Olms, 1971), 361.

36. See Beverley (75–76), who also cites Camões (*Lusiades*, 2.72–75) as a possible source: "Era no tempo alegre, quando entrava / no robador de Europa a la luz febea, / quando um e otro corno / he acquentava."

37. See "Menoscabo y grandeza" and "La nadería de la personalidad," in *Inquisiciones* (1925), where Borges proposes the notion of the universal author as a form of literary metempsychosis. Late in his life, Borges recalled: "When I was a young man, I was baroque. I did my best to be Sir Thomas Browne, Quevedo, or Lugones, or somebody else." See J. L. Borges, *Borges the Poet*, ed. Carlos Cortínez (Fayettville: University of Arkansas Press, 1986), 17.

38. From his *Carta echadiza*, reprinted in Emilio Orozco Diaz, *Lope y Góngora frente a frente* (Madrid: Gredos, 1973), 245.

39. Baltasar Gracián, *El Criticón, Obras Completas I* (Madrid: Turner, 1993), 10. For an incisive analysis of the role of *El Criticón* in the birth of modernity, see Alban K. Forcione, "At the Threshold of Modernity: Gracián's *El Criticón*," in *Rhetoric and Politics: Baltasár Gracián and the New World Order*, 3–70.

40. *El Criticón*, 10–11.

41. *El Criticón*, 16.

42. *El Criticón*, 10.

43. See Teresa Scott Soufas, *Melancholy and the Secular Mind in Spanish Golden Age Literature* (Columbia: University of Missouri Press, 1990).

44. Pedro Calderón de la Barca, *El mágico prodigioso*, ed. Bruce W. Wardrop' per (Madrid: Cátedra, 1985). All quotations are from this edition.

45. See also the Demonio's magnificent soliloquy (lines 1295–1418) describing his overreaching.

46. As Antonio Regalado affirms, in *Calderón: los orígenes de la modernidad en la España del Siglo de Oro*, 2 vols. (Madrid: Destino, 1995), the devil figure who tempts Cipriano also assumes a cosmic role: "El papel del demonio en el teatro de Calderón se ajusta al proceso de desorden inscrito en el universo . . . El demonio actualiza por medio de las relaciones que lo constituyen como personaje . . . la entropía del mundo creado" (1:876).

47. Garcilaso de la Vega, *Obra poética y textos en prosa*, ed. Bienvenido Morros (Barcelona: Crítica, 1995), 27. Morros traces the Phaeton theme, a theme also central to the final third of the *Primero sueño*.

48. Herrera praises Garcilaso's line ("Verso de grande i generoso espíritu i sonido") and blames the figure ("es demasiadamente común a los italianos, que no cansan en el contino trato i repetición d'ellos"). Fernando de Herrera, *Anotaciones a la poesía de Garcilaso*, ed. Inoria Pepe and José María Reyes (Madrid: Cátedra, 2001), 355–356.

49. Herrera, 360.

50. Herrera, 359.

51. Covarrubias's third definition for *fiar* is: "tener opinión de que no le han de engañar, como: Yo me fió de mi amigo."

52. The phrase is Garcilaso's from the *Égloga segunda* (lines 1539–1540), while Herrera's digressive commentary (899–905) aims to remedy a situation in which Italian cinquecento poetry embraces epic, despite lacking any recent martial exploits to imitate, whereas Spanish poetry eschews epic though potentially having ample martial deeds to represent.

53. *Autoridades* glosses *desvanecimiento* as "vanidad, presunción, altaneria, soberbia."

54. Robert Jammes, *La obra poética de Don Luis de Góngora y Argote*, tr. Manuel Moya (Madrid: Castalia, 1987); John Beverley, *Aspects of Góngora's "Soledades"* (Amsterdam: John Benjamins, 1980). See also the "Introducción" to Beverley's edition of the *Soledades*, 17–61; R. O. Jones's three articles "The Poetic Unity of the *Soledades*," *BHS* 31 (1954): 189–204; "Neoplatonism and the *Soledades*," *BHS* 40 (1963): 1–16; "Góngora and Neoplatonism Again," *BHS* 43 (1966): 117–120.

55. For a rigorous appraisal of the origins of the Neo-Baroque, see Gregg Lambert, *The Return of the Baroque in Modern Culture* (London: Continuum, 2004); also Walter Moser, "Résurgences baroques," in *Diskurse des Barocks:*

Dezentrierte oder rezentrierte Welt, ed. Joachim Küpper and Friedrich Wolfzettel (Munich: Wilhelm Fink, 2000), 655–680.

56. Dámaso Alonso, "Claridad y belleza de las Soledades," in *Estudios y ensayos gongorinos* (Madrid: Gredos, 1960), 83. See also his exhaustive *Góngora y el "Polifemo,"* 3 vols., 5th ed. (Madrid: Gredos, 1967).

57. In particular, see Jammes' chapter "El Elogio de los grandes" (207–256) where he discusses Góngora's 1617 "Panegírico al duque de Lerma." Also relevant is his section "El ideal de las *Soledades*," 497–508.

58. Daniel Javitch, *Poetry and Courtliness in Renaissance England* (Princeton: Princeton University Press, 1978), 4. Javitch also comments on the courtier's need for a savvy audience in order to employ hyperbole successfully (89–90).

59. For a moving lament on the courtier's life, see Góngora's 1609 poem in *tercetos*, "A lo poco que hay que fiar de los favores de los príncipes cortesanos: por lo cual se sale de la corte."

60. Francisco de Quevedo, *Poesía original completa*, ed. José Manuel Blecua (Barcelona: Planeta, 1996), #233. All poems from Quevedo's *obra* cited in the main text will be from this edition and will follow Blecua's numbering and editorial choices.

61. Like the "tenebrosas aves," which "ya mis musas serán, ya mis serenas," the stars are synecdoches for poetry itself — both birds and stars break the "silencio" (lines 15, 68) that haunts Quevedo here.

62. Sor Juana Inés de la Cruz, *Obras completas de Sor Juana Inés de la Cruz*, vol. 1., ed. Alfonso Méndez Plancarte (Mexico City: Fondo de Cultura Económica, 1951), #103. All poems of Sor Juana cited in the main text, unless otherwise noted, are from Plancarte's edition and follow his numbering.

CHAPTER FIVE: GÓNGORA'S ART OF ABUNDANCE

1. Jammes, *La obra poética de Don Luis de Góngora y Argote*, 450.

2. Antonio Vilanova, *Las fuentes y los temas del Polifemo de Góngora*, 2 vols. (Madrid: CSIC, 1957).

3. Ignacio Navarrete, *Orphans of Petrarch: Poetry and Theory in the Spanish Renaissance* (Berkeley: University of California Press, 1994), 195.

4. See Andres Sánchez Robayna, "Petrarquismo y parodía (Góngora y Lope)," *Revista de filología de la Universidad de la Laguna* 1 (1982): 25–45, where the "hyper-norm" of decadence introduced by Góngora is discussed.

5. Navarrete, 191.

6. Luis de Góngora, *Fábula de Polifemo y Galatea*, 5th ed., ed. Alexander Parker (Madrid: Cátedra, 1993). All citations from the poem are from this edition.

7. Vilanova, 2:33, 2:43–46.

8. See Antonio Carreira, "Defecto y exceso en la interpretación de Góngora," *Gongoremas* (Barcelona: Península, 1998), 47–74. Carreira rightly places Vilanova in the same camp as Góngora's original, learned defenders whose Herculean exegetical labors mining diachronic sources produce "disforme" (50) excess that often tends to obviate the hermeneutic task.

9. Jammes, 458. But inexplicably, Jammes also casts Góngora as a proponent of "clasicismo" who tries "evitar cualquier exceso" (477–478).

10. See Ovid, *Metamorphosis*, 13.738–897. David West, in *Fábula de Polifemo y Galatea*, ed. Alexander Parker, 5th ed. (Madrid: Cátedra, 1993), offers a brief, but incisive essay on Góngora's debt to Ovid, "La fuente ovidiana," 157–163.

11. See Edward C. Riley, "Aspectos del concepto de *admiratio* en la teoria literaria del Siglo de Oro," in *Homenaje ofrecido a Dámaso Alonso*, *Studia philologica* 3 (1963): 173–183.

12. Again Vilanova finds sources for Góngora's hyperboles: "Pese a las innumerables alusiones ovidianas de este tipo, en la poesía renancentista, esta ponderaciones hiperbólicas de tipo geográfico, en que se mencionan las más lejanas o encontradas partes del mundo, proceden fundamentalmente de Ariosto, aunque se encuentren ya en el Dante. Así en el *Orlando furioso*: 'Dall'iperboree nievi ai lidi rubri, / Dall'Indo ai monti ch'al tuo mar via danno.' (XII, 63)." For the central place of cartography in the early modern literary imagination, see Tom Conley, *The Self-Made Map: Cartographic Writing in Early Modern France* (Minneapolis: University of Minnesota Press, 1996).

13. See Jammes (463) on the agricultural "abundancia" in the poem.

14. Vilanova notes: "La desmesurada hipérbole con la cual Góngora pondera el inmenso peso del cíclope y su fuerza desmesurada, capaz de doblegar el pino que le servía de bastón, procede de un símil de la segunda parte de *La Araucana* de Ercilla describiendo el bastón del gigante Talcaguano" (1:465). The *cultismo* "eminente" means "alto" or "elevado," adds Vilanova, though it had not yet acquired any moral valuation.

15. Cited in Vilanova, 1:462.

16. *A Greek-English Lexicon* (Oxford: Clarendon Press, 1996), 1861.

17. While the *silva* has long been read as a prosodic form that encourages hyperbaton, this does not fully explain why Spanish poets cultivated hyperbaton far more than their French, German, or English counterparts who more fre-

quently choose parataxis and other figures of repetition to accompany hyperbolic conceits.

18. Vilanova (1:470) cites Virgil's description of Atlas (*Aen.* 4.246–251) as a possible source for Góngora's "pino." He also views Camões's Adamastor and a "monstruosa hipérbole" of Aldana's from *Todas las obras* (1593) as informing the octave.

19. In his edition of the *El Polifemo de Don Luis de Góngora* (Madrid, 1636), José García de Salcedo Coronel offers a possible etymology for "Pirineo" by linking the mountains to a myth about Hercules and "una donzella" named Pirene (327v).

20. See also octave 49 where Polifemo exclaims: "Sorda hija del mar, cuyas orejas / a mis gemidos son rocas al viento . . ."

21. Alonso, *Góngora y el "Polifemo,"* 3:241. For the emblematic importance of the peacock image, see Jean Rousset's *La littérature de l'âge baroque en France: Circe et Paon* (Paris: José Corti, 1954).

22. Pedro de Valencia, "Carta escrita a don Luis de Góngora en censura de sus poesías," in *La batalla en torno a Góngora*, ed. Ana Martínez Arancón (Barcelona: Antonio Bosch, 1978), 7.

23. Paul Celan, *Paul Celan: Selections*, tr. Pierre Joris (Berkeley: University of California Press, 2005), 165–166.

24. Cave, 325–330.

25. Cave, ix.

26. As Jammes comments: "En el plano ético, el autor insiste sobre el valor moral (entendido en un sentido amplio) de la vida en el campo por oposición a la vida en la cuidad, y más particularmente a la de la Corte" (497).

27. Beverley, *Aspects of Góngora's "Soledades,"* 23. For an insightful analysis of Góngora's lyric subjectivity, see Mary M. Gaylord, "Góngóra and the Footprints of the Voice," *MLN* 108 (1993): 230–253.

28. See Joaquín Roses Lozano, *Góngora:* Soledades *habitadas* (Malaga: Publicaciones de la Universidad de Málaga, 2007), 23.

29. All quotations from these texts are from *La batalla en torno a Góngora*, with the exception of Cascales's epistles 8–10, which appear in *Cartas filológicas* (Madrid: Espasa-Calpe, 1930) and Lope's two letters which appear in Emilio Orozco Díaz, *Lope y Góngora frente a frente* (Madrid: Gredos, 1973). For more recent reevaluations of the controversy see Joaquín Roses Lozano, *Una poética de la oscuridad: la recepción crítica de las* Soledades *en el Siglo XVII* (Madrid: Tamesis, 1994); Antonio Carreira, "La controversia en torno a las *Soledades*. Un parecer desconocido, y edición crítica de las primeras cartas," *Gongoremas*, 239–266;

Christopher Johnson, "*De Doctrina Gongorina*: Góngora's Defence of Obscurity," *Bulletin of Hispanic Studies* 77.1 (2000): 21–46.

30. Córdoba, 13.

31. Córdoba, 24.

32. Cascales, *Cartas filológicas*, 178–181.

33. Cascales, 182, 188, 214, 219. Covarrubias defines a *cosa peregrina* as a "cosa rara."

34. *Lope y Góngora frente a frente*, 175.

35. José Pellicer de Salas y Tovar, *Lecciones solemnes a las obras de Don Luis de Góngora y Argote* (Hildesheim and New York: Georg Olms, 1971). Almansa y Mendoza pens the fawning "Advertencias para la inteligencia de las *Soledades* de don Luis de Góngora" as the poems were still making the rounds at court.

36. José García de Salcedo Coronel, "Al Lector," *Soledades de D. Luis de Góngora* (Madrid, 1636), 1r.

37. Salcedo Coronel, "Al Lector," 4r–v.

38. Helmut Hatzfeld, *Estudios sobre el Barroco*, 3rd ed. (Madrid: Gredos, 1972), 342–348.

39. "Claridad y belleza de las *Soledades*," 83.

40. Juan Huarte de San Juan, *Examen de ingenios para las ciencias*, ed. Guillermo Serés (Madrid: Cátedra, 1989), 344–345. On the theme of solitude see Karl Vossler, *La soledad en la poesía lírica española* (Madrid: Revista de Occidente, 1941).

41. Huarte de San Juan, 345.

42. See Jammes, 506.

43. All Portugese citations from *Os Lusíades* are from the edition by Frank Pierce (Oxford: Clarendon Press, 1981). Richard Burton, who translates the *Lusiads*, writes also a wonderfully Borgesian commentary on the poem. On this passage, he observes: "The 'Old Man of Belem' is the people personified; and the episode and philippic containing the popular croaking is from Osorio. It is the 'Speech of Old Age' (*Pharsalia*, ii. 68–233) and the *Illi robur*, etc., of Horace (*Odes*, i. 3); but it is Lucan made cosmopolitan, and Horace set in personality, in movement; therefore, grander and more striking." See Richard T. Burton, *Camoens: His Life and His Lusiads. A Commentary*, 2 vols. (London: Bernard Quaritch, 1881).

44. David Quint reads the Adamastor episode as possessing "remarkable self-consciousness" and as ultimately pushing the epic toward romance. See *Epic and Empire: Politics and Generic Form from Virgil to Milton* (Princeton: Princeton University Press, 1993), 113–125.

45. Camões sailed for India in 1553 and then spent seventeen years in Goa, though he had a post in Macau for a time as well.

46. See also stanza 23 where similiar sentiments are expressed.

47. In addition to Jammes and Beverley, see Kenneth Krabbenhoft, "Góngora's Stoic Pilgrim," *BHS* 73 (1996): 1–12. By focusing on the *topoi* and content of the poem, more than its formal characteristics, Krabbenhoft argues that it deserves to be read in the context of Augustine's debt to Stoic philosophy and his battle against concupiscence.

48. A parallel treatment of the navigation theme is the soliloquy of the *peregrino* in lines 116–170 of the "Soledad segunda," a section of which I considered in chapter four.

49. Alonso seems unsure how to appreciate Góngora's hyperbolic rhetoric in the navigation-*exkursus*: "Góngora tal vez no se interesaba por el fondo de la cuestión, sino se dejaba llevar por un ejercicio retórico con evidentes modelos clásicos." See "Góngora y América," *Estudios y ensayos gongorinos* (Madrid: Gredos, 1960), 390.

50. See Góngora's "Égloga piscatoria" (1615) where the American empire is described as a corpse bleeding from violence and greed (which includes "interés ligurino").

51. Beverley, *Soledades*, 91n. In his discussion of the *exkursus*, Jammes (118) underscores "la influencia de Camões sobre Góngora." But he also would distinguish Camões's broad condemnation of "cobiça" or thirst for glory and fame from Góngora's narrower attack on the "codicia" for precious metals. Pellicer (429–480) cites Camões together with a bevy of other intertexts as possible sources for Góngora's invention. But the most complex reaction to Góngora's intertextuality is surely Salcedo Coronel's. By way of comment he first offers a sonnet of his own which links the gigantomachy with navigation. Then he cites the Bible (e.g., Ecclesiastes 43:23, Wisdom 14) to support this polemic, only to conclude by execrating scholarly gluttony: "No he querido valerme de los lugares comunes de Horat. Od. 3. lib. 1. ni de Seneca en Medea, ni de Propertio elegia 17. del libro 1. ni de otros muchos que se ha valido alguno. La lecion de muchos libros, ò noticia dellos, si falta la juizio, no sirve de otra cosa, que de manifestar la ignorancia del que los lee; que el acumular lugares sin proposito, es lo mismo que llenar desordenadamente el estomago de multitud de manjares . . ." (79r).

52. William S. Anderson, "Horace *Carm*. 1.14: What Kind of Ship?" *Classical Philology* 61 (1966): 84–98.

53. Hans Blumenberg, *Shipwreck with Spectator: Paradigm of a Metaphor for Existence*, tr. Stephen Rendall (Cambridge: The MIT Press, 1997), 12.

54. Stephen Greenblatt, *Marvelous Possessions* (Chicago: University of Chicago Press, 1991), 76.

55. Greenblatt, 54.

56. Cristóbal Colón, *Diario de a bordo*, ed. Luis Arranz Márquez (Madrid: Dastin, 2000), 287; *pezón* can also mean "nipple." See also the *primer viaje* where Columbus constantly tries out new analogies to express his wonder at the novelties he encounters even as he worries about being blamed for exaggerating the marvels his describes.

57. Pellicer, 429, 447. Similarly, Salcedo Coronel cites the *Aeneid* 2.780 ("et vastum maris aequor arandum") as a possible source for the metaphor "surcó."

58. Jacques Derrida, "La mythologie blanche: la métaphore dans le texte philosophique," *Marges de la philosophie* (Paris: Les éditions de minuit, 1972), 323.

59. Luis de Góngora y Argote, *Carta en respuesta*, in *Antología poética*, ed. Antonio Carreira (Madrid: Castalia, 1986), 341–344.

60. *De doctrina Gongorina*, 33–41. See also Beverley's *Aspects of Góngora's "Soledades"* (11–25) for further analysis of the "Carta en respuesta."

61. Here "leño" is at once a ship, but, as Pellicer comments, also the wooden horse at Troy. See also line 397 where Góngora seems to mean only ship by "leña"; "Frigio" is native of Frigia (ancient Asia).

62. Pellicer, 432–443.

63. Salcedo Coronel, 93. He cites various cosmographers, Homer, and Virgil as authorities, but then comments: "Este engaño de los antiguos siguió el moderno expositor destas Soledades, afirmando por verdad lo que D. Luis dixo por encarecimiento" (93r–94r).

64. Pellicer, 450–460. But Salcedo Coronel, after praising Columbus's "generosa ambicion, y magnanima osadia" (95r) blames Góngora: ". . . no dexaré de culpar a don Luis, pues atribuye a la codicia, y no a una ambicion prudente la dilacion de la Monarquia Española" (97r).

65. Pellicer, 458–459. His description of Grotius' *Mare liberum* (1609) is particularly hostile.

66. See Pellicer, 464.

67. José Lezama Lima, "Sierpe de Don Luis de Góngora," *Obras completas* (Mexico City: Aguilar, 1977), 2:207.

68. Pellicer, 465.

69. These lines occur in a *coro*, a shorter form that recalls Petrarch's sonnets.

70. In his commentary on these lines, Pellicer calls *Os Lusiades* "aquella grande obra en nada, mas de en el tiempo, inferior a la Eneyda" (471).

71. Regarding this extravagant metaphor, Salcedo Coronel observes: "En to-das estas Soledades no ay alusion mas dura a mi parecer" (114r).

72. Jáuregui (173) condemns the "buitres" — metaphor as misconceived but calls the earlier venerable metaphor of vultures as living tombs (line 440) a ". . . notable pensamiento e hipérbole."

73. Juan de Jáuregui, "Antidoto contra la pestilente poesía de las *Soledadas*," *La Batalla en torno a Góngora*, 155–190. Section numbers in the main text corre-spond to this edition.

74. Jáuregui, 9–10, 16.

75. Jáuregui, 17.

76. Jáuregui, 17.

77. Jáuregui, 17.

78. This is from Quintilian's discussion of the judicious use of figures (9.3.2–5). The remainder of the sentence, not quoted by Jáuregui, is: ". . . et se non obvias fuisse dicenti sed conquisitas et ex omnibus latebris extractas conges-tasque declarant."

79. Jáuregui, 32.

80. Jáuregui, 32.

81. It was first published in 1684.

82. Jáuregui, 34.

83. Jáuregui, 36.

84. Jáuregui, 35.

85. Jáuregui, 33.

86. Jáuregui, 42.

CHAPTER SIX: QUEVEDO'S POETICS OF DISILLUSION

1. Claudio Guillén, "Quevedo y los géneros literarios," in *Quevedo in Per-spective*, ed. James Iffland (Newark, DE: Juan de a Cuesta, 1982), 12. Para-phrasing Quevedo, Guillén analyses the "inmensa escritura" that comprises the Quevedian *obra*. While Guillén finds epic poetry wanting, Quevedo does pen a mock epic poem, "Poema heroico de las necedades y locuras de Orlando el en-amorado," which is filled with parodic hyperbole that depends for its success on the reader's knowledge of the epic tradition.

2. See Pablo Jauralde Pou's biography, *Francisco de Quevedo (1580–1645)* (Madrid: Castalia, 1999); the Introduction to *Selected Poetry of Francisco de Quevedo*, tr. and ed. Christopher Johnson (Chicago: University of Chicago Press, 2009).

3. *Aguja de navegar cultos con la receta de hacer* Soledades *en un día*, in *La batalla en torno a Góngora*, 75–76. Another ludic attack on the *culto* style is *La culta latiniparla* (1629).

4. Antonio Vilanova, "Preceptistas españoles de los siglos XVI y XVII," in *Historia general de las literaturas hispánicas*, ed. Guillermo Díaz-Plaja (Barcelona: Barna, 1953), 3:567–692; Alexander A. Parker, "La 'agudeza' in algunos sonetos de Quevedo: Contribución al estudio del Conceptismo," in *Francisco de Quevedo*, ed. Gonzalo Sobejano (Madrid: Taurus, 1978), 44–57; Mercedes Blanco, *Les rhétoriques de la pointe. Baltasar Gracián et le conceptisme en Europe* (Geneva: Éditions Slatkine, 1992), 1–19.

5. Francisco de Quevedo, *Preliminares literarios a las poesías de Fray Luis de León*, ed. Antonio Azaustre Galiana, in *Obras completas en prosa*, gen. ed. Alfonso Rey (Madrid: Castalia, 2003), 1.1:128, 144–145.

6. He approvingly cites Quintilian's praise (8.3) of Virgil's use of ornament, but he also invokes Statius, Propertius, and Martial as authorities in his condemnation of the *cultistas*.

7. Francisco de Quevedo, *Obras completas I, Obras en prosa*, ed. Luis Astraña Marin (Madrid: Aguilar, 1961), 1337. In *España defendida* (1609), Quevedo attacks Joseph Scaliger for his Protestantism ("mala fe") and for calling Quintilian, Lucan, and Seneca "Pingues isti cordubenses."

8. While Smith rightly points out the contradictions of using "silver" Latin tradition to defend the ideals of clarity and poetic decorum, he concludes rather hastily that since Quevedo disliked Scaliger, and Scaliger attacks Lucan, this is why Quevedo defends the "hyperbolic Lucan" (27). Quevedo cites Lucan approvingly three times in the *Sueños*, as well as praising him in the *Virtud Militante* and *Providencia de Dios*. For more on Quevedo's thoughts regarding Scaliger, see Jauralde Pou, *Francisco de Quevedo (1580–1645)*, 209–211.

9. J. L. Borges, *Inquisiciones* (Buenos Aires: Proa, 1925), 40.

10. "La metáfora es la figura que permite decir lo impossible, lo anómalo, es una forma de transgressión de las restricciones semánticas del sistema." Lía Schwartz Lerner, *Metáfora y sátira en la obra de Quevedo* (Madrid: Taurus, 1984), 187.

11. For invaluable analysis of the semantic, cultural, and conceptual aspects of Quevedian satiric verse, as well as commentary on this and other satiric sonnets, see Ignacio Arellano Ayuso, *Poesía satírico burlesca de Quevedo: Estudio y anotación filológica de los sonetos*, 2nd ed. (Madrid: Iberoamericana, 2003). See also James Iffland, *Quevedo and the Grotesque* (London: Tamesis, 1978). Iffland calls Quevedo "one of the most important figures in the history of the grotesque in literature" (14). He argues that the "grotesque image and situation" in Quevedo's

prose and poetry "generally involve a clash between the comic and something which is incompatible with the comic" (61). More locally, see Maurice Molho, "Una cosmogonía antisemita: 'Érase un hombre a un nariz pegado,'" *Quevedo in Perspective*, 57–80.

12. See Dámaso Alonso, "La angustia de Quevedo," in *Francisco de Quevedo*, 17–22.

13. Mikhail Bakhtin, *Rabelais and His World*, tr. Helene Iswolsky (Cambridge: The MIT Press, 1968), 19.

14. Essential for an understanding of Quevedo's perception of himself at court is his *comedia*, *Como ha de ser el Privado* (1629). See also #572, which contain the lines: "Ya dije a los palacios: 'Adiós, choza'. | Cualquiera pretensión tengo por maza . . ." For the best recent account of Quevedo as courtier, see Jauralde Pou, *Francisco de Quevedo (1580–1645)*, esp. 65–88, 174–175, 385–390, 459–463, 625–630, 821–827.

15. George Mariscal, *Contradictory Subjects: Quevedo, Cervantes, and Seventeenth-Century Spanish Culture* (Ithaca: Cornell University Press, 1991), 100.

16. See J. H. Elliott, "Quevedo and the Count-Duke of Olivares," in *Spain and its World*, 1500–1700 (New Haven: Yale University Press, 1989), 189–212. Tracing the intersections of literature and politics, Elliott argues that Quevedo and his Neo-Stoicism effected the Count-Duke's policies and decisions almost as much as the latter influenced the poet's circumstances and subjects.

17. J. L. Borges, "Quevedo," in *Francisco de Quevedo*, 23–28. Ever the transgressor of space and time, Borges argues: "En cuanto a la *sangrienta Luna*, mejor es ignorar que se trata del símbolo de los turcos, eclipsado por no sé que piraterías de don Pedro Téllez Girón" (27). For my part, following Gracián, I regard such factual information as increasing the complexity and thus the *agudeza* of the conceit.

18. Henry Ettinghausen, *Francisco de Quevedo and the Neostoic Movement* (Oxford: Oxford University Press, 1972), 15. Quevedo's correspondence with Lipsius is collected in *Epistolario de Justo Lipsio y los Españoles* (Madrid: Castalia, 1966). In letters 92–97, Lipsius good-naturedly chides Quevedo for his excessive praise ("sed cum nimia laudes mea"); they also discuss the progress of Quevedo's efforts to propagate Neo-Stoicism in Spain.

19. In terms of his *imitatio*, "Miré los muros de la patria mía" [#29] is heavily indebted to Seneca's *Epistulae Morales*, 1.12 ("Quocumque me verti, argumenta senectutis meae video," "Debeo hoc suburbano meo, quod mihi senectus mea, quocumque adverteram, apparuit"). It also, as Blecua notes, recalls Ovid, *Tristia*, 1.11.23: "Quocumque adspicio, nihil est, nisi mortis imago." As for "Cerrar podrá mis ojos la postrera" [#472], Borges in *Otras inquisiciones* (Buenos

Aires: Emece, 1964) detects the influence of Propertius, *Elegiae*, 1.19 ("Ut meus oblito pulvis amore jacet") on the last verse (61). As for the difficulty he had achieving the Stoic ideal, Jauralde Pou, in *Francisco de Quevedo (1580–1645)*, quotes from one of Quevedo's letters: "Yo no tengo suficienza de estoico, mas tengo afición a los estoicos. Ha me asistido su doctrina por guía en las dudas, por consuelo en las trabajos, por defensa en las persecuciones, que tanta parte han poseído de mi vida. Yo he tenido su dotrina por estudio continuo; no sé si ella ha tenido en mí buen estudiante" (287–288).

20. Cited in *La batalla en torno a Góngora*, 76.

21. Despite its limited focus, Elaine Hoover's *John Donne and Francisco de Quevedo: Poets of Love and Death* (Chapel Hill: University of North Carolina Press, 1978) sketches several lines of comparison.

22. Navarrete, 205–240. González de Salas's several *dissertaciones* on Quevedo's amorous verse place it in the context of Petrarchism.

23. J. L. Borges, *A Universal History of Infamy* (Prologue to 1954 edition), tr. Norman Thomas di Giovanni (London: Penguin Books, 1973), 11.

24. For example, de Salas entitles #294, "Ausente, se halla en pena más rigurosa que Tántalo"; #299, "Exageraciones de su fuego, de su llanto, de sus suspiros y de sus penas"; #312, "Encareciendo las adversidades de los Troyanos, exagera más la hermosura de Aminta"; #384, "Advierte la brevedad de la hermosura con exhortación deliciosa"; #485, "Persevera en la exageración de su afecto amoroso y en el exceso de su padecer."

25. In "Prevenciones al Letor," González de Salas comments: "La abundancia pues de el pensar, y enriquecer de conceptos sus Poesias, alcançó tan felizmente, que a mi entender no existe Escritor antiguo, ni moderno, que en ella le compita" (a4v). Although he later allows that Ovid might be considered Quevedo's equal.

26. See Mercedes Blanco's acute reading of this poem and its anagrams, i.e. *Etna = amante*, in *Introducción al comentario de la poesía amorosa de Quevedo* (Madrid: Arcos, 1998). These lines also resemble Segismundo's self-characterization: "En llegando a esta pasión, / un volcán, un Etna hecho, / quisiera sacar del pecho / pedazos del corazón" (163–166).

27. As Jauralde Pou notes (299–395), Quevedo was in Sicily (in the shadow of Etna) from 1613–1616, and he was in Naples (in the shadow of Vesuvius) from 1616–1618.

28. For a recent, comprehensive study of the history of the European sonnet and Quevedo's place in it, see Friedhlem Kemp, *Das europäische Sonett* (Munich: Wallstein, 2002), esp. 1:381–397.

29. See Roland Greene, *Post-Petrarchism: Origins and Innovations of the Western Lyric Sequence* (Princeton: Princeton University Press, 1991).

30. The hyperboles of #503 are literally "airado": "Mas en los Alpes de tu pecho airado, / no miro que tus ojos a los míos / regalen, siendo fuego, el yelo amado."

31. "Quevedo asume el exorbitante concepto de loco amor eterno y con pocos versos, medidos y desmedidos a la vez, en un relámpago de audacia, va más lejos que todos y que nadie. *Plus ultra*: Quevedo es el que va más lejos, hipérbole de una literatura" (Guillén, 16).

32. Oeta is a mountain in southern Thessaly where Hercules burnt himself to death.

33. Paul de Man, "The Rhetoric of Temporality," *Blindness and Insight*, 2nd ed. rev. (Minneapolis: University of Minnesota, 1983), 213.

34. Line 9 suddenly introduces the first person with the verb "lloro." See Maurice Mohlo's "Sobre un soneto de Quevedo: 'En crespa tempestad del oro undoso,'" in *Francisco de Quevedo*, 343–377. Likewise, #142 shows how exaggerated the speaker's pose can be: "Reina en ti propio, tú que reinar quieres, / pues provincia mayor que el mundo eres" (95–96).

35. Francisco de Quevedo, *Sueños y discursos*, ed. Felipe C. R. Maldonado (Madrid: Castalia, 1972), 97.

36. Again *codicia* calls for hyperbole: ". . . otros se pierden por la codicia, haciendo *amazonas* sus villas y ciudades a fuerza de grandes pechos, que en vez de criar, desustancian . . ." (*El alguacil endemoniado*, 97).

37. Covarrubias, *Tesoro de la lengua castellana o española*, 545.

38. Quevedo, *El mundo por de dentro*, 165.

39. Quevedo, *El mundo por de dentro*, 165.

40. "En el sistema de la sátira quevedesca, lo infernal es siempre el *non plus ultra* del horror, físico o moral y espiritual. Todo lo hiperbólicamente desagradable y condenable es demoníaco." Schwartz Lerner, *Metáfora y sátira en la obra de Quevedo*, 174.

41. "No puede ser casual que precisamente *este* tipo de comparación abunde tanto en Quevedo: el *más . . . que* de carácter aritmético se convierte así en signo de jactanciosa exageración numeral, pero también de esa grandiosidad sobrenatural e ilusionista tan perseguida por el Barroco." Leo Spitzer, "Sobre el arte de Quevedo en el *Buscón*," in *Francisco de Quevedo*, ed. Sobejano, 130. See also Ignacio Arellano Ayuso, *Poesía satírica burlesca de Quevedo*, on the use of the expression "más que" to achieve burlesque effects (285–286).

42. Cited in Spitzer, "Sobre el arte de Quevedo en el *Buscón*," 139.

43. See Alfonso Rey, *Quevedo y la poesía moral española* (Madrid: Castalia, 1995). Rey devotes a few pages to Quevedo's use of hyperbole in the moral poetry, which he reads as satirizing human actions, although sometimes as being employed "describir realidades independientes de la voluntad humana" such as the idea of time or the description of the natural world (164). However, in regard to Quevedo's *Polimnia* at least, hyperbole "tiene un papel secundario," as it fuels not so much his own invention but helps develop the "exageraciones que ya estaban en su modelo [the poetry of Martial and Propertius]" (165). See also his sections on "El tópico del navegante" (212–213) and "la codicia" (69–76).

44. Herrera, 273.

45. See his "dissertacion compendiosa" which prefaces the poem.

46. Likewise, in "¿Donde vas, ignorante navecilla?" [#138], Quevedo wittily imitates Horace's *Ode* 1.14 to amplify the idea that sailing is unnatural as he synecdochically warns the wood of a ship not to forsake its natural locus. Referring to Horace's *Ode* 1.14, Rey comments: "Tal composición, bien conocida en la época, fue objeto de divergentes traducciones por parte de fray Luis de León, el Brocense, Juan de Almeida y Alonso de Espinosa, pero no parece haber surgido ninguna creación tan singular como la de Quevedo, basada en la personificación del barco y en la sostenida contraposición entre su pasado como árbol y su presente en el mar" (213).

47. For more on the poem's many intertextual debts to Horace and other classical writers, see Alfonso Rey, "Tradición y originalidad en el *Sermón estoico*," *Edad de Oro* 6 (1987): 235–251.

48. Greenblatt, *Marvelous Possessions*, 64.

49. See also "Juntas grande tesoro, / y en Potosí y en Lima . . ." [#145.124–138].

50. A *mina* is a Greek coin but also a "mine."

51. Other moral poems infused with similar hyperbolic rhetoric include the superb poems on time [#139–341]; "Al inventor de la pieza de artillería" [#144]; "Juicio moral de los cometas" [#148], where Quevedo, intriguingly, refuses to confuse the sub- and superlunary.

52. Pico della Mirandola, "Oration on the Dignity of Man," tr. Elizabeth Forbes, in *The Renaissance Philosophy of Man*, ed. Ernst Cassirer, P. O. Kristeller, and J. H. Randall, Jr. (Chicago: University of Chicago Press, 1948), 228.

53. *Agudeza*, 1:51.

54. "Ponto" is a *cultísmo* for the sea; "robre" is a variant for "roble."

55. Calderón might call such unnatural, hyperbolic motion an "aborto." See *El mágico prodigioso* (lines 1203–1213) where the verb *abortar* signals a departure from the harmonious vision of the universe as a "fábrica gallarda."

56. *Obras completas I, Obras en prosa*, 357. On the ambiguities in and surrounding the production of this text, see Pablo Jauralde, "Aventura intelectual de Quevedo, *España defendida*," in *Quevedo a nueva luz: escritura y política*, ed. Lía Schwartz and Antonio de Carreira (Málaga: Universidad de Málaga, 1997), 45–58.

57. Confessor to Ferdinand and Isabella, Ximénez was a Franciscan, cardinal, and the Primate of Spain. As a Franciscan he wore the humble *cordón*, which *Autoridades* (1729) glosses as "la cuerda con que se ciñen los Religiosos de San Francisco, que regularmente es de esparto, pita, u otra cosa tosca y áspera." Compare this with the "cuerda," which at the end of "El mundo por de dentro" transforms, with "tales tropelías," appearances into realities.

58. Hernán Cortés, *Cartas de relación* (Madrid: Historia, 1985), 131.

CHAPTER SEVEN: EXORBITANT DESIRES

1. Sor Juana's first editor and biographer, Diego Calleja refers to the poem, which Sor Juana calls simply "El sueño," as *Primero sueño, que así intituló y compuso la Madre Juana Inés de la Cruz, imitando a Góngora*. But this only begs the question of the Mexican poet's debts to the author of the *Soledad primera*. See Calleja's hagiographic *Aprobación*, which he attaches to Sor Juana's *Fama y Obras Póstumas* (1700). For an invaluable interpretation of the Gongorist legacy in the New World, see Emilio Carilla, "Trayectoria del Gongorismo en Hispanoamerica," *Atenea* 142 (1961): 110–121.

2. José Pascual Buxó, *Sor Juana Inés de la Cruz: lectura barroca de la poesía* (Seville: Junta de Andalucía; Consejería de Cultura, 2006).

3. Sor Juana Inés de la Cruz, *Die Welt im Traum: Eine Dichtung der "zehnten Muse von Mexiko,"* ed. Karl Vossler (Berlin: Ulrich Riemerschmidt Verlag, 1941), 24.

4. Octavio Paz, *Sor Juana Inés de la Cruz o las trampas de la fe* (Barcelona: Editorial Seix Barral, 1992), 474; *Sor Juana or, The Traps of Faith*, tr. Margaret Sayers Peden (Cambridge: Harvard University Press, 1988), 371. Another fine literary biography is: Dario Puccini, *Una mujer en soledad: Sor Juana Inés de la Cruz, una excepción en la cultura y la literatura* (Madrid: Anaya & Mario Muchnik, 1996).

5. *Primero sueño*, line 818. All citations from the poem are from Sor Juana Inés de la Cruz, *Poesía Lírica*, ed. José Carlos González Boixo (Madrid: Cátedra, 1992). For a reading of the poem's hermetic elements, see Robert Ricard, *Une*

poétesse mexicaine du XVII siècle: Sor Juana Inés de la Cruz (Paris: Centre de Documentation Universitaire, 1953).

6. Sor Juana Inés de la Cruz, "Respuesta a sor Filotea," *Obras completas de Sor Juana Inés de la Cruz*, in *Comedias, sainetes y prosa*, ed. Alberto G. Salceda (Mexico City: Fondo de Cultura Económica, 1957), 4:470–471.

7. Lisa Rabin, "The Blason of Sor Juana Inés de la Cruz: Politics and Petrarchism in Colonial Mexico," *Bulletin of Hispanic Studies* 72.1 (1995): 28–39.

8. Braden, *Petrarchan Love and the Continental Renaissance* (New Haven: Yale University Press, 1999), 130. Braden notes that in one of Sor Juana's plays, Columbus exclaims: "¡Plus ultra! ¡Más mundos hay, / y ya venimos de verlos."

9. The frontispiece to González de Salas's 1652 edition of Quevedo's poetry, *El Parnasso Español*, likewise has Quevedo beneath the backdrop of the twin peaks of Parnassus.

10. "Sor Juana suele añadir referencias personales, creando un tono de familiaridad que sirve de contrapunto a los desmesurados elogios que prodiga a sus homenajeados." Introducción, *Poesía Lírica*, 54.

11. Paz, 233. For a more recent reading emphasizing how the text recasts the status of women in Baroque Mexico, see Virginia M. Bouvier, "La construcción de poder en *Neptuno alegórico* y *Ejercicios de la encarnación*," in *Aproximaciones a Sor Juana*, ed. Sandra Lorenzano (Mexico City: Fondo de cultura económica, 2005), 43–54.

12. Sor Juana Inés de la Cruz, *Inundación castálida* (Mexico City: UNAM, 1952), 366–367. (The *Neptuno* was published in the 1689 volume *Inundación castálida*.)

13. See, for example, the "Villancico de la ensaladilla" in *Inundación castálida*.

14. See *Obras completas*, ed. Méndez Plancarte, 2:17, 27, 41–42, 72–73, 98.

15. *Respuesta*, 4:447.

16. Ermilio Abreu Gómez attempts, in *Sor Juana Inés de la Cruz: bibliografía y biblioteca* (Mexico City: Monografías bibliográficas mexicanas, 1934), to reconstruct Sor Juana's library. He doubts that Sor Juana possessed the 4000 books that Calleja claims she sold in 1693 to provide assistance to the poor. Of the 173 books he lists, Latin and Greek authors make up half of this number. Elías Trabulse argues that she would have had access to all of Kircher's books published after 1641. See his "El tránsito del hermetismo a la ciencia moderna: Alejandro Fabián, Sor Juana Inés de la Cruz y Carlos de Sigüenza y Góngora (1667–1690)," *Caliope* 4.1–2 (1998): 56–69. See also Marie-Cécile Bénassy-Berling, *Humanisme et religion chez Sor Juana Inés de la Cruz: La femme et la culture au xviie siècle* (Paris: Éditions hispaniques, 1982). Bénassy-Berling notes that the "clas-

siques espagnols," above all Góngora and Calderón, had pride of place in her library, and that "Quevedo et Gracián lui sont également familiers" (117).

17. *Libra astronómica y filosófica*, ed. Bernabé Navarro (Mexico City: UNAM, 1959). Trabulse regards Sigüenza y Góngora as a proponent of the new methods of the materialistic philosophy (64–68). For two very different perspectives on Sigüenza y Góngora's life and work see Irving A. Leonard, *Don Carlos de Sigüenza y Góngora: A Mexican Savant of the Seventeenth Century* (Berkeley: University of California Press, 1929) and Kathleen Ross, *The Baroque Narrative of Carlos de Sigüenza y Góngora: A New World Paradise* (Cambridge: Cambridge University Press, 1993).

18. Paz, 335.

19. Bénassy-Berling, 23.

20. Kircher deduces, for example, that Confucius was a reincarnation of Thoth, the Egyptian god of writing. The Egyptians, he theorizes, inspired the construction of the Mexican pyramids and furnished the model for the Aztec priesthood.

21. See also Georgina Sabat de Rivers, *El "Sueño" de Sor Juana Inés de la Cruz: tradiciones literarias y originalidad* (London: Tamesis, 1977), 17.

22. I wonder if Sor Juana was also familiar with Kepler's dream narrative, *Somnium, seu de astronomia lunari* (1634).

23. *Respuesta*, 4:443, 444, 446, 447, 450, 459. For a valuable analysis of the letter's rhetoric, see Rosa Perelmuter, "La estructura retórica de la *Respuesta a Sor Filotea*," *Hispanic Review* 51.2 (1983): 147–158.

24. *Respuesta*, 4:452.

25. *Respuesta*, 4:454–455.

26. For other insights into the letter and its relation to the *Sueño*, see Electa Arenal, "Where Woman is the Creator of the Wor(l)d, or Sor Juana's Discourses on Method," in *Feminist Perspectives on Sor Juana Inés de la Cruz*, ed. Stephanie Merrim (Detroit: Wayne State University Press, 1991), 124–141; and in the same volume, Georgina Sabat de Rivers, "A Feminist Reading of Sor Juana's Dream," 142–161. For more recent work on Sor Juana and women in Baroque Mexico see the essays by Electa Arenal, Marie-Cécile Bénassy, Jennifer Cooley, and others in *Aproximaciones a Sor Juana*.

27. See Buxó (333–400) where the poets' debts to the humanist tradition are compared.

28. Gaston Bachelard, *Air and Dreams: An Essay on the Imagination of Movement*, tr. Edith R. and C. Fredrick Farrell (Dallas: Dallas Institute, 1988), 10. Jacqueline Nanfito cites this quote in "Sor Juana Inés de la Cruz's "El sueño": The Spatialization of Form in the Baroque Poetic Text," *Revista de estudios His-*

pánicos 23 (1989) 53–65; see also Nanfito's *El sueño: Cartographies of Knowledge and the Self* (New York: Peter Lang, 2000), which argues that the poem "reveals an essentially feminine space" that contains "shifting boundaries and alternative conceptual spaces" (1).

29. Bachelard, 5, 10–11.

30. Blumenberg, "Paradigmen zu einer Metaphorologie," *Archiv für Begriffs-geschichte* 6 (1960): 7–142; 9–11. See also his rethinking of this essay, "Prospect for a Theory of Nonconceptuality," in *Shipwreck with a Spectator: Paradigm of a Metaphor for Existence*, tr. Stephen Rendall (Cambridge: The MIT Press, 1997), 81–102.

31. Glossing *altivo*, *Autoridades* (1726) cites this sentence by Espinosa: "He venido de un extremo à otro, de áspera à amorosa, de desamorada à tibia, de sacudida à soberbia, y de *altiva* y desvanecida à rendida y sujeta."

32. See Patricia Parker, "Metaphor and Catachresis"; also Margo Glantz, "Dialectica de lo alto y de lo bajo: *El sueño*," in *Sor Juana Inés de la Cruz*, ed. Luis Sáinz de Medrano (Rome: Bulzoni, 1997), 47–66.

33. Jacques Derrida, "La mythologie blanche," *Marges de la philosophie* (Paris: Les Éditions de Minuit, 1972), 261.

34. Pedro Álvarez de Lugo Usodemar, *Ilustración al Sueño*, in *Para leer "Primero Sueño" de Sor Juana Inés de la Cruz*, ed. Andrés Sánchez Robayana (Mexico City: Fondo de Cultura Económica, 1991). The commentary reached only to line 233 before the author's demise. As for the belated historical position of Álvarez de Lugo (who was also a poet) vis-à-vis the flowering of the Baroque, Sánchez Robayana floridly comments: "Poeta del final de un tiempo, el tiempo hiperbólico de la sensibilidad barroca, Álvarez de Lugo se hallaba, como muchos de sus coetáneos, condenado a ser la débil, casi invisible estela última del fuego de artificio levantado por la gran poesía barroca" (20). Antonio Alatorre has edited an invaluable collection of texts constituting the reception history of Sor Juana's writing, including the *Ilustración* (slightly abridged) and Calleja's *Aprobación*: *Sor Juana a través de los siglos (1668–1910)*, 2 vols. (Mexico City: UNAM, 2007).

35. Álvarez de Lugo, 60.

36. Sabat de Rivers, 130. She largely follows Méndez Plancarte's divisions, though, her slight reorganization of these divisions, I agree, are "más organica." Compare this with Buxó's discussion of the poem's structure (102–107).

37. Sabat de Rivers, 142.

38. Antonio Alatorre, "Notas al *Primero Sueño* de Sor Juana," *NRFH* 43.2 (1995): 379–407.

39. "Pyramis est figura, quae in modum ignis ab amplo in acumen consur-git; ignis enim apud Graecos Pyr apellatur" (quoted by Álvarez de Lugo, Nota 1, 62). Since his commentary stops prematurely, he did not have the opportunity to appreciate how these symbolic pyramids later are transformed into an "ambi-ciosa llama ardiente" in line 405.

40. Álvarez de Lugo, Nota 2, 63–64. The references are to *Aen.* 8.728 and Statius' *Sylvae* 1.

41. I discuss this at length in "Clavius's Number and Its Early Modern Af-terlife," in *Arts of Calculation: Numerical Thought in Early Modern Europe*, ed. David Glimp and Michelle Warren (New York: Palgrave Macmillan, 2004), 67–92.

42. See Ruth Hill, *Sceptres and Sciences in the Spains: Four Humanists and the New Philosophy (ca. 1680–1740)* (Liverpool: Liverpool University Press, 2000). Hill makes Sor Juana a reader of Gassendi and thus also of Epicurus through the mediation of Sigüenza y Góngora's texts and personal influence (46–47). She reads the details and themes of the *Sueño* as an "imitation or fiction of the activity of the philosophers who inspired her practical ethics and her understanding of the cosmos and microcosmos, the Christian epicureans" (43).

43. Méndez Plancarte cites Statius' "To Sleep" (*Silvae*, 4.4) as a possible in-fluence on lines 80–150; if this is correct, then Sor Juana emulates the Roman's predilection for exaggeration and anaphora as well as his theme.

44. This echoes those fabulously gloomy lines from the *Polifemo*, octavo 2 ("infame turba de nocturnas aves, / gimiendo tristes y volando graves"), lines that Quevedo also reworks in "Himno a las estrellas": "Las tenebrosas aves, / que el silencio embarazan con gemido, / volando torpes y cantando graves . . ." Paul B. Dixon, in "Balances, Pyramids, Crowns, and the Geometry of Sor Juana Inés de la Cruz, *Hispania* 67 (1984): 560–566, observes: "The image of the eagle is concerned with *limits*, boundaries beyond which everything is excess . . ." (565).

45. Reading lines 220–221, Méndez Plancarte refers to Galen's theory of vi-tal spirits.

46. Vossler (112) notes that the "intelectuales claras . . . Estrellas" are "die himmlischen Intelligenzen oder Engel, durch die man sich die Bewegungen der Himmelsphären bzw. der Sterne geregelt dachte."

47. The same holds for her diction ("el modo posible," "del reino casi de Neptuno todo," "todas de las cosas," "todas las criaturas" and "siempre"). While noting that Sor Juana's notion of science often seems to correspond to "la expresión de conceptos escolásticos," Sabat de Rivers comments: ". . . hay que reconocer que el lenguaje gongorino es aquí, en efecto, científicamente analítico y exacto . . ." (136).

48. *Respuesta*, 4:460.

49. Explaining why all forms of knowledge are connected and mutually il-luminating, Sor Juana in the *Respuesta* turns to the commonplace of the *cadena*: ". . . quisiera yo persuadir a todos con mi experiencia a que no sólo no estorban [the study of diverse subjects], pero se ayudan dando luz y abriendo camino las unas para las otras, por variaciones y ocultos engarces — que para esta cadena universal les puso la sabiduría de su Autor — de manera que parece se corre-sponden y están unidas con admirable trabazón y concierto. Es la cadena que fin-gieron los antiguos que salía de la boca de Júpiter, de donde pendían todas las cosas eslabonadas unas con otras" (4:450).

50. Bénassy-Berling, 149. But see also Verónica Grossi, *Siglosos v(u)elos epis-temológicos en Sor Juana Inés de la Cruz* (Madrid: Iberoamericana, 2007). Grossi reads the "vuelo" in the *Sueño* as an allegory that bridges the poet's social-political circumstances and her thirst for knowledge. "El *Sueño* retrata el proceso de la creación poética como una actividad hiperbólicamente transgresiva, como una batalla titánica e invencible que amenaza el orden reinante . . ." (33).

51. And yet as Alatorre colorfully observes, in lines 301–306 the ultimate emphasis is on terrestrial not celestial things (392).

52. See *Discurso III*, where Gracian writes that "agudeza verbal" consists "más en la palabra; de tal modo que, si aquélla se quita, no queda alma, ni se pueden éstas traducir en otra lengua; de este género son los equívocos . . ." See also his discussion and examples in *Discurso XXXI*, "De la agudeza nominal," and *Discurso XXXII*, "De la agudeza por paranomasia, retruécano y jugar del vocablo." Curtius in *ELLMA* writes: "Since the composition of poetry was a part of rhetoric, and since etymology was among the fundamentals of grammar and rhetoric, it was and remains an obligatory 'ornament' of poetry" (497).

53. Frederick Ahl, *Metaformations: Soundplay and Wordplay in Ovid and Other Classical Poets* (Ithaca: Cornell University Press, 1985).

54. Alatorre (392) notes that such clouds are a *locus communis* originating in Homer. Méndez Plancarte sends us to the *Soledad primera* (*Ded.* 8): "bates los montes que, de nieve armados, / gigantes de cristal los teme el cielo . . ."

55. As Sabat de Rivers notes, the gerunds convey an uncompleted action "de un esfuerzo también repetido" (137). But the manner the present participle of *pretender* yields to the past participle, together with the way the physical is defeated by the abstract in the verses (". . . [the eagle] ha pretendido, / tejiendo de los áto-mos escalas, / que con su inmunidad rompan sus dos alas"), also produces a chill-ing effect.

56. Rosa Perelmuter demonstrates how hyperbaton is essential to the poem's *dianoia*. See *Noche intelectual, la oscuridad idiomática en el* Primero sueño (Mexico City: UNAM, 1982), 99–176.

57. See my comments on Aristotle in chapter one. Obviously, quantities such as meter, stanza length, etc., are also intrinsic to creating poetry's sensual, emotional effects.

58. The pun of "despeñada" and "peña" recalls Calderón's *La vida es sueño*, especially the opening scene. For line 359, Méndez Plancarte sends us to the *Soledad primera* (1048), where the sight "cojea el pensamiento . . ."

59. Vossler (115) cites Macrobius' *Conviviorum primi diei saturnaliorum* (5.3.16) as a possible source for Sor Juana's take on Homer.

60. Alatorre (393) cites the *Carta atenagórica*: "Aunque ya se vio que una [mu- jer] quitó la clava de las manos de Alcides, siendo uno de los tres imposibles que veneró la antigüedad."

61. Vossler, 22.

62. See Jean Céard, "De Babel à la Pentecôte: La transformation du mythe de la confusion des langues au XVIe siècle," *Bibliotheque d'Humanisme et Renais- sance* 42 (1980): 577–594.

63. This emblemizes the struggle for divine knowledge as the intersection of two cones, one superlunary and luminous, the other terrestrial and obscure, but both circumscribed by a hermetic circle. See Vossler, 113–114; Paz, 485–486.

64. See Sabat de Rivers, 13. Mabel Velasco argues that the poem's structure is indebted to the Aztec archetypal notion of the four cardinal directions; see "La cosmologia azteca en el Primero sueño de Sor Juana Inés de la Cruz, *Revista Ib- eramericana*, 50.127 (1984): 539–548.

65. Athanasius Kircher, *Oedipus aegyptiacus* (Rome, 1654), 1:422.

66. Consider also "dimidiaba" (152), a *cultismo* which Alatorre affirms is unique to Sor Juana. The verb *medir* can also mean to scan a verse — exactly what Sor Juana does when reading Homer. *Autoridades* (1734) notes that "me- dida" can "[m]etaphoricamente significa cordúra, prudencia y tolerancia."

67. See Ovid's version of the myth in *Metamorphoses* (8.195–235). The noun *alarde* is a "boast" or "brag"; here it puns on "ala."

68. Ludwig Pfandl's overly psychologized portrait of Sor Juana, *Sor Juana Inés de la Cruz. La décima musa de México: Su vida, su poesía, su psique* (Mexico City: UNAM, 1963), offers the first extended treatment of melancholy in the poem.

CHAPTER EIGHT: A DREAM DEFERRED

1. See Kurt Flasch, "Nikolaus von Kues: Die Idee der Koinzidenz," *Philosophie des Altertums und des Mittelalters*, ed. Josef Speck (Göttingen: Vanden-hoeck & Ruprecht, 2001), 214–254.

2. Elías Trabulse, *El círculo roto: Estudios históricos sobre la ciencia en México* (Mexico City: Fondo de Cultura Económica, 1982); "El universo científico de Sor Juana Inés de la Cruz," *Colonial Latin American Review* 4.2 (1995): 41–50; *El hermetismo y Sor Juana Inés de la Cruz: Orígenes e interpretación* (Mexico City: Litografía Regina de los Ángeles, 1980); Sabat de Rivers, "Sor Juana y su *Sueño*: antecedentes científicos en la poesía del Siglo de Oro," *Cuadernos Hispanoameri-canos* 3 (1976): 186–204.

3. Ruth Hill, *Sceptres and Sciences in the Spains: Four Humanists and the New Philosophy (ca. 1680–1740)* (Liverpool: Liverpool University Press, 2000), 55.

4. Echoes of lines 566–570, Méndez Plancarte notes, are also to be found in *Sol.* 2.386–387. The wordplay with "grado" seems meant to recall Góngora's de-votion to "paso," i.e., "Pasos de un peregrino son errante . . ." At 594 Sor Juana writes "grado a grado," and at 619 "del ínfimo grado," all of which is wittily re-fashioned as "al gusto grato" at 613. A similar polyptoton occurs with "graduá" (181) and "graduara" (428). And stressing the methodical character of such de-duction, "grado a grado" amplifies "astilla a astilla" (570).

5. Compare also with "los altos escalones ascendiendo" (608). In one of the definitions offered by *Autoridades*, "altiva" describes "la persona, ò cosa sobérbia, orgúllosa, de pensamientos y operaciones desordenadas."

6. Petrarch initiates the Renaissance *topos* of the ascent of the mountain as a spiritual ascent. In addition to "Ascent of Mont Ventoux," see his *Africa* where Truth sits atop Mount Atlas.

7. See John R. Cole, *The Olympian Dreams and Youthful Rebellion of René Descartes* (Urbana and Chicago: University of Illinois Press, 1992), 26–27. See also Francisco López Camara, "El cartesianísmo en Sor Juana y Sigüenza y Góngora," *FYL* 20 (1950): 107–131; Juan Manuel Silva Camerena, "Dos sueños y una pesadilla: la modernidad y el saber en Descartes y Sor Juana," *Aproximaciones a Sor Juana*, 371–380.

8. See Méndez Plancarte's explanation of these four operations (596).

9. Giovanni Pico della Mirandola, *De dignitate hominis* (Bad Homburg: Gehlen, 1968). "Quis hunc nostrum chamaeleonta non admiretur . . . Invadat animum sacra quaedam ambitio ut mediocribus non contenti anhelemus ad summa . . ." (30–32) Although Abréu Gómez does not include Pico in Sor

Juana's library, Sabat de Rivers (16) reads Sor Juana's epistemological project in the light of Pico's humanism. See Rocío Olivares Zorrilla, "Los tópicos del *Sueño* y del microcosmos: la tradición de Sor Juana Inés de la Cruz," in *Sor Juana Inés de la Cruz y las vicisitudes de la crítica*, ed. Jose Pascual Buxó (Mexico City: UNAM, 1998), 179–211. "No es fácil afirmar que Sor Juana consultó las Con-clusiones de Pico para escribir *El sueño*, pero es indudable que fue parte de su tradición cultural" (190).

10. "Tu, nullis angustiis coercitus, pro tu arbitrio, in cuius manu te posui, tibi illam praefinies" (*De dignitate hominis*, 28).

11. Relevant also is the repetition of "eminente" — a *cultísmo* appearing also in lines 29, 308, 431, and 648. See my discussion above of Quevedo's "Estatua de Nabuco" [#181].

12. Paz, *Sor Juana or, the Traps of Faith*, 358.

13. Hill, 62, 50, 52. Hill thus rejects Calleja's attempts in the *Aprobación* to link the two poets (80), though, as she acknowledges, this flies in the face of al-most all criticism, to say nothing of the poem's style.

14. *Obras completas*, 4.447.

15. See Sabat de Rivers's discussion of these figures, 85–86.

16. Lucretius ends his poem with the horrific description of the Athenian plague, which most commentators have read as a Stoic allegory warning against the pleasures of the flesh and moral decadence.

17. Alatorre comments on line 779: ". . . lo que Sor Juana está diciendo es que 'para Atlante y Hércules sería abrumadora la máquina de la máquina.' Parece que se le enredaron los hilos."

18. See Sabat de Rivers (86–96) on Phaeton.

19. Compare lines 792–794 with *Soledad primera*, 446–449: "No le bastó . . . / con tantas del primer atrevimiento / señas . . . para con éstas . . . / temeridades en-frenar segundas . . ."

20. Alatorre, 405.

21. Méndez Plancarte, 601. Concerning lines 805–810 and their possible debts to Góngora, Méndez Plancarte notes allusions to Icarus in *Sol.* 2.141–143; 148–149.

22. The "linterna mágica" was a much-publicized novelty in mid-seventeenth-century Europe. Kircher describes its workings in *Ars Magna lucis et umbrae* (1646) where Sor Juana would have encountered it.

23. Alatorre (406) glosses the textual history of the word *Tithón*. The linger-ing confusion whether she meant "Tithón," "Titón," or "Titán" is fostered, he suggests, by Sor Juana herself.

24. Thomas Browne, *Religio Medici and Other Works*, ed. L. C. Martin (Oxford: At the Clarendon Press, 1964), 174–175.

25. Sabat de Rivers writes: "Estos versos finales dan un nuevo enfoque levemente irónico a todas las ilusiones que los anteceden, al hacernos salir por fin del marco ficcional del *Sueño*" (129).

26. Friedrich Schlegel, "Philosophische Lehrjahre," 1796–1806, *Kritische Ausgabe*, 17.2 (I), ed. Ernst Behler (Paderborn: Schöningh, 1958), 128.

27. See Stephen Toulmin, *Cosmopolis: The Hidden Agenda of Modernity* (Chicago: University of Chicago Press, 1990). Discussing, among other texts, Donne's *Anniversaries* and a poem by a very young Descartes, Toulmin argues that contemporary philosophy should return to those skeptical, humanist, and nonsystemizing roots so prevalent in the late sixteenth and early seventeenth century.

28. *Carta a Padre Nuñoz*, cited in Boixo, 30–31.

29. Francis Bacon, *The Advancement of Learning*, ed. Michael Kiernan (Oxford: Clarendon Press, 2000), 126.

30. *The Advancement of Learning*, 125, 126.

31. See Karlheinz Stierle, "Translatio Studii and Renaissance: From Vertical to Horizontal Translation," *The Translatability of Cultures: Figurations of the Space Between*, ed. Sanford Burdick and Wolfgang Iser (Stanford: Stanford University Press, 1996), 55–67. Stierle's notion of "horizontal" translation, or synchronic and geographical translation, helps to situate Bacon, who, from his corner of Europe, rejects the weight of ancient authority.

32. For an incisive rethinking of cartographic discourse see Richard Helgerson, "The Folly of Maps and Modernity," *Literature, Mapping, and the Politics of Space in Early Modern Britain*, ed. Andrew Gordon, Bernhard Klein (Cambridge: Cambridge University Press, 2001), 241–262.

33. See Richard F. Jones, *Ancients and Moderns: A Study of the Rise of the Scientific Movement of Seventeenth-Century England* (New York: Dover, 1982). "The enormous expansion in geographical learning was not without effect in militating against the standing of antiquity . . . and nowhere did it show its influence more significantly than in the numerous geographical figures of speech with which the moderns urged their claims upon mankind" (11).

34. *The Advancement of Learning*, 321–322.

35. Jonathan Goldberg, *James I and the Politics of Literature* (Stanford: Stanford University Press, 1989), 48, fig.11.

36. Quoted in *The Advancement of Learning*, 250. For the seventeenth-century afterlife of this motif in the English context, see Joseph Glanvill's *Plus Ultra: Or, the Progress and Advancement of Knowledge since the Days of Aristotle* (1668) and

Henry Stubbes's *The Plus Ultra Reduced to a Non Plus; or a Specimen of some ani-madversions upon the Plus Ultra of Mr. Glanvill* (1670). Glanvill champions Bacon and the Royal Society, while Stubbes plays the cranky skeptic.

37. See R. F. Jones, *Ancients and Moderns: A Study of the Rise of the Scientific Movement in Seventeenth-Century England* (Berkeley: University of California Press, 1961), 44.

38. Francis Bacon, *Novum Organum, with Other Parts of the Great Instauration*, tr. and ed. Peter Urbach and John Gibson (Chicago: Open Court, 1994). The Latin text of the *Organum* appears in *The Works of Francis Bacon*, ed. James Spedding, Robert L. Ellis, and Douglas D. Heath (Reprinted, Stuttgart: Frommann Verlag, 1989), 1:119–148.

39. *The Advancement of Learning*, 70–71.

40. *Georgics*, 1.247.

41. *The Advancement of Learning*, 71.

42. Bacon, "To Our Most Serene and Mighty Prince and Lord, James," *Novum Organum, with Other Parts of the Great Instauration*, 6. Kiernan also notes that Puttenham's *Arte of English Poesie* may have been another source for Bacon's use of *Plus ultra*. If so, it would further deepen Bacon's debts to the rhetorical tradition. For Bacon and rhetoric, see Brian Vickers, *Francis Bacon and Renaissance Prose* (Cambridge: Cambridge University Press, 1968); "Bacon and Rhetoric," *Cambridge Companion to Francis Bacon*, ed. Markku Peltonen (Cambridge: Cambridge University Press, 1996); Lisa Jardine, *Francis Bacon: Discovery and the Art of Discourse* (Cambridge: Cambridge University Press, 1974); John C. Briggs, *Francis Bacon and the Rhetoric of Nature* (Cambridge: Harvard University Press, 1989).

43. *The Advancement of Learning*, 249. Kiernan cites Pliny's *Nat. Hist.*, iii, proem.

44. Blumenberg, in *The Legitimacy of the Modern Age* (340), suggests that it is Ulysses' ship going through the pillars; if this is so, it would be yet another anachronism.

45. Spedding, 4:82, 4:102. Apropos of the question of self-representation, in their edition of the *Novum Organon*, Urbach and Gibson (xxviii) note that the *GI* is itself a Herculean labor which defied completion given the ambitiousness of Bacon's plan. Consider also the hubris of his titles: *The Great Instauration*, *Novum Organon* (i.e., Aristotle superseded), *The Advancement of Learning*.

46. *Novum Organum, with Other Parts of the Great Instauration*, 3–4.

47. For the moral, political, and natural philosophical aspects of such "progress" see Robert K. Faulkner, *Francis Bacon and the Project of Progress* (Lan-

ham, MD: Rowman and Littlefield, 1993). The *OED* definitions for *progress* in-clude: 1) "The action of stepping or marching forward or onward; onward march; journeying, travelling, travel; a journey, an expedition." 2) "A state jour-ney made by a royal or noble personage, or by a church dignitary; a visit of state; also, the official tour made by judges and others, a circuit; an official visitation of its estates by a college." 3) "Onward movement in space; course, way."

48. *Novum Organum, with Other Parts of the Great Instauration*, 7. He also com-pares the contemporary state of the sciences to "the Scylla of fable" — another classical image signaling the perils of navigation (8). Extending the logic of his metaphor, Bacon later contrasts the "whirl of arguments" with the "eaves of ex-perience" (11).

49. *Novum Organum, with Other Parts of the Great Instauration*, 14. He further amplifies the navigation metaphor when he compares "a better and more perfect method of using the human mind and understanding" to the use of the compass which was the reason why "the ocean could be crossed and the regions of the new world discovered" (13).

50. *Novum Organum, with Other Parts of the Great Instauration*, 15.

51. *Novum Organum, with Other Parts of the Great Instauration*, 15, 16.

52. *The Advancement of Learning*, 22.

53. *The Advancement of Learning*, 23.

54. Harry Levin, *The Overreacher: A Study of Christopher Marlowe* (Cam-bridge: Harvard University Press, 1952), 108–135.

55. *Respuesta*, 4:455. The Latin is from Martial's *Epigrams*, 8.8.

CHAPTER NINE: STAGING HYPERBOLE, SKEPTICISM, AND STOICISM

1. Stanley Cavell, *Disowning Knowledge in Seven Plays of Shakespeare*, updated ed. (Cambridge: Cambridge University Press, 2003), 9.

2. Timothy Gould, "The Literal Truth: Cavell on Literality in Philosophy and Literature," paper given at *Stanley Cavell and Literary Criticism* conference, May 9–11, 2007, Edinburgh, UK.

3. Cavell glosses this "phenomenon" as "determining the data from which philosophy proceeds and to which it appeals, and specifically the issue is one of placing the words and experiences with which philosophers have always begun in alignment with human beings in particular circumstances who can be imag-ined to be having those experiences and saying and meaning those words. This is all that 'ordinary' in the phrase 'ordinary language philosophy' means, or ought to mean" (*Disowning Knowledge*, 42).

4. *Disowning Knowledge*, 82; *This New Yet Unapproachable America: Lectures after*

Emerson after Wittgenstein (Albuquerque: Living Batch Press, 1989), 37. In the context of the latter text, I take it that this melodrama is akin to what Cavell calls Wittgenstein and Heidegger's "fervor" or "pathos," which he tentatively links to the "moral judgment or religious aspiration," but which also is a question of literary style and the "sociality or geniality" of the text (11–15). Later, commenting on the *Philosophical Investigations*, Cavell grants that the "intellectual fervor" with which Wittgenstein urges a return to the ordinary is susceptible to charges of "charlatanry" (67).

5. Cavell, "Benjamin and Wittgenstein: Signals and Affinities," *Critical Inquiry* 25 (1999): 235–246; quotation from 237.

6. *Disowning Knowledge*, 5–6, 36.

7. Stanley Cavell, *The Claim of Reason: Wittgenstein, Skepticism, Morality, and Tragedy* (Oxford: Oxford University Press, 1979), 180.

8. Cavell, *Disowning Knowledge*, 118–121.

9. Cavell, *Disowning Knowledge*, 42.

10. Ludwig Wittgenstein, *Tractatus Logico-Philosophicus*, tr. C.K. Ogden (London and New York: Routledge & Kegan Paul, 1981), 7. This, of course, is the concluding proposition of the *Tractatus*.

11. *Tractatus*, 6.522.

12. Stanley Cavell, "Aesthetic Problems of Modern Philosophy," in *Must We Mean What We Say?* 2nd ed. (Cambridge: Cambridge University Press, 2002), 94.

13. See *Disowning Knowledge* (11–12) where he outlines these cruxes.

14. Cavell, *Disowning Knowledge*, 82.

15. Cavell's notion of complicity echoes Wittgenstein's insistence on seeing all the possibilities inherent in language games; for Cavell the medium of tragedy "is one which keeps all significance continuously before our senses, so that when it comes over us that we have missed it, this discovery will reveal our ignorance to have been willful, complicitous, a refusal to see" (85).

16. Because it hews more closely to the original manuscript and to how the play would have first been performed, I have chosen to use almost exclusively the 1608 Quarto version of the play, published in the edition by Stanley Wells as *The History of King Lear* (Oxford: Oxford University Press, 2000). For a discussion of some of the many valuable questions raised by scholars associated with the so-called New Textualism in the 1990s, see Wells's Introduction, 3–9.

17. Cavell, *Disowning Knowledge*, 1. Anthony Cascardi considers but quickly rejects this possibility in his essay "*Disowning Knowledge*: Cavell on Shakespeare,"

in *Stanley Cavell*, ed. Richard Eldridge (Cambridge: Cambridge University Press, 2003), 190–205. Cascardi distills Cavell's method with this formulation: "Shakespearean tragedy . . . is a form of drama in which language is drawn to extremes, but the force of Cavell's work is to magnify the intensities within Shakespeare's work rather than to submit them to anything like a 'philosophical' point of view extraneous to it" (191).

18. Cavell, *Disowning Knowledge*, 8. Cavell's most extended treatment of the differences between external world skepticism and "the problem of other minds" is the chapter "Between Acknowledgment and Avoidance" in *The Claim of Reason*, 329–496.

19. Cavell, *The Claim of Reason*, 90.

20. Cavell, *Disowning Knowledge*, 138, 136.

21. Richard Eldridge, "Introduction: Between Acknowledgement and Avoidance," in *Stanley Cavell*, 2.

22. There are, however, are a few tantalizingly moments when Cavell meditates on how Shakespearean tragedy might relate to historical contexts; for example, see *Disowning Knowledge* (35n) for his thoughts on Shakespeare and early modern science, and 93–94 for how *Lear* marks the difference between Renaissance and modern epistemology. But Michael Fischer, in *Stanley Cavell and Literary Skepticism* (Chicago: University of Chicago Press, 1989), notes: "As if aware of the apparent unlikelihood of a connection between Lear's tragedy and skepticism, Cavell makes the historical point that replacing acknowledgment with knowledge in the (vain) hope that we can save our lives only by knowing them is also a legacy of modern epistemology, which begins in the writings of Galileo, Bacon, and Descartes, Shakespeare's contemporaries" (84–85). Another reader troubled by Cavell's lack of historical engagement is William M. Hamlin. See his *Tragedy and Scepticism in Shakespeare's England* (New York: Palgrave Macmillan, 2005). For a more intellectual-historical account of Renaissance skepticism, see Charles B. Schmitt, *Cicero Scepticus: A Study of the Influence of the Academica in the Renaissance* (The Hague: Martinus Nijhoff, 1972).

23. Cavell, *Disowning Knowledge*, 3.

24. Cascardi, 192.

25. Otto Regenbogen, "Schmerz und Tod in den Tragödien Senecas," in *Vorträge 1927–1928 zur Geschichte des Dramas* (Leipzig: B. G. Teubner, 1930), 172.

26. See A. J. Boyle, *Tragic Seneca: An Essay in the Theatrical Tradition* (London and New York: Routledge, 1997). Boyle considers Senecan tragedy, its influence on Renaissance drama, and how European scholarship has frequently objected to both on grounds of taste. For studies dedicated mainly to Seneca, his drama,

thought, and historical-cultural context see: Wolf-Lüder Liebermann, Margerethe Billerbeck, and Ernst A. Schmidt, eds., *Sénèque: le tragique* (Geneva: Fondation Hardt, 2004), esp. Liebermann's "Senecas Tragödien: Forschungsüberblick und Methodik" (1–48), which examines recent approaches and issues in Seneca stud-ies; Michael von Albrecht, *Wort und Wandlung: Senecas Lebenskunst* (Leiden: Brill, 2004); C. A. J. Littlewood, *Self-Representation and Illusion in Senecan Tragedy* (Oxford: Oxford University Press, 2004); Alessandro Schiesaro, *The Passions in Play: Thyestes and the Dynamics of Senecan Drama* (Cambridge: Cambridge University Press, 2003); Manfred Fuhrmann, *Seneca und Kaiser Nero: Eine Biographie* (Berlin: Alexander Fest Verlag, 1997); Florence Dupont, *Les monstres de Sénèque: pour une dramaturgie de la tragédie romaine* (Paris: Éditions Belin, 1995); Charles Se-gal, *Language and Desire in Seneca's Phaedra* (Princeton: Princeton University Press, 1986); Otto Zwierlein, *Senecas Hercules im Lichte kaiserzeitlicher und spätantiker Deutung* (Wiesbaden: Academie der Wissenschaften und der Literatur, 1984) and *Kritischer Kommentar zu den Tragödien Senecas* (Mainz: Academie der Wis-senschaften und der Literatur, 1986); Pierre Grimal, *Sénèque, ou la conscience de l'Empire* (Paris: Société d'Édition, 1979).

27. T. S. Eliot, Introduction to *Seneca: His Tenne Tragedies, Translated into En-glish by Thomas Newton anno 1581* (Reprinted: Bloomington & London: Indiana University Press, 1964), and "Shakespeare and the Stoicism of Seneca," *Selected Essays, 1917–1932* (New York: Harcourt, Brace and Company, 1938), 107–120.

28. Eliot, "Shakespeare and the Stoicism of Seneca," 109.

29. Eliot, "Shakespeare and the Stoicism of Seneca," 109. Eliot traces the development of blank verse back to Marlowe's desire to imitate the Senecan iamb.

30. Eliot, "Shakespeare and the Stoicism of Seneca," 112.

31. Eliot, "Shakespeare and the Stoicism of Seneca," 110. Eliot touches upon two principal preoccupations of Renaissance commentators on Seneca: the need to distinguish between the philosopher and dramatist, and the striking way that the actions and language of the heroes in Seneca's plays often defy Stoic doctrine. Summing up these tensions, he archly notes: "The influence of Seneca is much more apparent in the Elizabethan drama than it is in the plays of Seneca" (113).

32. English tastes, Eliot notes, tend precipitously to dismiss Seneca's ver-bosity and monotony of voice, a tendency not alleviated by the Tudor translations that cast his Latin pentameters into ungainly "fourteeners." And while Seneca's so-called stylistic faults (in translation) may also be ascribed to the "peculiarities of Latin," looking more closely at his rhetoric, Eliot regards the curt, aphoristic

Senecan style as having an "oratorical impressiveness" perfectly suited to Elizabethan culture (*Introduction* to *Seneca*, xii, xvii).

33. Eliot, *Introduction* to *Seneca*, xxxvii–xxxviii.

34. In addition to the criticism discussed in this chapter, see Silvia Locati, *La rinascita del genere tragico nel Medioevo: l'Ecerinis di Albertino Mussato* (Florence: F. Cesati, 2006); Gianni Guastella, *L'ira e l'onore. Forme della vendetta nel teatro senecano e nella sua tradizione* (Palermo: Palumbo, 2001), esp. 155–208; *Séneca, dos mil años después: actas del congreso internacional conmemorativo del bimilenario de su nacimiento*, ed. Miguel Rodríguez-Pantoja (Córdoba: Publicaciones de la Universidad de Cór-doba, 1997); Charles and Michelle Martindale, *Shakespeare and the Uses of Antiq-uity* (London and New York: Routledge, 1994); *Der Einfluß Senecas auf das europäische Drama*, ed. Eckard Lefèvre (Darmstadt: Wissenschaftliche Buchge-sellschaft, 1978); Karl Alfred Blüher, *Seneca in Spanien. Untersuchungen zur Geschichte der Seneca-Rezeption in Spanien vom 13. bis 17. Jahrhundert* (Munich: A. Francke, 1969); Jean Jacquot, "Sénèque, la renaissance et nous," in *Les tragédies de Sénèque et le théâtre de la renaissance*, ed. Jean Jacquot (Paris: CNRS, 1964), 271–307; J. W. Cunliffe, *Influence of Seneca on Elizabethan Tragedy* (London: Macmil-lan, 1893), which was the primary impetus for Eliot's essays.

35. An important feature of this debate both in recent scholarship, as well as in the late Renaissance, is whether Seneca's dramas were performed or merely re-cited, as mere recitation tends to loosen decorum's reigns.

36. Gordon Braden, *Renaissance Tragedy and the Senecan Tradition: Anger's Privilege* (New Haven: Yale University Press, 1985), 40.

37. Braden, 28.

38. Braden, 30.

39. For a comparatist study finely attuned to the modalities of linguistic ex-cess and potency, see Michael Edwards, *Racine et Shakespeare* (Paris: PUP, 2004).

40. Braden, 57.

41. Littlewood, 20.

42. Thomas G. Rosenmeyer, *Senecan Drama and Stoic Cosmology* (Berkeley: University of California Press, 1989).

43. Calling the end of *Hercules furens* (lines 1278–1294) "the most hyperbol-ically theatrical statement of the play," Rosenmeyer compares it to Othello's last speech (53).

44. Rosenmeyer, 74.

45. Braden discusses the divergence between Lipsius's reception of Seneca's plays and philosophy (69).

46. Rosenmeyer, 33.

47. Seneca, *Ad Lucilium epistulae morales* (92.2). Latin text is from Seneca, *Epistles*, tr. R. M. Gummere (Cambridge: Harvard University Press, 1996), 3.446–448.

48. As the epistle cites the *Aeneid* three times, Seneca seems to imply both that the reading of epic poetry may be conducive to virtue and that Virgil championed Stoic ethics.

49. Rosenmeyer, 141, 145. His note on 145 focuses on the diction of exaggeration.

50. C. J. Herington, "Senecan Tragedy," *Arion* 5.6 (1966): 422–471; quotation from 443. Herington's essay remains one of the best general introductions to the subject. While celebrating Eliot's reading of the tragedies, Herington insists that criticism should focus on "the terrible moral sensitivity which imperiously compelled their creation" and "that concrete, pictorial imagination which brought them into shape" (428). For an incisive analysis of Seneca's Stoicism and his penchant for *Übersteigerung*, see Max Pohlenz, *Die Stoa: Geschichte einer geistigen Bewegung* (Göttingen: Vandenhoeck & Ruprecht, 1984), 303–327.

51. Seneca, *De beneficiis*, in *Moral Essays III*, tr. John W. Basore (Cambridge: Harvard University Press, 1935), 508–511.

52. Herington, 448.

53. "Der Autor und seine Geschöpfe sind immer auf der Suche nach dem Ungewöhnlichen (*insolitum*), dem noch nicht Gewagten (*inausum*), auf der Jagd nach etwas, das alles bisher Dagewesen übertrifft, nach dem *maius aliquid*, dem Größeren, Gewaltigeren, Furchtbaren, Gräßlicheren. Die senecanische Komparativ, wie man diese Erscheinung mit einem Begriff bezeichnen könnte, spielt in allen Stücken eine mehr oder weniger bedeutungsvolle Rolle." Bernd Seidensticker, "Senecas *Thyestes* oder die Jagd nach der Außergewöhnlichen," in *Thyestes*, tr. Durs Grünbein (Frankfurt am Main: Insel, 2002), 115. The lucid, playful translation by Grünbein makes a powerful case for the lasting power of Seneca's hyperboles. So for that matter does Caryl Churchill's 1995 translation and Introduction.

54. Quintilian's comments on Seneca are at once admiring and dismissive: "Cuius et multae alioqui et magnae virtutes fuerunt, ingenium facile et copiosum, plurimim studii, multa rerum cognitio . . . Tractavit etiam omnem fere studiorum materiam: nam et orationes eius et poemata et epistulae et dialogi feruntur. In philosophia parum diligens, egregius tamen vitiorum insectator fuit. Multae in eo claraeque sententiae, multa etiam morum gratia legenda, sed in eloquendo corrupta pleraque, atque eo perniciosissima quod abundant dulcibus vitiis" (10.1.128–130). He goes on to accuse Seneca of perversity and a lack of

judgment. And while Seneca is not blamed for his hyperbole, and his tragedies are only obliquely mentioned (Quintilian alludes to "poemata"), clearly his "extremely decadent" [*perniciosissima*] style points towards the *ultra modum*.

55. Seidensticker, 116.

56. All citations from the Latin text are from Seneca, *Tragedies*, 2 vols., tr. F. J. Miller (Cambridge: Harvard University Press, 1987, 1998). I have chosen to provide the Tudor translations — here Jasper Heywood translates — as a historicist way to prepare the ground for a reading of *King Lear*, but also because their *copia* anticipates certain aspects of Baroque aesthetics. Herington, who also uses these translations, opines: "To read through these translations is in fact no great aesthetic pleasure. Pleasure one feels, but it is akin to the pleasure of ruins — of early Elizabethan ruins, rambling, whimsical, repetitive in their effects, wavering still in provincial uncertainty between Gothic and Renaissance" (426). I have silently changed *i* to *j* and *u* to *v* for clarity's sake. For more contemporary English versions of the plays, see Miller's revised translations cited above. See also Frederick Ahl's lucid, idiomatic verse translations of *Trojan Women*, *Medea*, and *Phaedra* in *Three Tragedies* (Ithaca: Cornell University Press, 1986).

57. See also Seneca, *Seneca's Thyestes*, ed. R. J. Tarrant (Atlanta: Scholars Press, 1985). Tarrant's Introduction and Commentary are invaluable; see esp. his thoughts on Seneca's predilection for *sententiae* and debts to declamatory oratory (19–22).

58. Schiesaro reads these opening lines as metaliterary, as commenting on "theatrical essence" and thus the possibility of a certain kind of "self-reflexive" drama (26–27).

59. The *great chain of being*, as Tillyard and others have shown, is, of course, an idea heavily indebted to Platonic and Neo-Platonic antecedents as well. In Manilius' *Astronomica* (1.247–254) it is the "vis animae divina" which creates "mutua . . . foedera" in the universe.

60. As Samuel Sambursky notes in regard to Virgil and Lucan, the manner in which outrage is felt simultaneously in the ethical and cosmographical spheres characterizes much of classical thought: "[t]he dynamic continuum not only had a profound influence on epistemology in the Hellenistic period, but it also molded some of the basic ideas in the later teachings of Stoic ethics." See Samuel Sambursky, *Physics of the Stoics* (Princeton: Princeton University Press, 1987), viii; John M. Rist, *Stoic Philosophy* (Cambridge: Cambridge University Press, 1969); Anthony Long, "The Stoics on World-Conflagration and Everlasting Recurrence," *Southern Journal of Philosophy* 23 (1985): 13–38. Long would disagree with my emphasis on quantity even as we concur that Stoic physics influ-

enced other discourses: "Stoic physics . . . just because it lacks any precisely es-tablished concepts on quantifiable measures of change, is a theory whose ex-planatory power is partly metaphorical; it can be compared to a translation system whereby physical processes are converted into terms which are wider in their sig-nificance than the physical domain that they primarily name" (20–21). This helps explains why the *translatio* of Stoic physics to the stage seems so effortless.

61. Timothy Reiss, *Mirages of the Selfe: Patterns of Personhood in Ancient and Early Modern Europe* (Stanford: Stanford University Press, 2003), 139, 151.

62. Compare this with the simile I quoted earlier: "Hoc . . . adversus vir-tutem possunt calamitates et damna et iniuriae, quod adversus solem potest nebula" (*Ep.* 92.18). Although here because neither brother is virtuous, the sim-ile's logic is reversed; once a hint of vice appears the entire cosmos is shaken. See Schiesaro (172–173) on the "chorus's belief that the end of the universe is imminent."

63. Herington, 428, 428. But H. J. Rose, expressing a long-standing school of thought in his *A Handbook of Latin Literature* (New York: E. P. Dutton & Co., 1960), accuses Seneca of hypocrisy and bad faith. Herington, for his part, dis-misses such accusations from those who have not endured at close hand — tyranny, matricide, infanticide, madness, etc. — such as Seneca did under Caligula and Nero.

64. Herington, 430.

65. One of the constellations is Leo which he mistakes for the Nemean lion he slew. Such errors are predicted by Seneca when in *De ira* he pithily observes that *ira* is "brevem insaniam" (1.1.2–3).

66. This image recalls one of Demetrius' examples of rhetoric that lacks decorum: a rock so large that it has goats browsing on it.

67. Jasper Heywood is again the translator.

68. These lines are echoed in Macbeth's exclamations: "What hands are here? Ha! they pluck out mine eyes! / Will all great Neptune's ocean wash this blood / Clean from my hand? No. This my hand will rather / The multitudinous seas incarnadine, / Making the green one red" (2.2.78–81).

69. Erich Burck, *Vom römischen Manierismus: von der Dichtung der frühen röm-ischen Kaiserzeit* (Darmstadt: Wissenschaftliche Buchgesellschaft, 1971), esp. 14–18, 92–100.

70. Braden, 20.

71. As Rosenmeyer comments: "above all they are the old dramatic mecha-nism for evoking the interconnectedness of causes in a resistant cosmos" (82). This might help to explain their constant, but vain invocation in *Lear*.

72. See Rosenmeyer, 172, 175.

73. The nurse's fluvial metaphor ("ubi se iste fluctus franget? Exundat furor") (392) also helps establish an objective, cosmic basis for Medea's passions.

74. Schiesaro: "The certainty of her *furor* is rooted in the certainty of natural events" (212).

75. See my discussion in chapters 5 and 6 of Quevedo and Góngora's versions of the navigation *topos*.

76. Commenting on *Naturales quaestiones* (4.2.24; 1.*Pr*.13) and analogous cartographical moments in the tragedies, Herington observes that "[s]uch Senecan passages, taken together, convey perhaps as vividly as anything in Latin writing the sheer immensity of the Imperial Roman World" (438). Celebrating Seneca's "truly ecumenical poetry," Herington ascribes to him "the power of projecting himself imaginatively into regions which he could never see" (438–439).

77. Heywood's translation of "everso cardine mundus" (*Thy.* 877–878).

78. Rosenmeyer, 187. He identifies six rhetorical aspects of the tirade or what he calls "deflection" — that is, from self to world and back again: imperatives, jussives and injunctives, use of *debet* or *decet* (thereby creating a kind of "demonic decorum"!), exclamatory questions, pure exclamation, and future indicatives. And while the metapoetic elements in the passages make me balk at Rosenmeyer's claim that "Senecan rhetoric does not recognize tropes as tropes" (194), Senecan hyperbole, simile, analogy, and other forms of comparison and amplification clearly spring from a coherent, compelling emotional and conceptual worldview.

79. Schiesaro compares these lines and the thirst for "immortal fame" they convey to *Titus Andronicus*, 3.1.133–135: "What shall we do? Let us have our tongues / Plot some device of further misery / To make us wondered at in times to come." Thus such rhetoric is the flipside of the hyperbolism in the Sonnets either urging the young man to reproduce or claiming immortality (*aere perennis*) for Shakespeare's verse.

80. See also the Chorus's refashioning of the gigantomachy at 804–812.

81. The dynamic of outbidding in Senecan drama, however, can also be explicitly intertextual: Seneca's *Medea* must compete with Euripides', even while Medea herself strives for knowledge and power in a hostile world. The famous stichomythic exchange between the nurse and Medea (168–173) expresses in dialogic form this will to self-mastery: "Medea, / Fiam." As for Thyestes, Schiesaro comments: "His deeds will have to be sublime, literally exceeding human bound-

aries . . . above all, they will have to outdare all precedents, just as the Fury de-manded . . ." (52).

82. *Erotesis* or *interrogatio* is a rhetorical question; *diacope* is the repetition of a word with one or a few words in between.

83. Cavell, *The Claim of Reason*, 496.

CHAPTER TEN: GOING BAROQUE IN SHAKESPEAREAN DRAMA

1. Gordon Braden, *Renaissance Tragedy and the Senecan Tradition: Anger's Priv-ilege* (New Haven: Yale University Press, 1985), 62. Thus "the needs of rhetorical self-aggrandizement" (170) must be considered alongside the question of *imitatio*. Seneca's "dead end" also helps explain why late Renaissance and Baroque hy-perbolists often turn to genres other than drama to pursue their ambitions. Shake-speare begins writing the *Sonnets* near the time he pens the Senecan *Titus Andronicus*. And as we saw in Spanish Baroque lyric, the dynamics of ambition are crucial for the imitators of the Petrarchan tradition as well; in fact, there the awareness may be even stronger given the continuous presence of the lyric "I" which habit-ually reflects on the nature and limits of the means of expression at its disposal.

2. Braden, 209, 215, 216. But Braden, who ultimately offers a reading of Senecan tragedy through the lens of Hegel's "unhappy consciousness," also sometimes engages in creative anachronism.

3. See Leonard Forster, "La renaissance du stoïcisme," *L'époque de la Re-naissance (1400–1600). Tome IV: Crises et essors nouveaux (1560–1610)*, ed. Tibor Klaniczay, Eva Kushner, and Paul Chavy (Amsterdam and Philadelphia: John Benjamins, 2000), 121–138.

4. Aside from *Lear*, all citations from Shakespeare's dramatic works unless otherwise noted are from *The Norton Shakespeare*, gen. ed. Stephen Greenblatt (New York: W. W. Norton & Co., 1997).

5. Calderón, for instance, gives us Segismundo, who in *La vida es sueño* be-gins as an object of scorn and fear because of his volatile emotions, but ends as an exemplum of Christian Stoicism and patience.

6. G. E. Lessing, *Laokoon*, in *Werke*, ed. Kurt Wölfel (Frankfurt am Main: Insel, 1982), 3:13. Kant, as we will see below, prizes *Verwunderung* over *Bewun-derung* in the third *Critique* (§29).

7. Likewise, just before he is stabbed he asks his petitioners: "Wilt thou lift Olympus?" (3.1.74).

8. See, for example, 1.33 where the "rudesse Stoïque" is viewed as in need of Christian moderation. For an account of the philosophical influences on Mon-

taigne, see Hugo Friedrich, *Montaigne*, tr. Dawn Eng (Berkeley: University of California Press, 1991), esp. 60–61.

9. Cited by Friedrich (172) from the "Apology."

10. Michel de Montaigne, *Essais* (Paris: Flammarion, 1979), 2:156; *The Essayes of Michael Lord Of Montaigne*, tr. John Florio (New York: E. P. Dutton, 1927), 2:188. However, later in the "Apology," Florio-Montaigne praises "the serenity and tranquility of [the] souls" of the "natives of Brazil," even as he notes that the futility of Stoic philosophy led Sextus to suicide. Further complicating the picture, Montaigne praises Lipsius as "le plus sçavant homme qui nous reste" (2:243).

11. *Essais*, 2:115; *The Essayes*, 2:137.

12. Jill Kraye, "Moral Philosophy," in *The Cambridge History of Renaissance Philosophy*, ed. Charles B. Schmitt and Quentin Skinner (Cambridge: Cambridge University Press, 1988), 303–386; quotation from 366. Kraye underscores the importance of "De l'inconstance de nos actions" and "De mesnager sa volonté."

13. *Essais*, 2:268; *The Essayes*, 2:325–326. Curiously, Florio ignores Montaigne's "extraordinairement."

14. Forster asserts: "C'est avec Lipse que commence le néo-stoïcisme, ou stoïcisme renaissant" (125). Forster (127–128) also discusses Lipsius' European-wide influence. The title of Lipsius' book, first published in Antwerp in 1584, derives from Seneca's *De Constantia*. Lipsius also wrote the influential *Physiologia stoicorum* (1604), an elaborate scholarly attempt to place Stoic physics in a Christian frame.

15. *Two Bookes of Constancie*, 14. Consider also his metaphorics of the heliotrope and labyrinth: "As the Marigold and other flowers are by nature always enclined towards the sunne: so hath Reason a respect unto God . . ." (11); ". . . whoso hath this thred of *Theseus* may passe without straying through all the laberinths of this life . . ." (12).

16. *Two Bookes of Constancie*, 19.

17. Likewise, in Thomas James's dedication to his 1598 translation of Guillame Du Vair's *The Moral Philosophie of the Stoicks*, we read: "Let it not seeme strange unto us that Philosophie should be a meanes to help Divinitie, or that Christians may profit by the Stoicks. Indeed the licentious loosenes of our times cannot well brooke the strictness of this sect. The Stoicks are as odious unto some men, as they themselves are hated of others: they call the professors hereof in their gibing manner stockes, and not Stoicks, because of the affinitie of their names . . . but no kinde of philosophie is more profitable and neerer approching unto Christianitie (as *S. Hierome* saith) then the philosophie of the Stoicks." Gui-

llaume Du Vair, *The Moral Philosophie of the Stoicks. Englished by Thomas James*, ed. Rudolf Kirk (New Brunswick, NJ: Rutgers University Press, 1951), 45. I won, der if the gibe mentioned here inspired Shakespeare to put the Stoic Kent in the stocks. See also Jill Kraye (367–374) for the convergences and divergences of Neo,Stoicism and Christianity in the Renaissance.

18. *Two Bookes of Constancie*, 32, 46–47.

19. *Two Bookes of Constancie*, 34–35. The phrase "breathing spirite" glosses *pneuma*.

20. *Two Bookes of Constancie*, 39.

21. *Two Bookes of Constancie*, 41.

22. *Two Bookes of Constancie*, 44–45.

23. Forster observes: ". . . le livre avait, aux yeux des contemporains, les défauts de ses qualités, dont le principal était l'absence de toute transcendance" (125).

24. Quoted in Robert S. Miola, *Shakespeare and Classical Tragedy: The Influ, ence of Seneca* (Oxford: Clarendon Press, 1992), 2n. Miola's source is Lipsius' *Animadversiones*, which was appended to *L. Annaei Senecae Cordubensis Tragoediae* (Heidelberg, 1589). But here, perhaps, the traditional distinction between *lexis* and *dianoia* needs to be revised somewhat, as *sonus* depends on the auricular figures of speech which, as Shakespeare will show with his mastery of stichomythia, is not tied to any particular subject matter but rather to the expression of great emotion.

25. Scaliger, 5.274. Scaliger goes on to explain why he doesn't expand on these all,too,brief comments: "Quare ipsum quoque intactum relinquamus. Non quod omnino desperemus quaedam melius dici posse, sed quia ex aliis tribus [Valerius Flaccus, Statius, and Lucan] satis erit nobis suppeditatum, unde poeta noster quid fugiat, quid sequatur intellegere queat."

26. Newton, 4–5.

27. Eliot in his Introduction to *Seneca: His Tenne Tragedies*, after citing some particularly awful lines from *Locrine*, a play he attributes to Greene, comments: "This is the proper Ercles bombast, ridiculed by Shakespeare, Jonson, and Nashe" (xxxiii). Wells, in his note, sends us to Rolfe's study, which cites two pas, sages from Studley's 1581 translation of *Hercules Oeteaus* (a play no longer as, cribed to Seneca) that Bottom conflates.

28. Wells notes the common emendation of "stones" for "storms," and cites *Julius Caesar* (3.2.223–225) where Antony: "a tongue / . . . that should move / The stones of Rome." This line is variously refashioned in *Lear*.

29. See Charles Frey's chapter "Shakespeare's Bombast," in *Experiencing Shakespeare* (Columbia: University of Missouri Press, 1988), 144–160. As Frey

observes, the issue of Shakespeare's "bombast" has long been at the heart of the critical tradition, from Greene and Jonson (who would that Shakespeare "had blotted a thousand" lines, to Dryden, who laments Shakespeare's "serious swelling into bombast," to Pope, who blames his "verbose and bombast expression," and to the present day when teachers and critics of Shakespeare neglect to consider how the dramatist's Latin grammar school "*forced* Shakespeare to write ornate, Latinate, inflated oratorical discourse" (151).

30. Boyle, *Tragic Seneca*, 160.

31. The dimeter appears to play on Senecan infamous terseness and ellipticality. See Miola who devotes an entire chapter (175–214) to what he calls "light Seneca."

32. Jean Howard, headnotes to *The Second Part of Henry IV*, 1298.

33. Both "Herod" and "Termagant" were stock characters in medieval English drama. Herod was known for his ranting, while Termagant was an idol worshipped by the Muslims and so made to speak in a vociferous, violent manner.

34. See John Erskine Hankins, *Backgrounds of Shakespeare's Thought* (Hamden, CT: Archon Press, 1978). Hankins (26) glosses the "burning zone" as a hyperbole explained by the diffuse influence of classical cosmology on Shakespeare. He also compares it to Puck's remark: "I'll put a girdle around about the earth / In forty minutes" (2.1.175–176).

35. G. Wilson Knight, "*King Lear* and the Comedy of the Grotesque," in *The Wheel of Fire: Interpretations of Shakespearian Tragedy* (London: Methuen, 1986), 175.

36. Ben Ross Schneider reads *De beneficiis* as informing *King Lear*'s plot and explaining Shakespeare's depiction of flattery and its effects. See "*King Lear* in its Own Time: The Difference that Death Makes," *ELMS* 1.1 (1995): 1–49; reference is to 13.

37. William R. Elton, *King Lear and the Gods* (San Marino: The Huntington Library, 1968), 122. The initial thirst for quantities ultimately yields to "cosmic ambiguity" (124). Elton's invaluable monograph demonstrates the syncretism of sources and ideas that may have directly and indirectly influenced Shakespeare. It also helps put the language, philosophy, and theology of the tragedy into an intellectual, historicist framework. See also Nick Davies, *Stories of Chaos: Reason and its Displacement in Early Modern English Narrative* (Aldershot, England: Ashgate, 1999), which examines "the assessment of the properties and worth of things by means of mathematical calculation ('numbers')" (121). Beginning with Cordelia's initial "Nothing," Davies traces the play's many allusions to the "algoristic zero" (133).

38. Cavell, 58.

39. Recalling that the Stoic king is a "constant" topic for Seneca, Rosenmeyer notes the parodic effects of the maxim, "the more violent the king, the kinglier he is" (89). He also underscores "the usefulness of the royal cypher" especially in a "diseased" universe (90).

40. See Curtius, *ELLMA* (165), on *taceat* as a rhetorical formula integral to panegyric and the inexpressibility *topoi*.

41. Cavell, *Disowning Knowledge*, 64. "The truth is she *could* not flatter; not because she was too proud or too principaled, though these might have been the reasons for a different character; but because nothing she could have done would have *been* flattery — at best it would have been *dissembled flattery*" (65).

42. Wells notes (104) that this idea was proverbial.

43. See Scodel, *Excess and the Mean in Early Modern English Literature*, 1–18.

44. The rhetoric of the curse in Shakespearean tragedy is ubiquitous; for a fine example, see Lady Anne's *imprecatio* in *Richard III* (1.2).

45. Harry Levin's reading of Marlowe offers several instructive points of comparison: "Marlowe habitually prefers the invidious comparison to the more usual kind of simile. Similes and metaphors are links, explicit or implicit, which connect the plane of literal reality with a plane of figurative cross-reference. Marlowe's habit is to abolish the boundaries between these two planes, elevating the human to the divine or vice versa, and freely and frankly pitting the moderns against the ancients. He restores the classical pantheon only to despoil it; he seeks out the great archetypes of humanity in order to challenge them, one by one, on the very grounds of their mythological fame. He storms the heavens by piling Pelion on Ossa" (20). Further afield, in *La vida es sueño*, Rosaura serves as Segismundo's necessary interlocutor, thereby mediating his Baroque absolutism.

46. Miola observes that Regan's later speeches in the scene ("O sir, you are old . . ."; "Give eare, sir, to my sister . . .") "misuses Stoic language and principle" (156). But if this is so, then together Kent and Regan provide a Stoic frame to Lear's gathering storm even as they, because of Kent's marginality and Regan's bad faith, effectively undermine it.

47. Elton (121–125) discusses the important role of numbers and quantities in the scene and the entire play. "Gonoril and Regan move within a universe of confused proportions in which the only unit of measurement is quantitative, and the main value word, 'more.'" But Elton also gestures at how such quantitative reasoning may speak to the period's more general *episteme*: ". . . despite his occasional bad dreams, mathematical man bounded himself, relatively, in a nutshell and counted himself a king of infinite space." For a fine recent study of the early

modern sublime, see David L. Sedley, *Sublimity and Skepticism in Montaigne and Milton* (Ann Arbor: University of Michigan Press, 2005).

48. Henry Peacham, *The Garden of Eloquence* (1577, revised in 1593), ed. Beate-Maria Koll (Frankfurt am Main: Peter Lang Verlag, 1996). Rather than simply treating hyperbole as a means of creating *energeia* or vividness, Peacham treats hyperbole as a way of scaling and so circumscribing the "greatest" and "highest things": "The use hereof serveth most fitly for amplification, and that especially when matters require either to be amplified in the greatest degree, or diminished in the least: by this figure the Orator either lifteth up high or casteth downe low, either stretcheth things to the uttermost length, or presseth them to the least quantitie: so high is the reach, so wide is the compasse of this figure, that it mounteth to the highest things, compasseth the widest, and comprehendeth the greatest" (40).

Michael Witmore acutely interprets the tensions in the play between quantitative and qualitative ways of perceiving the world in *Shakespeare's Metaphysics* (London: Continuum, 2008). His reading of the play's metaphysics privileges a Deleuzian "immanence" over a more traditional "punctualism." In so doing, he attends to the play's textual history and leans on the philosophy of Bergson to help illuminate the play's language, actions, and gestures: "In contrast to the zero-sum logic of substance that infects Lear's conception of himself — one in which any division of substance (kingship, majesty, paternity) leads to a corresponding diminution of that substance — we glimpse at the end of *Lear* an alternative, comic metaphysics in which time is boundlessly unfolding new kinds of beings and feelings rather than destroying static versions of "older" ones. Here each moment would be a new species of time and feeling, a constantly ripening, immanent flux rather than a diminishing record of previous moments and passions" (21).

49. Stanley Cavell, "The Interminable Shakespearean Text," *Philosophy the Day after Tomorrow* (Cambridge: Harvard University Press, 2005), 37. The essay reads the question of praise in the light of criticism of Shakespeare by Burke, Empson, Fineman, Emerson, and Wittgenstein.

50. Clearly Edmund's take on astrology and the way his skepticism is complicated by the play's dramatic action relate to the larger question of the survival of the Stoic notion of *sumpatheia* in the Baroque. Lipsius, in *De constantia libri duo*, tends to explain astrological causation as a form of Stoic *sumpatheia*. See also Kent's comments at 18.32–36, which suggest that astrology is the last recourse for meaning in a world otherwise emptied of it.

51. Its connotations are further increased by typographic play of the pathetic

exclamations: "O, Regan . . . O, Regan!" (7.290–298), wherein the "O" serves as a cipher for the "naught" she has become for him. I will discuss a more extensive instance of this in the next chaper.

52. Elton, 122.

53. Braden, 216. Compare this with Craig Kallendorf who, in "*King Lear* and the Figures of Speech," *Landmark Essays on Rhetoric and Literature*, ed. Craig Kallendorf (Mahwah, NJ.: Hermagoras Press, 1999), 101–118, echoes Margreta de Grazia's warning against the tendency to see the play as representing "the inadequacy of all language to express what the characters think and feel" (102). Instead, he proposes that *Lear* offers various instances of what he intriguingly calls the "opaque style."

54. Braden, 216. See also Miola 156–157 on Shakespeare's use of the Senecan *nescio quid* and its Greek antecedents: "In the world of the play Senecan anger appears to be even more complex and ambivalent than Stoical patience . . . Lear's adoption of Senecan rhetoric and *ira* is a troubled and complex accommodation." Miola also notes that Lewis Theobald as early as 1773 saw these lines as an *imitatio* of Seneca (he also points to Ovid, *Met.* 6.619–674).

CHAPTER ELEVEN: SAYING THE "WORST" IN *LEAR*

1. Mark Morford maps this *topos* in *The Poet Lucan: A Study in Rhetorical Epic* (Oxford: Basil Blackwell, 1967), 30–31.

2. *The Tempest*, 1.2.2. Gonzalo imagines a Christian Stoic death, but on land: "Now would I give a thousand furlongs of sea for an acre of barren ground: long heath, broom, furze, anything. The wills above be done, but I would fain die a dry death" (1.1.58–60).

3. The storm scene is probably best read as confirmation of what Thomas Greene describes as the indirect nature of Renaissance *imitatio*; it depends, that is, on commonplaces more than specific textual sources.

In the seventeenth century, the *OED* notes, *pother* could mean "a choking smoke or atmosphere of dust"; "disturbance, commotion, turmoil, bustle"; "a tumult, uproar; a noise, din"; and by transference "a verbal commotion, stir, or fuss"; or a "mental perturbation or tumult . . . display of sorrow or grief." Thus "dreadful pother" nicely captures the storm's psychological and physical aspects.

4. Cordelia at the beginning of Scene 18 likewise fuses the nautical and terrestrial, the internal and external: "Why, he was met even now, / As mad as the racked sea, singing aloud, / Crowned with rank fumitor and furrow weeds, / With burdocks, hemlock, nettles, cuckoo-flowers, / Darnel, and all the idle

weeds that grow / In our sustaining corn" (18.1–6). Her simile is joined with the *copia* of words and things to produce extravagant *affectus*.

5. Wells cites Psalms, 46:2–3; but the passage also recalls numerous passages in Job and the Book of Revelations.

6. Lipsius, 40.

7. Miola, 146. But they also resemble the *Aeneid*, 1.249 (". . . fluctus ad sidera tollit").

8. While Elton observes that ". . . the Fool, in his pointed worldly prudence, is the counterpoise to the thunder in its cosmic ambiguity" (200), this is true at first only for the audience who hears both voices along with the storm.

9. Compare this to Othello's hyperbole: "When I love thee not, Chaos is come again" (3.3.92), which depends on the microcosmic-macrocosmic analogy as well as Petrarchan subjectivity.

10. Miola (160) hears echoes of Hercules' tirade in *Hercules furens*: "Nunc parte ab omni, genitor, iratus tona; / oblite nostri, uindica sera manu / saltem nepotes, stelliger mundus sonet / flammasque et hic et ille iaculetur polus" (1202–1205). See also Madeleine Doran, *Shakespeare's Dramatic Language* (Madison: University of Wisconsin Press, 1976). Her chapter, "Command, Question, and Assertion in *King Lear*," examines the "rhetoric of fiat, pronouncement, objurgation, imprecation, petition, interrogation."

11. See Seneca's *Naturales quaestiones* (2.59.11–12) for another important parallel. Elton (202–204) summarizes traditional views from Cicero and Seneca to La Primaudaye and Marlowe on how thunder causes belief, or at least accompanies it. Conversely, he charts the more skeptical, naturalistic views of Democritus, Pliny, Aristotle, Epicurus, Lucretius, and Dolet on the matter.

12. Elton, 212.

13. Miola, 163. As in the Sonnets, Shakespeare would show that hyperbole can be witty and self-referential; consider the conceit on his own family name lurking in the phrase "thou all-shaking thunder, / Smite flat the thick rotundity of the world," i.e., *shake* + *sphere*. There are permutations on *shake* at 9.6, 9.55, and 11.32.

14. As Elton comments: "Lear's speech is *in extremis*, pitiful and self-pitying, far from the confidence of Act 1. Peripeteia and anagnorisis coincide; suffering becomes 'knowledge,' *pathema*, *mathema*" (199).

15. Cavell, 79.

16. Ultimately, Cavell notes, Lear will make a scapegoat of himself (78).

17. Elton, 97.

18. Richard Strier, "Against the Rule of Reason: Praise of Passion from Petrarch to Luther to Shakespeare to Herbert," in *Reading the Early Modern Passions: Essays in the Cultural History of Emotion*, ed. Gail Kern Paster, Katherine Rowe, and Mary Floyd-Wilson (Philadelphia: University of Pennsylvania Press, 2004), 23–42; quotation from 36. See also Erasmus, *Laus stultitae*, ch. 30, where he inquires what the result would be if Seneca's demands that the emotions be conquered were met. The answer, Erasmus concludes, would be an artificial, untenable half-god, half-man that has never existed and never will exist, in short, a motionless statue of stone. Jill Kraye cites the view of the Florentine humanist, Leonardo Bruni, that Stoic impassivity in the face of suffering was more fitting for a rock than a man ("Moral Philosophy," 362). Reading Scaliger, Braden notes "the *actio* of a play is described as simply the means, for which the affectus is the end" (231).

19. The first drop in the seas of Shakespearean criticism was spilled in 1592 when Robert Greene mocked Shakespeare as an "upstart Crow, beautified with our feathers, that, with his Tiger's heart wrapt in a Player's hide, supposes he is as well able to bombast out a blank verse as the best of you." *Bombast* was the Elizabethan terms for the "padding" of a costume and only later became a catachresis for an actor's padded, extravagant rhetoric. Likewise, when Nashe, apropos of Marlowe, writes of "the swelling bumbast of bragging blanke verse," the sartorial and scenographic connotations should not be forgotten.

20. The interior roof of the Globe was apparently painted with stars. For a powerful, largely dramaturgical and thematic reading of "extremity" in *Lear*, see Richard Fly, *Shakespeare's Mediated World* (Amherst: University of Massachusetts Press, 1976), esp. chapter four, "Beyond Extremity: *King Lear* and the Limits of Poetic Drama." Fly reads the play as the ultimate expression of Shakespeare's poetic ambitions. Of the plot's harrowing trajectory, he observes that its "progressions suggest a compulsion to press beyond extremity by stripping away all that mediates between man and a direct encounter with his universe" (92).

21. Wilson Knight, 171.

22. S. T. Coleridge, *Shakespeare Criticism*, ed. T. M. Raysor (New York: Dutton, 1960), 1:51.

23. Rosenmeyer, 147.

24. In addition to Greenblatt's *Marvelous Possessions*, see Lorraine Daston, Katherine Park, *Wonders and the Order of Nature, 1150–1750* (New York: Zone Books, 1998); Jean Céard, *La nature et les prodiges: L'insolite au XVIe siècle* (Geneva: Droz, 1977).

25. See, for example, Montaigne's "D'un enfant monstreux" as well as, of course, "Apologie de Raimond Sebond."

26. This echoes earlier Lear's complaint of his daughters' "monster ingratitude" (5.36).

27. Walter Benjamin, *The Origin of German Tragic Drama*, tr. John Osborne (New York: Verso, 1985), 137.

28. See Harry Levin, "The Heights and Depths: A Scene from *King Lear*," in *More Talking of Shakespeare*, ed. John Garret (London: Longmans, Green, 1959), 87–103; Stephen Orgel, "Shakespeare Imagines a Theater," *Poetics Today* 5.3 (1984): 549–561; Jonathan Goldberg, "Perspectives: Dover Cliff and the Conditions of Representation," *Shakespeare and Deconstruction*, ed. G. Douglas Atkins and David M. Bergeron (New York: Peter Lang, 1988), 245–265.

29. Orgel, 556.

30. George Puttenham's idiosyncratic discussion, in *The Arte of English Poesie* (1589), of *enargeia* as appealing to the ear rather than the eye, casts a curious light on this scene. Poetic "ornament," Puttenham writes: ". . . is of two sorts, one to satisfy the ear only by good outward show set upon the matter, with words and speeches smoothly and tunable running; another by certain intendements or sense of such words and speeches inwardly working a stir to the mind. The first quality the Greeks call *enargeia*, of this word *argos*, because it giveth a glorious lustre and light. The latter they called *energeia*, of *ergon*, because it wrought with a strong and virtuous operation." *English Renaissance Literary Criticism*, ed. Brian Vickers (Oxford: Oxford University Press, 2003), 224–225. Edgar's description possesses enormous *enargeia* and *energeia*, but in so far as the former, also called *illustratio*, means "vividness."

31. Goldberg, 250–256. See also Ernest Gilman, *The Curious Perspective: Literary and Pictorial Wit in the Seventeenth Century* (New Haven: Yale University Press, 1978), for a more extensive reading of anamorphotic wit.

32. The verb *trifle* links this scene with the play's last where Albany, after learning of Cordelia's death and witnessing Lear's sorrow, hears of Edmund's death and responds: "That's but a trifle here" (20.290). Glossed in the *OED* as the act of treating "with a lack of seriousness or respect; to play or dally with," to *trifle* may also mean to "cheat, delude, befool, or to mock." The noun denotes a "thing of slight value, or small importance." It thus points to a scale of values as well as a certain lack of truth and seriousness. In other words, the "trifle" of Edmund's death helps to measure the tragedy that is Cordelia's. Whereas for Edgar to call his theatrical production starring his unwitting father a "trifle" is to push it toward comedy. In this way the scene's hyperboles signal the kind of *engaño* and

desengaño common to Spanish baroque drama, for instance, in *La vida es sueño*. Another parallel is with the deception of Quixote and Sancho by the Duke and Duchess when they are made to believe they are riding a flying horse (2.41), though in Quixote's case, the deception only deepens his own self-delusion.

33. As Wilson Knight comments: "The grotesque merged into the ridiculous reaches a consummation in this bathos of tragedy: it is the furthest, most exaggerated, reach of the poet's towering fantasticality" (171).

34. Wells, 232n.

35. Levin's reading of the scene's resolution is theological: "Providence must be at work, after all; and if we discern the workings of cosmic design in our personal destinies, then no man has the right to take his own life; he must bear the slings and arrows of fortune, however outrageous they seem. To the Stoic argument for suicide Edgar would oppose the Christian attitude . . ." (99).

36. Lipsius, 30.

37. For more on Demetrius see fn. 94 in chapter one. In *Directions for Speech and Style* (ca. 1599), ed. Hoyt H. Hudson (Princeton: Princeton University Press, 1935), John Hoskins writes of hyperbole: "Sometimes it expresseth a thing in the highest degree of possibility, beyond the truth, that it descending thence may find the truth; sometimes in flat impossibility, that rather you may conceive the unspeakableness than the untruth of the relation" (29).

38. In *Must We Mean What We Say?*, updated edition (Cambridge: Cambridge University Press, 2002), reading *Endgame*, Cavell also rejects this dichotomy by showing the theatrical depth and utter contingency of Beckett's "strategy of literalization" (126). Earlier in the same book, in the "Aesthetic Problems of Modern Philosophy" (73–82), he discusses how metaphor and not literal language is endlessly paraphrasable. This is difficult to reconcile, though, with the assertion, in *The Claim of Reason*, that metaphor is "unnatural" (189–190).

39. Or as Rosenmeyer notes, "The Senecan view of the world simply cannot accept the fixity of the natural law upon which the figure of the *impossible* is founded" (197).

40. Elton, 270.

41. Braden observes: "Beyond madness and the worst life can do waits recognition that our isolation is a shared nakedness. The Senecan world of the closed self is here transfigured; these moments mirror some of the most powerful scenes on the Greek stage" (209).

42. Miola persuasively shows that "Lear's awakening reactions and his acceptance of guilt contrast sharply with the grand *furor* of Seneca's Hercules" (168). The manner in which the "romance reunion" of Lear and Cordelia will

presently be curtailed by another species of *furor* ("Had I your tongues and eyes, I would use them so / That Heaven's vault should crack.") that reanimates Shakespeare's dialogue with the Senecan tradition.

43. Cavell, *Disowning Knowledge*, 72–73.

44. For an extended consideration of the nature of Lear's desire see Coppélia Kahn, "The Absent Mother in *King Lear*," *Rewriting the Renaissance: The Discourse of Sexual Difference in Early Modern Europe,* ed. Margaret Ferguson, Maureen Quilligan, and Nancy J. Vickers (Chicago: University of Chicago Press, 1986), 33–49.

45. His moving similes in the last scene: "like birds i'th' cage"; "As if we were God's spies"; and his epitaph for Cordelia, "Her voice was ever soft, / Gentle, and low," suggest that if he had but lived, he might have proved a master of such qualification. Witmore reads the prison scene as instituting "a realm of pure quality" (84), though he seems to be already looking forward to the *romance* world of the *Tempest* rather than meditating on the play's bleak final scenes.

46. Wells promotes an alternate reading that omits the comma after *amplify*, and thus clarifies the sense, i. e., "another*"* is Kent who comes to tell the story of Lear's defeat.

47. In this sense, the play, with its multiple subjectivities in dialogue with one another, complicates and even challenges Joel Fineman provocative claims, in *Shakespeare's Perjured Eye: The Invention of Poetic Subjectivity in the Sonnets* (Berkeley: University of California Press, 1986), concerning the shift from a poetics of vision to the poetics of the "I" in the sonnets. I hear in Albany's "see, see" an attempt, however vain, to salvage something of the poetics of vision. The result, though, is that vision produces an ironic if tragic spectacle.

48. Greenblatt calls "Never, never, never, never, never," in the First Folio (5.3.284), the "bleakest pentameter line Shakespeare ever wrote" and "the climax of an extraordinary poetics of despair." See his headnotes to the play in *The Norton Shakespeare*, 2311. Witmore discusses the differences between the Quarto and Folio at length in his reading of the play's metaphysics. He surmises that Shakespeare increased verbal repetitions in the Folio not only because of its dramatical "effect" but also because it heightened the "intensity" of the qualitative aspects of Shakespeare's thought (77–79).

49. For a compelling reading of quantification in *Lear*, see Brian Rotman, *Signifying Nothing: The Semiotics of Zero* (Stanford: Stanford University Press, 1987), 78–86.

50. Reading the last scenes, Fly offers another interpretation of hyperbole's trajectory: "The use of language to defiantly 'outface,' 'outscorn,' and 'outjest'

soul-crushing experiences is clearly an important humanistic weapon in the play's defense against an encroaching darkness . . . When brought face to face with an inconceivable horror, the characters have to abandon the 'outdoing' *topos* and fall back on the simplest units of expression, causing bare and humble words to be suddenly charged with miraculously expressive power" (100).

51. For a fine psychoanalytic, deconstructive take on the play's rhetoric of "nothing," see David Wilbern, "Shakespeare's Nothing," *Representing Shakespeare: New Psychoanalytic Essays*, ed. Murray M. Schwartz and Coppélia Kahn (Baltimore: The Johns Hopkins University Press, 1980), 244–263.

52. Fly, 108.

53. Benjamin calls the Baroque an "age of bombast" (60); he underscores the "eccentric features" (58) and the "unremitting artistic will" (55) of the Baroque *Trauerspiele*. Significantly, Optiz's *Die Troerinnen*, a 1625 translation of Seneca's *Troades* into German alexandrines, began the period that Benjamin treats as "Baroque."

54. Benjamin, *Origin*, 38. This is not the place to parse what Benjamin means by "origin" and how it shapes his idiosyncratic history of ideas. A sense of what is at stake, though, can be gleaned in the *Epistemo-Critical Prologue*: "Philosophical history, the science of origin, is the form which, in the remotest extremes and the apparent excesses of the process of development, reveals the configuration of the idea — the sum total of all possible meaningful juxtapositions of such opposites. The representation (*Darstellung*) of an idea can under no circumstances be considered successful unless the whole range of possible extremes it contains has been virtually explored" (47). For an acute analysis of this crux, see Beatrice Hanssen, "Philosophy at Its Origin: Walter Benjamin's Prologue to the *Ursprung des deutschen Trauerspiels*," *MLN* 110 (1995): 809–833.

55. Cavell, "Benjamin and Wittgenstein: Signals and Affinities," 236.

56. Benjamin, *Origin*, 55; *Ursprung des deutschen Trauerspiels* (Frankfurt am Main: Suhrkamp, 1963), 42. The distinctions between *Trauerspiel* and tragedy are central to his conception of allegory — Benjamin, as George Steiner observes, also cultivates a critical dialectic of silence and hyperbole: "Tragedy posits an aesthetic of reticence; the 'sorrow-play' is emphatically ostentatious, gestural, and hyperbolic." See Steiner's Introduction, 18.

57. Benjamin, *Origin*, 173.

58. Benjamin, *Origin*, 139.

59. Benjamin, *Origin*, 210, 67. Helga Geyer-Ryan, in "Abjection in the Texts of Walter Benjamin," in *Walter Benjamin: Appropriations*, ed. Peter Osborne (London: Routledge, 2005), 261–279, writes: "Benjamin interprets the bombast of the

baroque as a sign of linguistic natural longing for nature whose tone of language must nevertheless burden itself with cultural significance" (272). Thus bombast, or what I am calling hyperbole, is a longing for, what Benjamin calls in numerous places, a "reine Sprache," albeit one that does not nostalgically forget history.

60. Their inability to lose their immanence is ascribed to Stoicism (73). The figure of the monarch-tyrant-martyr thus displaces the martyred Christ. In addition to the monarchs that people the mourning plays, one thinks here of actual late Renaissance rulers like Rudolf II, but also of literary figures such as Calderón's Segismundo, Basilieus, and Cipriano, and, of course, Shakespeare's Richard II, Hamlet, and Lear.

61. Benjamin, *Origin*, 157; *Ursprung*, 171.

62. Benjamin borrows from Panofsky and Saxl's discussion of melancholy as a form of allegorical *extremitas* in Renaissance emblematics and Dürer's *Melancholia I* (149, 160).

63. Benjamin, *Origin*, 185. See Bainard Cowan, "Walter Benjamin's Theory of Allegory," *New German Critique* 22 (1981): 109–122; Nina Zimnik, "Allegorie und Subjektivität in Walter Benjamins *Ursprung des deutschen Trauerspiels*," *The Germanic Review* 72 (1997): 285–302.

64. Benjamin, *Origin*, 162, 34–36, 36, 49, 56; on 48 he writes of a "metaphysics of form."

65. See Cowan, 118.

66. Benjamin, *Origin*, 216.

67. See especially the last section of the *Ursprung*, which is entitled "Ponderación misteriosa" after Calderón's *autos* and *comedias religiosas* (233–235).

68. Benjamin, *Origin*, 231–232.

69. Benjamin links the "miracle" to the Baroque conception of "fate" (129). See Cowan (117–118) on the "miracle" and why Benjamin identifies it as an "inorganic" feature of the "non-dialectical" *Trauerspiel*.

70. Benjamin, *Origin*, 81, 231.

71. Benjamin, *Origin*, 180–181.

72. Benjamin, *Origin*, 182.

73. Benjamin, *Origin*, 35; *Ursprung*, 16.

74. Benjamin, *Origin*, 57–58.

75. Benjamin, *Origin*, 58.

76. Benjamin, 160. See Hans-Georg Gadamer's programmatic essay, "Philosophy and Poetry," *The Relevance of the Beautiful and Other Essays* (Cambridge: Cambridge University Press, 1986), 131–139.

77. Benjamin, *Origin*, 54.

78. Benjamin, *Origin*, 136. Given that Gryphius's most celebrated tragedies is *Cardenio und Celinde*, it is worth recalling that Shakespeare is presumed to have written with John Fletcher a now-lost play entitled *The History of Cardenio*.

79. Benjamin, *Origin*, 157–158.

80. Benjamin, *Origin*, 108. But see also his comments on p.109. Benjamin's reading of how Renaissance theories of tragedy influenced the Baroque is anchored in Scaliger's emphasis on the emotions (*affectus*) over action (98–99). Much of what he writes here about the tyrant, his "will," "sensibility," and "madness" could well apply to *Lear*.

81. Cavell, *Disowning Knowledge*, 73–80.

82. Benjamin, *Origin*, 228.

83. Gordon Teskey, in *Allegory and Violence* (Ithaca: Cornell University Press, 1996), persuasively describes both the hermeneutic "capture" and psychological-phenomenological causes of allegory in terms of "violence" (6).

CHAPTER TWELVE: FABULOUS DISCOURSE

1. Cavell, *Disowning Knowledge*, 122.

2. For a compelling analysis of Cartesian metaphysics as a form of onto-theology, see Jean-Luc Marion, *Sur le prisme métaphysique de Descartes: Constitution et limites de l'onto-théo-logie dans la pensée cartésienne* (Paris: PUF, 1986); *On Descartes' Metaphysical Prism*, tr. Jeffrey L. Koskey (Chicago: University of Chicago Press, 1999).

3. "*Cogito* est *l'extrémité* même, si l'on entend désormais ce mot comme une qualité et non comme une position . . . A l'extrémité même où la feinte s'aveugle (dans la fiction de ne voir aucun monde), *la feinte s'illumine* . . . Au point du cogito — pointe de la feinte — la pensée ne s'identifie que par cette structure de l'*extrême retranchement*." Jean-Luc Nancy, *Ego Sum* (Paris: Flammarion, 1979), 115–118.

4. René Descartes, *Meditations on First Philosophy*, in *The Philosophical Writings of Descartes*, tr. John Cottingham, Robert Stoothoff, and Dugald Murdoch (Cambridge: Cambridge University Press, 1984); 2:6, 2:8. All English citations from Descartes are from this edition, hereafter referred to as CSM. All citations from Descartes' French and Latin texts are from *Œuvres de Descartes,* 11 vols., ed. Charles Adam and Paul Tannery (Paris: Vrin, 1971–1986). Hereafter referred to as AT.

5. Martial Gueroult, *Descartes' Philosophy Interpreted According to the Order of Reasons, The Soul and God*, tr. Roger Ariew (Minneapolis: University of Minnesota Press, 1984), 1:15. In "Descartes' Use of Doubt," David Owens notes

that doubt is only used against belief and judgments; see *A Companion to Descartes*, ed. Janet Broughton and John Carriero (Oxford: Blackwell, 2008), 164–178. Michael Della Rocca, in "Judgment and Will," observes that Descartes insists in the First Meditation that he has good "*reasons* for doubt" and thus is not just exercising "a simple mental fiat." See *The Blackwell Guide to the Meditations*, ed. Stephen Gaukroger (Oxford: Blackwell, 2006), 142–159; quotation from 149.

6. René Descartes, *Discours de la méthode*, in *Œuvres philosophiques*, ed. Ferdinand Alquié (Paris: Bordas, 1988), 1:605n.

7. Janet Broughton, *Descartes's Method of Doubt* (Princeton: Princeton University Press, 2002), 7.

8. Broughton, 11–12. Stephen Gaukroger demonstrates at length, in *Descartes' System of Natural Philosophy* (Cambridge: Cambridge University Press, 2002), how Cartesian metaphysics and the search for first principles had as their ultimate aim the more secure grounding of a system of natural philosophy.

9. *Meditationes de prima philosophia*, AT 7:89.

10. For Descartes' relation to Stoicism, see Etienne Gilson's *Commentaire Historique* in his edition of the *Discours de la méthode* (Paris: Vrin, 1925), 130–131, 226, 231–233, 246–254; Victor Brochard, "Descartes stoïcien," in *Etudes de philosophie ancienne et de philosophie moderne* (Paris: Vrin, 1926); Pierre Mesnard, *Essai sur la morale de Descartes* (Paris: Bolvin, 1936); Henri Gouhier, *La pensée métaphysique de Descartes* (Paris: Vrin, 1962), 31–40; E. M. Curley, *Descartes against the Skeptics* (Cambridge: Harvard University Press, 1978); Richard H. Popkin, *History of Scepticism: from Erasmus to Bayle* (Berkeley: University of California Press, 1979); Richard Davies, *Descartes, Scepticism and Virtue* (London: Routledge, 2001); Casey Perrin, "Descartes and the Legacy of Ancient Skepticism," in *A Companion to Descartes*, 52–65.

11. See Popkin, 173. Pierre Charron's, *De la sagesse* (1601), especially Book II, chs. 1–2, bear on Descartes' First Meditation as Charron writes of the need to make oneself clear, like a white sheet, of all popular belief and passions, in order to attain to wisdom. Likewise, the thought of Francisco Sánchez is essential to any consideration of the skeptical legacy such as Descartes encountered it. See his *Quod nihil scitur (That Nothing is Known)*, ed. Elaine Limbrick, tr. Douglas F. S. Thomson (Cambridge: Cambridge University Press, 1988).

12. Jacques Lezra, *Unspeakable Subjects: The Genealogy of the Event in Early Modern Europe* (Stanford: Stanford University Press, 1997). "For if the systematic (demonstrative) and the performative (rhetorical) readings of the *Meditations* are not rigidly distinguished, then the truth to be experienced in the first case does not

differ from the system of modifications of the second, which means ascribing to it the epistemologically neutral status of an act (the act of stating "cogito, ergo sum," for instance, which can easily be parroted by an automaton) or an event" (91). That Lezra himself eventually finds such a distinction untenable, and thus a "novelistic reading" of Descartes unavoidable, raises the question whether Descartes successfully strips his rhetoric, its metaphorics and hyperbolics, of all epistemological and ontological value.

13. CSM 2:61; AT 7:89.

14. ". . . j'oserais espérer ensuite une langue universelle fort aisée à apprendre, à prononcer et à écrire, et ce qui est le principal, qui aiderait au jugement, lui représentant si distinctement toutes choses qu'il lui serait presque impossible de se tromper . . . Or je tiens que cette langue est possible, et qu'on peut trouver la Science de qui elle dépend, par le moyen de laquelle les paysans pourraient mieux juger de la vérité des choses, que ne font maintenant les philosophes. Mais n'espérez pas de la voir jamais en usage; cela présuppose de grands changements en l'ordre des choses, et il faudrait que tout le Monde ne fût qu'un paradis terrestre, ce qui n'est bon à proposer que dans le pays de romans." René Descartes, "Lettre à Mersenne" (November 20, 1629), *Correspondance*, ed. C. Adam and G. Milhaud (Paris: Félix Alcan, 1936), 1:93.

15. See also *La pensée métaphysique de Descartes* (75), where Gouhier observes how great is Descartes' faith that translation will not disfigure the exact meaning of his texts, given that it is the "pensée" and not the "signe" that matters.

16. Timothy Reiss, "The Word/World Equation," *Yale French Studies* 49 (1974): 3–12; 8.

17. Jacques Derrida, "Cogito and the History of Madness," in *Writing and Difference*, tr. Alan Bass (Chicago: University of Chicago Press, 1978), 53.

18. See Descartes' "Letter to Abbé Picot," which recommends an initial, cursory, novelistic reading of the *Principia* to be followed by second and third readings that will yield increased understanding. Studies examining the complex role of rhetoric in Descartes' thinking include: Peter France, *Rhetoric and Truth in France* (Oxford: Clarendon Press, 1972), esp. his chapter "Descartes: la recherche de la vérité," 40–67; Sylvie Romanowski, *L'illusion chez Descartes: la structure du discours cartésien* (Paris: Klincksieck, 1974); Timothy J. Reiss, "Cartesian Discourse and Classical Ideology," *Diacritics* 6.4 (1976): 19–27; L. Aryeh Kosman, "The Naive Narrator: Meditation in Descartes' *Meditations*," in *Essays on Descartes' Meditations*, ed. A. O. Rorty (Berkeley: University of California Press, 1986), 21–44; Thomas M. Carr, Jr., *Descartes and the Resilience of Rhetoric:*

Varieties of Cartesian Rhetorical Theory (Carbondale: Southern Illinois University Press, 1990), esp. 26–61; John D. Lyons, "Rhétorique du discours cartésien," *Cahiers de littérature de XVIIe siècle* 8 (1986): 125–47; Claudia Brodsky Lacour, *Lines of Thought: Discourse, Architectonics, and the Origin of Modern Philosophy* (Durham N.C.: Duke University Press, 1996).

19. CSM 1:112.

20. Thus Wittgenstein's criticism of the distinction between private and public language is aimed at philosophers like Descartes who would substitute the former for the latter in the name of philosophical absolutism.

21. CSM 1:112; AT 6:4. In Part VI, after tepidly supporting Galileo's "physical theory," he notes "the great care I had always taken never to adopt any new opinion for which I had no certain demonstration . . .") (CSM 1:142).

22. AT 6:5–6. ". . . que l'éloquence a des forces et des beautés incomparables; que la poésie a des délicatesses et des douceurs très ravissantes . . ." (AT 6:5–6). But then he observes that he has already given enough time to the study of classical languages and texts "et à leur histoires, et à leur fables" (AT 6:6). For such study, he continues, is comparable to constantly traveling without ever coming to know one's own country, that is, without ever knowing oneself. Both eloquence (rhetoric) and poetry, moreover, are treated as "dons de l'esprit, plutôt que des fruits de l'étude" (AT 6:7). Thus despite the full year devoted to the study of rhetoric at La Fléche (see Gouhier, 96), Descartes implicitly casts the rhetoric of his *Discours* as natural and spontaneous.

23. CSM 1:114; AT 6:7.

24. CSM 1:114; AT 6:7. Translation slightly modified.

25. Nancy writes: "L'extravagance des fables se définit donc trés exactement par l'omission de ce que n'omet pas la fable du *Discours*. Le *Discours* rapporte tout; la fable de la franchise est une fable franche. Elle est plus fidèle que 'les histoires les plus fidèles' — elle est véridique" (111).

26. CSM 1:123. "Et entre plusiers opinions également reçues, je ne choisissais que les plus modérées: tant à cause que ce sont toujours les plus commodes pour la pratique, et vraisemblablement les meillures, tous excès ayant coutume d'être mauvais" (AT 6:23).

27. AT 6:26–27; CSM 1:124.

28. For Descartes' use of metaphor, in addition to the works on Cartesian rhetoric cited above, see Jacques Lezra's book, the Derrida essays discussed below, as well as: Théodule Spoerri, "La puissance métaphorique chez Descartes," in *Descartes* (Paris: Éditions de Minuit, 1957); Antonio Negri, *Descartes Politico* (Milan: Feltrinelli Editore, 1970), 9–60; Jeanette Bicknell, "Descartes's Rheto-

ric: Roads, Foundations, and Difficulties in the Method," *Philosophy and Rhetoric* 36.1 (2003): 22–38.

29. AT 6:31–32; CSM 1:126–127 (translation slightly modified).

30. See *This New Yet Unapproachable America* (9) where Cavell quotes Emerson's "I embrace the common" as the motto for his own philosophical project that seeks to moderate or reverse the Romantic thirst for transcendence. Likewise citing Descartes' distrust of ordinary language in the Second Meditation where he discusses the piece of wax, Cavell offers Wittgenstein's *Philosophical Investigations* as a counter-model since it recognizes "that refusing or forcing the ordinary is a cause of philosophical emptiness (say avoidance) and violence" (33).

31. AT 6:32; CSM 1:127.

32. Peter Markie, "The Cogito and its Importance," in *The Cambridge Companion to Descartes*, ed. John Cottingham (Cambridge: Cambridge University Press, 1992), 140–173; quotation from 145. Markie concludes that this juxtaposition of intuition ("Descartes' appeal to the intuition is unclear") and inference is unsatisfactory as it stands. Instead, he offers this gloss: "He does not just 'intuit' that he thinks and immediately infer that he exists. He first discovers a mental attribute, determines that it is a thought, decides that one and only one thing has it, and then concludes, 'I think,' or more properly, 'The thing with this thinks,' where 'this' refers to the thought. Only then does he immediately infer, 'I exist,' or more properly, 'The thing with this exists'" (163).

33. See A. J. Ayer, "I think, therefore I am," in *The Problem of Knowledge* (New York: St. Martin's Press, 1956), 45–54.

34. Markie, 163: ". . . what is it about Descartes' self-awareness when he clearly and distinctly perceives that he thinks makes his awareness an awareness of *him*? Is he directly acquainted with himself in the same way he is directly acquainted with an idea, like a pain sensation? Is he aware of himself by virtue of conceiving a particular concept of himself? If so, what concept?"

35. "He nowhere proves that thoughts need a thinker, nor is there reason to believe this except in a grammatical sense." Bertrand Russell, "Descartes," in *History of Western Philosophy* (London: Allan and Unwin, 1946), 589.

36. CSM 1:123; AT 6:24–25.

37. *The Search for Truth*, CSM 2:408; *Recherche de la vérité*, AT 10: 512–513.

38. CSM 2:408–409; AT 10:512–513.

39. Broughton observes that Descartes does not fully use the method of radical doubt in the *Discourse* (5).

40. Descartes, Letter to P. Vatier, February 22, 1638, *Correspondance* (AT 1:560).

41. "Quant à la feinte dont parlait le *Discours*, elle se détache du moment où s'opère la généralisation: une hypothèse métaphysique n'est pas une fiction; mais une fiction la double avec l'artifice du Malin génie" (Gouhier, 67). There is no agreement as to when the *Recherche* was composed. See CSM 2:359, for the attempts to date the *Recherche*. Alquié conjectures that the *Recherche* is from 1641 (2:1102–1104).

42. Gouhier, 94.

43. Fifth Set of Objections, CSM 2:180; Objectiones quintae, AT 7:258.

44. Gassendi's skepticism and its attendent incredulity may though also inform his disdain for Cartesian ornament. Gouhier, intriguingly, stresses "la modestie de [Gassendi's] exigences quant à la vérité" (33).

45. Gouhier, 105.

46. See Lezra, 99.

47. Second Set of Replies, CSM 2:110; Secundae responsiones, AT 7:156. The glosses in the parenthesis occur in the French translation by the Duc de Lynes (1647), see Réponses aux Secondes Objections (Alquié, 2:582), which was probably authorized by Descartes. For a recent appraisal of Descartes' use of analysis and synthesis, see Murray Miles, "Descartes' Method," in *A Companion to Descartes*, 145–163. Miles distinguishes between implicit truths (e.g., axioms such as the light of reason) and explicit ones (e.g., the *cogito*) in the process of analysis. The former are not produced by hyperbolic doubt.

48. CSM 2:110; AT 7:155.

49. CSM 2:111; AT 7:156. The geometers use only synthesis in their writings but this is not because they are ignorant of analysis, but "because they had such a high regard for it that they kept it to themselves like a sacred mystery" (CSM 2:111). Thus by analogy, Descartes' revelation of his analysis acquires a certain hermetic flavor.

50. CSM 2:111; AT 7:156. Summing up his reading of the final pages in the Second Set of Replies, Gouhier remarks: "Psychologie, métaphysique et méthode apparaissent dans leur unité, chacune étant condition des autres" (108).

51. CSM 2:111.

52. See, though, Lezra's reading (116–134) of the phrase "dans les déserts les plus écartés," which ends the second part of the *Discours*; a *tmesis* that not only contains Descartes' proper name, it also is an "event" whose literariness and "signature" complicate the pretensions of the method per se.

53. See Gouhier, 75–76. With this said, Descartes is often very reluctant to credit his predecessors. The most (in)famous example of this concerns the extent to which Descartes owed Augustine for the *cogito*.

54. Gouhier, 76.

55. Gouhier, 79–80.

56. In the Thirteenth Objection of the Third Set of Objections and Replies, Hobbes writes: "The phrase 'a great light in the intellect' [*magna lux in intellectu*] is metaphorical, and so has no force in the argument . . ." Descartes replies: "It is quite irrelevant whether the phrase 'a great light' has force in the argument or not; what matters is whether it helps explain matters — and it does . . ." (CSM 2:134–135).

57. See Broughton's rehearsal of the "circle" objection (and her solution to it) (*Descartes's Method of Doubt*, 175–202); also illuminating is E. M. Curley's chapter on the subject (96–124) where, by demonstrating that "Descartes is not the theist and dualist he appears to be, but an atheist and materialist" (98), the circle is also broken; Peter Markie's chapter, "The Mind, Clear and Distinct Perception, and Certainty," in *Descartes's Gambit* (Ithaca: Cornell University Press, 1986), 151–195, traces the intricacies of Descartes' logical failure. The volume, *Eternal Truths and the Cartesian Circle: A Collection of Studies*, ed. Willis Doney (New York: Garland, 1987), brings together important articles on the question. A more recent reappraisal is: John Carriero, "The Cartesian Circle and the Foundations of Knowledge," in *A Companion to Descartes*, 302–318.

58. See Hans-Georg Gadamer, *Truth and Method*, esp. 405–438.

59. I am thinking here, of course, of Deleuze's reading of Spinoza and Descartes, in *Expressionism in Philosophy: Spinoza* (New York: Zone Books, 1992). Deleuze reads Spinoza's "doctrine of truth" as wanting "*to substitute a conception of adequacy for the Cartesian conception of clarity and distinctiveness*" (151). For Deleuze, Spinoza's adequate ideas *express* rather than *represent* their content.

60. CSM 2:12; AT 7:17.

61. CSM 2:12; AT 7:18.

62. In the *Rules for the Direction of the Mind*, Descartes glosses this species of intuition: "By 'intuition' I do not mean the fluctuating testimony of the senses or the deceptive judgment of the imagination as it botches things together [*vel male componentis imaginationis judicium fallax*], but the conception of a clear and attentive mind [*mentis purae & attentae*], which is so easy and distinct that there can be no room for doubt about what we are understanding. Alternatively, and this comes to the same thing, intuition is the indubitable conception of a clear and attentive mind [*mentis purae & attentae non dubium conceptum*], which proceeds solely from the light of reason [*qui a sola rationis luce nascitur*]. Because it is simpler, it is more certain than deduction, though deduction . . . is not something a man can perform wrongly" (CSM 1:14; AT 10:368).

63. CSM 1:25. If so, then such "enumeration," which Descartes explicates as a form of deduction, would follow from "first and self-evident principles" already derived from an intuition that presumably occurred before the *Meditations* proper begin. In other words, his hyperbole would be a remedy for a defective memory: ". . . deduction sometimes requires such a long chain of inferences that when we arrive at such a truth it is not easy to recall the entire route which led us to it. That is why we say that a continuous movement of thought is needed to make good any weakness of memory . . . In this way our memory is relieved, the sluggishness of our intelligence redressed, and its capacity in some way enlarged" (CSM 1:25). Again the proleptic specter of Spinoza's third kind of knowledge seems present here. Also in the same Rule he links "enumeration" with "induction" (CSM 1:27).

64. Seventh Set of Objections and Replies, CSM 2:348–349; AT 7:512. See also AT 7:481 where the same analogy is used. The Seventh Set of Objections and Replies is published in the Second Edition (1642) of the *Meditations*.

65. Gouhier, 26. In *Demons, Dreamers, and Madmen: The Defense of Reason in Descartes's* Meditations (Indianapolis: Bobbs-Merrill, 1970), Harry Frankfurt further underscores the artifice of the hyperbole here: "The basket-of-apples analogy suggests that emptying one's mind is a rather headlong and indiscriminate affair. The process of examining and evaluating the mind's former contents, on the other hand, plainly requires meticulous discrimination and careful argument. This makes it far more plausible to suppose that Descartes' skeptical arguments have to do with the task of deciding which of his former opinions are worthy of being reinstated than to suppose that they are designed to bring about the general overthrow of his beliefs" (20).

66. Kosman, 22. See Kosman on the way Descartes refashions the concerns of religious meditative literature (22–23).

67. CSM 2:13, CSM 2:13, AT 7:19, AT 9:14.

68. CSM 2:13.

69. *The Passions of the Soul*, CSM 1:350; *Les passions de l'ame*, AT 11:373.

70. Daston and Park, *Wonders and the Order of Nature*, 311.

71. CSM 2:14.

72. CSM 2:14. AT 7:21.

73. CSM 2:15; AT 7:21

74. AT 7:22, CSM 2:15.

75. CSM 2:151.

76. CSM 2:172; AT 7:247. Arnauld writes: ". . . I rather think that the First Meditation should be furnished with a brief Preface which explains that

there is no serious doubt cast on these matters but that the purpose is to isolate temporarily those matters which leave room for even the 'slightest' and most 'exaggerated' doubt (as the author himself puts it elsewhere); it should be explained that this is to facilitate the discovery of something so firm and stable that not even the most perverse sceptic will have even the slightest scope for doubt. Following on from this point, where we find the clause 'since I did not know the author of my being,' I would suggest a substitution of the clause 'since I was pretending that I did not know [*ignorare me fingerem*] ...'" (CSM 2:151; AT 7:215). As CSM notes, for once Descartes heeds his readers' advice and adds a qualification in the main text, though significantly in the Sixth not the First Meditation.

77. Broughton, 31–32.

78. Broughton, x.

CHAPTER THIRTEEN: HYPERBOLE AND DESCARTES' WILL TO REASON

1. Following tradition, I retain this English phrase for Descartes' "genium ... malignam." In CSM it is translated as "malicious demon."

2. CSM 2:15; AT 7:22–23. The Duc de Lynes' 1647 French translation seems to mimic "Je pense, donc je suis": "Je supposerai donc qu'il y a, non point un vrai Dieu ..." (AT 9.1:17). The effect in both cases is neatly to balance thought and being.

3. Gouhier, 119.

4. CSM 2:15; AT 7:23.

5. CSM 2:16; AT 7:24. De Lynes' translation engages in some suggestive wordplay. Descartes would emulate Archimedes who "ne demandait rien qu'un point qui fût fixe et assuré," which inverts the anaphora in the First Meditation, where he imagines himself "n'ayant point de mains, point d'yeux, point de chair, point de sang."

6. CSM 2:18; AT 7:27.

7. This phrase is added in the French version.

8. CSM 2:18 (translation slightly modified); AT 7:27.

9. CSM 2:18–19; AT 7:27–28.

10. AT 7:28.

11. CSM 2:21. "... pudeat supra vulgus sapere cupientem, ex formis loquendi quas vulgus invenit dubitationem quaesivisse" (AT 7:32).

12. Quoted by Karsten Harries, in "Metaphor and Transcendence," *Critical Inquiry* 5.1 (1978): 73–90; 82. And while Harries would temper his Nietzschean reading of the *cogito* by arguing that Valéry "misreads Descartes" by insisting on this radical isolation of the self, and by forgetting how Descartes will quickly

parlay the *cogito* into a reconciliation with the universal, he uses this misreading to suggest that Valéry's Descartes is "the precursor of the modern poet" in "his insistence to be the author of his own thoughts, his refusal to owe anything to the world, to others, and to God, a will to power that refuses to acknowledge its own final impotence" (83). This interpretation neatly resembles Cavell's comments on the absolutism of the lyric poet.

13. CSM 2:39–40; AT 7:56–57.

14. William Dilthey, in *Weltanschauung und Analyse des Menschen seit Renaissance und Reformation*, makes a strong case for the central role that the Stoic conception of the will play in Renaissance philosophical thought and beyond. See *Gesammelte Schriften* (Stuttgart: B. G. Teubner, 1957), esp. 2:14–18; see also *Discours de la Méthode*, ed. Etienne Gilson (Paris: Vrin, 1925), 130–131, 226, 231–233, 246–254.

15. In particular, I am thinking of Nicholas of Cusa's notion of *docta ignorantia*, which yields the strategy of accommodation between an individual's limited ability to know God and the transcendent meaning of the divine object itself. But Montaigne's *Apologie de Raymond Sebond* is also relevant here.

16. CSM 2:39.

17. Gueroult, xviii.

18. Gueroult, 18.

19. Gueroult, 20.

20. Gueroult, 20–21, 19, 19. Gueroult argues for the word "opinion" because, as of this stage in Descartes' analysis, there is no certain knowledge — not of God's existence, nor his omnipotence, nor his goodness or his willingness or unwillingness to play the deceiver or allow a deceiver to exist.

21. Gueroult, 19.

22. Lezra, 134. See also his two chapters devoted to *Don Quixote*, 135–256.

23. CSM 1:4; AT 10:217.

24. Norman Kemp Smith, *New Studies in the Philosophy of Descartes* (London: Macmillan, 1966), 7.

25. See Roger Ariew, "The *Meditations*, *Objections*, and *Replies*," in *The Blackwell Guide to Descartes' Meditations*, 6–16; Jean-Luc Marion, "The Place of the *Objections* in the Developement of Cartesian Metaphysics," in *Descartes and his Contemporaries: Meditations, Objections, and Replies*, ed. Roger Ariew and Marjorie Grene (Chicago: University of Chicago Press, 1995), 7–20; Jean-Marie Beyssade, "Méditer, objecter, répondre," *Descartes: Objecter et répondre*, ed. Jean-Marie Beyssade and Jean-Luc Marion (Paris: PUP, 1994), 21–38. Summing up his argument, Ariew writes: "All in all, Descartes' bloc of certainty [an allusion

to Gueroult's "internal, non-developmental" reading of the *Meditations*] looks more like a sedimentary rock; that is, a geological stratum with cracks and fissures, able to be read in historical terms" (14).

26. See Popkin, 205–207. The curtness of his replies to Hobbes, especially concerning the unexamined status of the language in the *Meditations*, is indicative of what I have been calling, perhaps too baldly, Descartes' solipsism.

27. Reiss, in *Mirages of the Selfe*, defines "passage technique" as "a philosophical — or other — means to get from one way of thinking about things to another, using, reordering elements present in that earlier way to respond to new exigencies of context and practice; a means, not an end. A passage technique is not a 'working theory.' Acting as a *bridge* to get from *a* to *b*, it offers no hypothesis about *b*. Rather does it offer a liberating context in which it is eventually possible to formulate such hypotheses" (469–470).

28. CSM 2:16. See Rule Sixteen in the *Regulae* (CSM 1:66–70).

29. Thus Russell's insight, repeated and amplified by Ayer, that *je pense donc je suis* assumes a thinking subject, whereas Descartes' reasoning only proves that thought and not the individual exists.

30. CSM 2:46.

31. "Literature . . . utilizes postulated beginnings and principles of coherence, most clearly illustrated by geometry, as consistently as rhetoric and philosophy. In each case, the self-consistency of mathematical demonstration lends, like a common denominator, its structural stability and coherence to rhetorical, philosophical, and literary arguments . . . The solution of a 'question' — philosophical or rhetorical or both — by means of a fiction, 'posited' like the *archai* of a geometrical proof, suggests the ways in which formal, cognitive, and judicative hypotheses combine their energies in the literary hypothesis of fiction." Wesley Trimpi, *Muses of One Mind: The Literary Analysis of Experience and Its Continuity* (Princeton: Princeton University Press, 1983), 28, 30. For a different perspective on how Descartes mined the resources of his humanist education to pursue mathematical and philosophic aims, see Matthew L. Jones, *The Good Life in the Scientific Revolution: Descartes, Pascal, Leibniz and the Cultivation of Virtue* (Chicago: University of Chicago Press, 2006).

32. Hans Blumenberg, *The Genesis of the Copernican World*, tr. Robert M. Wallace (Cambridge: The MIT Press, 1987), 313–314.

33. See Descartes' letters to Beeckman, 1628–1629 (AT 10:335–346). Francesco Barozzi's *Admirandum illud geometricum problemata tredecim modis demonstratum* [That Wonderful Geometrical Proposition with Thirty Demonstrations] (Venice, 1586) explores how a hyperbolic curve and asymptote (two nonparallel,

infinite lines) can lie on the same plane and never meet in order to show larger truths about the validity of mathematical reasoning in the face of an apparent physical impossibility. Girard Desargues' pamphlet *Brouillon project d'un atteinte aux evenmens des rencontres du Cone avec un plan*, [Rough Draft of an Essay on the Results of Taking Plane Sections of a Cone] (Paris, 1639) is considered by many the beginning of the modern study of projective geometry, a branch of geometry that has its origins in the study of perspective by Renaissance painters. He glosses the word hyperbola as "outrepassement ou excedement." Pascal's *Essay pour les coniques* (Paris, 1639), a response to Desargues, consists of several theorems accompanied by only the briefest suggestions as to how they should be proved. For Pascal, the various conic sections have no hierarchy of importance; they are simply images of one another. Accordingly, the hyperbola may be extended infinitely in space, thus creating "two infinite spaces" even though it is generated by a finite figure. Blaise Pascal, *Essai pour les coniques*, in *Œuvres complètes*, ed. Jean Mesnard (Paris: Desclée De Brouwer, 1970), 2.220–235. He also later composed a longer *Traité des coniques*, which has only been partially reconstructed from notes that Leibniz took from it in 1676.

34. Explaining to Gassendi how the suspension of judgment in hyperbolic doubt is an act of will, Descartes offers this metaphor: "in order to straighten out a curved stick, we [bend] it round in the opposite direction" (CSM 2:242).

35. Quoted in Fernand Hallyn, *The Poetic Structure of the World: Copernicus and Kepler* (New York: Zone Books, 1993), 225. Hallyn places Mersenne's exploration of the figurative value of geometry in the context of related observations by Pascal, Tesauro, Kepler, and Galileo.

36. Transforming himself into a latter day Mersenne, Jacques Lacan famously figures the Imaginary as the asymptote that the hyperbolic subject forever approaches but never reaches.

37. See the *Préface* to *Les principes de la philosophie*, AT 9.2:1–20.

38. CSM 2:50.

39. There the verb "imaginabor" is repeated twice in the same passage that discounts the knowledge produced by the imagination (AT 7:27–28).

40. CSM 2:50; AT 7:72. For an extensive discussion of this distinction and the Cartesian imagination more generally, see Dennis L. Sepper, *Descartes's Imagination: Proportion, Images, and the Activity of Thinking* (Berkeley: University of California Press, 1996), esp. 239–284.

41. CSM 2:51. This prefigures Kant's interpretation of the two faculties in the third *Critique*.

42. CSM 2:55; CSM 2:57; CSM 2:58; AT 7:84.

43. Or, as Foucault describes this epistemic "discontinuity" in *The Order of Things*: "At the beginning of the seventeenth century, during that period that has been termed, rightly or wrongly, the Baroque, thought ceases to move in the element of resemblance. Similitude is no longer the form of knowledge but rather the occasion of error . . ." (51).

44. CSM 2:59; AT 7:85.

45. CSM 2:61; AT 7:89; AT 9.1:71–72. See also AT 7:226 where Descartes outlines the structure of all six meditations and reveals that the cornerstone is indeed hyperbole: "Sed, quia inter hyperbolicas illas dubitationes, quas in prima Meditatione proposui, una eousque processit ut de hoc ipso . . . certus esse non possem, quandiu authorem meae originis ignorare me supponebam, idcirco omnia quae de Deo & de veritate in tertia, quarta & quinta Meditatione scripsi, conferunt ad conclusionem de reali *mentis* a *corpore* distinctione, quam demum in sexta Meditatione perfeci."

46. "Et certe cum nullam occasionem habeam existimandi aliquem Deum esse deceptorem, nec quidem adhuc satis sciam utrum sit aliquis Deus, valde tenuis & ita loquar, Metaphysica dubitandi ratio est, quae tantum ex ea opinione dependet" (AT 7:36). But see also AT 10:513 and AT 7.172: ". . . partim etiam ut ostenderem quam firmae sint veritates quas postea propono, quandoquidem ab istis Metaphysicis dubitationibus labefactari non possunt."

47. CSM 2:372–373; AT 7:546. As Alquié notes, "est l'un des rares [passages] où Descartes justifie le caractère hyperbolique de son doute par la nécessité de combattre le scepticisme" (2:1060n).

48. Bourdin writes: "Ars illa peccat excessu. Hoc est, plus molitur quam ab ea prudentiae leges exigant, plus quam ab ea quisquam mortalium deposcat" (AT 7:547).

49. CSM 2:375; AT 7:549.

50. Jean de Sponde, *D'amour et de mort* (Giromagny: Orphée, 1989), 39.

51. Cavell, "The Avoidance of Love," 107.

52. Cavell, Introduction, *Disowning Knowledge*, 18.

53. Descartes scathingly responded with the so-called *Letter to Voetius* (AT 8.2:41). For more on this controversy, see Stephen Gaukroger, *Descartes: An Intellectual Biography* (Oxford: Oxford University Press, 1995).

54. Popkin, 210. Popkin refers to the Objectiones septimae (AT 7:473–477); Objectiones tertiae (AT 7:171–172); *Letter to Dinet* (AT 7:573–574); *Comments on a Certain Broadsheet Published in Belgium* (AT 8.2:367–368).

55. Popkin writes: ". . . it was precisely in the movement from subjective certainty to objective truth that Descartes and his philosophy, as well as Calvin and

Calvinism, met their most serious opposition, opposition that was to change the Cartesian triumph into tragedy. The enemies fought to show that though a truth might have been found, the heroic effort of Descartes was either no effort at all, or was a complete failure, leaving the *crise pyrrhonienne* unsolved and insoluble at the base of all of modern philosophy" (192).

56. Jacques Derrida, "Cogito and the History of Madness," *Writing and Difference*, tr. Alan Bass (Chicago: University of Chicago Press, 1978), 31–63; "Cogito et histoire de la folie," *L'écriture et la différence* (Paris: Éditions du seuil, 1967), 51–97.

57. Shoshana Felman, *Writing and Madness (Literature/ Philosophy /Psychoanalysis)*, tr. Martha Noel Evans and the author with the assistance of Brian Massumi (Ithaca: Cornell University Press, 1985), 35–55.

58. Michel Foucault, *Historie de la Folie* (Paris: Gallimard, 1972), 56–59. See also Foucault's stinging response to Derrida's critique in this edition, Appendice II: "Mon corps, ce papier, ce feu" (583–603). Mining Descartes' text for evidence, Foucault rejects Derrida's claim that Descartes' dream-argument hyperbolizes the madness-argument; instead, they are "à la fois parallèles et différents" (589), or chiasmic rather than logically dependent (594). In brief, Foucault refuses to ascribe to the *cogito* the "folie totale" (601) that Derrida discovers there.

59. Rejecting Socrates' and thereby also Foucault's attempts to make madness the "contrary" of reason, Derrida also challenges the latter's conception of a historical event because of its metaphysical presumptions: "The attempt to write the history of the decision, division, difference runs the risk of construing the division as an event or a structure subsequent to the unity of an original presence, thereby confirming metaphysics in its fundamental operation" ("Cogito and the History of Madness," 40). But as Felman notes: "Foucault, of course, was fully aware of the impossibility of his task" (44).

60. "Cogito and the History of Madness," 48, 46, 50–52.

61. Felman, 48.

62. Jacques Derrida, "White Mythology: Metaphor in the Text of Philosophy," *Margins of Philosophy*, tr. Alan Bass (Chicago: University of Chicago Press, 1982), 243–254.

63. "White Mythology," 268. The "abyss" here is specifically Cartesian as Derrida is quoting Descartes "Entretien avec Burman": ". . . And as for the cataracts of the abyss, this is a metaphor, but this metaphor escapes us."

64. "White Mythology," 266–267.

65. As Derrida writes: "By virtue of what we might entitle . . . tropic supplementarity, since the extra turn of speech becomes the missing turn of speech,

the taxonomy or history of philosophical metaphors will never make a profit . . . The field is never saturated" ("White Mythology," 220).

66. "Cogito and the History of Madness," 48.

67. "Cogito and the History of Madness," 53. Gueroult is cited on 223, though Derrida mentions no specific work.

68. "Cogito and the History of Madness," 54.

69. "Cogito and the History of Madness," 54.

70. "Cogito and the History of Madness," 55. Derrida is playing on Foucault's chapter title "Le grand renfermement."

71. Later in the essay Derrida writes that Descartes' "system of certainty" and all that it has come to represent, would "inspect, master, and limit hyperbole" (59). For it uses axioms exempt from doubt — such as the natural light of reason, the notion that the effect must have at least as much reality as the cause — to moderate the "extremity of hyperbole" after it has achieved its goals (60). Further, he discovers this same dialectic in the Augustinian and Husserlian *cogito* (60). In sum, any account of the history or structure of Western thought must be punctuated by those crises of reason marked by the eruption of hyperbole.

72. "Cogito and the History of Madness," 56.

73. H. G. Liddell and Robert Scott, *A Greek-English Lexikon* (Oxford: Clarendon Press, 1996), 132.

74. "Cogito and the History of Madness," 56.

75. "Cogito and the History of Madness," 56.

76. "Cogito and the History of Madness," 56. Intriguingly, given my comments on Descartes's *superbia*, in subsequent comments Derrida subordinates the hubris of the philosopher to this world-denying "demonic hyperbole."

77. "Cogito et histoire de la folie," 88; "Cogito and the History of Madness," 57.

78. "Cogito et histoire de la folie," 96; "Cogito and the History of Madness," 62.

79. I take my cue here from Felman: "Metaphor, pathos, fiction: without being named, it is *literature* which has surreptitiously entered the debate. The discussion about madness and its relation to philosophy has thus indirectly led us to the significant question of literature; and the way in which madness displaces, blocks, and opens up questions seems to point to the particular nature of the relationship between literature and philosophy" (47).

80. "Cogito and the History of Madness," 61.

CHAPTER FOURTEEN: BETWEEN RHETORIC AND GEOMETRY:

1. Blaise Pascal, *Pensées*, ed. Philippe Sellier (Paris: Bordas, 1991). All citations of the *Pensées* in the main text are indicated by Sellier's numbering. All
English translations are from *Pensées*, tr. Roger Ariew (Indianapolis: Hackett,
2005). For a fine recent biography of Pascal, see Jacques Attali, *Blaise Pascal, ou,
le génie français* (Paris: Fayard, 2000).

2. Patricia Topliss, *The Rhetoric of Pascal* (Leicester: Leicester University Press,
1966), 288. Commenting on Pascal's *Provinciales*, Topliss writes: "In the fire of
his impassioned eloquence, scorn, indignation, anger and the *libido dominandi* impose on his language their customary distortions. Thus he lapses into *hyperbole*.
This figure has an obvious affinity with the trenchant imperiousness of his nature
and his dramatic sense of the importance of the issues he habitually discusses;
none is more characteristic of the style he adopts whenever he sets out to persuade,
be it in the role of correspondent, disputant or apologist. In the polemics of the
Provinciales, where objectivity is not to be looked for, his exaggerations are less unfortunate than they are . . . in the *Pensées*" (117).

3. Topliss, 290.

4. Topliss, 290.

5. Of course, strictly speaking, the third office for Cicero is *movere*. Pascal
would have also been familiar with these offices from Augustine's *De doctrina
Christiana*, 4.12.27. As for hyperbole, Sellier observes in 1991: "L'écriture pascalienne demeure aujourd'hui encore mal connue. Nous manquons le plus souvent à la fois de monographies sur ses caractéristiques les plus voyantes (le
fragment ou l'hyperbole, par exemple) et de vues synthétiques . . ." (60). More
provocatively, Sellier adds: "L'hyperbole, déjà souveraine dans les *Provinciales*, ne
frappe pas moins dans les *Pensées* . . . Cette seule figure mériterait toute une
étude . . . Bien plus, aucun écrivain français, semble t-il, n'a recouru à cette figure
avec autant de constance et d'efficacité." This and the following chapter aim to
remedy the absence of such an "étude" (71–72).

6. Stéphane Natan, *Les* Pensées *de Pascal. D'un projet apologétique à un texte poétique* (Paris: Connaissance et savoirs, 2004). See esp. his section on "Le style hyperbolique" (321–343), where he describes how hyperbole variously effects "une
globalisation totale," "surenchérissement," and "la négation exceptive." He divides his broader analysis of Pascal's rhetoric into three sections: *la rhétorique du la
clarté* (114–232), *la rhétorique du martèlement* (233–289), and *la rhétorique du la force*
(290–406).

7. His polemic continues later in the *pensée*: "Rien ne fait mieux entendre combien un faux sonnet est ridicule que d'en considérer la nature et le modèle, et de s'imaginer ensuite une femme ou une maison faite sur ce modèle-là ... On ne passe point dans le monde pour se connaître en vers si l'on n'a mis l'enseigne de poète, de mathématicien, etc. Mais les gens universels ne veulent point d'enseigne, et ne mettent guère de différence entre le métier de poète et celui de brodeur."

8. Consider, for example, the opening quatrain of Tristan's "Les cheveux blonds": "Fin or, de qui le prix est sans comparaison, / Clair rayons d'un soleil, douce et subtile trame / Dont la molle étendue a des ondes de flamme / Où l'Amour mille fois a noyé ma raison ..."

9. This *pensée* also treats Descartes' *Meditations* and his "démon méchant" as exemplary of the "pyrrhoniens."

10. Similarly, though without the semantic play on "face," in #228 he writes: "Rien ne montre mieux la vanité des hommes que de considérer quelle cause et quels effets de l'amour, car tout l'univers en est changé. La nez de Cléopâtre." Other examples of epigrammatic, hyperbolic *pensées* include: #102, #78, #33.

11. For more on Pascal's views of "eloquence" see also #481 and #485.

12. Sellier, 72.

13. Michel de Certeau, *The Mystic Fable. Volume One: The Sixteenth and Seventeenth Centuries*, tr. Michael B. Smith (Chicago: University of Chicago Press, 1992). His analysis (29–72) of how the tension between the desire for "rapture"' and the pleasures of "rhetoric" shaped early modern mysticism nicely corresponds to what I will call the apophatic and cataphatic tendencies in Pascal.

14. Pascal's so-called *nuit de feu* refers to the moment of his final conversion to Jansenism, November 23–24, 1654, the ardor of which is recorded in the "Mémorial" (#742), a document found sown into his clothes at the time of his death ("Joie, joie, joie, pleurs de joie ... Mon Dieu, me quitterez vous?"). See Topliss (136–151) on other "psychological" seventeenth-century apologies.

15. Blaise Pascal, "De l'esprit géométrique," in *Œuvres complètes*, ed. Jean Mesnard (Paris: Desclée de Brouwer, 1964–1992), 3:390–428. *De l'esprit géométrique* consists of two manuscript fragments entitled *Réflexions sur la géométrie en général* and *De l'art de persuader*. See Mesnard's introduction to *De l'esprit géométrique*, 3:360–389, for a commentary and comprehensive discussion of textual and chronological issues.

16. *De l'esprit géométrique*, 3:391, 400, 402.

17. *De l'esprit géométrique*, 3:410, 411, 393. To experience these infinities, he urges readers to avail themselves of telescopes, microscopes, and to undertake an experiment, taken from Cartesian optics, which demonstrates how a receding boat seen through a lens ("un verre") will never seem to reach the vanishing point.

18. *De l'esprit géométrique*, 3:413. Later Pascal writes of "un balancement douteux entre la vérité et la volupté," that is, between the objects proper to these two faculties.

19. *De l'esprit géométrique*, 3:413, 416.

20. *De l'esprit géométrique*, 3:414.

21. *De l'esprit géométrique*, 3:416–417.

22. Compare "la manière d'agréer" here with "l'agrément, qui est l'objet de la poésie," which he dismisses in #486. Nicholas Hammond regards this passage as crucial to an understanding the trajectory of Pascal's intellectual career: "Although Pascal felt incapable of defining rules for such an art in *De l'esprit géométrique*, I contend that the *Pensées* represent a different attempt to understand this other aspect of persuasion, through his use and analysis of language. The complexity of achieving this aim is reflected in the *Pensées* in the multiplicity of voices and the fragmentation and constant preoccupation with the diverse meanings of words . . ." *Playing with Truth: Language and the Human Condition in Pascal's* Pensées (Oxford: Clarendon Press, 1994), 17.

23. *De l'esprit géométrique*, 3:413. Likewise, a bit further on, Pascal writes: "Je ne parle donc que des vérités de notre portée . . ." (3:414). In part this is because God, in order "humilier cette superbe puissance du raisonnement" has made his truths accessible to the "heart" and not to the "mind" (3:413).

24. *De l'esprit géométrique*, 3:418.

25. See Paul de Man, "Pascal's Allegory of Persuasion," *Aesthetic Ideology* (Minneapolis: University of Minnesota Press, 1996), 51–69. After establishing the "heterogeneous" and "nameless" quality of zero in *De l'esprit géométrique* (59), de Man turns to the *Pensées* and compares Pascal's difficulties in defining zero with the figure of irony, a "term not susceptible to nominal or real definition." Thus he suggests that the "order of figure and the order of reality are really heterogeneous."

26. *De l'esprit géométrique*, 3:421.

27. *De l'esprit géométrique*, 3:418.

28. *De l'esprit géométrique*, 3:424.

29. Thomas Parker, in *Volition, Rhetoric, and Emotion in the Work of Pascal* (London: Routledge, 2008), writes: "Pascal's explanation of effective rhetorical language corresponds to his theories of knowledge. Some discourses are designed

to convince the rational mind, while others transcend reason to please the heart and impart wisdom to the soul. Pascal shows how the adversary's will must be taken into consideration when one undertakes to convince him or her of a proposition" (5).

30. *De l'esprit géométrique*, 3:427–428. Mesnard (3:427) hears in these last paragraphs echoes of Montaigne's "De l'experience."

31. This road is lexical as well as conceptual. For example, "s'abaisser" anticipates "forcé à s'abaisser" in "Disproportion de l'homme" and the infamous "vous abêtira" in "Le pari" (#681).

32. *Playing with Truth*, 17.

33. *Descartes and the Resilience of Rhetoric*, 81–82.

34. Quoted in Sellier, 61. Sellier discovers eight "techniques" structuring Pascal's rhetoric of *force*: 1) "la recherche du discontinu et de la cassure" 2) "privilégier une panoplie de figures que la plupart des théoriciens du temps dénonçaient comme excessives" 3) "l'imitation originale des prophètes d'Israël" 4) "l'usage de la citation comme coup de fouet ou coup de massue" 5) "le réglage du rire" 6) "la mathématisation des images et des arguments" 7) novel application of *dispositio* and 8) *memoria*.

35. By "Baroque" I mean more than the primarily stylistic traits ably traced, for example, by Sister Mary Maggioni in *The 'Pensées' of Pascal: A Study in Baroque Style* (Washington: The Catholic University of America Press, 1950). Specifically, I have in mind how Jean Rousset makes Bernini's aesthetic a model for evaluating Baroque literature and thought in France. Distilling this aesthetic into four essential elements — instability, mobility, metamorphosis, and the prevalence of ornament — Rousset discovers in the *Pensées* many of these same elements he finds in the poetry of Sponde, d'Aubigné, Théophile, Saint Amant, Crashaw, Quevedo, and Marino. Conceding that Pascal undoubtedly would have despised Bernini's art, Rousset, nonetheless, uses Bernini's observation, "man never resembles himself better than when he is in movement," to epitomize Pascal's philosophy. Jean Rousset, *La littérature de l'âge baroque en France: Circe et Paon* (Paris: José Corti, 1954), 141.

36. Sara Melzer, *Discourses of the Fall: A Study of Pascal's* Pensées (Berkeley: University of California Press, 1986), 4. She adds: "Pascal's notion of an epistemological fall from truth into language generates an aporia, two irreconcilable interpretations, within his text" (3).

37. In *L'ordre du cœur: la théologie et mystique dans les* Pensées de Pascal (Paris: Honoré Champion, 1996), Hélène Michon notes that given our fallen state and thus fallen language, "la figure fonctionne comme le contrepoint de la vérité"

(167). Figures in the Old Testament (see #11) are only redeemed by the advent of Christ (see #8).

38. For the many textual and editorial issues that concern the *Pensées*, see Pol Ernst, *Les* Pensées *de Pascal, géologie et stratigraphie* (Paris: Universitas; Oxford: Voltaire Foundation, 1996); Jean Mesnard, *Les* Pensées *de Pascal*, revised edition (Paris: SEDES, 1993); Anthony Pugh, *The Composition of Pascal's Apologia* (Toronto: University of Toronto Press, 1984).

39. See Topliss for a thorough analysis of Pascal's rhetoric in these epistles.

40. Friedrich Nietzsche, *Ecce Homo*, in *Kritische Studienausgabe*, ed. Giorgio Colli and Mazzino Montinari (Munich: DTV, 1988), 6:285.

41. In "Variation sur une pensée," in *Œuvres* (Paris: Gallimard, 1957), Valéry offers a vivid, scathing psychological portrait of Pascal and his religious logic, which he sees as imbued with a strong current of self-hate and fear: "Le cœur finit presque toujours, dans sa lutte contre la figure effrayante du monde, par susciter, à force de désir, l'idée de quelque Être assez puissant pour contenir, pour avoir construit, ou pour émettre, ce monstre d'étendue et de rayonnements qui nous produit, qui nous alimente, qui nous enferme, qui nous menace, qui nous fascine, qui nous intrigue et nous dévore. Et cet Être, ce sera même une Personne, c'est-à-dire qu'il y aura quelque ressemblance entre lui et nous, et je ne sais quel espoir d'une entente indéfinissable. Voilà ce que le cœur *trouve*. Il tend à se répondre par un dieu" (470).

42. Sellier, 53. See also Sellier, *Pascal et saint Augustin* (Paris: Armand Colin, 1970).

43. See Sellier, 46–47.

44. Stanley Cavell, "Philosophy and the Arrogation of the Voice," in *A Pitch of Philosophy: Autobiographical Exercises* (Cambridge: Harvard University Press, 1994), 3.

45. Hammond calls the primary speaker in the *Pensées* the "dialectician" (8).

46. By "dogmatists" Pascal generally means the Neo-Stoics and Neo-Epicureans.

47. See #669 where *extravaguer* is also employed.

48. For a fine analysis examining the subtleties of imperative rhetoric in the *Pensées*, see Gilles Magniont, *Traces de la voix Pascalienne. Examen des marques de l'énonciation dans les* Pensées (Lyon: Presses universitaires de Lyon, 2003), 95–121.

49. As Melzer puts it: "As long as one is limited to one of these two orders, one is locked within the hermeneutic circle" (46).

50. Sellier, borrowing from the anthropologist Gilbert Durand, praises the "diurnal (or heroic) regime" of Pascal's imagination whereby imagery of the fall,

darkness, and death is countered by those of combat, ascension, and eternal illu-mination (63).

51. Gérard Bras and Jean-Pierre Cléro, *Pascal: Figures de l'imagination* (Paris: PUF, 1994).

52. *Pascal: Figures de l'imagination*, 36–37.

53. See #679. Pascal also refers to the "l'esprit de finesse" by the synonym "l'esprit de justesse."

54. The *pensée* is entitled: "Différence entre l'esprit de géométrie et l'esprit de finesse"; see also #671.

55. See among other *pensées* #19, #31, and #149.

56. See, for instance, *De doctrina Christiana*, 2.6.7–8. For Augustine's perva-sive influence in seventeenth-century France, see Fumaroli, *L'âge de l'éloquence*, esp. 70–76.

57. Augustine, *On Christian Doctrine*, tr. D. W. Robertson (New York: Macmillan, 1958), (1.6.6), 10–11. The English translation necessarily loses much of Augustine's remarkable wordplay in the face of the ineffable. See *De doctrina Christiana*, in *Sancti Aurelli Augustini Opera: Corpus Christianorum*, vol. 32 (Turnhout, Belgium: Brepols, 1962), 9–10.

58. See Jean Mesnard, "La théorie des figuratifs chez Pascal," *Revue d'His-toire de la Philosophie et d'Histoire générale* 35 (1943): 219–259; Erec R. Koch, *Pascal and Rhetoric: Figural and Persuasive Language in the Scientific Treatises, the* Provinciales, *and the* Pensées (Charlottesville: Rockwood Press, 1997). Koch, taking a largely de Manian approach, focuses on "tropes as agents of semantic displacement" such that neither a positivist (Edouard Morot-Sir) nor a negative theological ap-proach (Sara Melzer) to a reading of Pascal's figures can be said to produce sta-ble meaning (xx). For her part, Melzer stresses the influence of another member of Port-Royal, the Augustinian Martin de Barcos, on Pascal: "Barcos and Pascal put obscurity and distance at the center of their linguistic theory" (27). To think otherwise, she notes, was to be guilty of *superbia*. And yet this stance has its theo-logical advantages as well: ". . . precisely because language is uncontrollably fig-urative, it opens up the possibility of slipping past human meaning and of turning toward Redemption" (30).

59. In "Variation sur une pensée," Valéry writes: "Elle [Pascal's intellect] se ressent, elle se peint, et se lamente, comme une bête traquée; mais de plus, qui se traque elle-même, et qui excite les grandes ressources qui sont en elle, les puis-sances de sa logique, les vertus admirable de sa langage, à corrompre tout ce qui est visible et qui n'est point desolant" (461).

60. For Pascal as a negative theologian, see Michon (139–172; 241–356);

Dawn M. Ludwin, *Blaise Pascal's Quest for the Ineffable* (New York: Peter Lang, 2001). For a general, but still rigorous treatment of Pascal's religious beliefs, see Jean Mesnard, *Pascal* (Paris: Desclée de Brouwer, 1965). A thorough treatment of Pascal's Jansenism and the question of grace is Jan Miel, *Pascal and Theology* (Baltimore: The Johns Hopkins University Press, 1969). Finally, there is Lucien Goldmann's idiosyncratic, Marxist take on Jansenism in *Le Dieu cachée: Étude sur la vision tragique dans les* Pensées *de Pascal et dans le théatre de Racine* (Paris: Gallimard, 1955).

61. Michon argues that Pascal envisions a "Dieu caché" as a means for our salvation (327); see also Bernard Grasset, *Les* Pensées *de Pascal, une interprétation de l'écriture* (Paris: Kimé, 2003), 121–157.

62. Michon, 158–160.

63. See also #182.

64. Ludwin, 24. Ludwin's use of Dionysius to read Pascal challenges the critical commonplace that Augustine was the main theological-mystical influence on Pascal. (Pascal cites Dionysius just once in the *Pensées*: "Denys a la charité, il était en place" (#629).) Ludwin acknowledges the paucity of textual evidence showing that Pascal was directly influenced by Dionysius' writings. Michon, by contrast, reads Pascal's mysticism mainly in light of Aquinas and Karl Barth.

65. Denys Turner, *The Darkness of God: Negativity in Christian Mysticism* (Cambridge: Cambridge University Press, 1995), 20.

66. Turner, 32. Or put another way: ". . . the sheer crassness of the signs is a goad so that even the materially inclined cannot accept that it could be permitted or true that the celestial and divine sights could be conveyed by such shameful things" (25).

67. Pseudo-Dionysius, *The Divine Names*, in *The Complete Works*, tr. Colm Luibheid (New York: Paulist Press, 1987), 54.

68. *The Divine Names*, 54, 54.

69. *The Divine Names*, 56–57.

70. "Given that the Good transcends everything . . . its nature, unconfined by form, is the creator of all form. In it nonbeing is really an excess of being. It is not *a* life, but is, rather, superabundant Life. It is not *a* mind, but is superabundant wisdom" (73). Augustine, in *De doctrina Christiana* (4.19.38), urges the "grand style" if an orator is trying to convert adverse minds or if he is praising God, although he notes that such praise will always be lacking.

71. Ludwin, 58.

72. Ludwin, 98. For a thorough consideration of religious hyperbole as a form of excess without the traditional frames of apophasis and cataphasis, see

Stephen J. Webb *Blessed Excess: Religion and the Hyperbolic Imagination* (Albany: SUNY Press, 1993). Webb reads hyperbole as crucial to the religious imagination in the face of still-lingering Enlightenment prejudices: "As religion has withered away in modern Western culture, so has hyperbole, and the demise of hyperbole goes pretty far in explaining the demise of religion . . . I want to affirm that religion today is exaggeration, an excess that is a surplus, supererogatory, something that inefficiently exceeds the cautious boundaries of the utilitarian mentality, the rational, the expected" (xii–xiii).

73. The phrase is Ludwin's (56).

74. But Ludwin, after considering Pascal's excessive nominalism as a form of apophasis (though technically it also participates in cataphasis), considers paradox as his second main apophatic strategy. Unfortunately, Ludwin's reading of hyperbole largely ignores Pascal's own writings and focuses instead on how the "grotesque" is cultivated in a series of letters by his sister describing in horrific detail how his niece's infected eye was cured in the "Miracle of the Holy Thorn."

75. See Jacques Derrida, "How to Avoid Speaking: Denials," "Post Scriptum: Aporias, Ways and Voices," in *Derrida and Negative Theology*," ed. Harold Coward and Toby Foshay (Albany: SUNY Press, 1992), 73–142, 283–323. Derrida later amplifies "Post-Scriptum" as *Sauf le nom* (Paris: Galilée, 1993). Although I shall be discussing only Marion's *In Excess: Studies of Saturated Phenomena*, tr. Robyn Horner and Vincent Berraud (New York: Fordham University Press, 2002), see also his "In the Name: How to Avoid Speaking of Negative Theology," in *God, The Gift, and Postmodernism*, ed. John D. Caputo and Michael J. Scanlon (Bloomington: Indiana University Press, 1999), 20–42, with a response by Derrida (42–53), but also in the same volume, Caputo's "Apostles of the Impossible: On God and The Gift in Derrida and Marion," 185–223.

76. "How to Avoid Speaking: Denials," 76.

77. "How to Avoid Speaking: Denials," 77. Marion will object strongly to Derrida's apparent reification of the *hyperousia*. Later in the essay, it seems that Derrida presents the "secret" as an alternative to hyper-essentiality, thus his "digression" on the secret and his extravagant claim: "To keep something to oneself is the most incredible and thought-provoking power" (87). Derrida will subsequently devote considerable energy to (re)thinking the secret; see, for example, Jacques Derrida and Maurizio Ferraris, *A Taste for the Secret*, tr. Giacomo Donis (Cambridge, England: Polity Press, 2001).

78. "How to Avoid Speaking: Denials," 78.

79. "How to Avoid Speaking: Denials," 80–81, 81. He picks up the Wittgensteinian thread on p. 99.

80. "How to Avoid Speaking: Denials," 91.

81. "How to Avoid Speaking: Denials," 101–102.

82. "How to Avoid Speaking: Denials," 102.

83. "How to Avoid Speaking: Denials," 110.

84. "How to Avoid Speaking: Denials," 130.

85. "Post-Scriptum," 287, 294–295, 298, 300.

86. *The Darkness of God*, 39.

87. *The Mystical Theology*, in *The Complete Works*, 135.

88. "Post-Scriptum," 290, 304.

89. "Post-Scriptum," 306.

90. See my diagram of *the quantity of expressibility* in the Introduction. My hyperbole is also in response to Derrida's: "Negative theology, we have said this enough, is also the most economical and most powerful formalization, the greatest reserve of language possible in so few words. Inexhaustible literature, literature for the desert, for the exile, always saying too much and too little, it holds desire in suspense" (321–322).

91. See "Post-Scriptum," 320.

92. *In Excess*, xxi. See also *Reduction and Givenness: Investigations of Husserl, Heidegger, and Phenomenology*, tr. Thomas A. Carlson (Evanston: Northwestern University Press, 1998); *Being Given: Toward a Phenomenology of Givenness*, tr. Jeffrey L. Kosky (Stanford: Stanford University Press, 2002). For a recent appraisal of Marion's theology, see Robyn Horner, *Jean-Luc Marion: A Theo-logical Introduction* (Burlington VT: Ashgate, 2005).

93. Translator's Introduction, *In Excess*, xv.

94. *In Excess*, 17–18.

95. As the Translator's Introduction phrases it: "Now, the striking thing about *In Excess* is that its phenomenological analyses are riddled with *différance* even where it is not so named" (xiv).

96. *In Excess*, 33; *Post-Scriptum*, 305.

97. *In Excess*, 139.

98. *In Excess*, 139.

99. *In Excess*, 141. See Kevin Hart, *The Trespass of the Sign: Deconstruction, Theology and Philosophy*, 2nd ed. (New York: Fordham University Press, 2000).

100. *In Excess*, 132.

101. *In Excess*, 132.

102. *In Excess*, 139.

103. *The Divine Names*, 80.

CHAPTER FIFTEEN: DISPROPORTION AND TASTE

1. Derrida does mention Pascal once: "Pascal, in whom one could at times discern the genius or the machine of apophatic dialectics," but otherwise in the two essays discussed in the previous chapter he passes over the *Pensées* in silence" ("Post-Scriptum," 312).

2. G. W. Leibniz, "Double infinité chez Pascal et monade," *Textes inédits*, ed. Gaston Grua (Paris: PUP, 1948), 2:553.

3. For Senecan parallels with "Disproportion de l'homme" see *Naturales quaestiones* (1. Pr. 8–11) and *Epistles* (88.13).

4. Michon argues that Pascal replaces the scholastic *analogia entis* with an "*analogia caritatis*," which appeals to the *ordre du cœur* (344). Thus to be interpreted hyperbole requires Augustinian charity.

5. See Magniont's analysis of "l'exhortation indirecte" in *Traces de la voix Pascalienne*, 103–106.

6. Perhaps, "idée" should be taken also in its etymological sense of a "thing seen."

7. J. L. Borges, "Pascal's Sphere," in *Borges: A Reader*, ed. E. R. Monegal and Alastair Reid (New York: E. P. Dutton, 1981), 240. Borges, though, also offers a historicist and psychological interpretation: "In that jaded century the absolute space that inspired the hexameters of Lucretius, the absolute space that had been a liberation for Bruno, was a labyrinth and abyss for Pascal. He hated the universe, and yearned to adore God. But God was less real to him than the hated universe" (241). See also Karsten Harries, "The Infinite Sphere: Comments on a History of a Metaphor," *Journal of the History of Philosophy* 13.1 (1975): 5–15.

8. See #195–196 for other uses of the "cachot" image.

9. See Morris Croll, *Style, Rhetoric, and Rhythm*, ed. J. Max Patrick and Robert Evans (Princeton: Princeton University Press, 1966). For more on Pascal's use of other rhetorical figures see Topliss, Demorest, and Maggioni.

10. Although Robert Hooke probably did not read Pascal, the former's description in *Micrographia* (London, 1665) of insects and especially the eye of the fly demonstrates that the desire to use "Mechanical helps for the senses, both in the surveying the already visible world, and for the discovery of many others hitherto unknown . . ." was not in vain.

11. Note the rare qualifier "presque" here. Sellier, discussing the way Pascal rhetoric imitates that of Old Testament prophets, underlines "le refus presque total des modalisateurs" (73).

12. Pascal's fascination with titles speaks to his preoccupation with the figurative nature of language, of the gulf between the mere signifier (nowhere made more material and empty than on a title page) and the signified (here scientific truth, but elsewhere divine truth). Or to modify the cliché: every book's cover lies.

13. For more on *misère*, see #19, 22–24, 30–35, 48, 86, 89, 103, 155, 223, 225, 229, 384, 526, 689, 690.

14. See George Lakoff and Mark Johnson, *Metaphors We Live By* (Chicago: University of Chicago Press, 1980).

15. Elsewhere Pascal purposefully flirts with Pyrrhonism to highlight the virtues of his belief. In #570, for example, he writes: "Le pyrrhonisme est le vrai. Car après tout les hommes, avant Jésus-Christ, ne savient où ils en étaient, ni s'ils étaient grands ou petits . . ."

16. See Blumenberg's discussion, in *Shipwreck with Spectator,* of the shipwreck metaphor in Lucretius and briefly in Pascal (18–19). Pascal, of course, uses the trope of navigation to begin "Le pari" ("Vous êtes embarqué . . .").

17. For the *topos* of inconstancy see Rousset, *La littérature de l'âge baroque en France*, esp. parts I and II. See also *pensées* #87–89. In the next paragraph, Pascal writes: "Notre raison est toujours deçue par l'inconstance des apparences, rien ne peut fixer le fini entre les deux infinis qui l'enferment et le fuient."

18. See Matthew L. Jones's chapter, "The Anthropology of Disproportion," in *The Good Life in Scientific Revolution: Descartes, Pascal, Leibniz and the Cultivation of Virtue* (Chicago: University of Chicago Press, 2006). In the next chapter, I will compare such images with Kant's description of how the experience of the sublime proves the imagination's inadequacy.

19. Augustine is cited to argue (in an implicit rebuke to Descartes and his infamous theory of the pineal gland) that we cannot know how the soul and body are linked: "Modus quo corporibus adhaerent spiritus comprehendi ab hominibus non potest, et hoc tamen homo est" (*City of God*, xxi.10). As Sellier notes, Montaigne (*Essais*, 2.12) also quotes this passage.

20. For Pascal's notion of grace see his posthumously published (and entitled) *Écrits sur la grâce*, as well as #164, 203, 544, 581, 665, 756. See Melzer (42–49, 75–81) on the double hermeneutic circle the reader of the *Pensées* encounters as a result of this condition.

21. As Ricoeur recounts in *The Rule of Metaphor* (21), many students of metaphor have used Gilbert Ryle's notion of a "category mistake" as the basis for their analysis. Such terminology, though, tends to emphasize the logical violence rather than the "semantic gain" in the metaphorical process.

22. This and an observation a few paragraphs earlier ("De la vient...") would seem to make Pascal an enemy of metaphor, which as Quintilian and others have defined it, is the ability to see inanimate thing in terms of animate ones and vice versa.

23. See Hugh Davidson, *The Origins of Certainty: Means and Meanings in Pascal's* Pensées (Chicago: University of Chicago Press, 1979). Davidson distinguishes between different kinds of proofs in the *Pensées*: "geometric" (as in "Disproportion de l'homme"), "syllogistic," "dialectical," and "pragmatic" (12–27).

24. Bachelard might say that it becomes psychoanalytical. Yet given his polemic against the *superbia* of the philosophers, I wonder whether Pascal himself is hubristically usurping the role of Scripture with his absolutist itinerary of abysses and infinite spaces.

25. Valéry writes: "Cette phrase, dont la force de ce qu'elle veut imprimir aux âmes et la magnificence de sa forme ont fait une des paroles les plus fameuses qui aient jamais été articulées, est un *Poème*, et point du tout une *Pensée*" (458).

26. See Dorothea Singer, *Giordano Bruno: His Life and Thought with an Annotated Translation of his Work, On the Infinite Universe and Worlds* (New York: Henry Schuman, 1950); Hilary Gatti, *Giordano Bruno and Renaissance Science* (Ithaca: Cornell University Press, 1999).

27. See *Expériences nouvelles touchant le vide* (1647) and the never completed *Traité du vide* of which remains only fragments; see also #795. For a broader perspectives on Pascal's vacuuism, see Roger Ariew, "Descartes and Pascal," *Perspectives on Science* 15.4 (2007): 397–409.

28. Similarly, see #164.

29. *See*, for example Quirinus Kuhlmann, *Himmlische Libes-küsse*, 1671 [reprint], ed. Birgit Biehl-Werner (Tübingen: Niemeyer, 1971).

30. I owe this insight to Ludwin (126–127), who obliquely links Pascal's scientific work on the void to the rhetoric of hyperbole. See also David Castillo, "Horror (Vacui): The Baroque Condition," in *Hispanic Baroques: Reading Cultures in Context*, ed. Nicholas Spadaccini and Luis Martin-Estudillo (Nashville: Vanderbilt University Press, 2005), 87–106. Vincent Carraud, in *Pascal: Des connaissances naturelles à l'étude de l'homme* (Paris: Vrin, 2007), traces the metaphysical heritage and implications of Pascal's notion of the "néant" (163–176).

31. Sellier, 72. Sellier notes that Pascal privileges "une panoplie de figures que la plupart des théoriciens du temps dénonçaient comme excessives" (68). More to the point, he reminds us: "... cette omniprésence de l'hyperbole contredit les vœux des théoriciens du temps (Bouhours, l'abbe de Villars, Brette-

ville . . .) . . . De lá, sans doute, pour une part, la toujours renaissante accusation de véhemence et de recours à la force."

32. For an analysis of the origins and aims of French neoclassical rhetoric, see Gilles Declerq, "La rhétorique classique entre évidence et sublime (1650–1675), in *Histoire de la rhétorique dans l'Europe moderne, 1450–1950*, ed. Marc Fumaroli, 629–706.

33. Koch, xvi.

34. Antoine Arnauld and Pierre Nicole, *La logique ou l'art de penser* (1683), ed. Pierre Clair and François Girbal (Paris: Vrin, 1981), 29; *Logic or the Art of Thinking*, tr. and ed. Jill Vance Buroker (Cambridge: Cambridge University Press, 1996), 16. All English translations are from this edition.

35. *La logique*, 277; *Logic*, 216.

36. *La logique*, 278; *Logic*, 216.

37. *La logique*, 267; *Logic*, 208.

38. *La logique*, 267; *Logic*, 208.

39. The first publication of the *Pensées*, *Pensées de Monsieur Pascal sur la Religion et sur quelque autres sujets*, the so-called Port-Royal edition, was in 1670. Arnauld and Nicole participated in preparing the manuscript.

40. *La logique*, 295; *Logic*, 230. Pascal's "Disproportion de l'homme" is briefly paraphrased just afterwards.

41. L'Abbé de Villars, *La première critique des "Pensées": Texte et commentaire du cinquième dialogue du* Traité de la délicatesse *de l'abbé de Villars* (1671), ed. Dominique Descotes (Paris: CNRS, 1980). Descotes notes in his Introduction: "Quel que soit le verdict du lecteur, il faut constater que ce reproche est l'un des thèmes constants du courant antipascalien: Voltaire et, avant lui, les Jésuites de 1656 ont reproché à Pascal de faire passer des arguments fallacieux sous une rhétorique brillante: s'en prendre au style de Pascal, c'est souvent le moyen de discréditer sa pensée et de neutraliser ses arguments" (24–25).

42. *Traité de la délicatesse*, 54–55. Somewhat earlier Aliton-Abbé, after quoting from #230, ironically offers Pascal his consolation: "Alors je le consoleray de cette misere si affligeante, de ne pouvoir rien connoistre . . ." (53).

43. Dominique Bouhours, *La manière de bien penser dans les ouvrages d'esprit. Dialogues* [1688, 2nd ed.](Hildesheim and New York: George Olms Verlag, 1974), vii.

44. Bouhours, v.

45. Bouhours, 100.

46. Bouhours, 2. See also his discussion of the merits of Lucan (9–12).

47. Bouhours, 20.

48. Bouhours, 30–31.

49. 8.7.75. But he does cite from the same section in the *Institutio oratoria*: "Monere satis est mentiri hyperbolem, nec ita ut mendacio fallere possit." Likewise, he later adds: "Ces hyperboles, selon Quintilien, mentent sans tromper; & selon Séneque, elles ramenent l'esprit à la vérité par le mensonge, en faisant concevoir ce qu'elles signifient, à force de l'exprimer d'une maniére que semble le rendre incroyable" (31–32).

50. Bouhours, 32–33.

51. Bouhours, 34.

52. He also quotes a passage from Seneca's *De beneficiis* (7.23.2) on why hyperbole should be believed.

53. Bouhours, 36.

54. Though Tesauro employs a *remedium*, Bouhours notes, this still does not excuse the hyperbole.

55. Bouhours, 39. In allying hyperbole so closely with irony Bouhours nicely prefigures the approaches of Gans and Perrin.

56. César Chesneau Dumarsais-Pierre Fontanier, *Les tropes* [1818], 2 vols., ed. Gérard Genette (Geneva: Slatkine Reprints, 1984).

57. Dumarsais, 1.147.

58. Here the inexpressibility *topos* neatly merges with the world-as-a-book *topos*. Dumarsais quotes the Latin: "Sunt autem alia multa quae fecit Jesus, quae si scribantur per singula, nec ipsum arbitror mundum capere posse eos, qui scribendi libros."

59. Dumarsais, 1.149.

60. Dumarsais, 1.149–150. Although he seems to reopen the door slightly for hyperbole from the likes of Rabelais and Molière: "On en trouve quelques exemples dans le style satirique et badin, et quelquefois même dans le style sublime et poétique."

61. Dumarsais, 1.150. Dumarsais gives his source as: "*Traité de la vraie et de la fausse beauté dans le ouvrages d'esprit*. C'est une traduction que [Pierre] Richelet nous a donnée de la dissertation que Messieurs de P. R. [Arnauld and Nicole], ont mise à la tête de leur *Deléctus Epigrámmatum*." The actual title of the treatise, now thought to be authored by Nicole alone, is: *Dissertatio de vera pulchritudine & adumbrata, in qua ex certis principiis, rejectiones ac selectionis Epigrammatum causae redduntur.* The full title of the edition I consulted is *Epigrammatum delectus, ex omnibus, tum veteribus, tum recentioribus poetis accurate decerptus . . .* (London: Mosis Pitt, 1683). Curiously, Boileau is not quoted here so either Richelet or Dumarsais must have interpolated the verses.

62. Pierre Fontanier, who edits and comments on *Les tropes* in his *Commen-*

taire raisonné (1818), reclaims hyperbole for the French and the grand style; indeed, he nearly makes hyperbole synonymous with metaphor itself: "On ne sera convaincu, si l'on veut faire attention qu'il n'y a presque pas une seule mé-taphore qui ne soit plus ou moins hyperbolique, et qu'il y a bien peu de discors de quelque genre que ce soit, où il n'entre plus ou moins de métaphores" (2.153). He also views hyperbole from the perspective of what in today's parlance would be called "reader-response" theory. Rather than being proper only to peasants' banter, hyperbole demands a savvy, judicious audience: ". . . l'hyperbole, pour être une beauté d'expression et pour plaire, doit porter le caractère de la bonne foi et la franchise, et ne paraître de la part de celui qui parle que la langage même de la persuasion. Ce n'est pas tout: il faut que celui qui écoute puisse partager jusqu'à un certain point l'illusion, et ait besoin peut-être d'un peu de réflexion pour n'être pas dupe, c'est-à-dire, pour réduire les mots à leur juste valeur. Tout cela suppose que l'hyperbole, en passant la croyance, ne doit passer la mesure; qu'elle ne doit pas heurter la vraisemblance, en heurtant la vérité" (2.148). But by making verisimilitude the commonground — later he calls it the "pierre de touche" — of hyperbole, he devalues the idiosyncratic ingenuity native to Baroque hyperbole. He also seems to remove hyperbole from the satirist's arsenal, as he makes "la bonne foi et la franchise" the conditions enabling hyperbole. That the hyperbolist may be "frappé" by an idea that shocks his reader's expectations is not admitted as a possibility. See Perrin's discussion of Fontanier (15–18, 52–83).

63. Nicolas Boileau, "L'art poétique," *Œuvres complètes* (Paris: Gallimard, 1966), 158.

64. Jean Racine, *Phèdre*, ed. Raymond Picard (Paris: Gallimard, 2000). Quibbling with Dumarsais' definition of hypotypose, Fontanier writes: "L'hy-potypose consiste, non pas à donner pour présente une chose passée ou une chose future, mais à peindre les faits ou les objets d'une manière si vive et si énergique, qu'on les mette en quelque sorte sous les yeux, et qu'on semble donner l'original même pour la copie" (2.159). Thus the hyperbolic is again contained within a vi-sual poetics.

65. For accounts of this controversy see Carlos Lynes Jr., "A Defense of the 'Récit de Théramène,'" *MLN* 59.6 (1944): 387–391; Leo Spitzer, "The 'Récit de Théramène,'" *Linguistics and Literary History: Essays in Stylistics* (Princeton: Princeton University Press, 1967), 87–134; Amy Wygant, "Leo Spitzer's Racine," *MLN* 109.4 (1994): 632–649.

66. Spitzer, 119.

67. Spitzer, 117.

68. Spitzer, 123. For a detailed reevaluation of Racine's rhetoric in the light of French classicism, see Gerhild Schulz, *Rhetorik im Zeichen sprachlicher Transparenz: Racine – Lessing* (Dresden: Thelem, 2003).

69. Wygant, 641; Spitzer, 100.

70. Spitzer, 105.

71. Spitzer, 113.

CHAPTER SIXTEEN: CRITIQUE OF HYPERBOLIC REASON

1. Max Horkheimer and Theodor W. Adorno, *Dialectic of Enlightenment*, tr. Edmund Jephcott (Stanford: Stanford University Press, 2002), 35–36.

2. Immanuel Kant, *Critique of the Power of Judgment*, ed. Paul Guyer; tr. Paul Guyer and Eric Matthews (Cambridge: Cambridge University Press, 2001), §53, 205. All German quotations are from Immanuel Kant, *Kritik der Urteilskraft*, in *Werke* (Wiesbaden: Insel Verlag, 1957), 10.2:431.

3. For a rigorous reappraisal of Kant's theory of taste and the notion of "free play" that distinguishes it, see Henry Allison, *Kant's Theory of Taste: A Reading of the Critique of Aesthetic Judgment* (Cambridge: Cambridge University Press, 2001).

4. *Critique of the Power of Judgment*, §23, 128. Though I shall endeavor to show why it is not the case, it might well be objected that I am exaggerating the role of the *Analytic of the Sublime* in Kant's critical project, especially in light of the scant attention he gives it in the two Introductions, and given assertions such as the "theory of the sublime [is] a mere appendix to the aesthetic judging of the purposiveness [*Zweckmässigkeit*] of nature" (§23, 120), for, unlike in judgments of beauty, in judgments of the sublime we never escape ourselves to perceive Nature's (i.e., God's) teleology and order.

5. *Critique of the Power of Judgment*, §53, 204.

6. *Critique of the Power of Judgment*, §53, 205; *Kritik der Urteilskraft*, 10.2:431.

7. See Introduction (1793), *Critique of the Power of Judgment*, 64–65; also Guyer's Introduction, xiv, xxiii. Paul de Man, "Phenomenality and Materiality in Kant," in *Aesthetic Ideology*, 90, 87.

8. Introduction, *Critique of the Power of Judgment*, IX, 80.

9. Introduction, *Critique of the Power of Judgment*, IX, 81; Einleitung, *Kritik der Urteilskraft*, 10.1:270.

10. *Critique of the Power of Judgment*, §29, 153. For the larger context in which the Analytic of the Sublime operates and how it contrasts with the Analytic of the Beautiful, which concerns aesthetic judgments of taste, see Eva Schaper, "Taste, Sublimity, and Genius: The Aesthetics of Nature and Art," in *The Cambridge*

Companion to Kant, ed. Paul Guyer (Cambridge: Cambridge University Press, 1992), 367–393; also see Paul Crowther, *The Kantian Sublime: From Morality to Art* (Oxford: Clarendon Press, 1989).

11. *Critique of the Power of Judgment*, §25, 134; *Kritik der Urteilskraft*, 10.2:335–336.

12. *Critique of the Power of Judgment*, §24, 130–131.

13. Schaper, 383.

14. See Crowther, 41–44; 99–100.

15. *Critique of the Power of Judgment*, §28, 144–145; *Kritik der Urteilskraft*, 10.2:349.

16. *Critique of the Power of Judgment*, §29, 148; *Kritik der Urteilskraft*, 10.2:354. See also p. 142 on the "violence" [*Gewalt*] done to the imagination by the experience of the sublime.

17. *Critique of the Power of Judgment*, §29, 152. The pathos inherent in such "sacrifice" is explored by de Man (87) and Lyotard in *Leçons sur l'Analytique du sublime* (Paris: Galilée, 1991), 226–230.

18. *Critique of the Power of Judgment*, §29, 151. "The satisfaction in the sublime in nature is thus only *negative* (whereas that in the beautiful is *positive*), namely a feeling of the deprivation of the freedom of the imagination by itself, insofar as it is purposively determined in accordance with a law other than that of empirical use."

19. *Critique of the Power of Judgment*, §29, 154.

20. De Man, "Phenomenality and Materiality in Kant," 89–90.

21. De Man, "Phenomenality and Materiality in Kant," 77–79.

22. De Man (78) cites the passage where Pascal describes the insufficiency of our senses ("Nos sens n'aperçoivent rien d'extrême . . ."); though given his notion that both Pascal and Kant necessarily resort to "the model of discourse," another moment comes to mind: ". . . et que le dernier objet où il peut arriver soit maintenant celui de notre discours."

23. *Critique of the Power of Judgment*, §29, 154; *Kritik der Urteilskraft*, 10.2:363.

24. *Critique of the Power of Judgment*, §26, 136. This is analogous to the discussion and devaluation of "adherent beauty" in the *Analytic of the Beautiful*, that is, beauty which has a concept as its end, and so hinders "the purity of the judgment of taste" (§16, 114).

25. *Critique of the Power of Judgment*, §29, 153.

26. *Critique of the Power of Judgment*, §29, 152.

27. *Critique of the Power of Judgment*, §51, 198; *Kritik der Urteilskraft*, 10.2:422–423. For a broad historical analysis of the concept of taste, see Franz

Schümmer, "Die Entwicklung des Geschmacksbegriff in der Philosophie des 17. und 18. Jahrhunderts," *Archiv für Begriffsgeschichte* 1 (1955): 120–141.

28. *Critique of the Power of Judgment*, §49, 196.

29. *Kritik der Urteilskraft*, 10.2:360; *Critique of the Power of Judgment*, §29, 153. See also Kant's famous praise of the "art of poetry (which owes its origin almost entirely to genius, and will be guided least by precept or example) . . ." Aside from its philosophic, schematic value, such poetry, unlike "deceiving" rhetoric, "plays with the illusion which it produces at will, yet without thereby being de-ceitful . . ." (§53, 203–204).

30. *Critique of the Power of Judgment*, §29, 157.

31. Or as Paul Guyer comments: "[Kant's] account of the mathematical sublime is organized around the concepts of quantity and quality while the dis-cussion of the dynamical sublime represents the application of the concepts of re-lation and modality" (xxx–xxxi).

32. *Critique of the Power of Judgment*, §25, 131–132; *Kritik der Urteilskraft*, 10.2:333.

33. But as Kant (§26) distinguishes between the mathematical estimation and the aesthetic intuition ("measured by eye") of a magnitude, he discovers, much like Pascal in *De l'esprit géométrique*, that even numerical measurement ulti-mately depends on an initial intuition.

34. *Critique of the Power of Judgment*, §26, 139.

35. *Kritik der Urteilskraft*, 10.2:345–348; *Critique of the Power of Judgment*, §27, 141–143. Crowther (81, 121–128) deftly analyses the ambiguity of whether these emotions are successive or alternating.

36. *Critique of the Power of Judgment*, §26, 136.

37. *Critique of the Power of Judgment*, §26, 136; *Kritik der Urteilskraft*, 10.2:339.

38. Derrida discusses this "beinahe" at length in the section dedicated to the colossal in "Parergon," in *The Truth in Painting*, tr. Geoff Bennington and Ian McLeod (Chicago: University of Chicago Press, 1987), 119–147.

39. Andrzej Warminski, "Returns of the Sublime: Positing and Performa-tive in Kant, Fichte, and Schiller," *MLN* 116 (2001): 964–978. Warminski also places such disjunction in the larger context of Kant's critical project: "For if the project and task of the third *Critique* is in fact, in the end, to ground transcenden-tally the subject of the critical philosophy itself, i.e., the critical subject itself, and if the specific place of *this* specific project in the third *Critique* is in fact the "Ana-lytic of the Sublime". . . then the self-disarticulation of the sublime in the apo-ria of the disjunction between cognitive and performative signifies the radical *un*-grounding (or "abyssing," as it were, *ab-gründen*) and disarticulation of the

critical system itself and its demand for an articulation between the supersensuous underlying nature and the supersensuous underlying freedom, between first and second *Critiques*" (967–968).

40. *Critique of the Power of Judgment*, §26, 138.

41. As Guyer notes (355n), Burke and Addison make "grandeur" one of the fundamental aspects of their aesthetic.

42. *Critique of the Power of Judgment*, §27, 142; §28, 144–145.

43. *Critique of the Power of Judgment*, §26, 134. Schaper summarizes these four moments in the feeling of the sublime: "Regarding quantity it must claim universality; regarding quality, it must be independent of interest; regarding relation, it must exhibit subjective finality; and regarding modality, it must be necessary" (383). See §23, 129 where Kant alerts his readers that aesthetic judgments of the sublime will eventually give way to teleological judgments of nature's purposiveness. Nature, as Guyer notes, is assumed by Kant to be systematic and teleological (xxv). Indeed, one might conclude that there persists in Kant's thought the *analogia entis* between mind and world that was discarded by Pascal.

44. *Critique of the Power of Judgment*, §26, 140; *Kritik der Urteilskraft*, 10.2:343–344.

45. Friedrich Hölderlin, "Über die Verfahrungsweise des poëtischen Geistes," *Sämtliche Werke und Briefe*, ed. Jochen Schmidt (Frankfurt am Main: DKV, 1994), 2:538–539. See Jan Mieszkowski's fine discussion, in *Labors of the Imagination: Aesthetics and Political Economy from Kant to Althusser* (New York: Fordham University Press, 2006), 75–110, of Hölderlin's essay in the context of Romantic aesthetics.

46. *Critique of the Power of Judgment*, §23, 129.

47. *Critique of the Power of Judgment*, §27, 141. Kant describes a "certain subreption" that allows us to substitute "a respect for the object instead of the idea of humanity in our subject." Subreption works backwards or metonymically from concept to phenomenon.

48. *Critique of the Power of Judgment*, §25, 133; *Kritik der Urteilskraft*, 10.2:335.

49. *Critique of the Power of Judgment*, §51, 199; *Kritik der Urteilskraft*, 10.2:423.

50. *Critique of the Power of Judgment*, §29, 153. The passage continues: "If, on the contrary, something else determines the judgment, whether it be a sensation of the senses or a concept of the understanding, then it is certainly lawful but not the judgment of a *free* power of judgment."

51. *Critique of the Power of Judgment*, §29, 148.

52. *Critique of the Power of Judgment*, §29, 148.

53. *Critique of the Power of Judgment*, §49, 194n. The quote is from Johannes Andreas Segner's *Einleitung in die Naturlehre* (1754).

54. *Critique of the Power of Judgment*, §26, 139.

55. *Critique of the Power of Judgment*, §27, 141; *Kritik der Urteilskraft*, 10.2:344–345.

56. Thus De Man (90) highlights the "bewildering alternation of the two terms, *Angemessen(heit)* and *Unangemessen(heit)*" in a crucial later passage in the "General Remark on the Exposition of Aesthetic Reflective Judgments." See *Critique of the Power of Judgment*, §29, 152; *Kritik der Urteilskraft*, 10.2:359.

57. *Critique of the Power of Judgment*, §29, 151. In *Metaphor and Continental Philosophy: From Kant to Derrida* (London: Routledge, 2007), Clive Cazeaux reads metaphor (and its cousin analogy) as the chief means by which Kant reconciles the sensible and the super-sensible in the third *Critique*. To which I would add that hyperbole is the condition of this schematic metaphor's possibility.

58. *Critique of the Power of Judgment*, §29, 151.

59. Kant announces at the beginning of *The Analytic of the Sublime* that his chief aim is to indicate how subjective "admiration or respect," which he equates with "negative pleasure," will eventually help us reach "ideas that contain a higher purposiveness" (§23, 129).

60. Crowther, 104–105.

61. By way of a remedy, Crowther identifies Kant's "austere thesis" in which "without any reference to infinity . . . the imagination simply proves inadequate to reason's demand that it present the object's phenomenal totality in a single whole of intuition" (104). Even so, as I suggest below, this austere thesis cannot account for all intuitions.

62. Crowther, 105–106, 133.

63. *Critique of the Power of Judgment*, §26, 140; *Kritik der Urteilskraft*, 10.2:344.

64. *Critique of the Power of Judgment*, §27, 141–142; *Kritik der Urteilskraft*, 10.2:345.

65. See *Critique of the Power of Judgment*, §25, 134.

66. Ludwig Wittgenstein, *Philosophische Untersuchungen*, in *Werkausgabe* (Frankfurt am Main: Suhrkamp, 1990), §38, 1:259. This volume also contains the *Tractatus logico-philosophicus*. Hereafter all references to the *Philosophische Untersuchungen* will appear in the main text by proposition number. All English translations are from *Philosophical Investigations*, tr. G. E. M. Anscombe (Oxford: Basil Blackwell, 1958) and *Tractatus Logico-Philosophicus*, tr. C.K. Ogden (London and New York: Routledge & Kegan Paul, 1981).

67. Cavell, "Work in Progress: An Introductory Report," *This New Yet Unapproachable America*, 1; "Declining Decline," 75.

68. "Declining Decline," 57.

69. Cavell, "Work in Progress," 14.

70. "Declining Decline," 30–31.

71. Though the passage and the context suggest that Cavell might balk at this reductive label, clearly his lifelong engagement with Wittgenstein's thought qualifies him as such. See Cavell's Foreword to *The Claim of Reason*, which de- scribes the decisive influence of the *Philosophic Investigations* (esp. xix–xxii). In an April 29, 2005 review in the *TLS*, Terry Eagleton playfully dubs Cavell "The high priest of literary Wittgensteinianism."

72. "Declining Decline," 37.

73. *Disowning Knowledge*, 122.

74. "Declining Decline," 38.

75. "Declining Decline," 38.

76. "Declining Decline," 38.

77. "Declining Decline," 38.

78. The question of delineating the various voices in the *Investigations* has long occupied commentators. Sometimes, for instance, the first voice sounds rather Cartesian, other times it echoes the point of view of the *Tractatus*. Like- wise, the second voice, often identified as expressing Wittgenstein's point of view, can seem at times more muddled than skeptical. Expanding upon Wittgenstein's comparison of his philosophy to therapy (§133, 255), Marie McGinn, in *Wittgenstein and the* Philosophical Investigations (New York: Routledge, 1997), comments: "Wittgenstein's use of the interlocutor's voice allows him to present this therapeutic process, not as a series of exchanges between a therapist and pa- tient, but in the form of an internal dialogue, in which Wittgenstein both gives expression to the temptations to misunderstand which our language presents to us and struggles to resist these misunderstandings" (29). Such a dialectic or, if you will, heteroglossia, confirms the difficulty of isolating a hyperbolic mode of thought in the *Investigations*.

79. "Declining Decline," 38–39.

80. The key proposition from the *Investigations* that informs Cavell's reading here is §116: "*Wir* führen die Wörter von ihrer metaphysischen, wieder auf ihre alltägliche Verwendung zurück." As the italicized "We" suggests, to succeed Wittgensteinian philosophy requires numerous hands: the philosopher, his imag- ined opponents, and of course potential readers like Cavell.

81. "Declining Decline," 46.

82. For exemplary versions of ordinary language criticism, see *Ordinary Language Criticism: Literary Thinking after Cavell after Wittgenstein*, ed. Kenneth Dauber and Walter Jost (Evanston: Northwestern University Press, 2003). In their Introduction, Dauber and Jost describe ordinary language criticism as "particular," "superficial," "empirical," "experiential," "dogged," "connective," "paratactic," "dialogic," "anthropocentric," "ethical," and "literary."

83. "Declining Decline," 58.

84. Cavell expresses his "differences with deconstruction" when he rejects its "extremes," specifically, the infinite deferral of the signified, in favor of "Wittgenstein's diurnalization of philosophy's ambitions" (23). See, though, Michael Fischer, *Stanley Cavell and Literary Skepticism* (Chicago: University of Chicago Press, 1989).

85. With this said, I wonder if Cavell's attempt, in "Performative and Passionate Utterance," in *Philosophy the Day after Tomorrow*, to widen the scope of Austin's *How To Do Things with Words* to include perlocutionary speech, is not implicitly also a philosophical attempt, and therefore also a psychological and rhetorical one (Aristotle's *Rhetoric* is cited on the opening page), to give legitimacy to certain hyperbolic forms of expression. "Perlocutionary acts make room for, and reward, imagination and virtuosity . . . that perlocutionary-like effects — for example, stopping you in your tracks, embarrassing or humiliating you — are readily, sometimes more effectively, achieved without saying anything, indicates the urgency of passion is expressed before and after words" (173). Casting his ideas as a "theory of expression" (186) and a "refusal of moralism" (187), Cavell concludes: "I might say that my view of the role of ordinary language in relation to the imperative of expression, is that it is less in need of weeding than of nourishment" (188).

86. In "Finding as Foundling: Taking Steps in Emerson's 'Experience,'" Cavell reiterates his oft-expressed contention that the *Investigations* is a "Kantian work" (87), as it also seeks a priori knowledge of what can be known and said. More specifically, I would add that whereas Kant explores in the third *Critique* non-conceivable ideas, i.e., ideas that do not rise to the status of concepts, Wittgenstein tries to distinguish between nonsense and sense.

87. See Bertrand Russell's Introduction to the English translation of the *Tractatus* (21–22).

88. I am thinking especially of Carnap, Neurath, and its greatest English apostle A. J. Ayer. See Ayer's *Language, Truth and Logic* (New York: Oxford

University Press, 1936) and *Wittgenstein* (Chicago: University of Chicago Press, 1985) for further development of the Wittgensteinian notions of certainty and verifiability. The logical-positivists chose to focus on propositions such as: "In fact, all the propositions of our everyday language, just at they stand, are in perfectly logical order" [*Alle Sätze unserer Umgangssprache sind tatsächlich, so wie sie sind, logisch vollkommen geordnet*] (5.5563).

89. As a starting point, see Scott R. Stripling, *The Picture Theory of Meaning: An Interpretation of Wittgenstein's Tractatus logico-philosophicus* (Washington, D.C.: University Press of America, 1978).

90. Preface, *Tractatus*, 9.

91. See the two preceding propositions, 6.53–6.54.

92. Quoted in Cyril Barrett, *Wittgenstein on Ethics and Religious Belief* (Oxford: Blackwell, 1991), x.

93. Barrett, 16.

94. See Brian Clack, *An Introduction to Wittgenstein's Philosophy of Religion* (Edinburgh: Edinburgh University Press, 1999), 35. Clack adds: "The picture theory of meaning, with its resultant banishment of theology to silence, is designed to protect 'what is higher' from the perverting, all too human encroaches of language."

95. See Norman Malcolm, *Wittgenstein: A Religious Point of View?* (Ithaca: Cornell University Press, 1994); Fergus Kerr, *Theology after Wittgenstein* (Oxford: Blackwell, 1986), esp. 64, 163; see also Clack, esp. 27–50. There has been a minor explosion of studies of Wittgenstein and religion; see especially: D. Z. Phillips, *Wittgenstein and Religion* (New York: St. Martin's Press, 1993); *Wittgenstein and Philosophy of Religion*, ed. Robert L. Arrington and Mark Addis (London: Routledge, 2001); *Der Denker als Seiltänzer: Ludwig Wittgenstein über Religion, Mystik und Ethik*, ed. Ulrich Arnswald, Anja Weiberg (Düsseldorf: Parerga, 2001); Tim Labron, *Wittgenstein's Religious Point of View* (London: Continuum, 2006).

96. Ludwig Wittgenstein, "A Lecture on Ethics," *The Philosophical Review* 74.1 (1965): 3–12; quotation from 8.

97. "A Lecture on Ethics," 11–12.

98. See *Philosophical Investigations*, 519–520.

99. "A Lecture on Ethics," 10; Marcus Hester, *The Meaning of Poetic Metaphor* (The Hague: Mouton, 1967).

100. Cavell, "Aesthetic Problems of Modern Philosophy," *Must We Mean What We Say?*, 80.

101. Cavell, "Performative and Passionate Utterance," 185.

102. "A Lecture on Ethics," 10.

103. In "A Lecture on Ethics," Wittgenstein asserts: "The truth is that the scientific way of looking at a fact is not the way to look at it as a miracle." See Barrett (72–90) for a full discussion of "the mystical."

104. Wittgenstein, "A Lecture on Ethics," 7.

105. Ludwig Wittgenstein, *Culture and Value: A Selection from the Posthumous Remains*, ed. Georg Henrik von Wright and Heikki Nyman, tr. Peter Winch (Oxford: Blackwell, 1998), 34–34e.

106. Cavell, "The Availability of Wittgenstein's Later Philosophy," *Must We Mean What We Say?*, 71.

107. Although he does mention a "hyperbola" when he considers the exclamation "Slab!" as a "'degenerated sentence' (as one speaks of a degenerate hyperbola)" (§20).

108. Closely related to this is: "Denn die philosophische Probleme entstehen, wenn die Sprache *feiert*. Und *da* können wir uns allerdings einbilden, das Benennen sei irgend ein merkwürdiger seelischer Akt, quasi eine Taufe eines Gegenstandes" (§38).

109. Barrett critiques §97: "The mistake Wittgenstein made was to treat these concepts as 'super-concepts' in trying to 'grasp the incomparable essence of language.' . . . Not all meaningful uses of language are pictorial . . . And, while the concepts of the sayable and the unsayable, the expressible and the inexpressible, may still have a limited application, it can no longer serve uniquely to distinguish expressions of value, propositions of logic and mathematics, tautologies and contradictions, from other forms of expression" (122–123).

110. See §103 where the metaphors reveal the tyranny of the "Ideal" and "Idee."

111. Compare with §110: "'Die Sprache (oder das Denken) ist etwas Einzigartiges' — das erweist sich als ein Aberglaube (nicht Irrtum!), hervorgerufen selbst durch grammatische Täuschungen. Und auf diese Täuschungen, auf die Probleme, fällt nun das Pathos zürück."

112. *Philosophical Investigations*, ix; *Philosophische Untersuchungen*, 1:231–232.

113. Quoted in Malcolm, 44.

114. See §371 ("Das Wesen ist in der Grammatik ausgesprochen.)" and §291 ("Wenn man an eine Beschreibung als ein Wortbild der Tatsachen denkt, so hat das etwas Irreführendes: Man denkt etwa nur an Bilder, wie sie an unseren Wänden hängen; die schlechtweg abzubilden scheinen, wie an Ding aussieht, wie es beschaffen ist. (Diese Bilder sind gleichsam müßig.")

115. Here I am referring to Wittgenstein's polemic against "private language," i.e., "Wie ein Wort funktioniert, kann man nicht erraten. Man muß

seine Anwendung *ansehen* und daraus lernen" (§340). See also §243 on the impossibility of a private language.

116. Umberto Eco, "The Scandal of Metaphor: Metaphorology and Semiotics," *Poetics Today* 4.2 (1983): 217–257. Although Wittgenstein had relatively
little to say about literature *per se*, his thoughts on language together with the aesthetic, indeed, literary qualities of his writing have increasingly become important for the philosophy of literature and the practice of literary criticism. See,
for example, *The Literary Wittgenstein*, ed. John Gibson and Wolfgang Huemer
(London: Routledge, 2004).

117. But nor are there "hyper-facts" to be represented. Clack recounts that in
the 1950's Rush Rhees, a friend of Wittgenstein, was concerned: ". . . to show
how mistaken it is to think of religious language as a form of discourse the purpose of which is to describe 'hyper-facts'" (78).

118. See Barrett (112) on how the approach in the *Investigations* seems to "undermine the distinction between fact and value"; also 116–117 where he distinguishes between "syntactical language-games" and "cultural language games."
Expressions of fact, syntactical expressions are sayable, and yet: "There is no reason to believe that, as a language-game, or set of language-games, expressions of
value become any more sayable in later Wittgensteinian thought than they were
earlier. They become more animated, that is all" (122).

119. See Barrett, 134–38.

120. In *Lectures & Conversations on Aesthetics, Psychology and Religious Belief*,
ed. Cyril Barrett (Berkeley: University of California Press, 1967), 64.

121. See §36.

122. The fact that the *Investigations* begins with a lengthy quotation from
Augustine's *Confessions* illustrating how a child learns language also suggests
that the metaphorics of the path structures Wittgenstein's book and notion of
Bildung.

123. See also §436 where "that dead-end in philosophy" [*jene Sackgasse des
Philosophierens*] is blamed.

124. See Wittgenstein's *Vorwort* (232) and "Declining Decline," 35. Intriguingly, Cavell proposes Heidegger as Wittgenstein's principal twentieth-century
analogue; specifically, the former's reading of Hölderlin's "Brot und Wein" (". . .
wozu Dichter in dürftiger Zeit?") corresponds to Cavell's reading of "impoverishment" in Wittgenstein. See also 46. But here one would also want to consider
Cavell's recent championing of what he calls "moral perfectionism," in *Cities of
Words: Pedagogical Letters on a Register of the Moral Life* (Cambridge: Harvard University Press, 2004).

125. As Wittgenstein announces in the opening sentences of the *Vorwort*: "In dem Folgenden veröffentliche ich Gedanken, den Niederschlag philosoph/ischer Untersuchungen, die mich in den letzten 16 Jahren beschäftigt haben. Sie betreffen viele Gegenstände: Den Begriff der Bedeutung, des Verstehens, des Satzes, der Logik, die Grundlagen der Mathematik, die Bewußtseinszustände und Anderes. Ich habe diese Gedanken alle als *Bemerkungen*, kürze Absätze, niedergeschrieben" (231).

126. Cavell affirms in "Declining Decline": "What [the *Investigations*] claims for itself is no more than poverty, not Platonic or Augustinian or Carte/sian or Kantian or Hegelian or Heideggerean lavishness" (72).

127. "Declining Decline," 67, 71.

128. See §89 where the sublime and the "Tiefe" are seen as improper pursuits of logic. Wittgenstein seems to suggest here that a grammatical rather than a philosophical (logical) approach to the objects and experiences of the sublime is the only one possible.

Bibliography

Abbot, Don. "La Retórica y el Renacimiento: An Overview of Spanish Theory," in *Renaissance Eloquence: Studies in the Theory and Practice of Renaissance Rhetoric*, ed. James J. Murphy, 95–104. Berkeley: University of California Press, 1983.

Abreu Gómez, Ermilio. *Sor Juana Inés de la Cruz: bibliografía y biblioteca*. Mexico City: Monografías bibliográficas mexicanas, 1934.

Agamben, Giorgio. *The Man without Content*, tr. Georgia Albert. Stanford: Stanford University Press, 1999.

Ahl, Frederick. *Metaformations: Soundplay and Wordplay in Ovid and Other Classical Poets*. Ithaca: Cornell University Press, 1985.

Alatorre, Antonio. "Notas al *Primero Sueño* de Sor Juana," *NRFH* 43.2 (1995): 379–407.

———, ed. *Aprobación: Sor Juana a través de los siglos (1668–1910)*, 2 vols. Mexico City: UNAM, 2007.

Albaladejo, Tomás, Emilio del Río, and José Antonio Caballero, eds., *Quintiliano: Historia y actualidad de la retórica*, 3 vols. Logroño: Ediciones Instituto de Estudios Riojanos,1998.

Alciato, Andrea. *Emblemata* (Lyon, 1550), ed. and tr. Betty I. Knott. Aldershot: Scolar Press, 1996.

Alighieri, Dante. *Inferno*, tr. John and Jean Hollander. New York: Random House, 2002.

Allison, Henry. *Kant's Theory of Taste: A Reading of the Critique of Aesthetic Judgment*. Cambridge: Cambridge University Press, 2001.

Alonso, Dámaso. *Estudios y ensayos gongorinos*. Madrid: Gredos, 1960.

———, *Góngora y el "Polifemo,"* 3 vols. 5th ed. Madrid: Gredos, 1967.

Álvarez de Lugo Usodemar, Pedro. *Ilustración al Sueño*, in *Para leer "Primero Sueño" de Sor Juana Inés de la Cruz*, ed. Andrés Sánchez Robayana. Mexico City: Fondo de Cultura Económica, 1991.

Anderson, William S. "Horace *Carm.* 1.14: What Kind of Ship?" *Classical Philology* 61 (1966): 84–98.

Anon. *Rhetorica ad Herennium*, tr. Harry Caplan. Cambridge: Harvard University Press, 2004.

Arancón, Ana Martínez, ed. *La batalla en torno a Góngora*. Barcelona: Antonio Bosch, 1978.

Arellano Ayuso, Ignacio. *Poesía satírico burlesca de Quevedo: Estudio y anotación filológica de los sonetos*, 2nd. ed. Madrid: Iberoamericana, 2003.

Arenal, Electa. "Where Woman is the Creator of the Wor(l)d, or Sor Juana's Discourses on Method," *Feminist Perspectives on Sor Juana Inés de la Cruz*, ed. Stephanie Merrim, 124–141. Detroit: Wayne State University Press, 1991.

Ariew, Roger. "The *Meditations, Objections,* and *Replies,*" in *The Blackwell Guide to Descartes' Meditations*, ed. Stephen Gaukroger, 6–16. Oxford: Blackwell, 2006.

———, "Descartes and Pascal," *Perspectives on Science* 15.4 (2007): 397–409.

Aristotle. *The Rhetoric of Aristotle with a Commentary*, 3 vols. ed. Edward M. Cope, rev. John E. Sandys. Cambridge: Cambridge University Press, 1877.

———, *Problems*, 2 vols. tr. W. S. Hett. Cambridge: Harvard University Press, 1953–57.

———, *On Poetics*, tr. Seth Benardette and Michael Davis. South Bend: St. Augustine's Press, 2002.

———, *On Rhetoric*, tr. George A. Kennedy. New York: Oxford University Press, 1991.

———, *Poetics*, ed. Stephen Halliwell. Cambridge: Harvard University Press, 1995.

Arnauld, Antoine, and Pierre Nicole, *La logique ou l'art de penser* (1683), ed. Pierre Clairand François Girbal. Paris: Vrin, 1981.

———, *Logic or the Art of Thinking*, tr. and ed. Jill Vance Buroker. Cambridge: Cambridge University Press, 1996.

Arnswald, Ulrich, and Anja Weiberg, eds. *Der Denker als Seiltänzer: Ludwig Wittgensteinüber Religion, Mystik und Ethik*. Düsseldorf: Parerga, 2001.

Arrington, Robert L., and Mark Addis, eds. *Wittgenstein and Philosophy of Religion*. London: Routledge, 2001.

Artaud, Antonin. "The Theater of Cruelty (First Manifesto)," *Selected Writings*, tr. Helen Weaver. Berkeley: University of California, 1988.

Attali, Jacques. *Blaise Pascal, ou, le génie français*. Paris: Fayard, 2000.

Augustine. *On Christian Doctrine*, tr. D. W. Robertson. New York: Macmillan, 1958.

————, *De doctrina Christiana*, in *Sancti Aurelli Augustini Opera: Corpus Christianorum*, vol. 32. Turnhout, Belgium: Brepols, 1962.

Ayer, A. J. *Language, Truth and Logic*. New York: Oxford University Press, 1936.

————, *The Problem of Knowledge*. New York: St. Martin's Press, 1956.

————, *Wittgenstein*. Chicago: University of Chicago Press, 1985.

Bachelard, Gaston. *Air and Dreams: An Essay on the Imagination of Movement*, tr. Edith R. and C. Fredrick Farrell. Dallas: Dallas Institute, 1988.

Bacon, Francis. *The Works of Francis Bacon*, 14 vols., ed. James Spedding, Robert L. Ellis, and Douglas D. Heath. Reprinted, Stuttgart: Frommann Verlag, 1989.

————, *Novum Organum, with Other Parts of the Great Instauration,* tr. and ed. Peter Urbach and John Gibson. Chicago: Open Court, 1994.

————, *The Advancement of Learning*, ed. Michael Kiernan. Oxford: Clarendon Press, 2000.

Bakhtin, Mikhail. *Rabelais and His World*, tr. Helene Iswolsky. Cambridge: The MIT Press, 1968.

Balavoine, Claudie. "La *Poétique* de J. C. Scaliger: Pour un *mimèsis* de l'imaginaire," in *La statue et l'empreinte: la poétique di Scaliger*, ed. Claudie Balavoine and Pierre Laurens, 107–129. Paris: Vrin, 1986.

Barner, Wilfried. *Barockrhetorik: Untersuchungen zu ihren geschichtlichen Grundlagen*. Tübingen: Max Niemeyer Verlag, 1970.

Barozzi, Francesco. *Admirandum illud geometricum problemata tredecim modisdemonstratum*. Venice, 1586.

Barrett, Cyril. *Wittgenstein on Ethics and Religious Belief*. Oxford: Blackwell, 1991.

Barthes, Roland. "The Old Rhetoric: an aide-mémoire," in *The Semiotic Challenge*, tr.Richard Howard. New York: Hill and Wang, 1988.

Bataillon, Marcel. "Plus Oultre: La cour découvre le nouveau monde," in *Fêtes et cérémonies au temps de Charles Quint*, ed. Jean Jacquot, 13–27. Paris: CNRS, 1960.

Bénassy-Berling, Marie-Cécile. *Humanisme et religion chez Sor Juana Inés de la Cruz: La femme et la culture au xviiᵉ siécle*. Paris: Éditions hispaniques, 1982.

Benjamin, Walter. *Ursprung des deutschen Trauerspiels*. Frankfurt am Main: Suhrkamp, 1963.

————, *The Origin of German Tragic Drama*, tr. John Osborne. New York: Verso, 1985.

Beverley, John. *Aspects of Góngora's "Soledades."* Amsterdam: John Benjamins, 1980.

————, "Going Baroque?" *Boundary 2* 15 (1988): 27–39.

Beyssade, Jean-Marie. "Méditer, objecter, répondre," in *Descartes: Objecter et répondre*, ed. Jean-Marie Beyssade and Jean-Luc Marion, 21–38. Paris: PUP, 1994.

Bicknell, Jeanette. "Descartes's Rhetoric: Roads, Foundations, and Difficulties in the Method," *Philosophy and Rhetoric* 36.1 (2003): 22–38.

Black, Max. *The Prevalence of Humbug and Other Essays*. Ithaca: Cornell University Press, 1983.

Blanco, Mercedes. *Les rhétoriques de la pointe: Baltasar Gracián et le conceptisme en Europe*. Geneva: Éditions Slatkine, 1992.

————, *Introducción al comentario de la poesía amorosa de Quevedo*. Madrid: Arcos, 1998.

Bloom, Harold. *Map of Misreading*. New York: Oxford University Press, 1975.

Blüher, Karl Alfred. *Seneca in Spanien. Untersuchungen zur Geschichte der Seneca-Rezeption in Spanien vom 13. bis 17. Jahrhundert*. Munich: A. Francke, 1969.

Blumenberg, Hans. "Paradigmen zu einer Metaphorologie," *Archiv für Begriffsgeschichte* 6 (1960): 7–142.

————, *The Legitimacy of the Modern Age*, tr. Robert M. Wallace. Cambridge: The MIT Press, 1983.

————, *The Genesis of the Copernican World*, tr. Robert M. Wallace. Cambridge: The MIT Press, 1987.

————, *Shipwreck with Spectator: Paradigm of a Metaphor for Existence*, tr. Stephen Rendall. Cambridge: The MIT Press, 1997.

Boileau, Nicolas. "L'art poétique," *Œuvres complètes*. Paris: Gallimard, 1966.

Borges, J. L. *Inquisiciones*. Buenos Aires: Editorial Proa, 1925.

————, *Labyrinths*. New York: New Directions, 1964.

————, *Otras inquisiciones*. Buenos Aires: Emece, 1964.

————, *A Universal History of Infamy*, tr. Norman Thomas di Giovanni. London: Penguin Books,1973.

————, *Borges: A Reader*, ed. E. R. Monegal and Alastair Reid. New York: E. P. Dutton, 1981.

————, *Borges the Poet*, ed. Carlos Cortínez. Fayettville: University of Arkansas Press, 1986.

————, *Historia de la eternidad*. Madrid: Alianza, 1996.

————, *This Craft of Verse*. Cambridge: Harvard University Press, 2000.

Bouhours, Dominique. *La manière de bien penser dans les ouvrages d'esprit. Dialogues* (1688). Hildesheim and New York: George Olms Verlag, 1974.

Bouillier, Victor. *Baltasar Gracián et Nietzsche*. Paris: Honoré Champion, 1926.

Bouvier, Virginia M. "La construcción de poder en *Neptuno alegórico* y *Ejercicios de la encarnación*, in *Aproximaciones a Sor Juana*, ed. Sandra Lorenzano, 43–54. Mexico City: Fondo de cultura económica, 2005.

Boyle, A. J. *Tragic Seneca: An Essay in the Theatrical Tradition*. London: Routledge, 1997.

Braden, Gordon. *Renaissance Tragedy and the Senecan Tradition: Anger's Privilege*. New Haven: Yale University Press, 1985.

———, *Petrarchan Love and the Continental Renaissance*. New Haven: Yale University Press, 1999.

Bras, Gérard, and Jean-Pierre Cléro. *Pascal: Figures de l'imagination*. Paris: PUF, 1994.

Briesemeister, Dietrich. "Rhetorik und Humanismus in Spanien," in *Renaissance-Poetik /Renaissance Poetics*, ed. Heinrich F. Plett, 92–106. Berlin: Walter de Gruyter, 1994.

Briggs, John C. *Francis Bacon and the Rhetoric of Nature*. Cambridge: Harvard University Press, 1989.

Broc, Numa. *La géographie de la Renaissance (1420–1620)*. Paris: Bibliothéque Nationale, 1980.

Brochard, Victor. *Études de philosophie ancienne et de philosophie moderne*. Paris: Vrin, 1926.

Brodsky Lacour, Claudia. *Lines of Thought: Discourse, Architectonics, and the Origin of Modern Philosophy*. Durham, N.C.: Duke University Press, 1996.

Brooke-Rose, Christine. *A Grammar of Metaphor*. London: Seckler & Warburg, 1958.

Broughton, Janet. *Descartes's Method of Doubt*. Princeton: Princeton University Press, 2002.

Browne, Thomas. *Religio Medici and Other Works*, ed. L. C. Martin. Oxford: Clarendon Press, 1964.

Bruni. Leonardo. *The Study of Literature* in *Humanist Educational Treatises*, ed. and tr. Craig Kallendorf. Cambridge: Harvard University Press, 2002.

Buci-Glucksmann, Christine. *La raison baroque: de Baudelaire à Benjamin*. Paris: Éditions Galilée, 1984.

Burck, Erich. *Vom römischen Manierismus: von der Dichtung der frühen römischen Kaiserzeit*. Darmstadt: Wissenschaftliche Buchgesellschaft, 1971.

Burke, Kenneth. *A Grammar of Motives*. Berkeley: University of California Press, 1969.

Burton, Richard T. *Camoens: His Life and His Lusiads. A Commentary*, 2 vols. London: Bernard Quaritch, 1881.

Burton, Robert. *The Anatomy of Melancholy*, 3 vols. Oxford: Clarendon Press, 1989.

Calabrese, Omar. *Neo-Baroque: A Sign of the Times*. Princeton: Princeton University Press, 1992.

Calderón de la Barca, Pedro. *El mágico prodigioso*, ed. Bruce W. Wardropper. Madrid: Cátedra, 1985.

————, *La vida es sueño*, ed. José M. Ruano de la Haza. Madrid: Castalia, 1994.

Calin, William. "Ernst Robert Curtius: The Achievement of a Humanist," *Studies of Medievalism* 9 (1997): 218–227.

Camões, Luis de. *Os Lusíades*, ed. Frank Pierce. Oxford: Clarendon Press, 1981.

Caputo, John D. "Apostles of the Impossible: On God and The Gift in Derrida and Marion," in *God, The Gift, and Postmodernism*, ed. John D. Caputo and Michael J. Scanlon, 185–223. Bloomington: Indiana University Press, 1999.

Carilla, Emilio. "Trayectoria del Gongorismo en Hispanoamerica," *Atenea* 142 (1961): 110–121.

Carillo y Sotomayor, Luis. *Libro de la erudición poética*, ed. Manuel Cardenal Iracheta. Madrid: CSIC, 1946.

Carr, Jr., Thomas M. *Descartes and the Resilience of Rhetoric: Varieties of Cartesian Rhetorical Theory*. Carbondale: Southern Illinois University Press, 1990.

Carraud, Vincent. *Pascal: Des connaissances naturelles à l'étude de l'homme*. Paris: Vrin, 2007.

Carreira, Antonio. *Gongoremas*. Barcelona: Península, 1998.

Carreño, Antonio. "Of 'Orders' and 'Disorders': Analogy in Spanish Baroque Poetry," in *The Image of the Baroque*, ed. Aldo Scaglione, 139–156. New York: Peter Lang, 1995.

Carriero, John. "The Cartesian Circle and the Foundations of Knowledge," in *A Companion to Descartes*, ed. Janet Broughton and John Carriero, 302–318. Oxford: Blackwell, 2008.

Carson, Anne. *Eros the Bittersweet*. Princeton: Princeton University Press, 1985.

————, *If Not Winter. Fragments of Sappho*. New York: Vintage, 2002.

Cascardi, Anthony. "Gracián and the Authority of Taste," in *Rhetoric and Politics: Baltasar Gracián and the New World Order*, ed. Nicholas Spadaccini and Jenaro Talens, 255–283. Minneapolis: University of Minnesota Press, 1997.

————, "*Disowning Knowledge*: Cavell on Shakespeare," in *Stanley Cavell*, ed. Richard Eldridge, 190–205. Cambridge: Cambridge University Press, 2003.

Castillo, David. "Horror (Vacui): The Baroque Condition," in *Hispanic Baroques: Reading Cultures in Context*, ed. Nicholas Spadaccini and Luis Martin-Estudillo, 87–106. Nashville: Vanderbilt University Press, 2005.

Cave, Terence. *The Cornucopian Text: Problems of Writing in the French Renaissance*. Oxford: Clarendon Press, 1979.

Cavell, Stanley. *The Claim of Reason: Wittgenstein, Skepticism, Morality, and Tragedy*. Oxford: Oxford University Press, 1979.

————, *This New Yet Unapproachable America: Lectures after Emerson after Wittgenstein*. Albuquerque: Living Batch Press, 1989.

————, *A Pitch of Philosophy: Autobiographical Exercises*. Cambridge: Harvard University Press, 1994.

————, "Benjamin and Wittgenstein: Signals and Affinities," *Critical Inquiry* 25 (1999): 235–246.

————, *Must We Mean What We Say?* 2nd ed. Cambridge: Cambridge University Press, 2002.

————, *Disowning Knowledge in Seven Plays of Shakespeare*, updated ed. Cambridge: Cambridge University Press, 2003.

————, *Cities of Words: Pedagogical Letters on a Register of the Moral Life*. Cambridge: Harvard University Press, 2004.

————, *Philosophy The Day after Tomorrow*. Cambridge: Harvard University Press, 2005.

Cazeaux, Clive. *Metaphor and Continental Philosophy: From Kant to Derrida*. London: Routledge, 2007.

Céard, Jean. *La nature et les prodiges: L'insolite au XVIe siècle*. Geneva: Droz, 1977.

————, "De Babel à la Pentecôte: La transformation du mythe de la confusion des langues au XVIe siècle," *Bibliotheque d'Humanisme et Renaissance* 42 (1980): 577–594.

Celan, Paul. *Paul Celan: Selections*, tr. Pierre Joris. Berkeley: University of California Press, 2005.

Celenza, Christopher. *The Lost Italian Renaissance: Humanists, Historians, and Latin's Legacy*. Baltimore: The Johns Hopkins University Press, 2004.

Certeau, Michel de. *The Mystic Fable. Volume One: The Sixteenth and Seventeenth Centuries*, tr. Michael B. Smith. Chicago: University of Chicago Press, 1992.

Chastel, André. "L'ennemi de la magnificence," in *Dix conférences sur Érasme: Eloges de la folie — Colloques*, 163–168. Paris: Champion; Geneva: Slatkine, 1986.

Chauveau, Jean Pierre, ed. *Anthologie de la poésie française de XVIIe siècle*. Paris: Gallimard, 1987.

Chomarat, Jacques. *Grammaire et rhétorique chez Erasme*, 2 vols. Paris: Société d'Édition "Les Belles Lettres," 1981.

Cicero. *Philippics*, tr. Walter C. A. Ker. Cambridge: Harvard University Press, 1969.

————, *De oratore*, 2 vols., tr. E. W. Sutton and H. Rackham. Cambridge: Harvard University Press, 2001.

————, *Topica*, tr. Tobias Reinhardt. Oxford: Oxford University Press, 2003.

Clack, Brian. *An Introduction to Wittgenstein's Philosophy of Religion*. Edinburgh: Edinburgh University Press, 1999.

Cole, John R. *The Olympian Dreams and Youthful Rebellion of René Descartes*. Urbana and Chicago: University of Illinois Press, 1992.

Coleridge, S. T. *Shakespeare Criticism*, 2 vols., ed. T. M. Raysor. New York: Dutton, 1960.

Colie, Rosalie. *Paradoxia Epidemica: The Renaissance Tradition of Paradox*. Princeton: Princeton University Press, 1966.

Colón, Cristóbal. *Diario de a bordo*, ed. Luis Arranz Márquez. Madrid: Dastin, 2000.

Conley, Thomas M. *Rhetoric in the European Tradition*. Chicago: University of Chicago Press, 1990.

Conley, Tom. *The Self-Made Map: Cartographic Writing in Early Modern France*. Minneapolis: University of Minnesota Press, 1996.

Cooper, David E. *Metaphor*. Oxford: Oxford University Press, 1986.

Cope, E. M. *An Introduction to Aristotle's Rhetoric*. London: Macmillan, 1867.

Cortés, Hernán. *Cartas de relación*. Madrid: Historia, 1985.

Cousin, Jean. *Études sur Quintilian*, 2 vols. Amsterdam: P. Schippers, 1967.

Covarrubias Orozco, Sebastian de. *Tesoro de la lengua castellana o española*. Madrid: Turner, 1979.

Cowan, Bainard. "Walter Benjamin's Theory of Allegory," *New German Critique* 22 (1981): 109–122.

Croce, Benedetto. "I trattatisti italiani del concettismo e Baltasar Gracián," in *Problemi di estetica: e contributi alla storia dell'estetica italiana*, 5th ed. Bari: G. Laterza, 1954.

Croll, Morris. *Style, Rhetoric, and Rhythm*, ed. J. Max Patrick and Robert Evans. Princeton: Princeton University Press, 1966.

Crowther, Paul. *The Kantian Sublime: From Morality to Art*. Oxford: Clarendon Press, 1989.

Cunliffe, J. W. *Influence of Seneca on Elizabethan Tragedy*. London and New York: Macmillan, 1893.

Curley, E. M. *Descartes against the Skeptics*. Cambridge: Harvard University Press, 1978.

Curtius, E. R. "Topik als Heuristik," in *Toposforschung*, ed. Max Baumer, 19–21. Darmstadt: Wissenschaftliche Buchgesellschaft, 1973.

———, *European Literature and the Latin Middle Ages*, tr. Willard R. Trask. Princeton: Princeton University Press, 1990.

D'Alton, J. F. *Roman Literary Theory and Criticism: A Study in Tendencies*. New York: Russell & Russell, 1962.

Daston, Lorraine and Katherine Park. *Wonders and the Order of Nature, 1150–1750*. NewYork: Zone Books, 1998.

Dauber, Kenneth, and Walter Jost, eds. *Ordinary Language Criticism: Literary Thinking after Cavell after Wittgenstein*. Evanston: Northwestern University Press, 2003.

Davidson, Hugh. *The Origins of Certainty: Means and Meanings in Pascal's* Pensées. Chicago: University of Chicago Press, 1979.

Davies, Nick. *Stories of Chaos: Reason and its Displacement in Early Modern English Narrative*. Aldershot, England: Ashgate, 1999.

Davies, Richard. *Descartes, Scepticism and Virtue*. London: Routledge, 2001.

De Man, Paul. *Blindness and Insight*, 2nd ed. rev. Minneapolis: University of Minnesota, 1983.

———, *Aesthetic Ideology*. Minneapolis: University of Minnesota Press, 1996.

Declerq, Gilles. "La rhétorique classique entre évidence et sublime (1650–1675), in *Histoire de la rhétorique dans l'Europe moderne, 1450–1950*, ed. Marc Fumaroli, 629–706. Paris: PUF, 1999.

Deleuze, Gilles. *The Fold: Leibniz and the Baroque*, tr. Tom Conley. Minneapolis: University of Minnesota Press, 1988.

———, *Expressionism in Philosophy: Spinoza*. New York: Zone Books, 1992.

Della Rocca, Michael. "Judgment and Will," in *The Blackwell Guide to the Meditations*, ed. Stephen Gaukroger, 142–159. Oxford: Blackwell, 2006.

Demetrius. *On Style*, tr. Doreen C. Innes. Cambridge: Harvard University Press, 1995.

Derrida, Jacques. *L'écriture et la différence*. Paris: Éditions du Seuil, 1967.

———, *Marges de la philosophie*. Paris: Les éditions de minuit, 1972.

———, *Writing and Difference*, tr. Alan Bass. Chicago: University of Chicago Press, 1978.

———, *Margins of Philosophy*, tr. Alan Bass. Chicago: University of Chicago Press, 1982.

————, *The Truth in Painting*, tr. Geoff Bennington and Ian McLeod. Chicago: University of Chicago Press, 1987.

————, *Derrida and Negative Theology*," ed. Harold Coward and Toby Foshay. Albany: SUNY Press, 1992.

————, *Sauf le nom*. Paris: Galilée, 1993.

————, *Of Grammatology*, tr. Gayatri Chakravorty Spivak. Baltimore: The Johns Hopkins University Press, 1997.

————, *Derrida and Negative Theology*," ed. Harold Coward and Toby Foshay. Albany: SUNY Press, 1992.

————, and Maurizio Ferraris. *A Taste for the Secret*, tr. Giacomo Donis. Cambridge, England: Polity Press, 2001.

Desargues, Girard. *Brouillon project d'un atteinte aux evenmens des rencontres du Cone avec un plan*. Paris, 1639.

Descartes, René. *Discours de la méthode*, ed. Etienne Gilson. Paris: Vrin, 1925.

————, *Correspondance*, ed. C. Adam and G. Milhaud, vol. 1. Paris: Félix Alcan, 1936.

————, *Œuvres philosophiques*, 2 vols., ed. Ferdinand Alquié. Paris: Bordas, 1988.

————, *The Philosophical Writings of Descartes*, 2 vols., tr. John Cottingham, Robert Stoothoff, and Dugald Murdoch. Cambridge: Cambridge University Press, 1984.

————, *Œuvres de Descartes,* 11 vols., ed. Charles Adam and Paul Tannery. Paris: Vrin, 1971-1986.

Dilthey, William. *Weltanschauung und Analyse des Menschen seit Renaissance und Reformation*, in *Gesammelte Schriften*, vol. 2. Stuttgart: B. G. Teubner, 1957.

Dixon, Paul B. "Balances, Pyramids, Crowns, and the Geometry of Sor Juana Inés de la Cruz, *Hispania* 67 (1984): 560–566.

Donato, Eugenio. "Tesauro's Poetics: Through the Looking Glass," *MLN* 78 (1963): 15–30.

Doney, Willis, ed. *Eternal Truths and the Cartesian Circle: A Collection of Studies*. New York: Garland, 1987.

Doran, Madeleine. *Shakespeare's Dramatic Language*. Madison: University of Wisconsin Press, 1976.

D'Ors, Eugenio. *Lo barroco*. Madrid: Aguilar, 1964.

Du Bellay, Joachim. *La défense et illustration de la langue française*, in *Les regrets*. Paris: Gallimard, 1967.

Du Vair, Guillaume. *The Moral Philosophie of the Stoicks. Englished by Thomas James*, ed. Rudolf Kirk. New Brunswick, N. J., Rutgers University Press, 1951.

Dumarsais, César Chesneau and Pierre Fontanier, *Les tropes* [1818], 2 vols., ed. Gérard Genette. Geneva: Slatkine Reprints, 1967.

Dupont, Florence. *Les monstres de Sénèque: pour une dramaturgie de la tragédie romaine.* Paris: Éditions Belin, 1995.

Eco, Umberto. "The Scandal of Metaphor: Metaphorology and Semiotics," *Poetics Today*, 4.2 (1983): 217–257.

Edwards, Michael. *Racine et Shakespeare.* Paris: PUP, 2004.

Egido, Aurora. *La rosa de silencio: Estudios sobre Gracián.* Madrid: Alianza, 1996.

Eldridge, Richard. "Introduction: Between Acknowledgement and Avoidance," in *Stanley Cavell*, ed. Richard Eldridge, 1–14. Cambridge: Cambridge University Press, 2003.

Eliot, T. S. *Selected Essays, 1917–1932.* New York: Harcourt, Brace and Company, 1938.

Elliott, J. H. "Self-Perception and Decline in Early Seventeenth-Century Spain," *Past and Present* 74 (1977): 41–61.

———, *Spain and its World, 1500–1700.* New Haven: Yale University Press, 1989.

Elton, William R. *King Lear and the Gods.* San Marino: The Huntington Library, 1968.

Erasmus, Desiderius. *On Copia of Words and Ideas*, tr. D. B. King and H. David Rix. Milwaukee: Marquette University Press, 1963.

———, *Copia: Foundations of the Abundant* Style, tr. Betty I. Knott, in *Literary and Educational Writings 2; De Copia / De Ratione Studii*, ed. Craig R. Thompson, *Collected Works of Erasmus*, vol. 24. Toronto: University of Toronto Press, 1978.

———, *Moriae encomium id est stultitiae laus*, ed. Clarence H. Miller, in *Opera omnia*, vol. 9. Amsterdam: North-Holland, 1979.

———, *De copia verborum ac rerum*, ed. Betty I. Knott, *Opera omnia*, vol. 17. Amsterdam: North-Holland, 1988.

———, *The Praise of Folly and Other Writings*, tr. Robert M. Adams. New York: Norton, 1989.

Ernst, Pol. *Les Pensées de Pascal, géologie et stratigraphie.* Paris: Universitas; Oxford: Voltaire Foundation, 1996.

Ettenhuber, Katrin. "Hyperbole: exceeding similitude," in *Renaissance Figures of Speech*, ed. Sylvia Adamson, Gavin Alexander, and Katrin Ettenhuber, 197–216. Cambridge: Cambridge University Press, 2007.

Ettinghausen, Henry. *Francisco de Quevedo and the Neostoic Movement.* Oxford: Oxford University Press, 1972.

Evans, Arthur R. *On Four Modern Humanists: Hofmannsthal, Gundolf, Curtius, Kantorowicz.* Princeton: Princeton University Press, 1970.

Faulkner, Robert K. *Francis Bacon and the Project of Progress.* Lanham, Maryland: Rowman and Littlefield, 1993.

Felman, Shoshana. *Writing and Madness (Literature/ Philosophy/ Psychoanalysis)*, tr. Martha Noel Evans, Shoshana Felman, with Brian Massumi. Ithaca: Cornell University Press, 1985.

Fernández López, Jorge. *Retórica, humanismo y filología: Quintiliano y Lorenzo Valla.* Logroño: Ediciones Instituto de Estudios Riojanos, 1999.

Fineman, Joel. *Shakespeare's Perjured Eye: The Invention of Poetic Subjectivity in the Sonnets.* Berkeley: University of California Press, 1986.

Fischer, Michael. *Stanley Cavell and Literary Skepticism.* Chicago: University of Chicago Press, 1989.

Flasch, Kurt. "Nikolaus von Kues: Die Idee der Koinzidenz," *Philosophie des Altertums und des Mittelalters*, ed. Josef Speck, 214–254. Göttingen: Vandenhoeck & Ruprecht, 2001.

Fly, Richard. *Shakespeare's Mediated World.* Amherst: University of Massachusetts Press, 1976.

Fontanier, Pierre. *Les figures de discours*, ed. Gérard Genette. Paris: Flammarion, 1968.

Forcione, Alban K. "At the Threshold of Modernity: Gracián's *El Criticón*," in *Rhetoric and Politics: Baltasár Gracián and the New World Order*, ed. Nicholas Spadaccini and Jenaro Talens, 3–70. Minneapolis: University of Minnesota Press, 1997.

Forster, Leonard. "La renaissance du stoïcisme," *L'époque de la Renaissance (1400–1600). Tome IV: Crises et essors nouveaux (1560–1610)*, ed. Tibor Klaniczay, Eva Kushner, and Paul Chavy, 121–138. Amsterdam and Philadelphia: John Benjamins, 2000.

Foucault, Michel. *Historie de la Folie.* Paris: Gallimard, 1972.

———, *The Order of Things: An Archaeology of the Human Sciences.* New York: Vintage, 1994.

France, Peter. *Rhetoric and Truth in France.* Oxford: Clarendon Press, 1972.

Frankfurt, Harry. *Demons, Dreamers, and Madmen: The Defense of Reason in Descartes's Meditations.* Indianapolis: Bobbs-Merrill, 1970.

———, *On Bullshit.* Princeton: Princeton University Press, 2005.

Frare, Pierantonio. *"Per istraforo di perspettiva":* il Cannochiale aristotelico *e la poesia del Seicento.* Pisa: Instituti editoriali e poligrafici internazionali, 2001.

Frey, Charles. *Experiencing Shakespeare*. Columbia: University of Missouri Press, 1988.

Friedrich, Hugo. *Montaigne*, tr. Dawn Eng. Berkeley: University of California Press, 1991.

Fuhrmann, Manfred. *Seneca und Kaiser Nero: Eine Biographie*. Berlin: Alexander Fest Verlag, 1997.

Fumaroli, Marc, *L'âge de l'éloquence: Rhétorique et "res literaria" de la Renaissance au seuil de l'époque classique*. Geneva: Droz, 1980.

———, ed. *Histoire de la rhétorique dans l'Europe moderne, 1450–1950*. Paris: PUF, 1999.

Gadamer, Hans-Georg. *The Relevance of the Beautiful and Other Essays*. Cambridge: Cambridge University Press, 1986.

———, *Truth and Method*, 2nd rev. ed. New York: Continuum, 1999.

Galand-Hallyn, Perrine, and Fernand Hallyn, eds. *Poétiques de la Renaissance: Le modèle italien, le monde franco-bourguignon et leur héritage en France au XVIe siècle*. Geneva: Droz, 2001.

Gans, Eric. "Hyperbole et ironie," *Poétique* 24 (1975): 488–494.

Gardner, Helen, ed. *The Metaphysical Poets*. London: Penguin Books, 1985.

Gatti, Hilary. *Giordano Bruno and Renaissance Science*. Ithaca: Cornell University Press, 1999.

Gaukroger, Stephen. *Descartes' System of Natural Philosophy*. Cambridge: Cambridge University Press, 2002.

Gaylord, Mary. "Góngora and the Footprints of the Voice," *MLN* 108 (1993): 230–253.

Genette, Gérard. *Figures*. Paris: Éditions du Seuil, 1966.

———, *Figures III*. Paris: Éditions du Seuil, 1972.

Geyer-Ryan, Helga. "Abjection in the Texts of Walter Benjamin," in *Walter Benjamin: Appropriations*, ed. Peter Osborne, 261–279. London and New York: Routledge, 2005.

Gibson, John, and Wolfgang Huemer, eds. *The Literary Wittgenstein*. London and New York: Routledge, 2004.

Gilman, Ernest. *The Curious Perspective: Literary and Pictorial Wit in the Seventeenth Century*. New Haven: Yale University Press, 1978.

Glantz, Margo. "Dialectica de lo alto y de lo bajo: *El sueño*," in *Sor Juana Inés de la Cruz*, ed. Luis Sáinz de Medrano, 47–66. Rome: Bulzoni, 1997.

Glare, P. G. W., ed. *Oxford Latin Dictionary*. Oxford: Clarendon Press, 2004.

Goldberg, Jonathan. "Perspectives: Dover Cliff and the Conditions of Representation,"*Shakespeare and Deconstruction*, ed. G. Douglas Atkins and David M. Bergeron, 245–265. New York: Peter Lang, 1988.

———, *James I and the Politics of Literature*. Stanford: Stanford University Press, 1989.

Goldmann, Lucien. *Le Dieu cachée: Étude sur la vision tragique dans les Pensées de Pascal et dans le théatre de Racine*. Paris: Gallimard, 1955.

Góngora y Argote, Luis de. *Soledades de D. Luis de Góngora. Comentadas de d. García de Salzedo Coronel*, ed. José García de Salcedo Coronel. Madrid, 1636.

———, *El Polifemo de Don Luis de Góngora, Comentado de don Garcia de Salcedo Coronel*, ed. José García de Salcedo Coronel. Madrid, 1636.

———, *Antología poética*, ed. Antonio Carreira. Madrid: Castalia, 1986.

———, *Fábula de Polifemo y Galatea*, 5th ed., ed. Alexander Parker. Madrid: Cátedra, 1993.

———, *Soledades*, ed. John Beverley. Madrid: Cátedra, 1995.

González de Cellorigo, Martin. *Memorial de la política necessaria y útil restauración a la República de España y estados de ella y del desempeño universal de estos Reinos* (1600), ed. José Luis Pérez de Ayala. Madrid: Instituto de cooperación iberoamericana, 1991.

Gouhier, Henri. *La pensée métaphysique de Descartes*. Paris: Vrin, 1962.

Gracián, Baltasar. *Oráculo manual y arte de prudencia*. Salamanca: Anaya, 1968.

———, *El Criticón, Obras Completas I*. Madrid: Turner, 1993.

———, *Agudeza y arte de ingenio*, 2 vols. Madrid: Castalia, 2001.

Grafton, Anthony. *Joseph Scaliger: A Study in the History of Classical Scholarship*, 2 vols. New York: Oxford University Press, 1983/93.

———, *Cardano's Cosmos: The Worlds and Works of a Renaissance Astrologer*. Cambridge: Harvard University Press, 1999.

Grasset, Bernard. *Les Pensées de Pascal, une interprétation de l'écriture*. Paris: Kimé, 2003.

Grassi, Ernesto. *Rhetoric as Philosophy: The Humanist Tradition*. University Park: Pennsylvania State University Press, 1980.

Green, Otis. *Spain and the Western Tradition*, 4 vols. Madison and Milwaukee: University of Wisconsin Press, 1965.

Greene, Roland. *Post-Petrarchism: Origins and Innovations of the Western Lyric Sequence*. Princeton: Princeton University Press, 1991.

Greenblatt, Stephen. *Marvelous Possessions*. Chicago: University of Chicago Press, 1991.

Grimal, Pierre. *Sénèque, ou la conscience de l'Empire*. Paris: Société d'Édition, 1979.

Grossi, Verónica. *Siglosos v(u)elos epistemológicos en Sor Juana Inés de la Cruz*. Madrid: Iberoamericana, 2007.

Guastella, Gianni. *L'ira e l'onore. Forme della vendetta nel teatro senecano e nella sua tradizione*. Palermo: Palumbo, 2001.

Gueroult, Martial. *Descartes' Philosophy Interpreted According to the Order of Reasons*, 2 vols., tr. Roger Ariew. Minneapolis: University of Minnesota Press, 1984.

Guillén, Claudio. "Quevedo y los géneros literarios," in *Quevedo in Perspective*, ed. James Iffland, 1–16. Newark, DE.: Juan de a Cuesta, 1982.

Gumbrecht, Hans Ulrich. *Vom Leben und Sterben der grossen Romanisten: Karl Vossler, Ernst Robert Curtius, Leo Spitzer, Erich Auerbach, Werner Krauss*. Munich: Carl Hanser Verlag, 2002.

Guzmán, Juan de. *Primera parte de la Rhetorica*, ed. Blanca Periñan. Pisa: Giardini, 1993.

Hallyn, Fernand. *The Poetic Structure of the World: Copernicus and Kepler*. New York: Zone Books, 1993.

Hamlin, William M. *Tragedy and Skepticism in Shakespeare's England*. New York: Palgrave Macmillan, 2005.

Hammond, Nicholas. *Playing with Truth: Language and the Human Condition in Pascal's* Pensées. Oxford: Clarendon Press, 1994.

Hampton, Timothy. "Introduction: Baroques," in *Baroque Topographies: Literature, History, Philosophy*, ed. Timothy Hampton, 1–9. New Haven: Yale University Press, 1991.

Hankins, John Erskine. *Backgrounds of Shakespeare's Thought*. Hamden, CT: Archon Press, 1978.

Hanssen, Beatrice. "Philosophy at Its Origin: Walter Benjamin's Prologue to the *Ursprung des deutschen Trauerspiels*," *MLN* 110 (1995): 809–833.

Hardie, Philip. *Virgil's* Aeneid: *Cosmos and Imperium*. Oxford: Clarendon Press, 1986.

Harries, Karsten. "The Infinite Sphere: Comments on a History of a Metaphor," *Journal of the History of Philosophy* 13.1 (1975): 5–15.

———, "Metaphor and Transcendence," *Critical Inquiry* 5.1 (1978): 73–90.

Hart, Kevin. *The Trespass of the Sign: Deconstruction, Theology and Philosophy*, 2nd ed. New York: Fordham University Press, 2000.

Hathaway, Baxter. *Marvels and Commonplaces: Renaissance Literary Criticism*. New York: Random House, 1968.

Hatzfeld, Helmut. *Estudios sobre el Barroco*, 3rd ed. Madrid: Gredos, 1972.

Haverkamp, Anselm. "Metaphora Dis/Continua: Base Respects of Thrift But

None of Love," *Die Aktualität der Rhetorik*, ed. Heinrich F. Plett, 176–189. Munich: Wilhelm Fink, 1997.

Heaney, Seamus. *District and Circle*. New York: Farrar, Straus & Giroux, 2006.

Helgerson, Richard. "The Folly of Maps and Modernity," *Literature, Mapping, and the Politics of Space in Early Modern Britain*, ed. Andrew Gordon and Bernhard Klein, 241–262. Cambridge: Cambridge University Press, 2001.

Herington, C. J. "Senecan Tragedy," *Arion* 5.6 (1966): 422–471.

Hermann, Gottfried. *Opuscula*, 8 vols. Leipzig, 1831; reprinted Hildesheim: G. Olms, 1970.

Hermogenes. *On Types of Style*, ed. and tr. Cecil W. Wooten. Chapel Hill: University of North Carolina Press, 1987.

Herrera, Fernando de. *Anotaciones a la poesía de Garcilaso*, ed. Inoria Pepe and José María Reyes. Madrid: Cátedra, 2001.

Hersant, Yves. *La métaphore baroque: D'Aristote à Tesauro. Extraits du* Cannochiale aristotelico *et autres textes*. Paris: Éditions du Seuil, 2001.

Hester, Marcus. *The Meaning of Poetic Metaphor*. The Hague: Mouton, 1967.

Hill, Ruth. *Sceptres and Sciences in the Spains: Four Humanists and the New Philosophy (ca. 1680–1740)*. Liverpool: Liverpool University Press, 2000.

Hölderlin, Friedrich. *Sämtliche Werke und Briefe*, 3 vols., ed. Jochen Schmidt. Frankfurt am Main: DKV, 1994.

Homer. *The Iliad*, tr. Richmond Lattimore. Chicago: University of Chicago Press, 1951.

Hooke, Robert. *Micrographia*. London, 1665.

Hoover, Elaine. *John Donne and Francisco de Quevedo: Poets of Love and Death*. Chapel Hill: University of North Carolina Press, 1978.

Horkeimer, Max, and Theodor W. Adorno. *Dialectic of Enlightenment*, tr. Edmund Jephcott. Stanford: Stanford University Press, 2002.

Horner, Robyn. *Jean-Luc Marion: A Theo-logical Introduction*. Burlington: Ashgate, 2005.

Hoskins, John. *Directions for Speech and Style*, ed. Hoyt H. Hudson. Princeton: Princeton University Press, 1935.

Howell, W. S. *Logic and Rhetoric in England, 1500–1700*. Princeton: Princeton University Press, 1956.

Huarte de San Juan, Juan. *Examen de ingenios para las ciencias*, ed. Guillermo Serés. Madrid: Cátedra, 1989.

Huidobro, Vicente. *Altazor*. Barcelona: Andres Bello, 2001.

Iffland, James. *Quevedo and the Grotesque*. London: Tamesis, 1978.

Inés de la Cruz, Sor Juana. *Die Welt im Traum: Eine Dichtung der "zehnten Muse von Mexiko,"* ed. Karl Vossler. Berlin: Ulrich Riemerschmidt Verlag, 1941.

———, *Obras completas de Sor Juana Inés de la Cruz,* 4 vols., ed. Alfonso Méndez Plancarte. Mexico City: Fondo de Cultura Económica, 1951; vol. 4, ed. Alberto G. Salceda, 1957.

———, *Inundación castálida.* Mexico City: UNAM, 1952.

———, *Poesía Lírica,* ed. José Carlos González Boixo. Madrid: Cátedra, 1992.

Irwin, T. H. "Ethics in the *Rhetoric* and in the Ethics," in *Essays on Aristotle's Rhetoric,* ed. A. O. Rorty, 142–172. Berkeley: University of California Press, 1996.

Jacquot, Jean. "Sénèque, la renaissance et nous," in *Les tragédies de Sénèque et le théâtre de la renaissance,* ed. Jean Jacquot, 271–307. Paris: CNRS, 1964.

Jammes, Robert. *La obra poética de Don Luis de Góngora y Argote,* tr. Manuel Moya. Madrid: Castalia, 1987.

Jardine, Lisa. *Francis Bacon: Discovery and the Art of Discourse.* Cambridge: Cambridge University Press, 1974.

Jaumann, Herbert. *Critica: Untersuchungen zur Geschichte der Literaturkritik zwischen Quintilian und Thomasius.* Leiden: Brill, 1995.

Jauralde Pou, Pablo. "Aventura intelectual de Quevedo, *España defendida,*" in *Quevedo a nueva luz: escritura y política,* ed. Lía Schwartz and Antonio Carreira, 45–58. Malaga: Universidad de Málaga, 1997.

———, *Francisco de Quevedo (1580–1645).* Madrid: Castalia, 1999.

Javitch, Daniel. *Poetry and Courtliness in Renaissance England.* Princeton: Princeton University Press, 1978.

Johnson, Christopher. "De Doctrina Gongorina: Góngora's Defense of Obscurity," *BHS* 77.1 (2000): 21–46.

———, "Clavius's Number and Its Early Modern Afterlife," in *Arts of Calculation: Numerical Thought in Early Modern Europe,* ed. David Glimp and Michelle Warren, 67–92. New York: Palgrave Macmillan, 2004.

Johnson, Samuel. *Selected Poetry and Prose,* ed. Frank Brady and W. K. Wimsatt. Berkeley: University of California Press, 1977.

Jones, Matthew L. *The Good Life in the Scientific Revolution: Descartes, Pascal, Leibniz and the Cultivation of Virtue.* Chicago: Univeristy of Chicago Press, 2006.

Jones, R. F. *Ancients and Moderns: A Study of the Rise of the Scientific Movement of Seventeenth-Century England.* Berkeley: University of California Press, 1961.

Jones, R. O. "The Poetic Unity of the *Soledades,*" *BHS* 31 (1954): 189–204.

———, "Neoplatonism and the *Soledades,*" *BHS* 40 (1963): 1–16.

———, "Góngora and Neoplatonism Again," *BHS* 43 (1966): 117–120.

Kahn, Coppélia. "The Absent Mother in *King Lear*," in *Rewriting the Renaissance: The Discourse of Sexual Difference in Early Modern Europe,* ed. Margaret Ferguson, Maureen Quilligan, and Nancy J. Vickers, 33–49. Chicago: University of Chicago Press, 1986.

Kallendorf, Craig. "*King Lear* and the Figures of Speech," in *Landmark Essays on Rhetoricand Literature,* ed. Craig Kallendorf, 101–118. Mahwah, NJ: Hermagoras Press, 1999.

Kant, Immanuel. *Kritik der Urteilskraft,* in *Werke,* 12 vols. Wiesbaden: Insel Verlag, 1957.

———, *Critique of the Power of Judgment,* ed. Paul Guyer; tr. Paul Guyer and Eric Matthews. Cambridge: Cambridge University Press, 2001.

Kemp, Friedhlem. *Das europäische Sonett,* 2 vols. Munich: Wallstein, 2002.

Kemp Smith, Norman. *New Studies in the Philosophy of Descartes.* London: Macmillan, 1966.

Kennedy, George A. "Theophrastus and Stylistic Distinctions," *Harvard Studies in Classical Philology* 62 (1957): 93–104.

———, *Quintilian.* New York: Twayne Publishers, 1969.

———, *Classical Rhetoric and its Christian and Secular Tradition from Ancient to Modern Times.* Chapel Hill: University of North Carolina Press, 1980.

Kerr, Fergus. *Theology after Wittgenstein.* Oxford: Blackwell, 1986.

Kessler, Eckhard and Ian Maclean, eds. *Res et Verba in der Renaissance.* Wiesbaden: Harrassowitz in Kommission, 2002.

Kircher, Athanasius. *Oedipus aegyptiacus,* 4 vols. Rome, 1654.

Knight, G. Wilson. *The Wheel of Fire: Interpretations of Shakespearian Tragedy.* London: Methuen, 1986.

Koch, Erec R. *Pascal and Rhetoric: Figural and Persuasive Language in the Scientific Treatises, the* Provinciales, *and the* Pensées. Charlottesville: Rockwood Press, 1997.

Kosman, L. Aryeh. "The Naive Narrator: Meditation in Descartes' *Meditations,*" in *Essays on Descartes' Meditations,* ed. A. O. Rorty, 21–44. Berkeley: University of California Press, 1986.

Krabbenhoft, Kenneth. "Góngora's Stoic Pilgrim," *BHS* 73 (1996): 1–12.

Kraye, Jill. "Moral Philosophy," in *The Cambridge History of Renaissance Philosophy,* ed. Charles B. Schmitt and Quentin Skinner, 303–386. Cambridge: Cambridge University Press, 1988.

Kuhlmann, Quirinus. *Himmlische Libes-küsse* (1671), ed. Birgit Biehl-Werner. Tübingen: Niemeyer, 1971.

Labron, Tim. *Wittgenstein's Religious Point of View.* London: Continuum, 2006.

Lakoff, George, and Mark Johnson. *Metaphors We Live By*. Chicago: University of Chicago Press, 1980.

Laks, André. "Substitution et connaissance: une interprétation unitaire (ou presque) de la théorie aristotélicienne de la métaphore," in *Aristotle's* Rhetoric: *Philosophical Essays*, ed. David J. Furley and Alexander Nehemas, 283–305. Princeton: Princeton University Press, 1994.

Lambert, Gregg. *The Return of the Baroque in Modern Culture*. London and New York: Continuum, 2004.

Lamberton, Robert. *Homer the Theologian: Neoplatonist Allegorical Reading and the Growth of the Epic Tradition*. Berkeley: University of California Press, 1986.

Landauer, Carl. "Ernst Robert Curtius and the Topos of the Book," ed. R. Howard Bloch and Stephen G. Nichols, *Medievalism and the Modernist Temper*. Baltimore: Johns Hopkins University Press, 1996.

Lanham, Richard. *A Handlist of Rhetorical Terms*. Berkeley: University of California Press, 1991.

Lausberg, Heinrich. *Ernst Robert Curtius (1886–1956)*, ed. Arnold Arens. Stuttgart: Steiner Verlag, 1993.

———, *Handbook of Literary Rhetoric: A Foundation for Literary Study*, ed. David E. Orton and R. Dean Anderson. Leiden: Brill, 1998.

Lefebvre, Henri. *The Production of Space*, tr. Donald Nicholson-Smith. Oxford: Blackwell Publishing, 1991.

Lefèvre, Eckard, ed. *Der Einfluß Senecas auf das europäische Drama*. Darmstadt: Wissenschaftliche Buchgesellschaft, 1978.

Leibniz, G. W. *Textes inédits*, 2 vols., ed. Gaston Grua. Paris: PUP, 1948.

Leonard, Irving A. *Don Carlos de Sigüenza y Góngora: A Mexican Savant of the Seventeenth Century*. Berkeley: University of California Press, 1929.

Lessing, G. E. *Laokoön*, in *Werke*, 12 vols., ed. Kurt Wölfel. Frankfurt am Main: Insel, 1982.

Lestringant, Frank. *Mapping the Renaissance World: The Geographical Imagination in the Age of Discovery*, tr. David Fausett. Berkeley: University of California Press, 1994.

Levin, Harry. *The Overreacher: A Study of Christopher Marlowe*. Cambridge: Harvard University Press, 1952.

———, "The Heights and Depths: A Scene from *King Lear*," in *More Talking of Shakespeare*, ed. John Garret, 87–103. London: Longmans, Green, 1959.

Lewis C. T., and Charles Short. *A Latin Dictionary*. Oxford: Clarendon Press, 1962.

Lezama Lima, José. *Obras completas*, 2 vols. Mexico City: Aguilar, 1977.

————, *La expresión americana*. Mexico City: Fondo de la cultura económica, 1993.

Lezra, Jacques. *Unspeakable Subjects: The Genealogy of the Event in Early Modern Europe*. Stanford: Stanford University Press, 1997.

Liddell, H. G., and Robert Scott. *A Greek-English Lexicon*. Oxford: Clarendon Press, 1996.

Liebermann, Wolf-Lüder, Margerethe Billerbeck, and Ernst A. Schmidt, eds. *Sénèque: le tragique*. Geneva: Fondation Hardt, 2004.

Lipsius, Justus. *De constantia libri duo. Qui alloquium praecipue continent in Publicis malis.* Antwerp, 1584.

————, *Two Bookes of Constancie*, tr. John Stradling. London, 1595.

————, *Epistolario de Justo Lipsio y los Españoles*. Madrid: Castalia, 1966.

Littlewood, C. A. J. *Self-Representation and Illusion in Senecan Tragedy*. Oxford: Oxford University Press, 2004.

Locati, Silvia. *La rinascita del genere tragico nel Medioevo: l'*Ecerinis *di Albertino Mussato*. Florence: F. Cesati, 2006.

Long, Anthony. "The Stoics on World-Conflagration and Everlasting Recurrence," *Southern Journal of Philosophy* 23 (1985): 13–38.

Longinus. *On the Sublime*, ed. and tr. W. Rhys Roberts. Cambridge: At the University Press, 1935.

————, *On the Sublime*, ed. D. A. Russell. Oxford: At the Clarendon Press, 1964.

————, *On the* Sublime, tr. and ed. James A. Arieti and John M. Crossett. New York: The Edwin Mellon Press, 1985.

————, *On the Sublime*, tr. W. H. Fyfe. Cambridge: Harvard University Press, 1995.

López Camara, Francisco. "El cartesianísmo en Sor Juana y Sigüenza y Góngora," *FYL* 20 (1950): 107–131.

Lopéz de Gómara, Francisco. *Historia general de las Indias*. Madrid: Iberia, 1982.

López Pinciano, Alfonso. *Philosophia antigua poética*, ed. Alfredo Carballo Picazo, vol. 3. Madrid: CSIC, 1953.

López Piñero, J. M. *Ciencia y técnica en la sociedad española de los siglos XVI y XVII*. Barcelona: Labor Universitaria, 1979.

Ludwin, Dawn M. *Blaise Pascal's Quest for the Ineffable*. New York: Peter Lang, 2001.

Lynes Jr., Carlos. "A Defense of the 'Récit de Théramène,'" *MLN* 59.6 (1944): 387–391.

Lyons, John D. "Rhétorique du discours cartésien," *Cahiers de littérature de XVIIe siècle* 8 (1986): 125–147.

Lyotard, Jean-François. *Leçons sur l'Analytique du sublime*. Paris: Galilée, 1991.

Mack, Peter. *Renaissance Argument: Valla and Agricola in the Tradition of Rhetoric and Dialectic*. Leiden: E. J. Brill, 1993.

————, *Elizabethan Rhetoric: Theory and Practice*. Cambridge: Cambridge University Press, 2002.

Maclean, Ian. "Foucault's Renaissance Episteme Reassessed: An Aristotelian Counterblast," *JHI* 59 (1998): 149–166.

Maggioni, Mary. *The 'Pensées' of Pascal: A Study in Baroque Style*. Washington: The Catholic University of America Press, 1950.

Magniont, Gilles. *Traces de la voix Pascalienne. Examen des marques de l'énonciation dans les* Pensées. Lyon: Presses universitaires de Lyon, 2003.

Malcolm, Norman. *Wittgenstein: A Religious Point of View?* Ithaca: Cornell University Press, 1994.

Maravall, José Antonio. *Culture of the Baroque: Analysis of a Historical Structure*, tr. Terry Cochran. Minneapolis: University of Minnesota Press, 1986.

Margolin, Jean-Claude. *Erasme: le prix des mots et de l'homme*. London: Variorum Reprints, 1986.

Marion, Jean-Luc. *Sur le prisme métaphysique de Descartes: Constitution et limites de l'onto-théo-logie dans la pensée cartésienne*. Paris: PUF, 1986.

————, "The Place of the *Objections* in the Developement of Cartesian Metaphysics," in *Descartes and his Contemporaries: Meditations, Objections, and Replies*, ed. Roger Ariew and Marjorie Grene, 7–20. Chicago: University of Chicago Press, 1995.

————, *Reduction and Givenness: Investigations of Husserl, Heidegger, and Phenomenology*, tr. Thomas A. Carlson. Evanston: Northwestern University Press, 1998.

————, "In the Name: How to Avoid Speaking of Negative Theology," in *God, The Gift, and Postmodernism*, ed. John D. Caputo and Michael J. Scanlon, 20–42. Bloomington: Indiana University Press, 1999.

————, *On Descartes's Metaphysical Prism*, tr. Jeffrey L. Koskey. Chicago: University of Chicago Press, 1999.

————, *Being Given: Toward a Phenomenology of Givenness*, tr. Jeffrey L. Kosky. Stanford: Stanford University Press, 2002.

————, *In Excess: Studies of Saturated Phenomena*, tr. Robyn Horner and Vincent Berraud. New York: Fordham University Press, 2002.

Mariscal, George. *Contradictory Subjects: Quevedo, Cervantes, and Seventeenth-Century Spanish Culture*. Ithaca: Cornell University Press, 1991.

Markie, Peter. *Descartes's Gambit*. Ithaca: Cornell University Press, 1986.

———, "The Cogito and its Importance," in *The Cambridge Companion to Descartes*, ed. John Cottingham, 140–173. Cambridge: Cambridge University Press, 1992.

Marsh, David. "Julius Caesar Scaliger's *Poetics*," *Journal of the History of Ideas* 65.4 (2004): 667–676.

Martindale, Charles and Michelle. *Shakespeare and the Uses of Antiquity*. London; New York: Routledge, 1994.

Mathieu-Castellani, Gisèle. "Baroque et maniérisme," in *Dictionnaire universel des littératures*, ed. Béatrice Didier, 1:342–345. Paris: PUF, 1994.

May, T. E. *Wit of the Golden Age*. Kassel: Reichenberger, 1986.

Mazzeo, Joseph. "Metaphysical Poetry and the Poetry of Correspondences," *JHI* 14 (1953): 221–235.

McGinn, Marie. *Wittgenstein and the* Philosophical Investigations. New York: Routledge, 1997.

McKeon, Richard. "Rhetoric in the Middle Ages," *Speculum* 17 (1942): 1–32.

McLaughlin, Martin L. *Literary Imitation in the Italian Renaissance: The Theory and Practice of Literary Imitation from Dante to Bembo*. Oxford: Clarendon Press, 1995.

Meerhoff, Kees. *Rhétorique et Poétique au XVIᵉ Siècle en France: Du Bellay, Ramus et les autres*. Leiden: Brill, 1986.

Melzer, Sara. *Discourses of the Fall: A Study of Pascal's* Pensées. Berkeley: University of California Press, 1986.

Mertner, Edgar. "Topos und Commonplace," in *Toposforschung*, ed. Peter Jehn, 20–68. Frankfurt am Main: Athenäum Verlag, 1972.

Mesnard, Jean. "La théorie des figuratifs chez Pascal," *Revue d'Histoire de la Philosophie et d'Histoire générale*, 35 (1943): 219–259.

———, *Pascal*. Paris: Desclée de Brouwer, 1965.

———, *Les* Pensées *de Pascal*, rev. ed. Paris: SEDES, 1993.

Mesnard, Pierre. *Essai sur la morale de Descartes*. Paris: Bolvin, 1936.

Meyer, Holt. "Jesuit Concedes Jesuit Conceits: A Hit on Sarbievius' Head," in *Gedächtnis und Phantasma: Festschrift für Renate Lachmann*, ed. Susi K. Frank et al., 372–389. Munich: Otto Sanger, 2001.

Michel, Alain. "La rhétorique, sa vocation et ses problèmes: sources antiques et médiévales," in *Histoire de la rhétorique dans l'Europe moderne, 1450–1950*, ed. Marc Fumaroli, 17–45. Paris: PUF, 1999.

Michon, Hélène. *L'ordre du cœur: la théologie et mystique dans les* Pensées *de Pascal*. Paris: Honoré Champion, 1996.

Miel, Jan. *Pascal and Theology.* Baltimore: The Johns Hopkins University Press, 1969.

Mieszkowski, Jan. *Labors of the Imagination: Aesthetics and Political Economy from Kant to Althusser.* New York: Fordham University Press, 2006.

Miles, Murray. "Descartes's Method," in *A Companion to Descartes*, ed. Janet Broughton and John Carriero, 145–163. Oxford: Blackwell, 2008.

Milton, John. *Complete Prose Works of John Milton*, 8 vols. New Haven: Yale University Press, 1953–1982.

Miola, Robert S. *Shakespeare and Classical Tragedy: The Influence of Seneca.* Oxford: Clarendon Press, 1992.

Mohlo, Maurice. "Sobre un soneto de Quevedo: 'En crespa tempestad del oro undoso,'"*Francisco de Quevedo*, ed. Gonzalo Sobejano, 343–377. Madrid: Taurus, 1978.

———, "Una cosmogonía antisemita: 'Érase un hombre a un nariz pegado,'" *Quevedo in Perspective*, ed. James Iffland, 57–80. Newark, Del.: Juan de a Cuesta, 1982

Monfasani, John. "Humanism and Rhetoric," in *Renaissance Humanism: Foundations, Forms, and Legacy*, vol. 3, ed. Albert Rabil, Jr., 171–235. Philadelphia: University of Pennsylvania Press, 1988.

Montaigne, Michel de. *The Essayes of Michael Lord Of Montaigne*, 3 vols., tr. John Florio. New York: E. P. Dutton, 1927.

———, *Essais*, 3 vols. Paris: Flammarion, 1979.

Moraleja, Alfonso, ed. *Gracián hoy*. Madrid: Cuaderno Gris, 2002.

Moran, Richard. "Artifice and Persuasion: The Work of Metaphor in the *Rhetoric*," in *Essays on Aristotle's* Rhetoric, ed. Amélie Oksenberg Rorty, 385–398. Berkeley: University of California Press, 1996.

Morford, Mark. *The Poet Lucan: A Study in Rhetorical Epic.* Oxford: Basil Blackwell, 1967.

Morpurgo Tagliabue, Guido. "Aristotelismo e barocco," in *Retorica e barocco. Atti del III Congresso internazionale di studi umanistici*, ed. Enrico Castelli, 119–195. Rome: Fratelli Boca, 1955.

Moser, Walter. "Barock," in *Asthetische Grundbegriffe: historisches Wörterbuch in sieben Bänden*, ed. Karlheinz Barck et al., 1:578–618. Stuttgart: J. B. Metzler, 2000–2005.

———, "Résurgences baroques," in *Diskurse des Barocks: Dezentrierte oder rezentrierte Welt*, ed. Joachim Küpper and Friedrich Wolfzettel, 655–680. Munich: Wilhelm Fink, 2000.

Moss, Anne. "Theories of Poetry: Latin Writers," in *The Cambridge History of*

Literary Criticism, vol. 3., ed. Glyn P. Norton, 98–105. Cambridge: Cambridge University Press, 1999.

Most, Glenn W. "The Uses of *Endoxa*: Philosophy and Rhetoric in the *Rhetoric*," in *Aristotle's* Rhetoric: *Philosophical Essays*, ed. David J. Furley and Alexander Nehemas, 167–190. Princeton: Princeton University Press, 1994.

Murphy, James J. *Rhetoric in the Middle Ages: A History of Rhetorical Theory from St. Augustine to the Renaissance*. Berkeley: University of California Press, 1974.

———, ed. *Renaissance Eloquence: Studies in the Theory and Practice of Renaissance Rhetoric*. Berkeley: University of California Press, 1983.

———, and Lawrence D. Green. *Renaissance Rhetoric Short-Title Catalogue 1460–1700*, 2nd ed. Burlington, VT: Ashgate, 2006.

Nancy, Jean-Luc. *Ego Sum*. Paris: Flammarion, 1979.

Nanfito, Jacqueline. "Sor Juana Inés de la Cruz's "El sueño": The Spatialization of Form in the Baroque Poetic Text," *Revista de estudios Hispánicos* 23 (1989) 53–65.

———, *El sueño: Cartographies of Knowledge and the Self*. New York: Peter Lang, 2000.

Natan, Stéphane. *Les* Pensées *de Pascal. D'un projet apologétique à un texte poétique.* Paris: Connaissance et savoirs, 2004.

Navarrete, Ignacio. *Orphans of Petrarch: Poetry and Theory in the Spanish Renaissance* Berkeley: University of California Press, 1994.

Negri, Antonio. *Descartes Politico*. Milan: Feltrinelli Editore, 1970.

Nicole, Pierre and Lancelot, Claude. *Epigrammatum delectus, ex omnibus, tum veteribus, tum recentioribus poetis accurate decerptus . . .* London, 1683.

Nietzsche, Friedrich. *Kritische Studienausgabe*, 15 vols., ed. Giorgio Colli and Mazzino Montinari. Munich: DTV, 1988.

———, *Nietzsche on Rhetoric and Language*, ed. and tr. Sander L. Gilman, Carole Blair, and David J. Parent. Oxford: Oxford University Press, 1989.

Norden, Eduard. "Die Composition und Literaturgattung der Horazischen Epistula ad Pisones," *Hermes* 40 (1905): 481–528.

Norton, Glyn P., ed. *Cambridge History of Literary Criticism: The Renaissance*, vol. 3. Cambridge: Cambridge University Press, 1999.

Olivares Zorrilla, Rocío. "Los tópicos del *Sueño* y del microcosmos: la tradición de Sor Juana Inés de la Cruz," *Sor Juana Inés de la Cruz y las vicisitudes de la crítica*, ed. Jose Pascual Buxó, 179–211. Mexico City: UNAM, 1998.

Ong, Walter F. *Ramus, Method, and the Decay of Dialogue: From the Art of Discourse to the Art of Reason*. Cambridge: Harvard University Press, 1983.

Orgel, Stephen. "Shakespeare Imagines a Theater," *Poetics Today* 5.3 (1984): 549–561.

Orozco Diaz, Emilio, ed. *Lope y Góngora frente a frente*. Madrid: Gredos, 1973.

Owens, David. "Descartes's Use of Doubt," in *A Companion to Descartes*, ed. Janet Broughton and John Carriero, 164–178. Oxford: Blackwell, 2008.

Padrón, Ricardo. "Mapping Plus Ultra: Cartography, Space and Hispanic Modernity," *Representations* 79 (2002): 28–60.

Pagden, Anthony. *Lords of All the World: Ideologies of Empire in Spain, Britain and France, c.1500–c.1850*. New Haven: Yale University Press, 1995.

Parker, Alexander. "La 'agudeza' in algunos sonetos de Quevedo: Contribución al estudio del Conceptismo," in *Francisco de Quevedo*, ed. Gonzalo Sobejano, 44–57. Madrid: Taurus, 1978.

———, "'Concept' and 'Conceit': An Aspect of Comparative Literary History," *MLR* 77.4 (1982): xxi–xxxv.

Parker, Patricia. "Metaphor and Catachresis," in *The Ends of Rhetoric: History, Theory, Practice*, ed. John Bender and David E. Wellbery, 60–73. Stanford: Stanford University Press, 1990.

Parker, Thomas, *Volition, Rhetoric, and Emotion in the Work of Pascal*. London: Routledge, 2008.

Pascal, Blaise. *Œuvres complètes*, 4 vols. ed. Jean Mesnard. Paris: Desclée De Brouwer, 1964–1992.

———, *Pensées*, ed. Philippe Sellier. Paris: Bordas, 1991.

———, *Pensées*, tr. Roger Ariew. Indianapolis: Hackett, 2005.

Patterson, Annabel. *Hermogenes and the Renaissance: Seven Ideas of Style*. Princeton: Princeton University Press, 1970.

Paz, Octavio. *Sor Juana or, The Traps of Faith*, tr. Margaret Sayers Peden. Harvard University Press, 1988.

———, *Sor Juana Inés de la Cruz o las trampas de la fe*. Barcelona: Editorial Seix Barral, 1992.

Peacham, Henry. *The Garden of Eloquence* (1577, revised 1593), ed. Beate-Maria Koll. Frankfurt am Main: Peter Lang, 1996.

Pellicer de Salas y Tovar, José. *Lecciones solemnes a las obras de Don Luis de Gongora y Argote*. Hildesheim: Olms, 1971.

Perelmuter, Rosa. *Noche intelectual, la oscuridad idiomática en el* Primero sueño. Mexico City: UNAM, 1982.

———, "La estructura retórica de la *Respuesta a Sor Filotea*," *Hispanic Review* 51.2 (1983): 147–158.

Perrin, Casey. "Descartes and the Legacy of Ancient Skepticism," in *A Companion to Descartes*, ed. Janet Broughton and John Carriero, 52–65. Oxford: Blackwell, 2008.

Perrin, Laurent. *L'ironie mise en trope: du sens des énoncés hyperboliques et ironiques*. Paris: Kimé, 1996.

Pfandl, Ludwig. *Sor Juana Inés de la Cruz. La décima musa de México: Su vida, su poesía, su psique*. Mexico City: UNAM, 1963.

Phillips, D. Z. *Wittgenstein and Religion*. New York: St. Martin's Press, 1993.

Phillips, Margaret Mann. *The "Adages" of Erasmus: A Study with Translations*. Cambridge: The University Press, 1964.

Pico della Mirandola, Giovanni. "Oration on the Dignity of Man," tr. Elizabeth Forbes, in *The Renaissance Philosophy of Man*, ed. Ernst Cassirer, P. O. Kristeller, and J. H.Randall, Jr. Chicago: University of Chicago Press, 1948.

————, *De dignitate hominis*. Bad Homburg: Gehlen, 1968.

Plett, Heinrich F. *Rhetoric and Renaissance Culture*. Berlin: Walter de Gruyter, 2004.

————, ed. *Renaissance-Rhetorik | Renaissance Rhetoric*. Berlin: Walter de Gruyter, 1993.

————, ed. *Renaissance-Poetik | Renaissance Poetics*. Berlin: Walter de Gruyter, 1994.

Pohlenz, Max. *Die Stoa: Geschichte einer geistigen Bewegung*. Göttingen: Vandenhoeck & Ruprecht, 1984.

Pope, Alexander. *Pastoral Poetry and An Essay on Criticism*, ed. Émile Audra and Aubrey Williams. New Haven: Yale University Press, 1961.

Popkin, Richard H. *History of Scepticism: from Erasmus to Bayle*. Berkeley: University of California Press, 1979.

Porqueras Mayo, Alberto, ed., *La teoría poética en el Renacimiento y manierismo españoles*. Barcelona: Puvill, 1986.

Pound, Ezra. *ABC of Reading*. New York: New Directions, 1960.

Praz, Mario. "The Flaming Heart: Richard Crashaw and the Baroque," *The Flaming Heart: Essays on Crashaw, Machiavelli, and Other Studies in the Relations between Italian and English Literature from Chaucer to T. S. Eliot*. Garden City, N.Y.: Doubleday, 1958.

Proctor, Robert E. "Emanuele Tesauro: A Theory of the Conceit," *MLN* 88.1 (1973): 68–94.

Pseudo-Dionysius. *The Divine Names*, in *The Complete Works*, tr. Colm Luibheid. New York: Paulist Press, 1987.

Puccini, Dario. *Una mujer en soledad: Sor Juana Inés de la Cruz, una excepción en la cultura y la literatura.* Madrid: Anaya & Mario Muchnik, 1996.

Pugh, Anthony. *The Composition of Pascal's Apologia.* Toronto: University of Toronto Press, 1984.

Putnam, Michael. *Virgil's Epic Designs: Ekphrasis in the* Aeneid. New Haven: Yale University Press, 1998.

Puttenham, George. *The Arte of English Poesie*, ed. Edward Arber. London: Alex. Murray &Son, 1869; reprint AMS Press, 1966.

Quevedo y Villegas, Francisco de. *El Parnasso español, monte en dos cumbres dividido, con las nuevas musas castellanas*, ed. José Antonio González de Salas. Madrid, 1648.

————, *The Dog & the Fever*, tr. W. C. Williams and R. H. Williams. Hamden, CT: The Shoe String Press, 1954.

————, *Obras completas I, Obras en prosa*, ed. Luis Astraña Marin. Madrid: Aguilar, 1961.

————, *Sueños y discursos*, ed. Felipe C. R. Maldonado. Madrid: Castalia, 1972.

————, *Poesía original completa*, ed. José Manuel Blecua. Barcelona: Planeta, 1996.

————, *Preliminares literarios a las poesías de Fray Luis de* León, ed. Antonio Azaustre Galiana, in *Obras completas en prosa*, vol.1.1, gen. ed. Alfonso Rey. Madrid: Castalia, 2003.

————, *Selected Poetry of Francisco de Quevedo*, tr. and ed. Christopher Johnson. Chicago: University of Chicago Press, 2009.

Quint, David. *Epic and Empire: Politics and Generic Form from Virgil to Milton.* Princeton: Princeton University Press, 1993.

Quintilian, *Institutio oratoria*, 5 vols., ed. and tr. Donald A. Russell. Cambridge: Harvard University Press, 2001.

Rabin, Lisa. "The Blason of Sor Juana Inés de la Cruz: Politics and Petrarchism in Colonial Mexico," *Bulletin of Hispanic Studies* 72.1 (1995): 28–39.

Racine, Jean. *Phèdre*, ed. Raymond Picard. Paris: Gallimard, 2000.

Randolph, Thomas. *The Poems of Thomas Randolph.* London: Etchells & Macdonald, 1929.

Real Academia Española, *Diccionario de Autoridades*, 3 vols. Madrid: Gredos, 1963.

Regalado, Antonio. *Calderón: los orígines de la modernidad en la España del Siglo de Oro*, 2 vols. Madrid: Destino, 1995.

Regenbogen, Otto. *Vorträge 1927–1928 zur Geschichte des Dramas.* Leipzig: B. G. Teubner, 1930.

Reiss, Timothy. "The Word/World Equation," *Yale French Studies* 49 (1974): 3–12.

———, "Cartesian Discourse and Classical Ideology," *Diacritics* 6.4 (1976): 19–27.

———, *Mirages of the Selfe: Patterns of Personhood in Ancient and Early Modern Europe*. Stanford: Stanford University Press, 2003.

Renaker, David. "Robert Burton and Ramist Method," *Renaissance Quarterly* 24.2 (1971): 210–220.

Rey, Alfonso. *Quevedo y la poesía moral española*. Madrid: Castalia, 1995.

Ricard, Robert. *Une poétesse mexicaine du XVII siècle: Sor Juana Inés de la Cruz*. Paris: Centre de Documentation Universitaire, 1953.

Richards, Earl J. "E. R. Curtius's Vermächtnis an die Literaturwissenschaft: Die Verbindung von Philologie, Literaturgeschichte und Literaturkritik," *Ernst Robert Curtius: Werk, Wirkung, Zukunftsperspektiven*, ed. Walter Berschin and Arnold Rothe, 249–269. Heidelberg: Carl Winter Universität Verlag, 1989.

Ricoeur, Paul. *The Rule of Metaphor*, tr. Paul Czerny. Toronto: University of Toronto Press, 1975.

Riley, Edward C. "Aspectos del concepto de *admiratio* en la teoria literaria del Siglo de Oro," in *Homenaje ofrecido a Dámaso Alonso, Studia philologica* 3 (1963): 173–183.

Rist, John M. *Stoic Philosophy*. Cambridge: Cambridge University Press, 1969.

Rodríguez-Pantoja, Miguel, ed. *Séneca, dos mil años después: actas del congreso internacional conmemorativo del bimilenario de su nacimiento*. Córdoba: Publicaciones de la Universidad de Córdoba, 1997.

Rohls, Jan. "Schrift, Wort und Sache in der frühen protestantischen Theologie," in *Res et Verba in der Renaissance*, ed. Eckhard Kessler and Ian Maclean, 241–272. Wiesbaden: Harrassowitz, 2002.

Romanowski, Sylvie. *L'illusion chez Descartes: la structure du discours cartésien*. Paris: Klincksieck, 1974.

Rose, H. J. *A Handbook of Latin Literature*. New York: E. P. Dutton & Co., 1960.

Rosenmeyer, Thomas G. *Senecan Drama and Stoic Cosmology*. Berkeley: University of California Press, 1989.

Rosenthal, Earl. "*Plus Ultra, Non Plus Ultra*, and the Columnar Device of Emperor Charles V," *Journal of the Warburg and Courtauld Institutes* 34 (1971): 204–228.

Roses Lozano, Joaquín. *Una poética de la oscuridad: la recepción crítica de las Soledades en el Siglo XVII*. Madrid: Tamesis, 1994.

————, *Góngora:* Soledades *habitadas*. Malaga: Publicaciones de la Universidad de Málaga, 2007.

Ross, Kathleen. *The Baroque Narrative of Carlos de Sigüenza y Góngora: A New World Paradise*. Cambridge: Cambridge University Press, 1993.

Rotman, Brian. *Signifying Nothing: The Semiotics of Zero*. Stanford: Stanford University Press, 1987.

Rousset, Jean. *La littérature de l'âge baroque en France: Circé et le paon*. Paris: José Corti, 1954.

————, *L'interieur et l'exterieur. Essais sur la poésie et sur le théatre*. Paris: José Corti, 1968.

Russell, Bertrand. *History of Western Philosophy*. London: Allan and Unwin, 1946.

Sabat de Rivers, Georgina. "Sor Juana y su *Sueño*: antecedentes científicos en la poesía del Siglo de Oro," *Cuadernos Hispanoamericanos* 3 (1976): 186–204.

————, Georgina. *El "Sueño" de Sor Juana Inés de la Cruz: tradiciones literarias y originalidad*. London: Tamesis, 1977.

————, "A Feminist Reading of Sor Juana's Dream," *Feminist Perspectives on Sor Juana Inés dela Cruz*, ed. Stephanie Merrim, 142–161. Detroit: Wayne State University Press, 1991.

Sambursky, Samuel. *Physics of the Stoics*. Princeton: Princeton University Press, 1987.

Sánchez, Francisco. *Quod nihil scitur (That Nothing is Known)*, ed. Elaine Limbrick, tr. Douglas F. S. Thomson. Cambridge: Cambridge University Press, 1988.

Sánchez Robayna, Andres. "Petrarquismo y parodía (Góngora y Lope)," *Revista de fililogía de la Universidad de la Laguna* 1 (1982): 25–45.

Sarduy, Severo. *Barocco*. Buenos Aires: Editorial Sudamericana, 1974.

Sarmiento, Edward. "On Two Criticisms of Gracián's *Agudeza*," *Hispanic Review* 3.1 (1935): 23–35.

Scaliger, Julius Caesar. *Poetices libri septem / Sieben Bücher über die Dichtkunst*, 5 vols. ed. and tr. Luc Dietz and Gregor Vogt-Spira. Stuttgart-Bad Cannstatt: frommann-holzboog, 1994.

Schaper, Eva. "Taste, Sublimity, and Genius: The Aesthetics of Nature and Art," in *The Cambridge Companion to Kant*, ed. Paul Guyer, 367–393. Cambridge: Cambridge University Press, 1992.

Schiesaro, Alessandro. *The Passions in Play:* Thyestes *and the Dynamics of Senecan Drama*. Cambridge: Cambridge University Press, 2003.

Schlegel, Friedrich. "Philosophische Lehrjahre," 1796–1806, *Kritische Ausgabe*, 17.2 (I), ed. Ernst Behler. Paderborn: Schöningh, 1958.

Schmitt, Charles B. *Cicero Scepticus: A Study of the Influence of the Academica in the Renaissance*. The Hague: Martin Nijhoff, 1972.

Schneider, Ben Ross. "*King Lear* in its Own Time: The Difference that Death Makes," *ELMS* 1.1 (1995): 1–49.

Schulz, Gerhild. *Rhetorik im Zeichen sprachlicher Transparenz: Racine — Lessing*. Dresden: Thelem, 2003.

Schümmer, Franz. "Die Entwicklung des Geschmacksbegriff in der Philosophie des 17. und 18. Jahrhunderts," *Archiv für Begriffsgeschichte* 1 (1955): 120–141.

Schwartz Lerner, Lía. *Metáfora y sátira en la obra de Quevedo*. Madrid: Taurus, 1984.

Scodel, Joshua. *Excess and the Mean in Early Modern English Literature*. Princeton: Princeton University Press, 2002.

Scott, Izora, ed. *Controversies over the Imitation of Cicero in the Renaissance*. Davis, CA: Hermagoras Press, 1991.

Scott, John A. "L'Ulisse dantesco," in *Dante magnanimo. Studi sula Commedia*. Florence: L.S. Olschki, 1977.

Screech, M. A. *Erasmus: Ecstasy and* The Praise of Folly. Harmondsworth: Penguin, 1988.

Sedley, David L. *Sublimity and Skepticism in Montaigne and Milton*. Ann Arbor: University of Michigan Press, 2005.

Seel, Otto. *Quintilian, oder Die Kunst des Redens und Schweigens*. Stuttgart: Klett-Cotta, 1977.

Segal, Charles. *Language and Desire in Seneca's Phaedra*. Princeton: Princeton University Press, 1986.

Seidensticker, Bernd. "Senecas *Thyestes* oder die Jagd nach der Außergewöhnlichen," in *Thyestes*, tr. Durs Grünbein. Frankfurt am Main: Insel, 2002.

Sellier, Philippe. *Pascal et saint Augustin*. Paris: Armand Colin, 1970.

Seneca. *De beneficiis*, in *Moral Essays III*, tr. John W. Basore. Cambridge: Harvard University Press, 1935.

———, *Seneca: His Tenne Tragedies, Translated into English by Thomas Newton anno 1581*, with Introduction by T. S. Eliot. (Reprinted) Bloomington: Indiana University Press, 1964.

———, *Naturales quaestiones*, 2 vols, tr. T. H. Corcoran. Cambridge: Harvard: Harvard University Press, 1972.

———, *Seneca's Thyestes*, ed. R. J. Tarrant. Atlanta: Scholars Press, 1985.

———, *Three Tragedies*, tr. Frederick Ahl. Ithaca: Cornell University Press, 1986.

————, *Tragedies*, 2 vols., tr. F. J. Miller. Cambridge: Harvard University Press, 1987, 1998.

————, *17 Letters*, tr. C. D. N. Costa. Warminster: Aris & Phillips Ltd., 1988.

————, *Epistles*, 3 vols., tr. R. M. Gummere. Cambridge: Harvard University Press, 1996.

Seneca the Elder. *Suasoriae*, ed. William A. Edward. Cambridge: University Press, 1928.

————, *Controversiae*, 2 vols. tr. Michael Winterbottom. Cambridge: Harvard University Press, 1974.

Sepper, Dennis L. *Descartes's Imagination: Proportion, Images, and the Activity of Thinking*. Berkeley: University of California Press, 1996.

Shakespeare, William. *The Norton Shakespeare*, gen. ed. Stephen Greenblatt. New York: W.W. Norton & Co., 1997.

————, *The History of King Lear*, ed. Stanley Wells. Oxford: Oxford University Press, 2000.

Shearman, John. *Mannerism*. Harmondsworth: Penguin, 1967.

Shepard, Sanford. *El Pinciano y las teórias literarias del siglo de oro*, 2nd ed. Madrid: Gredos, 1970.

Shuger, Debora K. *Sacred Rhetoric: The Christian Grand Style in the English Renaissance*.Princeton: Princeton University Press, 1988.

Sigüenza y Góngora, Carlos. *Libra astronómica y filosófica*, ed. Bernabé Navarro. Mexico City: UNAM, 1959.

Silva Camerena, Juan Manuel. "Dos sueños y una pesadilla: la modernidad y el saber en Descartes y Sor Juana," *Aproximaciones a Sor Juana*, 371–380. Mexico City: Fondo de cultura económica, 2005.

Singer, Dorothea. *Giordano Bruno: His Life and Thought with an Annotated Translation of his Work, On the Infinite Universe and Worlds*. New York: Henry Schuman, 1950.

Smith, Paul Julian. *Writing in the Margin: Spanish Literature of the Golden Age*. Oxford: Clarendon Press, 1988.

Soufas, Teresa Scott. *Melancholy and the Secular Mind in Spanish Golden Age Literature*. Columbia, MO: University of Missouri Press, 1990.

Spence, Sarah. *Figuratively Speaking: Rhetoric and Culture from Quintilian to the Twin Towers*. London: Duckworth, 2007.

Spies, Marjike. *Rhetoric, Rhetoricians, and Poets: Studies in Renaissance Poetry and Poetics*, ed. Henk Duits and Ton van Strien. Amsterdam: Amsterdam University Press, 1999.

Spitzer, Leo. *Linguistics and Literary History: Essays in Stylistics*. Princeton: Princeton University Press, 1967.

———, "The Spanish Baroque," *Representative Essays*, ed. Alban K. Forcione, Herbert Lindenberger, and Madeline Sutherland. Stanford: Stanford University Press, 1988.

Spoerri, Théodule. "La puissance métaphorique chez Descartes," in *Descartes*. Paris: Éditions de Minuit, 1957.

Sponde, Jean de. *D'amour et de mort*. Giromagny: Orphée, 1989.

Staten, Henry. *Wittgenstein and Derrida*. Oxford: Basil Blackwell, 1985.

Stierle, Karlheinz. "Translatio Studii and Renaissance: From Vertical to Horizontal Translation," *The Translatability of Cultures: Figurations of the Space Between*, ed. Sanford Burdick and Wolfgang Iser, 55–67. Stanford: Stanford University Press, 1996.

———, "Odysseus und Aeneas. Eine typologische Konfiguration in der *Commedia*," in *Das große Meer des Sinns. Hermenautische Erkundungen in Dantes' Commedia.* Munich: Wilhelm Fink, 2007.

Strier, Richard. "Against the Rule of Reason: Praise of Passion from Petrarch to Luther to Shakespeare to Herbert," in *Reading the Early Modern Passions: Essays in the Cultural History of Emotion*, ed. Gail Kern Paster, Katherine Rowe, and Mary Floyd-Wilson, 23–42. Philadelphia: University of Pennsylvania Press, 2004.

Stripling, Scott R. *The Picture Theory of Meaning: An Interpretation of Wittgenstein's Tractatus logico-philosophicus*. Washington, D.C.: University Press of America, 1978.

Tasso, Torquato. *Discourses on the Heroic Poem*, tr. Mariella Cavalchini and Irene Samuel. Oxford: Clarendon Press, 1973.

Tesauro, Emanuele. *Il Cannocchiale aristotelico* (1670), ed. August Buck. Bad Homburg: Gehlen, 1968.

Teskey, Gordon. *Allegory and Violence*. Ithaca: Cornell University Press, 1996.

Tetel, Marcel. "L'Eloge de la Folie: Captatio benevolentiae," in *Dix conférences sur Érasme: Eloges de la folie — Colloques*, 23–32. Paris: Champion; Geneva: Slatkine, 1986.

Topliss, Patricia. *The Rhetoric of Pascal*. Leicester: Leicester University Press, 1966.

Toulmin, Stephen. *Cosmopolis: The Hidden Agenda of Modernity*. Chicago: University of Chicago Press, 1990.

Trabulse, Elías. *El hermetismo y Sor Juana Inés de la Cruz: Orígenes e interpretación*. Mexico City: Litografía Regina de los Angeles, 1980.

————, *El círculo roto: Estudios históricos sobre la ciencia en México*. Mexico City: Fondo de Cultura Económica, 1982.

————, "El universo científico de Sor Juana Inés de la Cruz," *Colonial Latin American Review* 4.2 (1995): 41–50.

————, "El tránsito del hermetismo a la ciencia moderna: Alejandro Fabián, Sor Juana Inés de la Cruz y Carlos de Sigüenza y Góngora (1667–1690)," *Caliope* 4.1–2 (1998): 56–69.

Trimpi, Wesley. *Muses of One Mind: The Literary Analysis of Experience and Its Continuity*. Princeton: Princeton University Press, 1983.

Turner, Denys. *The Darkness of God: Negativity in Christian Mysticism*. Cambridge: Cambridge University Press, 1995.

Ueding, Gert, ed. *Historisches Wörterbuch der Rhetorik*, 8 vols. Tübingen: Max Niemayer, 1992–.

Valéry, Paul. "Variation sur une pensée," *Œuvres*. Paris: Gallimard, 1957.

Valla, Lorenzo. *Le postille all'Institutio oratoria di Quintiliano*, ed. L. C. Martinelli and Alessandro Perosa. Padua: Antenore, 1996.

Van Hook, J. W. "'Concupiscence of Witt': The Metaphysical Conceit in Baroque Poetics, *Modern Philology* 84.1 (1986): 24–38.

Vasoli, Cesare. *La dialettica e la retorica dell'umanesimo*. Milan: Feltrinelli, 1968.

Vega, Garcilaso de la. *Obra poética y textos en prosa*, ed. Bienvenido Morros. Barcelona: Crítica, 1995.

Velasco, Mabel. "La cosmologia azteca en el Primero sueño de Sor Juana Inés de la Cruz, *Revista Iberamericana*, 50.127 (1984): 539–548.

Vickers, Brian. *Francis Bacon and Renaissance Prose*, Cambridge: University Press, 1968.

————, "The 'Songs and Sonnets' and the Rhetoric of Hyperbole," in *John Donne: Essays in Celebration*, ed. A. J. Smith, 132–174. London: Metheun, 1978.

————, *Classical Rhetoric in English Poetry*, with a new preface and annotated bibliography. Carbondale: Southern Illinois University Press, 1986.

————, *In Defense of Rhetoric*. Oxford: Clarendon Press, 1988.

————, "Bacon and Rhetoric," *Cambridge Companion to Francis Bacon*, ed. Markku Peltonen. Cambridge: Cambridge University Press, 1996.

————, "'Words and Things' — 'Words, Concepts, and Things'? Rhetorical and Linguistic Categories in the Renaissance," in *Res et Verba in der Renaissance*, ed. Eckhard Kesslerand Ian Maclean, 287–336. Wiesbaden: Harrassowitz, 2002.

————, ed. *English Renaissance Literary Criticism*. Oxford: Oxford University Press, 2003.

Vilanova, Antonio. "Preceptistas españoles de los siglos XVI y XVII," in *Historia general de las literaturas hispánicas*, 6 vols., ed. Guillermo Díaz-Plaja, 3:567–692. Barcelona: Editorial Barna, 1953.

———, *Las fuentes y los temas del Polifemo de Góngora*, 2 vols. Madrid: CSIC, 1957.

Villars, L'Abbé de. *La première critique des "Pensées": Texte et commentaire du cinquième dialogue du* Traité de la délicatesse *de l'abbé de Villars (1671)*, ed. Dominique Descotes. Paris: CNRS, 1980.

Virgil. *The Aeneid*, tr. David West. New York: Penguin, 1990.

———, *Eclogues, Georgics, Aeneid I–VI*, tr. H. Rushton Fairclough; rev. ed. G. P. Goold. Cambridge: Harvard University Press, 1999.

Volkmann, Richard. *Die Rhetorik der Griechen und Römer*. Hildesheim: Georg Olms, 1963.

Von Albrecht, Michael. *Wort und Wandlung: Senecas Lebenskunst*. Leiden: Brill, 2004.

Vossler, Karl. *La soledad en la poesía lírica española*. Madrid: Revista de Occidente, 1941.

Vuilleumier, Florence. "Les conceptismes," in *Histoire de la rhétorique dans l'Europe moderne*, ed. Marc Fumaroli, 517–537. Paris: PUF, 1999.

Ward, John O. "Cicero and Quintilian," *Cambridge History of Literary Criticism: The Renaissance*, vol. 3, ed. Glyn P. Norton, 77–87. Cambridge: Cambridge University Press, 1999.

Warminski, Andrzej. "Returns of the Sublime: Positing and Performative in Kant, Fichte, and Schiller," *MLN* 116 (2001): 964–978.

Webb, Stephen J. *Blessed Excess: Religion and the Hyperbolic Imagination*. Albany: SUNY Press, 1993.

Weinberg, Bernard. "Scaliger versus Aristotle on Poetics," *Modern Philology* 39 (1942): 337–360.

———, *A History of Literary Criticism in the Italian Renaissance*, 2 vols. Chicago: University of Chicago Press, 1961.

Wellek, René. *Concepts in Criticism*. New Haven: Yale University Press, 1963.

Wilbern, David. "Shakespeare's Nothing," in *Representing Shakespeare: New Psychoanalytic Essays*, ed. Murray M. Schwartz and Coppélia Kahn, 244–263. Baltimore: The Johns Hopkins University Press, 1980.

Wilde, Oscar. *The Artist as Critic: Critical Writings of Oscar Wilde*, ed. Richard Ellmann. Chicago: University of Chicago Press, 1982.

Winterbottom, Michael. *Problems in Quintilian*. London: University of London, 1970.

Witmore, Michael. *Shakespeare's Metaphysics*. London: Continuum, 2008.

Wittgenstein, Ludwig. *Philosophical Investigations*, tr. G. E. M. Anscombe. Oxford: Basil Blackwell, 1958.

————, "A Lecture on Ethics," *The Philosophical Review* 74.1 (1965): 3–12.

————, *Lectures & Conversations on Aesthetics, Psychology and Religious Belief*, ed. Cyril Barrett. Berkeley: University of California Press, 1967.

————, *Tractatus Logico-Philosophicus*, tr. C.K. Ogden. London and New York: Routledge & Kegan Paul, 1981.

————, *Philosophische Untersuchungen*, in *Werkausgabe*, 8 vols. Frankfurt am Main: Suhrkamp, 1990.

————, *Culture and Value: A Selection from the Posthumous Remains*, ed. Georg Henrik von Wright and Heikki Nyman, tr. Peter Winch. Oxford: Blackwell, 1998.

Wölfflin, Heinrich. *Renaissance and Baroque*, tr. Kathrin Simon. Ithaca: Cornell University Press, 1966.

Woods, M. G. *The Poet and the Natural World in the Age of Gongora*. Oxford: Oxford University Press, 1978.

Wygant, Amy. "Leo Spitzer's Racine," *MLN* 109.4 (1994): 632–649.

Yates, Frances. "Charles Quint et L'idée d'empire," in *Fêtes et cérémonies au temps de Charles Quint*, ed. Jean Jacquot, 57–97. Paris: CNRS, 1960.

Zárate Ruiz, Arturo. *Gracián, Wit, and the Baroque Age*. New York: Peter Lang, 1996.

Zimnik, Nina. "Allegorie und Subjektivität in Walter Benjamins *Ursprung des deutschen Trauerspiels*," *The Germanic* Review 72 (1997): 285–302.

Zwierlein, Otto. *Senecas Hercules im Lichte kaiserzeitlicher und spätantiker Deutung*. Wiesbaden: Academie der Wissenschaften und der Literatur, 1984.

————, *Kritischer Kommentar zu den Tragödien Senecas*. Mainz: Academie der Wissenschaften und der Literatur, 1986.

Author Index